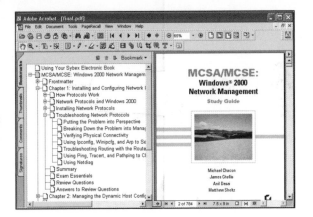

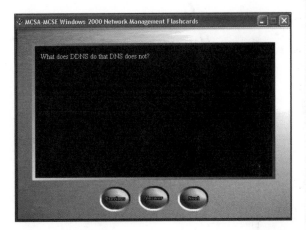

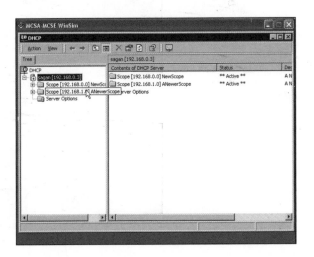

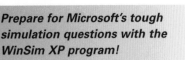

SYBEX

MCSA/MCSE: Windows 2000® Network Management Study Guide

Exam 70-218: *Managing a Microsoft Windows 2000 Network Environment*

OBJECTIVE	CHAPTER
Creating, Configuring, Managing, Securing, and Troubleshooting File, Print, and Web Resources	
Publish resources in Active Directory. Types of resources include printers and shared folders	5
Perform a search in Active Directory Users and Computers; Configure a printer object	5
Manage data storage; Considerations include file systems, permissions, and quotas	9
Implement NTFS and FAT file systems; Enable and configure quotas; Implement and configure Encrypting File System (EFS); Configure volumes and basic and dynamic disks; Configure file and folder permissions; Manage a domain-based distributed file system (DFS); Manage file and folder compression	9
Create shared resources and configure access rights; Shared resources include printers, shared folders, and Web folders	9
Share folders and enable Web sharing; Configure shared folder permissions; Create and manage shared printers; Configure shared printer permissions	9
Configure and troubleshoot Internet Information Services (IIS)	12
Configure virtual directories and virtual servers; Troubleshoot Internet browsing from client computers; Troubleshoot intranet browsing from client computers; Configure authentication and SSL for Web sites; Configure FTP services; Configure access permissions for intranet Web servers	12
Monitor and manage network security; Actions include auditing and detecting security breaches	6, 7, 9
Configure user-account lockout settings; Configure user-account password length, history, age, and complexity; Configure Group Policy to run logon scripts; Link Group Policy objects; Enable and configure auditing; Monitor security by using the system security log file	6, 7, 9
Configuring, Administering, and Troubleshooting the Network Infrastructure	
Troubleshoot routing; Diagnostic utilities include the **tracert** command, the **ping** command, and the **ipconfig** command	1
Validate local computer configuration by using the **ipconfig**, **arp**, and **route** commands; Validate network connectivity by using the **tracert**, **ping**, and **pathping** commands	1
Configure and troubleshoot TCP/IP on servers and client computers; Considerations include subnet masks, default gateways, network IDs, and broadcast addresses	1, 2
Configure client computer TCP/IP properties; Validate client computer network configuration by using the **winipcfg**, **ipconfig**, and **arp** commands; Validate client computer network connectivity by using the **ping** command	1, 2
Configure, administer, and troubleshoot DHCP on servers and client computers	1, 2
Detect unauthorized DHCP servers on a network; Configure authorization of DHCP servers; Configure client computers to use dynamic IP addressing; Configure DHCP server properties; Create and configure a DHCP scope	1, 2
Configure, administer, and troubleshoot DNS	3
Configure DNS server properties; Manage DNS database records such as CNAME, A, and PTR; Create and configure DNS zones	3
Troubleshoot name resolution on client computers; Considerations include WINS, DNS, NetBIOS, the Hosts file, and the Lmhosts file	1, 3
Configure client computer name resolution properties; Troubleshoot name resolution problems by using the **nbtstat**, **ipconfig**, **nslookup**, and **netdiag** commands; Create and configure a Hosts file for troubleshooting name resolution problems; Create and configure an Lmhosts file for troubleshooting name resolution problems	1, 3
Managing, Securing, and Troubleshooting Servers and Client Computers	
Install and configure server and client computer hardware	9
Verify hardware compatibility by using the qualifier tools; Configure driver signing options; Verify digital signatures on existing driver files; Configure operating system support for legacy hardware devices	9
Troubleshoot starting servers and client computers; Tools and methodologies include Safe Mode, Recovery Console, and parallel installations	9

SYBEX

Exam objectives are subject to change at any time without prior notice and at Microsoft's sole discretion. Please visit Microsoft's Training & Certification website (www.microsoft.com/traincert) for the most current listing of exam objectives.

SYBEX

MCSA/MCSE:
Windows 2000
Network Management
Study Guide

MCSA/MCSE:
Windows® 2000
Network Management
Study Guide

Michael Chacon

James Chellis

Anil Desai

Matthew Sheltz

San Francisco • London

SYBEX

Associate Publisher: Neil Edde
Acquisitions and Developmental Editor: Jeff Kellum
Editor: Linda Recktenwald
Production Editor: Dennis Fitzgerald
Technical Editors: Jeff Durham, Kevin Lundy
Book Designer: Bill Gibson
Graphic Illustrator: Tony Jonick
Electronic Publishing Specialist: Nila Nichols
Proofreaders: Emily Hsuan, Dave Nash, Yariv Rabinovitch, Nancy Riddiough
Indexer: Nancy Guenther
CD Coordinator: Dan Mummert
CD Technician: Kevin Ly
Cover Designer: Archer Design
Cover Photographer: Natural Selection

Library of Congress Card Number: 2002101983

ISBN: 0-7821-4105-6

SYBEX

To Our Valued Readers:

Since its inception nearly ten years ago, Microsoft's MCSE program has established itself as the premier computer and networking industry certification, with nearly half a million IT professionals having attained this elite status. And with Microsoft's recent creation of the MCSA program, IT professionals can now choose to pursue the certification that best suits their career goals. Microsoft developed the MCSA certification to address demands from the IT industry for a mid-level administrator certification. This new program has met with considerable enthusiasm in the IT arena, both from certification candidates and corporations seeking individuals possessing the skills required for today's competitive job market.

Sybex is proud to have helped thousands of Microsoft certification candidates prepare for their exams over the years, and we are excited about the opportunity to continue to provide computer and networking professionals with the skills they'll need to succeed in the highly competitive IT industry.

The authors and editors have worked hard to ensure that the Study Guide you hold in your hand is comprehensive, in-depth, and pedagogically sound. We're confident that this book will exceed the demanding standards of the certification marketplace and help you, the Microsoft certification candidate, succeed in your endeavors.

As always, your feedback is important to us. Please send comments, questions, or suggestions to support@sybex.com. At Sybex we're continually striving to meet the needs of individuals preparing for IT certification exams.

Good luck in pursuit of your Microsoft certification!

Neil Edde
Associate Publisher—Certification
Sybex, Inc.

Software License Agreement: Terms and Conditions

Dedicated to my loving family

-Matt

Acknowledgments

First I need to thank Anil Desai. His writing and contributions truly made this book a reality. Anil's knowledge of all things Windows 2000 should be an inspiration to any aspiring MCSA or MCSE. Michael Chacon's long-time real world experience also added valuable insight to the development of this book. Michael's knowledge of many aspects of Windows 2000 network management provided direction that you will use almost every day as an administrator.

I would especially like to thank James Chellis for being a mentor and inspirational leader. James is the backbone of the MCSA/MCSE series at Sybex, and his support through this project was always welcome.

Of course, the editors at Sybex are always meticulous, and without them this book would not have been possible. Jeff Kellum was instrumental in conceptual development at the beginning, and he supported the project until the end. Dennis Fitzgerald and Linda Recktenwald fine-tuned the content to perfection. Jeff Durham and Kevin Lundy ensured that the book is technically sound and relevant. Thanks to all of the editors for their excellent work.

I would like also to thank you, the aspiring MCSA or MCSE. You are the future of the IT industry, and you know how important it is to be fully prepared for your job. I am confident that books such as this one and all of the other MCSE Study Guides produced by Sybex will prepare you for a successful career as an IT administrator.

I must include a special thanks to my wife Tara for supporting me in everything I do.

Matthew Sheltz

Contents at a Glance

Contents

Table of Exercises

Introduction

The Microsoft Certified Systems Administrator (MCSA) certification is currently the hottest certification in the computer industry. Designed for computer industry professionals who implement, manage, and trouble-shoot computer networks, it is the ideal first credential for demonstrating proficiency with Windows 2000.

The MCSA is part of Microsoft's Microsoft Certified Professional (MCP) program. This is the premier certification program for computer industry professionals. Covering the core technologies around which Microsoft's future will be built, the MCP program provides powerful credentials for career advancement.

This book builds upon the knowledge and skills you gathered completing the other two MCSA core requirements exams: Windows 2000 Professional and Windows 2000 Server. It has been developed to give you the critical skills and knowledge you need to prepare for one of the core requirements for the MCSA certification: *Managing a Microsoft Windows 2000 Network Environment* (Exam 70-218).

This exam also serves as an elective for the Windows 2000 Microsoft Certified Engineer (MCSE) credential!

The Microsoft Certified Professional Program

Since the inception of its certification program, Microsoft has certified almost 1.5 million people. As the computer network industry grows in both size and complexity, this number is sure to grow—and the need for *proven* ability will also increase. Companies rely on certifications to verify the skills of prospective employees and contractors.

Microsoft has developed its Microsoft Certified Professional program to give you credentials that verify your ability to work with Microsoft products effectively and professionally. Obtaining your MCP certification requires that you pass any one Microsoft certification exam. Several levels of certification are available based on specific suites of exams. Depending on your areas of interest or experience, you can obtain any of the following MCP credentials:

Microsoft Certified System Administrator (MCSA) The MCSA certification is the latest certification track from Microsoft. This certification targets network and systems administrators with roughly 6 to 12 months of desktop and network administration experience. The MCSA can be considered the entry-level certification. You must take and pass a total of four exams to obtain your MCSA.

Microsoft Certified System Engineer (MCSE) on Windows 2000 This certification track is designed for network and systems administrators, network and systems analysts, and technical consultants who work with Microsoft Windows 2000 Professional and Server software. You must take and pass seven exams to obtain your MCSE.

MCSE versus MCSA

In an effort to provide those just starting off in the IT world a chance to prove their skills, Microsoft recently announced its Microsoft Certified System Administrator (MCSA) program.

Targeted at those with less than a year's experience, the MCSA program focuses primarily on the administration portion of an IT professional's duties. The requirements for the MCSA are:

- One client operating system exam, including the Windows 2000 Professional exam.

- Two networking system exams, including the *Windows 2000 Server* and *Managing a Microsoft Windows 2000 Network Environment* exams.

- One elective, including many of the MCSE exams or a combination of either the CompTIA A+ and Network+ exams or the A+ and Server+ exams.

Of course, it should be any MCSA's goal to eventually obtain his or her MCSE. The good news is that as many as all four of the MCSA exams can count toward the seven exams required for MCSE certification! However, keep in mind that the MCSE certification is an advanced certification that requires network design and hands-on skills beyond those of the MCSA.

Microsoft Certified Solution Developer (MCSD)   This track is designed for software engineers and developers and technical consultants who primarily use Microsoft development tools. Currently, you can take exams on Visual Basic, Visual C++, and Visual FoxPro. However, with Microsoft's pending release of Visual Studio 7, you can expect the requirements for this track to change. You must take and pass four exams to obtain your MCSD.

Microsoft Certified Database Administrator (MCDBA)   This track is designed for database administrators, developers, and analysts who work with Microsoft SQL Server. As of this printing, you can take exams on either SQL Server 7 or SQL Server 2000, but Microsoft is expected to announce the retirement of SQL Server 7. You must take and pass four exams to achieve MCDBA status.

Microsoft Certified Trainer (MCT)   The MCT track is designed for any IT professional who develops and teaches Microsoft-approved courses. To become an MCT, you must first obtain your MCSE, MCSD, or MCDBA, and then you must take a class at one of the Certified Technical Training Centers. You will also be required to prove your instructional ability. You can do this in various ways: by taking a skills-building or train-the-trainer class, by achieving certification as a trainer from any of several vendors, or by becoming a Certified Technical Trainer through CompTIA. Last of all, you will need to complete an MCT application.

How Do You Become an MCSA?

Attaining any MCP certification has always been a challenge. In the past, students have been able to acquire detailed exam information—even most of the exam questions—from online "brain dumps" and third-party "cram" books or software products. For the new MCSA exams, however, this is simply not the case.

Microsoft has taken strong steps to protect the security and integrity of the new MCSA track. Prospective MCSAs must complete a course of study that develops detailed knowledge about a wide range of topics. It supplies them with the true skills needed, derived from working with Windows 2000 and related software products.

The MCSA Windows 2000 program is heavily weighted toward hands-on skills and experience. Microsoft has stated that "nearly half of the core required exams' content demands that the candidate have troubleshooting skills acquired through hands-on experience and working knowledge."

The Sybex *MCSA: Windows 2000 Virtual Lab* is an excellent tool that will allow you to accumulate necessary "hands-on" experience, without having to put in the time and resources needed set up an expensive computer training network. This product is available through bookstores worldwide.

Fortunately, if you are willing to dedicate the time and effort to learn Windows 2000, you can prepare yourself well for the MCSA exams. By working through this book and utilizing the proper study tools, you can successfully meet the exam requirements to pass the MCSA exams.

This book is best employed *after* you have completed the *Windows 2000 Server* and *Windows 2000 Professional* exams. It presumes that you already have knowledge and skills in those areas.

This book is part of a complete series of MCSA/MCSE Study Guides, published by Sybex Inc., that together cover the MCSA requirements needed to complete your MCSA track. Study Guide titles include the following:

- *MCSE: Windows 2000 Professional Study Guide,* Second Edition, by Lisa Donald with James Chellis (Sybex, 2001)

- *MCSE: Windows 2000 Server Study Guide,* Second Edition, by Lisa Donald with James Chellis (Sybex, 2001)

- *MCSE: Windows 2000 Network Infrastructure Administration Study Guide,* Second Edition, by Paul Robichaux with James Chellis (Sybex, 2001)

Exam Requirements

Candidates for MCSA certification on Windows 2000 must pass four exams, including one client operating system exam, two networking system exams, and one elective, as shown in the following graphic.

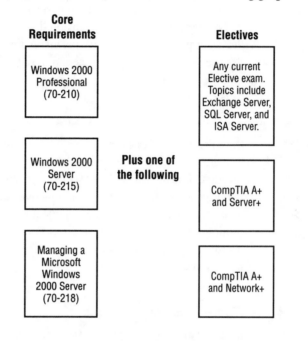

Core Requirements

| Windows 2000 Professional (70-210) |

| Windows 2000 Server (70-215) |

Plus one of the following

| Managing a Microsoft Windows 2000 Server (70-218) |

Electives

| Any current Elective exam. Topics include Exchange Server, SQL Server, and ISA Server. |

| CompTIA A+ and Server+ |

| CompTIA A+ and Network+ |

For a more detailed description of the Microsoft certification programs, including a list of current and future MCSA electives, check Microsoft's Training and Certification website at www.microsoft.com/traincert.

The *Managing a Microsoft Windows 2000 Network Environment* Exam

The *Managing a Microsoft Windows 2000 Network Environment* exam focuses on your ability to administer, maintain, and troubleshoot computer networks that use Windows 2000. It emphasizes the following elements of Windows 2000 Professional and Server support:

- Managing file, print, and web resources

- Managing a network infrastructure, including TCP/IP, DNS, WINS, and DHCP

- Maintaining and troubleshooting client and server computers

- Managing Active Directory organizational units and Group Policy

- Managing remote access

This exam is quite specific regarding Windows 2000 Professional and Server requirements and operational settings, and it can be particular about how administrative tasks are performed within the operating system. It also focuses on fundamental concepts of Windows 2000 operations. Careful study of this book, along with hands-on experience, will help you prepare for this exam.

Microsoft provides exam objectives to give you a general overview of possible areas of coverage on the Microsoft exams. For your convenience, this Study Guide includes objective listings positioned within the text at points where specific Microsoft exam objectives are discussed. Keep in mind, however, that exam objectives are subject to change at any time without prior notice and at Microsoft's sole discretion. Please visit Microsoft's Training and Certification website (www.microsoft.com/traincert) for the most current listing of exam objectives.

Types of Exam Questions

In an effort to both refine the testing process and protect the quality of its certifications, Microsoft has focused its Windows 2000 exams on real experience and hands-on proficiency. There is greater emphasis on your past working environments and responsibilities and less emphasis on how well you can memorize. In fact, Microsoft says an MCSA candidate should have at least six months of hands-on experience.

Microsoft accomplishes its goal of protecting the exams' integrity by regularly adding and removing exam questions, limiting the number of questions that any individual sees in a beta exam, limiting the number of questions delivered to an individual by using adaptive testing, and adding new exam elements.

Exam questions may be in a variety of formats: Depending on which exam you take, you'll see multiple-choice questions, as well as select-and-place and prioritize-a-list questions. Simulations and case study–based formats are included as well. You may also find yourself taking what's called an *adaptive format exam*. Let's take a look at the types of exam questions and examine the adaptive testing technique, so you'll be prepared for all of the possibilities.

Microsoft no longer offers a score indicating how close you were to passing or failing an exam. Now you will be told only whether you pass or fail.

For more information on the various exam question types, go to www.microsoft.com/traincert/mcpexams/policies/innovations.asp.

MULTIPLE-CHOICE QUESTIONS

Multiple-choice questions come in two main forms. One is a straightforward question followed by several possible answers, of which one or more are correct. The other type of multiple-choice question is more complex and based on a specific scenario. The scenario may focus on several areas or objectives.

SELECT-AND-PLACE QUESTIONS

Select-and-place exam questions involve graphical elements that you must manipulate to successfully answer the question. For example, you might see a diagram of a computer network, as shown in the following graphic taken from the select-and-place demo downloaded from Microsoft's website.

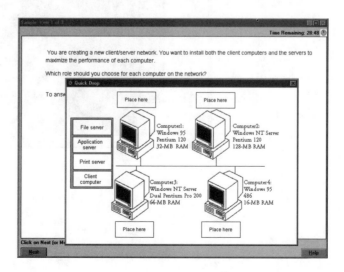

A typical diagram shows computers and other components next to boxes that contain the text "Place here." The labels for the boxes represent various computer roles on a network, such as a print server and a file server. Based on information given for each computer, you are asked to select each label and place it in the correct box. You need to place *all* of the labels correctly. No credit is given for the question if you correctly label only some of the boxes.

In another select-and-place problem, you might be asked to put a series of steps in order by dragging items from boxes on the left to boxes on the right and placing them in the correct order. One other type requires that you drag an item from the left and place it under an item in a column on the right.

SIMULATIONS

Simulations are the kinds of questions that most closely represent actual situations and test the skills you use while working with Microsoft software interfaces. These exam questions include a mock interface on which you are asked to perform certain actions according to a given scenario. The simulated interfaces look nearly identical to what you see in the actual product, as shown in this example:

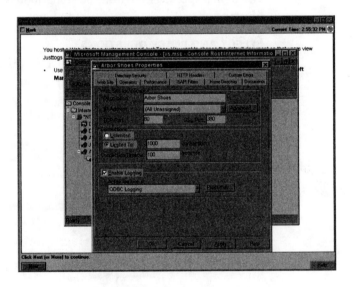

Because of the number of possible errors that can be made on simulations, be sure to consider the following recommendations from Microsoft:

- Do not change any simulation settings that don't pertain to the solution directly.

- When related information has not been provided, assume that the default settings are used.

- Make sure that your entries are spelled correctly.

- Close all the simulation application windows after completing the set of tasks in the simulation.

The best way to prepare for simulation questions is to spend time working with the graphical interface of the product on which you will be tested.

We recommend that you study with the WinSim 2000 product, which is included on the CD that accompanies this Study Guide. By completing the exercises in this Study Guide and working with the WinSim 2000 software, you will greatly improve your level of preparation for simulation questions.

CASE STUDY–BASED QUESTIONS

Case study–based questions first appeared in the MCSD program. These questions present a scenario with a range of requirements. Based on the information provided, you answer a series of multiple-choice and select-and-place questions. The interface for case study–based questions has a number of tabs, each of which contains information about the scenario.

At present, this type of question appears only in most of the Design exams.

ADAPTIVE EXAM FORMAT

Microsoft presents many of its exams in an *adaptive* format. This format is radically different from the conventional format previously used for Microsoft certification exams. Conventional tests are static, containing a fixed number of questions. Adaptive tests change depending on your answers to the questions presented.

The number of questions presented in your adaptive test will depend on how long it takes the exam to ascertain your level of ability (according to the statistical measurements on which exam questions are ranked). To determine a test-taker's level of ability, the exam presents questions in an increasing or decreasing order of difficulty.

Unlike the earlier test format, the adaptive test does *not* allow you to go back to see a question again. The exam only goes forward. Once you enter your answer, that's it—you cannot change it. Be very careful before entering your answers. There is no time limit for each individual question (only for the exam as a whole). Your exam may be shortened by correct answers (and lengthened by incorrect answers), so there is no advantage to rushing through questions.

Microsoft will regularly add and remove questions from the exams. This is called *item seeding*. It is part of the effort to make it more difficult for individuals to merely memorize exam questions that were passed along by previous test-takers.

Exam Question Development

Microsoft follows an exam-development process consisting of eight mandatory phases. The process takes an average of seven months and involves more than 150 specific steps. The MCP exam development consists of the following phases:

Phase 1: Job Analysis Phase 1 is an analysis of all the tasks that make up a specific job function, based on tasks performed by people who are currently performing that job function. This phase also identifies the knowledge, skills, and abilities that relate specifically to the performance area being certified.

Phase 2: Objective Domain Definition   The results of the job analysis phase provide the framework used to develop objectives. Development of objectives involves translating the job-function tasks into a comprehensive package of specific and measurable knowledge, skills, and abilities. The resulting list of objectives—the *objective domain*—is the basis for the development of both the certification exams and the training materials.

Phase 3: Blueprint Survey   The final objective domain is transformed into a blueprint survey in which contributors are asked to rate each objective. These contributors may be MCP candidates, appropriately skilled exam-development volunteers, or Microsoft employees. Based on the contributors' input, the objectives are prioritized and weighted. The actual exam items are written according to the prioritized objectives. Contributors are queried about how they spend their time on the job. If a contributor doesn't spend an adequate amount of time actually performing the specified job function, his or her data are eliminated from the analysis. The blueprint survey phase helps determine which objectives to measure, as well as the appropriate number and types of items to include on the exam.

Phase 4: Item Development   A pool of items is developed to measure the blueprinted objective domain. The number and types of items to be written are based on the results of the blueprint survey.

Phase 5: Alpha Review and Item Revision   During this phase, a panel of technical and job-function experts reviews each item for technical accuracy. The panel then answers each item and reaches a consensus on all technical issues. Once the items have been verified as being technically accurate, they are edited to ensure that they are expressed in the clearest language possible.

Phase 6: Beta Exam   The reviewed and edited items are collected into beta exams. Based on the responses of all beta participants, Microsoft performs a statistical analysis to verify the validity of the exam items and to determine which items will be used in the certification exam. Once the analysis has been completed, the items are distributed into multiple parallel forms, or *versions*, of the final certification exam.

Phase 7: Item Selection and Cut-Score Setting The results of the beta exams are analyzed to determine which items will be included in the certification exam. This determination is based on many factors, including item difficulty and relevance. During this phase, a panel of job-function experts determines the *cut score* (minimum passing score) for the exams. The cut score differs from exam to exam because it is based on an item-by-item determination of the percentage of candidates who answered the item correctly and who would be expected to answer the item correctly.

Phase 8: Live Exam In the final phase, the exams are given to candidates. MCP exams are administered by Prometric and Virtual University Enterprises (VUE).

Tips for Taking the MCSA Exams

Here are some general tips for achieving success on your certification exam:

- Arrive early at the exam center so that you can relax and review your study materials. During this final review, you can look over tables and lists of exam-related information.

- Read the questions carefully. Don't be tempted to jump to an early conclusion. Make sure you know *exactly* what the question is asking.

- Answer all questions. Remember that the adaptive format does *not* allow you to return to a question. Be very careful before entering your answer. Because your exam may be shortened by correct answers (and lengthened by incorrect answers), there is no advantage to rushing through questions.

- On simulations, do not change settings that are not directly related to the question. Also, assume default settings if the question does not specify or imply which settings are used.

- For questions you're not sure about, use a process of elimination to get rid of the obviously incorrect answers first. This improves your odds of selecting the correct answer when you need to make an educated guess.

Exam Registration

You may take the Microsoft exams at any of more than 1000 Authorized Prometric Testing Centers (APTCs) and VUE Testing Centers around the world. For the location of a testing center near you, call Prometric at 800-755-EXAM (755-3926), or call VUE at 888-837-8616. Outside the United States and Canada, contact your local Prometric or VUE registration center.

Find out the number of the exam you want to take, and then register with the Prometric or VUE registration center nearest to you. At this point, you will be asked for advance payment for the exam. The exams are $100 each and you must take them within one year of payment. You can schedule exams up to six weeks in advance or as late as one working day prior to the date of the exam. You can cancel or reschedule your exam if you contact the center at least two working days prior to the exam. Same-day registration is available in some locations, subject to space availability. Where same-day registration is available, you must register a minimum of two hours before test time.

You may also register for your exams online at www.prometric.com or www.vue.com.

When you schedule the exam, you will be provided with instructions regarding appointment and cancellation procedures, ID requirements, and information about the testing center location. In addition, you will receive a registration and payment confirmation letter from Prometric or VUE.

Microsoft requires certification candidates to accept the terms of a Non-Disclosure Agreement before taking certification exams.

Is This Book for You?

If you want to acquire a solid foundation in Windows 2000 Professional and Windows 2000 Server management, and your goal is to prepare for the exam by learning how to use and manage the new operating system, this book is for you. You'll find clear explanations of the fundamental concepts you need to grasp and plenty of help to achieve the high level of professional competency you need to succeed in your chosen field.

If you want to become certified as an MCSE or MCSA, this book is definitely for you. However, if you just want to attempt to pass the exam without really understanding Windows 2000, this Study Guide is *not* for you. It is written for people who want to acquire hands-on skills and in-depth knowledge of Windows 2000.

How to Use This Book

What makes a Sybex Study Guide the book of choice for over 100,000 MCSEs? We took into account not only what you need to know to pass the exam, but what you need to know to take what you've learned and apply it in the real world. Each book contains the following:

Objective-by-objective coverage of the topics you need to know   Each chapter lists the objectives covered in that chapter, followed by detailed discussion of each objective.

Assessment Test   Directly following this introduction is an Assessment Test that you should take. It is designed to help you determine how much you already know about Windows 2000. Each question is tied to a topic discussed in the book. Using the results of the Assessment Test, you can figure out the areas where you need to focus your study. Of course, we do recommend you read the entire book.

Exam Essentials   To highlight what you learn, you'll find a list of Exam Essentials at the end of each chapter. The Exam Essentials section briefly highlights the topics that need your particular attention as you prepare for the exam.

Key Terms and Glossary   Throughout each chapter, you will be introduced to important terms and concepts that you will need to know for the exam. These terms appear in italic within the chapters, and a list of the Key Terms appears just after the Exam Essentials. At the end of the book, a detailed Glossary gives definitions for these terms, as well as other general terms you should know.

Review Questions, complete with detailed explanations   Each chapter is followed by a set of Review Questions that test what you learned in the chapter. The questions are written with the exam in mind, meaning that they are designed to have the same look and feel as what you'll see on the exam. Question types are just like the exam, including multiple choice, exhibits, select-and-place, and prioritize-a-list.

Hands-on exercises   In each chapter, you'll find exercises designed to give you the important hands-on experience that is critical for your exam preparation. The exercises support the topics of the chapter, and they walk you through the steps necessary to perform a particular function.

Real World Scenarios   Because reading a book isn't enough for you to learn how to apply these topics in your everyday duties, we have provided Real World Scenarios in special sidebars. These explain when and why a particular solution would make sense, in a working environment you'd actually encounter.

Interactive CD   Every Sybex Study Guide comes with a CD complete with additional questions, flashcards for use with an interactive device, a Windows simulation program, and the book in electronic format. Details are in the following section.

The topics covered in this Study Guide map directly to Microsoft's official exam objectives. Each exam objective is covered completely.

What's on the CD?

With this new member of our best-selling MCSA/MCSE Study Guide series, we are including quite an array of training resources. The CD offers numerous simulations, bonus exams, and flashcards to help you study for the exam. We have also included the complete contents of the Study Guide in electronic form. The CD's resources are described here:

The Sybex Ebook for the *Managing a Microsoft Windows 2000 Network Environment* **exam**   Many people like the convenience of being able to carry their whole Study Guide on a CD. They also like being able to search the text via computer to find specific information quickly and easily. For these reasons, the entire contents of this Study Guide are supplied on the CD, in PDF. We've also included Adobe Acrobat Reader, which provides the interface for the PDF contents as well as the search capabilities.

WinSim 2000   We developed the WinSim 2000 product to allow you to experience the multimedia and interactive operation of working with Windows 2000 Professional and Server. WinSim 2000 provides both audio/video files and hands-on experience with key features of Windows 2000 Professional and Server. Built around the Study Guide's exercises, WinSim 2000 will help you attain the knowledge and hands-on skills you must have in order to understand Windows 2000 (and pass the exam). Here is a sample screen from WinSim 2000:

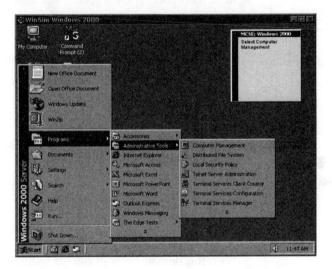

The Sybex EdgeTests The EdgeTests are a collection of multiple-choice questions that will help you prepare for your exam. There are four sets of questions:

- Two bonus exams designed to simulate the actual live exam.

- An adaptive test simulator that will give the feel for how adaptive testing works.

- All the questions from the Study Guide, presented in a test engine for your review. You can review questions by chapter or by objective, or you can take a random test.

- The Assessment Test.

Here is a sample screen from the Sybex EdgeTests:

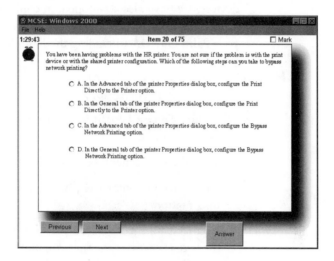

Sybex Flashcards for PCs and Handheld Devices   The "flashcard" style of question offers an effective way to quickly and efficiently test your understanding of the fundamental concepts covered in the exam. The Sybex MCSA/MCSE Flashcards set consists of more than 150 questions presented in a special engine developed specifically for this Study Guide series. Here's what the Sybex MCSA/MCSE Flashcards interface looks like:

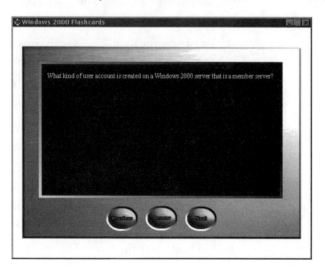

Because of the high demand for a product that will run on handheld devices, we have also developed, in conjunction with Land-J Technologies, a version of the flashcard questions that you can take with you on your Palm OS PDA (including the PalmPilot and Handspring's Visor).

How Do You Use This Book?

This book provides a solid foundation for the serious effort of preparing for the exam. To best benefit from this book, you may wish to use the following study method:

1. Take the Assessment Test to identify your weak areas.

2. Study each chapter carefully. Do your best to fully understand the information.

3. Complete all the hands-on exercises in the chapter, referring back to the text as necessary so that you understand each step you take. If you don't have access to a lab environment in which you can complete the exercises, install and work with the exercises available in the WinSim 2000 software included with this Study Guide.

To do the exercises in this book, your hardware should meet the minimum hardware requirements for Windows 2000 Server.

4. Read over the Real World Scenarios to improve your understanding of how to use what you learn in the book.

5. Study the Exam Essentials and Key Terms to make sure you are familiar with the areas you need to focus on.

6. Answer the review questions at the end of each chapter. If you prefer to answer the questions in a timed and graded format, install the EdgeTests from the book's CD and answer the chapter questions there instead of in the book.

7. Take note of the questions you did not understand, and study the corresponding sections of the book again.

8. Go back over the Exam Essentials and Key Terms.

9. Go through the Study Guide's other training resources, which are included on the book's CD. These include WinSim 2000, electronic flashcards, the electronic version of the chapter review questions (try taking them by objective), and the two bonus exams.

To learn all the material covered in this book, you will need to study regularly and with discipline. Try to set aside the same time every day to study, and select a comfortable and quiet place in which to do it. If you work hard, you will be surprised at how quickly you learn this material. Good luck!

Contacts and Resources

To find out more about Microsoft Education and Certification materials and programs, to register with Prometric or VUE, or to obtain other useful certification information and additional study resources, check the following resources:

Microsoft Training and Certification Home Page
www.microsoft.com/traincert
This website provides information about the MCP program and exams. You can also order the latest Microsoft Roadmap to Education and Certification.

Microsoft TechNet Technical Information Network
www.microsoft.com/technet
800-344-2121
Use this website or phone number to contact support professionals and system administrators. Outside the United States and Canada, contact your local Microsoft subsidiary for information.

PalmPilot Training Product Development: Land-J
www.land-j.com
407-359-2217
Land-J Technologies is a consulting and programming business currently specializing in application development for the 3Com PalmPilot Personal Digital Assistant. Land-J developed the Palm version of the EdgeTests, which is included on the CD that accompanies this Study Guide.

Prometric
www.prometric.com
800-755-3936
Contact Prometric to register to take an MCP exam at any of more than 800 Prometric Testing Centers around the world.

Virtual University Enterprises (VUE)

www.vue.com

888-837-8616

Contact the VUE registration center to register to take an MCP exam at one of the VUE Testing Centers.

MCP Magazine Online

www.mcpmag.com

Microsoft Certified Professional Magazine is a well-respected publication that focuses on Windows certification. This site hosts chats and discussion forums, and tracks news related to the MCP program. Some of the services cost a fee, but they are well worth it.

Windows & .NET Magazine

www.windows2000mag.com

You can subscribe to this magazine or read free articles at the website. The study resource provides general information on Windows 2000.

Cramsession on Brainbuzz.com

cramsession.brainbuzz.com

Cramsession is an online community focusing on all IT certification programs. In addition to discussion boards and job locators, you can download one of several free cram sessions, which are nice supplements to any study approach you take.

Assessment Test

1. Which of the following are benefits of using Active Directory? (Choose all that apply.)

   A. Hierarchical object structure

   B. Fault-tolerant architecture

   C. Ability to configure centralized and distributed administration

   D. Flexible replication

2. The AcmeToyStore Corporation is configuring a website using IIS. This website will allow the public to access the company's online toy catalog. Which of the following directory security options should be configured?

   A. Anonymous access

   B. Basic access

   C. Remote access

   D. Public access

3. Which of the following default Active Directory containers includes the Print Operators and Server Operators groups?

   A. Builtin

   B. Users

   C. Foreign Security Principals

   D. Windows NT

4. Which of the following disk configurations are supported as basic storage on Windows 2000 Server? (Choose all that apply.)

   A. Primary partition

   B. Extended partition

   C. Mirrored volume

   D. RAID-5 volume

5. When running in native mode, which of the following group scope changes *cannot* be performed?

   A. Universal to Global

   B. Domain Local to Universal

   C. Global to Universal

   D. Domain Local to Global

6. You have just attached your server to a dedicated connection between a satellite and your company's home office. The dedicated connection is providing you with three addresses. All clients must have direct access to a DOS-based database to enter and retrieve information. What is the best way to attach your 18 clients to the database?

   A. ICS

   B. Proxy DNS

   C. Proxy server

   D. NAT

7. The DHCP relay agent serves which function on the network?

   A. It listens for DHCP messages on a network and forwards them to a DHCP server on another network.

   B. It accepts DHCP messages from multiple networks and consolidates them for a single DHCP server.

   C. It allows DHCP clients to use WINS services.

   D. It relays DHCP requests to a Dynamic DNS server.

8. You have finally completed your migration from Windows NT Servers to Windows 2000 Servers. You have upgraded all the services necessary to maintain the existing Windows NT services, and you plan to deploy Active Directory after you finish migrating all the clients. You also are planning to move from your current static addressing and implement DHCP before you start the Active Directory deployment. Thus, you take the time to build all the necessary scopes, and you take advantage of redesigning the IP address space using the large network's private 10.0.0.0 address. Since you have the DHCP server all ready to go, you test it from one of your Windows workstations by selecting the DHCP option at the client. You restart the workstation, and it obtains the address from the DHCP server. Since you are not yet ready to move to DHCP, you select the other option and shut down the machine. When the user comes back the next day, she cannot connect to anything on the network. What is the most likely cause of this problem?

   A. You need to edit the Registry to remove the DHCP information.

   B. You have to restart the machine twice to reset the IP configuration.

   C. When you change the static IP option to DHCP, you lose most of your static information.

   D. The DHCP server on the network is conflicting with the static IP addresses of the clients.

9. You configure a member server in your domain as a DHCP server. You find that the server is not issuing any IP information to clients. What final step must you take in order for your DHCP server to work properly?

   A. You must manually authorize the DHCP server in the domain.

   B. You must wait a few minutes for the DHCP server to be automatically authorized.

   C. DHCP doesn't work on member servers.

   D. The DHCP server needs to be unauthorized from the domain.

10. You want to make your new antivirus software available to all users. You publish the application, but it doesn't show up in the Programs menu, and users complain that they can't find the software. What is most likely the cause of the problem?

   A. All of the users should install the software manually from the installation CD-ROM.

   B. All of the users should install the software with the Add/Remove Programs Control Panel applet.

   C. Only administrators can install published applications.

   D. You should assign the application rather than publish it.

11. Which of the following features of DNS can be used to improve performance? (Choose all that apply.)

   A. Caching-only servers

   B. DNS forwarding

   C. Secondary servers

   D. Zone delegation

12. If settings on a local machine conflict with settings assigned by a DHCP server, which of the following statements are *not true*? (Choose all that apply.)

   A. None of the conflicting settings will apply.

   B. The DHCP-assigned settings override the locally assigned settings.

   C. Whichever settings are applied first take effect.

   D. The locally assigned settings override the DHCP-assigned settings.

13. Which of the following is the standard used by Active Directory to query Active Directory information?

   A. NetBEUI

   B. NetBIOS

   C. LDAP

   D. IPX/SPX

14. Which of the following operations *cannot* be performed using the Active Directory Users and Computers tool?

   A. Creating shared folders

   B. Creating printers

   C. Creating domains

   D. Creating organizational units

15. Where should you install a parallel installation?

   A. On the same partition as the main installation

   B. On a different partition from the main installation

   C. On a striped volume

   D. On a mirrored volume

16. Which of the following statements regarding auditing and Active Directory is false?

   A. Auditing prevents users from attempting to guess passwords.

   B. Systems administrators should regularly review audit logs for suspicious activity.

   C. Auditing information can be generated when users view specific information within Active Directory.

   D. Auditing information can be generated when users modify specific information within Active Directory.

17. Which of the following is *not* a valid type of resource record (RR)?

   A. SRV

   B. PTR

   C. A

   D. MX

   E. PDC

18. Which of the following access permissions can be assigned to a website? (Choose all that apply.)

   A. Read

   B. Write

   C. Full Control

   D. Directory Browsing

19. Which of the following tools can be used to create GPO links to Active Directory? (Choose all that apply.)

   A. Active Directory Users and Computers

   B. Active Directory Domains and Trusts

   C. Active Directory Sites and Services

   D. Delegation of Control Wizard

20. To reject any incoming call from a client that can't use a specified level of encryption, you would do which of the following?

   A. Turn off the No Encryption check box on the Encryption tab of the remote access policy's profile.

   B. Turn off the No Encryption check box on the Security tab of the server's Properties dialog box.

   C. Create a new remote access profile named Require Encryption.

   D. Check the Require Encryption check box in each user's profile.

21. Darryl wants to use Terminal Services to remotely administer 25 servers within his organization. He wants to ensure that he meets all of the proper licensing agreements for Terminal Services. Which license does he need in order to run Terminal Services in remote administration mode?

   A. Windows 2000 Terminal Services Client Access license

   B. Windows 2000 Terminal Services Internet Connector license

   C. Windows 2000 Server license

   D. Windows 2000 Professional license

22. What are the three private address ranges? (Choose all that apply.)

    A. 10.x.y.z

    B. 168.192.x.y

    C. 172.16.x.y

    D. 192.168.x.y

23. A GPO at the domain level sets a certain option to Disabled, while a GPO at the OU level sets the same option to Enabled. No other GPOs have been created. Which option can a systems administrator use to ensure that the effective policy for objects within the OU is Enabled?

    A. Block Policy Inheritance on the OU

    B. Block Policy Inheritance on the site

    C. Set No Override on the OU

    D. Set No Override on the site

24. Which of the following operations is not supported by Active Directory?

    A. Assigning applications to users

    B. Assigning applications to computers

    C. Publishing applications to users

    D. Publishing applications to computers

25. You want to assign multiple logical subnet addresses to DHCP clients on a single physical network. What must you configure in order to do this?

    A. A subscope

    B. A superscope

    C. A scope

    D. Exclusions

26. Which of the following is used to automatically assign TCP/IP information to clients?

   A. WINS

   B. DNS

   C. DHCP

   D. RRAS

27. Which of the following statements is true regarding the actions that occur when a software package is removed from a GPO that is linked to an OU?

   A. The application will be automatically uninstalled for all users within the OU.

   B. Current application installations will be unaffected by the change.

   C. The systems administrator may determine the effect.

   D. Each user that the application is published or assigned to may determine the effect.

28. If you had a striped volume set with five 10GB drives, how much space would be available to store data?

   A. 40GB

   B. 45GB

   C. 48GB

   D. 50GB

29. What button on the TCP/IP Properties screen would you click to manually configure more than two DNS servers?

   A. Use The Following IP Address

   B. Obtain DNS Server Address Automatically

   C. OK

   D. Advanced

30. How do you start the Recovery Console? (Choose all that apply.)

   A. Run the `WINNT32 /CMDCONS` command from the Windows 2000 Server CD-ROM. Then choose Recovery Console from the Startup Options menu.

   B. Use the Windows 2000 Server Setup disks.

   C. Use the Windows 2000 Server boot disk.

   D. Select Start ➢ Programs ➢ Administrative Tools ➢ Recovery Console.

31. Which of the following is a valid role for a Windows 2000 Server computer? (Choose all that apply.)

   A. Stand-alone server

   B. Member server

   C. Domain controller

   D. Active Directory controller

32. The process through which authority for a portion of a DNS zone is assigned to another DNS server is known as what?

   A. Zone transfer

   B. Forwarding

   C. Delegation

   D. Promotion

33. To convert an existing RRAS server into a VPN server, you must do which of the following? (Choose all that apply.)

   A. Enable remote access on the server's General Properties tab.

   B. Add L2TP or PPTP ports.

   C. Disable IP routing.

   D. Enable the DHCP relay agent.

34. You administer a network that assigns IP addresses via DHCP. You want to make sure that one of the clients always receives the same IP address from the DHCP server. You create an exclusion for that address, but you find that the computer isn't being properly configured at bootup. What's the problem?

A. You excluded the wrong IP address.

B. You need to make a reservation for the client that ties the IP address to the computer's MAC address. Then you must delete the exclusion.

C. You need to create a superscope for the address.

D. You must configure the client manually. You cannot assign the address via the DHCP server.

35. The Active Directory database is stored in which type of servers on the network?

A. Web servers

B. Domain controllers

C. Stand-alone servers

D. Mainframe servers

36. Which of the following types of server configurations *cannot* be used within a single DNS zone?

A. A single primary server with no secondary servers

B. Multiple primary servers

C. A single primary server with a single secondary server

D. A single primary server with multiple secondary servers

E. A single primary server and multiple caching-only servers

37. You can control VPN access through which of the following mechanisms? (Choose two.)

A. Individual user account properties

B. Remote access policies

C. Remote access profiles

D. Group Policy objects

38. Group Policy can be linked to which of the following Active Directory objects?

A. Organizational units (OUs)

B. Users

C. Computers

D. Groups

39. To enable dial-up users to get a fixed IP address, you must do which of the following?

A. Define an address pool on the IP tab of the server's Properties dialog box.

B. Define an address pool in the remote access policy.

C. Add a DHCP address range for the dial-up users.

D. Disable the DHCP address allocator.

40. Which of the following services is not considered a part of Internet Information Services (IIS)?

A. SMTP

B. SNMP

C. NNTP

D. HTTP

41. Which of the following is *not* considered a security principal?

   A. Users

   B. Security groups

   C. Distribution groups

   D. Computers

42. Which of the following file extensions is used primarily for backward compatibility with non–Windows Installer setup programs?

   A. .msi

   B. .mst

   C. .zap

   D. .aas

43. A GPO at the domain level sets a certain option to Disabled, while a GPO at the OU level sets the same option to Enabled. All other settings are left at their default. Which setting will be effective for objects within the OU?

   A. Enabled

   B. Disabled

   C. No Effect

   D. Not Configured

44. Shared Folder objects can refer to which of the following types of shares? (Choose all that apply.)

   A. Existing Windows NT shares

   B. Existing Windows 2000 shares

   C. Printer shares

   D. File shares

Answers to Assessment Test

1. **A, B, C, D.** All of the options listed are benefits of using the Active Directory. See Chapter 4 for more information.

2. **A.** If the public will access your website, you should configure anonymous access. See Chapter 12 for more information.

3. **A.** The Builtin container contains the default groups that are available within the domain. See Chapter 5 for more information.

4. **A, B.** Mirrored volumes and RAID-5 volumes are supported disk configurations for Windows 2000 Server, but they are dynamic storage, not basic storage. See Chapter 9 for more information.

5. **A.** The scope of universal groups cannot be changed. See Chapter 6 for more information.

6. **D.** Because transparent access to a database is required, the best solution is NAT. ICS would change port addresses, which would be unacceptable in a database access. A proxy server is normally used for caching and single-address access and is incompatible with non-ODBC–compliant databases. See Chapter 11 for more information.

7. **A.** The DHCP relay agent allows you to use a DHCP server that resides on one network with clients that live on a separate network. See Chapter 10 for more information.

8. **C.** The static IP configuration information is lost when you select the Obtain An IP Address Automatically radio button. If you plan to go back to the static address, make sure that you write down the IP information before you change this setting. You don't need to edit the Registry to modify IP address configuration. You do have to restart the machine when changing back to a static address, but you don't need to do it twice. DHCP servers don't conflict with static addresses. It's very common to have static IP addresses on certain machines while the others receive their IP configuration from the DHCP server. See Chapter 1 for more information.

9. A.   The server must be authorized in Active Directory or it won't issue any leases. See Chapter 2 for more information.

10. D.   Applications that you want to be available to all users should be assigned rather than published. Published applications are available only to users you specify. See Chapter 8 for more information.

11. A, B, C, D.   One of the major design goals for DNS was support for scalability. All of the features listed can be used to increase the performance of DNS. See Chapter 3 for more information.

12. A, B, C.   Local settings always override settings specified by the DHCP server. See Chapter 1 for more information.

13. C.   Active Directory uses the Lightweight Directory Access Protocol. See Chapter 4 for more information.

14. C.   Domains can be created only through the use of the Active Directory Installation Wizard. See Chapter 5 for more information.

15. B.   You should always install a parallel installation on a separate partition. Otherwise, both installations could end up overwriting necessary files in the Program Files and Documents and Settings folders. See Chapter 9 for more information.

16. A.   The purpose of auditing is to monitor and record actions taken by users. Auditing will not prevent users from attempting to guess passwords (although it might discourage them from trying, if they are aware it is enabled). See Chapter 6 for more information.

17. E.   There is no PDC type of resource record. All of the other options are standard DNS RRs. See Chapter 3 for more information.

18. A, B, D.   You cannot assign Full Control access to a website. See Chapter 12 for more information.

19. A, C.   Both the Active Directory Users and Computers tool and the Active Directory Sites and Services tool can be used to create GPO links to Active Directory. See Chapter 7 for more information.

20. A. The profile associated with each remote access policy controls whether that policy will require, allow, or disallow encryption. To force encryption, create a policy that disallows using No Encryption. See Chapter 10 for more information.

21. C. You do not need any special Terminal Services licenses in order to run Terminal Services in remote administration mode. See Chapter 12 for more information.

22. A, C, D. The private address ranges are $10.x.y.z$, $172.16.x.y$, and $192.168.x.y$. The private address ranges will not be forwarded by a router. See Chapter 11 for more information.

23. A. By blocking policy inheritance on the OU, you can be sure that other settings defined at higher levels do not change the settings at the OU level. However, this will work only if the No Override option is not set at the site level. See Chapter 7 for more information.

24. D. Applications cannot be published to computers. See Chapter 8 for more information.

25. B. A superscope is just a convenience for the administrator—it's a way to pass out a consistent group of options to multiple scopes. See Chapter 2 for more information.

26. C. The Dynamic Host Configuration Protocol (DHCP) automatically assigns TCP/IP address information to clients. Optionally, DHCP information can be used to automatically update DNS databases. See Chapter 3 for more information.

27. C. The systems administrator can specify whether the application will be uninstalled or if future installations will be prevented. See Chapter 8 for more information.

28. D. Striped volume sets do not contain parity information and are not fault tolerant. You can use the entire striped volume set to store data. See Chapter 9 for more information.

29. D.   Click the Advanced button to display the Advanced TCP/IP Settings dialog box. You can then configure DNS information in the DNS tab of that dialog box. See Chapter 1 for more information.

30. A, B.   In order to access the Recovery Console, you must first run the WINNT32 /CMDCONS command from the Windows 2000 Server CD-ROM. This adds the Recovery Console option to the Startup Options menu. Alternatively, you can run the console from the Windows 2000 Server Setup disks. See Chapter 9 for more information.

31. A, B, C.   Based on the business needs of an organization, a Windows 2000 Server computer can be configured in any of the first three roles. See Chapter 4 for more information.

32. C.   Delegation is used to break zones apart into smaller units for performance or manageability. See Chapter 3 for more information.

33. A, B.   RRAS includes the needed components to act as a VPN server, but you have to enable them and then create appropriate VPN ports. See Chapter 11 for more information.

34. B.   Excluded addresses are just marked as excluded; the DHCP server doesn't maintain any information about them. Reserved addresses are marked as reserved. See Chapter 2 for more information.

35. B.   Domain controllers are stored in the Active Directory database. See Chapter 4 for more information.

36. B.   DNS does not allow for the use of more than one primary server per zone. See Chapter 3 for more information.

37. A, B.   You can allow users to make VPN connections by modifying individual account properties; if you're using a native-mode Windows 2000 domain, you can also use remote access policies. See Chapter 11 for more information.

38. A.   Group Policy settings are linked at the OU level and may affect other object types within that OU. See Chapter 6 for more information.

39. A. To assign static IP addresses to dial-up clients, you have to define a pool of addresses on the server; this pool is used instead of allowing DHCP assignments to clients. See Chapter 10 for more information.

40. B. The Simple Network Management Protocol (SNMP) is not installed as a part of IIS. See Chapter 12 for more information.

41. C. Permissions and security settings cannot be made on distribution groups. Distribution groups are used only for the purpose of sending e-mail. See Chapter 6 for more information.

42. C. Initialization ZAP files are used primarily to point to older programs that do not use Windows Installer. See Chapter 8 for more information.

43. A. Assuming that the default settings are left in place, the Group Policy setting at the OU level will take effect. See Chapter 7 for more information.

44. A, B. A Shared Folder object refers to resources by its UNC name and can point to a Windows NT or Windows 2000 share. See Chapter 5 for more information.

Installing and Configuring Network Protocols

MICROSOFT EXAM OBJECTIVES COVERED IN THIS CHAPTER:

✓ **Troubleshoot routing. Diagnostic utilities include the tracert command, the ping command, and the ipconfig command.**

- Validate local computer configuration by using the ipconfig, arp, and route commands.
- Validate network connectivity by using the tracert, ping, and pathping commands.

✓ **Configure and troubleshoot TCP/IP on servers and client computers. Considerations include subnet masks, default gateways, network IDs, and broadcast addresses.**

- Configure client computer TCP/IP properties.
- Validate client computer network configuration by using the winipcfg, ipconfig, and arp commands.
- Validate client computer network connectivity by using the ping command.

✓ **Configure, administer, and troubleshoot DHCP on servers and client computers.**

- Detect unauthorized DHCP servers on a network.
- Configure authorization of DHCP servers.
- Configure client computers to use dynamic IP addressing.
- Configure DHCP server properties.
- Create and configure a DHCP scope.

✓ **Troubleshoot name resolution on client computers. Considerations include WINS, DNS, NetBIOS, the Hosts file, and the Lmhosts file.**

- Configure client computer name resolution properties.
- Troubleshoot name resolution problems by using the nbtstat, ipconfig, nslookup, and netdiag commands.
- Create and configure a Hosts file for troubleshooting name resolution problems.
- Create and configure an Lmhosts file for troubleshooting name resolution problems.

Only the "Configure client computers to use dynamic IP addressing" subobjective under the "Configure, administer, and troubleshoot DHCP on servers and client computers objective is covered in this chapter. The subobjectives related to DHCP are covered in Chapter 2, "Managing the Dynamic Host Configuration Protocol." In addition, the nbtstat and nslookup commands, as well as the Hosts and Lmhosts files, are covered in Chapter 3, "Windows 2000 Name Resolution."

Network protocols are the most fundamental part of the network that you will need to know for the exam. With the release of Windows 2000, Microsoft heavily endorsed the ubiquitous TCP/IP protocol. NetBIOS, implemented with NetBEUI in Windows 2000, is an aging protocol that is nonetheless still supported by Microsoft. You will need to understand both of these protocols in order to pass the exam. But before you dive into the specifics of network protocols, you should understand what protocols are and why you need to know how they work. The first section of this chapter gives you an overview of protocols in general. Then you will learn about the specific protocols that are typically used in Windows 2000. Finally, you will learn how to install, configure, and troubleshoot TCP/IP, which is the most commonly used and accepted network protocol today.

How Protocols Work

A *protocol* is a set of basic steps that both parties (or computers) must perform in the right order. For instance, for one computer to send a message to another computer, the first computer must perform the steps given in the following general example:

1. Break the data into small sections called packets.

2. Add addressing information to the packets, identifying the destination computer.

3. Deliver the data to the network card for transmission over the network.

The receiving computer must perform the inverse of these steps:

1. Accept the data from the network adapter card.

2. Remove the transmitting information that was added by the transmitting computer.

3. Reassemble the packets of data into the original message.

Each computer needs to perform these steps, in the same way and in the correct order, so that the data will arrive and be reassembled correctly. If one computer uses a protocol with different steps or even the same steps with different parameters (such as different sequencing, timing, or error correction), the two computers won't be able to communicate with each other.

Network Packets

Networks primarily send and receive small chunks of data called *packets*. Network protocols construct, modify, and disassemble packets as they move data across the network. Packets have the following components:

- A source address specifying the sending computer

- A destination address specifying where the packet is being sent

- Instructions that tell the computer how to pass the data along

- Reassembly information (if the packet is part of a longer message)

- The data to be transmitted to the remote computer (often called the *packet payload*)

- Error-checking information to ensure that the data arrives intact

These components are assembled into slightly larger chunks; each packet contains three distinct parts, listed below, and each part contains some of the components listed above.

Header A typical header includes an alert signal to indicate that the data is being transmitted, source and destination addresses, and clock information to synchronize the transmission.

Data This is the actual data being sent. It can vary (depending on the network type) from 48 bytes to 4 kilobytes.

Trailer   The content of the trailer (or even the existence of a trailer) varies among network types, but it typically includes a cyclic redundancy check (CRC). The CRC helps the network determine whether a packet has been damaged in transmission.

Network Protocols and Windows 2000

Microsoft networking products come with four network transports, and each is intended for networks of different sizes with different requirements. Each network transport has various strengths and weaknesses. In general, *NetBEUI* is intended for small, single-server networks. *NWLink* is intended for networks that require access to Novell NetWare file servers. AppleTalk's primary use is interoperating with Macintosh computers (a topic that's too specialized to discuss further here). TCP/IP is a complex transport sufficient for globe-spanning networks such as the Internet, and Microsoft is doing everything possible to position TCP/IP as a one-size-fits-all network protocol. In Windows 2000, TCP/IP is required to use Active Directory and is the default protocol for Windows 2000.

Microsoft
✓ ***Exam***
Objective

Troubleshoot routing. Diagnostic utilities include the `tracert` command, the `ping` command, and the `ipconfig` command.

Configure and troubleshoot TCP/IP on servers and client computers. Considerations include subnet masks, default gateways, network IDs, and broadcast addresses.

NetBEUI

NetBEUI stands for NetBIOS Enhanced User Interface. (NetBIOS, in turn, stands for Network Basic Input Output System. NetBEUI implements the NetBIOS Frame (NBF) transport protocol, which was developed by IBM in the mid-1980s to support LAN workgroups under OS/2 and LAN Manager.

When IBM developed NetBEUI, they didn't intend for it to allow networked PCs to have enterprise-wide connectivity. Instead, NetBEUI was developed for workgroups of 2 to 200 computers. NetBEUI traffic can't be routed between networks, so it's constrained to small local area networks consisting of relatively small numbers of clients and servers.

NetBEUI has a number of advantages, including these:

- It's fast on small networks, because it has very low overhead.

- It's easy to set up and implement.

- It's largely self-tuning.

NetBEUI has some drawbacks, too:

- NetBEUI cannot be routed between networks. This makes it totally unsuitable for large-scale networks.

- There are few management or maintenance tools for NetBEUI, which makes it difficult to troubleshoot.

- NetBEUI offers very little cross-platform support.

- Microsoft is trying to do away with NetBEUI in favor of TCP/IP.

- NetBEUI consumes an inordinate amount of network bandwidth.

Because it's not widely used, there is—outside the realm of Microsoft operating systems—very little software available to help you analyze Net-BEUI problems. However, there's an alternate flavor of NetBEUI called *NBT* (which stands for NetBIOS over TCP/IP). NBT is routable, and because it uses TCP/IP as its transport, it gains all the advantages of TCP/IP. However, Microsoft is trying to kill off NBT, too.

NWLink

NWLink is Microsoft's implementation of Novell's IPX/SPX protocol stack, which is used in Novell NetWare. In fact, it's fair to say that NWLink is nothing more than IPX for Windows NT. IPX is the protocol; NWLink is the networking component that implements it.

IPX is included with Windows 2000 primarily to allow Windows 2000 clients and servers to interconnect with older Novell NetWare servers and clients. Microsoft clients and servers can then be added to existing network installations, over time easing the migration between platforms and obviating the need for a complete cutover from one networking standard to another. (IPX is also a popular protocol for networked games, guaranteeing its appearance in future Microsoft operating systems for some years to come.)

The advantages of NWLink include the following:

- It's easy to set up and manage.

- It's routable.

- It's easy to connect to installed NetWare servers and clients.

NWLink provides a reasonable middle ground between the simple, non-routable NetBEUI transport protocol and the complex, routable TCP/IP protocol. Like NetBEUI, IPX has many self-tuning characteristics, and it requires little administrative knowledge or skill to set up. However, NWLink has some disadvantages, such as these:

- It is difficult to exchange traffic with other organizations that aren't using IPX/SPX.

- It has limited support in Windows 2000.

- It doesn't support standard network management protocols.

Truly large networks (networks that connect many organizations) may find that NWLink is difficult to work over IPX, because there is no effective central IPX addressing scheme—as there is with TCP/IP—to ensure that two networks don't use the same address numbers. IPX doesn't support the wide range of network management tools available for TCP/IP.

You do not need to know how to work with NWLink for the MCSA exam. However, it is useful to understand why Microsoft included NWLink with Windows 2000.

TCP/IP

TCP/IP is actually two sets of protocols bundled together: the *Transmission Control Protocol (TCP)* and the *Internet Protocol (IP)*. TCP/IP, and a suite of related protocols, was developed by the Department of Defense's Advanced Research Projects Agency (ARPA, or later DARPA) beginning in 1969. Their original goal was to develop network protocols that were robust enough to route around damage caused by nuclear war. Happily, that design goal was never tested, but some aspects of that design have led to the redundant, distributed whole we call the Internet.

TCP/IP is by far the most widely used protocol for interconnecting computers, and it is the protocol of the Internet. This is because, although ARPA originally created TCP/IP to connect military networks together, it provided the protocol standards to government agencies and universities free of charge. The academic world leapt at the chance to use a robust protocol to interconnect their networks, and the Internet was born. Many organizations and individuals collaborated to create higher-level protocols for everything from newsgroups, mail transfer, and file transfer to printing, remote booting, and even document browsing.

To support NetBIOS over TCP/IP, Microsoft has included NBT. If you're already using a TCP/IP network, supporting NBT allows older clients to use NetBIOS-based services without actually allowing any NetBEUI traffic across your network.

TCP/IP is currently the protocol king because of its rapid and widespread adoption. It also brings some significant advantages to the table, including the following:

- Broad connectivity among all types of computers and servers, including direct access to the Internet

- Strong support for routing, using a number of flexible routing protocols

- Support for advanced name and address resolution services (which will be covered in more depth in the next chapter): the Domain Name Service (DNS), the Dynamic Host Configuration Protocol (DHCP), and the Windows Internet Name Service (WINS)

- Support for a wide variety of Internet-standard protocols, including protocols for mail transport, web browsing, and file and print services

- Centralized network number and name assignment, which facilitates internetworking among organizations

If you have a network that spans more than one metropolitan area, or if you want to connect to (or over) the Internet, you'll need to use TCP/IP. It's not fast or easy to use, but it can carry an immense amount of payload and it's mechanically very robust.

TCP/IP also has some disadvantages:

- It's harder to set up than NetBEUI or IPX.

- Its routing and connectivity features impose relatively high overhead.

- It's slower than IPX and NetBEUI.

Even given these disadvantages, we'll all have to learn to live with TCP/IP, since it's the core protocol that Windows 2000 depends on for all its network services.

Understanding IP Addressing

Understanding IP addressing is critical to understanding how IP routing works. An IP address is a numeric identifier assigned to each machine on an IP network. It designates the location of the device it is assigned to on the network. This type of address is a software address, not a hardware address, which is hard-coded into the machine or network interface card.

We're going to assume you're comfortable with binary notation and math for the remainder of this section. You will need this knowledge for the exam.

The Hierarchical IP Addressing Scheme

An IP address is made up of 32 bits of information. These bits are divided into four sections (sometimes called octets or quads) containing one byte (8 bits) each. There are three methods for specifying an IP address:

- Dotted-decimal, as in 130.57.30.56

- Binary, as in 10000010.00111001.00011110.00111000

- Hexadecimal, as in 82 39 1E 38 (rarely used)

All of these examples represent the same IP address.

The 32-bit IP address is a structured or *hierarchical address,* as opposed to a flat or nonhierarchical one. Although IP could have used either flat or hierarchical addressing, its designers chose hierarchical addressing—for a very good reason, as it turns out.

The good news about flat addressing is that it can handle a large number of addresses, namely 4.3 billion (a 32-bit address space with two possible values for each position—either zero or one—giving you 2^{32}, which equals approximately 4.3 billion). The bad news—and the reason why flat addressing isn't used in IP—relates to routing. If every address were totally unique, every router on the Internet would need to store the address of each and every *other* machine on the Internet. It would be fair to say that this would make efficient routing impossible, even if only a fraction of the possible addresses were used.

The solution to this dilemma is to use a hierarchical addressing scheme that breaks the address space into ordered chunks. Instead of treating the entire 32 bits as a unique identifier, one part of the IP address is designated as the *network address* and the other part as a *node address*, giving it a layered, hierarchical structure.

The Network Address   The network address uniquely identifies each network. Every machine on the same network shares that network address as part of its IP address. In the IP address 130.57.30.56, for example, the 130.57 is the network address.

The Node Address   The node address is assigned to, and uniquely identifies, each machine on a network. This part of the address must be unique because it identifies a particular machine—an individual, as opposed to a network that is a group. This number can also be referred to as a host address. In the sample IP address 130.57.30.56, the .30.56 is the node address.

The designers of the Internet decided to create classes of networks based on network size. For the small number of networks possessing a very large number of nodes, they created the Class A network. At the other extreme is the Class C network, reserved for the numerous networks with a small number of nodes. The class distinction for networks in between very large and very small is predictably called the Class B network. How you would subdivide an IP address into a network and node address is determined by the class designation of your network. Table 1.1 provides a summary of the three classes of networks, which will be described in more detail in the following sections.

TABLE 1.1   Network Address Classes

Class	Leading Bit Pattern	Decimal Range of First Byte of Network Address	Maximum Number of Networks	Maximum Nodes per Network
A	0	1–127	127	16,777,214
B	10	128–191	16,384	65,534
C	110	192–223	2,097,152	254

To ensure efficient routing, Internet designers defined a mandate for the leading bits section of the address for each different network class. For example, since a router knows that a Class A network address always starts with a zero, the router might be able to speed a packet on its way after reading only the first bit of its address. Table 1.1 illustrates how the leading bits of a network address are defined.

Some IP addresses are reserved for special purposes and shouldn't be assigned to nodes by network administrators. Table 1.2 lists the members of this exclusive little club, along with their reason for being included in it.

TABLE 1.2   Special Network Addresses

Address	Function
Network address of all zeros	Interpreted to mean "this network."
Network address of all ones	Interpreted to mean "all networks."
Network address 127	Reserved for loopback tests. Designates the local node and allows that node to send a test packet to itself without generating network traffic.
Node address of all zeros	Interpreted to mean "this node."
Node address of all ones	Interpreted to mean "all nodes" on the specified network; for example, 128.2.255.255 means "all nodes" on network 128.2 (Class B address).
Entire IP address set to all zeros	Used to designate the default route.
Entire IP address set to all ones (same as 255.255.255.255)	Broadcast to all nodes on the current network; sometimes called an "all ones broadcast."

Subnetting a Network

If an organization is large and has numerous computers, or if its computers are geographically dispersed, it makes good sense to divide a colossal network into smaller ones connected by routers. These smaller nets are called *subnets*. The benefits to using subnets include the following:

- Reduced network traffic: We all appreciate less traffic of any kind, and so do networks. Without routers, packet traffic could choke the entire network. With routers, most traffic stays on the local network—only packets destined for other networks pass through the router and over to another subnet. This traffic reduction also improves overall performance.

- Simplified management: It's easier to identify and isolate network problems in a group of smaller interconnected networks than within one gigantic one.

One problem with the original IP addressing scheme is that a single network address can be used to refer to multiple physical networks. An organization can request individual network addresses for each of its physical networks. If these requests were granted, there wouldn't be enough addresses to go around. Another problem relates to routers—if each router on the Internet needed to know about every physical network, routing tables would be impossibly huge. There would be an overwhelming amount of administrative overhead to maintain those tables, and the resulting physical overhead on the routers would be massive (CPU cycles, memory, disk space, and so on). Because routers exchange routing information with each other, an additional, related consequence is that a terrific overabundance of network traffic would result.

Although there's more than one way to approach this tangle, the principal solution is the one that we'll cover in this section—*subnetting*. As you might guess, *subnetting* is the process of carving a single IP network into smaller logical subnetworks. This trick is achieved by subdividing the host portion of an IP address to create something called a *subnet address*. The actual subdivision is accomplished through the use of a *subnet mask*.

SUBNET MASKS

For the subnet address scheme to work, every machine on the network must know which part of the host address will be used as the subnet address. This is accomplished by assigning each machine a subnet mask.

The network administrator creates a 32-bit subnet mask comprised of ones and zeros. The ones in the subnet mask represent the positions that refer to the network or subnet addresses. The zeros represent the positions that refer to the host part of the address. This combination is illustrated in Figure 1.1.

FIGURE 1.1   The subnet mask revealed

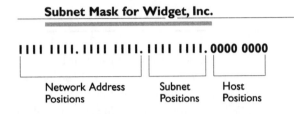

Subnet Mask Code

1s = Positions representing network or subnet addresses
0s = Positions representing the host address

Subnet Mask for Widget, Inc.

1111 1111. 1111 1111. 1111 1111. 0000 0000

Network Address   Subnet   Host
Positions   Positions   Positions

In order to subnet a Class B network, for example, the first two bytes of the subnet mask are ones, formatted as Net.Net.Node.Node. The third byte, normally assigned as part of the host address, is now used to represent the subnet address. Hence, those bit positions are represented with ones in the subnet mask. The fourth byte is the only part in our example that represents the unique host address.

The subnet mask can also be expressed using the decimal equivalents of the binary patterns. The binary pattern of 1111 1111 is the same as decimal 255. Consequently, the subnet mask in our example can be denoted in two ways, as shown in Figure 1.2.

FIGURE 1.2   Different ways to represent the same mask

Subnet Mask in Binary: 1111 1111. 1111 1111. 1111 1111. 0000 0000

Subnet Mask in Decimal: 255 .   255 .   255 .   0

(The spaces in the above example are only for illustrative purposes.
The subnet mask in decimal would actually appear as 255.255.255.0.)

Not all networks need to have subnets and therefore don't need to use subnet masks. In this event, they are said to have a *default subnet mask*. This is basically the same as saying they don't have a subnet address. The default subnet masks for the different classes of networks are shown in Table 1.3. (Now you know where the familiar "255.255.255.0" comes from!)

TABLE 1.3 Special Network Addresses

Class	Format	Default Subnet Mask
A	Net.Node.Node.Node	255.0.0.0
B	Net.Net.Node.Node	255.255.0.0
C	Net.Net.Net.Node	255.255.255.0

Once the network administrator has created the subnet mask and assigned it to each machine, the IP software applies the subnet mask to the IP address to determine its subnet address. The word "mask" carries the implied meaning of "lens" in this case—the IP software looks at its IP address through the lens of its subnet mask to see its subnet address. An illustration of an IP address being viewed through a subnet mask is shown in Figure 1.3.

FIGURE 1.3 Applying the subnet mask

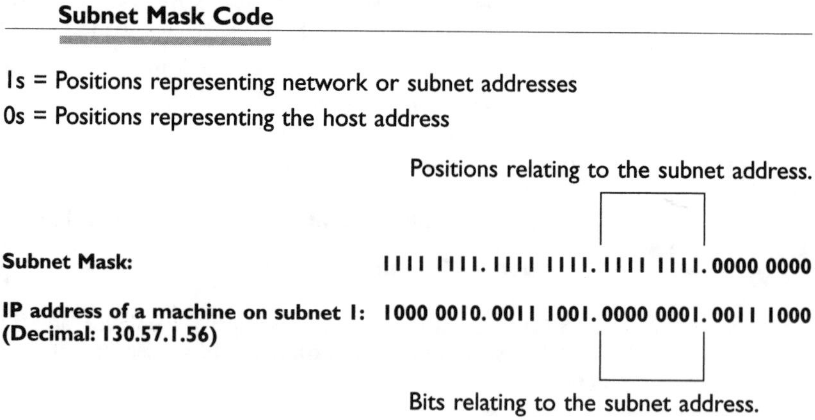

Subnet Mask Code

Is = Positions representing network or subnet addresses
0s = Positions representing the host address

Positions relating to the subnet address.

Subnet Mask: IIII IIII. IIII IIII. IIII IIII. 0000 0000

IP address of a machine on subnet I: 1000 0010. 0011 1001. 0000 0001. 0011 1000
(Decimal: 130.57.1.56)

Bits relating to the subnet address.

In this example, the IP software learns through the subnet mask that, instead of being part of the host address, the third byte of its IP address is now going to be used as a subnet address. The IP software then looks at the bit positions in its IP address that correspond to the mask, which are 0000 0001.

The final step is for the subnet bit values to be matched up with the binary numbering convention and converted to decimal, as illustrated in Figure 1.4.

FIGURE 1.4   Converting the subnet mask to decimal

Binary Numbering Convention

	128	64	32	16	8	4	2	1
Position / Value: ← (continued)	128	64	32	16	8	4	2	1
Widget third byte:	0	0	0	0	0	0	0	1
Decimal Equivalent:							0 + 1 = 1	
Subnet Address:								1

By using the entire third byte of a Class B address as the subnet address, it is easy to set and determine the subnet address. If the Class B network in our example above wants to have a Subnet 6, the third byte of all machines on that subnet will be 0000 0110 (decimal 6 in binary).

Using the entire third byte of a Class B network address for the subnet allows for a fair number of available subnet addresses. One byte dedicated to the subnet provides eight bit positions. Each position can be either a one or a zero, so the calculation is 2^8, or 256. Because you cannot use the two patterns of all zeros and all ones, you must subtract two for a total of 254. Thus, our Class B network can have up to 254 total subnetworks, each with 254 hosts.

Although the official IP specification limits the use of zero as a subnet address, some products actually permit this usage. Microsoft's TCP/IP stack allows it, as does the software in most routers (provided you enable this feature). This gives you one additional subnet. However, you should not use a subnet of zero (all zeros) unless all of the software on your network recognizes this convention.

How Routing Works

In this section, we'll confine the discussion of routing theory and practice to IP routing, even though the same concepts apply to IPX/SPX and AppleTalk routing. The underlying idea is that each packet on a network has a source address and a destination address, which means that any device that receives the packet can inspect its headers to determine where it came from and where it's going. If such a device also has some information about the network's design and implementation—like how long it takes packets to travel over a particular link—it can intelligently change the routing to minimize the total cost, which refers to the time it takes a packet to travel from the source to the destination.

Although Windows 2000 supports routing IPX, AppleTalk, and IP, only IP routing will be covered in this section. It's the most widely used, and it's the one you're most likely to see on the test.

Figure 1.5 shows an imaginary network made up of six interconnected local networks. These networks, imaginatively named A through F, are connected by links of varying speeds and costs. This accurately mirrors what happens in the real world, where it's common for internal networks (or Internet providers) to have multiple ways to establish a link between two points.

FIGURE 1.5 An example network

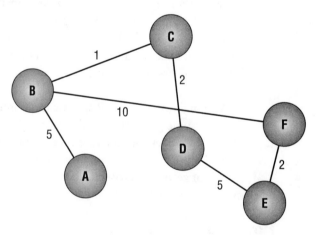

Imagine that a client machine on network B wants to send traffic to a machine on network E. The most obvious route would probably be B to F to E, but you could also use B to C to D to E. Notice the costs: B-F-E has a total cost of 12, while the seemingly longer B-C-D-E actually has a lower cost of

8! That doesn't appear to make sense, since the latter route has a longer path. When you consider what "cost" really means, though, things get better. Assigning link costs is entirely up to you. Normally, you assign costs that reflect your preference for how you want traffic to flow. An expensive or slow link would probably deserve a higher cost than a cheaper or faster link; by assigning your most-expensive links (say, a metered ISDN connection) a high cost, you'd make them too expensive to use if there were less-expensive links available.

Now, revisit Figure 1.5 with the assumption that each circle is really a router. After all, you can hide all the complexity of the network behind a router, since only the router is in charge of moving packets. Call your client machine "X" and your server "Y." When X wants to send traffic to Y, it already knows the destination IP address of its target. X will build a packet, including its IP address as the source and Y's address as the destination. X will then use its default gateway setting to send that packet to router B.

Technically, a gateway and a router are two different things. However, Microsoft uses the terms interchangeably, and so will we.

Router B receives the packet and has both source and destination address information. By examining the IP addresses, it can determine that it doesn't "know" a direct route to the network where Y is located. However, there are two intermediate nodes that claim to know how to reach Y: C and F. Since C has the lowest link cost, the router at B will send the packet to C in a simple routing algorithm. When C receives it, it will go through the same process, forwarding the packet on to D, and so on. Eventually, the packet gets where it's going.

Static Routing

Static routing systems make no attempt to discover other routers or systems on their networks. Instead, you tell the routing engine how to get data to other networks; specifically, you tell it which other networks are reachable from your network by specifying their network addresses and subnet masks, along with a metric for that network. This information goes into the system's routing table, a big list of known routes to other networks. When an outgoing packet arrives at the routing engine, the engine can examine the routing table to select the lowest-cost route to the destination. If there's no explicit entry in the routing table for that network, the packet goes to the default gateway, which is then entrusted with getting the packet where it needs to go.

Static routing is faster and more efficient than dynamic routing. Static routing works well when your network doesn't change much. You can identify the remote networks to which you want to route and then add static routes to them to reflect the costs and topology of your network. In Windows 2000, you maintain static routes with the `route` command, which allows you to either see the contents of the routing table or modify it by adding and removing static routes to individual networks. The `route` command is explained in detail later in this chapter.

Dynamic Routing

By contrast with static routing, *dynamic routing* doesn't depend on your adding fixed, unchangeable routes to remote networks. Instead, a dynamic routing engine can discover its surroundings by finding and communicating with other nearby routers in an internetwork.

This process, usually called *router discovery,* enables a newly added (or rebooted) router to configure itself. This is roughly equivalent to the process that happens when you move into a new neighborhood. Within a short time of your arrival, you'll probably meet most of the people who live nearby, either because they come to you or because you go to them. At that point, you have useful information about the surrounding environment that could come only from people who were already there.

The two major dynamic routing protocols in Windows 2000 are the Routing Information Protocol (RIP) and the Open Shortest Path First (OSPF) protocol. Each has its advantages and disadvantages, but they share some common features and functionality. Each router (whether a hardware device, a Windows 2000 machine, or whatever) is connected to at least two separate physical networks. When the router starts, the only information it has is drawn from its internal routing table. Normally, that means it knows about all the attached networks plus whatever static routes have been previously defined. The router then receives configuration information that tells it about the state and topology of the network.

As time goes on, the network's physical topology can change. For example, take a look at the network in Figure 1.6. If network G suddenly dropped out of the air, the routers in sites A, D, and E would need to readjust their routing tables since they could no longer route traffic directly to G. The process by which this adjustment happens is what makes routing dynamic, and it's also the largest area of difference between the two major dynamic routing protocols for IP.

FIGURE 1.6 A more complex, dynamically routed network

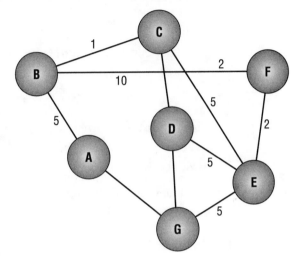

Installing Network Protocols

Windows 2000 supports a wide range of network protocols, both in the set provided with Windows 2000 itself and from third-party vendors. In brief, any vendor who wants to write an NDIS-compatible driver can do so; in theory, any network protocol could potentially have a Windows 2000 version. Microsoft ships protocol stacks for TCP/IP, NetBEUI, Novell's IPX/SPX (which Microsoft calls NWLink), AppleTalk, and DLC. You install or remove all of these protocols using the same interface; once you actually install the protocol, you will still have to configure it.

Installation Basics

You install network protocols through the Local Area Connection Properties dialog box, which lists all of the known protocols on your Windows 2000 machine. Protocols marked with a check indicate that they're bound to the adapter whose properties you're inspecting. Figure 1.7 shows an example of what this dialog box might look like on your machine.

Microsoft ✓ *Exam* *Objective*

Configure and troubleshoot TCP/IP on servers and client computers. Considerations include subnet masks, default gateways, network IDs, and broadcast addresses.

- Configure client computer TCP/IP properties.

Configure, administer, and troubleshoot DHCP on servers and client computers.

- Configure client computers to use dynamic IP addressing.

Troubleshoot name resolution on client computers. Considerations include WINS, DNS, NetBIOS, the Hosts file, and the Lmhosts file.

- Configure client computer name resolution properties.

FIGURE 1.7 The Local Area Connection Properties dialog box shows you which protocols are already installed.

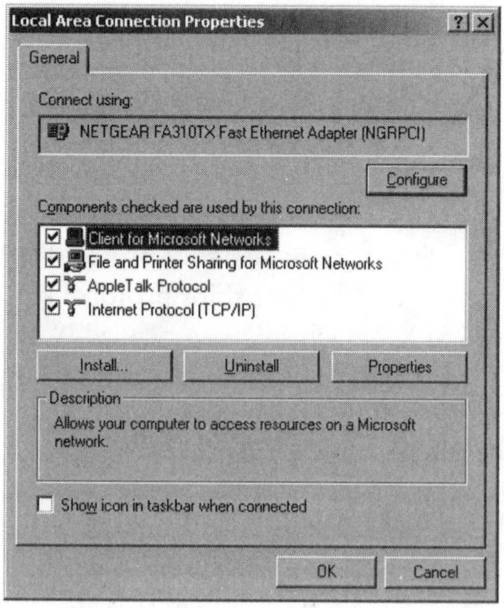

Installing and Configuring TCP/IP

TCP/IP is normally installed as part of the Windows 2000 setup process. This is no accident, since Microsoft would much rather have all its Windows 2000 customers use TCP/IP than NetBIOS. If you need to install TCP/IP manually, you still can. The process for installing it is very similar to the process required to install NWLink, as you can see in Exercise 1.1.

EXERCISE 1.1

Installing TCP/IP

Follow these steps to install the TCP/IP protocol:

1. Open the Network and Dial-Up Connections folder (Start ➤ Settings ➤ Network and Dial-Up Connections).

2. Right-click the Local Area Connection icon and choose Properties. The Local Area Connection Properties dialog box appears, as shown earlier in Figure 1.7.

3. Click the Install button. The Select Network Component Type dialog box appears. Select Protocol and click the Add button.

4. The Select Network Protocol dialog box appears. Choose Internet Protocol (TCP/IP); then click the OK button.

5. If prompted, insert your Windows 2000 CD and click OK.

6. Click the Close button in the Local Area Connection Properties dialog box.

When you install TCP/IP, it defaults to using DHCP for automatic configuration. If you want to use DHCP for automatic configuration you certainly can, but it's always useful to know how to manually configure a TCP/IP connection (especially since Microsoft will be asking you to prove you know how to as part of the exam!). Now you'll see what that configuration process entails.

See Chapter 2 for more information on DHCP.

Configuring Basic TCP/IP Settings

If you've bought into the rap that TCP/IP is convoluted and difficult to configure, Windows 2000's basic TCP/IP Properties dialog box may surprise you. TCP/IP actually requires only two pieces of information to function: the IP address you want to use for this system and the subnet mask that corresponds to the network subnet the client is on. For example, in the Windows 2000 classes we teach, we set up an in-classroom network that doesn't connect to any outside networks, including the Internet. We don't need a *default gateway* since that's used for routing, and we don't set up DNS until later in the class. With only these two parameters, machines can communicate with each other (although not having DNS is inconvenient, since it means we have to enter IP addresses by hand).

Figure 1.8 shows the Internet Protocol (TCP/IP) Properties dialog box. You reach this dialog box by opening the Local Area Connection icon, selecting the Internet Protocol (TCP/IP), and clicking the Properties button. Of course, if you have multiple network adapters in a single computer, you can set independent TCP/IP properties for each adapter. Depending on what you want to do, you'll use either the automatic configuration buttons or the text fields.

FIGURE 1.8 The basic TCP/IP Properties dialog box

Internet Protocol (TCP/IP) Properties	? |X|

General

You can get IP settings assigned automatically if your network supports this capability. Otherwise, you need to ask your network administrator for the appropriate IP settings.

○ Obtain an IP address automatically
● Use the following IP address:

IP address:	192 . 168 . 0 . 144
Subnet mask:	255 . 255 . 255 . 0
Default gateway:	192 . 168 . 0 . 1

○ Obtain DNS server address automatically
● Use the following DNS server addresses:

| Preferred DNS server: | 192 . 168 . 0 . 144 |
| Alternate DNS server: | 208 . 147 . 155 . 2 |

Advanced...

OK   Cancel

If You Want to Use DHCP

If you're configuring a Windows 2000 Professional machine, chances are probably pretty good that you're using DHCP with it. In that case, the default TCP/IP settings will work fine for you, since they configure the TCP/IP stack to get configuration parameters from any available DHCP server. Remember that you can mix and match DHCP and non-DHCP machines; on a single client, you can use DHCP to get everything except DNS server addresses if you want to. You have two basic choices:

- To configure a client to get its TCP/IP configuration information from a DHCP server, leave the Obtain An IP Address Automatically radio button selected.

- If you're using DHCP for basic IP addressing and you want to accept DNS server addresses from the DHCP server, leave the Obtain DNS Server Address Automatically radio button selected.

If You Don't Want to Use DHCP

We recommend against using DHCP on servers, since they're not nearly as dynamic as clients. Ideally, you won't reboot servers unless they *need* it, and you won't be moving them around. Therefore, the "dynamic" in DHCP isn't really useful, and its other benefits are outweighed by the comfort that comes from knowing that your server has a correct and unchanging IP configuration. If you want to configure the TCP/IP settings yourself, start by selecting the Use The Following IP Address radio button, and then fill in the following fields:

- In the IP Address field, enter the IP address you want to use for this machine. Remember that Windows 2000 won't do any kind of sanity checking. The most common mistake people make with this field is to enter an address that doesn't match the address range they're using on their network.

- In the Subnet Mask field, enter the appropriate subnet mask for your network.

- If you want this machine to be able to route packets to other networks, enter the gateway or router address you want it to use in the Default Gateway field. Again, remember that Windows 2000 will slavishly use whatever address you enter here, so make sure it's right.

- If you're using DNS on your network, enter the first DNS server you want this client to talk to in the Preferred DNS Server field. It's critical to get this right on a Windows 2000 network since DNS is required for Active Directory services. If you want to specify another server to use when the preferred server is unavailable or can't resolve a DNS query, enter it in the Alternate DNS Server field. (You can also specify additional servers, as you'll see in the following section on the Advanced TCP/IP Properties dialog box.)

Configuring Advanced TCP/IP Settings

The Advanced button in the TCP/IP Properties dialog box brings up something that looks more like what you'd expect from TCP/IP. The Advanced TCP/IP Properties dialog box contains four tabs that let you extend and override the settings from the simpler dialog box shown in Figure 1.8.

Expanding the Basic Settings

The basic configuration dialog box you saw earlier lets you enter one IP address, one subnet mask, and one default gateway. For the majority of systems that's enough, but what if you want to configure a machine that can communicate on multiple IP addresses? For example, if you're setting up an Internet Information Services (IIS) server, you may want it to answer to multiple IP addresses on a single physical network connection (such as the connection that links your server to the Internet). Adding multiple IP addresses in this manner is called multi-homing. You may also want to specify multiple gateways so that an outbound packet sent by your systems can be sent to whichever gateway is "cheapest" (more on what "cheap" means in a minute). The IP Settings tab of the Advanced TCP/IP Properties dialog box allows you to do both of these things. Figure 1.9 shows what it looks like.

FIGURE 1.9   The IP Settings tab of the Advanced TCP/IP Settings dialog box

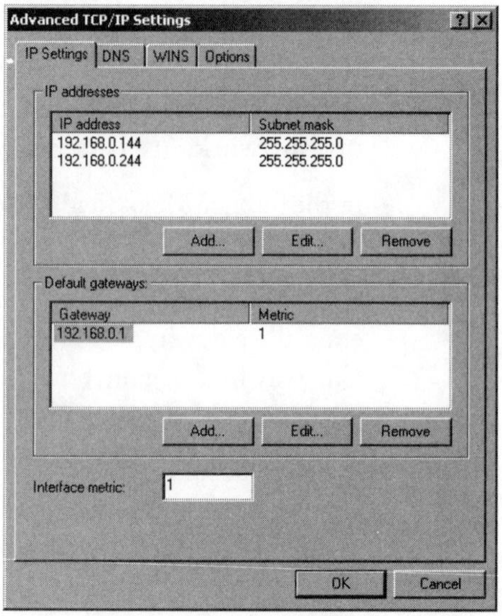

Your options on the IP Setting tab include the following:

- The IP Addresses control group lists the IP addresses currently defined for this network adapter. You can add new address bindings, edit existing bindings, or remove an address with the buttons at the bottom of the control group. Once you add an address here and close all open network properties dialog boxes (including the Local Area Connection dialog box), any changes you make here take effect.

- The Default Gateways control group shows the routing gateways that are currently defined *for this computer only*. Each gateway has an IP address (to which the client sends outbound packets) and an associated metric, or cost. When deciding where to send packets bound for other networks, Windows 2000 examines its internal TCP/IP routing table to see whether it already "knows" how to get packets to the destination network. If so, it uses that route. If not, it uses the default gateway. If you specify more than one default gateway, the system chooses a gateway by selecting the one that has the lowest cost. If that gateway is down, or if it can't get packets to the destination system, Windows 2000 tries the next-most-expensive gateway. This process repeats until the packets arrive at their destination or until the system runs out of gateways to try.

Expanding DNS and WINS Settings

If all you want to do is configure your clients to use two DNS servers, you can use the Preferred and Alternate Server Configuration fields in the basic TCP/IP Properties dialog box. The DNS tab of the Advanced TCP/IP Properties dialog box allows you to specify more than two servers; in addition, you can control which DNS domain names are appended to search queries when you don't specify a fully qualified domain name. However, we want to point out the most salient feature here as well: The DNS Server Addresses, In Order Of Use field (and its associated buttons) lets you specify multiple DNS servers. When the client resolver needs an address looked up, it starts by querying the server at the top of this list and working down the list until it finds an answer or runs out of servers to query. Adding servers to this list is a quick way to improve your clients' fault tolerance, since losing the preferred and alternate DNS servers will otherwise result in a loss of DNS service to the clients. Figure 1.10 shows the DNS tab.

DNS and WINS are explained in detail in Chapter 3.

FIGURE 1.10 The DNS tab of the Advanced TCP/IP Properties dialog box

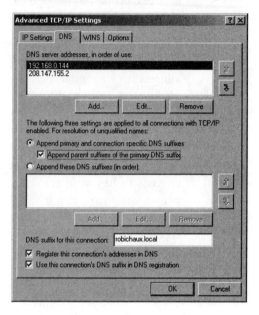

Likewise, the WINS tab (not shown here) allows you to specify multiple WINS servers. In fact, the only place where you can specify which WINS servers to use is in this tab, because Microsoft is trying to move you away from using WINS (and NetBIOS!) to using pure TCP/IP and DNS. Finally, the Options tab lets you configure protocol-specific options, including whether the IP Security (IPSec) extensions are used and whether any type of packet filtering is enabled.

Before attempting Exercise 1.2 on your network, be sure to choose an IP address *not* in use by any other host or device on your network!

EXERCISE 1.2

Configuring TCP/IP Settings

Follow these steps to add a second IP address to your existing NIC. Note that this exercise assumes that you're not using DHCP on that NIC, since you can't assign additional addresses to a DHCP-enabled NIC.

1. Choose an IP address on your network that's not currently in use by another device (e.g., 169.254.0.202). Make sure you know the correct subnet mask to use with that IP address (e.g., 255.255.255.0).

2. Open the Network and Dial-Up Connections folder (Start ➢ Settings ➢ Network and Dial-Up Connections).

3. Right-click the Local Area Connection icon and choose Properties. The Local Area Connection Properties dialog box appears, as shown earlier in Figure 1.7.

4. Select Internet Protocol (TCP/IP) in the Components list, and then click the Properties button. The Internet Protocol (TCP/IP) Properties dialog box appears.

5. Click the Advanced button. The Advanced TCP/IP Properties dialog box appears.

6. Click the Add button in the IP Addresses control group. The TCP/IP Address dialog box appears.

7. Type in the IP address and subnet mask you chose in Step 1.

8. Click the OK button in the Advanced TCP/IP Settings dialog box.

9. Click the OK button in the Internet Protocol (TCP/IP) Properties dialog box.

10. Click the OK button in the Local Area Connection Properties dialog box.

Installing NetBEUI

What about NetBEUI? Up to now, you've been reading that Microsoft is trying its darnedest to drive a pointed wooden stake through NetBEUI and replace it with TCP/IP. Although that's a lofty goal, there are still lots of NetBEUI networks and seats out there in the world, and it's important to know how to install NetBEUI in case you ever need it on a network. The good news is that there's virtually nothing new to learn by this point, because you install NetBEUI using steps that are almost identical to what you've already done while installing NWLink and TCP/IP. In this case, there are actually three separate pieces you may need to install to use NetBEUI:

- You need the NetBEUI protocol itself, which you install using the steps outlined in Exercise 1.1. Note that NetBEUI isn't installed by default on any version of Windows 2000.

- The Client for Microsoft Networks client allows your client machine to attach to shares and printers on other servers, no matter which transport protocol you're using. This is actually the Workstation service, which you may recognize from Windows NT 4.0.

- The File and Print Sharing for Microsoft Networks service allows your machine to act as a server, sharing resources with other machines just like the Server service in Windows NT 4.0.

NetBEUI is designed to be self-tuning, so there are no properties to set for it. However, do you remember the WINS tab on the Advanced TCP/IP Properties dialog box? You can use a radio button there to turn off the use of NetBEUI over TCP/IP. As an alternative, you can remove the protocol or selectively unbind it from some or all of your network adapters.

Real World Scenario

Multiple Protocols Are Nice but Inefficient

Your company has been running Windows NT, Novell NetWare, and even some Banyan that has been floating around for years. There are also connections to old mainframe controllers that still use DLC. Over the years, the connections to these various operating systems have been accomplished piecemeal by adding the clients and protocols at each workstation. This is a common approach, particularly on networks that have grown over time as each special-interest group kept control over its piece of the network. The interoperability features of Windows 2000 (as well as Windows NT before it), specifically the ability to run multiple protocols, are phenomenal. With the NDIS (Network Driver Interface Specification) and TDI (Transport Data Interface), you can run just about as many protocols as you would like. But the ease of this functionality can also cause problems at the other end, because running multiple protocols creates multiple bandwidth consumption and multiple points of management.

Although you can't just throw out the other systems (well, maybe you can throw out the Banyan), there are other ways to approach this interoperability. With the global acceptance of TCP/IP, every major operating system today supports this protocol. This provides an opportunity to remove the other protocols on the network, such as IPX and NetBEUI, which are fading out of use. Each protocol stack brings its own overhead to the network. If you have Windows NT or Windows 9.*x* machines on your network with multiple protocols, you also have multiple instances of services that ride on top of those protocols. For example, if you're running NWLink and TCP/IP, there is a complete browser service (not the Internet kind of browser) that handles NetBIOS requests. This type of redundancy isn't efficient—it just provides another level of complexity where something can go wrong, thus adding to support efforts.

In the future, you'll see the maturity of protocol interoperability applied at the other end of the OSI stack. Using technologies such as XML and HTTP, the network client is becoming simply the browser (yes, the Internet kind) that can be used to access information across different underlying platforms. Until then, the best practice is to work toward the goal of a unified client and to minimize the number of protocols on your network, as well as the number of clients, if possible. Although the functionality is there to support more protocols and more clients, this is another case where more is not necessarily better.

The reality of today is that you will be supporting TCP/IP and for this reason you need to be able to support the basic configurations at the client. You also need to understand how a particular address relates to the network-addressing scheme for your network as a whole. You will not be able to troubleshoot an address problem if you do not understand how a particular address fits into the network and what will happen if it is not appropriate for the subnet.

Troubleshooting Network Protocols

In a perfect world, troubleshooting would never be necessary. However, in the real world, we troubleshoot things constantly to solve problems—such as, why the microwave isn't working (because lightning hit the power line last night) or why one workstation can't see others on the network (its network cable was unplugged).

Microsoft ✓ *Exam* *Objective*

Troubleshoot routing. Diagnostic utilities include the `tracert` **command, the** `ping` **command, and the** `ipconfig` **command.**

- Validate local computer configuration by using the `ipconfig`, `arp`, and `route` commands.

- Validate network connectivity by using the `tracert`, `ping`, and `pathping` commands.

Configure and troubleshoot TCP/IP on servers and client computers. Considerations include subnet masks, default gateways, network IDs, and broadcast addresses.

- Validate client computer network configuration by using the `winipcfg`, `ipconfig`, and `arp` commands.

- Validate client computer network connectivity by using the `ping` command.

Troubleshoot name resolution on client computers. Considerations include WINS, DNS, NetBIOS, the Hosts file, and the Lmhosts file.

- Troubleshoot name resolution problems by using the `nbstat`, `ipconfig`, `nslookup`, and `netdiag` commands.

Knowing how to effectively troubleshoot network problems is an essential part of managing even small networks, and Microsoft expects you to understand basic troubleshooting principles and how to apply them in Windows 2000 networking. Fortunately, you probably already know *what* to check; now you'll read about a set of tools that you can use to verify the proper functioning of your network. More important, you'll learn how to use those tools the right way at the right time.

Putting the Problem into Perspective

When someone complains that their network is broken, your first impulse should be to ask, "Well, what changed?" This might seem weird, but it's actually very practical. If a system is working and then it stops working, obviously something has changed somewhere—either as the result of an explicit change or by accident. Once you can identify what has, or has not, changed, you're ready to start looking for effects of the change and ways to fix whatever's gone wrong.

For example, one of the servers in our home office is a reliable old Intergraph TD-30. Even though it's been running Windows 2000 Advanced Server since very early in the beta cycle, it just keeps trucking along, never giving us any trouble. It happens to have a front-mounted power switch. When we can't contact it, our first suspicion is that it's been powered off.

The first sign of network trouble is usually pretty obvious, too: One machine can't talk to another. Using the above example, if we look at the back panel of *hawk*, our primary Windows 2000 Server, we can see that its NIC has some LEDs that indicate network activity. Just because we see those lights blinking, that doesn't tell us anything about what kind of network data is being carried by the Transport, Application, Session, or Presentation layers of the OSI model—all it tells us is that the Physical-layer components are sending and receiving *something*.

Breaking Down the Problem into Manageable Chunks

You can often save yourself a lot of unnecessary time and effort when troubleshooting a problem by doing something simple: stopping to think. It's hard to keep your wits about you when something's wrong with your network and end users are clamoring for your head on a stick, but if you can clearly identify the problem source, you're well on your way to being able to effectively resolve it without any time-wasting detours.

What Kind of Problem Is It?

Sometimes this can be the most frustrating part of troubleshooting. Getting a phone call or a pager message that says, "The network is down," doesn't tell you much. Is it your connection to the Internet? Your e-mail server? A file server somewhere on your LAN? Without knowing what specific service or connection is unavailable, you won't know what to start fixing.

Some types of problems immediately suggest a solution. For example, if a client calls us and says they get DNS errors when trying to connect to websites, our first two thoughts are that someone's changed their DNS settings or that their DNS servers are down. Likewise, if a user reports a problem reaching a particular share on a server, the problem may be on the client, the server, or the intervening network. If you can, arm yourself with as many details about how the problem is manifesting itself (including exact error messages), when it started, and whether or not it's consistent before you try to figure out what the problem is. Knowing these things beforehand can guide you to an easy, quick solution if it's a problem you've seen and fixed before—but only if you *know* you've seen it before!

Who's Having the Problem?

Knowing which users or computers are affected by a problem is very important since that gives you insight into possible causes (including user mistakes) and helps you select a course of action.

If One User Reports a Problem

If one user on our network has a problem, our experience has been that more often than not the problem stems from some change the user made. Windows contains a lot of interrelated components, and it's not evident to most people that a simple change they made in component A may have unexpected side effects on component B. When troubleshooting an end-user problem, your first question should always involve whether or not they've changed anything on the machine. This includes changing Control Panel settings, installing or removing software, rebooting, or any other action that might have directly or indirectly changed the state of the machine. If you can find out what's changed, that will give you a list of potential places to start looking.

For example, in a class we recently taught, one user complained that he could no longer see the network after doing one of the labs. As it turned out, he had turned his machine into a DHCP server while experimenting, which meant that his previously assigned DHCP address could no longer be used. He'd picked another IP address at random, which turned out not to work with our classroom network configuration. Knowing what changed let us pinpoint and fix the problem quickly.

If Several Users Report the Same Problem

Multiuser troubleshooting is, paradoxically, both easier and harder than single-user troubleshooting. Most of the time, one user can't change anything that will affect other users on the network, so you generally don't have to worry about that variable. On the other hand, the kinds of changes that can accidentally affect connectivity for many users at once are more likely to be things *you've* changed. The first step in fixing this kind of problem is identifying its scope. Is everyone on the network affected? Are only people in one workgroup or on one floor of a building affected? Is the problem limited to the lack of one key service (like DNS), or is all network traffic hosed? Answering this type of question helps you isolate where the problem's occurring so you can concentrate your efforts on that area.

Verifying Physical Connectivity

Physical-layer connectivity is absolutely critical. If you don't have a physical connection to the network you want to talk to, how can you send packets to it? This might seem like an obvious question to ask, but the number of times that we've seen people forget to ask it and look for a more complex—and ultimately nonexistent—problem would boggle your mind. So, when you first notice a network problem, be sure to verify that all of your network cables are correctly connected; that your hub, router, or switch has power; and so on. Take a look at the activity or "heartbeat" lights on your NIC, hub, or switch to see whether the Physical layer is reporting any type of activity.

Knowing something about the scope of the outage helps, too—if all your users begin complaining at once that the network is down, it's unlikely to be the fault of one user's network cable. Contrariwise, if a single user is having trouble with the network, it's unlikely that a router or switch is to blame. If you've properly identified exactly who's having trouble, that may suggest a cause based on your knowledge of the physical topology. When we worked at Intergraph, for example, we used wall-mounted routers that plugged into ordinary power outlets. Every so often, someone on the cleaning crew would unplug a router at night to plug in a floor polisher or vacuum cleaner and then forget to plug it back in. Result: No one in that area would have network access the next morning!

If you verify that all of the physical connections are okay, with power and cabling all in good order, and you *still* have no connectivity, it indicates that the problem probably resides within a higher layer.

Using *Ipconfig, Winipcfg, and Arp* to See What's What

If your problem persists even after you've verified that the physical aspects of the network are all in order, you will need to dig a little deeper using some of the tools that are built into Windows 2000. Ipconfig, winipcfg, and arp are tools you can use to verify that the local computer's configuration information is correct. You might spot a problem in the output of one of these commands and quickly resolve the issue with a simple configuration change.

Ipconfig

Windows 2000 includes a useful tool called ipconfig. As its name implies, it's used to see the configuration of TCP/IP interfaces on your local machine. Typing **ipconfig** into a Windows 2000 command-prompt window presents you with a neat summary of your current IP configuration, including the local DNS name, the IP addresses, and the subnet masks configured for all adapters on the computer. Figure 1.11 shows an example of this output. You can use ipconfig in this mode to get a quick snapshot of its IP configuration, even if it's using DHCP. For example, if you see that the problem machine has no IP address assigned, even though there's a DNS server, it suggests the possibility that the DHCP server isn't authorized in Active Directory.

The ipconfig command does not work on Windows 95/98/Me computers. Use the winipcfg command instead, with the same switches and parameters that you would use with ipconfig.

FIGURE   1.11   The output from *ipconfig*

```
E:\W2KSRV\System32\cmd.exe

E:\temp>ipconfig

Windows 2000 IP Configuration

Ethernet adapter Local Area Connection:

        Connection-specific DNS Suffix  . : robichaux.local
        IP Address. . . . . . . . . . . . : 192.168.0.244
        Subnet Mask . . . . . . . . . . . : 255.255.255.0
        IP Address. . . . . . . . . . . . : 192.168.0.144
        Subnet Mask . . . . . . . . . . . : 255.255.255.0
        Default Gateway . . . . . . . . . : 192.168.0.1

E:\temp>_
```

In addition to the DHCP-related switches that you'll see in Chapter 2, there's another switch of interest to troubleshooters: /all. As you might expect, adding the /all switch causes ipconfig to spill its guts and display everything it knows about the current IP configuration on all installed adapters. In addition to the DNS information and IP address that it ordinarily displays, you'll also get the MAC address of each NIC, the present WINS configuration (if any), and the IP addresses being used for the preferred and alternate DNS servers. Figure 1.12 shows an example of the ipconfig /all output.

FIGURE 1.12   The output from *ipconfig /all*

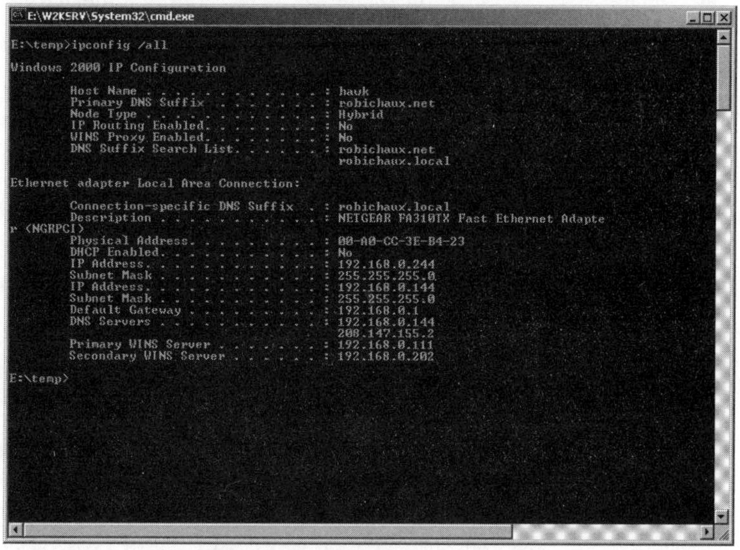

What can you do with all this information? It depends. If you're familiar enough with your network to know what IP address configurations should look like, often a quick check with ipconfig will tell you where the problem lies. For example, you might notice that an adapter that should be DHCP-enabled isn't, or vice versa. Even if you're not familiar with the details of your network, though, knowing how to find the IP addresses and subnet masks in use on your computers can be very valuable. Exercise 1.3 demonstrates how to check configurations with ipconfig.

EXERCISE 1.3

Checking Configurations with *Ipconfig*

Follow these steps to run ipconfig and analyze its output:

1. Open a command window (Start ➤ Run; then enter **cmd** in the Run dialog box and click OK).

2. At the command prompt, type **ipconfig**. Notice that you see an abbreviated display containing the machine's connection-specific DNS suffix, its IP address, subnet mask, and default gateway.

3. Type **ipconfig /all**. Note that a great deal more information is displayed, including information on multiple adapters (if you have more than one).

ARP

Before diving into the specifics of the arp command, you should understand what a MAC address and the Address Resolution Protocol (ARP) are.

Defining the MAC Address and the ARP

Every network adapter is given a unique 12-digit hexadecimal hardware address from the factory called the MAC address. The MAC address can never be changed, so no two network cards will ever have the same hardware identifier (people have reported duplicate addresses, but this is only due to errors on the part of the hardware manufacturer).

ARP maps node names (i.e., MAC addresses) to IP addresses. It equates logical and physical device addresses. ARP maintains tables of name-to-address mappings and can send out discovery packets if a desired name or address is not currently in its table. The discovery packet requests that the entity corresponding to the known name or address respond with the needed information. A copy of this table is stored on the local machine for easy access in the arp cache.

A related protocol, RARP (Reverse Address Resolution Protocol), performs the same function in reverse; that is, given an IP address, it determines the corresponding node name.

The *Arp* Command

The arp command allows you to view and modify the arp cache. You might want to do this if two computers are unable to connect to each other. You can run the arp -a command on each machine to see if they have the correct MAC address listed in cache for each other. You can determine the correct MAC address using the ipconfig /all command, explained in the preceding section. A sample output of the arp -a command is shown here:

```
C:\> arp -a
Interface 66.127.67.40 on interface 0x1000002
Internet Address        Physical Address      Type
66.127.67.41           00-10-67-00-a2-93     dynamic
66.127.67.42           00-80-ad-88-6a-79     dynamic
```

If any of the physical addresses listed in the table are not correct for that IP address, you should run the arp -d *ipaddress* command, where *ipaddress* is the IP address of the offending entry. This command deletes the entry from the cache. The next time the local machine attempts to access that IP address, it won't find an entry in the cache and will broadcast a new arp request. The new IP-to-MAC mapping will then be placed in cache. Table 1.4 lists all of the ARP switches and their functions.

TABLE 1.4 ARP Switches

Switch	Name	Function
-d ipaddress	Delete	Deletes an entry in the arp cache.
-s macaddress	Static	Adds a new static mapping to the arp cache.
-N interface IP address	Interface	Displays the contents of the arp cache for the interface specified. This is useful if you have more than one network adapter installed on your machine.

TABLE 1.4 ARP Switches *(continued)*

Switch	Name	Function
-a	Display	Displays the contents of the arp cache for all interfaces.
-g	Display	Displays the contents of the arp cache for all interfaces (yes, exactly the same as -a).

Troubleshooting Routing with the *Route* Command

As you saw earlier in the chapter, the local host maintains a routing table of all its known routes. The route add command allows you to add new static routes; you can choose whether these routes remain in the routing table after the system reboots. Routes that stick around in this manner are called *persistent routes*. The command itself is simple:

```
route add <destination> mask <netMask> <gateway> <metric>
<interface>
```

You specify the destination, net mask, gateway, metric, and interface name on the command line. These parameters are all required, and route add does some basic sanity checking to make sure that the net mask and destination match and that you haven't left anything out. One speed bump: You have to specify the interface as a number, not as a name. However, the route print command lists its interfaces and the associated numbers.

The route print command can show you all or part of the routing table from the command line. Just typing **route print** into a command window will give you a complete dump of the entire routing table; adding a wildcard IP address (for example, **route print 206.151.***) will display only routes that match 206.151.

You can also use the route delete and route change commands to make changes to the routing table. The official syntax for the route command is route [-f] [-p] [*command* [*destination*]] [MASK *netmask*] [*gateway*] [metric *metric*] [if *interface*]. The switches are processed in order. Table 1.5 lists the various switches that can be used with the route command.

TABLE 1.5 *Route* Switches

Switch	Function
-f	Clears the routing table of all gateway entries.
-p	When used with the add command, this switch adds the route to the routing table and to the Windows 2000 Registry. The route is automatically added to the routing table each time TCP/IP is initialized. By default, routes added without the -p switch are only stored in the RAM-based IP routing table and are not preserved when TCP/IP is restarted. This option is ignored for all other commands.
Print <destination>	Displays a route to the host specified by destination.
Add <destination> Mask <netmask> <gateway> Metric <metric> if <interface>	Adds a route for the specified destination using the forwarding IP address of the gateway. The metric and if options are optional.
Delete <destination>	Deletes a route for the specified destination.
Change <destination> Mask <netmask> <gateway> Metric <metric> if <interface>	Changes an existing route.
Mask <netmask>	Indicates the network mask value. If you leave <netmask> blank, the default is 255.255.255.255.
Metric <metric>	Specifies the cost to reach the destination. Lower values prioritize the route over other similar routes with higher values.
if <interface>	Specifies the interface to use for the route.

Using *Ping, Tracert,* and *Pathping* to Check Connectivity between Network Hosts

The next step up from Physical layer troubleshooting is tracing the route that packets take, or are attempting to take, between the source and destination. Once you've verified that all of the physical connections are in good shape, you must see whether you can send *any* type of packet between points A and B.

TCP/IP includes a protocol called the *Internet Control Message Protocol (ICMP)*. ICMP is designed to pass control and status information between TCP/IP devices. One type of ICMP packet, popularly known as a *ping* packet, tells the receiving system to send back an ICMP response. This gives you confirmation of whether or not the ICMP ping packet reached the target, which in turn tells you whether or not you can get packets from place to place. Since name resolution and application services depend on lower-level protocols, this sort of "Is this thing on?" test is the next logical step after testing the underlying physical connection. The `ping` and `tracert` tools both use ICMP to help sniff out network problems.

The *Ping* Tool

When you ping a remote computer using the `ping` utility in its default mode, your computer sends out four ICMP ping packets and measures the time required before each packet's corresponding response arrives. When it finishes, `ping` gives you a helpful summary showing the number of packets sent and received; the minimum, maximum, and average round-trip times; and a percentage indicating how many ping packets got no response. The following is a sample session that pings the machine at IP address `206.151.234.1`:

```
F:\Shared\abi-0.7.8>ping 206.151.234.1

Pinging 206.151.234.1 with 32 bytes of data:

Reply from 206.151.234.1: bytes=32 time=125ms TTL=250
Reply from 206.151.234.1: bytes=32 time=110ms TTL=250
Reply from 206.151.234.1: bytes=32 time=110ms TTL=250
Reply from 206.151.234.1: bytes=32 time=110ms TTL=250

Ping statistics for 206.151.234.1:
Packets: Sent = 4, Received = 4, Lost = 0 (0% loss),
Approximate round trip times in milli-seconds:
Minimum = 110ms, Maximum = 125ms, Average = 113ms
```

What does this tell you? First of all, you can see that all of the packets you sent arrived, and there are approximately five hops in between this machine and your target. You know the latter because the time to live, or TTL, value is 250. By default, the TTL on the packets that ping sends out is set to 255, and each routing device that routes the packets subtracts one from the TTL value. When a packet's TTL hits zero, it is dropped.

More importantly, this ping session shows that data is flowing normally between your machine and the target. Since all of the ping packets got there (notice the "0% loss" line near the bottom), you can comfortably say that any network problems on this link aren't because of a routing problem. Packets are flowing normally between here and there.

How would you identify a problem using this data? The most obvious way to tell is when ping times out without getting *any* packets back from the remote end. That's a big red flag indicating either that you typed the IP address incorrectly or that something is blocking traffic between the two ends of the connection. Likewise, high rates of packet loss signal that something may be wrong somewhere along the path between the machines.

The *Tracert* Tool

When your plumbing is stopped up, you can tell because your sink, toilet, or shower won't drain—but knowing that it won't drain doesn't tell you where the blockage is. Likewise, the ping utility can tell you whether packets are flowing, but it won't necessarily tell you where the problem is. Windows 2000 includes a tool called tracert (pronounced "traceroute" after the original Unix version) that takes advantage of the TTL in each IP packet to map out the path that the packets are taking as they flow to a remote system. Recall that each device that routes a packet decrements its TTL. Tracert begins by sending one ICMP ping packet with a TTL of 1. That means that the first router or gateway to encounter it sends an ICMP response, decrements the ping packet's TTL, notices that the TTL is now zero, and drops the packet. At that point, tracert sends a second packet with a TTL of 2. The first device responds, decrements the TTL, and then routes the packet to the next hop. The next device in the chain responds to the ping, decrements the TTL, and drops the original packet. This process continues with tracert gradually incrementing the TTL until the packet finally reaches the desired destination host.

As it sends these packets, tracert keeps a running log of which hosts along the route have responded and which ones haven't. You can use this information to figure out where the stoppage is. For example, take a look at this `tracert` session:

```
F:\>tracert www.microsoft.com

Tracing route to microsoft.com [207.46.131.137]
over a maximum of 30 hops:

1    <10 ms    <10 ms    <10 ms    ELGRANDE [192.168.0.1]
2    *         *         *         Request timed out.
3    *         *         *         Request timed out.
4    *         *         *         Request timed out.
5    *         *         *         Request timed out.
```

You can clearly see that the problem lies at the first hop away from your machine, a machine named ELGRANDE running the Routing and Remote Access Services (RRAS) package, or that the router at the second hop has gone down. You know this because the trace shows no response from any machine "downstream" of ELGRANDE. (Just for fun, while writing this section we did a second `tracert` on a Unix box outside our network at the same time and found that connectivity to Microsoft's website was blocked by a problem with an intermediate router in California!) In this case, it's easy to fix the problem on your end by restarting the RRAS service on ELGRANDE, but you wouldn't know that you needed to do that unless you did a `tracert`. However, if the router at hop 2 has failed, you might not be able to fix the problem.

The *Pathping* Tool

The `pathping` tool provides the functionality of both `ping` and `tracert` and adds some of its own features into the mix as well. A sample `pathping` output is shown in Figure 1.13. The first list in the output is the route that the packet takes to reach the destination. This is similar to the output of the `tracert` command. You will have to wait for several seconds (25 per hop, to be exact) until the next list appears. The two rightmost columns provide the most useful information. The Address column indicates the address of the node or link that the hop went to. The This Node/Link Lost/Sent% column indicates the packet loss that occurred at that point in the route. Typically the packet loss should be 0, but if you are having routing problems, you might spot a malfunctioning router by seeing where along the line you are losing packets.

FIGURE 1.13   Pathping output

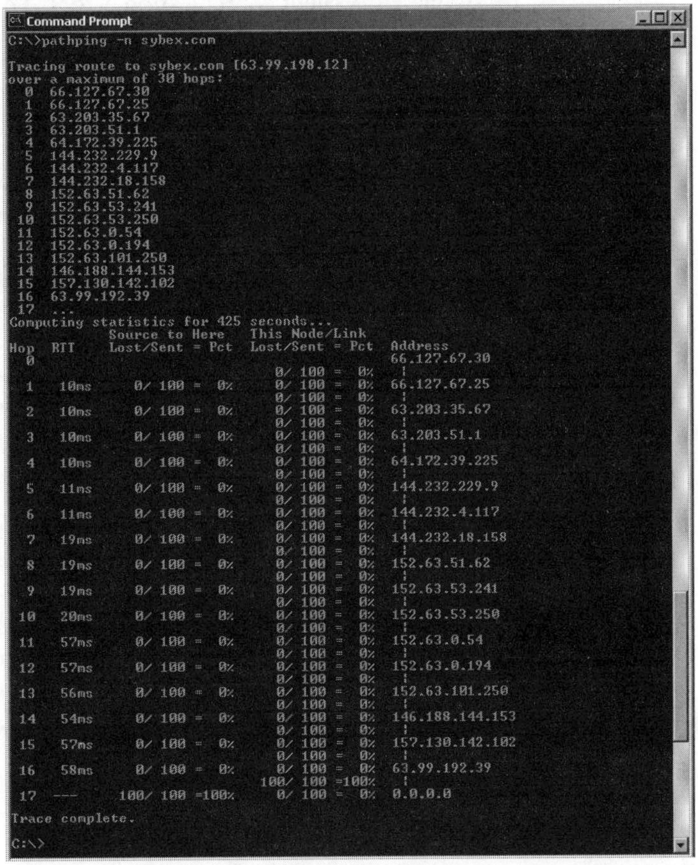

```
Command Prompt                                                    _ □ ×
C:\>pathping -n sybex.com

Tracing route to sybex.com [63.99.198.12]
over a maximum of 30 hops:
  0  66.127.67.30
  1  66.127.67.25
  2  63.203.35.67
  3  63.203.51.1
  4  64.172.39.225
  5  144.232.229.9
  6  144.232.4.117
  7  144.232.18.158
  8  152.63.51.62
  9  152.63.53.241
 10  152.63.53.250
 11  152.63.0.54
 12  152.63.0.194
 13  152.63.101.250
 14  146.188.144.153
 15  157.130.142.102
 16  63.99.192.39
 17  ...
Computing statistics for 425 seconds...
                  Source to Here   This Node/Link
Hop  RTT     Lost/Sent = Pct    Lost/Sent = Pct   Address
  0                                                66.127.67.30
                                  0/ 100 =  0%    |
  1  10ms    0/ 100 =  0%        0/ 100 =  0%    66.127.67.25
                                  0/ 100 =  0%    |
  2  10ms    0/ 100 =  0%        0/ 100 =  0%    63.203.35.67
                                  0/ 100 =  0%    |
  3  10ms    0/ 100 =  0%        0/ 100 =  0%    63.203.51.1
                                  0/ 100 =  0%    |
  4  10ms    0/ 100 =  0%        0/ 100 =  0%    64.172.39.225
                                  0/ 100 =  0%    |
  5  11ms    0/ 100 =  0%        0/ 100 =  0%    144.232.229.9
                                  0/ 100 =  0%    |
  6  11ms    0/ 100 =  0%        0/ 100 =  0%    144.232.4.117
                                  0/ 100 = 0%    |
  7  19ms    0/ 100 =  0%        0/ 100 =  0%    144.232.18.158
                                  0/ 100 =  0%    |
  8  19ms    0/ 100 =  0%        0/ 100 =  0%    152.63.51.62
                                  0/ 100 =  0%    |
  9  19ms    0/ 100 =  0%        0/ 100 =  0%    152.63.53.241
                                  0/ 100 =  0%    |
 10  20ms    0/ 100 =  0%        0/ 100 =  0%    152.63.53.250
                                  0/ 100 =  0%    |
 11  57ms    0/ 100 =  0%        0/ 100 =  0%    152.63.0.54
                                  0/ 100 =  0%    |
 12  57ms    0/ 100 =  0%        0/ 100 =  0%    152.63.0.194
                                  0/ 100 =  0%    |
 13  56ms    0/ 100 =  0%        0/ 100 =  0%    152.63.101.250
                                  0/ 100 =  0%    |
 14  54ms    0/ 100 =  0%        0/ 100 =  0%    146.188.144.153
                                  0/ 100 =  0%    |
 15  57ms    0/ 100 =  0%        0/ 100 =  0%    157.130.142.102
                                  0/ 100 =  0%    |
 16  58ms    0/ 100 =  0%        0/ 100 =  0%    63.99.192.39
                                100/ 100 =100%    |
 17  ---    100/ 100 =100%       0/ 100 =  0%    0.0.0.0

Trace complete.

C:\>
```

The most useful switch to know is the -n switch, which only displays the
IP address of each hop rather than resolving each name.

Using *Netdiag*

Netdiag is a tool that shows you just about everything about the state of the
local computer's network configuration. The output that results from running the netdiag command can be quite daunting because of its sheer
length, but if you break it down into manageable pieces, it can provide you
with the information you need to fix connectivity problems. Netdiag
requires no switches, but several optional switches are available to fine-tune

the output. The most commonly used switch is the /fix switch, which will fix simple DNS client configuration errors. You must install the Windows 2000 Support Tools provided on the Windows 2000 CD to use netdiag. Table 1.6 explains the various tests that netdiag performs.

TABLE 1.6 Netdiag Tests

Test	Name	Explanation
NDIS	Network Adapter Status	Shows the details related to the network adapter such as the MAC address and the adapter name. If the adapter does not respond, the remaining tests will not run.
IPConfig	IP Configuration	This provides similar information to the ipconfig /all command. In addition, it pings the DHCP and WINS servers and verifies that the default gateway is on the same subnet as the local IP address.
Member	Domain Membership	Displays information regarding the local machine's domain membership.
NetBTTransports	Transports Test	Displays information about the NBT transport. If no NBT transport is found, it gives an error message.
Automatic Private IP Addressing (APIPA)	APIPA Address	Checks to see if any of the network adapters on the local machine are Automatic Private IP Addressing.

TABLE 1.6   Netdiag Tests *(continued)*

Test	Name	Explanation
IPLoopBk	IP Loopback Ping	Pings the IP loopback address of 127.0.0.1.
DefGw	Default Gateway	Pings all the default gateways for each interface.
NbtNm	NetBT Name Test	This test is similar to the nbtstat -n command, discussed in Chapter 3.
WINS	WINS Service Test	Sends NetBT queries to all WINS servers.
Winsock	Winsock Test	Fetches available transport protocols for use with Windows Sockets.
DNS	DNS Test	Verifies the DNS configuration of the local computer. If the /fix option is used, the test tries to re-register with the DNS server.
Browser	Redirector and Browser Test	Checks the status of the Workstation service. Queries the redirector and the browser for transport lists. Checks the NBT transports test to see if the NBT transports are present. Verifies that the browser is bound to all of the NBT transports. Verifies that the local machine can send mailslot messages.

TABLE 1.6   Netdiag Tests *(continued)*

Test	Name	Explanation
DsGetDc	DC Discovery Test	Finds any random domain controller, and then finds the primary domain controller. The test then attempts to find a Windows 2000–based domain controller. Checks the local GUID against the domain controller's GUID and verifies their integrity. If the /fix switch is used, the test attempts to fix problems with the local GUID.
DcList	DC List Test	Displays a list of all the domain controllers in the domain.
Trust	Trust Relationship Test	Tests the state of the trust relationships if the computer is connected to a domain.
Kerberos	Kerberos Test	Tests Kerberos if the computer is connected to a domain and the user is not logged on locally.
LDAP	Lightweight Directory Access Protocol (LDAP) Test	Tests LDAP on all active domain controllers if Active Directory is present.
Route	Route test	Performs a test similar to the route command explained earlier in the chapter.
NetStat	NetStat test	Performs a test similar to the netstat tool explained in Chapter 3.

TABLE 1.6 Netdiag Tests *(continued)*

Test	Name	Explanation
Bindings	Bindings test	Lists details about network bindings.
WAN	WAN test	Tests the current remote access connection.
Modem	Modem test	Tests all of the computer's modem devices and displays configuration information.
NetWare	NetWare test	Tests the status of NetWare.
IPX	IPX test	Tests and displays the current IPX configuration.
IPSec	IP Security test	Tests IPSec and displays a list of the currently active IPSec policies.

Summary

In this chapter, you learned:

- Which network protocols are included with Windows 2000 and what they do
- How TCP/IP works, including IP addresses and subnet masks
- How to install network protocols, including NetBEUI and TCP/IP
- How to troubleshoot network problems

Exam Essentials

Know what protocols are and how they work.   Protocols are an agreed-upon way in which two objects (people, computers, home appliances, or whatever) can exchange information. It is the protocols at a particular level in the OSI model that provide that level's functionality.

Know which major network protocols Windows 2000 supports. Microsoft networking products come with four network transports, which are intended for networks of different sizes with different requirements. In general, NetBEUI is intended for small, single-server networks. NWLink is intended for medium-sized networks (in a single facility, perhaps) or for networks that require access to Novell NetWare file servers. AppleTalk's primary use is interoperating with Macintosh computers. TCP/IP is a complex transport sufficient for globe-spanning networks such as the Internet.

Understand the difference between Class A, Class B, and Class C networks.   In a Class A network, the first byte is the network address, and the three remaining bytes are used for the node addresses. In a Class B network, the first two bytes are assigned to the network address, and the remaining two bytes are used for node addresses. The first three bytes of a Class C network are dedicated to the network portion of the address, with only one byte remaining for the node address.

Understand what subnetting is and when to use it.   If an organization is large and has many computers, or if its computers are geographically dispersed, it's sensible to divide its large network into smaller ones connected by routers. These smaller nets are called subnets. Subnetting is the process of carving a single IP network into smaller, logical subnetworks.

Understand subnet masks.   For the subnet address scheme to work, every machine on the network must know which part of the host address will be used as the subnet address. The network administrator creates a 32-bit subnet mask consisting of ones and zeros. The ones in the subnet mask represent the positions that refer to the network or subnet addresses. The zeros represent the positions that refer to the host part of the address.

Understand how routing works.   Each packet on a network has a source address and a destination address, which means that any device that receives the packet can inspect its headers to determine where it came from and where it's going. If such a device also has some information about the network's design and implementation—like how long it takes packets to travel over a particular link—it can intelligently change the routing to minimize the total cost, which refers to the time it takes a packet to travel from the source to the destination.

Know how to install network protocols.   You install network protocols through the Local Area Network Connection Properties dialog box, which lists all of the known protocols on your Windows 2000 machine. Protocols marked with a check indicate that they're bound to the adapter whose properties you're inspecting.

Know how to configure TCP/IP settings.   TCP/IP requires only two pieces of information to function: the IP address you want to use for the system and the subnet mask that corresponds to the network subnet the client is on. If you're configuring a Windows 2000 Professional machine, you're probably using DHCP with it. In that case, the default TCP/IP settings will work fine, since they configure the TCP/IP stack to get configuration parameters from any available DHCP server.

Know the steps for troubleshooting network protocols.   First, figure out what the problem is. Arm yourself with as many details as possible about how the problem is manifesting itself (including exact error messages), when it started, and whether or not it's consistent. Knowing which users or computers are affected by a problem is very important, since that gives you insight into possible causes (including user mistakes) and helps you select a course of action. When you first notice a network problem, be sure to verify that all of your network cables are correctly connected; that your hub, router, or switch has power; and so on.

Know how to use the *ipconfig* tool.   Ipconfig is used to view and, with switches such as `renew` and `release`, modify the configuration of TCP/IP interfaces on your local machine. Typing **ipconfig** *without the switches* into a Windows 2000 command prompt window produces a neat summary of your current IP configuration, including the local DNS name, the IP addresses, and the subnet masks configured for all adapters on the computer.

Know how to use the *arp* tool. The `arp` command allows you to view and modify the arp cache. The arp cache stores logical-to-physical-address mappings.

Know how to use the *route* command. The `route` command allows you to view and change the local static routing table. The two most commonly used `route` switches are `route add`, which creates a new static route, and `route print`, which displays the current routing table.

Know how to use the *ping* tool. When you ping a remote computer using the `ping` utility in its default mode, your computer sends out four ICMP ping packets and measures the time required before each packet's corresponding response arrives. When it finishes, `ping` gives you a helpful summary showing the number of packets sent and received; the minimum, maximum, and average round-trip times; and a percentage indicating how many ping packets got no response.

Know how to use the *tracert* tool. The `tracert` tool takes advantage of the TTL in each IP packet to map out the path that the packets are taking as they flow to a remote system.

Know how to use the *pathping* tool. The `pathping` tool provides the functionality of both `ping` and `tracert` and adds some of its own features. The tool displays the packet loss at each hop in a route.

Know how to use the *netdiag* command. `Netdiag` is a tool that shows you just about everything about the state of the local computer's network configuration. The most commonly used switch is the `/fix` switch, which fixes simple DNS client configuration errors.

Key Terms

Before you take the exam, be certain you are familiar with the following terms:

default gateway	node address
default subnet mask	NWLink
dynamic routing	packet payload
hierarchical address	packets
Internet Control Message Protocol (ICMP)	`ping`
Internet Protocol (IP)	static routing
`ipconfig`	subnet address
NBT	subnet mask
NetBEUI	subnets
network address	Transmission Control Protocol (TCP)

Review Questions

1. You are working at a manufacturing company that occupies an entire city block. Management informs you that they have acquired another business on the other side of town that previously had been a supplier to your company. The Windows 2000 network that you have been supporting now needs to be connected to the new location through a router. You also have several NetBIOS applications that need to continue functioning properly. What protocols are available for you to use to ensure that these criteria are met? (Choose all that apply.)

   A. NWLink

   B. TCP/IP

   C. XNS

   D. NetBEUI

2. The company you work for manufactures handballs and has an Intel PC–based Windows 2000 network. To cut packaging costs, the management of the company has acquired a graphics arts company. Their network is entirely Macintosh-based and is currently using AppleTalk as the protocol to communicate among workstations. You have to integrate the two networks so that they can easily share information. What protocols must you have on your network for communication among all the workstations on this network?

   A. AppleTalk

   B. TCP/IP

   C. NWLink

   D. NetBEUI

3. Your multinational company has a Windows NT and Novell NetWare network that is built on several subnetworks. To provide interoperability, you have been using NWLink on the NT network and IPX for the NetWare network. You have been told that the Windows NT network must be migrated to Windows 2000 because it's less expensive to administer. You know that the administrative cost benefits are a result of utilizing Active Directory, so you include this service in your migration plan. What are you going to have to do immediately in order to install and begin using Active Directory on this network?

A. Change the protocol to TCP/IP.

B. Make sure that you install a copy of Active Directory on the NetWare servers as well as on the Windows 2000 Servers.

C. As you upgrade the Windows NT Servers, make sure that you choose to upgrade some of them as domain controllers so that you can install Active Directory on them.

D. Install NetBEUI in order to provide connectivity for the NetBIOS components of Windows 2000.

4. Your company just purchased a new router. The router's address is 173.24.12.2/24 and your computer's address is 173.24.12.3/24. You want to test the router's performance by routing all information to the 173.25.14.3/24 IP address through the new router. What command should you use before performing the test?

A. route delete 173.24.12.2

B. route add 173.24.12.2 mask 255.255.255.0 173.25.14.3

C. route print 173.25.14.3

D. route add 173.25.14.3 mask 255.255.255.0 173.24.12.2

5. Recently you have been experiencing performance problems with network traffic between your computer and several other computers on the network. Your company manages several routers between your host and the troublesome section of the network. You suspect that one of the routers along the line is dropping packets, but you want to be sure. What is the best command to use for obtaining detailed information about packet loss at each hop in a network transmission?

   A. `ping`

   B. `ipconfig`

   C. `winipcfg`

   D. `pathping`

   E. `tracert`

   F. `netdiag`

6. For several years you have been administering a small network that is fully contained in one building. You recently finished the migration from Windows NT to Windows 2000 and changed the protocol from NetBEUI to TCP/IP. You have just learned that a very large company that houses a network that contains several subnets connected by routers has acquired your company. Since you are not fully up to speed on all the details of TCP/IP, the acquiring company's IS department is going to send you a preconfigured router with the network address that you provided to them. After the line is installed, you receive the router and power it up. The network administrator of your new IS department checks out the router connections, and everything looks good. However, when you try to connect to resources on the other networks, the attempts fail. All the local workstations continue to function properly, but none of them can access anything across the router. When you ping the router interface, however, you get the proper response. What is most likely the problem?

   A. You have provided an incorrect subnet mask.

   B. You are running the wrong version of TCP/IP.

   C. You have not provided a default gateway address.

   D. You have not provided any DNS information.

   E. You have provided an incorrect IP address.

7. You have spent a great deal of time upgrading your 500-node network from Windows NT to Windows 2000. During the migration you finally took advantage of the centralized management that DHCP brings to TCP/IP by redesigning your IP subnets and creating the scope necessary to cover all the workstations. You have activated the scope. You haven't implemented Active Directory yet, but you plan to do that after you confirm that everything works fine. During the weekend of the final rollover, at each workstation you run a script that edits the Registry to convert the IP configuration from static IP addressing to support DHCP; then you reboot all the machines. You test a few random machines and connect them to resources across your routers, and they all connect to the servers appropriately. On Monday morning you receive a flurry of phone calls from users who complain that the Internet connection is down. You check the Internet connection from your Windows 2000 Server, and the connection is fine. What is the probable cause of this problem?

A. The subnet mask is incorrect on some of the workstations.

B. The default gateway is incorrect.

C. The DNS configuration on the workstations is overriding the configuration in the DHCP server.

D. The IP address scheme that you created is not valid.

E. The WINS server is not configured properly.

8. You administer a computer lab for a university. The lab consists entirely of Macintosh computers that use the AppleTalk protocol. You want to add a single Windows 2000 Server computer to the lab, and it needs to be able to talk to the other computers that are there. Where should you click in the following exhibit in order to accomplish this?

   A. Install

   B. Uninstall

   C. Properties

   D. Configure

9. You are helping the lead systems engineer design a network for a new company location. You determine that in the future the company could conceivably grow to include as many as 200 different networks. Each network could also contain as many as 1,000 clients. Your boss insists that he doesn't want to subnet the network. Which network address class should you use?

   A. Class A

   B. Class B

   C. Class C

   D. Class D

Question to go over

10. You work for Carpathian Worldwide Enterprises, which has more than 50 administrative and manufacturing locations around the world. The size of these organizations varies greatly, with the number of computers per location ranging from 15 to slightly fewer than 1,000. The sales operations use more than 1,000 facilities, each of which contains two to five computers. Carpathian is also in merger talks with another large organization; if the merger materializes as planned, you will have to accommodate another 100 manufacturing and administrative locations, each with a maximum of 600 computers, as well as 2,000 additional sales facilities. You don't have any numbers for the future growth of the company, but you are told to keep growth in mind. You decide to implement a private addressing plan for the entire organization. More than half of your routers don't support variable subnet masking. What subnet masks would work for this situation? (Choose all that apply.)

A. 255.255.224.0

B. 255.255.240.0

C. 255.255.248.0

D. 255.255.252.0

E. 255.255.254.0

11. For several years you have been administering a small network that is fully contained in one building. You recently finished the migration from Windows NT to Windows 2000 and changed the protocol from NetBEUI to TCP/IP. You have just learned that a very large company that houses a network that contains several subnets connected by routers has acquired your company. Since you are not fully up to speed on all the details of TCP/IP, the corporate administrators are going to send you a pre-configured router with the network address that you provided to them. After the line is installed, you receive the router and power it up. The network administrator of your new IS department checks out the router connections, and everything looks good. However, when you try to connect to resources on the other networks, the attempts fail. All the local workstations continue to function properly, but none of them can access anything across the router. What tool would you use to troubleshoot this problem?

A. `netstat -a`

B. `nslookup`

C. `ipconfig`

D. `winipcfg`

E. `nbtstat`

12. You want to install two network cards on one computer. You definitely want to configure the IP address of one of the cards manually. How must you configure the other card?

A. Both cards must be configured manually.

B. Both cards must be configured dynamically.

C. One card must be configured manually, and the other must be configured dynamically.

D. Both cards can be configured either manually or dynamically.

Question
13 go over

13. The company you work for is growing dramatically via acquisitions of other companies. As the network administrator, you need to keep up with the changes because they affect the workstations and you need to support them. When you started, there were 15 locations connected via routers, and now there are 25. As new companies are acquired, they are migrated to Windows 2000 and brought into the same domain as another site. Management says that they are going to acquire at least 10 more companies in the next two years. The engineers have also told you that they are redesigning the company's Class B address into an IP addressing scheme that will support these requirements and that there will never be over 1000 network devices on any subnet. What will be the appropriate subnet mask to support this network when the changes are completed?

A. 255.255.252.0   63N   1023

B. 255.255.248.0   31N   2047

C. 255.255.255.0   254   255

D. 255.255.255.128   511N   127w

14. The company that you work for has two separate divisions: one that handles sporting event ticketing and the other that handles leasing event venues. They are completely separate from a financial operations perspective, but they are located in the same building, connected by a single router. You are the administrator for both divisions. Even though the companies are managed separately, they share some of their IS resources, such as their Internet connection and an IIS server that is physically on the ticketing side of the company. One of the workstations in the venue side of the house cannot connect to any of the resources on the other side, including the Internet. The following machines are configured as follows:

IIS server:

Node address	192.23.64.23/24
Gateway	192.23.64.1/24

Router:

Ticketing interface	192.23.64.1/24
ISP interface	10.2.223.23/28
Venue interface	204.45.36.1/24

Problem workstation:

Node address	204.45.36.2/24
Gateway	10.2.223.23/28

What do you need to do to allow the workstation to access the Internet?

A. Change the IIS server gateway to 10.2.223.23/28.

B. Change the ISP interface to 192.23.64.1/24.

C. Change the workstation gateway to 204.45.36.1/24.

D. Change the workstation gateway to 192.23.64.1/24.

15. You are the administrator of a network that has completed its migration from Windows NT. The entire company is located in one building, and the network has been a flat subnet until recently. The company has experienced accelerated growth, and there are now more than 1,000 users on the network. The network engineers have decided to break the network into two segments separated by a multi-homed Windows 2000 Server. One NIC has an address of 172.160.0.1, and the other NIC has an address of 172.150.0.1. The workstations have been largely divided between the two segments and have been configured by the engineer. You immediately start getting calls from users on both sides, stating that they cannot reach the other side of the router. You run the `route print` command, and it displays the following information:

Destination	Netmask	Gateway	Interface
172.160.0.0	255.255.0.0	172.160.0.1	172.160.0.1
172.160.0.1	255.255.255.255	127.0.0.1	127.0.0.1
172.150.0.0	255.255.0.0	172.150.0.11	172.150.0.1
172.150.0.1	255.255.255.255	127.0.0.1	127.0.0.1

What **route** command do you need to execute on the router to resolve the address resolution problem?

A. route delete 172.160.0.0
route -p add 172.160.0.0 mask 255.255.0.0 172.160.0.1

B. route delete 172.160.0.1
route -p add 172.160.0.1 mask 255.255.255.255
172.160.0.1

C. route delete 172.150.0.
route -p add 172.150.0.0 mask 255.255.0.0 172.150.0.1

D. route delete 172.150.0.1.
route -p add 172.150.0.1 mask 255.255.255.255
172.150.0.1

Answers to Review Questions

1. A, B. Both NWLink and TCP/IP are routable and both can function properly with NetBIOS applications, since they are both Microsoft's versions and have the interface for proper communication. XNS is a routable protocol but is not provided with Windows 2000. With the overwhelming popularity of TCP/IP, XNS is generally no longer used in networks. NetBEUI, although it supports the NetBIOS programs, is not routable.

2. B. Although Macintosh computers can use AppleTalk to communicate with each other, these computers can also run TCP/IP, so AppleTalk won't be necessary when these two networks are merged. You could add AppleTalk to the servers in the network, and the two machine types could share files back and forth, but if you can reduce the number of protocols on any network, it's best practice to do so.

3. A. Active Directory requires TCP/IP in order to function. Even though you can have TCP/IP and IPX coexisting on the same network, it's not beneficial to have multiple protocols, as they increase the level of support necessary for the network. Active Directory does not run on NetWare, and NetBEUI is not required for NetBIOS communication. Finally, Active Directory can be installed and uninstalled on any Windows 2000 Server computer. It's a service that is added rather than a particular type of server that is installed, as with Windows NT.

4. D. The `route add` command is used to add a static route to the local routing table. The correct syntax for the route add command is `route add <destination> mask <netMask> <gateway> <metric> <interface>`.

5. D. `Pathping` is similar to `tracert` but gives more detailed information about each hop. For example, you can see exactly how many packets each router drops.

6. C. You need to provide a default gateway address so that the computer can route packets to other subnets and networks. When a packet is formed and is addressed to a different subnet, the local IP stack looks to a special address in its configuration to forward the packet to. This is called the default gateway. If the default gateway isn't configured, all local IP traffic will function properly, but the machines missing this gateway configuration won't be able to reach any other networks.

If the subnet mask or IP addresses were incorrect, local communication would not work properly. The DNS configuration is used for name resolution and would not result in this type of failure.

7. C. A static DNS configuration can override the DHCP configuration that negotiated with the DHCP client. Since the Registry was edited from static IP to DHCP, the DNS information wasn't changed and is still entered as static information, overriding the DHCP configuration. With the incorrect DNS configuration, the workstations cannot resolve a URL into the IP addresses necessary to connect to resources on the Web. If the subnet mask and IP addresses were incorrect, they would not be able to communicate on the local network. The default gateway is accurate because you were able to make connections across the routers. WINS is not involved with web services browsing.

8. A. The new Windows computer needs to have AppleTalk installed in order to communicate with the Macintosh machines in the lab. To install any services or protocols, you need to click the Install button in the Local Area Connection Properties dialog box.

9. B. Class A networks can have a maximum of 127 networks. Class C networks can have a maximum of 254 nodes per network. Class D networks are used for multicasting only.

10. B, C, D. When you add up the locations that currently need to be given a network address, the total is 3,150, and the maximum number of hosts at any one of these locations is less than 1,000. The subnet masks need to support those requirements. Each of the subnet masks given in the second, third, and fourth answers will provide the address space to support the requirements outlined above. The subnet mask 255.255.240.0 supports more than 4,000 subnets and 4,000 hosts. The subnet mask 255.255.248.0 supports more than 8,000 subnets and more than 2,000 hosts. The subnet mask 255.255.252.0 supports more than 16,000 subnets and more than 1,000 hosts.

Although each of these subnet masks will work, at the rate that this company is growing, 255.255.252.0 is probably the best mask to prepare for the future. It's unlikely that there will ever be more than 1,000 hosts on any given network. In fact, that number would probably cause performance problems on that subnet. Therefore, it's better to have more subnets available to deploy as the company grows.

The subnet mask 255.255.224.0 supports more than 2,000 subnets—an insufficient number to cover the locations. The subnet mask 255.255.254.0 supports more than 32,000 subnets but only 500 hosts, which is not enough hosts to cover all the locations.

11. C. Ipconfig displays the configuration information of the IP stack of the machine you run it on. To view the details of the IP configuration, including the DNS information, you need to add the /all switch to the command.

Netstat shows active TCP connections, and nbtstat shows similar information for NetBIOS connections. Winipcfg is a similar command for TCP/IP configurations, but it runs on Windows 9.*x*. Nslookup is used to discover DNS name resolution problems.

12. D. Any adapter can use either DHCP or manual addressing without reference to what the other adapters are using.

13. A. The network mask applied to an address determines which portion of that address reflects the number of hosts available to that network. The balance with subnetting is always between the number of hosts and individual subnetworks that can be uniquely represented within one encompassing address. The number of hosts and networks that are made available depends upon the number of bits that can be used to represent them. This scenario requires more than 35 networks and fewer than 1000 workstations on each network. If you convert the subnet masks as described in the chapter, you will see that the mask in option A allows for more than 60 networks and more than 1000 hosts. All of the other options are deficient in either the number of networks or hosts that they represent.

14. C. The workstation gateway address is the address that IP uses to send packets that are off the network. Regardless of whether the ultimate destination is to the IIS server on the other LAN or an address somewhere on the Internet, the only way packets can reach this destination is if they first reach the gateway that can contact other routers to forward the packets. You do not make the gateway address the address of a particular machine that you want to reach.

15. C. The host ID or network ID is displayed in the Destination field. The Netmask column places the correct mask that is used to define the relationship between the network ID and the range of host IDs. The important column here is Gateway, which shows where packets will be sent if their destination is off the network. The Interface column shows the IP address that is configured for this device, which is the router. The command in the C option corrects a problem where the router is forwarding packets to the wrong address. It needs to send the packets to the address that represents the interface of the network that it is trying to reach.

Managing the Dynamic Host Configuration Protocol

MICROSOFT EXAM OBJECTIVES COVERED IN THIS CHAPTER:

✓ **Configure and troubleshoot TCP/IP on servers and client computers. Considerations include subnet masks, default gateways, network IDs, and broadcast addresses.**

- Configure client computer TCP/IP properties.
- Validate client computer network configuration by using the winipcfg, ipconfig, and arp commands.
- Validate client computer network connectivity by using the ping command.

✓ **Configure, administer, and troubleshoot DHCP on servers and client computers.**

- Detect unauthorized DHCP servers on a network.
- Configure authorization of DHCP servers.
- Configure client computers to use dynamic IP addressing.
- Configure DHCP server properties.
- Create and configure a DHCP scope.

This chapter covers the ipconfig command only in how it relates to DHCP. The rest of the subobjectives concerning TCP/IP were covered earlier in Chapter 1, "Installing and Configuring Network Protocols." Also, the "Configure client computers to use dynamic IP addressing" subobjective was covered in Chapter 1.

The Dynamic Host Configuration Protocol is designed to automate configuration of TCP/IP clients. In theory, you can put one or more DHCP servers on your network, program them with a range of network addresses and other configuration parameters, and let clients automatically obtain IP addressing information without manual intervention. While theory and practice often diverge (especially when software is involved), DHCP pretty much delivers on this promise. With appropriate DHCP configurations, your TCP/IP clients—running any OS that has DHCP support—can be configured with little or no manual intervention from you.

An Overview of DHCP

DHCP's job is to centralize the process of IP address and option assignment. What does this mean? Simply put, you can configure a DHCP server with a range of addresses and then sit back and let it assign IP parameters like addresses, default gateways, DNS server addresses, and so on. DHCP is defined by a series of RFCs, notably 2132, 1534, 2131, and 1542. In brief, the DHCP process goes like this: When TCP/IP starts up on a DHCP-enabled host, a special message is sent out requesting an IP address and a subnet mask from a DHCP server.

Any DHCP server that hears the request checks its internal database and then replies with a message containing the information the client requested. The contents of this message vary, depending on how the DHCP server is configured—there are numerous different pieces of information that you can specify to pass to the client on a Windows 2000 DHCP server. When the client accepts the IP offer, it is then extended to the client for a specified period of time, called a *lease*. If the DHCP server has given out all the IP addresses in its range, it won't make an offer; if no other servers make an offer, the client's TCP/IP initialization will fail.

Microsoft ✓ *Exam* *Objective*

Configure and troubleshoot TCP/IP on servers and client computers. Considerations include subnet masks, default gateways, network IDs, and broadcast addresses.

- Validate client computer network configuration by using the `winipcfg`, `ipconfig`, and `arp` commands.

Advantages of DHCP

DHCP seems like just the kind of helpful, unobtrusive tool we all want to use to simplify our network management tasks. It has some significant advantages, such as the following:

- DHCP capability is bundled with Windows 2000, so adding it to your network costs nothing extra.

- Once you enter the IP configuration information in one place—the server—it's automatically propagated to clients, eliminating the chance that a user will fat-finger some parameters and require you to fix it.

- Configuration problems are minimized, clearing up a labyrinth of possible situations that lead to big messes and obscure, hard-to-find problems.

- IP addresses are conserved, since DHCP assigns them only when a client requests one. A pool of 254 Class C addresses lasts a lot longer when they can be reused.

- IP configuration becomes almost completely Plug and Play. In most cases, you can unbox and plug in a new system (or move one) and then watch as it magically receives a configuration from the server.

Disadvantages of DHCP

Lest you think that DHCP is the best thing for network administrators since Diet Mountain Dew, let me point out a few actual and potential drawbacks of DHCP:

- Not all DHCP client implementations work properly with Windows 2000's DHCP server. It's an open question of whether this is the fault of Microsoft or the other vendors, since the DHCP RFCs leave some areas open to interpretation.

- "Garbage in, garbage out" still rules. If you put incorrect information into your DHCP server, it will automatically be blasted onto all your DHCP clients, meaning you may have to clean up after yourself by reconfiguring the DHCP server and renewing every lease on the misconfigured network.

- If you're not careful, DHCP can become a single point of failure for your network. If you have only one DHCP server and it's not available, clients won't be able to request or renew leases.

- If you want to use DHCP on a multisegment network, you must either put a DHCP server on each segment, ensure that your router can forward BootP broadcasts, or enable a relay agent.

How DHCP Works

DHCP is a pretty simple process; at the end of the process (and if all goes well), the client will have an IP address and whatever other parameters the DHCP server owner wanted to supply. Since an IP address is required to communicate with other devices on a TCP/IP network, the DHCP negotiation happens very early in the Windows 2000 boot cycle.

Each network adapter in a system has its own IP address. However, you may have multiple NICs that are configured to use DHCP. In the following sections, you'll see the process happening once for each DHCP-configured NIC.

Stage One: IP Discovery

The first step in the DHCP mating dance is the *discovery* stage. It's triggered the first time a client's DHCP-configured TCP/IP stack starts or when you switch from using an assigned IP address to using DHCP. Just to complicate things further, it can also occur when a specific IP address is requested but unavailable or immediately after a formerly used IP address is released.

At the time of the lease request, the client doesn't know what its IP address is, nor does it know the IP address of the server. To work around this, the client uses 0.0.0.0 as its address and 255.255.255.255 for the server's address; then it sends out a broadcast *DHCP discover message* on UDP ports 67 and 68. The discover message contains the hardware MAC address and NetBIOS name of the client.

Once the first discover message is sent, the client waits one second for an offer. If no DHCP server responds within that time, the client repeats its request three more times at 9-, 13-, and 16-second intervals. If the client still doesn't hear an answer, it continues to broadcast discover messages every five minutes until it gets an answer. If no DHCP server ever becomes available, no TCP/IP communications will be possible. The Windows 2000 client will automatically pick what it thinks is an unused address (from the 169.254.xy address block) instead of waiting indefinitely for an answer. Even though a static address has been assigned, the DHCP client will continuously poll every five minutes for a DHCP server and then switch back to using a DHCP-assigned address when the server becomes available.

Remember that the discover message broadcasts won't be heard outside the client's local subnet unless your routers support BootP forwarding or the DHCP relay agent.

Stage Two: IP Lease Offer

In the second phase of the DHCP process, any DHCP server that received the discover message broadcast and that has valid address information to offer responds with an *offer message*. (This feature allows you to configure multiple DHCP servers so that you're protected against a single-point failure.) The Windows 2000 DHCP server registers itself in Active Directory, and it won't begin offering leases until it successfully registers in the directory. The offer message is a proposal from the server to the client, and it contains an IP address, a subnet mask, a lease period (in hours), and the IP address of the

DHCP server offering the proposal. The IP address being offered is temporarily reserved so that the server doesn't offer the same address to multiple clients. All offers are sent directly to the requesting client's hardware MAC address.

Stage Three: IP Lease Selection

Once the client has received at least one offer, the third phase of the DHCP process begins. In this phase, the client machine selects an offer from those it received. Windows 2000 always accepts the first offer that arrives; to signal acceptance, the client broadcasts an acceptance message containing the IP address of the server it selected. It has to be broadcast so that the servers whose offers weren't selected can un-reserve (pull back) the addresses they offered.

Stage Four: IP Lease Acknowledgment

Once the chosen DHCP server receives the acceptance message from the client, it marks the selected IP address as leased and then sends an acknowledgment message, called a *DHCPACK*, back to the client. It's also possible that the server might send a negative acknowledgment, or *DHCPNACK*, to the client; DHCPNACKs are most often generated when the client is attempting to renew a lease for its old IP address after that address has been reassigned elsewhere. Negative acceptance messages can also mean that the requesting client has an inaccurate IP address resulting from physically changing locations to an alternate subnet.

The DHCPACK message includes any DHCP options specified by the server, along with the IP address and subnet mask. When the client receives this message, it stuffs the parameters into the TCP/IP stack, which can then proceed just as though the user had manually given it new configuration parameters.

Manually configured entries on the client override any DHCP-supplied entries.

This four-step process may seem overly complicated, but each step is necessary. The aggregate result of these steps is that one server assigns one address to one client. For example, if each server offering a lease immediately assigned an IP address to a requesting workstation, there would soon be no numbers left to assign. Likewise, if the DHCP client controlled whether it accepted or rejected the lease (instead of waiting for a DHCPACK or DHCP-NACK message), a slow client could cause the server to mark an assigned address as free and then assign it somewhere else—leaving two clients with the same offer.

DHCP Lease Renewal

Nothing lasts forever, not even DHCP leases. That raises the question of what happens when the lease expires or needs to be renewed. No matter how long the lease period is, the client sends a new lease request message to the DHCP server when the lease period is half over. If the server hears the request message, and there's no reason to reject it, it sends a DHCPACK to the client. This resets the lease period, just like signing a renewal rider on a car lease.

If the DHCP server isn't available, the client receives an "eviction notice" indicating that the lease can't be renewed. The client can then use the address for the rest of the lease period; once 87.5 percent of the lease period has elapsed, the client sends out another renewal request. At that point, any DHCP server that hears the renewal could respond to this *DHCP request message* with a DHCPACK and renew the lease.

Any time the client gets a DHCPNACK message, it must stop using its IP address immediately and start the leasing process over from the beginning by requesting a brand-new lease.

When a client initializes TCP/IP, it always attempts to renew its old address. Just like any other renewal, if the client has time left on the lease, it continues to use the lease until its end. If the client is unable to get a new lease by that time, all TCP/IP functions stop until a new, valid address can be obtained.

DHCP Lease Release

Although leases can be renewed repeatedly, at some point they're likely to run out. Furthermore, the lease process is an "at will" process—the client or server can cancel the lease before it ends. In addition, if the client doesn't succeed in renewing the lease before it expires, out it goes! This release process is an important function that's useful for reclaiming extinct IP addresses formerly used by systems that have moved or switched to a non-DHCP address.

DHCP Terminology

From the previous section, you should have a solid understanding of the lease process. To properly learn how to configure your servers to hand out those leases, though, you need to have a bigger vocabulary. You can start with the concept of a *scope*, which is nothing more than a contiguous range of addresses. There's usually one scope per physical subnet, and a scope can cover a Class A, Class B, or Class C network address. DHCP uses scopes as the basis for managing and assigning IP addressing information.

A *superscope* is an administrative convenience. It allows you to group two or more scopes together even though they're actually separate. In reality, a superscope is just a list of its child scopes. Microsoft's DHCP snap-in allows you to manage IP address assignment in the superscope, though you must still configure other scope options individually for each child scope.

Each scope has a set of parameters you can set. These parameters, or scope options, control what data are delivered to DHCP clients to complete the DHCP negotiation process with that particular server. For example, the DNS server name, default gateway, and default network time server are all separate options that can be assigned. More properly, these settings are called option types; you can use any of the types provided with Windows 2000 or you can roll your own.

What about IP addresses? Aren't they the *raison d'etre* of DHCP? You bet. The scope defines what addresses could potentially be assigned, but you can influence the assignment process in two additional ways by specifying the following:

- Any IP addresses within the range that you *never* want automatically assigned. These addresses are called excluded addresses or just *exclusions*, and they're off-limits to DHCP. You'll typically use exclusions to tag any addresses that you never want the DHCP server to assign.

- Any IP addresses within the range for which you want a permanent DHCP lease. These addresses are known as *reservations*, since they essentially reserve a particular IP address for a particular device.

How do you know whether to use a reservation or an exclusion? The key is what you want to do with the addresses. Obviously, you don't want them assigned to "ordinary" clients, but why not? Any addresses that are configured manually on individual hosts should be excluded so that they are not assigned by DHCP. If you're using devices like laptops, and you want them to get DHCP settings without getting a new address each time they restart, you can use reservations.

The range of IP addresses that the DHCP server can actually assign is called its *address pool*. For example, say you set up a new DHCP scope covering the 192.168.0 subnet; that gives you 255 IP addresses in the pool. After adding an exclusion from 192.168.0.240 to 192.168.0.254, you're left with 255 − 14 = 241 IP addresses in the pool. That means (in theory, at least) that you can service 241 unique clients at one time before you run out of IP addresses.

Installing DHCP

Installing DHCP is easy, since it uses the new Windows 2000 installation mechanism. Unlike some of the other services you'll see in this book, the actual installation installs just the service and its associated snap-in, starting it when it's done. At that point, it's not delivering any DHCP service, but you don't have to reboot or answer a bunch of intrusive wizard questions. Exercise 2.1 explains how to do the installation.

Microsoft ✓ *Exam Objective*

Configure, administer, and troubleshoot DHCP on servers and client computers.

- Detect unauthorized DHCP servers on a network.
- Configure authorization of DHCP servers.

EXERCISE 2.1

Installing the DHCP Service

Follow these steps to install the DHCP server. Note that this exercise works only on computers running Windows 2000 Server or Advanced Server.

1. Open the Windows Components Wizard by opening the Add/Remove Programs in Control Panel (Start ➢ Settings ➢ Control Panel ➢ Add/Remove Programs).

2. Click the Add/Remove Windows Components icon. The Installation Wizard opens and lists all the components that it knows how to install or remove.

3. Select the Networking Services item from the component list; then click the Details button.

4. When the Subcomponents Of Network Services list appears, make sure that Dynamic Host Configuration Protocol (DHCP) is selected; then click the OK button.

5. If prompted, enter the path to the Windows 2000 distribution files.

When you install the DHCP server, you get the DHCP snap-in installed, too; you can open it by choosing Start ➤ Programs ➤ Administrative Tools ➤ DHCP. The snap-in is shown in Figure 2.1; as you can see, it follows the standard MMC model. The left-hand pane shows you which servers are available; you can connect to servers other than the one you're already talking to. Each server contains subordinate items grouped into folders. Each scope has a folder, which is named after the scope's IP address range. There's also a separate folder, Server Options, which holds options that are specific to a particular DHCP server. Within each scope, there are four subordinate views that show you interesting things about the scope such as the following:

- The Address Pool view shows you what the address pool looks like.

- The Address Leases view contains one entry for each current lease. Each lease shows the computer name to which the lease was issued, the corresponding IP address, and the current lease expiration time.

- The Reservations view shows you which IP addresses are reserved and which devices hold them.

- The Scope Options view lists the set of options you've defined for this scope. For example, Figure 2.1 shows three options: the default gateway (003 Router), the default DNS server (006 DNS Servers), and the default DNS domain name (015 DNS Domain Name).

FIGURE 2.1   The DHCP snap-in

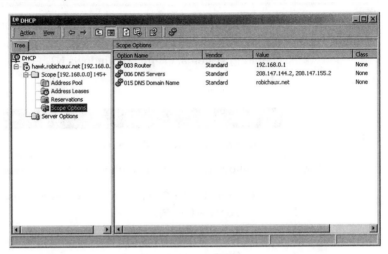

Authorizing DHCP for Active Directory

Once you've installed a server, your next step is to authorize the DHCP server in Active Directory. *Authorization*, which actually creates an Active Directory object representing the new server, helps keep unauthorized servers off your network. These renegade servers can cause two separate kinds of problems: They may hand out bogus leases, or they may fraudulently deny renewal requests from legitimate clients. How can you prevent this? You might start with threatening your end users with banishment back to Windows for Workgroups and then review how Active Directory can help.

When you install a DHCP server using Windows 2000 and if Active Directory is present on your network, the server won't be allowed to provide DHCP services to clients until it's been authorized. If you install DHCP on a member server in an Active Directory domain or on a stand-alone server, you'll have to manually authorize the server. When you authorize a server, you're really adding its IP address to the Active Directory object that contains a list of the IP addresses of all authorized DHCP servers. At start time, each DHCP server queries the directory, looking for its IP address on the "authorized" list. If it can't find the list, or if it can't find its IP address on the list, the DHCP service fails to start. Instead, it logs an event log message indicating that it couldn't service client requests because it wasn't authorized. Exercise 2.2 shows you how to authorize a DHCP server.

This mechanism works only with Windows 2000 DHCP servers; there's no way to monitor or restrict the presence of DHCP servers running under other operating systems, including Windows NT.

EXERCISE 2.2

Authorizing a DHCP Server

Follow these steps to authorize a DHCP server in Active Directory:

1. Open the DHCP snap-in (Start ➢ Programs ➢ Administrative Tools ➢ DHCP).

2. Right-click the server you want to authorize and choose Authorize from the context menu.

3. Wait a short time (30–45 seconds) to allow the authorization to take place.

4. Right-click the server again. Verify that the Unauthorize command appears in the context menu; this indicates that the server is now authorized.

You can unauthorize a previously authorized server by right-clicking it and choosing Unauthorize.

Creating and Managing DHCP Scopes

Earlier, we tantalized you by claiming that you can use any number of DHCP servers on a single physical network. This is possible if you divide the range of addresses you want assigned into multiple scopes. Each scope contains a number of useful pieces of data, but before you can find out what they are, you need another DHCP vocabulary lesson.

Microsoft ✓ *Exam* *Objective*	**Configure, administer, and troubleshoot DHCP on servers and client computers.**
	• Configure DHCP server properties.
	• Create and configure a DHCP scope.

Creating a New, Plain-Vanilla Scope

Like many other things in Windows 2000, the process of creating a new scope is driven by a wizard. In this case, the New Scope Wizard does the dirty deed. The overall process is simple, as long as you know beforehand what the wizard is going to ask. If you think about what defines a scope, you'll be well prepared. You need to know the following:

- The IP address range for the scope you want to create

- Which IP addresses, if any, you want to exclude from the address pool

- Which IP addresses, if any, you want to reserve

- Values for the DHCP options you want to set, if any

This last item isn't strictly necessary for creating a scope, since the wizard doesn't ask for any options. However, to leave scopelessness behind and create a useful scope, you'll need to have *some* options to specify for the clients.

To create a scope, select a superscope or DHCP server in the DHCP snap-in and then use the Action ➤ New Scope command. That starts the New Scope Wizard, whose operation we'll now discuss in detail, with each wizard page in its own section.

The Boring Stuff

The first two wizard pages are pretty useless; the first page just tells you that you've launched the New Scope Wizard, and the second allows you to enter a name and description for your scope. These tidbits will be displayed by the DHCP snap-in, so it's a good idea to pick a sensible name for your scopes so that other administrators will be able to figure out what the scope is *for*.

Defining the IP Address Range

The next wizard page, the IP Address Range page (Figure 2.2), is where you enter the start and end IP addresses for your range. The wizard does minimal checking on the addresses you enter, but it does automatically calculate the appropriate subnet mask for the address range you enter. You can modify the subnet mask if you know what you're doing.

FIGURE 2.2   The IP Address Range page of the New Scope Wizard

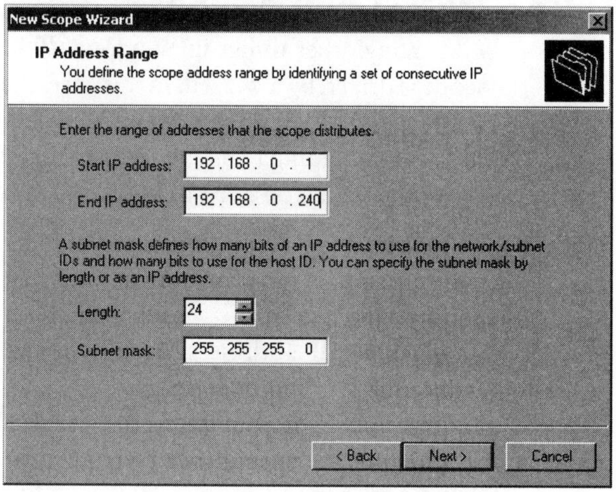

Adding Exclusions

The Add Exclusions page (Figure 2.3) allows you to create exclusion ranges as part of the scope-creation process. To exclude one address, put it in the Start IP Address field; to exclude a range, fill in a starting and ending address. Remember that you can always add exclusions later, but it's best to include them when you create the scope so that no excluded addresses are ever passed out to clients.

FIGURE 2.3   The Add Exclusions page of the New Scope Wizard

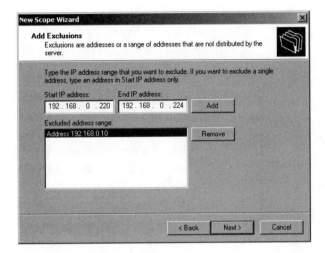

Setting a Lease Duration

The Lease Duration page (not shown) allows you to set the lease duration. By default, new leases start with a duration of eight days and zero hours. This isn't a bad default, but you may find that a shorter or longer duration makes sense for your network. If your network is highly dynamic, with lots of arrivals, departures, and moving computers, set the lease duration to be short; if it's less active, set it for longer. Remember that renewal attempts begin when half of the lease period is over, so don't set them *too* short.

Configuring Basic DHCP Options

The Configure DHCP Options page (not shown) allows you to choose whether you want to configure basic DHCP options (including the default gateway and DNS settings). If you choose to configure these options, you'll have to go through some additional pages, all of which are pretty simple. If you choose not to configure options, you can go back and do so later; if you choose to take that route, make sure you don't activate the scope until you've configured the options you want assigned.

Configuring a Router

The first option configuration page is the Router (Default Gateway) page (Figure 2.4), which allows you to enter the IP addresses of one or more routers that you want to use as gateways for outbound traffic. Type in the IP addresses of the routers you want to use, and then use the Up and Down buttons to put the list in the order you want clients to use when attempting to send outgoing packets.

Providing DNS Settings

The Domain Name And DNS Servers page (Figure 2.5) lets you specify the set of DNS servers and the parent domain you want passed down to DHCP clients. Normally, you'll need to specify at least one DNS server by filling in its DNS name or IP address; you can also specify the domain you want Windows 2000 to use as its base domain for all connections that don't have their own connection-specific suffixes defined.

FIGURE 2.4 The Router (Default Gateway) page of the New Scope Wizard

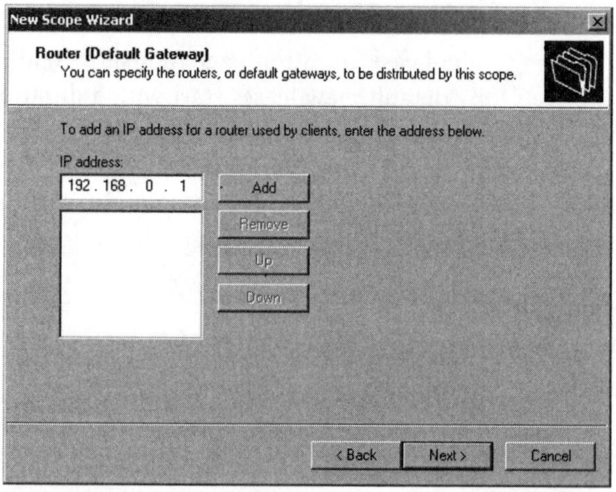

FIGURE 2.5   The Domain Name And DNS Servers page of the New Scope Wizard

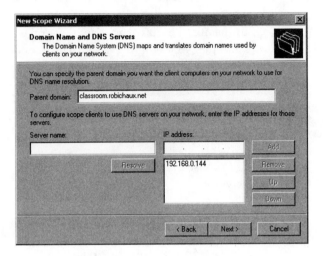

Providing WINS Settings

If you're still using WINS on your network, you can configure DHCP so that it passes WINS server addresses to your Windows clients (though if you want the Windows clients to honor it, you'll also need to define the WINS/NBT Node Type option for the scope). Like the DNS server page, on this page (Figure 2.6) you can enter the addresses of several servers, moving them into the order in which you want clients to try them. You may enter the DNS or NetBIOS name of each server, or you can enter an IP address.

FIGURE 2.6   The WINS Servers page of the New Scope Wizard

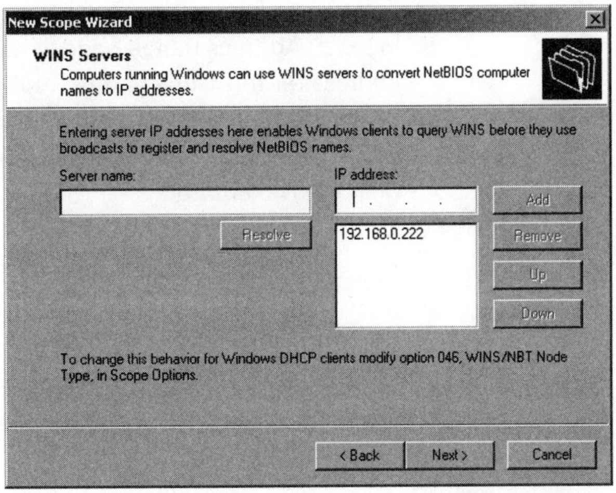

Activating the Scope

The final page allows you to activate the scope immediately after creating it. By default, the wizard assumes that you want the scope activated unless you select the No, I Will Active [sic] This Scope Later radio button, in which case the scope will remain dormant until you manually activate it.

WARNING Be sure to verify that there are no other DHCP servers assigned to the address range you choose!

Exercise 2.3 shows the steps to create a new scope for a private Class C network.

EXERCISE 2.3

Creating a New Scope

Follow these steps to create a new scope for the 193.169.0 private Class C network:

1. Open the DHCP snap-in (Start ➤ Programs ➤ Administrative Tools ➤ DHCP).

2. Right-click the server on which you want to create the new scope, and choose New Scope. The New Scope Wizard appears.

3. Click the OK button to dismiss the first (worthless) wizard page.

4. Enter a name and a description for your new scope, and then click the Next button.

5. In the IP Address Range page, enter **193.169.0.1** as the start IP address for the scope and **193.169.0.254** as the end IP address. Leave the subnet mask controls alone (though when creating a scope on a production network, you might need to change them). Click the Next button.

6. In the Add Exclusions page, click Next without adding any excluded addresses.

7. In the Lease Duration page, set the lease duration to three days; then click the Next button.

8. In the Configure DHCP Options page, click the Next button to indicate that you want to configure default options for this scope.

9. Enter a router IP address (e.g., **193.169.0.1**) in the IP Address field, and then click the Add button. Once the address is added, click the Next button.

10. In the Domain Name And DNS Servers page, enter the IP address of a DNS server on your network in the IP Address field; then click the Add button. When you've finished, click the Next button.

11. On the WINS Servers page, click the Next button to leave the WINS options unset and display the Activate Scope page.

12. If your network is currently using the 193.169.0.x range, select the No, I Will Active [sic] This Scope Later radio button. Click the Next button. When the Wizard Summary page appears, click the Finish button to create the scope.

Changing Your Mind Later

Each scope has a set of properties associated with it. Except for the set of options assigned by the scope (more about this in the next section), these properties are exposed in the General tab of the Scope Properties dialog box (Figure 2.7). Some of these properties, like the Scope Name and Description fields, are self-explanatory. Others require a little more exposition:

- The Start IP Address and End IP Address fields allow you to set the size of the scope. The subnet mask is automatically calculated for you based on the IP addresses you enter.

- The controls in the Lease Duration For DHCP Clients group determine how long leases in this scope remain valid. Your two choices are set by the Limited To and Unlimited radio buttons. If you choose to set lease duration limits, you use the Days, Hours, and Minutes controls to govern how long the leases remain in use.

FIGURE 2.7 The General tab of the Scope Properties dialog box

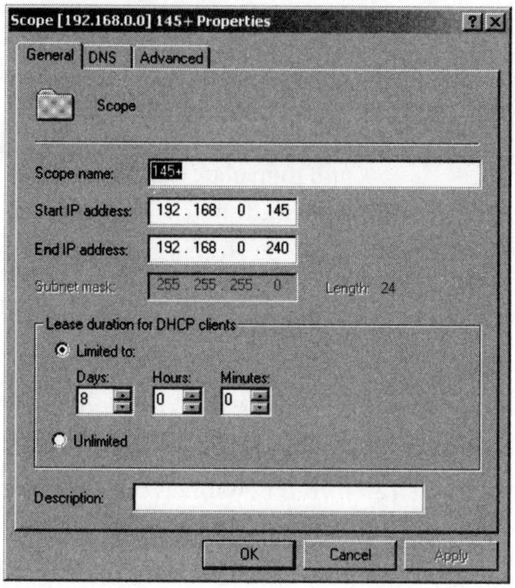

> Don't confuse the process of setting properties of the scope with setting the options associated with the scope—they're two entirely different operations.

When you make changes to these properties, bear in mind that they have no effect on existing leases. For example, say you create a scope from 172.30.1.1 to 172.30.1.199. You use that scope for a while and then edit its properties to reduce the range from 172.30.1.1 to 172.30.1.150. If a client has, say, 172.30.1.180–an address legal under the scope before you changed it—the client will retain that address but will not be able to renew the address.

Managing Reservations and Exclusions

After defining the address pool, the next step is to create whatever reservations and exclusions you want used to reduce the size of the pool.

Adding and Removing Exclusions

When you want to exclude an entire range of IP addresses, you need to add that range as an exclusion. Normally, you'll want to do this before you enable a scope, since that prevents you from accidentally issuing any of the excluded IP addresses. In fact, you can't create an exclusion that includes a leased address—you have to get rid of the lease first.

Here's how to add an exclusion range:

1. Open the DHCP snap-in and find the scope to which you want to add an exclusion.

2. Expand the scope so you can see its Address Pool item.

3. Right-click Address Pool and choose New Exclusion Range. (You can use the Actions ➤ New Exclusion Range command instead.)

4. When the Add Exclusion dialog box appears (see Figure 2.8), use it to enter the IP addresses you want to exclude. To exclude a single address, type it into the Start IP Address field; to exclude a range, put the ending address of the range into the End IP Address field.

5. Click the Add button to add the exclusion.

FIGURE 2.8 The Add Exclusion dialog box

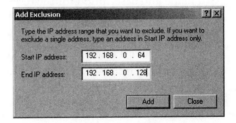

When you add exclusions, they appear in the Address Pool node under the scope where you add them. To remove an exclusion, just right-click it and use the Delete command. After confirming your command, the snap-in removes the excluded range and it becomes immediately available for issuance.

Adding and Removing Reservations

Adding reservations is simple, as long as you have the MAC address of the device for which you want to create a reservation. Since reservations belong to a single scope, you create and remove them within the Reservations node beneath each scope. You add reservations by right-clicking the scope and choosing New Reservation; that displays the New Reservation dialog box shown in Figure 2.9.

FIGURE 2.9 The New Reservation dialog box

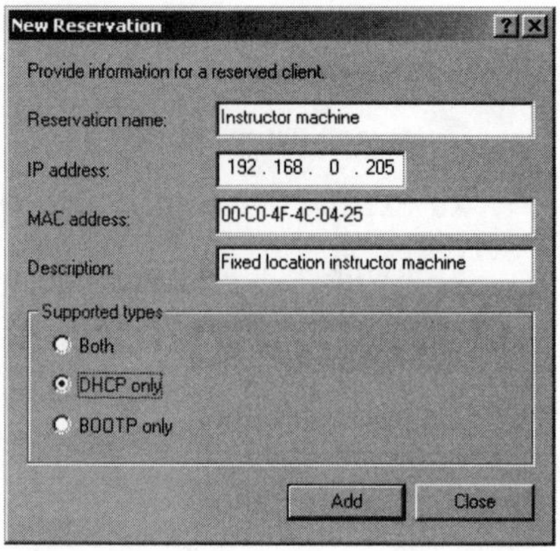

At a minimum, when you create a new reservation you must enter the IP address and MAC address for the reservation. If you like, you can also enter a name and description for the reservation. You can also choose whether the reservation will be made by DHCP only, BOOTP only (useful for remote-access devices that use BOOTP), or both.

To remove a reservation, right-click it and use the Delete command. This removes the reservation but does nothing to the client device (after all, it doesn't have a lease to revoke!).

There's no way to change a reservation once it's been created—you'll have to delete it and re-create it to change any of the associated settings.

Setting Options for a New Scope

Once you've installed a server, authorized it in Active Directory, and fixed up the address pool, the next step is to set the options you want sent out to clients. You *must* configure the options you want sent out before you activate a scope; if you don't, clients may register in the scope without getting any options, rendering them useless.

Understanding Option Assignment

There are actually five different (and slightly overlapping) ways to control which DHCP options are doled out to clients.

Predefined Options

You predefine options so that they'll be available in the Server, Scope, or Client Options dialog boxes. Think of predefining options like the process of printing a restaurant menu—you have to pick the dishes you want to appear before diners can select from them.

Server Options

Server options are assigned to all scopes and clients of a particular server. That means if there's some setting you want *all* clients of a DHCP server to have, no matter what scope they're in, this is where you'd assign them. However, note that more specific options (like those that are set at the class, scope, or client level) override server-level options. That gives you an escape valve; it's a better idea, though, to be careful about which options you assign if your server manages multiple scopes.

Scope Options

If you want a particular option value assigned only to those clients in a certain subnet, select that scope as the base for the option. For example, it's common to specify different routers for different physical subnets; if you have two scopes corresponding to different subnets, each scope would probably have a separate value for the router option.

Class Options

The idea behind class options is that you should be able to assign different options to clients in different classes. For example, Windows 2000 machines recognize a number of DHCP options that Windows 98 and Mac OS machines ignore. By defining a new Windows 2000 class, you could assign those options only to machines that report themselves as being in that class. The problem is that you need to have clients that are smart enough to do so, and most of them aren't.

Client Options

If you want to force certain options onto a specific client, you can do so—provided the client is using a DHCP reservation. You actually attach client options to a particular reservation; they'll override any scope, server, or class option. In fact, the only way to override a client option is to manually configure the client. The DHCP server manages client options.

Assigning Options

You can use the DHCP snap-in to assign options at the scope, server, reserved address, or class level (although we're now going to start pretending that the class options don't exist). The mechanism you use to assign these options is identical; the only difference is where you set the options. When you create an option assignment, remember that it applies to all the clients in the server or the scope *from that point forward*. Option assignments aren't retroactive, and they don't migrate from one scope to another.

To actually *create* a new option and have it assigned, select the scope or server where you want the option assigned; then select the corresponding Options node and choose Action ➢ Configure Options. (To set options for a reserved client, right-click its entry in the Reservations node and use the Configure Options command from there.) You'll then see the Scope Options dialog box (Figure 2.10), which lists all of the options you might potentially want to configure. To select an individual option, check the box next to it and then use the controls in the Data Entry control group to enter the value you want associated with the option. Continue to add options until you've specified all the ones you want attached to the server or scope; then click the OK button.

FIGURE 2.10   The Scope Options dialog box

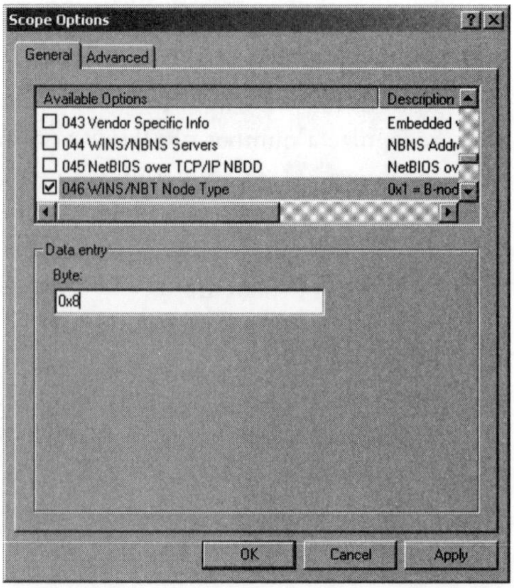

Activating and Deactivating Scopes

When you've completed the preceding steps and you're ready to unleash your new scope so that it can be used to make client assignments, the final required step is activating the scope. Activating a scope just tells the server that it's okay to start handing out addresses from that scope's address pool. As soon as you activate a scope, addresses from its pool may be assigned to clients. Of course, this is a necessary precondition to getting any use out of your scope.

If you later want to stop using a scope, you can, but beware: It's a permanent change. You turn off a scope by deactivating it, but when you do, DHCP tells all clients registered with the scope that they need to release their leases and renew them someplace else—the equivalent of a landlord who evicts his tenants when the building is condemned! Don't deactivate a scope unless you want clients to stop using it immediately.

Creating a Superscope

A superscope allows the DHCP server to provide multiple logical subnet addresses to DHCP clients on a single physical network. You create superscopes with the New Superscope command. It shouldn't surprise you to learn that this triggers the New Superscope Wizard. However, this particular wizard is so simple that it didn't really need to be a wizard.

To create a superscope, follow the steps in Exercise 2.4.

You can only have one superscope per server.

EXERCISE 2.4

Creating a New Superscope

Follow these steps to create a superscope:

1. Open the DHCP snap-in (Start ➤ Programs ➤ Administrative Tools ➤ DHCP).

2. Follow the instructions in Exercise 2.3 to create two scopes: one for 192.168.0.1–192.168.0.127 and one for 192.168.0.128–192.168.0.240.

3. Right-click your DHCP server and choose the New Superscope command. The New Superscope Wizard appears. Dismiss the first wizard page by clicking the Next button.

4. In the Superscope Name page, name your superscope and then click the Next button.

5. The Select Scopes page appears, showing a list of all scopes on the current server. Select the two scopes you created in step 2 and then click the Next button.

6. The Wizard Summary page appears; click the Finish button to create your scope.

7. Verify that your new superscope appears in the DHCP snap-in.

You may notice that you can delete a superscope by right-clicking it and choosing the Delete command. Since a superscope is just an administrative fantasy, you can safely delete one at any time—it doesn't affect the "real" scopes that make up the superscope.

Adding and Removing Children

Adding a scope to an existing superscope is trivial—find the scope you want to add and then right-click it and choose Action ≻ Add To Superscope. This causes the snap-in to show you a dialog box listing all of the superscopes known to this server; pick the one you want the current scope appended to and click the OK button.

If you later want to remove a scope from a superscope, open the superscope and right-click the target scope. The context menu provides a Remove From Superscope command that will do the deed.

Activating and Deactivating Superscopes

Just as with regular scopes, you can activate and deactivate superscopes. The same restrictions and guidelines apply: To wit, you must activate a superscope before it can be used, and you must not deactivate it until you want all your clients to lose their existing leases and be forced to request new ones.

Creating Multicast Scopes

IP multicasting is becoming increasingly common as the amount of network bandwidth available on the average network increases. It's much more efficient to *multicast* a video or audio stream to multiple destinations than it is to broadcast it to the same number of clients, and the increased demand for multicast-friendly network hardware has resulted in some head scratching about how to automate the multicast configuration.

MADCAP

DHCP is normally used to assign IP configuration information for *unicast* (or one-to-one) network communications. It turns out that there's a separate type of address space assigned just for multicasting: 224.0.0.0–239.255.255.255. However, multicast clients also need to have an "ordinary" IP address; clients can participate in a multicast just by knowing (and using) the multicast address for the content they want to receive.

How do they know what address to use? Ordinary DHCP won't help, since it's designed to assign IP addresses and option information to one client at a time. Realizing this, the IETF defined a new protocol, the *Multicast Address Dynamic Client Allocation Protocol (MADCAP)*. MADCAP provides an analogy to DHCP, but for multicast use. A MADCAP server issues leases for multicast addresses only. MADCAP clients can request a multicast lease when they want to participate in a multicast.

There are some important differences between DHCP and MADCAP. First, you have to realize that the two are totally separate. A single server can be a DHCP server, a MADCAP server, or *both*; there's no implied or actual relation between the two. Likewise, clients can use DHCP and/or MADCAP at the same time—the only requirement is that every MADCAP client has to get a unicast IP address from *somewhere*.

Next, remember that DHCP can assign options as part of the lease process, but MADCAP cannot. The only thing MADCAP does is dynamically assign multicast addresses.

The Windows 2000 Server online help has a comprehensive checklist that covers how to set up IP multicasting, just in case you're interested.

Building Multicast Scopes

When you want to create a new multicast scope, right-click the server where you want the scope created and choose the New Multicast Scope option. Most of the steps you go through when creating a multicast scope are identical to those required for an ordinary unicast scope, so you'll see the differences highlighted in Exercise 2.5.

EXERCISE 2.5

Creating a New Multicast Scope

Follow these steps to create a new multicast scope:

1. Open the DHCP snap-in (Start ➢ Programs ➢ Administrative Tools ➢ DHCP).

2. Right-click your DHCP server and choose New Multicast Scope. The New Multicast Scope Wizard appears. Dismiss the first wizard page by clicking the Next button.

3. In the Multicast Scope Name page, name your multicast scope (and add a description if you'd like); then click the Next button.

4. The IP Address Range page appears. Enter a start IP address of `224.0.0.0` and an end IP address of `224.255.0.0`. Adjust the TTL to 1 to make sure that no multicast packets escape your local network segment. Click the Next button when you've finished.

5. The Add Exclusions page appears; click its Next button.

6. The Lease Duration page appears. Normally you leave multicast scope assignments in place somewhat longer than their unicast brethren, hence the default lease length of 30 days. Click the Next button.

7. The wizard asks you if you want to activate the scope now. Click the No radio button and then the Next button.

8. The Wizard Summary page appears; click the Finish button to create your scope.

9. Verify that your new multicast scope appears in the DHCP snap-in. Delete it at your convenience.

Setting Multicast Scope Properties

Once you create a multicast scope, you can adjust its properties by selecting it and using the standard (and by now, very familiar) Properties command. The Multicast Scope Properties dialog box has two tabs. The General tab allows you to change the scope's name, its start or end address, its TTL value, its lease duration, and its description—in essence, all of the settings you provided when you created it in the first place. The Lifetime tab (see Figure 2.11) allows you to limit how long your multicast scope will hang around. By default, a newly created multicast scope will live forever, but if you're creating a scope to provide MADCAP assignments for a single event (or a set of events that cover a limited duration), you can specify an expiration time for the scope. When that time is reached, the scope disappears from the server, but not before making all its clients give up their multicast address leases. This is a nice way to make sure the lease cleans up after itself when you've finished with it.

FIGURE 2.11   The Lifetime tab of the Multicast Scope Properties dialog box

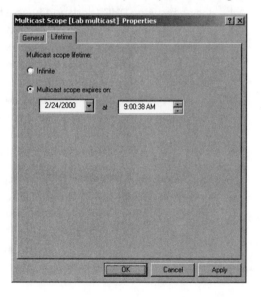

🌐 Real World Scenario

Deciding to Implement DHCP in a Static IP Environment

You work for a company that has a static IP environment. Everything about the IP configuration is currently stable, and you have a clearly written procedure for adding new workstations to the network, including the IP configuration. You have read a great deal about DHCP and are interested in it, but you subscribe to the time-tested philosophy that if something isn't broken, don't fix it.

At least, that was your philosophy until you were told yesterday that your company has decided to change its ISP because the CFO cut a deal that will save the company a lot of money over a two-year period. One thing that she hasn't considered, however, is the time that it will take you to change the DNS entry at every workstation in your network.

Much has been written about how simple it is to change an IP subnetting design by using DHCP and modifying it by modifying the scope. This is true, but in practice you don't actually change your subnet designs very often. However, DHCP really pays off even when you only have to make small changes to the IP configuration. A simple change like adding a new DNS server can be completed within seconds with DHCP, but, alas, with a static network you have to visit and touch every IP stack in your network. As you can imagine, this is going to take at least several minutes for each machine. The more workstations you have, the greater the cost you will pay, measured against the savings earned by using DHCP.

Now that you've calculated the cost in your head, here is a tip: The best time to move from static IP to DCHP is when there is no major change in the works. Just create your current environment using scopes in DHCP, test it in a lab, and then touch your workstations for the last time as you move them from static addresses to the automatic addresses available with DHCP.

Monitoring and Troubleshooting DHCP

DHCP doesn't require a lot of ongoing care. However, it's useful to know how to monitor and troubleshoot it for those rare occasions when something does go wrong (apart from the fact that monitoring and trouble-shooting are covered on the exam!).

Microsoft ✓ **Exam Objective**

Configure, administer, and troubleshoot DHCP on servers and client computers.

Monitoring DHCP Leases

You monitor which DHCP leases have been assigned using the Address Lease view associated with a particular scope. When you open the scope and choose this view, you'll see an easy-to-read list of all the leases currently in force for that scope. This view will show you the client IP address, the client DNS name, the lease's duration, and the client's unique DHCP ID (if there is one).

Removing Client Leases

If you want to remove a client lease, you can do so by right-clicking it and choosing Delete. This actually removes the lease, but not before canceling it. Normally, it's better to let leases expire rather than manually canceling them, but sometimes circumstances dictate otherwise.

In Exercise 2.6, we create a text file that contains information about all leases in a scope.

EXERCISE 2.6

Inspecting Leases

Follow these steps to create a tab-delimited text file containing infor-mation about all leases in a scope. You can use this file for analysis or record keeping.

1. Open the DHCP snap-in (Start ➢ Programs ➢ Administrative Tools ➢ DHCP).

2. Expand the target server's node in the MMC until you see the Address Leases node.

EXERCISE 2.6 *(continued)*

3. Right-click the Address Leases node and choose Export List.

4. When the Save As dialog box appears, select a location for the list file. Type a meaningful name in the Filename field and click the Save button.

5. Open the file you just created with WordPad, Word, Excel, or any other tool that honors tab settings. Notice that the contents of the file mirror exactly what you saw in the DHCP snap-in.

Using *Ipconfig* to Renew and Release a Lease

Ipconfig has some options that make it particularly handy for DHCP clients: the /renew and /release switches. These switches allow you to request renewal of, or give up, your machine's existing address lease. This might not seem that useful since you can essentially do the same thing by toggling the Obtain An IP Address Automatically button, but it is—especially when you're setting up a new network.

For example, we spend about a third of our time teaching Windows 2000 classes in temporary classrooms set up at conferences, hotels, and so on. These classes use laptops, with one brawny laptop set up as a DNS/DHCP/DC server. Occasionally, a balky client will lose its DHCP lease (or not get one, perhaps because a cable has come loose or something), and the quickest way to fix it is to pop open a command-line window and type **ipconfig / renew**. As if you couldn't guess by now, the switches do the following:

ipconfig /renew   Instructs the DHCP client to request a lease renewal. If it already has a lease, it requests a renewal from the server, which issued the current lease. This is exactly equivalent to what happens when the client reaches the half-life of its lease. If the client *doesn't* currently have a lease, the process is identical to what happens when you boot a DHCP client for the first time: It initiates the DHCP mating dance, listens for lease offers, and chooses one it likes.

ipconfig /release   Forces the client to immediately give up its lease by sending the server a DHCP release notification. The server updates its status information and marks the client's old IP address as "available," leaving the client with no address bound to its network interface. When you use this command, most of the time it will be immediately followed by `ipconfig /renew`; the combination releases the existing lease and gets a new one, probably with a different address. (It's also a handy way to force your client to get a new set of settings from the server before lease-expiration time.)

If you have multiple network adapters in a single machine, you can provide the name of the adapter (or adapters) you want the command to work on, including an asterisk (*) as a wildcard. For example, one of our servers has two network cards: One's an Intel EtherExpress, and one's a generic 100Mbps card from Best Buy. If we want to renew DHCP settings for both adapters, we can type **`ipconfig /renew *`**; if we just want to renew the generic card, we can type **`ipconfig /renew ELNK1`**.

Working with the DHCP Database Files

The following are true of DHCP database files:

- DHCP uses a set of database files to maintain its knowledge of scopes, superscopes, and client leases. These files, which live in `%systemroot%\system32\DHCP`, are always open when the DHCP service is running, and you shouldn't modify or alter them when the service is stopped. The primary database file is `dhcp.md`–it has all the goodies in it.

- `Dhcp.tmp` is a backup copy of the database file created during re-indexing of the database. You normally won't see this file, but if the service fails during re-indexing, it may not remove the file when it should.

- `J50.log` (plus a number of files named `J50xxxxx.log`) is a log file that stores changes before they're written to the database. The DHCP database engine can recover some changes from these files when it restarts.

- `J50.chk` is a checkpoint file that tells the DHCP engine which log files it still needs to recover.

Removing the Database Files

If you're convinced that your database is corrupt because the lease information you see doesn't match what's on the network, the easiest repair mechanism is to remove the database files and start over with a clean slate. (On the other hand, if you're convinced that it's corrupt because the DHCP service failed at startup, you should check the event log.) To start over, stop the DHCP service and remove all of the files from `%systemroot%\system32\DHCP`, and then restart the service. Once you've done so, you can reconcile the scope (as described in the next section) to rebuild the database contents.

Changing the Database Backup Interval

By default, the DHCP service backs up its databases every 15 minutes. You can adjust this setting by editing the Backup Interval value under `HKEY_LOCAL_MACHINE\SYSTEM\CurrentControlet\Services\DHCPServer\Parameters`. This allows you to make backups either more frequently (if your database changes a lot, or if you seem to have ongoing corruption problems) or less often (if everything seems to be on an even keel).

Reconciling DHCP Scopes

As time passes, you may experience what we call DHCP drift, or when the contents of your DHCP database no longer reflect accurately what's on your network. Although Microsoft doesn't make any prominent mention of this fact in the DHCP documentation, the DHCP server actually records lease information in two places: the DHCP database *and* the server's Registry. When you reconcile a scope, the DHCP server cross-checks the database contents with the contents of the Registry, reporting (and fixing) any inconsistencies it finds. You can also reconcile scopes to recover from a corrupt DHCP database. You first remove the database files, then reconcile the server's scopes, and off you go.

Exercise 2.7 details the steps necessary to reconcile a single scope.

EXERCISE 2.7

Reconciling a Scope

Follow these steps to reconcile a single scope on your server:

1. Open the DHCP snap-in (Start ➢ Programs ➢ Administrative Tools ➢ DHCP).

EXERCISE 2.7 *(continued)*

2. Expand the target server's node in the MMC until you see the target scope.

3. Right-click the target scope and choose Reconcile.

4. The Reconcile dialog box appears, but it's empty. To start the reconciliation, click the Verify button.

5. If the database is consistent, you'll see a dialog box telling you so. If there are any inconsistencies, the dialog box will list them and allow you to repair them.

You can use a similar procedure to reconcile all scopes on a server. You just right-click the DHCP server and choose Reconcile All Scopes instead of reconciling the individual scope. To recover a broken DHCP server the preferred way, you first remove the database files, and then you reconcile all scopes on the server to rebuild the database.

Real World Scenario

DHCP Options

The network you are administering covers several locations and is growing at a steady clip. You were part of the team that helped implement the design that the engineering staff planned. During that implementation, your main role was to make sure that the workstations were changed from static IP addresses to the dynamic option after the DHCP infrastructure was put into place. While you were working on this, you discovered that there were a great many options at the DHCP server that were not being used. When you brought this up to the team, you were told that only the options in the design were available and not to "redesign" the network as you deployed it. After the migration settled down, you decided as the administrator that you wanted to add some of the options in the DHCP server. In that vein, you looked at the scope for the subnet you are responsible for and started adding the options that seemed appealing to you. When you finished, you had added the Time Offset, Time Server, and Cookie Server options. You start testing your work and you discover that none of the changes have shown up at the client.

RFC 1497 originally defined the BootP Vendor Information Extensions for the DHCP protocol. There are many options specified, and the list grows constantly. However, these options are not mandatory, so all implementations of DHCP support only those options that the vendors thinks appropriate for their product. While Microsoft's DHCP server supports may of these options, the Microsoft DHCP client supports only the Subnet Mask, Router (Default Gateway), DNS Server, and DNS Domain Name options. This is because they are all Microsoft needs in order to deliver the services necessary to support their products. For example, a Microsoft client gets it time from the servers in a proprietary manner. Clients from other vendors can use other options stored in the DHCP server.

Many services work in harmony to provide the infrastructure that provides higher-level services to the users. Understanding how these layers upon layers of services work is critical to supporting the overall network. However, you must consider that not every option in every service is available or perhaps even desirable in the Windows 2000 environment. Before you start going down any sort of experimental road, it is important that you first test the options in a lab environment.

Summary

D HCP is an important administrative aid because it prevents you from having to configure every machine on the network individually. You will need to spend some time setting up your DHCP server initially, but once you do, DHCP requires little in the way of administration.

The first part of this chapter consisted of an overview of DHCP terms and how the lease process works. Then we dealt with installing the DHCP service and configuring scopes. Finally, you learned how to monitor and troubleshoot DHCP.

Exam Essentials

Know how to install and authorize a DHCP server.   You install the DHCP service using the Add/Remove Windows Components Wizard. You authorize the DHCP server using the DHCP snap-in. When you authorize a server, you're actually adding its IP address to the Active Directory object that contains a list of the IP addresses of all authorized DHCP servers.

Know how to create a DHCP scope.   You use the New Scope Wizard to create a new scope. Before you start, you'll need to know what the IP address range is for the scope you want to create, which IP addresses, if any, you want to exclude from the address pool, which IP addresses, if any, you want to reserve, and the values for the DHCP options you want to set, if any.

Understand the different settings that can be assigned via DHCP.   A DHCP server can assign IP addresses, router information, DNS settings, and WINS settings.

Understand the difference between exclusions and reservations.   When you want to exclude an entire range of IP addresses, you need to add that range as an exclusion. Any IP addresses within the range for which you want a permanent DHCP lease are known as reservations.

Understand what a superscope is used for.   A superscope allows you to group two or more scopes together even though they're actually separate.

Key Terms

Before you take the exam, be sure you're familiar with the following terms:

address pool	exclusion
DHCP authorization	Multicast Address Dynamic Client Allocation Protocol (MADCAP)
DHCP integration	multicast scope
reservation	superscope
scope	unicast scope

Review Questions

1. The corporate network that you help administer is in the process of migrating from Windows NT, Windows 98, and NetWare to Windows 2000. The NetWare servers are almost gone, and your team wants to implement DHCP after they come up with an address scheme. Before this plan was put into place, the network was a hodge-podge of protocols, including TPC/IP, but it was all statically addressed. The team has charged you with recommending how to deploy DHPC so that it will support all the workstations now and then how to migrate it in the future as the entire network is consolidated on Windows 2000. On which of the following machines would your recommend installing DHCP servers in order to support the existing workstations? (Choose all that apply.)

   A. NetWare server with DHCP

   B. Windows NT domain controller

   C. Windows NT member server

   D. Windows NT stand-alone server

   E. Windows 2000 standalone server

   F. Windows 2000 member server

   G. Windows 2000 Professional Server

   H. Windows 2000 domain controller

2. You work for a trucking company that has a flat network supporting the dispatchers, accounting staff, and mechanics, all of whom are in a single location. There are no plans to add any other facilities in the future. You currently have a Windows NT network; when you installed it, you migrated over to TCP/IP with a Class C address of `192.168.1.0`. You are now going to upgrade to Windows 2000, and you want to include DHCP. Because you want to make sure that the addresses are supplied, you want to have two DHCP servers in case one of them fails. How would you configure the two DHCP servers to supply the addresses for this subnet in case one of the DHCP servers goes down?

A. Install both DHCP servers and configure the scope to cover `192.168.1.1` through `192.168.1.254`. Also configure the two servers for push/pull updates so that each DHCP server is aware of the addresses that the other has leased to the Windows 2000 workstations.

B. Install both DHCP servers and configure the scope to cover `192.168.1.11` through `192.168.1.254` so that you exclude 10 addresses for the file and print servers. Also configure the two servers for push/pull updates so that each DHCP server is aware of the addresses that the other has leased to the Windows 2000 workstations.

C. Install both DHCP servers and configure the scope to cover `192.168.1.1` through `192.168.1.254`. Exclude addresses 192 `.168.1.1` through `192.168.1.10` and reserve them for the file and print servers. Also configure the two servers for push/pull updates so that each DHCP server is aware of the addresses that the other has leased to the Windows 2000 workstations.

D. Install both DHCP servers; on one server create a scope with an address range of `192.168.1.11–175`, and on the other server create a scope with an address range of `192.168.1.176–254`. The first 10 addresses are implicitly excluded for the file and print servers.

3. You administer a Windows 2000 network with two locations. The St. Louis office has four Windows 2000 Servers and 150 workstations. The Chicago office has seven Windows 2000 Servers and 300 work-stations. You have been presented with an implementation to support that has one DHCP server in the Chicago office. The two offices do not have a direct connection, but they frequently communicate over the Internet. You have been told to modify the clients to obtain their IP addresses using the DHCP service to finish the rollout of the service. You have completed the Chicago office and have started on the St. Louis office. As you begin to make the changes, it is obvious that these clients are not obtaining their address appropriately. What is the most likely reason that the workstations in St. Louis are not working correctly?

A. The scope on the DHCP server has not been activated.

B. The clients in St. Louis are not configured to use the DHCP relay agent.

C. The St. Louis office needs a DHCP server of its own in order for the St. Louis clients to use DHCP.

D. The DHCP has not been authorized for the other subnet.

4. You are in the process of upgrading your network to Windows 2000, and during the process, you are including DHCP to help manage the IP addressing. You have created the scope with your 10.0.0.0/16 private address range. You now have 50 Windows Professional workstations completed. You still have 100 Windows 95 workstations to migrate over to Windows 2000. Everything went smoothly during the migration and has worked properly for a month. When you arrived at the office this morning, however, there was havoc everywhere. You were told that the Windows 95 workstations can no longer connect to the Windows 2000 Servers, and the Windows 2000 workstations cannot access the servers, but they can communicate peer to peer. When you look at one of the Windows 2000 workstations, you notice that the address is 169.254.0.27. What is the next step you should take to resolve this problem?

A. Install the DHCP relay agent on a Windows 2000 Professional workstation.

B. Attempt to ping the DHCP server from a client with a valid IP address.

C. Enable the conflict-resolution protocol on the DHCP server.

D. Enable the APIPA protocol on the Windows 95 clients.

E. Enable the APIPA protocol on the Windows 2000 clients.

5. You are the network administrator of a company with locations in Atlanta and Baltimore. These locations are the result of a merged organization a few years ago. The Baltimore location was a NetWare environment that was migrated over to Windows NT a few years ago. Both LANS have since been a fully functioning Windows NT network, each running DHCP, DNS, and WINS. The DHCP servers each have their own scopes for their local clients. You have just helped the deployment team migrate all of the servers to Windows 2000 including Active Directory. The team is now completing migrating the workstations in the Atlanta office to Windows 2000 Professional. The team is on its way to Atlanta, and you are there over the weekend to prepare for their efforts. As you evaluate the machines, you realize that the workstations are no longer obtaining their addresses, but there are no reports of problems in the Baltimore office. What is the most probable reason for the new problems in the Atlanta location?

A. You need a DHCP relay agent until the workstations in Atlanta are upgraded.

B. You need one server running Window NT with DHCP to support the Windows NT Workstations in Atlanta.

C. The DHCP server in Atlanta is not authorized in the directory.

D. You need a WINS server running on Windows NT to support the Windows NT clients in Atlanta.

6. Your DHCP server crashed in the middle of the day. You rebooted the server and got it running within five minutes, and nobody but you seemed to notice that it had gone down at all. What additional steps must you take?

A. None. If there were no lease renewal requests during the five-minute period in which the DHCP server was down, none of the clients will ever know that it went down.

B. You need to renew all the leases manually.

C. None. The DHCP server automatically assigned new addresses to all the clients on the network transparently.

D. You must reboot all the client machines.

7. Your employer, the Huggy Buggy Bear Company, has used network-ing for years, starting with LAN Manager in the early 1990s. You migrated to Windows NT as an early adopter, and recently you migrated to Windows 2000. You are using DHCP on your newly upgraded Windows 2000 network, and you still have 100 Windows NT Workstations to migrate before you're finished. You have added a new DNS server to the network and modified the scope on the DHCP server to reflect the new addition. You want to manually renew the lease on the DHCP clients. What command should you use?

A. `w2kipcfg /renew`

B. `ipconfig /renew`

C. `dhcpcfg /renew`

D. `tcpcfg /renew`

E. `winipcfg /renew`

8. You assigned two DNS server addresses as part of the options for a scope. Later you find a client workstation that isn't using those addresses. What's the most likely cause?

A. The client didn't get the option information as part of its lease.

B. The client has been manually configured with a different set of DNS servers.

C. The client has a reserved IP address in the address pool.

D. One of the DNS servers has failed.

9. Your Dead Flowers Florist Company in Las Vegas has been migrated to Windows 2000 using Active Directory to manage the users and desktops with Group Policies. The company is in one location, and all the machines are on the same subnet. Recently, you decided to use DHCP to manage the address space more efficiently, and so you installed the DHCP server on one of the Windows 2000 Servers. The scope was created and activated for use. You also configured all the Windows 2000 Professional workstations to use DHCP. However, when you reboot the Windows 2000 Professional workstations, they cannot obtain an IP address from the DHCP server. What is the most likely reason for the problem on this network?

   A. The DHCP relay agent has not been enabled for this subnet.

   B. The DHCP server has not been authorized to provide addresses in Active Directory.

   C. The DHCP relay agent needs to be installed on the DHCP server to pass the requests to the DHCP service.

   D. The Windows 2000 Server that hosts the DHCP server needs to be rebooted before the DHCP service will start.

10. You are working on a client machine that gets its IP configuration via DHCP. You notice that the client received different configuration information the last few times its lease was renewed. Which of the following would cause this to occur?

   A. The DHCP server is not working properly.

   B. Another computer on the network has taken over your machine's configuration information since the last renewal.

   C. The client is receiving only the information that has changed since the last renewal. An administrator is changing the configuration information between lease renewals.

   D. When clients renew their leases, they receive all of their configuration information. An administrator is changing the configuration information between lease renewals.

11. You have recently been experiencing strange problems with your DHCP server that you can't solve using the traditional commands such as `ipconfig` and `ping`. Sometimes machines get valid leases, and sometimes they don't, seemingly at random. What is the next step you should take?

    A. Reconcile the scope.

    B. Remove the scope and create a new one.

    C. Authorize the server.

    D. Move the DHCP service to another computer.

12. You have a Windows 2000 network that supports a medium-sized business that refurbishes bowling balls for the Rock & Bowl Lanes in Cleveland, Ohio. You decide to finally take the plunge and use DHCP to help manage the IP addresses. You configure the DHCP server, two DNS servers, nine file and print servers, and the IIS server with static IP addresses from your private address range of 192.168.1.1 through 192.168.1.254. When you bring up the workstations over the weekend to test your new DHCP network, everything appears to be working fine; but on Monday you receive calls from some of the users, complaining that they cannot access their servers. What is the most likely cause of this sporadic networking problem?

    A. You didn't create client reservations for the static IP addresses in the scope.

    B. You didn't create a separate scope for the servers that have been configured with the static IP addresses.

    C. You didn't exclude the IP addresses of the servers that have been configured with the static IP addresses.

    D. You didn't configure the servers that have been configured with static IP addresses, for interoperability with a DHCP server.

13. You administer a network that consists of 300 Windows 2000 machines, all on a single subnet. You are deploying DHCP using two Windows 2000 DHCP servers named Dynamo1 and Dynamo2. Dynamo1 will assign IP addresses in the range 208.45.231.1 through 208.45.231.254. Dynamo2 will assign IP addresses in the range 208.45.232.1 through 208.45.232.254. What should you do to ensure that each DHCP client always receives its IP address from the same DHCP server?

A. Configure each DHCP server with one superscope and two member scopes. Configure the first member scope on each server with the range 208.45.231.1 through 208.45.231.254, and the second member scope on each server with the range 208.45.232.1 through 208.45.232.254. On Dynamo1, exclude the range 208.45.232.1 through 208.45.232.254. On Dynamo2, exclude the range 208.45.231.1 through 208.45.231.254.

B. Configure a scope on Dynamo1 with the range 208.45.231.1 through 208.45.231.254. Configure a scope on Dynamo2 with the range 208.45.232.1 through 208.45.232.254.

C. Configure a scope on both servers with the range 208.45.231.1 through 208.45.232.254. Exclude the range 208.45.232.1 through 208.45.232.254 on Dynamo1, and exclude the range 208.45.231.1 through 208.45.231.254 on Dynamo2.

D. Configure one superscope and two member scopes on each DHCP server. Configure the first member scope on each server with the range 208.45.231.1 through 208.45.231.254 and the second member scope on each server with the range 208.45.232.1 through 208.45.232.254.

14. Your network consists of three logical subnets named Subnet A, Subnet B, and Subnet C. They are all on the same physical network. Subnet A contains addresses in the range 208.44.0.1–208.44.0.50, Subnet B contains addresses in the range 208.44.0.60–208.44 .0.100, and Subnet C contains addresses in the range 208.44.0 .110–208.44.0.120. You are setting up a single DHCP server that will provide DHCP services for Subnet A and Subnet B only. The address of the server must be set to 208.44.0.10.

In the following exhibit, each address listed in the Choices column on the left will fit into only one of the empty boxes in the other two columns. Select each address and place it in its appropriate position within the network.

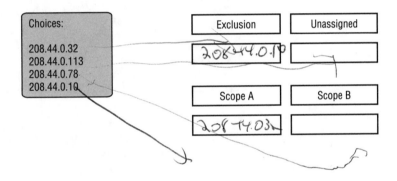

15. Your network consists of 100 Windows 2000 Professional machines, two Windows 2000 Server machines, and three NetWare clients. All the machines need to access resources on the Windows 2000 Server. You want to use TCP/IP with all the Windows computers and IPX/SPX on all the NetWare computers. You also want to minimize setup time as much as possible.

In the following exhibit, the items in the Choices box represent various configuration options for the three different machine types. Select the configuration options and place them in their appropriate places within the network.

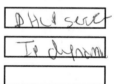

Windows 2000 Server

Choices:

IP addresses assigned dynamically
DHCP server
Static IP address
Network settings configured manually

DHCP server

IP dynami

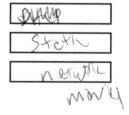

3 NetWare clients

100 Windows 2000
Professional machines

dynam

DHCP

Static

network

manly

Answers to Review Questions

1. F, H. The best choices in this scenario are Windows 2000 machines that participate in Active Directory. While DHCP is a recognized standard and will run on other platforms when the service is associated with Windows 2000, the service must be authorized in order to run. This eliminates problems such as rogue servers causing trouble on your network. It also make little sense to install a new service on platforms that you plan to migrate away from in the near future. As a standard, it is not necessary to run DHCP on the particular platform, such as Windows NT, in order for that service to function properly.

2. D. DHCP servers don't automatically share information. If you want to build a backup server, you must divide the available addresses between the servers. It is recommended that you place 75 percent of the addresses on one server and the other 25 percent of the addresses on the second server, because you'll use the second server only when the first server goes down. In reality, you'll lease an address from the DHCP server that first responds to your request.

3. C. DHCP does not assign addresses across the Internet unless you have set up a special configuration called a *relay agent*, discussed later in this book. DHCP-enabled clients broadcast requests to the local network and wait for a response from a DHCP server.

4. B. When a DHCP-enabled Windows 2000 workstation cannot locate a DHCP server, it automatically configures itself with an address in the 169.254.0.0/16 address range. If you cannot ping the DHCP server from a correctly configured machine, it's likely that the DHCP server is down—which is why the Windows 2000 machines have auto-configured themselves. In this particular situation, the Windows 2000 Servers have configured themselves using APIPA, which is why the other workstations can see the servers. Since the Windows 95 machines didn't participate in the APIPA configuration, they were left without an IP address.

   A conflict-resolution protocol on a DHCP server is used to determine duplicate addresses, not bad ones. APIPA is already enabled on the Windows 2000 machines, which is why the network is behaving in the manner described. The DHCP relay agent is used to pass requests through routers that don't support BootP for DHCP broadcasts.

5. C. Windows NT does not have the concept of authorization. When the servers were migrated, the Atlanta DHCP server was not authorized. You do not need a WINS server for DHCP to operate in either Windows NT or Windows 2000. You also do not need DHCP running on Windows NT to support Windows NT clients. The relay agent is necessary only when you do not have a DHCP server either on the local subnet or on the router between the servers and the client does not support BootP.

6. A. When the DHCP server crashed, the scope was effectively deactivated. Deactivating a scope has no effect on the client until it needs to renew the lease.

7. B. `Ipconfig /renew` command immediately renews the client's DHCP lease. `Winipcfg` is exclusive to Windows 95/98 machines, as you saw in the last chapter, and the other commands are invalid.

8. B. Manual settings override DHCP options.

9. B. When you install a DHCP server using Windows 2000 and Active Directory, the server won't be permitted to provide DHCP services until it has been authorized. When you authorize a server, you are actually adding its IP address to the Active Directory object that contains a list of DHCP servers. If the address of the server isn't on the list, the DHCP service will fail. DHCP relay agents are used to send DHCP requests across routers that don't support BootP. Windows 2000 Servers don't need to be rebooted after DHCP has been installed in order to start the service.

10. D. During lease renewal, the client gets *all* configuration information offered by the server, not a subset of that information.

11. A. Reconciling the scope can fix DHCP scope drift, a phenomenon that occurs over time. You should reconcile the scope if your DHCP server is performing erratically.

12. C. If you configure static IP addresses and then don't exclude those addresses from the scope in the DHCP server, the same addresses will be available to be delivered to clients and will thus create conflicts. The best practice is to exclude a block of addresses large enough to cover all the devices on your network that should be static. Having just one block also makes it easier for you to recognize the excluded addresses when you're looking at network traffic.

Client reservations are used to deliver the same address to the same machine each time and are not used to recognize statically configured clients. A scope identifies a subnet, and the servers and the workstations exist on the same subnet. There is no configuration for a static IP address to interoperate with a DHCP server.

13. A. A superscope allows the DHCP server to provide multiple logical subnet addresses to DHCP clients on a single physical network. By creating a superscope on each server with two member scopes, you will ensure that each DHCP client will always receive its IP address from the same server. In each superscope, you should exclude the range of addresses that you want the other server to assign.

14. See the exhibit below.

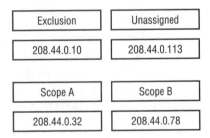

The address 208.44.0.10 needs to be excluded so that the DHCP server can use it. 208.44.0.113 is part of Subnet C and is not assigned by the DHCP server. 208.44.0.32 is part of Scope A, and 208.44.0.78 is part of Scope B.

15. See the exhibit below.

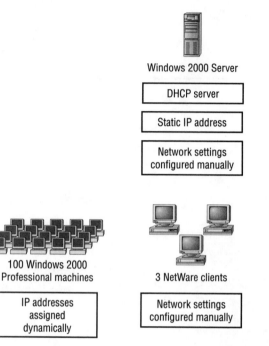

Windows 2000 Server

DHCP server

Static IP address

Network settings configured manually

100 Windows 2000 Professional machines

IP addresses assigned dynamically

3 NetWare clients

Network settings configured manually

Since you have a large number of Windows clients that need to use TCP/IP, you should assign IP addresses to them dynamically. To do this, the Windows 2000 Server computer needs to be configured as a DHCP server, and its IP address needs to be assigned manually. The NetWare clients will not use TCP/IP, so their network settings cannot be assigned via DHCP.

Windows 2000 Network Naming Services

MICROSOFT EXAM OBJECTIVES COVERED IN THIS CHAPTER:

✓ **Configure, administer, and troubleshoot DNS.**

- Configure DNS server properties.
- Manage DNS database records such as CNAME, A, and PTR.
- Create and configure DNS zones.

✓ **Troubleshoot name resolution on client computers. Considerations include WINS, DNS, NetBIOS, the Hosts file, and the Lmhosts file.**

- Configure client computer name resolution properties.
- Troubleshoot name resolution problems by using the nbtstat, ipconfig, nslookup, and netdiag commands.
- Create and configure a Hosts file for troubleshooting name resolution problems.
- Create and configure an Lmhosts file for troubleshooting name resolution problems.

The netdiag portion of the "Troubleshoot name resolution problems by using the nbtstat, ipconfig, nslookup, and netdiag commands" subobjective is covered in Chapter 1, "Installing and Configuring Network Protocols."

In Chapter 1, we looked at the protocols and low-level network infrastructure that are needed to get a network up and running. Theoretically, you could access each computer on the network using its IP address. Realistically, you would have a hard time remembering all of the IP addresses for the machines that you need to connect to. That's where network-naming services come in; they map easy-to-remember names to IP addresses. Windows 2000 ships with support for DNS and WINS, the two most common naming services. DNS is particularly important because understanding it is a prerequisite for using Active Directory, which is the new administrative super-tool that was released with Windows 2000.

You will learn about Active Directory in depth in Chapters 4 through 8.

Understanding DNS is vital to the deployment of Active Directory and is a prerequisite for installing and configuring domain controllers. A common mistake made by systems administrators is underestimating the importance and complexity of DNS. The Active Directory itself relies on DNS in order to find clients, servers, and network services that are available throughout your environment. Clients rely on DNS in order to find the file, print, and other resources they require to get their jobs done. Fully understanding DNS is not an easy task, especially for those who have limited experience with *Transmission Control Protocol/Internet Protocol (TCP/IP)*. However, the understanding and proper implementation of DNS is vital to the use of Active Directory.

We'll begin this chapter by looking at how DNS works. Then, we'll move on to look at how Microsoft's implementation of DNS can be used for name resolution. Finally, we'll look at the integration between Active Directory and DNS, and we'll explore the other major name resolution service, WINS.

DNS Overview

When dealing with large networks, it is vital for both users and network administrators to be able to locate the resources they require with a minimal amount of searching. From a user's standpoint, the actual physical or logical network address of the machine is unimportant. They just want to be able to connect to it using a simple name. From a network administrator's standpoint, however, each machine must have its own logical address that makes it part of the network on which it resides. Therefore, some method for resolving a machine's logical name to an IP address is required. DNS was created to do just that.

DNS is a hierarchical naming system that contains a distributed database of name-to-IP-address mappings. A DNS name is much friendlier and easier to remember than an IP address. For example, every time you enter a URL (such as `www.microsoft.com`), your computer makes a query to a DNS server that resolves it to an IP address. From then on, all communications between your computer and Microsoft's web server take place using the IP address. The beauty of the system is that it's transparent to users. The scalability and reliability of DNS can easily be seen by its widespread use on the Internet.

From a network and systems administration standpoint, however, things are considerably more complex. Active Directory itself is designed to use DNS to locate servers and clients. Microsoft has included a DNS server service with the Windows 2000 operating system. As we'll see, Microsoft has also included many advanced features (some of which are not yet part of the IETF-approved standard DNS) in order to reduce the complexity of maintaining DNS databases.

We'll begin this chapter by looking at how DNS works. Then, we'll move on to see how Microsoft's implementation of DNS can be used for name resolution. Finally, we'll examine the integration between Active Directory and DNS.

DNS Namespace

In the real world, technological and other limitations force network and systems administrators to create and adhere to their own specific set of names and network addresses. Hierarchical names are extremely useful and necessary when participating in a worldwide network such as the Internet. For example, if you have a computer called Workstation1, there must be some way to distinguish it from another computer with the same name at a different company. Similar to the way Active Directory uses hierarchical names for objects, DNS allows for the use of a virtually unlimited number of machines. In this section, we'll look at how these friendly names are structured.

The Anatomy of a DNS Name

We already mentioned that DNS is designed to resolve network addresses with friendly names. DNS names take the form of a series of alphanumeric strings separated by decimal points. Together, the various portions of a DNS name form what is called the *DNS namespace,* and each address within it is unique. All of the following examples are valid DNS names:

- `microsoft.com`

- `www.microsoft.com`

- `sales.microsoft.com`

- `engineering.microsoft.com`

The left-most portion of the name is called the hostname and refers to the actual name of a machine. The remaining portions are part of the domain name and uniquely specify the network on which the host resides. The full name is referred to as the fully qualified domain name (FQDN). For example, the hostname might be `engineering`, whereas the FQDN is `engineering` `.microsoft.com`.

There are several features and limitations to note about a DNS name:

The name is hierarchical.   The domains listed at the right-most side of the address are higher-level domains. As you move left, each portion zooms in on the actual host. In other words, as you read from left to right, you are moving from the specific hostname to its various containers.

The name is case-insensitive.   Although DNS names are sometimes printed in mixed case for clarity, the case of the characters has no relevance.

Each FQDN on a given network must be unique.   Typically, no two machines on the same network, or the Internet for that matter, may have the same FQDN. This requirement ensures that each machine can be uniquely identified.

Round robin DNS can be used to assign a single DNS name to more than one machine. Typically the machines contain the same content, such as mirrored web servers.

Only certain characters are allowed.   Each portion of the DNS name may include only standard English characters, decimal numbers, and dashes.

There are maximum lengths for addresses.   A DNS address can have a maximum length of 255 characters, and each name within the full name can have up to 63 characters.

Figure 3.1 shows an example of a valid hierarchical domain name.

FIGURE 3.1   A sample DNS namespace

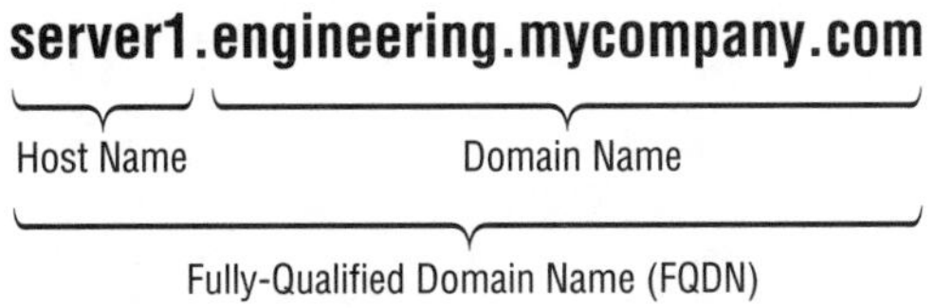

Now that we know the structure of a DNS name, let's move on to look at how the name is actually composed in the real world.

The Root

In order to be able to resolve friendly names with IP addresses, we must have some starting point. All DNS names originate from one address known as the *root*. This address typically does not have a name and is represented in the DNS as a ".". Until recently, there were only nine root DNS servers in the world. After the last Internet brownout, this number was increased and their administration policies were modified. Registered in the root servers are the standard top-level domains with which most people are familiar. It is possible to create your own root-level domain, and this mistake is often made during the installation of Windows 2000. If the Windows 2000 DNS is configured in this manner, then name resolution will occur only within the network controlled by the root-level DNS.

Many organizations worldwide require domain names to be resolved starting at the proper root. That is the purpose of the top-level domains. On the Internet, there are several established top-level domains. Table 3.1

provides a list of the common North American top-level domains. Each domain space is reserved for a particular type of user, also shown in the table.

TABLE 3.1 North American Top-Level Domain Names

Top-Level Domain	Typical Users
.com	Commercial organizations
.edu	Educational institutions
.gov	U.S. governmental organizations
.int	International organizations
.mil	U.S. military organizations
.net	Large network providers (such as Internet service providers)
.biz	Companies doing business online
.info	Organizations providing information
.org	Nonprofit organizations

In addition to these top-level domain names, there are many country codes for top-level domains throughout the world. Each is managed by its own authority. For example, a DNS name that is based in the United Kingdom may have a domain name of mycompany.co.uk. If you require a foreign domain name registration, you should inquire with the country's name service provider.

In order for an organization's own domain name to be resolved on the Internet, it must request that a second-level domain name be added to the global top-level DNS servers. Several registrars can perform this function.

For more information on registering a domain name for your own organization, see www.internic.net. There you will find a list of common registrars available worldwide. There is a nominal charge for each domain name you register.

The name that is registered on the Internet is known as a second-level domain name. `Company1.com`, for example, would be considered a second-level domain name. Within an organization, however, all of the domain names would be subdomains of this one. Figure 3.2 provides an example of how the various levels of DNS domain names form a hierarchy.

FIGURE 3.2   A DNS name hierarchy

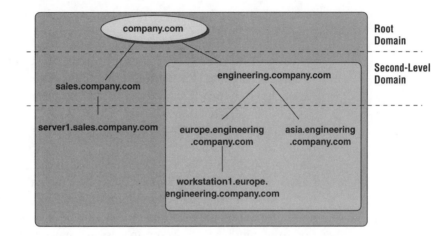

A major consideration of DNS namespace configuration is whether you want to trust public Internet service providers (ISPs) for name resolution. If not, the alternative is to host your own domain name (which can consist of any top-level domain name you choose), but unless you register a standard top-level domain name, your servers cannot be made directly accessible on the Internet. For example, you might choose to use the names `sales.mycompany` and `engineering.mycompany`. Although these are perfectly valid DNS names for internal use, Internet users will not be able to access them. On the other hand, you could trust public Internet authorities and use names such as `sales.mycompany.com` and `engineering.mycompany.com` (as long as you are the registered owner of the `mycompany.com` domain name). In this last scenario, you would need to rely on the DNS servers managed by your ISP for external name resolution.

Parent and Child Names

Once an organization has registered its own domain name, it must list that name on a DNS server. This might be a server controlled by the organization, or it might be one controlled by a third party such as an ISP that hosts the name. In either case, systems and network administrators can start adding names to their DNS servers using this top-level domain name.

If, for example, you have three computers that you want to make available on the Internet, you would first need to register a second-level domain name, such as `mycompany.com`. You could then choose to add your own host names, such as the following:

- `www.mycompany.com`

- `mail.mycompany.com`

- `computer1.northamerica.sales.mycompany.com`

Each of these domain names must be listed on the DNS server as a *resource record (RR)*. The records themselves consist of a domain-name-to-IP-address mapping. When users try to access one of these machines (through a web browser, for example), the name will be resolved with the appropriate TCP/IP address.

DNS servers themselves are responsible for carrying out various functions related to name resolution. One of their functions is related to fulfilling DNS name-mapping requests. If a DNS server has information about the specific hostname specified in the request, it simply returns the appropriate information to the client that made the request. If, however, the DNS server does not have information about the specific hostname, it must obtain that information from another DNS server. In this case, name resolution is required. In order to resolve names of which it has no knowledge, the DNS server queries other DNS servers for that information. As a result, you can see how a worldwide network of names can be formed. Later in this chapter, we'll see the various steps required to ensure that DNS servers are communicating worldwide.

Overview of DNS Zones

DNS servers work together to resolve hierarchical names. If they already have information about a name, they simply fulfill the query for the client; otherwise, they query other DNS servers for the appropriate information. The system works well as it distributes the authority of separate parts of the DNS structure to specific servers. A DNS *zone* is a portion of the DNS namespace over which a specific DNS server has authority. In this section, we'll see how the concept of zones is used to ensure accurate name resolution on the Internet.

In order to ensure that naming remains accurate in a distributed network environment, one DNS server must be designated as the master database for a specific set of addresses. It is on this server that updates to hostname-to-IP-address mappings can be updated. Whenever a DNS server is unable to resolve a specific DNS name, it simply queries other servers that can provide the information. Zones are necessary because many different DNS servers could otherwise be caching the same information. If changes are made, this information could become outdated. Therefore, one central DNS server must assume the role of the ultimate authority for a specific subset of domain names.

 There is an important distinction to make between DNS zones and Active Directory domains. Although both use hierarchical names and require name resolution, DNS zones do not map directly to DNS domains.

As shown in Figure 3.3, a zone may be an entire domain or represent only part of one.

FIGURE 3.3   The relationship between DNS domains and zones

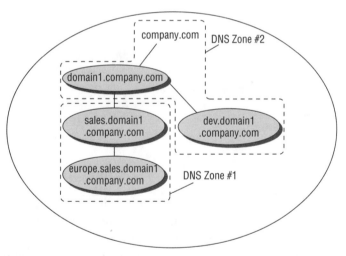

With this information in mind, let's take a more detailed look at the actual process of DNS name resolution.

DNS Name Resolution

When using the Internet, DNS queries are extremely common. For example, every time you click a link to visit a website, a DNS query must be made. In the simplest scenario, the client computer requests a DNS address from its designated DNS server. The DNS server has information about the IP address for the specified hostname, it returns that information to the client, and the client then uses the IP address to initiate communications with the host. This process is shown in Figure 3.4.

FIGURE 3.4 A simple DNS name resolution process

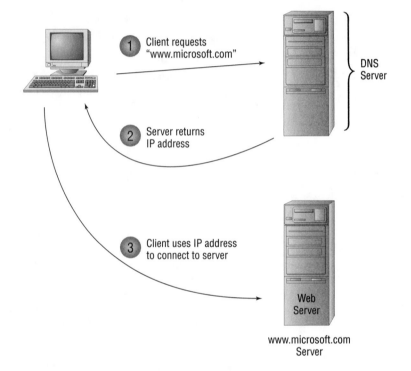

What happens, though, if the DNS server does not contain information about the specific host requested? In this case, the DNS server itself initiates a query to another DNS server, which thereby assumes responsibility for ultimately resolving the name. If the second DNS server is unable to fulfill the request, it, in turn, queries another. This process is known as *recursion*. In the process of recursion, one DNS server will contact another, which will then contact another, until one of the servers is able to resolve the hostname. The name resolution process usually begins with a query to the top-level DNS servers and continues downward through the domain hierarchy until the resource is reached. If, at this point, the name still cannot be resolved, an error is returned to the client. Figure 3.5 illustrates the process of recursion. Usually, DNS servers include information about the root- and top-level DNS servers. This information is configured during the initial configuration of the server.

FIGURE 3.5 DNS name resolution through recursion

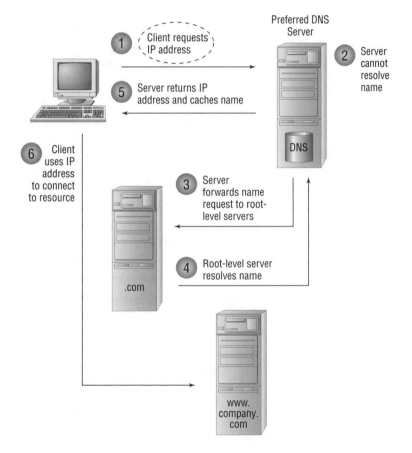

Because recursion is such an important process, let's look at an example. Suppose you want to connect to the DNS name `computer1.sales` `.somecompany.com`. The following steps will occur to make this happen:

1. The client requests information from its preferred DNS server.

2. The preferred DNS server is unable to find a resource record for this information in its own cache and must therefore query another server.

The DNS server first queries a root server and then sends a query to the top-level domain server and requests information about the server that has authority over the `somecompany.com` domain.

3. Once the information is obtained, the preferred DNS server then queries the `somecompany.com` DNS server for information about the `computer1` hostname within the sales domain.

4. The client's preferred DNS server then returns the IP address of the hostname to the client. It can then use the IP address to communicate with the host. The preferred DNS server may choose to cache a copy of the resource record information just in case additional requests for the domain name are made.

A client may also be configured to query multiple DNS servers for names. This process is known as *iteration*. Iteration is normally used when a client queries DNS servers but instructs them not to use recursion. Alternatively, systems administrators may configure the DNS servers themselves not to perform recursion. For example, we may configure all DNS servers to forward resolution requests to one DNS server on our network. This will direct all DNS traffic through this one server, thereby reducing network traffic and allowing us to secure DNS requests.

In the iteration process, the DNS server fulfills a request if it is able to do so based on the information in its own database. If it cannot, it will either return an error or point the client to another DNS server that may be able to resolve the name. Iteration requires the client to remain responsible for ultimately resolving the name request.

Usually, the client is configured with multiple DNS servers that are utilized according to a certain search order. One way this is useful is if different DNS servers are required to resolve intranet and Internet names. For example, a client may use one DNS server to resolve names for a specific department within the organization and another DNS server to resolve names of public websites. This method places the burden of finding the right name server on the client. In certain configurations, though, you may want to reduce network traffic with DNS *forwarding*, which allows you to specify exactly which DNS servers will be used for resolving names. For example, if you have multiple DNS servers located on a fast network (such as a LAN), you may want each of them to request DNS information from only a few specific DNS servers that can then gain information from other DNS servers on the network. Figure 3.6 provides an example of how DNS forwarding can be used.

FIGURE 3.6   Using DNS forwarding to reduce network traffic

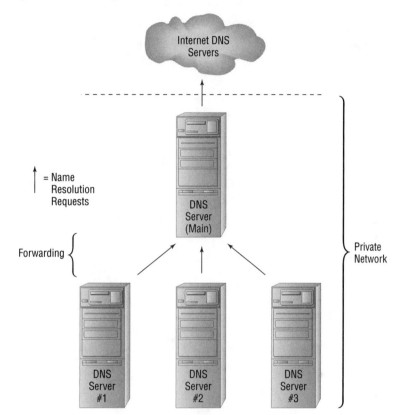

Another feature of DNS servers is their ability to cache information. As you can imagine, going through the recursion process each time a DNS query is initiated can place a significant load on servers worldwide. In order to limit some of this traffic, DNS servers usually save information about mapped domain names in their own local database. If future requests are made for the same host and domain names, this cached information is usually used. To ensure that the cached information is reasonably up-to-date, a time to live (TTL) value is attached to each cached DNS record. Typical TTL values range from three to seven days. Once this time limit is exceeded, the cached value is no longer used, and the next request for the information will result in going through the entire recursion process again.

Since DNS names are updated on a pull basis, it can take time for some DNS servers to update their databases. If you are required to make changes to a DNS entry, be sure to allow sufficient time for all of the name servers on the Internet to be updated. Usually, this should take only a few days, but, in some cases, it may take more than a week.

Although the most common DNS functions involve the mapping of DNS names to IP addresses, certain applications might require the opposite functionality—the resolution of an IP address to a DNS name. This is handled through a *reverse lookup zone* in the DNS server. Reverse lookup zones start with a special Internet authority address and allow the DNS server to resolve queries for specific TCP/IP addresses. As we'll see later in this chapter, reverse lookup zones are configured similarly to standard *forward lookup zones*.

In order to determine from which DNS server specific information can be found, zones must be used. Let's now examine the process of establishing authority for specific DNS zones.

Delegating Authority in DNS Zones

Every DNS server can be configured to be responsible for one or more DNS domains. The DNS server is then known as the authoritative source of address information for that zone. Generally, if you are using only a single DNS domain, you will have only one zone. Remember that there can be a many-to-many relationship between domains (which are used to create a logical naming structure) and zones (which refer primarily to the physical structure of a DNS implementation).

When you add subdomains, however, you have two options. You can allow the original DNS server to continue functioning as the authority for the *parent* and *child domains*. Or, you can choose to create another DNS zone and give a different server authority over it. The process of giving authority for specific domains to other DNS servers is known as *delegation*. Figure 3.7 shows how delegation can be configured.

The main reasons for using delegation are performance and administration. Using multiple DNS servers in a large network can help distribute the load involved in resolving names. It can also help in administering security by allowing only certain types of records to be modified by specified systems administrators.

FIGURE 3.7   Delegating DNS authority to multiple DNS servers

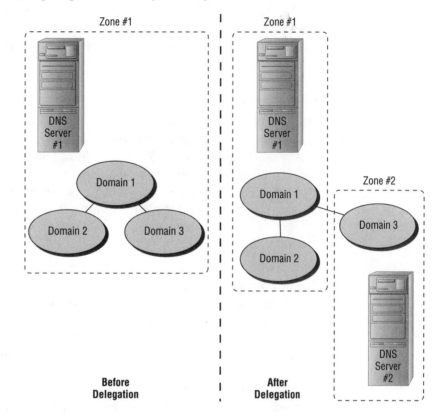

DNS Server Roles

One of the potential problems with configuring specific DNS servers as authorities for their own domains is fault tolerance. What happens if an authoritative server becomes unavailable? Normally, none of the names for the resources in that zone could be resolved to network addresses. This could be a potentially serious problem for networks of any size. For example, if the primary server for the `sales.mycompany.com` zone becomes unavailable (and there are no secondary servers in that zone), users will not be able to find resources such as `server1.sales.mycompany.com` or `workstation1.sales.mycompany.com`. In order to prevent the potential network problems of a single failed server, the DNS specification allows for supporting multiple servers per zone.

To maintain a distributed and hierarchical naming system, DNS servers can assume several different roles at once. In this section, we'll look at the various roles that DNS servers can assume within a zone. In later sections of this chapter, we'll see how Windows 2000 Server computers can assume these roles.

Primary Server

Each DNS zone must have one *primary DNS server*. The primary server is responsible for maintaining all of the records for the DNS zone and contains the primary copy of the DNS database. In addition, all updates of records occur on the primary server. You will want to create and add primary servers whenever you create a new DNS domain. When creating child domains, however, you may want to use the primary server from the parent domain.

Secondary Server

A *secondary DNS server* contains a database of all of the same information as the primary name server and can be used to resolve DNS requests. The main purpose of a secondary server is to provide for fault tolerance. That is, in case the primary server becomes unavailable, name resolution can still occur using the secondary server. Therefore, it is a good general practice to ensure that each zone has at least one secondary server to protect against failures.

Secondary DNS servers can also increase performance by offloading some of the traffic that would otherwise go to the primary server. Secondary servers are also often placed within each location of an organization that has high-speed network access. This prevents DNS queries from having to run across slow wide area network (WAN) connections. For example, if there are two remote offices within the mycompany.com organization, we may want to place a secondary DNS server in each remote office. This way, when clients require name resolution, they will contact the nearest server for this IP address information, thus preventing unnecessary WAN traffic.

Although it is a good idea to have secondary servers, having too many of them can cause increases in network traffic due to replication. Therefore, you should always weigh the benefits and drawbacks and properly plan for secondary servers.

Master Server

Master DNS servers are used in the replication of DNS data between primary and secondary servers. Usually, the primary server also serves as the master server, but these tasks can be separated for performance reasons. The master server is responsible for propagating any changes to the DNS database to all secondary servers within a particular zone.

Caching-Only Server

Caching-only DNS servers serve the same function as primary DNS servers in that they assist clients in resolving DNS names to network addresses. The only differences are that caching-only servers are not authoritative for any DNS zones and they don't contain copies of the zone files. They only contain mappings as a result of resolved queries and, in fact, they will lose all of their mapping information when the server is shut down. Therefore, they are installed only for performance reasons. A caching-only DNS server may be used at sites that have slow connectivity to DNS servers at other sites.

🌐 Real World Scenario

Optimizing DNS Performance

As the DNS administrator for your network environment, you are responsible for ensuring that DNS is working optimally. Recently, you've received several complaints that DNS queries are taking a long time and that sometimes client applications time out when trying to reach a remote server. The network is fairly large and includes three large offices and 25 remote sites.

So far, you have attempted to keep the DNS infrastructure design as simple as possible to ease administration. The current DNS environment consists of a single forward lookup zone that includes a primary server and two secondary servers. The primary server is located in one large office, and the secondary servers are located in the other two large offices. This design is simple and easy to administer, but the performance problem must be solved. So, what's the easiest way to do this?

Fortunately, DNS has been designed from the ground up to offer scalability and high performance for even the most distributed networks. In this instance, you could choose to redesign the DNS infrastructure. For example, you could break a single zone down into multiple smaller zones and then implement additional DNS servers for those zones. However, this would require a considerable amount of effort for planning, design, and implementation. It might also be more difficult to administer. Since performance is currently the only complaint, let's look at another solution.

Another option is to create additional secondary servers and place them in areas where users are complaining about the performance of DNS queries. For example, you might decide that you need to deploy DNS servers in several of the larger remote offices and remote offices that are located across slow or unreliable WAN links. There is a potential problem with implementing additional secondary servers: This can increase the amount of network traffic that flows between the DNS servers when updates are made. However, you'll probably find that it's a worthwhile trade-off.

There's one more option that's easy to implement and can help increase performance: caching-only DNS servers. These servers are particularly helpful in environments that consist of multiple DNS zones. They're easy to administer since they don't contain authoritative copies of your DNS databases, and they can improve performance by providing a quicker way to resolve DNS queries for remote clients.

As you can see, DNS is powerful and flexible enough to offer you many different types of solutions to performance problems. Be sure to keep this in mind as you work with DNS in the real world!

Zone Transfers

Similar to the situation with domain controllers and Active Directory, it is important to ensure that DNS zone information is consistent between the primary and secondary servers. The process used to keep the servers synchronized is known as a *zone transfer*. When a secondary DNS server is configured for a zone, it first performs a zone transfer, during which it obtains a copy of the primary server's address database. This process is known as an *all-zone transfer (AXFR)*.

In order to ensure that information is kept up-to-date after the initial synchronization, *incremental zone transfers (IXFRs)* are used. Through this process, the changes in the DNS zone databases are communicated between primary and secondary servers. IXFRs use a system of serial numbers to determine which records are new or updated. This system ensures that the newest DNS record is always used, even if changes were made on more than one server.

Not all DNS servers support IXFRs. Windows NT 4's DNS services and earlier implementations of other DNS services require a full-zone transfer of the entire database in order to update their records. This can sometimes cause significant network traffic. As with any software implementation, you should always verify the types of functionality supported before deploying it.

Zone transfers may occur in response to the following different events:

- The zone refresh interval has been exceeded.
- A master server notifies a secondary server of a zone change.
- A secondary DNS server service is started for the zone.
- A DNS zone transfer is manually initiated (by a systems administrator) at the secondary server.

An important factor regarding zone transfers is that secondary servers always initiate them. This type of replication is commonly known as a *pull operation*. Normally, a zone transfer request is made when a refresh interval is reached on the secondary server. The request is sent to a master server, which then sends any changes to the secondary server. Usually the primary server is also configured as a master server, but this can be changed for performance reasons.

One of the problems with pull replication is that the information stored on secondary servers can sometimes be out-of-date. For example, suppose an IXFR occurs today, but the refresh interval is set to three days. If you make a change on the primary DNS server, this change will not be reflected on the secondary server for at least several days. One potential way to circumvent this problem is to set a very low refresh interval (such as a few hours). However, this can cause a lot of unnecessary network traffic and increased processing overhead.

In order to solve the problems related to keeping resource records up-to-date, a feature known as *DNS notify* was developed. This method employs push replication to inform secondary servers whenever a change is made. When secondary servers receive the DNS notify message, they immediately initiate an IXFR request. Figure 3.8 shows how DNS notify is used to keep secondary servers up-to-date. This method ensures that compatible DNS servers are updated immediately whenever changes are made.

FIGURE 3.8 Using DNS notify to update secondary servers

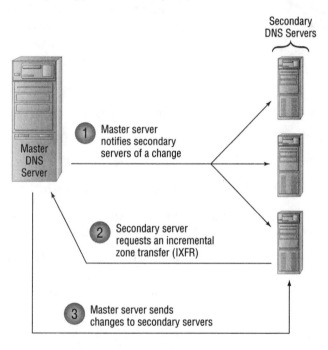

Managing DNS Resource Records

So far, we have looked at various ways in which DNS servers remain synchronized with each other. Now, it's time to look at the actual types of information stored within the DNS database. Table 3.2 provides a list of the types of records that are used within the DNS database. Each of these records is important for ensuring that the proper type of resource is made available. For example, if a client is attempting to send e-mail, the DNS server should respond with the IP address corresponding to the Mail Exchanger (MX) record of the domain.

TABLE 3.2 DNS Resource Record Types

Resource Record Type	Meaning	Notes
A	Address	Used to map hostnames to IP addresses. Multiple A records may be used to map to a single IP address.
CNAME	Canonical Name	Used as an alias or a nickname for a host (in addition to the A record).
MX	Mail Exchanger	Specifies the Simple Mail Transfer Protocol (SMTP) e-mail server address for the domain.
NS	Name Server	Specifies the IP address of DNS servers for the domain.
PTR	Pointer	Used for reverse lookup operations.
RP	Responsible Person	Specifies information about the individual who is responsible for maintaining the DNS information.
SOA	Start of Authority	Specifies the authoritative server for a zone.
SRV	Service	Specifies server services available on a host; used by Active Directory to identify domain controllers. The standard for SRV records has not yet been finalized.

In addition, certain conventions are often used on the Internet. For example, the hostnames mail, www, ftp, and news are usually reserved for e-mail, World Wide Web, file transfer protocol, and USENET news servers, respectively.

Now that you have a good understanding of the purpose and methods of DNS, let's move on to looking at how Microsoft's DNS service operates.

Installing and Configuring a DNS Server

Microsoft has made the technical steps involved in installing the DNS service extremely simple. This, however, is not an excuse for not thoroughly understanding and planning for a DNS configuration. In this section, we'll cover the actual steps required to install and configure a DNS server for use with Microsoft's Active Directory.

Microsoft ✔ *Exam* *Objective*

Configure, administer, and troubleshoot DNS.

- Configure DNS server properties.

- Manage DNS database records such as CNAME, A, and PTR.

Exercise 3.1 walks you through the steps required to install the DNS service.

EXERCISE 3.1

Installing the DNS Service

This exercise walks you through the steps required to install the DNS service:

1. Choose Start ➢ Settings ➢ Control Panel, and then double-click the Add/Remove Programs icon.

2. Select Add/Remove Windows Components.

3. Click the Components button to access a list of services and options available for installation on Windows 2000.

4. In the Windows 2000 Components Wizard, select Networking Services, and then click Details.

5. Place a check mark next to the option titled Domain Name System (DNS).

Networking Services   ☒

To add or remove a component, click the check box. A shaded box means that only part of the component will be installed. To see what's included in a component, click Details.

Subcomponents of Networking Services:

☐ 🖳 COM Internet Services Proxy	0.0 MB
☑ 🖳 Domain Name System (DNS)	1.1 MB
☐ 🖳 Dynamic Host Configuration Protocol (DHCP)	0.0 MB
☐ 🖳 Internet Authentication Service	0.0 MB
☐ 🖳 QoS Admission Control Service	0.0 MB
☐ 🖳 Simple TCP/IP Services	0.0 MB
☐ 🖳 Site Server ILS Services	1.5 MB

Description: Sets up a DNS server that answers query and update requests for DNS names.

Total disk space required: 2.0 MB
Space available on disk: 1968.9 MB   [Details...]

[OK]   [Cancel]

6. Click OK to accept your choice, and then click Next to continue with the wizard.

Once you have installed the DNS service, you are ready to begin configuring the server for Active Directory.

Adding DNS Zones

First, you'll need to configure DNS for your specific environment. The most important aspect of configuring DNS properly is planning. Based on the information presented in the previous sections, you should be aware of how you plan to configure DNS zones for your Active Directory environment.

The technical implementation process is quite easy, thanks to the Configure DNS Server Wizard. Exercise 3.2 walks you through the process used to configure DNS zones.

EXERCISE 3.2

Using the Configure DNS Server Wizard

In this exercise, you will configure basic DNS zones, including a standard primary forward lookup zone. This exercise assumes that you have already installed the DNS service and that no configuration options have been set.

1. Open the DNS snap-in in the Administrative Tools program group.

2. In the DNS administrative tool, right-click the name of your local server and select Configure The Server. The introduction page informs you that the Configure DNS Server Wizard will help you configure DNS zones for this server. Click Next to begin the process.

3. Create a forward lookup zone by choosing Yes, Create A Forward Lookup Zone, and then click Next.

4. Select the type of DNS zone you want to create. The available options include Active Directory-Integrated (available only if Active Directory is installed), Standard Primary, and Standard Secondary. Select Standard Primary, and click Next.

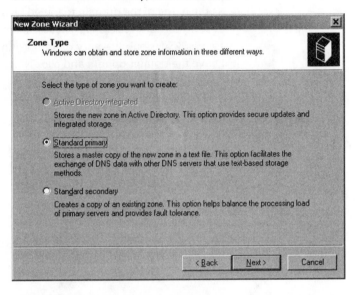

5. Enter the zone name by typing in the name of the DNS zone for which you want to record addresses. For example, you might type `test.mycompany.com`. Click Next.

6. Once you have determined the name for the DNS domain, you can choose either to create a new local DNS file or to use an existing DNS file. DNS zone files are standard text files that contain mappings of IP addresses to DNS names. Usually, zone files are named as the name of the domain followed by a .dns suffix (for example, test.mycompany.com.dns). These files must be stored in the system32\dns subdirectory of your Windows 2000 system root. Leave the default option, and click Next.

```
New Zone Wizard                                                    [X]

  Zone File
    You can create a new zone file or use a file copied from another computer.


    Do you want to create a new zone file or use an existing file that you have copied from
    another computer?

    ( • ) Create a new file with this file name:

        test.mycompany.com.dns

    (  ) Use this existing file:



    To use an existing file, you must first copy the file to the %SystemRoot%\system32\dns
    folder on the server running the DNS service.



                              < Back        Next >        Cancel
```

7. Although reverse lookup zones are not required for basic DNS functionality and are, therefore, optional, you will probably want to create one. Reverse lookup zones are used to map IP addresses to DNS names and are required for the proper operation of some TCP/IP applications. Select Yes, Create A Reverse Lookup Zone, and click Next.

8. Choose the reverse lookup zone type. The options are similar to those for the forward lookup zone. Select Standard Primary, and click Next.

9. Specify the reverse lookup zone. In order for reverse lookups to work properly, you must specify the network to which the zone applies. You can specify the value using a network ID or the name of the reverse lookup zone. The value you enter will be based on the subnet(s) for which this DNS server will provide reverse lookup information. Enter **169** for the Network ID, and click Next to continue.

10. Select a reverse lookup zone file. Reverse lookup zone files are created and managed similarly to forward lookup zone files. Choose the default option, and click Next.

11. To finalize the settings made by the wizard, click Next. The wizard will automatically create the forward and reverse lookup zones based on the information you specified.

If your network environment will require this DNS server to manage multiple zones, you can run the Configure DNS Server Wizard again. Alternatively, if you are comfortable with the options available, you can right-click the name of your server and select New Zone.

Configuring DNS Zone Properties

Once you have properly configured forward and reverse lookup zones for your DNS server, you can make additional configuration settings for each zone by right-clicking its name within the DNS administrative tool and selecting Properties. The following tabs and settings are available for forward lookup zones:

General The General tab allows you to set various options for the forward lookup zone. Using this tab (see Figure 3.9), you can pause the DNS service. When the service is paused, it continues to run, but clients cannot complete name resolution requests from this machine. The second option is to change the type of the zone. Choices include Primary, Secondary, and Active Directory–Integrated (available only if Active Directory is installed). You can also specify the name of the DNS zone file. Allowing dynamic updates is extremely useful for reducing the management and administration headaches associated with creating resource records. Finally, you can specify aging and scavenging properties for this zone.

FIGURE 3.9 Setting zone properties with the General tab

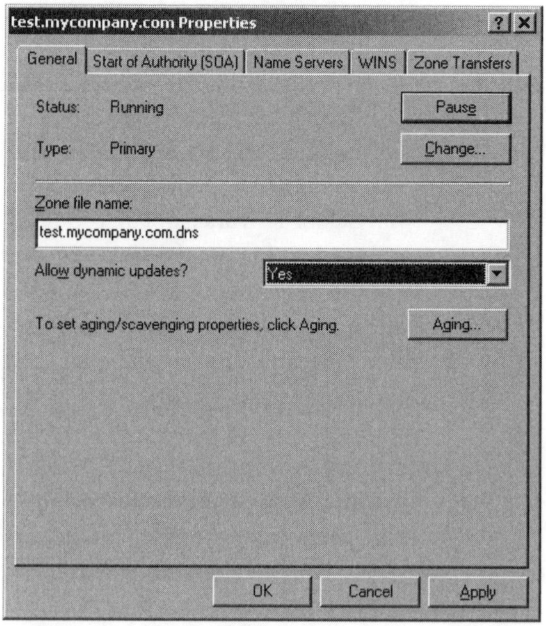

Start Of Authority (SOA)   The SOA tab allows you to specify information regarding the authority of the DNS server (see Figure 3.10). The Serial Number text box is used to determine whether a zone transfer is needed to keep any secondary servers up-to-date. For example, if a secondary server has a serial number of 6, but the SOA serial number is set to 7, the secondary server will request a zone transfer. The Primary Server text box allows you to designate the primary DNS server for the zone. The Responsible Person text box allows you to specify contact information for the systems administrator of the DNS server. The Refresh Interval text box and drop-down menu are used to specify how often a secondary zone should verify its information. Lower times ensure greater accuracy but can cause increased network traffic. The Retry Interval text box and drop-down menu are used to specify how often zone transfers will be requested. The Expires After text box and drop-down menu allow you to specify how long secondary DNS servers must try to request updated information before resource records expire. The Minimum (Default) TTL text box is used to specify how long a resource record will be considered current. If you are working in an environment where many changes are expected, a lower TTL value can help in maintaining the accuracy of information.

FIGURE 3.10   Setting zone properties with the SOA tab

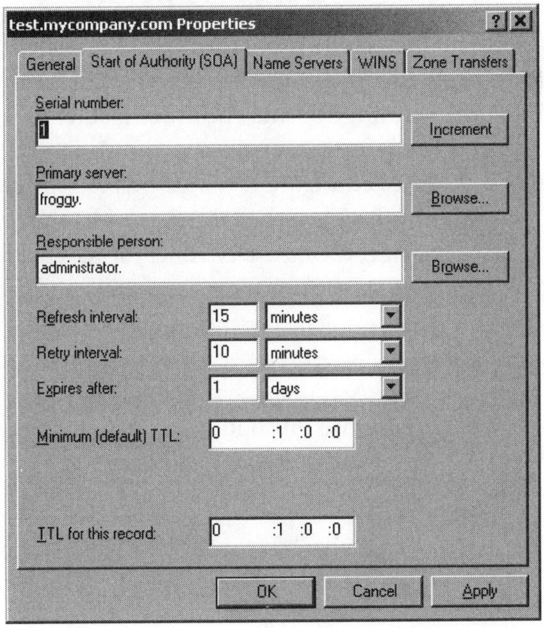

Name Servers The Name Servers tab shows a list of DNS servers for the specified domain. You can add specific DNS servers based on the configuration of your network. Generally, the list of name servers includes the primary name server and any secondary name servers for that zone.

WINS This tab allows you to set options for allowing *Windows Internet Name Service (WINS)* lookups to resolve DNS names. WINS and DNS issues are covered later in this chapter.

Zone Transfers Using the options on this tab, you can select which servers will be allowed to serve as a secondary server for the forward lookup zones specified in the properties for the zone. The default option allows any server to request a zone transfer, but you can restrict this by indicating specific IP addresses or allowing only the name servers listed on the Name Servers tab to request transfers. Setting restrictions on zone transfers can increase security by preventing unauthorized users from copying the entire DNS database.

The ability to set each of these options gives systems administrators the power to control DNS operations and resource record settings for their environment.

Configuring DNS Server Options

DNS record databases would tend to become disorganized and filled with outdated information if processes that periodically removed unused records were not present. The process of removing inactive or outdated entries in the DNS database is known as *scavenging*. Systems administrators use scavenging to configure DNS records to require refreshing based on a certain time setting. When the DNS record has not been refreshed for a certain amount of time, the next DNS query forces the record to be updated. By default, the DNS server is not configured to perform this process at all.

To implement scavenging in the DNS snap-in, you should right-click the name of the server or DNS zone for which you want the settings to apply and choose Set Aging/Scavenging. For example, if you right-click the server name and choose this option, the aging and scavenging settings you specify will apply to all of the DNS zones managed by that server. As shown in Figure 3.11, you can specify two different options:

No-Refresh Interval This allows you to specify the *minimum* amount of time that must elapse before a DNS record is refreshed. Higher values can reduce network traffic but may cause outdated information to be returned to clients.

Refresh Interval This allows you to specify the amount of time between when the no-refresh interval expires and when the resource record information may be refreshed. Lower values can provide for greater accuracy in information but may increase network traffic.

FIGURE 3.11 Setting aging and scavenging options

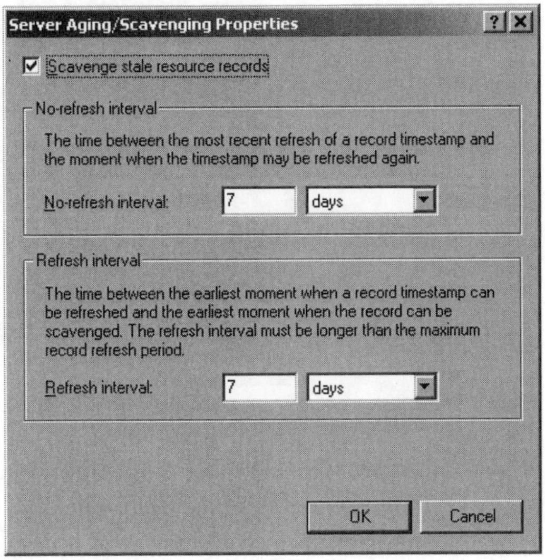

There are also several other DNS server options that can be set to maximize performance functionality in your network environment. To access the properties of the DNS server using the DNS snap-in, right-click the name of the server and choose Properties. The following tabs will be available:

Interfaces On servers that are enabled with multiple network adapters, you might want to provide DNS services on only one of the interfaces. The default option is to allow DNS requests on all interfaces, but you can limit operations to specific adapters by clicking the Only The Following IP Addresses option (see Figure 3.12).

FIGURE 3.12 Selecting DNS server interfaces

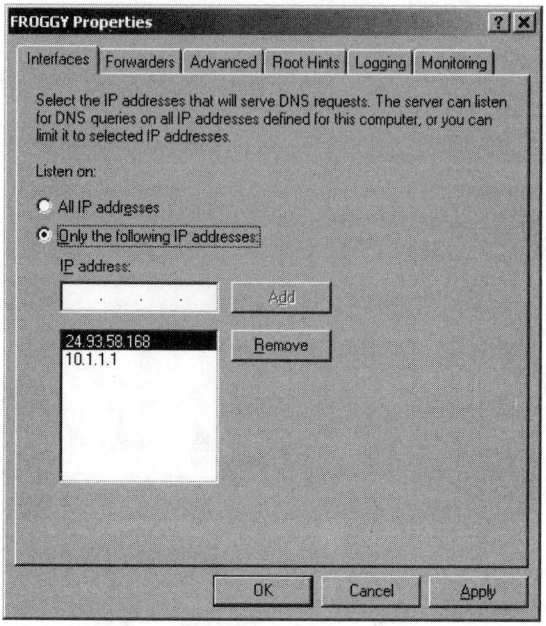

Forwarders DNS forwarding can be configured to relay all DNS requests that cannot be resolved by this server to one or more specific machines. To configure forwarders, check the box and specify the IP address of one or more DNS servers. If you check the Do Not Use Recursion option, name resolution will occur only through the configured forwarders.

Advanced The DNS service has several advanced options (see Figure 3.13). For example, you can disable DNS recursion for the entire server by checking the appropriate box. We'll cover specific options as they pertain to Active Directory later in this chapter.

Root Hints In order to resolve domain names on the Internet, the local DNS server must know the identities of the worldwide root servers. By default, the Microsoft DNS server is configured with several valid root IP addresses (see Figure 3.14). In addition, you can add or modify the root hints as needed, but you should do this only if you are sure of the configuration information.

FIGURE 3.13   Advanced DNS server configuration options

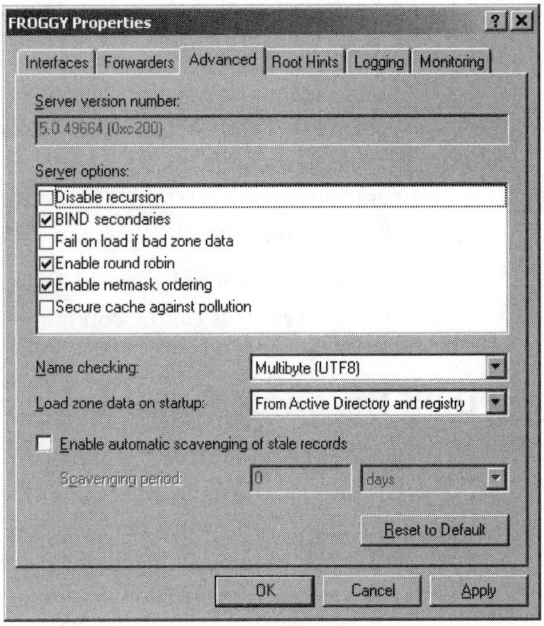

FIGURE 3.14   Viewing default DNS server root hints

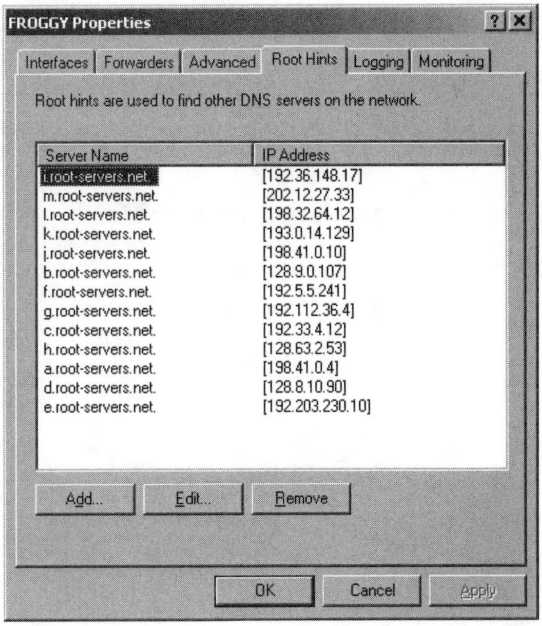

Logging   Logging various DNS operations can be useful for monitoring and troubleshooting the DNS service. You can select various events to monitor using the properties on this tab.

Monitoring   The Monitoring tab is useful for performing a quick check to ensure that the DNS service is operating properly. Using this tab, you are able to perform a simple query as well as a recursive request. If both operations are successful, you can be reasonably sure that the DNS server is functioning properly.

Once you are satisfied with the DNS server settings, it's time to look at how resource records can be configured.

Creating DNS Resource Records

The main functionality of a DNS server is based on the various resource records present within it. If Active Directory was configured to automatically integrate DNS at installation time, then the resource records listed in Table 3.3 will be created. Each of these records is of the type SRV (Service). The *Domain* and *DomainTree* specifiers will be based on the DNS domain name for the local domain controller, and the *Site* specifier will be based on your site configuration.

TABLE 3.3   Default Active Directory DNS Resource Records

Resource Record	Purpose
_ldap._tcp.*Domain*	Enumerates the domain controllers for a given domain.
_ldap._tcp.*Site*.sites.*Domain*	Allows clients to find domain controllers within a specific site.
_ldap._tcp.pdc.ms-dcs.*Domain*	Provides the address of the server acting as the Windows NT Primary Domain Controller (PDC) for the domain.
_ldap._tcp.pdc.ms-dcs.*DomainTree*	Enumerates the Global Catalog servers within a domain.

TABLE 3.3 Default Active Directory DNS Resource Records *(continued)*

Resource Record	Purpose
_ldap._tcp.*Site.gc* *.ms-dcs.DomainTree*	Allows a client to find a Global Catalog server based on site configuration.
_ldap._tcp.*GUID.domains* *.ms-dcs.DomainTree*	Used by computers to locate machines based on the Global Unique Identifier (GUID).
_ldap._tcp.writable *.ms-dcs.Domain*	Enumerates the domain controller(s) that hold(s) modifiable copies of Active Directory.
_ldap._tcp.*site.sites.writable* *.ms-dcs.Domain*	Enumerates domain controller(s) based on sites.

In addition to the default DNS records, you will likely want to create new ones to identify specific servers and clients on your network. Exercise 3.3 provides a walk-through of the creation of a DNS A record. Although different resource record types require different pieces of information, the process is similar for other types of records.

EXERCISE 3.3

Creating a DNS Host (A) Record

In this exercise, you will specify a new DNS host record. This exercise assumes that you have installed the DNS service and have configured at least one forward lookup zone.

1. Open the DNS snap-in in the Administrative Tools program group.

2. Expand the forward lookup zones folder for the local server.

3. Right-click the name of a zone and select New Host.

4. Specify the host record options. You'll need to configure a few options for the host record. The options are as follows:

   - Hostname

EXERCISE 3.3 *(continued)*

- IP address of the host

- Whether or not to add an associated pointer (PTR) record

5. When you are ready to create the record, click Add Host. This will add the host record to the forward lookup zone specified in step 3. Click Cancel to close the Add Host dialog box and return to the DNS administrative tool.

Real World Scenario

Implementing DNS for Multiple Mail Servers

You are a systems administrator for a medium-sized organization. One of your responsibilities is managing the DNS configuration for the entire domain. You have already implemented and configured DNS, including forward and reverse lookup zones. Currently, the environment consists of a single e-mail server (called mail.xyzservices.com). This mail server (and the corresponding DNS MX record) has been working properly. However, messaging traffic has been increasing, and users commonly report that the mail server is unavailable or that they must sometimes make multiple attempts before messages are sent.

To help alleviate some of the problems, another systems administrator has set up a second mail server. She wants you to create a DNS record for this second mail server, but she wants this server to be contacted only if the primary mail server is unavailable.

The appropriate steps can be taken quite easily using Windows 2000's DNS features. First, you must create a new Address (A) record within the domain. You will need to give this server a DNS name (such as mail2.xyzservices .com). Next, you must edit the properties of the domain's MX. Within the MX record, you can add both servers to the list and assign priorities for the servers. Since you want the original mail server to be the primary machine, set its priority to 1. For the second server, set the priority to 2. (Note that only the relative values are the important point. You could have just as easily chosen larger numbers such as 50 and 100 in order to have more flexibility in the future when adding new priorities.)

Now users should be able to access the second mail server when the first mail server is unavailable. Similar techniques can be used for other types of TCP/IP-based servers. For example, web servers (but not mail servers) can take advantage of "round-robin" DNS to help distribute load among multiple servers. In this configuration, clients will be directed to different web servers, although they will always connect to the same DNS name. This technique is used, for example, to allow multiple servers to respond to connection requests for www.microsoft.com.

Managing DNS Servers

Once your DNS server is installed and configured properly, you will need to manage various settings. In the previous section, we looked at the various options and features available within the DNS service. In this section, we'll focus on some specific operations that are required for working with Active Directory. The exercises should be helpful in learning your way around the various operations.

Microsoft ✓ **Exam Objective**

Configure, administer, and troubleshoot DNS.

- Create and configure DNS zones.

Configuring Zones for Automatic Updates

By allowing automatic updates to DNS zones, you will be able to dramatically reduce the administrative burden of managing resource records. Exercise 3.4 shows how to enable this option.

EXERCISE 3.4

Allowing Automatic Updates

This exercise assumes that you have properly installed and configured the DNS service and have configured at least one forward lookup zone.

EXERCISE 3.4 *(continued)*

1. Open the DNS snap-in in the Administrative Tools program group.

2. Expand the forward lookup zones folder under the name of the current server.

3. Right-click the name of a zone and select Properties.

4. Change the Allow Dynamic Updates option to Yes.

5. Click OK to accept and commit the setting.

Creating Zone Delegations

When you configure a DNS server as a primary server for a zone, that server is responsible for performing name resolution for all of the resources within that zone. In some cases, you might want to delegate authority for a portion of the zone to another DNS server. Exercise 3.5 shows how this can be done.

EXERCISE 3.5

Creating a Zone Delegation

This exercise delegates authority for a DNS zone to another DNS server. This exercise assumes that you have already created at least one DNS zone. In addition, this server must be the primary DNS server for at least one zone.

1. Open the DNS administrative tool and expand the branch for the local server.

2. Right-click the name of a zone for which the machine is the primary server, and select New Delegation.

3. This opens the New Delegation Wizard. Click Next.

4. Enter the name of the delegated domain. The delegated domain must be a subdomain of the domain you selected in step 2. For example, if the domain name is activedirectory.test, the subdomain might be domain2. This will make the fully qualified domain name domain2.activedirectory.test. Click Next.

New Delegation Wizard

Delegated Domain Name
Specify the name of the domain you want to create.

Authority for the domain you create will be delegated to a different zone.

Delegated domain:

domain2

Fully qualified domain name:

domain2.activedirectory.test

< Back   Next >   Cancel

5. Specify the name server(s) to which you want to delegate authority for the domain. To add servers to the list, click Add. You will be able to browse a list of available name servers or specify one by name or IP address. You can also click Edit to change the properties for servers you have already added to the delegation list.

6. Click Next to accept the setting, and then click Finish to create the new delegation.

Managing DNS Replication

Managing DNS replication is an important concern. If optimal settings are not chosen, you might encounter too much replication traffic. Alternatively, you might have the opposite problem—updates are not occurring frequently enough. Earlier in this chapter, we looked at ways to configure the DNS notify properties within a zone. In this section, we'll see what is required to enable DNS replication.

Exercise 3.6 walks through the steps required to configure DNS replication.

EXERCISE 3.6

Configuring DNS Replication

In this exercise, you will configure various DNS replication options. This exercise assumes that you have already created at least one DNS zone and that the local server is the primary DNS server for at least one zone.

1. Open the DNS administrative tool, and expand the branch for the local server.

2. Right-click the name of a zone for which this machine is the primary server, and select Properties.

3. Select the Zone Transfers tab.

4. Place a check mark in the Allow Zone Transfers box.

5. Choose whether you want to allow zone transfers from any server (the default setting), only servers specified on the Name Servers tab, or specific DNS servers based on their IP addresses. It is recommended that you choose one of the latter two options because these provide greater security.

6. Click the Notify button. Place a check mark in the Automatically Notify box. You can choose to automatically notify the servers listed on the Name Servers tab, or you can specify DNS servers by IP addresses. Each of these servers will be notified automatically whenever a change to the DNS database is made.

7. Click OK twice to save the settings.

Managing DNS Interoperability

In a pure Windows 2000 environment, you would probably choose to use only Microsoft's DNS service. However, in the real world (and especially in larger environments), you might require the DNS service to interact with other implementations of DNS. A common Unix implementation of DNS is known as the Berkeley Internet Name Domain (BIND) service. Active Directory mandates the use of SRV records and optionally supports DNS dynamic updates. The minimum version of BIND that supports both is version 8.2.1. When using a BIND server as the DNS server for Active Directory, it must be running version 8.2.1 or greater. Such features as the support of the underscore are not enabled in the default configuration. Before you can configure various DNS server settings for interoperability, you must know which features are supported by the non-Microsoft DNS system you are using.

Exercise 3.7 shows you how to set up a Windows 2000 DNS server to interoperate with non–Windows 2000 DNS servers.

EXERCISE 3.7

Enabling DNS Interoperability

This exercise assumes that you have properly installed and configured the DNS service and have configured at least one forward lookup zone. It also assumes that you know the various features supported by the types of DNS servers in your environment.

1. Open the DNS snap-in in the Administrative Tools program group.

2. Right-click the name of the local server, and choose Properties.

3. Click the Advanced tab. You will see a list of the various settings that can be enabled and disabled. Place a check mark next to a feature to enable it, or remove the check mark to disable it. For more information about the various options, click the Question Mark icon and then click the option.

4. Click OK to save the changes.

Managing DNS Interoperation with DHCP

It doesn't take much imagination to see how DHCP information can be used to populate a DNS database. The DHCP service already records all of the IP address assignments within its own database. In order to reduce manual administration of DNS entries for client computers, Windows 2000's DNS implementation can automatically create Address (A) records for hosts based on DHCP information. When Windows 2000 dynamic updates are enabled, the client updates the A record and the DHCP server updates the client's pointer (PTR) record. However, the method in which DHCP information is transmitted to the DNS server varies based on the client. There are two different modes of DHCP/DNS integration based on the client type:

For Windows 2000 Clients   Windows 2000 DHCP clients have the ability to automatically send updates to a dynamic DNS server as soon as they receive an IP address. This method places the task of registering the new address on the client. It also allows the client to specify whether the update of the DNS database should occur at all.

For Earlier Clients   The DHCP client code for Windows 95/98 and Windows NT 4 computers does not support dynamic DNS updates. Therefore, the DHCP server itself must update the DNS A and PTR records.

Figure 3.15 illustrates the two different methods of Dynamic DHCP/DNS updates based on the different client types.

FIGURE 3.15   Dynamic DHCP/DNS updates

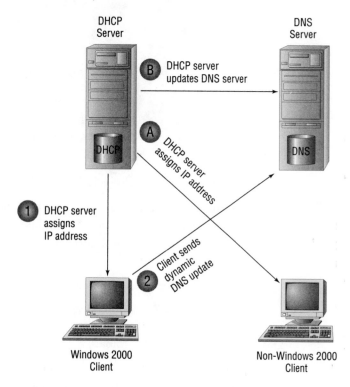

To implement dynamic updates of DNS using information from DHCP, open the DHCP administrative tool. Right-click the name of the server and choose Properties, and then select the DNS tab (see Figure 3.16).

FIGURE 3.16 Setting DNS options using the DHCP administrative tool

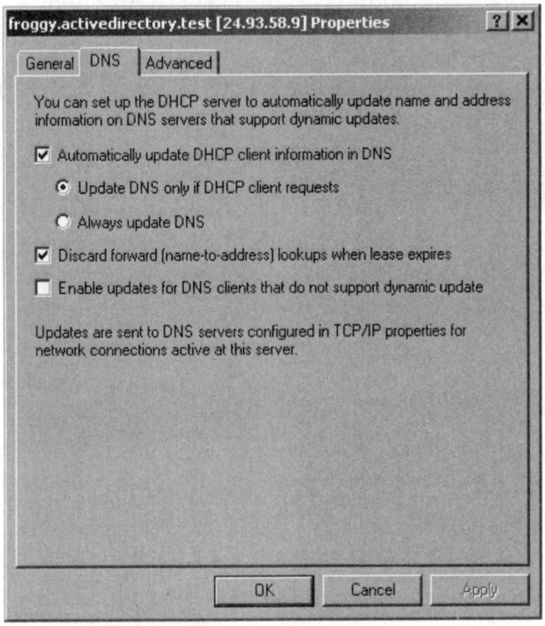

The options on this tab include the following:

Automatically Update DHCP Client Information In DNS This option allows you to enable dynamic DNS updates from the client. This selection applies only to Windows 2000 clients. Systems administrators can choose between two options:

- The client can decide whether or not the update is made.

- DNS is always updated.

Discard Forward (Name-To-Address) Lookups When Lease Expires When this option is checked, DNS entries for clients are automatically removed if a lease is not renewed in time. This is a useful option because it ensures that outdated entries no longer exist in the DNS database.

Enable Updates For DNS Clients That Do Not Support Dynamic Update If you are using Windows NT 4, Windows 95, or Windows 98 DHCP clients and want dynamic updates of DNS, you should choose this option. When it is set, the DHCP server is responsible for updating the DNS database whenever a new IP address is assigned.

By using the DHCP/DNS integration features of Windows 2000, you can automate what can be a very tedious process—managing client hostname address mappings.

Troubleshooting DNS

Name resolution problems are extremely common when working with distributed networks. If, for example, we are unable to connect to a specific hostname, it could be due to various reasons. First, the host itself may be unavailable. This could occur if a server has gone down or if a client computer is not online. In other cases, we may be receiving an incorrect IP address from a DNS server. Usually, the most common symptom of a DNS configuration problem is the ability to connect to a host using its IP address but not its hostname. In this section, we'll look at some ways in which you can troubleshoot client and server DNS problems.

Microsoft
✓ *Exam*
Objective

Configure, Administer, and Troubleshoot DNS.

Troubleshoot name resolution on client computers. Considerations include WINS, DNS, NetBIOS, the Hosts file, and the Lmhosts file.

- Troubleshoot name resolution problems by using the `nbtstat`, `ipconfig`, `nslookup`, and `netdiag` commands.

- Create and configure a Hosts file for troubleshooting name resolution problems.

Troubleshooting Clients

The most common client-side problem related to DNS is incorrect TCP/IP configuration. For example, if the DNS server values are incorrect or the default gateway is set incorrectly, clients may not be able to contact their DNS server. Consequently, they will be unable to connect to other computers using DNS names.

One of the fundamental troubleshooting steps in diagnosing network problems is to determine whether the problem is occurring on the client side or is the fault of the server side. The most common way to determine this is by testing whether other clients are having the same problem. If, on the one hand, a whole subnet is having problems resolving DNS names, it is very likely that a server or network device is unavailable or improperly configured. On the other hand, if only one or a few clients are having problems, then it is likely that the clients are misconfigured.

You should use the ipconfig, ping, and tracert commands to diagnose most TCP/IP and DNS errors. These tools were discussed in detail in Chapter 1. In the following section, we'll look at the nslookup utility, which is used exclusively to diagnose DNS-related problems. Then we'll see how to configure the Hosts file, which is used to manually map DNS names to IP addresses.

What's Your Name Again?

Part of troubleshooting network problems involves understanding how and when network name resolution is used, as well as how to test whether it's working properly. You already understand how DNS resolution works, and you understand the importance of making sure the DNS server addresses are set properly. Naturally, that should be the first thing you check when you notice that a client's getting DNS-related error messages. It's usually a good idea to check whether other clients are having related problems, too, since losing your DNS servers won't necessarily manifest itself at once. Windows 2000 DNS resolvers can maintain a cache of addresses, so if the DNS server dies after the address is stored in the cache, the client won't have a problem until the cached record reaches its TTL and expires.

The *nslookup* tool allows you to query a DNS server to see what information it holds for a host record. You can query for a single piece of information from the command line, as in this example:

```
F:\>nslookup mail.chellis.net
Server:  hawk.chellis.net
Address:  192.168.0.144
Name:  mail.chellis.net
Address:  209.68.1.225
```

Note that this session tells you which DNS server the query was made against, as well as what the answer is. If you run nslookup with no command-line arguments, it goes into interactive mode, in which you can make several queries in a row:

```
F:\>nslookup

Default Server:  hawk.chellis.net

Address:  192.168.0.144

> www.naismith-engineering.com

Server:  hawk.chellis.net

Address:  192.168.0.144

Non-authoritative answer:
Name:  www.hosting.swbell.net
Addresses:  216.100.99.6, 216.100.98.4, 216.100.98.6
Aliases:  www.naismith-engineering.com

> fly.hiwaay.net
Server:  hawk.chellis.net
Address:  192.168.0.144

Non-authoritative answer:
Name:  fly.hiwaay.net
Address:  208.147.154.56

> www.apple.com
Server:  hawk.chellis.net
Address:  192.168.0.144

Non-authoritative answer:
Name:  www.apple.com
Address:  17.254.0.91
```

You can use the `server ipAddress` command to switch resolution to the server at the specified IP address. That's very useful when your regular DNS server is down or can't seem to resolve a particular address. For example, look at this `nslookup` session, which begins when you switch to an (improperly configured) DNS server named minuteman:

```
> server minuteman

Default Server:  minuteman.chellis.net

Address:  192.168.0.201

> www.chellis.net

Server:  minuteman.chellis.net

Address:  192.168.0.201

DNS request timed out.

timeout was 2 seconds.

DNS request timed out.

timeout was 2 seconds.
*** Request to minuteman.chellis.net timed-out
```

So, minuteman can't find the answer. No problem; switch to an alternate server named hawk:

```
> server hawk

DNS request timed out.

timeout was 2 seconds.
*** Can't find address for server hawk: Timed out
```

Since minuteman is misconfigured, it can't find hawk's address. Try again with the IP address:

```
> server 192.168.0.144

DNS request timed out.

timeout was 2 seconds.

Default Server:  [192.168.0.144]
Address:  192.168.0.144

> www.chellis.net
Server:  [192.168.0.144]
Address:  192.168.0.144

Name:  www.chellis.net
Address:  209.68.1.225
```

Exercise 3.8 provides an example of how to use nslookup to verify the DNS server settings on the local machine.

EXERCISE 3.8

Using the *Nslookup* Command to Verify DNS Configuration

In this exercise, we'll use the nslookup command to verify the proper operation of the DNS server on the local machine. This exercise assumes that you have already installed and configured DNS.

1. Open a command prompt by clicking Start ➤ Programs ➤ Accessories ➤ Command Prompt. Alternatively, you can click Start ➤ Run and type **cmd**.

2. At the command prompt, type **nslookup** and press Enter. This runs the nslookup command and presents you with a > prompt. This prompt indicates that nslookup is awaiting a command.

3. To activate the local DNS server, type **Server 127.0.0.1**.

4. Type **set type = SRV** to filter resource records to only SRV types, and press Enter. If the command is successful, you will receive another > prompt.

5. To verify a resource record, simply type its FQDN. For example, if our domain name is activedirectory.test, we would type **_ldap._tcp.activedirectory.test**. You should receive information about the hostname that is mapped as a domain controller for this domain.

6. If you want to test other resources, simply type the names of the resources. You should receive valid responses. Table 3.3 provided a list of the default resource records that should be present.

7. When you are finished using nslookup, type **exit** and then press Enter. This returns you to the command prompt. To close the command prompt, type **exit** again and hit Enter.

Unfortunately, the nslookup command is not as user-friendly as it could be. It requires that you learn several different commands and use them in a specific syntax. Nevertheless, the nslookup command is an invaluable tool for troubleshooting DNS configuration issues.

Using *Ipconfig*

You can use the command-line tool ipconfig to view your DNS client settings, to view and reset cached information used locally for resolving DNS name queries, and to register the resource records for a dynamic update client. If you use ipconfig with no parameters, it displays DNS information for each adapter, including the domain name and DNS servers used for that adapter. Table 3.4 shows some command-line options available with ipconfig.

TABLE 3.4 Command-Line Options Available for the *Ipconfig* Command

Command	What It Does
Ipconfig /all	Displays additional information about DNS, including the FQDN and the DNS suffix search list.

TABLE 3.4 Command-Line Options Available for the *Ipconfig* Command *(continued)*

Command	What It Does
`Ipconfig /flushdns`	Flushes and resets the DNS resolver cache. For more information about this option, see the section "Installing and Configuring a DNS Server" earlier in this chapter.
`Ipconfig /displaydns`	Displays the contents of the DNS resolver cache. For more information about this option, see "Installing and Configuring a DNS Server" earlier in this chapter.
`Ipconfig /registerdns`	Refreshes all DHCP leases and registers any related DNS names. This option is available only on Windows 2000–based computers that run the DHCP Client service.

The Hosts File

The Hosts file is used to manually map DNS names to IP addresses. The Hosts file is not dynamic, so you will typically want to use this file only for testing purposes. A sample Hosts file is installed with Windows into the `\%systemroot%\system32\drivers\etc` folder. You can edit this file, which is really nothing more than a host table, with a text editor such as Notepad or WordPad. An entry in the Hosts file is defined by an IP address, followed by one or more spaces, followed by the hostname. So an entry for IP address `206.45.135.25` and hostname `computer1.mycompany.com` would look like this:

```
206.45.135.25   computer1.mycompany.com
```

Exercise 3.9 shows you how to edit the Hosts file.

EXERCISE 3.9

Editing the Hosts File

In this exercise, you will open the sample Hosts file and edit it in Notepad.

EXERCISE 3.9 *(continued)*

1. Open Windows Explorer by selecting Start ➢ Programs ➢ Accessories ➢ Windows Explorer.

2. Navigate to the Windows System folder (most likely C:\WINNT or C:\WIN2K) and open the \system32\drivers\etc\ folder.

3. Double-click the Hosts file. You will be prompted to select a program to open this file with. Select Notepad from the list of programs and click OK.

4. You should see the following data in the Hosts file:

```
# Copyright (c) 1993-1999 Microsoft Corp.

#

# This is a sample HOSTS file used by Microsoft TCP/IP
for Windows.

#

# This file contains the mappings of IP addresses to host
names. Each entry should be kept on an individual line.
The IP address should be placed in the first column
followed by the corresponding host name. The IP address
and the host name should be separated by at least one
space.

#

# Additionally, comments (such as these) may be inserted
on individual lines or following the machine name denoted
by a '#' symbol.

#

#

# For example:

#

#      102.54.94.97      rhino.acme.com           # source
server
```

```
#        38.25.63.10      x.acme.com              # x
client host
```

```
127.0.0.1       localhost
```

A # sign indicates the start of a comment line. As you can see, only one entry in the file is valid:

```
127.0.0.1       localhost
```

Create a new entry at the end of the file for a known IP address and hostname.

5. Select Save from the File menu, and close Notepad.

Troubleshooting DNS Servers

The symptoms related to DNS server problems generally include the inability to perform accurate name resolution. Provided that the DNS server has been installed, some troubleshooting steps to take include the following:

1. Verify that the DNS service has started. By using the DNS administrative tool, you can quickly determine the status of the DNS server.

2. Check the Event Viewer. Especially if you are having intermittent problems with the DNS server or the service has stopped unexpectedly, you can find more information in the Windows NT Event Log.

3. Verify that the DNS server is accessible to clients. A simple check for network connectivity between clients and the DNS server can eliminate a lot of potential problems. Browsing the network and connecting to clients or using the ping command is the easiest way to do this. Note, however, that if name resolution is not occurring properly, you may not be able to connect to clients.

4. Verify operations with the nslookup command. The nslookup command provides several very powerful options for testing recursion and other features of Microsoft's DNS.

5. Verify the DNS configuration. If the DNS server is providing inaccurate or outdated results, you may need to manually change the server settings or retire individual records. If outdated records are truly the problem, it is likely that users are able to get to many other machines (on the LAN or the Internet) but cannot connect to one or more specific computers.

In addition, if you're using implementations other than Microsoft DNS, you should consult the documentation that accompanies that product. Although DNS is an Internet standard, various DNS server software applications function quite differently from one another.

Monitoring DNS Servers

It's always a good idea to know how your network services are performing at any given moment. Monitoring performance allows you to adequately determine the load on current servers, evaluate resource usage, and plan for any necessary upgrades. After you install the DNS service, you will be able to select the DNS object in the Windows 2000 System Monitor. This object contains many different counters that are related to monitoring DNS server performance and usage.

Using System Monitor, you can generate statistics on the following types of events:

- AXFR requests (all-zone transfer requests)

- IXFR requests (incremental zone transfer requests)

- DNS server memory usage

- Dynamic updates

- DNS notify events

- Recursive queries

- TCP and UDP statistics

- WINS statistics

- Zone transfer issues

All of this information can be analyzed easily using the Chart, Histogram, or Report views of System Monitor. You can also use the Alerts function to automatically notify you (or other systems administrators) whenever certain performance statistic thresholds are exceeded. For example, if the total number of recursive queries is very high, you might want to be notified so you can examine the situation. Finally, information from Performance Logs and Alerts utility can be stored to a log data file.

The System Monitor application in Windows 2000 is an extremely powerful and useful tool for managing and troubleshooting systems. You should become familiar with its various functions to ensure that system services are operating properly. For more information on using Windows 2000 System Monitor, see Chapter 9, "Managing Server and Client Computers."

NetBIOS Name Resolution

NetBIOS works by broadcasting tons of network resource information—such as which shares a server offers and where the domain master browser is—so that any client can hear what its peers have to offer. Broadcasts work okay for smaller networks, but they generate a lot of unnecessary and undesirable clutter in larger networks. Since NetBIOS packets aren't routable, the problem is even worse: Not only do all those broadcasts clutter the network, they don't even do any good, since only machines on the local subnet can hear them!

Microsoft solved the routability problem by offering NetBIOS over TCP/IP, or NBT. However, NBT still sends out broadcasts. While NBT broadcasts do allow NetBIOS-style name resolution on TCP/IP networks, Microsoft's designers realized that it was possible to come up with a better solution, and the *Windows Internet Name Service (WINS)* was born.

Microsoft Exam Objective

Troubleshoot name resolution on client computers. Considerations include WINS, DNS, NetBIOS, the Hosts file, and the Lmhosts file.

- Troubleshoot name resolution problems by using the nbtstat, ipconfig, nslookup, and netdiag commands.

- Create and configure an Lmhosts file for troubleshooting name resolution problems.

Windows Internet Name Service

WINS essentially serves as a clearinghouse for NetBIOS naming information. In this role, it listens to NBT broadcasts and collates them in a central source. When you consider how NBT works, this makes a lot of sense. A pure NetBIOS network can use NetBIOS addresses. When one machine wishes to communicate with another, it can use information broadcast by its local master browser to find the address of the target machine. That approach doesn't work as well in TCP/IP, since the source machine has to already know the target's IP address to be talking to it!

NOTE WINS is documented in RFCs 1001 and 1002.

Think back to what you know about DNS. When a TCP/IP application needs an address, it calls the resolver, which uses the DNS query mechanism to obtain an IP address. The application then uses the address to open a communication channel. If you apply this same model to the crusty old NBT protocol, you'll see how WINS works: It provides a service that maps NetBIOS names to IP addresses. This service works in three simple steps:

1. Each time a WINS client (e.g., a machine that's been given the address of a WINS server) starts up, it registers its NetBIOS name and IP address with the WINS server.

2. When a WINS client wants to talk to another computer, the resulting NBT name query is sent directly to the WINS server instead of being broadcast all over the local network.

3. If the WINS server finds the destination host's NetBIOS name and IP address in its database, it returns this information directly to the WINS client. If it doesn't, the WINS server can then make a standard NBT broadcast (if necessary) to hunt down the necessary address.

Because the WINS server receives updates from each WINS client as it starts up, its database entries are always current. You can set up multiple WINS servers on a network so that queries and answers are distributed; the servers can replicate their database entries according to the method and schedule you specify.

WINS and Windows 2000

The WINS implementation in Windows 2000 is largely unchanged from what Microsoft shipped with Windows NT 4.0. The biggest difference is that Microsoft is pushing DNS and TCP/IP as the linchpins of Active Directory–based networks, so WINS is being shoved off to the side and used as a service to help in the migration to Windows 2000. However, there are some interesting Windows 2000 features to consider about WINS.

First, WINS is integrated with DNS. What that means is that DNS-capable clients such as web browsers can transparently take advantage of WINS resolution (provided you've turned this integration on). That allows you to fetch a web page, or other resource, from a machine when all you know is its NetBIOS name. Your application uses the resolver, which makes a DNS query; the DNS server can ask the WINS server for the address after it fails to find it in its local zone.

How WINS Works

When a WINS client starts, the client exchanges WINS messages with its designated WINS server. Each client can actually hold addresses for a primary and a secondary WINS server; the secondary will be used if the primary doesn't answer. The intent of these messages is to allow the client to register its address with the server, without allowing name or address duplication. This message exchange occurs in four phases, which we call the "Four Rs": name registration, name renewal, name release, and name resolution. Let's see what those steps entail.

Name Registration

When a client starts in a WINS network, it's required to register its name and IP address with its designated WINS server. When the WINS server gets a name registration request, it has to evaluate it by asking two questions:

Is the name unique? Duplicate names are undesirable, since they make it impossible to tell which computer *really* has a particular name—sort of the computer equivalent of cloning. If the WINS server receives a request to register a name that it already has in its database, it will send a challenge to the currently registered owner of the disputed name. The challenge message is repeated three times, at 500-millisecond (half-second) intervals—less if the server receives a reply. If the current owner of the name responds (saying, in effect, "Hey, that's still my name!"), the WINS server rejects the new request by sending a negative name request back to the machine attempting to claim the already-in-use NetBIOS name. If the currently registered owner *doesn't* reply, then the name is deleted from the database, and a positive acknowledgment is sent to the requesting machine.

Is the name valid? NetBIOS names have restrictions: Their length must be 15 or fewer characters, and they can't contain certain characters. The WINS server will reject any registration request for an invalid name.

Assuming the WINS server gets a request for a unique, valid name, it registers the name in its database and returns a message confirming the registration. This confirmation includes a time to live (TTL) for the WINS record; this TTL functions exactly as the TTL on a DNS record.

What happens if the client sends a request to its primary WINS server and never gets an answer back? Simple: The client tries again. After three tries, the client will then make three attempts to contact the secondary WINS server, if one is configured. If that fails, too, the client will attempt to register its name the old-fashioned way: by sending out an NBT broadcast.

Name Renewal

WINS clients have to renew their names with the server every so often. With WINS, the client has to notify the server that it wants to continue using its registered name so that the server will reset the TTL.

When the TTL has reached 50 percent of its original value, the WINS client sends a name renewal message to the primary WINS server. This message contains the client's name, the source, and the destination IP addresses for the client and the server. If there's no response, the message will be resent once more when one-eighth of the original TTL remains. If there's *still* no response from the primary server, the client will then attempt renewal through the secondary WINS server, if one is configured. If the effort is successful, the WINS client will attempt to register with the secondary server as though it was the first attempt. If, after three attempts, the WINS client fails to contact the secondary WINS server, it will switch back to the primary one.

Once successful contact is made, either the primary or secondary WINS server responds by sending the client a new TTL period. This process continues as long as the client computer is powered on and as long as it remains a WINS client.

Name Release

A WINS client can relinquish ownership of its name at any time by sending a name release message, which contains its IP address and name. However, this is most often done when the client machine is cleanly shut down. When the server receives a name release message, it deletes the client's information from its database and returns a positive release message composed of the released name and a new TTL of zero. At this point, the client stops responding to its former NetBIOS name.

If the IP address and name sent by the client don't match the WINS database, the WINS server will return a negative release message. If the client doesn't get either a positive or negative release message, it will send up to three B-node broadcasts notifying all other systems, including non-WINS clients, to remove the now-invalid name from their NetBIOS name caches.

Name Resolution

So far, you've learned about the communications only between a WINS-enabled computer and a WINS server. How do regular network clients get information from the WINS database? The basic idea is that the client should try to exhaust other methods of resolution before it resorts to blasting out network broadcasts (although, as you'll see, the process works a little differently in practice).

Here's how the process works, assuming you're trying to map a network drive on a server named TRIDENT:

1. You type **net use g: \\trident\public** into a command-line window.

2. NBT checks the system's local name cache to see if it already has an IP address on file for TRIDENT. If the name is found in the cache, the Address Resolution Protocol (ARP) is then used to turn the name into a hardware address. This deftly avoids adding unnecessary traffic on the network.

3. If the name isn't in the local cache, the name query goes directly to the primary WINS server. If the primary server is up and the name is found in its database, the information is returned to the requestor, where it's added into the local cache. If the server fails to respond, the request is repeated twice before the client switches to the secondary WINS server and starts over.

4. If neither the primary nor secondary WINS server can resolve the name, the client reverts to making a broadcast. If another system hears the broadcast and returns an address for the requested name, it goes into the local cache.

5. If the broadcast doesn't generate a useful answer, NBT searches the Lmhosts file for an answer. If that fails, it then checks the Hosts file and, finally, DNS. If none of these works, the command fails.

Real World Scenario

Windows Naming Services

You have just been hired as a network administrator for a large organization with offices in over 25 locations. The company is a decentralized organization with local administrators dealing with day-to-day support issues. The support staff developed this way during the heavy use of Windows NT. In the interest of lowering the support costs and increasing efficiency, the engineering staff is in the process of migrating to Windows 2000. The ability to centrally manage the network holds great promise for lower administrative costs, and this benefit grows dramatically the closer you get to a complete Windows 2000 network. Migrating any platform to a new version is no trivial task, and Windows 2000 is no exception, even though Microsoft has gone to great lengths to ease this process.

The main benefit comes from tying together management tasks and monitoring via Active Directory. However, when a significant percentage of legacy Windows platforms participate in the network, you need to maintain the supporting infrastructure. The biggest problem with the previous version of Windows was it reliance on NetBIOS to name resources. This created a need to resolve those names and pass that information to transport protocols. As the networks grew larger, this problem grew disproportionately since NetBIOS was never designed to support large networks, especially routed networks.

WINS was designed to help with this problem. It maintains a database of name-to-IP matchings so the clients need not search the entire network to find another workstation. While this helps stem the bleeding of a NetBIOS-based network, it is something everything network manager wants to move away from. Until you have eliminated the need for this service, you will have issues that will impact the entire network. And the users will not blame NetBIOS for the problem; they will simply blame the network administrator. You need to be up to speed on WINS and even its unwieldy predecessor, Lmhosts files. In some cases, particularly if you have only spot needs for NetBIOS name resolution, it makes more sense to use the Lmhosts file instead of dealing with a WINS server. The reality is that Windows 2000 network administrators must have a thorough understanding of NetBIOS name resolution and how to manage it appropriately.

The Lmhosts File

The *Lmhosts file* is similar to the Hosts file that you saw earlier in the chapter, except that it maps NetBIOS names to IP addresses. The Lmhosts file is actually called `LMHosts.sam` and is created by default in the `\%systemroot%\system32\drivers\etc` folder when Windows is installed. You can open this file in Notepad just like you would open the Hosts file. Entries in the Lmhosts file are made in much the same way that you add entries in the Hosts file. For example, if a machine has an IP address of 204.35.24.84 and a NetBIOS name of computer2, then an Lmhosts entry for this mapping would look like this:

```
204.35.24.84  computer2
```

The contents of the sample Lmhosts file included with Windows 2000 are shown here. The sample file includes detailed descriptions of all of the special commands that you can use, such as #PRE and #INCLUDE.

```
# Copyright (c) 1993-1999 Microsoft Corp.
#
# This is a sample LMHOSTS file used by the Microsoft TCP/
IP for Windows.
#
# This file contains the mappings of IP addresses to
computernames (NetBIOS) names.  Each entry should be kept
on an individual line. The IP address should be placed in
the first column followed by the corresponding
computername. The address and the computername should be
separated by at least one space or tab. The "#" character
is generally used to denote the start of a comment (see
the exceptions below).
#
# This file is compatible with Microsoft LAN Manager 2.x
TCP/IP lmhosts files and offers the following extensions:
#
#       #PRE
#       #DOM:<domain>
#       #INCLUDE <filename>
#       #BEGIN_ALTERNATE
#       #END_ALTERNATE
#       \0xnn (non-printing character support)
#
# Following any entry in the file with the characters
"#PRE" will cause the entry to be preloaded into the name
cache. By default, entries are not preloaded, but are
parsed only after dynamic name resolution fails.
#
# Following an entry with the "#DOM:<domain>" tag will
associate the entry with the domain specified by <domain>.
This affects how the browser and logon services behave in
TCP/IP environments. To preload the host name associated
with #DOM entry, it is necessary to also add a #PRE to the
line. The <domain> is always preloaded although it will
not be shown when the name cache is viewed.
```

```
#
# Specifying "#INCLUDE <filename>" will force the RFC
NetBIOS (NBT) software to seek the specified <filename>
and parse it as if it were local. <filename> is generally
a UNC-based name, allowing a centralized lmhosts file to
be maintained on a server. It is ALWAYS necessary to
provide a mapping for the IP address of the server prior
to the #INCLUDE. This mapping must use the #PRE directive.
In addition the share "public" in the example below must
be in the LanManServer list of "NullSessionShares" in
order for client machines to be able to read the lmhosts
file successfully. This key is under
#
\machine\system\currentcontrolset\services\lanmanserver\pa
rameters\nullsessionshares
# in the registry. Simply add "public" to the list found
there.
#
# The #BEGIN_ and #END_ALTERNATE keywords allow multiple
#INCLUDE statements to be grouped together. Any single
successful include will cause the group to succeed.
#
# Finally, non-printing characters can be embedded in
mappings by first surrounding the NetBIOS name in
quotations, then using the \0xnn notation to specify a hex
value for a non-printing character.
#
# The following example illustrates all of these
extensions:
#
# 102.54.94.97      rhino          #PRE #DOM:networking
#net group's DC
# 102.54.94.102     "appname  \0x14"
#special app server
# 102.54.94.123     popular        #PRE
#source server
# 102.54.94.117     localsrv       #PRE
#needed for the include
#
# #BEGIN_ALTERNATE
# #INCLUDE \\localsrv\public\lmhosts
```

```
# #INCLUDE \\rhino\public\lmhosts
# #END_ALTERNATE
#
# In the above example, the "appname" server contains a
special character in its name, the "popular" and
"localsrv" server names are preloaded, and the "rhino"
server name is specified so it can be used to later
#INCLUDE a centrally maintained lmhosts file if the
"localsrv" system is unavailable.
#
# Note that the whole file is parsed including comments on
each lookup, so keeping the number of comments to a
minimum will improve performance. Therefore it is not
advisable to simply add lmhosts file entries onto the end
of this file.
```

You can use the Lmhosts file as a backup NBT resolver in case the WINS server goes down. If you decide to do this, then you should take measures to maintain the contents of the file. You should update the file with new entries any time a computer on the network changes its hostname or IP address. You should also place frequently used NBT mappings at the top of the list since the Lmhosts file is searched one line at a time, starting from the top. For client machines, the most useful special command is probably the #INCLUDE function, which pulls NBT information from another file, most likely a master Lmhosts file that is stored on a server computer.

Exercise 3.10 shows you how to edit the Lmhosts file.

EXERCISE 3.10

Editing the Lmhosts File

In this exercise, you will open the sample Lmhosts file and edit it in Notepad:

1. Open Windows Explorer by selecting Start ➤ Programs ➤ Accessories ➤ Windows Explorer.

2. Navigate to the Windows system folder (most likely C:\WINNT or C:\WIN2K) and open the \system32\drivers\etc\ folder.

EXERCISE 3.10

3. Double-click the LMHosts.sam file. You will be prompted to select a program to use to open this file. Select Notepad from the list of programs and click OK.

4. You should see the following data in the Lmhosts file:

A # sign indicates the start of a comment line. The sample file includes examples of special modifiers that you can use to change the way the mappings work, but these go beyond the scope of this book. Type a new entry at the end of the file for a known IP address and NetBIOS name.

5. Select Save from the File menu, and close Notepad.

Using the *Nbtstat* Command

During normal operation, NBT resolves NetBIOS names to IP addresses. The local machine uses one of several possible sources for this: local cache lookup, WINS server query, broadcast, Lmhosts lookup, Hosts lookup, and DNS server query. The *nbtstat* command can help you diagnose and correct errors that occur in NBT at any of these lookup points. Nbtstat is run at the command prompt, and you must use several case-sensitive switches to get meaningful results from the command. For example, entering

```
nbtstat /?
```

at the command prompt lists the available options. Table 3.5 lists the nbtstat switches and their functions.

TABLE 3.5   *Nbtstat* Switches

Switch	Name	Function
-a <name>	adapter status	Displays the NetBIOS name table and MAC address of the address card for the computer name specified.
-A <IP address>	Adapter status	Displays the same information as -a but uses the target's IP address.

TABLE 3.5   *Nbtstat* Switches *(continued)*

Switch	Name	Function
-c	cache	Displays the contents of the NetBIOS name cache.
[Number]	Interval	The number you enter indicates the interval, in seconds, in which to redisplay selected statistics, pausing between each display. Press Ctrl+C to stop redisplaying statistics.
-n	names	Lists the names registered locally by NetBIOS applications.
-r	resolved	Shows a count of all names resolved by broadcast or WINS server.
-R	Reload	Purges the name cache and reloads all #PRE entries from Lmhosts.
-RR	ReleaseRefresh	Releases and reregisters all names with the name server.
-s	sessions	Lists the NetBIOS sessions table converting destination IP addresses to computer NetBIOS names.
-S	Sessions	Lists the current NetBIOS sessions and their status, with the IP address.
/?	Help	Displays this list.

Exercise 3.11 shows you how to use the nbtstat command.

EXERCISE 3.11

Using the *Nbtstat* command

In this exercise, you will use the nbtstat command to check the status of your NBT resolvers:

1. Open the command prompt by selecting Start ➢ Programs ➢ Accessories ➢ Command Prompt.

2. At the command prompt, enter **nbtstat /?**. You should see the list of switches shown in Table 3.5.

3. Now enter **nbtstat -a** *name*, where *name* is the NetBIOS name of your computer. You should see output displaying the NetBIOS name table and MAC address of the local computer.

4. Try entering **nbtstat -c**. If you have tried to access any computers by their NetBIOS name recently, then the output should include a list of names. If you haven't, then the output will just say "No names in cache."

5. If step 4 returns at least one name, then you can see how nbtstat is used to clear the nbt cache. Change the IP address of one of the machines that was listed in the output of step 4, and then try pinging the NetBIOS name of that machine. You should receive a timeout message since the cache is pointing to an IP address that is no longer valid for that machine. Now enter **nbtstat -R** to purge the cache, and then try pinging the NetBIOS name of that machine again. You should get a response.

Summary

In this chapter, we looked at name resolution in Windows 2000, focusing on DNS and WINS. DNS was designed to be a robust, scalable, high-performance system for resolving friendly names to TCP/IP host addresses. We started by giving an overview of the basics of DNS and how DNS names are generated. We then looked at the many features available in Microsoft's version of DNS and focused on how to install, configure, and manage the necessary services. We finished the chapter with an overview of WINS and techniques on how to troubleshoot NBT problems.

Important points to remember include the following:

- DNS is based on a widely accepted standard. It is designed to resolve friendly network names to IP addresses.

- DNS names are hierarchical and are read from left (most-specific) to right (least-specific).

- DNS zones are created to hold a database of authoritative information for the hosts in a specific domain.

- Within DNS zones, servers can assume various roles.

- Through the use of replication, multiple DNS servers can remain synchronized.

- WINS acts as a clearinghouse for NBT resolution, making NBT more reliable.

Understanding DNS is extremely important for using Active Directory, so if you aren't yet comfortable with the concepts described in this chapter, be sure to review them before going on.

Exam Essentials

Know how to troubleshoot DNS.   Know what to do with the information gleamed from the nslookup tool in order to resolve DNS communication problems. This includes understanding the configuration of the client in order to find the proper DNS server to provide name resolution. It also covers understanding the proper response to communication problems between DNS servers.

Understand design goals and features of DNS.   DNS has been designed as a distributed database that allows for scalability, performance, and maintainability of a large number of records. It is based on a widely accepted and formalized set of standards.

Be able to identify portions of a DNS name.   DNS names are hierarchical and include information about the names of various networks resources (such as mail and web servers), as well as the networks on which they reside.

Understand the purpose of DNS zones.   Be able to decide when multiple DNS zones should be implemented and how they can be created from existing zones. Also understand how the zones are transferred and how this can impact the performance and reliability of the overall DNS service.

Be able to choose DNS server roles.   A DNS server can be designated as a master, primary, secondary, or caching-only server for a particular zone. DNS servers can assume multiple roles for other DNS zones as well. Be sure you understand the differences between these roles and how they can be used to optimize DNS performance and reliability. And be sure you know the advantages of integrating DNS with Active Directory for simplifying management and for performance reasons.

Manage DNS replication.   You should understand how DNS replication (zone transfer) operations work, potential issues that might occur due to network traffic, and how to monitor and troubleshoot DNS.

Troubleshoot DNS problems.   Understand the tools that are available for isolating and fixing DNS name resolution issues. Various methods are available for troubleshooting client- and server-side issues. Know how to read the results of `nslookup` queries and how to modify configurations based upon them.

Understand the purpose of WINS.   WINS serves as a reliable way to resolve NetBIOS names to IP addresses. Without WINS, you would need to send broadcast information out to the network to resolve NetBIOS names, which is inefficient.

Know how to edit the Lmhosts file.   The Lmhosts file is used to resolve NetBIOS names to IP addresses when a WINS server is not available. You can make entries in the file using a standard text editor.

Know how to use the `nbtstat` command.   The `nbtstat` command is used to diagnose problems related to NBT resolution. You must run the command at the command prompt and use various switches to display meaningful information and make changes to NBT data.

Key Terms

Before you take the exam, be certain you are familiar with the following terms:

caching-only DNS server	parent domain
child domain	primary DNS server
delegation	recursion
DNS namespace	resource record (RR)
Domain Name System (DNS)	reverse lookup zone
forward lookup zone	root domain
forwarding	secondary DNS server
iteration	Windows Internet Name Service (WINS)
Lmhosts file	zone
master DNS server	zone transfer
nbtstat	

Review Questions

1. You're the DNS administrator for your organization's network. Thus far, the network has included three different DNS zones:

   - research.mycompany.com

   - development.mycompany.com

   - engineering.mycompany.com

   Recently, the organization has acquired another company. Since the organizations will be operated independently, you must provide DNS support for a new domain called newcompany.com. Which two of the following steps must you perform? (Choose all that apply.)

   A. Create a new DNS zone called newcompany.com.

   B. Remove all host records from the existing DNS zone.

   C. Create resource records (RRs) for the resources that are available in the new domain.

   D. Add the new domain to the research.mycompany.com zone.

2. You have just made a change to a resource record in the DNS database on a master server. Which two of the following processes may the server use to alert secondary servers that a change has been made and then copy the data to the secondary server? (Choose all that apply.)

   A. Zone transfer

   B. Forwarding

   C. Recursion

   D. Iteration

   E. DNS notify

3. A large organization has implemented 12 DNS zones and has configured at least two DNS servers in each zone. Recently, users in one department within the organization have reported intermittent problems connecting to portions of the organization's intranet. A systems administrator suspects that there is a problem with the configuration of one of the organization's DNS servers. Which of the following tools can she use to determine the source of the problem? (Choose all that apply.)

   A. Event Viewer

   B. System Monitor

   C. DNS administrative tool

   D. The `nslookup` command

4. The process that occurs when a DNS server cannot return enough information to fully resolve a DNS name to a TCP/IP addresses is known as what?

   A. Recursion

   B. Iteration

   C. Zone transfer

   D. Dynamic DNS update

5. Your organization has implemented several DNS servers in multiple zones, including a master server, a primary server, and two secondary servers. Users are complaining about performance problems related to DNS. You must solve the problem, but you have the following constraints:

   - The new server must improve DNS performance for multiple zones.

   - The new server must not be an authority for any DNS zone.

   - Due to budget constraints, you can only implement one new server.

You determine that you need to add an additional server to the environment. Which of the following types of DNS servers should you implement?

A. Master server

B. Caching-only server

C. Primary server

D. Secondary server

6. Recently, you've experienced problems in communications between domain controllers. For example, when you log on from some locations throughout the network, you are unable to access a domain controller. Also, when you examine the Directory Services log information through the Event Viewer tool, you see that there have been several failed communication attempts between domain controllers. It is likely that this problem is caused by the lack of which of the following types of DNS resource records (RRs)?

A. SRV

B. PTR

C. A

D. MX

7. The process by which one or more DNS servers use a specified DNS server for all recursive lookups is known as what?

A. Recursion

B. Iteration

C. DNS notify

D. Forwarding

8. Which of the following resource records (RRs) indicates the zone(s) for which a DNS server is an authority?

A. SRV

B. PTR

C. SOA

D. MX

9. A systems administrator for a small network has completed the upgrade of all clients and servers on the network to Windows 2000. She also has ensured that none of the applications on her network rely on NetBIOS names and that they use DNS names for finding network resources. Which of the following name resolution methods should she disable?

   A. DNS

   B. DHCP

   C. WINS

   D. IPX/SPX

10. You are configuring DNS replication for your zone. You want to notify all of the servers listed on the Name Servers tab of the Zone Properties dialog box whenever the zone changes. Where would you click in the following exhibit in order to accomplish this?

   A. The To Any Server radio button

   B. The Only To Servers Listed On The Name Servers Tab radio button

   C. The Notify button

   D. The Only To The Following Servers radio button

11. The following diagram outlines DNS name resolution through recursion. Move each item into the correct position so that the flow of DNS traffic is correct.

> Choices:
>
> Client uses IP address to connect to www.company.com.
> Root-level server resolves name.
> Server returns IP address and caches name.
> Client requests IP address.
> Server cannot resolve name. Forwards request.

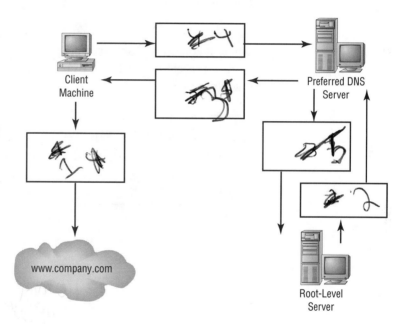

12. Your company needs to upgrade all of its Windows NT 4 machines to Windows 2000. You need to maintain the four DNS zones that are currently in place: San Jose, San Francisco, San Diego, and Los Angeles. The Los Angeles zone uses a Unix-based primary DNS server, and the administrator at that site insists that it remain in place in its current role. The other sites all use Windows-based primary and secondary DNS servers. The San Diego zone has a very unreliable WAN connection, so you decide that it will be worthwhile to use this machine to complete name resolution requests. For ease of administration, however, you do not want the San Francisco server to store a copy of the zone file.

You need to configure Windows 2000 Servers at each site. Drag the different zone types to their appropriate places within the diagram. Note that each item can be used more than once, and some items might not be used at all.

Choices:

Standard Primary Zone
Standard Secondary Zone
Caching-Only Server
Active Directory–Integrated Zone

San Francisco

San Jose

Los Angeles

San Diego

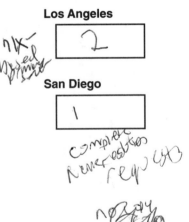

13. You are the administrator on a network that is being merged with another network. Your network is based upon Windows NT and is located entirely in one location. It consists of four Windows NT Servers and 200 Windows workstations. The new network consists of two Windows NT Servers and three Windows 2000 Servers. While 150 of the workstations have already been upgraded to Windows 2000 Professional, another 150 are running Windows NT Workstation. The new network is going to be connected to your network with a router. The plan is for both networks to migrate to Windows 2000 and utilize Active Directory. When you connect the two networks, the machines on each side of the network cannot see the other side. What must you install in order for the two networks to be able to locate resources on the other side of the routers?

A. You need to install DNS for name resolution on both sides of the network.

B. You need to install WINS on at least one side of the network.

C. You need to install a Unix server and install DNS on that machine until the migration to Windows 2000 is complete.

D. You only need to configure the router properly to support the Windows NT name resolution.

14. You have just completed the migration of single LAN network from Windows NT to Windows 2000. The network consists of four Windows 2000 Servers along with several hundred Windows Professional workstations. You have also installed Active Directory to help manage the accounts and plan to develop global policies to centrally manage them. During the installation of Active Directory, you also installed DNS. Lately, the users have been complaining that the network is much slower than it used to be and is degrading. Using Network Monitor, you narrow the problem to a significant amount of traffic between all of the workstations and the DNS server. What tool should you now use to determine the nature of the traffic between the machines in order to rectify the problem?

A. Event Viewer

B. `nslookup`

C. System Monitor

D. Task Manager

E. Performance Monitor

15. The company you work for has six locations around the country. You are part of the administrative team based in the central office, and you have finished upgrading the workstations and servers to Windows 2000. Your team is now in the process of deploying DNS in order to support your manager's planned implementation of a single Active Directory tree so you can support the network from your central location. Since you must support name resolution for six offices, you want to provide an efficient and responsive service for the users. Which of the following is the best approach to support your plans for a single Active Directory tree and provide the efficiency and responsiveness for the users in this situation?

   A. Create a single second-level name and maintain all the DNS servers at your central office to ease administration.

   B. Create a single second-level name and deploy a DNS server at each location in the network.

   C. Create a second-level name for each city and maintain all the DNS servers at your central office to ease administration.

   D. Create a second-level name for each city and deploy a DNS server at each location in the network.

Answers to Review Questions

1. A, C. Since the new domain is not part of the namespace of any existing zones, you must create a new zone. Then you must add information about network resources to this zone. There's absolutely no reason to remove host records, and newcompany.com needs its own domain space, so options B and D are incorrect.

2. A, E. A DNS notify message can be sent by a master server to notify secondary servers that changes have been made to the DNS database and that they should request an update. A zone transfer is the process by which information is replicated between master and secondary DNS servers.

3. A, B, C, D. All of the above tools can be used to view performance or operational information about the DNS service. She could use Event Viewer to check for logged error or informational events; she could use System Monitor to monitor network traffic; she could use the DNS administrative tool to verify that the DNS configuration is correct; and she could use the nslookup tool to query the DNS server.

4. B. In the process of iteration, a DNS server returns its best guess about a domain name, but the client is responsible for ultimately resolving the name. Recursion occurs when the DNS server passes the query on to a higher-level DNS server. Zone transfers and dynamic updates are used to update the DNS server's database.

5. B. Of the choices, only a caching-only server meets the requirements. All of the other server types contain information about specific DNS zones.

6. A. Active Directory domain controllers and client computers use SRV records to find domain controllers for a specific domain. If this record were missing or incorrect, it would cause problems when attempting to communicate with domain controllers.

7. D. Forwarding can be used to route all recursive DNS requests through specific DNS servers. This is often used to reduce network traffic across slow links. Forwarding is a part of recursion, so option A really isn't the best answer. Iteration occurs when the DNS server isn't sure how to resolve the name. DNS notify is used to notify compatible secondary servers that DNS information has been updated.

8. C. The Start of Authority (SOA) record indicates that a server is considered an authority for a specific zone. SRV records specify server services available on the host. PTR records are used only for reverse lookup operations. MX records are Mail Exchanger records, so they don't really apply here.

9. C. Windows 2000's support for WINS is primarily included for backward compatibility with legacy applications that rely on the use of NetBIOS names. Since this is no longer required, the systems administrator can reduce network traffic and increase performance by relying primarily on DNS for name resolution.

10. C. In order to notify any servers of zone updates, you need to click the Notify button. From the Notify dialog box, you can choose to notify all of the servers listed on the Name Servers tab or only particular servers that you specify.

11.

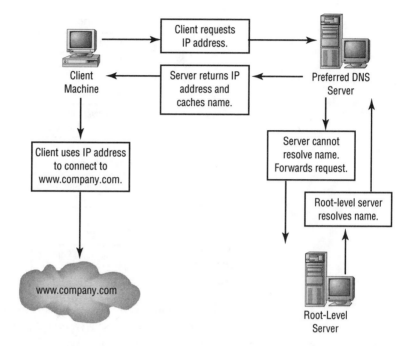

The client machine places its request with its preferred DNS server. If the DNS server doesn't have an entry in its DNS database, then it forwards the request to a root-level server. The root-level server resolves the name and sends it back to the preferred DNS server. The DNS server caches the name so that any future requests don't need to be forwarded, and then it sends the IP address to the client. The client then uses the IP address to reach the intended target.

12.

San Francisco

Active Directory–
Integrated Zone

San Jose

Active Directory–
Integrated Zone

Los Angeles

Standard Secondary
Zone

San Diego

Standard Primary
Zone

Secure DNS updates can be run only on Active Directory–integrated zones. San Diego should use a standard primary server because it won't be reliably available for Active Directory–integrated DNS updates. The Los Angeles site is using a Unix primary DNS server, so the best you can do there is run a standard secondary zone.

13. B. Since you don't have Active Directory installed yet, DNS is not a requirement for name resolution. However, before you complete the migration, you will still need some form of NetBIOS name resolution to pass through the router. You can best provide this through a WINS server on at least one side of the network. You can configure the clients on the other side of the router to locate the WINS server. It is possible to configure a router to pass NetBIOS traffic, but this is not recommended, particularly since the problem can be resolved so easily with WINS. Once the migration is complete, DNS will provide the name resolution and WINS will no longer be required.

14. C. System Monitor is the Windows 2000 replacement for Windows NT Performance Monitor and is used to monitor the various components of network services and subsystems. This allows the administrator to drill down into services and determine the demands placed upon them. Event Viewer is more of an alert mechanism that provides a historical log of various system events. Task Manager shows which services are running and basic data like how much memory and the number of threads each task is consuming. Nslookup is a utility that queries DNS servers and obtains information about the configuration records instantiated in the server.

15. B. Installing a DNS server at each city as well as the central office allows the workstations in each city to obtain their name resolution from local servers, thereby providing good response time. If all the DNS servers were in the central office, name resolution would have to cross the routers, introducing latency and the potential for no service if the link ever went down. The namespace in a single Active Directory tree must be contiguous. If you create a second-level domain for each city, you would need to create multiple Active Directory trees.

Active Directory's Logical and Physical Structure

MICROSOFT EXAM OBJECTIVES COVERED IN THIS CHAPTER:

✓ **Diagnose Active Directory replication problems.**

- Diagnose problems related to WAN link connectivity.
- Diagnose problems involving replication latency. Problems include duplicate objects and the LostandFound container.

Managing users, computers, applications, and network devices can seem like a never-ending process, especially to systems administrators. Nevertheless, there's a great need for organization, especially when it comes to some of the most fundamental yet tedious tasks we perform every day. That's where the concept of *directory services* comes in.

Microsoft's Active Directory technology is designed to store information about all of the objects within your network environment, including hardware, software, network devices, and users. Furthermore, it is designed to increase capabilities while it decreases administration through the use of a hierarchical structure that mirrors a business's logical organization. In other words, it forms the universal "phone book" we so badly need in the network world!

The Managing a Microsoft Windows 2000 Network Environment exam has an underlying assumption that you understand the overall purpose and functionality of Active Directory. You should have a solid understanding of what Active Directory is and how it can benefit your organization so that you can properly plan and implement Active Directory on your network.

Once you have determined exactly *what* your Active Directory should look like, it's time to find out *how* to configure it to best support the administration of the directory and hence the network resources. And that's what we'll cover throughout the next few chapters in this book. Specifically, we'll talk about the various methods for implementing the tools and services of Windows 2000 that support the directory based on your company's business and technical requirements. Despite the underlying complexity of all of the features of Active Directory and its supporting services, Microsoft has gone to great lengths to ensure that the implementation and management of Active Directory are intuitive and straightforward, for no technology is useful if no one can figure out how to use it appropriately.

In this chapter, we'll take a look at some of the many benefits of using a directory services system and, specifically, Microsoft's Active Directory. We'll cover basic information regarding the various concepts related to Microsoft's Active Directory. The emphasis will be on addressing why the entire idea of directory services came about and how it can be used to improve operations in your environment. We'll then look at the various logical objects created in Active Directory and the ways in which you can configure them to work with your network environment. Finally, we'll cover the details related to mapping your organization's physical network infrastructure to the directory services architecture and show you how directory replication is tied to this physical structure. The goal is to describe the framework on which Active Directory is based.

With that goal in mind, let's get started!

An Overview of Active Directory

Most businesses have created an organizational structure in an attempt to better manage their environments. For example, companies often divide themselves into departments (such as Sales, Marketing, and Engineering), and individuals fill roles within these departments (such as managers and staff). The goal is to add constructs that help coordinate the various functions required for the success of the organization as a whole.

The Information Technology (IT) department in these companies is responsible for maintaining the security of the company's information. In modern businesses, this involves planning for, implementing, and managing various network resources. Servers, workstations, and routers are common tools that are used to connect users with the information they need to do their jobs. In all but the smallest environments, the effort required to manage each of these technological resources can be great.

That's where Windows 2000 and Microsoft's Active Directory come in. In its most basic definition, a *directory* is a repository that records information and makes it available to users. The overall design goal for Active Directory was to create a single centralized repository of information that securely manages a company's resources. User account management, security, and applications are just a few of these areas. Active Directory is a data store that allows administrators to manage various types of information within a single distributed database, thus solving one of the problems we stated earlier. This is no small task, but as you will see in the next section, there are many features of this directory services technology that allow it to meet the needs of organizations of any size.

Active Directory's Logical Structure

Database professionals often use the term *schema* to describe the structure of data. A schema usually defines the types of information that can be stored within a certain repository and includes special rules on how the information is to be organized. Within a relational database or Microsoft Excel spreadsheet, for example, we might define tables with columns and rows and formatted for numbers or dates. Similarly, the Active Directory schema specifies the types of information that are stored within a directory. By default, the schema supports information regarding usernames, passwords, and permissions. The schema itself also describes the structure of the information stored within the Active Directory data store. The Active Directory data store resides on one or more domain controllers that are deployed throughout the enterprise. In this section, we'll take a look at the various concepts that are used to specify how Active Directory is logically organized.

An Overview of Active Directory Domains

In Windows 2000 Active Directory, a *domain* is a logical security boundary that allows for the creation, administration, and management of related resources. You can think of a domain as a logical division, such as a neighborhood within a city. Although each neighborhood is part of a larger group of neighborhoods (the city), it may carry on many of its functions independently of the others. For example, resources such as tennis courts and swimming pools may be made available only to members of the neighborhood, while resources such as electricity and water supplies would probably be shared among neighborhoods. So, think of a domain as a grouping of objects that utilizes resources exclusive to its domain, but keep in mind that those resources can also be shared *among* domains. Active Directory domains can be combined together into *forests* and *trees* to form hierarchical structures. Before going into the details, let's discuss the concept of domains.

Within most business organizations, network and systems administration duties are delegated to certain individuals and departments. For example, a company might have a centralized IT department that is responsible for all implementation, support, and maintenance of network resources throughout the organization. In another example, network support may be largely decentralized—that is, each department, business unit, or office may have its own IT support staff. Both of these models may work well for a company, but implementing such a structure through directory services requires the use of logical objects.

Domains are composed of computers and resources that share a common security database. An Active Directory domain contains a logical partition of users, groups, and other objects within the environment. Objects within a domain share several characteristics, including the following:

Group Policy and Security Permissions   Security for all of the objects within a domain can be administered based on one set of policies. Thus, a domain administrator can make changes to any of the settings within the domain. These settings can apply to all of the users, computers, and objects within the domain. For more granular security settings, however, permissions can be granted on specific objects, thereby distributing administration responsibilities and increasing security. Domains are configured as a single security entity. Objects, permissions, and other settings within a domain do not automatically apply to other domains.

Hierarchical Object Naming   All of the objects within an Active Directory container share a common namespace. When domains are combined, however, the namespace is hierarchical. For example, a user in one department might have an object name called `janedoe@engineering.microsoft.com` while a user in another department might have one called `johndoe@sales.microsoft.com`. The first part of the name is determined by the name of the object within the domain (in these examples, the username). The suffix is determined by the organization of the domains. The hierarchical naming system allows each object within Active Directory to have a unique name.

Hierarchical Properties   Containers called *organizational units (OUs)* (described in the next chapter) can be created within a domain. These units are used for creating a logical grouping of objects within Active Directory. Lower-level objects can inherit the specific user settings and permissions that are assigned to these objects. For example, if we have an organizational unit for the North America division within our company, we can set user permissions on this object. All of the objects within the

North America object (such as the Sales, Marketing, and Engineering departments) would automatically inherit these settings. This makes administration easier, but inheritance is an important concept to remember when implementing and administering security since it results in the implicit assignment of permissions. The proper use of hierarchical properties allows systems administrators to avoid inconsistent security policies (such as a minimum password length of six characters in one object and a minimum password length of eight characters in another).

Trust Relationships   In order to facilitate the sharing of information between domains, transitive trust relationships are automatically created between them. In addition, the administrator can break and establish trust relationships based on business requirements. A trust relationship allows two domains to share security information and objects but does not automatically assign permissions to these objects. This allows users who are contained within one domain to be granted access to resources in other domains. To make administrating trust relationships easier, Microsoft has made transitive two-way *trusts* the default relationship between domains. As shown in Figure 4.1, if Domain A trusts Domain B and Domain B trusts Domain C, Domain A implicitly trusts Domain C.

FIGURE 4.1   Transitive two-way trust relationships

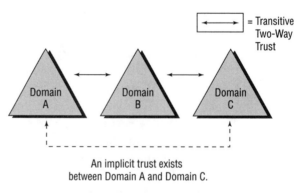

An implicit trust exists
between Domain A and Domain C.

Generally, triangles are used to represent Active Directory domains (thereby indicating their hierarchical structure), and circles are used to represent flat domains (such as those in Windows NT).

Overall, the purpose of domains is to ease administration while providing for a common security and resource database.

Using Multiple Domains

Although the flexibility and power afforded by the use of an Active Directory domain will meet the needs of many organizations, there are reasons for which companies might want to implement more than one domain. For now, however, it is important to know that domains can be combined into domain trees.

Domain trees are hierarchical collections of domains that are designed to meet the organizational needs of a business (see Figure 4.2). Trees are defined by the use of a contiguous namespace. For example, the following domains are all considered part of the same tree:

- `microsoft.com`
- `sales.microsoft.com`
- `research.microsoft.com`
- `us.sales.microsoft.com`

Notice that all of these domains are part of the `microsoft.com` domain. Domains within trees still maintain separate security and resource databases, but they can be administered together through the use of trust relationships. By default, trust relationships are automatically established between parent and child domains within a tree.

FIGURE 4.2   A domain tree

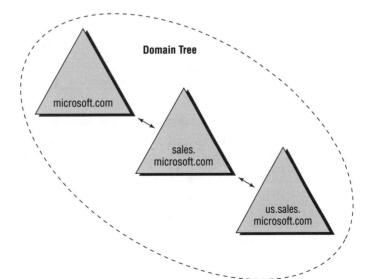

Although single companies will often want to configure domains to fit within a single namespace, noncontiguous namespaces may be used. When domain trees are combined into noncontiguous groupings, they are known as forests (see Figure 4.3). Forests often contain multiple noncontiguous namespaces consisting of domains that are kept separate for technical or political reasons. Just as trust relationships are created between domains within a tree, trust relationships are also created between trees within a forest so resources can be shared between them.

FIGURE 4.3 An Active Directory forest

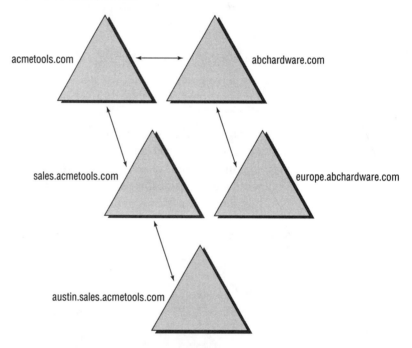

Physically, domains are implemented and managed by the use of domain controllers. We'll cover this topic later in this chapter. Now that we've seen the organizational concepts behind Active Directory, let's move on to looking at logical structure and features that are used to implement these concepts.

Components and Mechanisms of Active Directory

In order to maintain the types of information and to ensure that it is available throughout the forest in a manner required to support an entire organization, Active Directory must provide for many different types of functionality. These include the following:

Data Store   When you envision Active Directory from a physical point of view, you probably imagine a set of files stored on the hard disk that contain all of the objects within it. The term *data store* is used to refer to the actual structure that contains the information contained within Active Directory. The data store is implemented as just that—a set of files that reside within the file system of a domain controller. This is the fundamental structure of Active Directory.

The data store itself has a structure that describes the types of information it can contain. Within the data store, data about objects is recorded and made available to users. For example, configuration information about the domain topology, including trust relationships (which we'll cover later in this chapter), is contained within Active Directory. Similarly, information about users, groups, and computers that are part of the domain is also recorded.

Schema   The Active Directory schema consists of rules on the types of information that can be stored within the directory. The schema is made up of two types of objects: attributes and classes. *Attributes* define a single granular piece of information stored within Active Directory. First Name and Last Name, for example, are considered attributes, which may contain the values of Bob and Smith. *Classes* are objects that are defined as collections of attributes. For example, a class called Employee could include the First Name and Last Name attributes.

It is important to understand that classes and attributes are defined independently and that any number of classes can use the same attributes. For example, if we create an attribute called Nickname, this value could conceivably be used to describe a User class and a Computer class. By default, Microsoft has included several different schema objects. In order to support custom data, however, applications developers can extend the schema by creating their own classes and attributes. The entire schema is replicated to all of the domain controllers within the environment to ensure data consistency among them.

The overall result of the schema is a consistent centralized data store that can contain information about many different types of objects—including users, groups, computers, network devices, applications, and more.

Global Catalog The *Global Catalog* is a database that contains all of the information pertaining to objects within all domains in the Active Directory environment. One of the potential problems with working in an environment that contains multiple domains is that users in one domain may want to find objects stored in another domain, but they may not have any additional information about those objects.

The purpose of the Global Catalog is to index information stored in Active Directory so that it can be more quickly and easily searched. In order to store and replicate all of this information, the Global Catalog can be distributed to servers within the network environment. That is, network and systems administrators must specify which servers within the Active Directory environment should contain copies of the Global Catalog. This decision is usually made based on technical considerations (such as network links) and organizational considerations (such as the number of users at each remote site). You can think of the Global Catalog as a universal phone book. Such an object would be quite large and bulky, but also very useful. Your goal (as a systems administrator) would be to find a balance between maintaining copies of the phone book and making potential users of the book travel long distances to use it.

This distribution of Global Catalog information allows for increased performance during companywide resource searches and can prevent excessive traffic across network links. Since the Global Catalog includes information about objects stored in all domains within the Active Directory environment, its management and location should be an important concern for network and systems administrators.

Searching Mechanisms The best-designed data repository in the world is useless if users can't access the information stored within it. Active Directory includes a search engine that users can query to find information about objects stored within it. For example, if a member of the Human Resources department is looking for a color printer, they can easily query Active Directory to find the one located closest to them. Best of all, the query tools are already built into Windows 2000 operating systems and are only a few mouse clicks away.

Replication Although it is theoretically possible to create a directory service that involves only one central computer, there are several problems with this configuration. First, all of the data is stored on one machine. This server would be responsible for processing all of the logon requests and search queries associated with the objects that it contained. Although this scenario might work well for a small network, it would create a tremendous load on servers in larger environments. Furthermore, clients that are located on remote networks would experience slower response times due to the pace of network traffic. Another drawback is that the entire directory would be stored in only one location. If this server became unavailable (due to a failed power supply, for example), network authentication and other vital processes could not be carried out. To solve these problems, Active Directory has been designed with a replication engine. The purpose of *replication* is to distribute the data stored within the directory throughout the organization for increased availability, performance, and data protection. Systems administrators can tune replication to occur based on their physical network infrastructure and other constraints.

Each of these components must work together to ensure that Active Directory remains accessible to all of the users who require it and to maintain the accuracy and consistency of its information.

🌐 Real World Scenario

Administrative Advantages of Active Directory

You are a systems administrator for a fairly large company consisting of several physical locations, a few different domains, and a couple thousand employees. You have been called into a meeting of administrators and managers to discuss the future of the company's network. You are asked to voice your opinion on whether it's worthwhile to update the network to Active Directory. You explain how the following administrative advantages would immediately improve the efficiency of the network:

- Currently, I have to make administrative changes in several places in order to manage the day-to-day changes that occur in the network, unnecessarily contributing to the time and cost of network administration. With Active Directory, I would be able to centrally and granularly make administrative changes throughout every domain that exists in the company's forest.

- Currently, in order to delegate administrative control to localized areas, I need to give people a higher level of permission than necessary to perform their assigned tasks. This creates unnecessary security risks. With Active Directory, I could easily delegate administrative tasks to other employees who are explicitly focused on the assigned tasks.

- The Active Directory client configuration management tools would allow me to deal with client machines much more efficiently. If a machine crashed, I wouldn't have to spend very much time restoring the computer to its previous state. Almost all administrative functions related to client machines take a lot less time with Active Directory.

- Expanding the company would not require a great deal of administrative overhead because of Active Directory's scalability. If we needed to add another 200 employees, I could easily integrate them into Active Directory.

- The users and administrators currently spend an unnecessary amount of time searching for information and resources on the network, adding to IT costs. With Active Directory, every resource on the network is stored in a central location, logically organized, and indexed so that anyone can locate it in a fraction of the time it takes on our current network.

As you can see from the points above, the main advantage of Active Directory is its increased efficiency over previous systems. Many administrative tasks can be performed in a fraction of the time it would take without Active Directory in place. Regardless of the technical advantage of Active Directory, the real attraction is how its implementation can directly contribute to the bottom line in lowering the cost of IT systems.

Active Directory Object Names

A fundamental feature of a directory service is that each object within the directory should contain its own unique name. For example, our organization may have two different users named John Smith (who may or may not be in different departments or locations within the company). There should be some unique way for us to distinguish these users (and their corresponding User objects).

Generally, this unique identifier is called the *distinguished name*. Within Active Directory, each object can be uniquely identified using a long name that specifies the full path to the object. Following is an example of a distinguished name:

```
/O=Internet/DC=Com/DC=MyCompany/DC=Sales
 /CN=Managers/CN=John Smith
```

In the above name, we have specified the following different types of objects:

Organization (O)   The company or root-level domain. In this case, the root level is the Internet.

Domain Component (DC)   A portion of the hierarchical path. DCs are used for organizing objects within the directory service. The DCs specify that the User object is located within the `sales.mycompany.com` domain.

Common Name (CN)   Specifies the names of objects in the directory. In this example, the user John Smith is contained within the Managers container.

When used together, the components of the distinguished name uniquely identify where the User object is stored. Instead of specifying the fully distinguished name, we might also choose to use a *relative distinguished name*. This name specifies only part of the path above and is relative to another object. For example, if our current context is already the Managers group within the `sales.mycompany.com` domain, we could simply specify the user as `CN=John Smith`.

Note that if we change the structure of the domain, the distinguished name of this object would also change. A change might happen if we rename one of the containers in the path or move the User object itself. This type of naming system allows for flexibility and the ability to easily identify the potentially millions of objects that might exist in Active Directory.

Active Directory's Physical Structure

So far, we have focused our attention on the logical units that make up Active Directory. That is, the ideas presented so far are designed to bring organization to the structure of the network. What we haven't discussed is exactly *how* domains, trees, forests, and Active Directory itself are created and managed. In this section, we'll see how various servers and network devices can be used to implement and manage the components of Active Directory.

Server Roles within Active Directory

The Active Directory data store is stored on one or more computers within an organization's network environment. All editions of the Windows 2000 Server platform are able to participate in Active Directory domains under the following roles:

Domain Controllers The heart of Active Directory's functionality resides on *domain controllers*. These machines are responsible for maintaining the Active Directory data store, including all of its objects, and for providing security for the entire domain. Although an Active Directory configuration may involve only one domain controller, it is much more likely that organizations will have more servers in order to increase performance and establish fault tolerance. All of the information that resides within Active Directory is synchronized among the domain controllers, and most changes can be made at any of these servers. This functionality is referred to as *multi-master replication* and is the basis through which Active Directory information is distributed throughout an organization.

Member Servers Often, you will want to have servers that function as part of the domain but are not responsible for containing Active Directory information or authenticating users. Common examples include file/print, application, and web servers. A Windows 2000 Server computer that is a *member* of a domain but is not a domain controller itself is referred to as a *member server*. By using member servers, systems administrators can take advantage of the centralized security database of Active Directory without dedicating server processing and storage resources to maintaining the directory information.

Stand-Alone Servers It is possible to run Windows 2000 Server computers in a workgroup environment that does not include Active Directory functionality at all. These machines are known as *stand-alone servers*. They maintain their own security database and are administered independently of other servers, as no centralized security database exists. Stand-alone servers might be used for functions such as public web servers or in situations in which only a few users require resources from a machine and the administrative overhead for managing security separately on various machines is acceptable.

A major benefit in the Windows 2000 Server operating system is the ability to easily promote and demote domain controllers after the operating system has been installed. Unlike the situation with Windows NT 4, reinstallation of the entire operating system is no longer required to change the role of a server. Furthermore, by properly promoting and demoting domain controllers, you can effectively move them among domains, trees, and forests.

In addition to the various types of server roles that the Windows 2000 Server platform can take on within Active Directory domains, Active Directory requires systems administrators to assign specific functionalities to other servers. In discussing replication, certain servers might be referred to as *masters*. Masters contain copies of a database and generally allow both read and write operations. Some types of replication may allow multiple masters to exist, while others specify that only a single master be allowed. Certain tasks within Active Directory work well using multi-master replication. For example, the ability to update information at one or more of the domain controllers can speed up response times while still maintaining data integrity through replication. Other functions, however, better lend themselves to being defined centrally. These operations are referred to as *single-master operations* because the function supports modification on only a single machine in the environment. These machines are referred to as *Flexible Operations Master servers*. The role of these servers is to handle operations that are required to ensure consistency within an Active Directory environment. Some of these are unique within a domain, and others are unique within the tree or forest. The changes made on these machines are then propagated to other domain controllers as necessary. The various roles for Operations Master servers within Active Directory include the following:

Schema Master   As we mentioned earlier, one of the benefits of the Active Directory schema is that it can be modified. All changes to the schema, however, are propagated to all domain controllers within the forest. In order for the information to stay synchronized and consistent, it is necessary for one machine within the entire tree or forest to be designated as the Schema Master. All changes to the schema must be made on this machine. By default, the first domain controller installed in the tree or forest is the Schema Master.

Domain Naming Master   When creating, adding, or removing domains, it is necessary for one machine in the tree or forest to serve as a central authority for the Active Directory configuration. The Domain Naming Master ensures that all of the information within the Active Directory forest is kept consistent and is responsible for registering new domains.

Within each Active Directory domain, the following roles can be assigned to domain controllers:

Relative ID Master A fundamental requirement of any directory service is that each object must have a unique identifier. All users, groups, computers, and other objects within Active Directory, for example, are identified by a unique value. The Relative ID (RID) Master is responsible for creating all of these identifiers within each domain and for ensuring that objects have unique IDs between domains by working with RID Masters in other domains.

Primary Domain Controller (PDC) Emulator In order to support Windows NT, Windows 2000 Server must have the ability to serve as a Windows NT PDC. Microsoft has made a conscious decision to allow networks to work in a mixed mode of Windows NT domains and Active Directory domains in order to facilitate the migration process (and encourage more people to buy Windows 2000!). As long as there are computers in the environment running Windows NT 4, the PDC Emulator will allow for the transmission of security information between domain controllers. This provides for backward compatibility while an organization moves to Windows 2000 and Active Directory.

Infrastructure Master Managing group memberships is an important role fulfilled manually by systems administrators. In a potentially distributed Active Directory environment, though, it is important to make sure that group and user memberships stay synchronized throughout the network. In order to understand how information might become inconsistent, let's look at an example using two domain controllers named DC1 and DC2. Suppose we make a change to a user's settings on DC1. At the same time, suppose another systems administrator makes a change to the same user account but on DC2. There must be some way to determine which change takes precedence over the other. More important, all domain controllers should be made aware of these changes so that the Active Directory database information remains consistent. The role of the Infrastructure Master is to ensure consistency among users and their group memberships as changes, additions, and deletions are made.

If there is more than one domain controller in the domain, the Global Catalog should not reside on the same server as the Infrastructure Master. This would prevent it from seeing any changes to the data and would result in replication not occurring among the various domain controllers.

It is important to note that the above assignments are *roles* and that a single machine may perform multiple roles. For example, in an environment in which only a single domain controller exists, that server assumes all of the above roles by default. On the other hand, if multiple servers are present, these functions can be distributed among them for business and technical reasons. By properly assigning roles to the servers in your environment, you can ensure that single-master operations are carried out securely and efficiently.

Accessing Active Directory through LDAP

In order to insert, update, and query information from within Active Directory, Microsoft has chosen to employ the worldwide Internet Engineering Task Force (IETF) standard protocol called the *Lightweight Directory Access Protocol (LDAP)*. LDAP is designed to allow for the transfer of information between domain controllers and to allow users to query information about objects within the directory.

As LDAP is a standard, it also facilitates interoperability between other directory services. Furthermore, communications can be programmed using objects such as the Active Directory Services Interface (ADSI). For data transport, LDAP can be used over TCP/IP, thus making it an excellent choice for communicating over the Internet, as well as private TCP/IP-based networks.

Managing Replication

Even in the simplest of network environments, there is generally a need to have more than one domain controller. The major reasons for this include fault tolerance (if one domain controller fails, others can still provide network services) and performance (the load can be balanced among multiple domain controllers). Windows 2000 domain controllers have been designed to contain read/write copies of the Active Directory database. However, the domain controllers must also contain knowledge that is created or modified on other domain controllers since a systems administrator may make changes on only one out of many domain controllers. This raises an important point—how is information kept consistent among domain controllers?

The answer is *Active Directory replication*. Replication is the process by which changes to the Active Directory database are transferred among domain controllers. The end result is that all of the domain controllers within an Active Directory domain contain up-to-date information. Keep in mind that domain controllers may be located very near to each other (e.g., within the same server rack) or may be located across the world from each other. Although the goals of replication are quite simple, the real-world constraints of network connections between servers cause many limitations that must be accommodated.

Microsoft ✔ *Exam* *Objective*

Diagnose Active Directory replication problems.

- Diagnose problems related to WAN link connectivity.

- Diagnose problems involving replication latency. Problems include duplicate objects and the LostandFound container.

Sites

A common mistake made in planning Active Directory is to base its structure on the technical constraints of a network instead of on business practices. For instance, a systems administrator might recommend that a separate domain be placed at each of a company's three remote sites. The rationale for this decision is understandable—the goal is to reduce network traffic between potentially slow and costly remote links. However, the multidomain structure may not make sense for organizations that have a centralized IT department and require common security settings for each of the three locations.

In order to allow Active Directory to be based on business and political decisions while still accommodating network infrastructure issues, Windows 2000 supports the concept of *sites*. Active Directory sites are designed to define the physical layout of a company's network by taking into account multiple subnets, remote access links, and other network factors. You might want to limit bandwidth usage across a slow link when you perform vital functions between domain controllers. However, within your local area network (LAN) environment, you will want replication to occur as quickly as possible to keep machines synchronized.

Sites are usually defined as locations in which network access is quick and inexpensive. Windows 2000 uses sites to determine when and how information should be replicated between domain controllers and other machines within the environment. Figure 4.4 provides an example of how a distributed company might choose to implement sites.

FIGURE 4.4 A typical site configuration

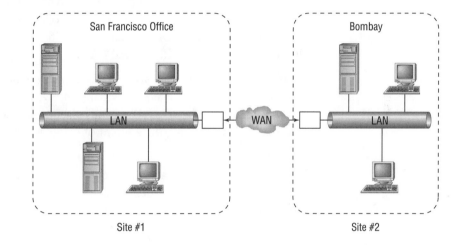

It is important to understand the distinction between logical and physical components of Active Directory. When planning your objects and domains, you will want to take into account the business requirements of your organization. This will create the logical structure of the directory. In planning for the implementation of Active Directory, however, you must take into account your network infrastructure—the physical aspects. Sites provide a great way to isolate these two requirements.

Configuring Replication

Sites are generally used to define groups of computers that are located within a single geographic location. In most organizations, machines that are located in close physical proximity (for example, within a single building or branch office) are well connected. A typical example is a LAN in a branch office of a company. All of the computers may be connected using Ethernet, and routing and switching technology may be in place to reduce network congestion.

Often, however, domain controllers are located across various states, countries, and even continents. In such a situation, network connectivity is usually much slower, less reliable, and more costly than that for the equivalent LAN. Therefore, Active Directory replication must accommodate accordingly. When managing replication traffic within Active Directory sites, there are two main areas of synchronization:

Intrasite *Intrasite replication* refers to the synchronization of Active Directory information between domain controllers that are located in the same site. In accordance with the concept of sites, these machines are usually well connected by a high-speed LAN.

Intersite *Intersite replication* occurs between domain controllers in different sites. Usually, this means that there is a WAN or other type of costly network connection between the various machines. Intersite replication is optimized for minimizing the amount of network traffic that occurs between sites.

In this section, we'll look at ways to configure both intrasite and intersite replication. In addition, we'll look at features of the Active Directory replication architecture that can be used to accommodate the needs of almost any environment.

Intrasite Replication

Intrasite replication is generally a simple process. One domain controller contacts the others in the same site when changes to its copy of Active Directory are made. It compares the logical sequence numbers in its own copy of Active Directory with that of the other domain controllers, then the most current information is chosen, and all domain controllers within the site use this information to make the necessary updates to their database.

Since it is assumed that the domain controllers within an Active Directory site are well connected, less attention to exactly when and how replication takes place is required. Communications between domain controllers occur using the *Remote Procedure Call (RPC) protocol*. This protocol is optimized for transmitting and synchronizing information on fast and reliable network connections. The actual directory synchronizing information is not compressed. Therefore, it provides for fast replication at the expense of network bandwidth.

Intrasite replication works well for domain controllers that are well connected. But what should be done about replication between sites? We'll cover this topic next.

Intersite Replication

Intersite replication is optimized for low-bandwidth situations and network connections that have less reliability.

Intersite replication offers several specific features that are tailored toward these types of connections. To begin with, there are two different protocols that may be used to transfer information between sites:

RPC over Internet Protocol (IP)   When connectivity is fairly reliable, the Internet Protocol is a good choice. IP-based communications require a live connection between two or more domain controllers in different sites and allow for the transfer of Active Directory information. RPC over IP was originally designed for slower WANs in which packet loss and corruption may occur often. As such, it is a good choice for low-quality connections involved in intersite replication.

Simple Mail Transfer Protocol (SMTP)   *Simple Mail Transfer Protocol (SMTP)* is perhaps best known as the protocol that is used to send e-mail messages on the Internet. SMTP was designed to use a store-and-forward mechanism through which a server receives a copy of a message, records it to disk, and then attempts to forward it to another mail server. If the destination server is unavailable, it will hold the message and attempt to resend it at periodic intervals.

This type of communication is designed for situations in which network connections are unreliable or not always available. If, for instance, a branch office in Peru were connected to the corporate office by a dial-up connection that is available only during certain hours, SMTP would be considered.

SMTP is an inherently insecure network protocol. You must, therefore, take advantage of Windows 2000's Certificate Services functionality if you use SMTP for Active Directory replication.

Other intersite replication characteristics that are designed to address low-bandwidth situations and less-reliable network connections include the compression of Active Directory information. This is helpful because changes between domain controllers in remote sites may involve a large amount of information and also because network bandwidth tends to be less available and more costly. Intersite replication topology is determined through the use of site links and site link bridges and can occur based on a schedule defined by systems administrators. All of these features provide for a high degree of flexibility in controlling replication configuration.

You can configure intersite replication by using the Active Directory Sites and Services tool. Select the name of the site for which you want to configure settings. Then right-click the NTDS (Windows NT Directory Services) Site Settings object in the right windowpane and select Properties. By clicking the Change Schedule button, you'll be able to configure how often replication between sites will occur (see Figure 4.5).

FIGURE 4.5 Configuring intersite replication schedules

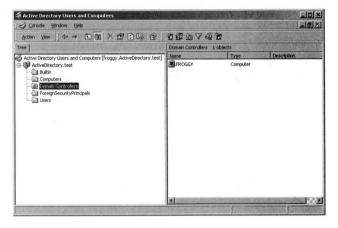

Creating Site Links and Site Link Bridges

The overall topology of intersite replication is based on the use of site links and site link bridges. *Site links* are logical connections that define a path between two Active Directory sites. Site links can include several descriptive elements that define their network characteristics. *Site link bridges* are used to connect site links so that the relationship can be transitive.

Figure 4.6 provides an example of site links and site link bridges.

FIGURE 4.6   An example of site links and site link bridges

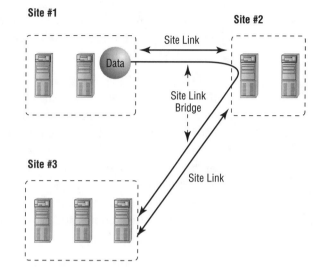

Both of these types of logical connections are used by the Active Directory services to determine how information should be synchronized among domain controllers in remote sites. So how is this information used? The Knowledge Consistency Checker (KCC) forms a replication topology based on the site topology created. This service is responsible for determining the best way to replicate information within and between sites.

When creating site links for your environment, you'll need to consider the following factors:

Transport   You can choose to use either RPC over IP or SMTP for transferring information over a site link. The main determination will be based on your network infrastructure and the reliability of connections between sites.

Cost   Multiple site links can be created between sites. Site links can be assigned a cost value based on the type of connection. The systems administrator determines the cost value, and the relative costs of site links are then used to determine the optimal path for replication. The lower the cost, the more likely the link is to be used for replication.

For example, a company may primarily use a T1 link between branch offices, but it may also use a slower dial-up Integrated Services Digital

Network (ISDN) connection for redundancy (in case the T1 fails). In this example, a systems administrator may assign a cost of 25 to the T1 line and a cost of 100 to the ISDN line. This will ensure that the more reliable and higher-bandwidth T1 connection is used whenever it's available but that the ISDN line is also available.

Schedule Once you've determined how and through which connections replication will take place, it's time to determine *when* information should be replicated. Replication requires network resources and occupies bandwidth. Therefore, you must balance the need for consistent directory information with the need to conserve bandwidth. For example, if you determine that it's reasonable to have a lag time of six hours between when an update is made at one site and when it is replicated to all others, you might schedule replication to occur once in the morning, once during the lunch hour, and more frequently after normal work hours.

Based on these factors, you should be able to devise a strategy that will allow you to configure site links.

Exercise 4.1 walks you through the process of creating site links and site link bridges.

The MCSA exam does not require that you know how to install Active Directory, so the exercises in this chapter assume that you have access to a pre-configured domain controller. You should be logged on as an Administrator in order to complete the exercises in this chapter. We will assume that your Active Directory configuration has three sites named Austin, CorporateHQ, and NewYork and that each site contains two domain controllers named <site-name>DC1 and <sitename>DC2. You can substitute these names with your actual site and domain controllers' names as needed.

EXERCISE 4.1

Creating Site Links and Site Link Bridges

In this exercise, you will create links between sites:

1. Open the Active Directory Sites and Services tool from the Administrative Tools program group.

2. Expand Sites ➤ Inter-Site Transports ➤ IP object. Right-click the DEFAULTIPSITELINK item in the right pane, and select Rename. Rename the object to **CorporateWAN**.

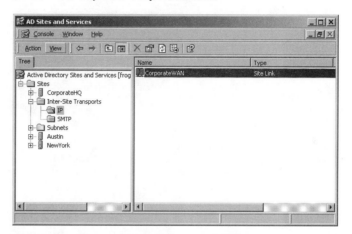

3. Right-click the CorporateWAN link and select Properties. For the description of the link, type **T1 connecting Corporate and New York offices**. Remove the Austin site from the link. For the Cost value, type **50**, and specify that replication should occur every 60 minutes. To create the site link, click OK.

EXERCISE 4.1 *(continued)*

---

4. Right-click the IP folder, and select New Site Link. For the name of the link, type **CorporateDialup**. Add the Austin and CorporateHQ sites to the site link, and then click OK.

5. Right-click the CorporateDialup link, and select Properties. For the description, type **ISDN Dialup between Corporate and Austin office**. Set the Cost value to **100**, and specify that replication should occur every 120 minutes.

6. To specify that replication should occur only during certain times of the day click the Change Schedule button. Highlight the area between 8:00 A.M. and 6:00 P.M. for the days Monday through Friday, and click the Replication Not Available option. This will ensure that replication traffic is minimized during normal work hours. Click OK to accept the new schedule, and then click OK again to create the site link.

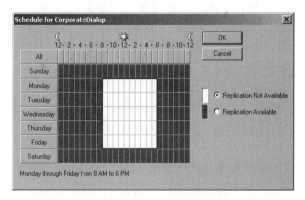

7. Right-click the IP object, and select New Site Link Bridge. For the name of the site link bridge, type **CorporateBridge**. Note that the CorporateDialup and CorporateWAN site links are already added to the site link bridge. Since there must be at least two site links in each bridge, you will not be able to remove these links. Click OK to create the site link bridge.

EXERCISE 4.1 *(continued)*

8. When finished, close the Active Directory Sites and Services tool.

Creating Connection Objects

Generally, it is a good practice to allow Active Directory's replication mechanisms to automatically schedule and manage replication functions. In some cases, however, you may want to have additional control over replication. Perhaps you want to replicate changes on demand (when you create new accounts). Or, you may want to specify a custom schedule for certain servers.

You can set up these different types of replication schedules through the use of *Connection objects*. Connection objects can be created with the Active Directory Sites and Services tool by expanding a Server object, right-clicking the NTDS Settings object, and selecting New Active Directory Connection (see Figure 4.7). Exercise 4.2 takes you through the steps for creating Connection objects in more detail.

You can see in the Connection object in the right pane of Figure 4.7. Within the properties of the Connection object, you can specify the type of transport to use for replication (RPC over IP or SMTP), the schedule for replication, and the domain controllers that will participate in the replication (see Figure 4.8). You will also have the ability to right-click the Connection object and select Replicate Now.

FIGURE 4.7   Creating a new Connection object

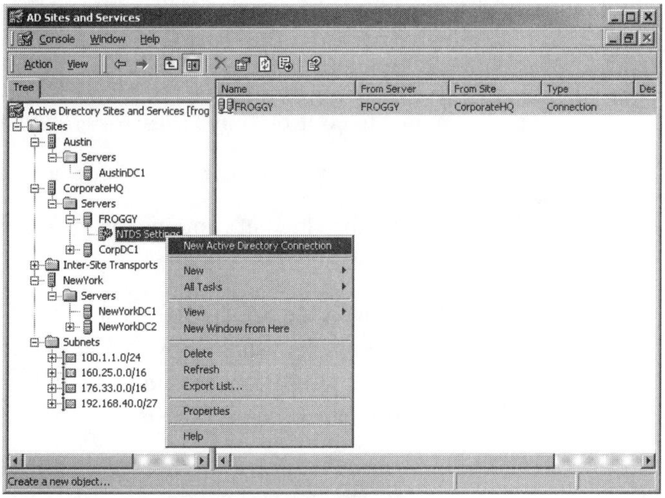

FIGURE 4.8   Viewing the properties of a Connection object

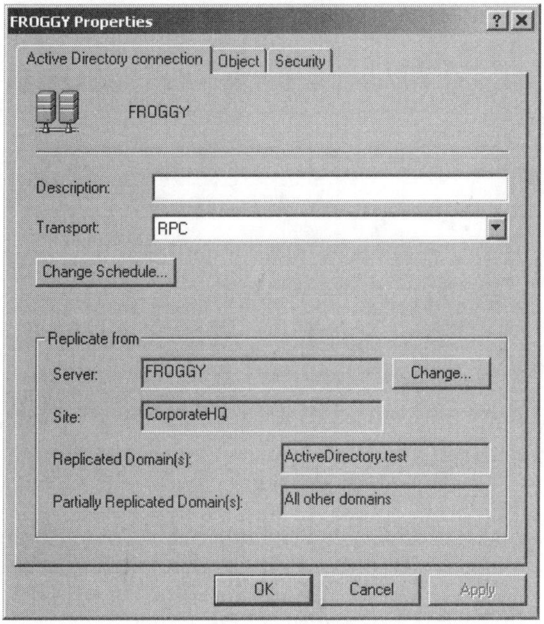

EXERCISE 4.2

Creating Connection Objects

In this exercise, you will create and configure a custom Connection object to control Active Directory replication:

1. Open the Active Directory Sites and Services tool.

2. Find the site that contains the local domain controller, and expand this object.

3. Expand the name of the local domain controller. Right-click NTDS Settings, and select New Active Directory Connection. The Find Domain Controllers dialog box will appear, showing a list of the servers that are available.

4. Highlight the name of the local server, and click OK.

5. For the name of the Connection object, type **Connection**. Click OK.

6. In the right pane of the window, right-click the Connection item, and select Properties.

7. For the description, type **After-hours synchronization**. For the Transport, choose IP.

Connection Properties	? X

Active Directory connection | Object | Security |

Connection

Description: After-hours synchronization

Transport: IP

Change Schedule...

Replicate from

Server: FROGGY   Change...

Site: CorporateHQ

Replicated Domain(s): ActiveDirectory.test

Partially Replicated Domain(s): All other domains

OK   Cancel   Apply

8. When finished, click OK to save the properties of the Connection object.

9. To modify the allowed times for replication, click the Change Schedule button. Highlight the area from 8:00 A.M. to 6:00 P.M. for all days, and then click the Once Per Hour item. This will reduce the frequency of replication during normal business hours. Click OK to save the schedule.

10. Close the Active Directory Sites and Services tool.

Moving Server Objects between Sites

Using the Active Directory Sites and Services tool, you can easily move servers between sites. To do this, simply right-click the name of a domain controller and select Move. You can then select the site to which you want to move the Domain Controller object.

Figure 4.9 shows the screen that you'll see when you attempt to move a server. After the server is moved, all replication topology settings will be updated automatically. If you want to choose custom replication settings, you'll need to manually create Connection objects (as described earlier). See Exercise 4.3 for a detailed explanation of the steps involved in moving Server objects between sites.

FIGURE 4.9   Choosing a new site for a specific server

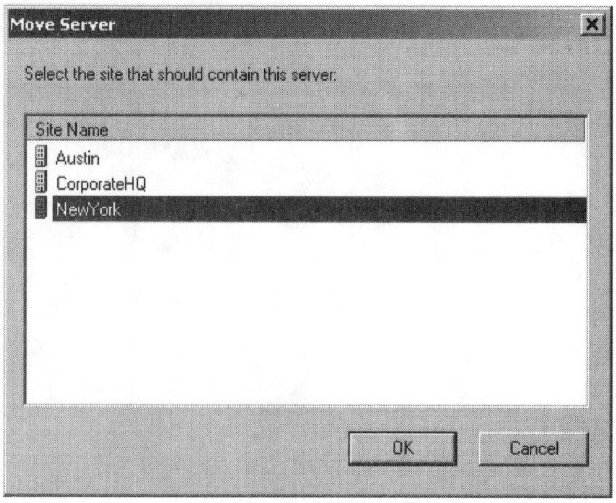

EXERCISE 4.3

Moving Server Objects between Sites

In this exercise, you will move a Server object between sites:

1. Open the Active Directory Sites and Services tool.

2. Right-click the server named NewYorkDC1, and select Move.

3. Select the Austin site, and then click OK. This will move this server to the Austin site.

4. To move the server back, right-click NewYorkDC1 (now located in the Austin site) and then click Move. Select New York for the destination site.

5. When finished, close the Active Directory Sites and Services tool.

Creating Bridgehead Servers

By default, all of the servers in one site communicate with the servers in another site. You can, however, further control replication between sites by using *bridgehead servers*. This method is useful for minimizing replication traffic in larger network environments and allows you to dedicate machines that are better connected to receive replicated data. Figure 4.10 provides an example of how bridgehead servers work.

FIGURE 4.10   A replication scenario using bridgehead servers

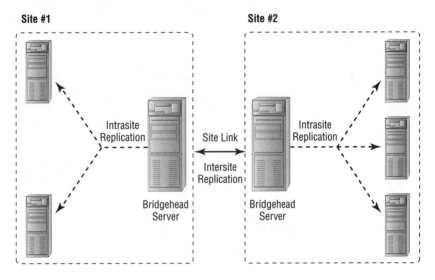

A bridgehead server is used to specify which domain controllers are preferred for transferring replication information between sites. Different bridgehead servers can be selected for RCP over IP and SMTP replication, thus allowing you to balance the load. To create a bridgehead server for a site, simply right-click a domain controller and select Properties (See Figure 4.11). Select any available transport and click the Add button to specify that the domain controller is a preferred bridgehead server for that transport.

FIGURE 4.11   Specifying a bridgehead server

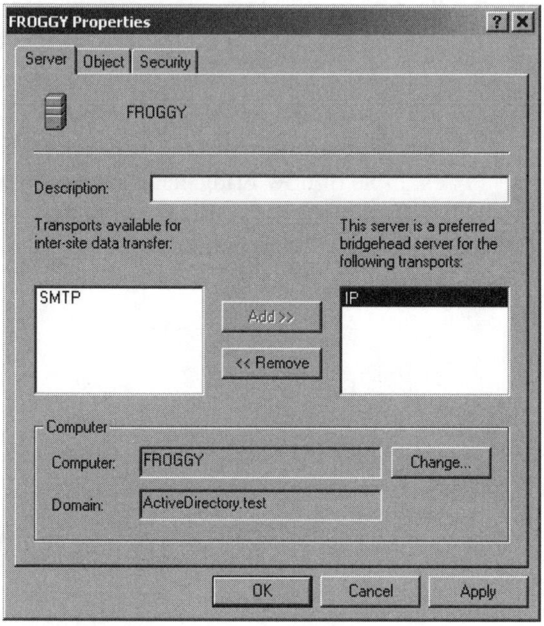

Configuring Server Topology

In environments that require the use of multiple sites, it is very important to consider the placement of servers. In so doing, you can greatly improve performance and end-user experience by reducing the time required to perform common operations such as authentication or searching Active Directory.

There are two main issues to consider when designing a distributed Active Directory environment. The first is the placement of domain controllers within the network environment. The second is managing the use of Global Catalog (GC) servers. Finding the right balance among servers, server resources, and performance can be considered an art form for network and systems administrators. In this section, we'll look at some of the important considerations that must be taken into account when designing a replication server topology.

Placing Domain Controllers

It is highly recommended that you have at least two domain controllers in each domain of your Active Directory environment. As mentioned earlier in this chapter, the use of additional domain controllers allows for enhanced performance (since the servers can balance the burden of serving client requests) and provides for fault tolerance (in case one domain controller fails, the other still contains a valid and usable copy of the Active Directory database). Furthermore, the proper placement of domain controllers can increase overall network performance since clients can connect to the server closest to them instead of performing authentication and security operations across a slow WAN link.

As we just mentioned, having too few domain controllers can be a problem. However, there is such a thing as *too many* domain controllers. Keep in mind that the more domain controllers you choose to implement, the greater the replication traffic will be. As each domain controller must propagate any changes to all of the others, you can probably see how this can result in considerable network traffic.

Placing Global Catalog Servers

A *Global Catalog (GC) server* is a domain controller that contains a copy of all the objects contained in all the domain controllers forest-wide that make up the Active Directory logical database. Making a domain controller a GC server is a very simple operation, and you can change this setting quite easily. That brings us to the harder part—determining which domain controllers should also be GC servers.

The placement of domain controllers and GC servers is an important issue. Generally, you will want to make GC servers available in every site that has a slow link. However, there is a trade-off that can make having too many GC servers a bad thing. The main issue is associated with replication traffic—each GC server within your environment must be kept synchronized with the other servers. In a very dynamic environment, the additional network traffic caused by the use of GC servers can be considerable. Therefore, you will want to find a good balance between replication burdens and GC query performance in your own environment.

To create a GC server, simply expand the Server object in the Active Directory Sites and Services tool, right-click NTDS Settings, and select Properties. To configure a server as a GC server, place a check mark in the Global Catalog box of the General tab of the Properties sheet (see Figure 4.12).

FIGURE 4.12 Enabling the Global Catalog on an Active Directory domain controller

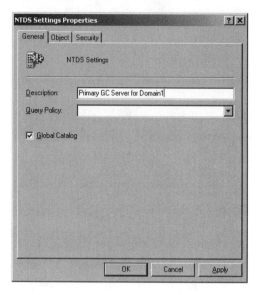

Real World Scenario

Accommodating a Changing Environment

You're part of the administrative team for a medium-sized business that consists of many offices located throughout the world. Some of these offices are well connected through the use of high-speed, reliable links, while others are not so fortunate. Overall, things are going well until your CEO announces that the organization will be merging with another large company and that the business will be restructured. The restructuring will involve the opening of new offices, the closing of old ones, and the transfer of employees to different locations. In addition, changes in the IT budget will affect the types of links that exist between offices. Your job as an administrator is to help ensure that the network environment—and, specifically, Active Directory—keeps pace with the changes.

An important skill for the effective administration of a network is the ability to quickly and efficiently adapt to a changing organization. When a business grows, restructures, or forms relationships with other businesses, there are often many IT-related changes that must also occur. Fortunately, Active Directory has been designed with these kinds of challenges in mind. For example, you can use the Active Directory Sites and Services administrative tool to reflect physical network changes in the Active Directory topology. If a site that previously had 64Kbps of bandwidth is upgraded to a T1 connection, you could change those characteristics for the Site Link objects. Conversely, if a site that was previously well connected is reduced to a slow, unreliable link, you could reconfigure the site, change the site link transport mechanisms (perhaps from IP to SMTP to accommodate a nonpersistent link), and create Connection objects (which would allow you to schedule replication traffic to occur during the least-busy hours). Or, suppose that many of your operations move overseas to a European division. This might call for designating specific domain controllers as preferred bridgehead servers to reduce the amount of replication traffic over costly and slow overseas links.

Sweeping organizational changes will inevitably require you to move servers between sites. For example, an office may be closed and its domain controllers moved to another region of the world. Again, you can accommodate this change through the use of Active Directory administrative tools. You may change your OU structure to reflect new logical and business-oriented changes, and you can move Server objects between sites to reflect physical network changes.

Rarely can the job of mapping a physical infrastructure to Active Directory be considered "complete." In most environments, it's safe to assume that there will always be changes required by business needs. Overall, however, you should feel comfortable that the physical components of Active Directory are at your side to help you accommodate the changes.

Monitoring and Troubleshooting Active Directory Replication

For the most part, domain controllers handle the processes involved with replication automatically. However, systems administrators still need to monitor the performance of Active Directory replication. Failed network links and incorrect configurations can sometimes prevent the synchronization of information among domain controllers.

There are several ways in which you can monitor the behavior of Active Directory replication and troubleshoot the process if problems occur.

Troubleshooting Replication

A common symptom of replication problems is that information is not updated on some or all domain controllers. For example, a systems administrator creates a user account on one domain controller, but the changes are not propagated to other domain controllers. In most environments, this is a potentially serious problem because it affects network security and can prevent authorized users from accessing the resources they require.

There are several steps that you can take to troubleshoot Active Directory replication:

Verify network connectivity.   The fundamental requirement for replication to work properly in distributed environments is network connectivity. Although the ideal situation would be that all domain controllers are connected by high-speed LAN links, this is rarely the case for larger organizations. In the real world, dial-up connections and slow connections are common. If you have verified that your replication topology is set up properly, you should confirm that your servers are able to communicate. Problems such as a failed dial-up connection attempt can prevent important Active Directory information from being replicated.

Verify router and firewall configurations.   Firewalls are used to restrict the types of traffic that can be transferred between networks. Their main use is to increase security by preventing unauthorized users from transferring information. In some cases, company firewalls may block the types of network access that must be available in order for Active Directory replication to occur. For example, if a specific router or firewall prevents data from being transferred using SMTP, replication that uses this protocol will fail.

Examine the event logs.   Whenever an error in the replication configuration occurs, events are written to the Directory Service event log. By using the Event Viewer administrative tool, you can quickly and easily view the details associated with any problems in replication. For example, if one domain controller is not able to communicate with another to transfer changes, a log entry will be created. Figure 4.13 shows an example of the types of events you will see in the Directory Service log, and Figure 4.14 shows an example of a configuration error.

FIGURE 4.13   Viewing entries in the Directory Service event log

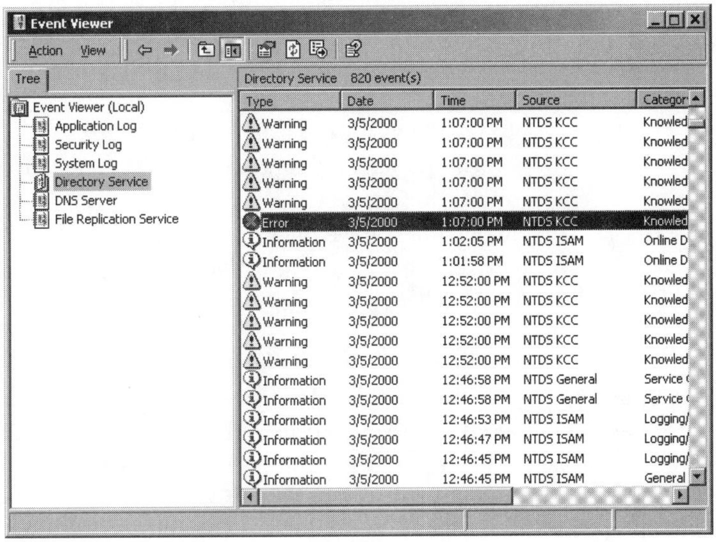

FIGURE 4.14   Examining the details of an event log entry

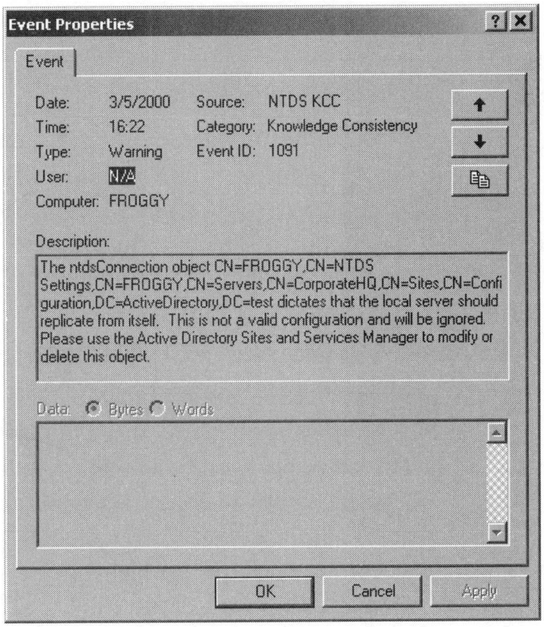

Verify site links.   Before domain controllers in different sites can communicate with one another, the sites must be connected by site links. If replication among sites is not occurring properly, verify that the proper site links are in place.

Verify that information is synchronized.   It's often easy to forget to perform manual checks regarding the replication of Active Directory information. One of the reasons for this is that Active Directory domain controllers have their own read/write copies of the Active Directory database. Therefore, you will not encounter failures in creating new objects if connectivity does not exist.

It is important to periodically verify that objects have been synchronized between domain controllers. The process might be as simple as logging on to a different domain controller and looking at the objects within a specific OU. This manual check, although it might be tedious, can prevent inconsistencies in the information stored on domain controllers, which, over time, could become an administration and security nightmare.

Verify authentication scenarios.   A common replication configuration issue occurs when clients are forced to authenticate across slow network connections. The primary symptom of the problem is that users complain about the amount of time that it takes to log on to Active Directory (especially during times of high volume of authentications, such as at the beginning of the workday).

Usually, this problem can be alleviated through the use of additional domain controllers or a reconfiguration of the site topology. A good way to test this is to consider the possible scenarios for the various clients that you support. Often, walking through a configuration, such as "A client in Domain1 is trying to authenticate using a domain controller in Domain2, which is located across a slow WAN connection," can be helpful in pinpointing potential problem areas.

Verify the replication topology.   The Active Directory Sites and Services tool allows you to verify that a replication topology is logically consistent. You can quickly and easily perform this task by right-clicking the NTDS Settings within a Server object and choosing All Tasks ➢ Check Replication Topology (see Figure 4.15). If any errors are present, a dialog box will alert you to the problem.

FIGURE 4.15   Verifying the Active Directory topology using the Active Directory Sites and Services tool

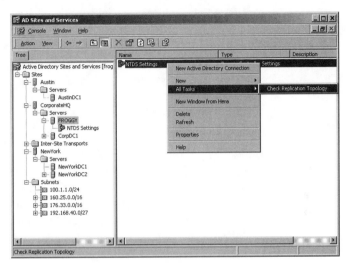

Replication Latency

Generally, replication ensures that all of the domain controllers are in sync. Replication does occur on a fixed schedule, so changes made on one domain controller aren't recognized by the other domain controllers until after the next replication cycle. The time between Active Directory replications is known as *replication latency*.

Theoretically, you could perform replication once a minute to reduce the problem of replication latency, but that would reduce your network traffic to a crawl and would be impractical. If you are on a 15-minute replication cycle, most latency issues aren't apparent. Even on this tight schedule, latency sometimes causes problems with directory synchronization. The two most common latency issues are covered in the following sections.

The LostAndFound Container

Normally, you create objects in containers, such as organizational units (OUs, described in detail in the Chapter 5, "Administering Active Directory"). The next time replication occurs, every domain controller in the domain is notified that a new object has been created in the container, and they update their databases accordingly. What happens if user Sam, on NewYorkDC1 creates an object in the NewYorkHR container, and user Bill, on NewYorkDC2, deletes the NewYorkHR container, all between replication cycles? Active Directory won't be able to place the object in the NewYorkHR container because it no longer exists. Instead, Active Directory will place the orphaned object into a special container called the *LostAndFound container*, which can be accessed through the Active Directory Sites and Services tool. If objects turn up missing, you should always check the LostAndFound container. You can then move the object to a different container that hasn't been deleted.

Duplicate Objects

As you saw earlier in this chapter, each object within Active Directory has a distinguished name consisting of the object's common name (CN), the CN of the object's container, and the domain components (DCs) for each part of the domain's name. Two objects with the same CN can peacefully coexist on the same domain as long as they are in different containers. Active Directory won't allow you to create two CNs in the same container, but what happens if Bill and Sam in the example above each create a user named Jodi Morris at the same time in the same container on their separate domain controllers? In a multi-master environment, Active Directory will attempt to replicate both objects across the two domain controllers, but since both users have the same CN, a conflict will occur. Both objects have unique GUIDs, so Active Directory knows that they aren't the same object and will rename the newer object. You can safely delete the renamed object, and the change will replicate itself across the domain controllers during the next replication cycle.

⊕ Real World Scenario

Analyzing Active Directory Replication Traffic

You are assigned to work in the central administrative facility for a worldwide company that has offices in over 50 locations. Ten of these locations have high-speed connections and contain hundreds of users. The other locations have from 10 to 100 users, and each has a wide range of connection speeds, depending upon the company policy that was published from the design document when the network was deployed. The design document also states that the users in all locations will be able to store personal information in the directory. As more and more people take advantage of the information in the directory, they add their own information to the directory. The growing success of the use of the directory has begun to have an effect on your support efforts. You are beginning to get calls that changes made in the directory are not showing up.

One of the most important things to remember when dealing with problems that begin to appear in a new system is not to jump to conclusions. There could be a simple explanation for the results that does not require any change to the system. For example, the logical database that supports the directory is consider a loosely consistent database. The reason for this is that it takes time for the database to converge when it is updated. It is possible that the users are looking for changes before the replication process is complete. You need to ask questions to determine that the user has not updated the database and immediately looked for the change.

If normal explanations do not resolve the problems, then you need to methodically apply troubleshooting tools to the situation. The best practice for this is to follow a written suite of activities to ensure that you have explored all avenues before bringing in other resources. For example, the first place to look is in Event Viewer to see if there have been any alerts regarding the replication of the directory. Then you can start to look at the site links and replication topology. The important thing here is to make sure that you baseline the environment with your troubleshooting tools so that you have something useful to compare with the results of any tests. As an administrator, it is in your best interests to understand how the replication is supposed to work so you can know when it is not working properly. Even more important, you must have a good idea of where it is broken so you can use the proper resources to resolve the situation.

Summary

In this chapter, we took a high-level overview of the concepts related to Active Directory, and we dove into the specifics of Active Directory replication. Specifically, we discussed the following:

- The benefits of implementing Active Directory

- How and why multiple Active Directory domains can be created

- The logical components of an Active Directory environment

- The physical components that make up an Active Directory environment

- The purpose of Active Directory replication

- The concepts behind Active Directory sites and how they affect replication and the accessibility of domain services

- Details about various Active Directory features that help optimize replication traffic based on the needs of various network environments. These features include sites, subnets, site links, and site link bridges.

- Connection objects that can be used to define replication behavior at a very granular level

- Bridgehead servers that can be used to reduce replication traffic across slow links

- The importance of domain controller and Global Catalog server placement and how it can affect overall Active Directory performance

- Several tools and methods that are available for monitoring and troubleshooting Active Directory replication

Although replication is a behind-the-scenes type of task, the optimal configuration of sites in distributed network environments will result in better use of bandwidth and faster response by network resources. For these reasons, you should be sure that you thoroughly understand the concepts related to managing replication for Active Directory.

Exam Essentials

Understand Active Directory design goals.   Active Directory should be structured to mirror an organization's logical structure. Understand the factors that you should take into account, including business units, geographic structure, and future business requirements.

Understand the features of Active Directory.   Understand how and why Microsoft has included features that allow for extensibility, centralized data storage, replication, ease of administration, security, and scalability.

Remember the Operations Master server roles that are required in an Active Directory environment. Operations Master roles are vital to the proper operations of Active Directory. Some of these roles must be present in each Active Directory domain, while for other roles, only one is required for the entire Active Directory environment.

Understand the basic domain structure for an Active Directory environment.   An Active Directory environment can consist of only a single domain, or it can include multiple domains that form a tree. Multiple trees can be combined into a forest.

Understand the purpose of Active Directory replication.   Replication is used to keep domain controllers synchronized and is important in Active Directory environments of all sizes.

Understand the differences between intrasite and intersite replication. Intrasite replication is designed to synchronize Active Directory information to machines that are located in the same site. Intersite replication is used to synchronize information for domain controllers that are located in different sites.

Implement site links, site link bridges, and Connection objects.   All three of these object types can be used to finely control the behavior of Active Directory replication and to manage replication traffic.

Determine where to place domain controllers and Global Catalog servers based on a set of requirements.   The placement of domain controllers and Global Catalog servers can increase the performance of Active Directory operations. However, in order to optimize performance, you should understand where the best places are to put these servers in a network environment that consists of multiple sites.

Monitor and troubleshoot replication.   Windows 2000's administrative tools include many methods for troubleshooting and monitoring replication.

Key Terms

Before you take the exam, be certain you are familiar with the following terms:

Active Directory replication	domain
bridgehead servers	domain controllers
Connection objects	forests
distinguished name	Global Catalog

Global Catalog (GC) server

intersite replication

intrasite replication

Lightweight Directory Access Protocol (LDAP)

LostAndFound container

member server

organizational units (OUs)

Remote Procedure Call (RPC) protocol

replication

replication latency

Simple Mail Transfer Protocol (SMTP)

site link bridges

sites

trees

trusts

Review Questions

1. Christina is responsible for managing Active Directory replication traffic for a medium-sized organization. Currently, the environment is configured with a single site and the default settings for replication. The site contains over 50 domain controllers, and the systems administrators often make changes to the Active Directory database. Recently, network administrators have complained that Active Directory traffic is consuming a large amount of network bandwidth between portions of the network that are connected by slow links. Ordinarily, the amount of replication traffic is reasonable, but recently users have complained about slow network performance during certain hours of the day.

   Christina has been asked to alleviate the problem while meeting the following requirements:

   - Be able to control exactly when replication occurs.

   - Be able to base Active Directory replication on the physical network infrastructure.

   - Perform the changes without creating or removing any domain controllers.

   Which two of the following steps can Christina take to meet these requirements? (Choose two.)

   A. Create and define Connection objects that specify the hours during which replication will occur.

   B. Create multiple site links.

   C. Create a site link bridge.

   D. Create new Active Directory sites that reflect the physical network topology.

   E. Configure one server at each of the new sites to act as a bridgehead server.

2. You have recently created a new Active Directory domain by promoting several Windows 2000 Server computers to domain controllers. You then use the Active Directory Sites and Services tool to configure sites for the environment. You soon find that changes that are made on one domain controller may not appear in the Active Directory database on another domain controller. By checking the Directory Service log using the Event Viewer application, you find that one of the domain controllers at a specific site is not receiving Active Directory updates. Which of the following are possible reasons for this? (Choose all that apply.)

   A. Network connectivity has not been established for this server.

   B. A firewall is preventing replication information from being transmitted.

   C. There are not enough domain controllers in the environment.

   D. There are too many domain controllers in the environment.

   E. You chose to disable Active Directory replication during the promotion of the machine to a domain controller.

3. You administer a network that consists of one domain that spans three physical locations: San Jose, Chicago, and Austin. All three locations contain domain controllers. You have a T1 line between San Jose and Chicago, with an ISDN for backup. The ISDN line must have the default site link cost assigned to it. You want Austin to always use San Jose for its replication communication, even though a link does exist between Austin and Chicago for other purposes.

In the diagram below, select and place the correct relative costs that should be assigned to the various site links. Each cost can only be used once.

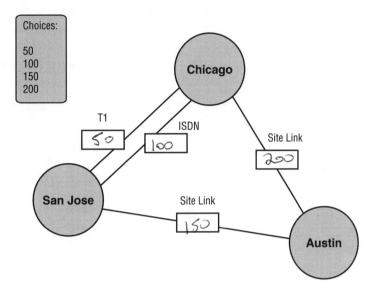

4. Which of the following is not a feature of Active Directory?

    A. The use of LDAP for transferring information

    B. Reliance on DNS for name resolution

    C. A flat domain namespace

    D. The ability to extend the schema

5. Which of the following is *false* regarding the naming of Active Directory objects?

    A. Active Directory relies on DNS for name resolution.

    B. Two objects can have the same relative distinguished name.

    C. Two objects can have the same distinguished name.

    D. All objects within a domain are based on the name of the domain.

6. Daniel is responsible for managing Active Directory replication traffic for a medium-sized organization that has deployed a single Active Directory domain. Currently, the environment is configured with two sites and the default settings for replication. Each site consists of 15 domain controllers. Recently, network administrators have complained that Active Directory traffic is using a large amount of available network bandwidth between the two sites. Daniel has been asked to meet the following requirements:

   - Reduce the amount of network traffic between domain controllers in the two sites.

   - Minimize the amount of change to the current site topology.

   - Require no changes to the existing physical network infrastructure.

   Daniel decides that it would be most efficient to configure specific domain controllers in each site that will receive the majority of replication traffic from the other site. Which of the following solutions will meet the requirements?

   A. Create additional sites that are designed only for replication traffic and move the existing domain controllers to these sites.

   B. Create multiple site links between the two sites.

   C. Create a site link bridge between the two sites.

   D. Configure one server at each site to act as a preferred bridgehead server.

7. Which of the following are possible roles for a Windows 2000 Server? (Choose all that apply.)

   A. Member server

   B. Primary Domain Controller

   C. Backup Domain Controller

   D. Stand-alone server

8. An organization uses 12 Active Directory domains in a single forest. How many Schema Masters must this environment have?

A. Zero

B. One

C. 12

D. More than 12

9. Which of the following features of Active Directory allows information between domain controllers to remain synchronized?

A. Replication

B. The Global Catalog

C. The schema

D. Synchronization

10. You have configured your Active Directory environment with multiple sites and have placed the appropriate resources in each of the sites. You are now trying to choose a protocol for the transfer of replication information between two sites. The connection between the two sites has the following characteristics:

- The link is generally unavailable during certain parts of the day due to an unreliable network provider.

- The replication transmission must be attempted whether the link is available or not. If the link was unavailable during a scheduled replication, the information should automatically be received after the link becomes available again.

- Replication traffic must be able to travel over a standard Internet connection.

Which of the following protocol(s) meets these requirements? (Choose all that apply.)

A. IP

B. SMTP

C. RPC

D. DHCP

11. Jane is a systems administrator for a large, multidomain, geographically distributed network environment. The network consists of a large central office and many smaller remote offices located throughout the world. Recently, Jane has received complaints about the performance of Active Directory–related operations from remote offices. Users complain that it takes a long time to perform searches for network resources (such as shared folders and printers). Jane wants to improve the performance of these operations. Which of the following components of Active Directory should she implement at remote sites to improve the performance of searches conducted for objects in *all* domains?

A. Data store

B. Global Catalog

C. Schema

D. Domain controller

12. You are the administrator of a medium-sized network that has just been upgraded to five Windows 2000 Server computers, 350 Windows 2000 Professional computers, and three Unix servers. You now want to implement Active Directory in order to obtain the efficiencies that are available with a centralized management system. All of the machines need to participate in the supporting services on the network. You know that you need to have name-to-IP-address resolution in order for Active Directory to work properly. Which of the following must be completed for Active Directory to function properly?

A. Install the DNS service on one of the Windows 2000 Server computers.

B. Install WINS on one of the Windows 2000 Server computers.

C. Install Microsoft's version of the DNS service on one of the Unix server computers.

D. Install DNS and WINS on one of the Windows NT Server computers.

13. A network administrator has decided that it will be necessary to implement multiple sites in order to efficiently manage your company's large Active Directory environment. Based on her recommendations, you make the following decisions:

    ▪ The best configuration involves the creation of four sites.

    ▪ The sites will be connected with site links and site link bridges.

    ▪ Two small offices must receive replication traffic only during non-business hours.

    ▪ The organization owns a single DNS name: `supercompany.com`.

    ▪ Administration should be kept as simple as possible, and you want to use the smallest possible number of domains.

    Based on this information, you must plan the Active Directory domain architecture. What is the minimum number of domains that must be created to support this configuration?

    A. Zero

    B. One

    C. Four

    D. Eight

14. Andrew is troubleshooting a problem with Active Directory. One systems administrator has told him that she made an update to a User object and that another systems administrator reported that he had not seen the change on another domain controller. It has been over a week since the change was made. Andrew further verifies the problem by making a change to another Active Directory object. Within a few hours, the change appears on a few domain controllers but not on all of them.

    Which of the following are possible causes for this problem? (Choose all that apply.)

    A. Network connectivity is unavailable.

    B. Connection objects are not properly configured.

    C. Sites are not properly configured.

    D. Site links are not properly configured.

    E. A WAN connection has failed.

    F. One of the domain controllers is configured for manual replication updates.

15. Your current network comprises three domains that have been used to control administrative rights to functions in the network, such as printer management, adding users, and creating file shares. Which of the following approaches takes advantage of the features of Windows 2000?

A. Duplicate the three domains in the Windows 2000 environment.

B. Create one domain in Windows 2000 and apply permissions through organizational units.

C. Migrate to Windows 2000 without domain controllers and manage the accounts and resources with a different administrator on each server.

D. Create additional domains to further distribute administration.

Answers to Review Questions

1. **A, D.** By creating new sites, Christina can help define settings for Active Directory replication based on the environment's network connections. She can use Connection objects to further define the details of how and when replication traffic will be transmitted among the domain controllers.

2. **A, B.** Since replication is occurring among most of the domain controllers, it is likely that a network problem is preventing this domain controller from communicating with the rest. A lack of network connectivity or the presence of a firewall can prevent replication from occurring properly. The number of domain controllers in an environment will not affect the replication of information, nor can replication be disabled during the promotion process.

3. See the following graphic.

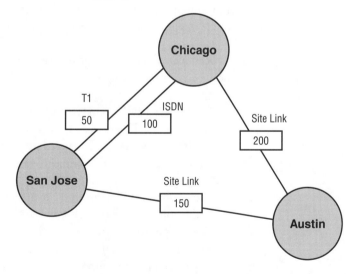

The ISDN line is required to have the default cost of 100. That means that the T1 line's cost must be lower than 100 in order for this connection to be used by preference, and the only choice is 50. That leaves costs of 150 and 200 for the Austin links. Since Austin will never get replication information from Chicago, that link's cost should be 200. That leaves only 150 for the cost of the link between Austin and San Jose.

4. C. Active Directory uses a hierarchical namespace for managing objects.

5. C. The distinguished name of each object in Active Directory must be unique, but the relative distinguished names may be the same. For example, we might have a User object named Jane Doe in two different containers.

6. D. Preferred bridgehead servers receive replication information for a site and transmit this information to other domain controllers within the site. By configuring one server at each site to act as a preferred bridgehead server, Daniel can ensure that all replication traffic between the two sites is routed through the bridgehead servers and that replication traffic flows properly between the domain controllers.

7. A, D. Primary Domain Controllers and Backup Domain Controllers are used only in Windows NT domains.

8. B. Only one Schema Master is allowed in an Active Directory environment, regardless of the number of domains.

9. A. Replication ensures that information remains synchronized between domain controllers.

10. B. The Simple Mail Transfer Protocol (SMTP) was designed for environments in which persistent connections may not always be available. SMTP uses the store-and-forward method to ensure that information is not lost if a connection cannot be made.

11. B. The Global Catalog contains information about multiple domains, and additional Global Catalog servers can greatly increase the performance of operations such as searches for shared folders and printers. The other options are features of Active Directory, but they are not designed for fast searching across multiple domains.

12. A. The clients use SRV records to locate the domain controller that contain the Active Directory service. While it is possible to use a Unix version of DNS as long as it supports SRV records and dynamic updates, there is no Microsoft version of DNS for Unix. WINS provides name resolution for Windows NT and other older clients, but it does not provide the type of name resolution necessary for Active Directory. Installing DNS and WINS on a Windows server will not provide the level of service required. While WINS will support Net-BIOS names for the clients, the version of DNS supported on the Windows NT Server platform will not support the SRV records or the dynamic updates required by Active Directory.

13. B. Since there is no relationship between domain structure and site structure, only one domain is required. Generally, if there is only one domain, there will be many domain controllers with at least one in each site.

14. A, B, C, D, E. Misconfiguring any of these components of Active Directory may cause a failure in replication.

15. B. One of the great advantages of Active Directory is the ability to create a hierarchical structure that you can then use to granularly apply administrative permissions. Duplicating the three flat domains from the Windows NT environment to the Windows 2000 Active Directory environment defeats a large purpose of the architecture. This would also apply if you don't install Active Directory, which is reflected by the domain controllers.

Administering Active Directory

MICROSOFT EXAM OBJECTIVES COVERED IN THIS CHAPTER:

✓ **Publish resources in Active Directory. Types of resources include printers and shared folders.**

- Perform a search in Active Directory Users and Computers.
- Configure a printer object.

✓ **Create, manage, and troubleshoot User and Group objects in Active Directory.**

- Create and configure user and computer accounts for new and existing users.
- Troubleshoot groups. Considerations include nesting, scope, and type.
- Configure a user account by using Active Directory Users and Computers. Settings include passwords and assigning groups.
- Perform a search for objects in Active Directory.
- Use templates to create user accounts.
- Reset an existing computer account.

✓ **Manage object and container permissions.**

- Use the Delegation of Control wizard to configure inherited and explicit permissions.
- Configure and troubleshoot object permissions by using object access control lists (ACLs).

n the previous chapter, you learned how to work with sites, as well as configure and troubleshoot Active Directory replication, but we still haven't talked about the lower-level objects that exist in Active Directory. In this chapter, we will look at the structure of the various components within a domain. We'll see how an organization's business structure can be mirrored within Active Directory through the use of *organizational units (OUs)*. Because the concepts related to OUs are quite simple, some systems administrators may underestimate their importance. Make no mistake—one of the fundamental components of a successful Active Directory installation is the proper design and deployment of OUs.

> **NOTE** The "Troubleshoot groups. Considerations include nesting, scope, and type," "Configure a user account by using Active Directory Users and Computers. Settings include passwords and assigning groups," and "Use templates to create user accounts" subobjectives, as well as more information on the "Create, manage, and troubleshoot User and Group objects in Active Directory" objective are presented in Chapter 6, "Active Directory Security." More information can be found on managing object and container permissions, including the "Configure and troubleshoot object permissions by using object access control lists (ACLs)" subobjective, in Chapter 6.

We'll also cover the actual steps required to create common Active Directory objects. Then, we'll see how these objects can be configured and managed. Finally, we'll look at ways to publish resources and methods for automating the creation of user accounts.

In order to perform the exercises included in this chapter, you must have access to Active Directory.

An Overview of OUs

Before we begin to look at how OUs can be used within an Active Directory domain, we should first take a look at what OUs are and how they can be used to organize an Active Directory structure.

First and foremost, the purpose of OUs is to logically group Active Directory objects, just as their name implies. They serve as containers within which other Active Directory objects can be created. OUs do not form part of the DNS namespace. They are used solely to create organization within a domain.

OUs can contain the following types of Active Directory objects:

User Objects   User objects are the fundamental security principals used in an Active Directory environment. A User object includes a username, a password, group membership information, and many customizable fields that can be used to describe the user (e.g., fields for a street address, a telephone number, and other contact information).

Group Objects   Group objects are logical collections of users that are used primarily for assigning security permissions to resources. When managing users, the recommended practice is to place users into groups and then assign permissions to the group. This allows for flexible management and prevents systems administrators from having to set permissions for individual users.

Computer Objects   Computer objects represent workstations that are part of the Active Directory domain. Every computer within a domain shares the same security database, including user and group information. Computer objects are useful for managing security permissions and enforcing *Group Policy* restrictions.

Shared Folders   One of the fundamental functions of servers is to make resources available to users. Often, shared folders are used to give logical names to specific collections of files. For example, systems administrators might create shared folders for common applications, user data, and shared public files. Shared folders can be created and managed within Active Directory.

Other Organizational Units   Perhaps the most useful feature of OUs is that they can contain *other* OUs. This allows systems administrators to hierarchically group resources and other objects in accordance with business practices. The OU structure is extremely flexible and, as we will see later in this chapter, can easily be rearranged to reflect business reorganizations.

Each type of object has its own purpose within the organization of Active Directory domains. We'll look at the specifics of User, Computer, Group, and Shared Folder objects later in this chapter. For now, let's focus on the purpose and benefits of using OUs.

The Purpose of OUs

The main purpose of OUs is to organize the objects within Active Directory. Before diving into the details of OUs, however, it is very important to understand how OUs, users, and groups interact. Perhaps the most important concept to understand is that OUs are simply containers that are used for logically grouping various objects. They are not, however, groups in the classical sense. That is, they do not contain users, groups, or computers and are not used per se for assigning security permissions. Another way of stating this is that the user accounts, computer accounts, and group accounts that are contained in OUs are considered *security principals* while OUs themselves are not.

It is important to understand that OUs do not take the place of standard user and group permissions (a topic we'll cover in Chapter 6). A good general practice is to assign users to groups and then place the groups within OUs. This enhances the benefits of setting security permissions and of using the OU hierarchy for making settings. Figure 5.1 illustrates this concept.

FIGURE 5.1   Using Users, Groups, and OUs

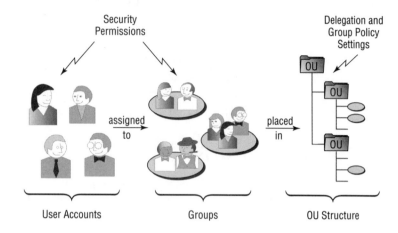

An organizational unit contains objects only from within the domain in which it resides. As we'll see later in this chapter, the OU is the finest level of granularity used for setting Group Policies and other administrative settings.

Benefits of OUs

There are many benefits of using OUs throughout your network environment:

- OUs are the smallest unit to which you can assign directory permissions.

- The OU structure can be easily changed, and OU structure is more flexible than domain structure.

- The OU structure can support many different levels of hierarchy.

- OU settings can be inherited by child objects.

- You can set Group Policy settings on OUs.

- Administration of OUs and the objects within them can be easily delegated to the appropriate users and groups.

Now that you have a good idea of why you should use OUs, let's look at some general practices for planning the OU structure.

Planning the OU Structure

One of the key benefits of Active Directory is the way in which it can bring organization to complex network environments. Before you can begin to implement OUs in various configurations, you must plan a structure that is compatible with business and technical needs. In this section, we'll look at several factors to consider when planning for the structure of OUs.

Logical Grouping of Resources

The fundamental purpose of using OUs is to hierarchically group resources that exist within Active Directory. Fortunately, hierarchical groups are quite intuitive and widely used in most businesses. For example, a typical manufacturing business might divide its various operations into different departments like the ones listed below:

- Sales

- Marketing

- Engineering

- Research and Development

- Support

- Information Technology (IT)

Each of these departments usually has its own goals and missions. In order to make the business competitive, individuals within each of the departments are assigned to various roles. Some types of roles might include the following:

- Managers

- Clerical staff

- Technical staff

- Planners

Each of these roles usually entails specific job responsibilities. For example, managers should be responsible for providing direction to general staff members. Note that the very nature of these roles suggests that employees may fill many different positions. That is, you might be a manager in one department and a member of the technical staff in another. In the modern workplace, such a situation is quite common.

So, how does all of this information help in planning for the use of OUs? First and foremost, the structure of OUs within a given network environment should map well to the needs of the business. This includes the political and logical structure of the organization, as well as its technical needs. Figure 5.2 provides an example of how a business organization might be mapped to the OU structure within an Active Directory domain.

FIGURE 5.2   Mapping a business organization to an OU structure

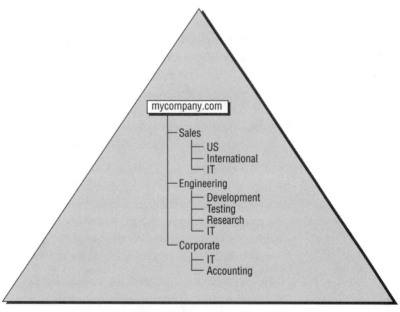

mycompany.com Domain

When naming OUs for your organization, you should keep several considerations and limitations in mind:

Keep it simple.   The purpose of OUs is to make administration and usage of resources simple. Therefore, it's always a good idea to keep the names of your objects simple and descriptive. Sometimes, finding a balance between these two goals can be a challenge. For example, although a printer name like "The LaserJet located near Bob's cube" might seem descriptive, it is certainly difficult to type. Imagine the naming changes that might be required if Bob moves (or leaves the company)!

Pay attention to limitations.   The maximum length for the name of an OU is 65 characters. In most cases, this should be adequate for describing OUs. Remember that the name of an OU object does not have to uniquely describe it because the OU will generally be referenced as part of the overall hierarchy. For example, you can choose to create an IT OU within two different parent OUs. Even though the OUs have the same name, users and administrators will be able to distinguish them based on their complete pathname.

Pay attention to the hierarchical consistency.   The fundamental basis of an OU structure is its relationship to a hierarchy. From a design standpoint, this means that you cannot have two OUs with the same name at the same level. However, you can have OUs with the same name at different levels. For example, we could create a Corporate OU within both the North America OU and the South America OU. This is because the fully qualified name includes information about the hierarchy. When an administrator tries to access resources in the Corporate OU, they must specify *which* Corporate OU they mean.

If, for example, you create a North America OU, the Canada OU should logically fit under it. If you decide that you want to separate them into completely different containers, then other names might be more appropriate. For example, North America could be changed to U.S. Users and administrators depend on the hierarchy of OUs within the domain, so make sure that it remains logically consistent.

Based on these considerations, you should have a good idea of how to best organize the OU structure for your domain.

Understanding OU Inheritance

When OUs are rearranged within the structure of Active Directory, several settings may be changed. Systems administrators must pay careful attention to changes in security permissions and other configuration options when moving and reorganizing OUs. By default, OUs will inherit the permissions of their new parent container when they are moved. Note that by using the built-in tools provided with Windows 2000 and Active Directory, you can move or copy OUs only within the same domain.

If you need to move an entire OU structure between domains, you can use the movetree command.

Delegation of Administrative Control

We already mentioned that OUs are the smallest component within a domain to which administrative permissions and Group Policy can be assigned. Now, let's look specifically at how administrative control is set on OUs.

The idea of *delegation* involves a higher security authority that can give permissions to another. As a real-world example, assume that you are the director of IT for a large organization. Instead of doing all of the work yourself (which would result in a very long workday!), you would probably assign roles and responsibilities to other individuals. For example, you might make one systems administrator responsible for all operations within the Sales domain and another responsible for the Engineering domain. Similarly, you could assign the permissions for managing all printers and print queues within the organization to one individual while allowing another to manage all security permissions for users and groups.

In this way, the various roles and responsibilities of the IT staff can be distributed throughout the organization. Businesses generally have a division of labor to handle all of the tasks involved in keeping the company's networks humming along. Network operating systems, however, often make it difficult to assign just the right permissions. Sometimes, the complexity is necessary to ensure that only the right permissions are assigned. A good general rule of thumb is to provide users and administrators the minimum permissions they require to do their jobs. This ensures that accidental, malicious, and otherwise unwanted changes do not occur.

In the world of Active Directory, the process of delegation is used to define the permissions for administrators of OUs. When considering implementing delegation, there are two main concerns to keep in mind:

Parent-Child Relationships The OU hierarchy you create will be very important when considering the maintainability of security permissions. As we've already mentioned, OUs can exist in a parent-child relationship. When it comes to the delegation of permissions, this is extremely important. You can choose to allow child containers to automatically inherit the permissions set on parent containers. For example, if the North America division of your organization contains 12 other OUs, you could delegate permissions to all of them by placing security permissions on the North America division. This feature can greatly ease administration, especially in larger organizations, but it is also a reminder of the importance of properly planning the OU structure within a domain.

You can delegate control only at the OU level and not at the object level within the OU.

Inheritance Settings   Now that we've seen how parent-child relationships can be useful for administration, we should consider the actual process of inheriting permissions. Logically, the process is known as *inheritance*. When permissions are set on a parent container, all of the child objects are configured to inherit the same permissions. This behavior can be overridden, however, if business rules do not lend themselves well to inheritance.

Application of Group Policy

One of the strengths of the Windows operating system is that it offers users a great deal of power and flexibility. From installing new software to adding device drivers, users can be given the ability to make many changes to their workstation configurations. This level of flexibility is also a potential problem. Inexperienced users might inadvertently change settings, causing problems that can require many hours to fix.

In many cases (and especially in business environments), users will require only a subset of the complete functionality provided by the operating system. In the past, however, the difficulty associated with implementing and managing security and policy settings has led to lax security policies. Some of the reasons for this are technical—it can be very tedious and difficult to implement and manage security restrictions. Other problems have been political—users and management might feel that they should have full permissions on their local machines, despite the potential problems this might cause.

One of the major design goals for the Windows 2000 platform (and specifically, Active Directory) was manageability. Although the broad range of features and functionality provided by the operating system can be helpful, being able to lock down types of functionality is very important.

That's where the idea of Group Policies comes in. Simply defined, *Group Policies* are collections of permissions that can be applied to objects within Active Directory. Specifically, Group Policy settings are assigned at the site, domain, and OU levels and can apply to user accounts, computer accounts, and groups. Examples of settings that a systems administrator can make using Group Policies include the following:

- Restricting access to the Start menu

- Disallowing the use of Control Panel

- Limiting choices for display and Desktop settings

We'll further cover the technical issues related to Group Policies in Chapter 7, "Managing Group Policy." In the following section, let's focus on how to plan OUs for the efficient use of policy settings.

Creating OUs

Now that we have looked at several different ways in which OUs can be used to bring organization to the objects within Active Directory, it's time to look at how OUs can be created and managed. In this section, we'll look at ways to create OUs.

Through the use of the Active Directory Users and Computers administrative tool, you can quickly and easily add, move, and change OUs. This graphical tool makes it easy to visualize and create the various levels of hierarchy required within an organization.

Figure 5.3 shows a geographically based OU structure that might be used by a multinational company. Note that the organization is based in North America and has a corporate office located there. In general, all of the other offices are much smaller than those located in North America.

FIGURE 5.3 A geographically based OU structure

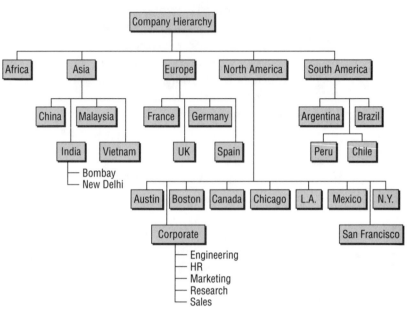

Also, it's important to note that this OU structure could have been designed in several different ways. For example, we could have chosen to group all of the offices located in the United States within a U.S. OU. However, due to the size of the offices, we chose to place these objects at the same level as the Canada and Mexico OUs. This prevents an unnecessarily deep OU hierarchy while still logically grouping the offices.

Exercise 5.1 walks you through the process of creating several OUs for a multinational business. We strongly recommend that you carry out this exercise since we'll be using this OU structure in later exercises within this chapter.

Creating OUs and other Active Directory objects can be a tedious process, especially for large organizations. A good way to speed up the process is to use keyboard shortcuts for creating objects instead of using the mouse. If your keyboard has a right-click key, be sure to use it. Also, learn the shortcuts for the context menus. For example, the *n* key automatically chooses the *New* selection and the *o* key specifies that you want to create an OU.

EXERCISE 5.1

Creating an OU Structure

In this exercise, we'll create an OU structure for a multinational company. In order to complete this exercise, you must have access to at least one domain and have permissions to administer the domain.

1. Open the Active Directory Users and Computers administrative tool.

2. Right-click the name of the local domain, and choose New ➤ Organizational Unit. You will see the dialog box shown in the following graphic. Notice that this box shows you the current context within which the OU will be created. In this case, we're creating a top-level OU, so the full path is simply the name of the domain.

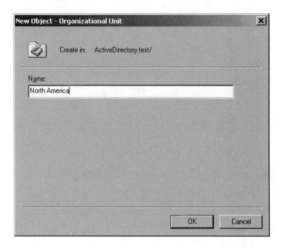

3. Type **North America** for the name of the first OU. Click OK to create this object.

4. Now, create the following top-level OUs by right-clicking the name of the domain and choosing New ➤ Organizational Unit:

> **Africa**
>
> **Asia**
>
> **Europe**
>
> **South America**

5. Note that the order in which OUs are created is not important. In this exercise, we are simply using a method that emphasizes the hierarchical relationship.

6. Now, create the following second-level OUs within the North America OU by right-clicking the North America OU and selecting New ≻ Organizational Unit:

   Austin

   Boston

   Canada

   Chicago

   Corporate

   Los Angeles

   Mexico

   New York

   San Francisco

7. Create the following OUs under the Asia OU:

   China

   India

   Malaysia

   Vietnam

8. Create the following OUs under the Europe OU:

   France

   Germany

   Spain

   UK

EXERCISE 5.1 *(continued)*

9. Create the following OUs under the South America OU:

   Argentina

   Brazil

   Chile

   Peru

10. Finally, it's time to create some third-level OUs. Right-click the India OU within the Asia OU, and select New ➢ Organizational Unit. Create the following OUs within this container:

    Bombay

    New Delhi

11. Within the North America Corporate OU, create the following OUs:

    Engineering

    HR

    Marketing

    Research

    Sales

12. When you have completed the creation of the OUs, you should have a structure that looks similar to the one in the following graphic.

Once you have created a logical OU structure, it's time to look at the various operations that are required to manage OUs.

Managing OUs

Managing network environments would be challenging enough if things rarely changed. However, in the real world, business units, departments, and employee roles change frequently. As business and technical needs change, so should the structure of Active Directory.

<table>
<tr>
<td>

Microsoft ✓ ***Exam*** ***Objective***

</td>
<td>

Manage object and container permissions.

- Use the Delegation of Control wizard to configure inherited and explicit permissions.

</td>
</tr>
</table>

Fortunately, changing the structure of OUs within a domain is a relatively simple process. In this section, we'll look at ways to delegate control of OUs and make other changes.

Moving, Deleting, and Renaming OUs

When you delete an OU, the various objects contained within it are deleted along with the OU itself. There are several reasons that you might need to delete OUs. First, changes in the business structure (such as a consolidation of departments) may make a specific OU obsolete. Or, you might choose to make changes to better reflect the changing needs of a business.

The process of moving OUs is an extremely simple one. Exercise 5.2 shows how you can easily change and reorganize OUs to reflect changes in the business organization. The specific scenario covered in this exercise includes the following changes:

- The Research and Engineering departments have been combined to form a department known as Research and Development (RD).

- The Sales department has been moved from the Corporate office to the New York office.

- The Marketing department has been moved from the Corporate office to the Chicago office.

EXERCISE 5.2

Modifying OU Structure

This exercise assumes that you have already completed the steps in the previous exercise within this chapter. In this exercise, we will make changes to the OUs as described in the text.

1. Open the Active Directory Users and Computers administrative tool.

2. To delete an OU, right-click the Engineering OU (located within North America ➤ Corporate) and click Delete. When prompted for confirmation, click Yes. Note that if this OU contained objects, all of the objects within the OU would have been automatically deleted as well.

3. Now, to rename an OU, right-click the Research OU and select Rename. Type **RD** to change the name of the OU and press Enter.

4. To move the Sales OU, right-click the Sales OU and select Move. In the Move dialog box, expand the North America branch and click the New York OU. Click OK to move the OU.

5. To move the Marketing OU, right-click the Marketing OU and select Move. In the Move dialog box, expand the North America branch and click the Chicago OU. Click OK to move the OU.

EXERCISE 5.2

6. When you have finished, you should see an OU structure similar to the one shown in the following screen shot. Close the Active Directory Users and Computers administrative tool.

Administering Properties of OUs

Although OUs are primarily created for the purpose of organization within the Active Directory environment, they have several settings that can be modified. To modify the properties of an OU using the Active Directory Users and Computers administrative tool, you can right-click the name of any OU and select Properties, and the Corporate Properties dialog box will appear. In the example shown in Figure 5.4, you see the options on the General tab.

In any organization, it's useful to know who is responsible for the management of an OU. This information can be set on the Managed By tab (see Figure 5.5). The information specified on this tab is very convenient because it is automatically pulled from the contact information on a user record. You should consider always having a contact for each OU within your organization so that users and other systems administrators will know whom to contact should the need for any changes arise.

FIGURE 5.4 Viewing OU general properties

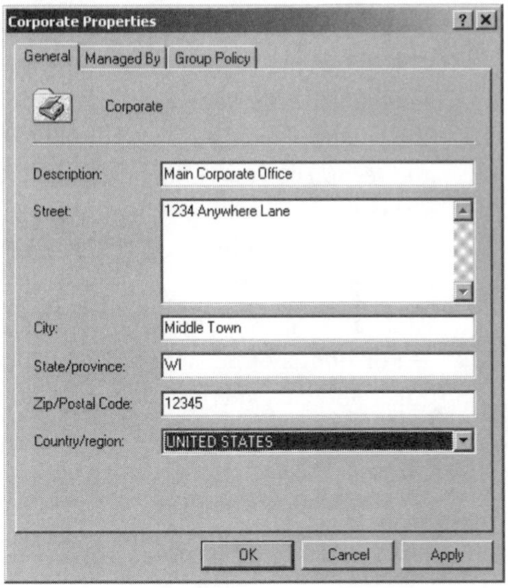

FIGURE 5.5 Setting OU Managed By properties

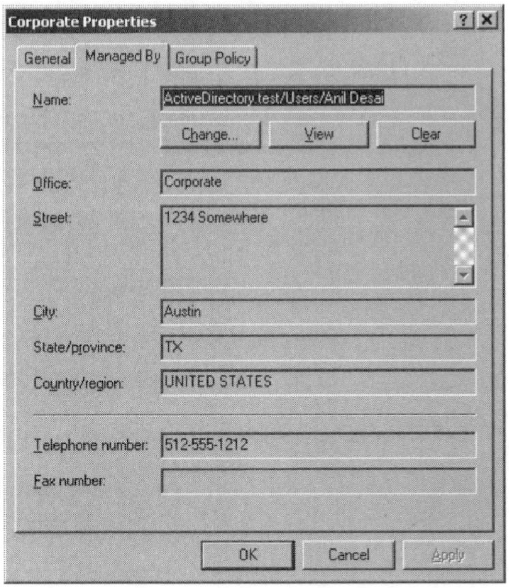

In addition, you can set Group Policy settings for the OU on the Group Policy tab. We'll cover this topic later in Chapter 7.

Delegating Control of OUs

In simple environments, one or a few systems administrators may be responsible for managing all of the settings within Active Directory. For example, a single systems administrator could be responsible for managing all users within all OUs in the environment. In larger organizations, however, roles and responsibilities may be divided among many different individuals. A typical situation is one in which a systems administrator is responsible for objects within only a few OUs in an Active Directory domain. Or, one systems administrator may be responsible for managing User and Group objects while another is responsible for managing file and print services.

Fortunately, the Active Directory Users and Computers tool provides a quick and easy method for ensuring that specific users receive only the permissions that they require. In Exercise 5.3, we will use the *Delegation of Control Wizard* to assign permissions to individuals.

EXERCISE 5.3

Using the Delegation of Control Wizard

In this exercise, we will use the Delegation of Control Wizard to assign permissions to specific users within Active Directory. In order to successfully complete these steps, you must first have created the objects in the previous exercises of this chapter.

1. Open the Active Directory Users and Computers administrative tool.

2. Right-click the Corporate OU (within the North America OU) and select Delegate Control. This will start the Delegation of Control Wizard. Click Next to begin configuring security settings.

3. In the Select Users, Computers, Or Groups dialog box, select the account for the Built-In Account Operators Group and click Add. Click OK to accept this item; then click Next to continue.

4. In the Tasks To Delegate window, select Delegate The Following Common Tasks, and place a check mark next to the following items:

    Create, Delete, And Manage User Accounts

    Reset Passwords On User Accounts

    Read All User Information

EXERCISE 5.3 *(continued)*

Create, Delete, And Manage Groups

Modify The Membership Of A Group

5. Click Next to continue.

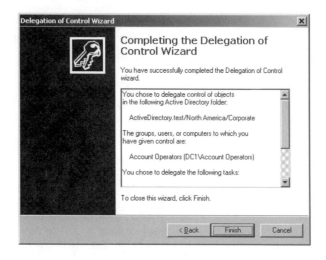

6. The Completing The Delegation Of Control Wizard dialog box will provide a summary of the operations you have selected. To implement the changes, click Finish.

Although the common tasks available through the wizard will be sufficient for many delegation operations, there might be cases in which you want more control. For example, you might want to give a particular systems administrator permissions to modify only Computer objects. Exercise 5.4 uses the Delegation of Control Wizard to assign more granular permissions.

EXERCISE 5.4

Delegating Custom Tasks

In this exercise, we will use the Delegation of Control Wizard to delegate custom tasks to specific users within Active Directory. In order to successfully complete these steps, you must first have created the objects in the previous exercises of this chapter.

1. Open the Active Directory Users and Computers administrative tool.

2. Right-click the Corporate OU (within the North America OU) and select Delegate Control. This will start the Delegation of Control Wizard. Click Next to begin making security settings.

3. In the Select Users, Computers, Or Groups dialog box, select the account for the Built-In Server Operators Group and click Add. Click OK to accept this item; then click Next to continue.

4. Select Create A Custom Task To Delegate, and click Next to continue.

5. In the Active Directory Object Type dialog box, choose Only The Following Objects In The Folder, and place a check mark next to the following items:

Computer Objects

Contact Objects

Group Objects

Organizational Unit Objects

Printer Objects

User Objects

6. Click Next to continue.

7. In the Permissions dialog box, place a check mark next to only the General option. Note that if the various objects within your Active Directory schema had property-specific settings, you would see those options here. Place a check mark next to the following items:

Create All Child Objects

Read All Properties

Write All Properties

8. Click Next to continue.

9. This will give the members of the Server Operators group the ability to create new objects within the Corporate OU and the permissions to read and write all properties for these objects. Click Next to continue.

10. The Completing The Delegation Of Control Wizard dialog box will provide a summary of the operations you have selected. To implement the changes, click Finish.

In addition to the basic types of security options we set in the exercise, you can create custom tasks and place permissions on specific types of objects within a container. We'll cover security permissions in greater detail in Chapter 6.

Real World Scenario

Delegation: Who's Responsible for What?

You're the IT director for a large, multinational organization. You've been with the company for quite a while, well since the time when the environment had only a handful of offices and a few network and systems administrators. But, times have changed. Systems administrators must now coordinate the efforts of hundreds of IT staffers in 14 countries.

When the environment ran under a Windows NT 4.0 domain environment, the network was set up with many domains. For security, performance, and distribution of administration, the computing resources in each major office were placed in their own domain. You have recently decided to move to Active Directory and to consolidate the numerous Windows NT domains into a single Active Directory domain. However, securely administering a distributed environment is still an important concern. So, the challenge is in determining how to coordinate the efforts of many different systems administrators.

Fortunately, through the proper use of OUs and delegation, you are given a lot of flexibility in determining how administration will be handled. There are several ways in which this may be structured. First, if you choose to create OUs based on geographic business structure, you could delegate control of these OUs based on the job functions of various systems administrators. For example, one user account may be used for administering the Europe OU. Within the Europe OU, this systems administrator could delegate control of offices represented by the Paris and London OUs. Within these OUs, you could further break down the administrative responsibilities for printer queue operators and security administrators.

Alternatively, the OU structure may create a functional representation of the business. For example, the Engineering OU might contain other OUs that are based on office locations such as New York and Paris. A systems administrator of the Engineering domain could delegate permissions based on geography or job functions to the lower OUs. Regardless of whether you build a departmental, functional, or geographical OU model, keep in mind that each model excludes other models. This is one of the most important decisions to make. The overriding concern when making this decision or modifying previous decisions is how will it affect the management and administration of the network. The good news is that with the many features of Active Directory, the model you choose can be based on specific business requirements rather than imposed by architectural constraints.

Troubleshooting OUs

In general, the use of OUs will be a straightforward and relatively painless process. With adequate planning, you'll be able to implement an intuitive and useful structure for OU objects.

The most common problems with OU configuration are related to the OU structure. When troubleshooting OUs, you should pay careful attention to the following factors:

Inheritance   By default, Group Policy and other settings are transferred automatically from parent OUs to child OUs and objects. This is an important point to consider. Even if a specific OU is not given a set of permissions, objects within that OU might still get them from parent objects.

Delegation of Administration   If the wrong user accounts or groups are allowed to perform specific tasks on OUs, you might be violating your company's security policy. Be sure to verify the delegations you have made at each OU level.

Organizational Issues   Sometimes, business practices may not easily map to the structure of Active Directory. A few misplaced OUs, user accounts, computer accounts, or groups can make administration difficult or inaccurate. In many cases, it might be beneficial to rearrange the OU structure to accommodate any changes in the business organization. In others, it might make more sense to change business processes.

If you make it a practice to regularly consider each of these issues when troubleshooting problems with OUs, you will be much less likely to make errors in Active Directory configuration.

Creating and Managing Active Directory Objects

We just looked at how a hierarchical structure could be created within a domain. If you are familiar with the task of creating OUs, creating other Active Directory objects will be quite simple. Let's look at the details.

Microsoft ✓ *Exam* *Objective*

Create, manage, and troubleshoot User and Group objects in Active Directory.

- Create and configure user and computer accounts for new and existing users.

- Reset an existing computer account.

Overview of Active Directory Objects

By default, after you install and configure a domain controller, you will see the following sections of organization within the Active Directory Users and Computers tool:

Built-In   The Built-In container includes all of the standard groups that are installed by default when you promote a domain controller. These groups are used for administering the servers in your environment. Examples include the Administrators group, Backup Operators, and Print Operators.

Computers   By default, the Computers container contains a list of the workstations in your domain. From here, you can manage all of the computers in your domain.

Domain Controllers   This container includes a list of all of the domain controllers for the domain.

Foreign Security Principals   Security principals are Active Directory objects to which permissions can be applied. They are used for managing permissions within Active Directory. We'll cover the details of working with security principals in Chapter 6.

Foreign security principals are any objects to which security can be assigned and that are not part of the current domain.

Users   The Users container includes all of the security accounts that are part of the domain. When you first install the domain controller, there will be several groups in this container. For example, the Domain Admins group and the Administrator account are created in this container.

There are several different types of Active Directory objects that you can create and manage. The following are specific object types:

Computer   *Computer objects* are used for managing workstations in the environment.

Contact   Contacts are not security principals like Users, but they are used for specifying information about individuals within the organization. *Contact objects* are usually used in OUs to specify the main administrative contact.

Group   Groups are security principals. That is, they are created for assigning and managing permissions. Groups contain user accounts.

Organizational Unit   An OU is created to build a hierarchy within the Active Directory domain. It is the smallest unit that can be used to create administrative groupings and can be used for assigning Group Policies. Generally, the OU structure within a domain reflects a company's business organization.

Printer   *Printer objects* map to printers.

Shared Folder   *Shared Folder objects* map to server shares. They are used for organizing the various file resources that may be available on file/print servers.

User   A *User object* is the fundamental security principal on which Active Directory is based. User accounts contain information about individuals, as well as password and other permission information.

We'll cover the security aspects related to the use of Active Directory objects in Chapter 6. For now, however, know that these objects are used to represent various items in your network environment. Through the use of these objects, you will be able to manage the content of your Active Directory.

Exercise 5.5 walks through the steps required to create various objects within an Active Directory domain.

EXERCISE 5.5

Creating Active Directory Objects

In this exercise, we will create some basic Active Directory objects. In order to complete this exercise, you must have first installed and configured at least one Active Directory domain.

1. Open the Active Directory Users and Computers tool.

2. Expand the current domain to list the objects currently contained within it. You should see folders similar to those shown.

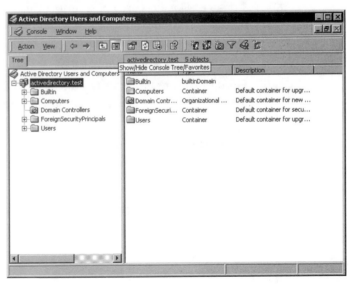

3. Create a new, top-level OU by right-clicking the name of the domain and selecting New ➢ Organizational Unit. When prompted for the name of the OU, type **Corporate** and click OK.

4. Repeat step 3 to create the following top-level OUs:

   Engineering

   HR

   IT

   Marketing

   Sales

5. Right-click the Corporate OU, and select New ➢ User. Fill in the following information:

   First Name: **Monica**

   Initials: **D**

   Last Name: **President**

   Full Name: (leave as default)

   User Logon Name: **mdpresident** (leave default domain)

   Click Next to continue.

EXERCISE 5.5

6. Enter a password for this user, and then confirm it. Note that you can also make changes to password settings here. Click Next. You will see a summary of the user information. Click OK to create the new user.

7. Create another user in the IT container with the following information:

First Name: **John**

Initials: **Q**

Last Name: **Admin**

Full Name: (leave as default)

User Logon Name: **jqadmin** (leave default domain)

Click Next to continue. Assign a password. Click Next, and then click Finish to create the user.

8. Right-click the IT OU, and select New ⮞ Contact. Use the following information to fill in the properties of the Contact object:

First Name: **Jane**

Initials: **R**

Last Name: **Admin**

Display Name: **jradmin**

Click OK to create the new Contact object.

9. Right-click the IT OU, and select New ➢ Shared Folder. Enter **Software** for the Name and **\\server1\applications** for the Network Path. Note that although this resource does not exist, the object can still be created. Click OK to create the Shared Folder object.

EXERCISE 5.5

10. Right-click the HR OU, and select New ➢ Group. Type **All Users** for the Group Name, and leave the Group Name (Pre-Windows 2000) field with the same value. For the Group Scope, select Global, and for the Group Type, select Security. To create the group, click OK.

11. Right-click the Sales OU and select New ➢ Computer. Type **Workstation1** for the name of the computer. Notice that the pre-Windows 2000 name will automatically be populated and that, by default, the members of the Domain Admins group will be the only ones who will be able to add this computer to the domain. Place a check mark in the Allow Pre-Windows 2000 Computers To Use This Account box, and then click OK to create the Computer object.

12. Close the Active Directory Users and Computers tool.

Now that you are familiar with the process of creating and managing objects, let's look at some additional properties that can be set for each of these items.

Managing Object Properties

Once you've created the necessary Active Directory objects, you'll probably need to make changes to their default properties. In addition to the settings you made when creating Active Directory objects, there are several more properties that can be configured. Exercise 5.6 walks you through setting various properties for Active Directory objects.

Although it may seem somewhat tedious, it's always a good idea to enter as much information as you know about Active Directory objects when you create them. Although the name Printer1 may be meaningful to you, users will appreciate the additional information when searching for objects.

EXERCISE 5.6

Managing Object Properties

In this exercise, we will modify the properties for Active Directory objects. In order to complete the steps in this exercise, you must have first completed Exercise 5.5.

1. Open the Active Directory Users and Computers tool.

2. Expand the name of the domain, and select the IT container. Right-click the John Q. Admin user account, and select Properties.

3. Here, you will see the various Properties tabs for the user account. The basic tabs include the following:

    General: General account information about this user

    Address: The physical location information about this user

    Account: User logon name and other account restrictions, such as workstation restrictions and logon hours

Profile: Information about the user's roaming profile settings

Telephones: Telephone contact information for the user

Organization: The user's title, department, and company information

Member Of: Group membership information for the user

Dial-In: Remote Access Service (RAS) permissions for the user

Environment: Logon and other network settings for the user

Sessions: Session limits, including maximum session time and idle session settings

Remote Control: Remote control options for this user's session

Terminal Services Profile: Information about the user's profile for use with Windows 2000 Terminal Services

Click OK to continue.

4. Select the HR OU. Right-click the All Users Group, and click Properties. In the dialog box that appears, you will be able to modify the membership of the group. Click the Members tab, and then click Add. Add the Monica D. President and John Q. Admin user accounts to the Group. Click OK to save the settings and then OK again to accept the group modifications.

5. Select the Sales OU. Right-click the Workstation1 Computer object. Notice that you can choose to disable the account or reset it (to allow another computer to join the domain under that same name). From the context menu, choose Properties. You'll see the properties for the Computer object. The various tabs in this dialog box include the following:

General: Information about the name of the computer, the role of the computer, and its description. Note that you can enable an option to allow the local system account of this machine to request services from other servers. This is useful if the machine is a trusted and secure computer.

Operating System: The name, version, and service pack information for the operating system running on the computer.

Member Of: The Active Directory groups that this Computer object is a member of.

Location: A description of where the computer is physically located.

Managed By: Information about the User or Contact object that is responsible for managing this computer.

After you have examined the available options, click OK to continue.

6. Select the Corporate OU. Right-click the Monica D. President user account, and choose Reset Password. You will be prompted to enter a new password and then asked to confirm it. Note that you can also force the user to change this password upon the next logon.

7. Close the Active Directory Users and Computers tool.

By now, you have probably noticed that there are many common options for Active Directory objects. For example, Group objects and Computer objects both have a Managed By tab. As was mentioned earlier, it's always a good idea to enter as much information as possible about an object. This will help systems administrators and users alike. On the downside, however, it will tell them who is to blame when a printer no longer works!

More Active Directory Management Features

The Active Directory Users and Computers tool has a couple of other features that come in quite handy when managing many objects. You can access the first by clicking the View menu in the MMC and choosing Filter Options. You'll see a dialog box similar to the one shown in Figure 5.6. Here, you can choose to filter objects by their specific types within the display. For example, if you are an administrator who works primarily with user accounts and groups, you can select those specific items by placing check marks in the list. In addition, you can create more complex filters by choosing Create Custom Filter. That will provide you with an interface that looks similar to that of the Find command.

FIGURE 5.6 Filtering objects using the Active Directory Users and Computers tool

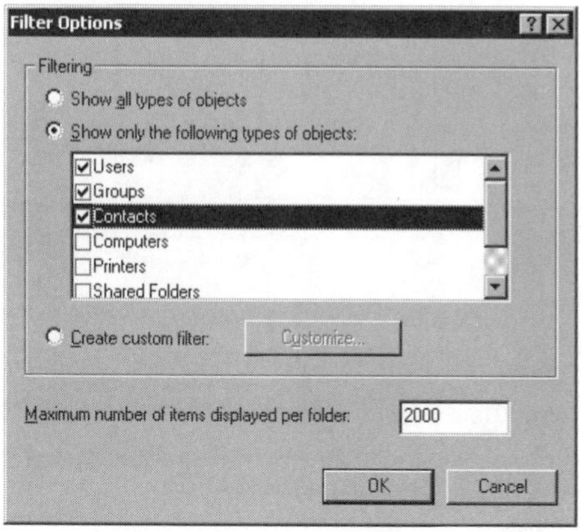

Another option in the Active Directory Users and Computers tool is to view Advanced options. You can enable the Advanced options by choosing Advanced Options in the View menu. This will add two top-level folders to the list under the name of the domain. The System folder (shown in Figure 5.7)

provides a list of some additional features that can be configured to work with Active Directory. For example, you can configure settings for the Distributed File System (DFS), IP Security policies, the File Replication Service, and more. In addition to the System folder, you'll see the LostandFound folder, which we first looked at in the previous chapter. This folder contains any files that may not have been replicated properly between domain controllers. You should check this folder periodically for any files so that you can decide whether you need to move them or copy them to other locations.

FIGURE 5.7 Advanced options in the Active Directory Users and Computers tool

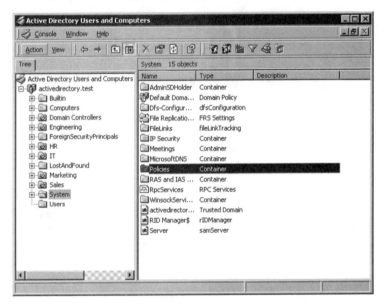

As you can see, managing Active Directory objects is generally a simple task. The Active Directory Users and Computers tool allows you to configure several objects. Let's move on to look at one more common administration function—moving objects.

Moving Active Directory Objects

One of the extremely useful features of the Active Directory Users and Computers tool is its ability to easily move users and resources.

Exercise 5.7 walks through the process of moving Active Directory objects.

EXERCISE 5.7

Moving Active Directory Objects

In this exercise, we will make several changes to the organization of Active Directory objects. In order to complete this exercise, you must have first completed Exercise 5.5.

1. Open the Active Directory Users and Computers tool, and expand the name of the domain.

2. Select the Sales OU, right-click Workstation1, and select Move. A dialog box will appear. Select the IT OU, and click OK to move the Computer object to that container.

3. Click the IT OU, and verify that Workstation1 was moved.

4. Close the Active Directory Users and Computers tool.

In addition to moving objects within Active Directory, you can also easily rename them by right-clicking an object and selecting Rename. Note that this option does not apply to all objects. For example, in order to prevent security breaches, Computer objects cannot be renamed. You can also remove objects from Active Directory by right-clicking them and choosing Delete.

WARNING Deleting an Active Directory object is an irreversible action. When an object is destroyed, any security permissions or other settings made for that object are removed as well. Since each object within Active Directory contains its own security identifier (SID), simply re-creating an object with the same name does not place any permissions on it. Before you delete an Active Directory object, be sure that you will never need it again.

Resetting an Existing Computer Account

Every computer on the domain establishes a discrete channel of communication with the domain controller at logon time. The domain controller stores a randomly selected password (different from the user password) for authentication across the channel, which is updated every 30 days. Sometimes the computer's password and the domain controller's password don't match, and communication between the two machines fails. Without the ability to reset the computer account, you wouldn't be able to connect the machine to the domain. Fortunately, you can use the Active Directory Users and Computers tool to reestablish the connection. Exercise 5.8 shows you how to reset an existing computer account.

EXERCISE 5.8

Resetting an Existing Computer Account

In this exercise, you will reset an existing computer account. You should have completed the previous exercises in this chapter before you begin this exercise.

1. Open the Active Directory Users and Computers tool, and expand the name of the domain.

2. Click the IT OU, and then right-click the Workstation1 computer account.

3. Select Reset Account from the context menu.

4. Resetting the account breaks the connection between the computer and the domain, so you will need to reconnect the computer after performing this exercise.

Publishing Active Directory Objects

One of the main goals of Active Directory is to make resources easy to find. Two of the most commonly used resources in a networked environment are server file shares and printers. These are so common, in fact, that most organizations will have dedicated File/Print Servers. When it comes to managing these types of resources, Active Directory makes it easy to determine which files and printers are available to users.

Microsoft ✓ *Exam Objective*

Publish resources in Active Directory. Types of resources include printers and shared folders.

- Perform a search in Active Directory Users and Computers.
- Configure a printer object.

With that said, let's look at how Active Directory manages the publishing of shared folders and printers.

Making Active Directory Objects Available to Users

An important aspect of managing Active Directory objects is that a systems administrator can control which objects users can see. The act of making an Active Directory object available is known as *publishing*. The two main publishable objects are Printer objects and Shared Folder objects.

The general process for creating server shares and shared printers has remained unchanged from previous versions of Windows. That is, the main method is to create the various objects (a printer or a file system folder) and then to enable it for sharing. To make these resources available via Active Directory, however, there's an additional step: Resources must be published. Once an object has been published in Active Directory, it will be available for use by clients.

You can also publish Windows NT 4 resources through Active Directory by creating Active Directory objects as we did in Exercise 5.5. When publishing objects in Active Directory, you should know the server name and share name of the resource. The use of Active Directory objects offers systems administrators the ability to change the resource to which the object points without having to reconfigure or even notify clients. For example, if we move a share from one server to another, all we need to do is update the Shared Folder object's properties to point to the new location. Active Directory clients will still refer to the resource with the same path and name as they used before.

Without Active Directory, Windows NT 4 shares and printers will be accessible only through the use of NetBIOS. If you're planning to disable the NetBIOS protocol in your environment, you must be sure that these resources have been published or they will not be accessible.

Publishing Printers

Printers can be published easily within Active Directory. Exercise 5.9 walks you through the steps required to share and publish a Printer object.

EXERCISE 5.9

Creating and Publishing a Printer

In this exercise, we will create and share a printer. Specifically, we will install and share a new, text-only printer. In order to complete the installation of the printer, you will require access to the Windows 2000 installation media (via the hard disk, a network share, or the CD-ROM drive).

1. Choose Start ➢ Settings ➢ Printers. Double-click Add New Printer. This will start the Add Printer Wizard. Click Next to begin.

2. In the Network Or Local Printer dialog box, select Local Printer. Uncheck the Automatically Detect And Install My Plug And Play Printer box. Click Next.

3. In the Select The Printer Port dialog box, select Use The Following Port. From the list below that option, select LPT1: Printer Port. Click Next.

EXERCISE 5.9

4. For the Manufacturer, select Generic, and for the printer, highlight Generic / Text Only. Click Next.

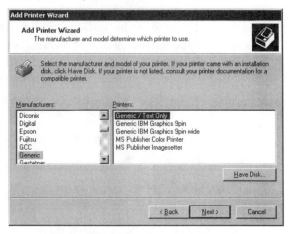

5. When asked for the name of the printer, type **Text Printer**. Click Next.

6. When prompted for the share name, select Share As and type **Text-Printer**. Click Next.

7. For the Location, type **Building 203** and add the comment **This is a text-only printer**. Click Next.

8. When prompted to print a test page, select No. Click Next.

9. You will see a confirmation of the printer options you selected. Click Finish to create the printer.

EXERCISE 5.9

10. Next, you will need to verify that you want the printer to be listed in Active Directory. In the Printers folder, right-click the Text Printer icon and select Properties. Next, select the Sharing tab, and ensure that the List In The Directory box is checked. Note that you can also add additional printer drivers for other operating systems using this tab. Click OK to accept the settings. Close the Printers window.

EXERCISE 5.9

11. Now that the printer has been created and shared, you need to verify that it is available for use. To do this, choose Start ➤ Search ➤ For Printers. In order to search for all printers, leave all of the options blank. Note that you can use the Features and Advanced tabs to restrict the list of printers to those that match certain requirements. Click Find Now. You should receive results that demonstrate that the printer is available through Active Directory.

12. When finished, exit the Find Printers dialog box.

Note that when you create and share a printer this way, an Active Directory Printer object is not displayed within the Active Directory Users and Computers tool. The printer is actually associated with the Computer object to which it is shared. Printer objects in Active Directory are manually created for sharing printers from Windows NT 4 and earlier shared printer resources.

Publishing Shared Folders

Now that we've created and published a printer, let's look at how the same thing can be done to shared folders. Exercise 5.10 walks through the steps required to create a folder, share it, and then publish it in Active Directory.

EXERCISE 5.10

Creating and Publishing a Shared Folder

In this exercise, we will create and publish a shared folder. This exercise assumes that you will be using the C: partition; however, you may want to change this based on your server configuration. This exercise assumes that you have completed Exercise 5.5.

1. Create a new folder in the root directory of your C: partition, and name it **Test Share**.

2. Right-click the Test Share folder, and select Sharing.

3. On the Sharing tab, select Share This Folder. For the Share Name, type **Test,** and for the Comment, enter **Share used for testing Active Directory**. Leave the User Limit, Permissions, and Caching settings as their defaults. Click OK to create the share.

4. To verify that the share has been created, choose Start ➤ Run, and type the UNC path for the local server. For instance, if the server was named DC1, you would type **\\DC1**. This will connect you to the local computer, where you can view any available network resources. Verify that the Test Share folder exists, and then close the window.

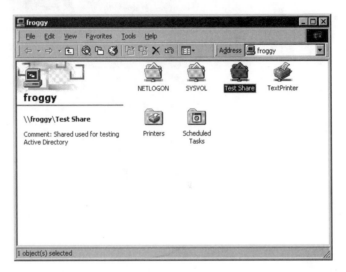

5. Open the Active Directory Users and Computers tool. Expand the current domain, and right-click the IT OU. Select New ➤ Shared Folder.

6. In the dialog box, type **Shared Folder Test** for the name of the folder. Then type the UNC path to the share (for example, **\\DC1\Test Share**). Click OK to create the share.

7. Now that we have created the shared folder in Active Directory, it's time to verify that it was created. To do this, right-click the name of the domain and select Find.

EXERCISE 5.10 *(continued)*

8. On the Find menu, select Shared Folders. Leave the remaining options blank to search for all Active Directory shares. (Notice that you can also use the Advanced tab to further specify information about the share you are searching for.) Click the Find Now button to obtain the results of the search.

9. Close the Find dialog box, and exit the Active Directory Users and Computers tool.

Once you have created and published the shared folder, clients can use the My Network Places icon to find this object. The shared folder will be organized based on the OU in which you created the Shared Folder object. Through the use of publication, you can see how this makes it easy to manage shared folders.

Once you have created resources, it is likely that you will want to restrict their use to only certain users and groups. We'll cover ways to do this in Chapter 6. In addition to setting permissions for end users, you can also use the Delegation of Control Wizard to assign management permissions to objects.

Searching Active Directory

So far we've created several Active Directory resources. One of the main benefits of having all of your resource information in Active Directory is that you should be able to easily find what you're looking for. Remember when we recommended that you should always enter as much information as possible when creating Active Directory objects? Well, this is where that extra effort begins to pay off.

Exercise 5.11 walks you through the steps required to find objects in Active Directory.

EXERCISE 5.11

Finding Objects in Active Directory

In this exercise, we will search for specific objects in Active Directory. In order to complete this exercise, you must have first completed Exercise 5.5.

1. Open the Active Directory Users and Computers tool.

2. Right-click the name of the domain, and select Find.

3. In the Find field, select Users, Contacts, And Groups. For the In setting, choose activedirectory. This will search the entire Active Directory environment for the criteria you enter. Note that if this is a production domain and if there are many objects, this may be a time-consuming and network-intensive operation.

4. In the Name field, type **admin** and then click Find Now to obtain the results of the search.

5. Now that we have found several results, let's narrow down the list. Click the Advanced tab. In the Field drop-down list, select User ≻ Last Name. For the Condition, select Starts With, and for the Value, type **Admin**. Click Add to add this item to the search criteria. Click Find Now. Notice that this time, only the User and Contact that have the last name Admin are shown.

6. To filter the result set even further, click the View menu and select Filter. The filter is displayed in the row just above the Results windows. In the Name field, type **John** and press Enter. Notice that this filters the list to only the John Q. Admin User object.

7. To view more information about the User object, you can right-click it and select Properties.

8. To quickly view (and filter) more information about multiple objects, select the View menu, and choose Select Columns. By selecting fields and clicking Add, you will be able to view more information about the retrieved objects. Click OK to add the information.

9. When you have finished searching, close the Find dialog box and exit the Active Directory Users and Computers tool.

Using the many options available in the Find dialog box, you can usually narrow down the objects you're searching for quickly and efficiently. Users and systems administrators alike will find this to be useful in environments of any size!

Summary

In this chapter, we examined the following topics:

- The purpose, function, and benefits of organizational units (OUs).

- Factors to consider when designing an OU structure. Based on this information, we created a sample OU structure for a geographically organized business.

- How to reorganize OUs, which can be a simple and painless process.

- How to use the Delegation of Control Wizard to assign administrative permissions to the objects within an OU.

- How to use the Active Directory Users and Computers tool to manage Active Directory objects. If you're responsible for day-to-day systems administration, there's a good chance that you are already familiar with using this tool.

- How to manage Active Directory objects such as users, computers, and groups.

- How to publish network resources (such as printers and shared folders) in Active Directory.

- How to search Active Directory for specific types of objects.

The concepts and operations we covered in this chapter will be instrumental in understanding the ideas behind other Active Directory topics. A prime example is the topic of Active Directory security, which we'll cover next!

Exam Essentials

Understand the purpose of organizational units (OUs). OUs are used to create a hierarchical, logical organization for objects within an Active Directory domain.

Know the types of objects that can reside within OUs. OUs can contain Active Directory User, Computer, Shared Folder, and other objects.

Understand the Delegation of Control Wizard. The Delegation of Control Wizard is used to assign specific permissions at the level of OUs.

Understand the concept of inheritance. By default, child OUs inherit permissions and Group Policy assignments set for parent OUs. However, these settings can be overridden for more granular control of security.

Understand how Active Directory objects work. Active Directory objects represent some piece of information about components within a domain. The objects themselves have attributes that describe details about them.

Understand how Active Directory objects can be organized. Through the use of the Active Directory Users and Computers tool, you can create, move, rename, and delete various objects.

Learn how resources can be published. A design goal for Active Directory was to make network resources easier for users to find. With that in mind, understand how the use of published printers and shared folders can simplify network resource management.

Key Terms

Before you take the exam, be certain you are familiar with the following terms:

Computer objects	organizational unit (OU)
Contact objects	Printer objects
delegation	publishing
Delegation of Control wizard	security principals
Group Policy	Shared Folder objects
inheritance	User objects

Review Questions

1. Gabriel is responsible for administering a small Active Directory domain. Recently, the Engineering department within his organization has been divided into two departments. He wants to reflect this organizational change within Active Directory and plans to rename various groups and resources. Which of the following operations *can* be performed using the Active Directory Users and Computers tool? (Choose all that apply.)

   A. Renaming an organizational unit

   B. Searching for resources

   C. Renaming a group

   D. Creating a computer account

2. You are a domain administrator for a large domain. Recently, you have been asked to make changes to some of the permissions related to OUs within the domain. In order to further restrict security for the Texas OU, you remove some permissions at that level. Later, a junior systems administrator mentions that she is no longer able to make changes to objects within the Austin OU (which is located within the Texas OU). Assuming no other changes have been made to Active Directory permissions, which of the following characteristics of OUs might have caused the change in permissions?

   A. Inheritance

   B. Group Policy

   C. Delegation

   D. Object properties

3. Isabel, a systems administrator, has created a new Active Directory domain in an environment that already contains two trees. During the promotion of the domain controller, she chose to create a new Active Directory forest. Isabel is a member of the Enterprise Administrators group and has full permissions over all domains. During the organization's migration to an Active Directory, there have been many updates to the information stored within the domains. Recently, users and other system administrators have complained about not being able to find specific Active Directory objects in one or more domains (although they exist in others).

In order to investigate the problem, Isabel wants to check for any objects that have not been properly replicated among domain controllers. If possible, she would like to restore these objects to their proper place within the relevant Active Directory domains.

Which two of the following actions should she perform to be able to view the relevant information? (Choose all that apply.)

A. Change the Active Directory permissions to allow viewing of object information in all domains.

B. Select the Advanced Options item in the View menu.

C. Promote a member server in each domain to a domain controller.

D. Rebuild all domain controllers from the latest backups.

E. Examine the contents of the LostandFound folder using the Active Directory Users and Computers tool.

4. You are a consultant hired to evaluate an organization's Active Directory domain. The domain contains over 200,000 objects and hundreds of OUs. You begin examining the objects within the domain, but you find that the loading of the contents of specific OUs takes a very long time. Furthermore, the list of objects can be very large. You want to do the following:

- Avoid the use of any third-party tools or utilities, and use the built-in Active Directory administrative tools.

- Be able to limit the list of objects within an OU to only the type of objects that you're examining (for example, only Computer objects).

- Prevent any changes to the Active Directory domain or any of the objects within it.

Which of the following actions meet the above requirements?

A. Use the Filter option in the Active Directory Users and Computers tool to restrict the display of objects.

B. Use the Delegation of Control Wizard to give yourself permissions over only a certain type of object.

C. Implement a new naming convention for objects within an OU and then sort the results using this new naming convention.

D. Use the Active Directory Domains and Trusts tool to view information from only selected domain controllers.

E. Edit the domain Group Policy settings to allow yourself to view only the objects of interest.

5. Your organization is currently planning a migration from a Windows NT 4 environment that consists of several domains to an Active Directory environment. Your staff consists of 25 systems administrators who are responsible for managing one or more domains. The organization is finalizing a merger with another company.

John, a technical planner, has recently provided you with a preliminary plan to migrate your environment to several Active Directory domains. He has cited security and administration as major justifications for this plan. Jane, a consultant, has recommended that the Windows NT 4 domains be consolidated into a single Active Directory domain. Which of the following statements provide a valid justification to support Jane's proposal? (Choose all that apply.)

A. In general, OU structure is more flexible than domain structure.

B. In general, domain structure is more flexible than OU structure.

C. It is possible to create a distributed systems administration structure for OUs through the use of delegation.

D. The use of OUs within a single domain can greatly increase the security of the overall environment.

6. Miguel is a junior-level systems administrator and has basic knowledge about working with Active Directory. As his supervisor, you have asked Miguel to make several security-related changes to OUs within the company's Active Directory domain. You instruct Miguel to use the basic functionality provided in the Delegation of Control Wizard. Which of the following operations are represented as common tasks within the Delegation of Control Wizard? (Choose all that apply.)

    A. Reset passwords on user accounts.

    B. Manage Group Policy links.

    C. Modify the membership of a group.

    D. Create, delete, and manage groups.

7. You are the primary systems administrator for a large Active Directory domain. Recently, you have hired another systems administrator to offload some of your responsibilities. This systems administrator will be responsible for handling help desk calls and for basic user account management. You want to allow the new employee to have permissions to reset passwords for all users within a specific OU. However, for security, reasons, it's important that the user not be able to make permissions changes for objects within other OUs in the domain. Which of the following is the best way to do this?

    A. Create a special administration account within the OU and grant it full permissions for all objects within Active Directory.

    B. Move the user's login account into the OU that he or she is to administer.

    C. Move the user's login account to an OU that contains the OU (that is, the parent OU of the one that he or she is to administer).

    D. Use the Delegation of Control Wizard to assign the necessary permissions on the OU that he or she is to administer.

8. You have been hired as a consultant to assist in the design of an organization's Active Directory environment. Specifically, you are instructed to focus on the OU structure (others will be planning for technical issues). You begin by preparing a list of information that you need to create the OU structure for a single domain. Which of the following pieces of information is not vital to your OU design?

    A. Physical network topology

    B. Business organizational requirements

    C. System administration requirements

    D. Security requirements

9. You want to allow the Super Users group to create and edit new objects within the Corporate OU. Using the Delegation of Control Wizard, you choose the Super Users group and arrive at the screen shown below. Where would you click in order to add the ability to create and edit new objects in the Corporate OU?

    A. Create, Delete, And Manage User Accounts

    B. Create, Delete, And Manage Groups

    C. Manage Group Policy Links

    D. Create A Custom Task To Delegate

10. A systems administrator is using the Active Directory Users and Computers tool to view the objects within an OU. He has previously created many users, groups, and computers within this OU, but now only the users are being shown. What is a possible explanation for this?

    A. Groups and computers are not normally shown in the Active Directory Users and Computers tool.

    B. Another systems administrator may have locked the groups, preventing others from accessing them.

    C. Filtering options have been set that specify that only User objects should be shown.

    D. The group and computer accounts have never been used and are, therefore, not shown.

11. The company you work for has a multilevel administrative team that is segmented by departments and locations. There are four major locations and you are in the Northeast group. You have been assigned to the administrative group that is responsible for creating and maintaining network shares for files and printers in your region. The last place you worked was a large Windows NT 4.0 network, where you had a much wider range of responsibilities. You are excited about the chance to learn more about Windows 2000. For your first task, you have been given a list of file and printer shares that need to be created for the users in your region. You ask how to create them in Windows 2000, and you are told that the process of creating a share is the same as with Windows NT. You create the shares and use NET USE to test them. Everything appears to work fine, so you send out a message that the shares are available. The next day, you start receiving calls from users who say that they cannot see any of resources that you created. What is the most likely reason for the calls from the users?

    A. You forgot to enable NetBIOS for the shares.

    B. You need to force replication for the shares to appear in the directory.

    C. You need to publish the shares in the directory.

    D. The shares will appear within the normal replication period.

12. Wilford Products has over 1,000 users in five locations across the country. The network consists of four servers and around 250 workstations in each location. One of the four servers in each location is a domain controller. As the new network administrator, you are now responsible for all aspects of the OUs within the directory. After meeting with the HR department, you have been informed that the vice president of sales has left the organization, and you are to remove his access to all resources on the network. You return to your office and remove his account from the directory. After you remove the account, you are immediately notified that you have been misinformed and the vice president of sales is not leaving the company. You quickly re-add him within the window of replication between the other domain controllers. What else must you do to reinstate his account and all his associated permissions?

A. Nothing. Since you re-created the account before the replication window opened, the account will remain in the directory.

B. Open the Tombstone folder and remove the object that is pending in order to remove the account before the replication window opens.

C. After replication occurs, you need to manually synchronize his account in the domain controllers.

D. You must reestablish every permission and setting manually.

13. You want to publish a printer to Active Directory. In the following screen, where would you click in order to accomplish this task?

A. The Sharing tab

B. The Advanced tab

C. The Device Settings tab

D. The Printing Preferences button

14. You have inherited the administrator position of a network that has already completed its migration from Windows NT to Windows 2000. The network consists of a single domain that serves two locations with five servers at each site. The replication topology has proven to be solid, and the monitoring tasks that were in place when you arrived show that there are no errors. Each site has two domain controllers for redundancy, and each one has a DNS server to support name resolution. Your first tasks are to learn how the directory has been designed and how the structure of the OUs is providing management capabilities to the domain. As you begin to settle in, you add some new users to the domain, but some of them complain that they cannot do what you have told them they could do. As you investigate the problem, you determine that Group Policy is not being applied when the users with the problems log on to the network. What are the possible reasons for this problem? (Choose all that apply.)

   A. The policy has been blocked for the OU of which the users are members.

   B. The users are not members of the OU that is subject to the Group Policy object.

   C. The users are members of a security group whose Apply Group Policy ACE is set to Deny.

   D. Policies must be applied to the specific OU that contains the users before they can applied.

15. A systems administrator creates a local Printer object, but it doesn't show up in Active Directory when a user executes a search for all printers. Which of the following are possible reasons for this? (Choose all that apply.)

   A. The printer was not shared.

   B. The List In Directory option is unchecked.

   C. The client does not have permissions to view the printer.

   D. The printer is malfunctioning

Answers to Review Questions

1. A, B, C, D. The Active Directory Users and Computers tool was designed to simplify the administration of Active Directory objects. All of the above operations can be carried out using the Active Directory Users and Computers tool.

2. A. Inheritance is the process by which permissions placed on parent OUs affect child OUs. In this example, the permissions change for the higher-level OU (Texas) automatically caused a change in permissions for the lower-level OU (Austin).

3. B, E. The LostandFound folder contains information about objects that could not be replicated among domain controllers. Enabling the Advanced Options item in the View menu will allow Isabel to see the LostandFound and System folders.

4. A. Through the use of the filtering functionality, you can choose which types of objects you want to see using the Active Directory Users and Computers interface. Several of the other choices may work, but they require changes to Active Directory settings or objects.

5. A, C. OUs can be easily moved and renamed without requiring the promotion of domain controllers and network changes. This makes OU structure much more flexible and a good choice since the company may soon undergo a merger. Since security administration is important, delegation can be used to control administrative permissions at the OU level.

6. A, B, C, D. All of the options listed are common tasks presented in the Delegation of Control Wizard.

7. D. The Delegation of Control Wizard is designed to allow administrators to set up permissions on specific Active Directory objects.

8. A. OUs are created to reflect a company's logical organization. Since your focus is on the OU structure, you should be primarily concerned with business requirements. Other Active Directory features can be used to accommodate the network topology and technical issues (such as performance and scalability).

9. D. When you choose to delegate custom tasks, you have many more options for what you can delegate control of and what permissions you can apply. In this case, you would delegate control of Organizational Unit objects and set the permissions to Create All Child Objects, Read All Properties, and Write All Properties.

10. C. The filtering options would cause other objects to be hidden (although they still exist). Another explanation (but not one of the choices) is that a higher-level systems administrator modified the administrator's permissions using the Delegation of Control Wizard.

11. C. You need to publish shares in the directory before they are available to the users of the directory. If NetBIOS is still enabled on the network, the shares will be visible to the NetBIOS tools and clients, but you do not have to enable NetBIOS on shares. While replication must occur before the shares are available in the directory, it is unlikely that the replication will not have occurred by the next day. If this is the case, then you have other problems with the directory as well.

12. D. When you delete an object in the directory, such as a user, it is gone and cannot be brought back. You could use a tape backup to bring an object back, but this would be a major undertaking for something like that and you would lose any other changes that occurred since the last backup. The best way to deal with an employee leaving the organization is to disable the account and wait for a specified period before permanently removing it. In many cases, the person who replaces them will need the same resources, so you can then simply rename the account, change the password, and re-enable the account for the new user.

13. A. The Sharing tab contains a check box that you can use to list the printer in Active Directory.

14. A, B, C. If you or a previous administrator has blocked policies from flowing to an OU, then it will not apply to users in the OU. If the users are not in an OU that is subject to the policy, then the users will not receive that policy. If the users are members of a security group with an ACE set to Deny The Apply Group Policy, then it will block the policy. In general, policies flow down the directory tree if they are not blocked, so you do not have to apply the policy to each individual OU.

15. A, B, C. The first three reasons listed are explanations for why a printer may not show up within Active Directory. The printer will appear as an object in AD even if it is malfunctioning.

Chapter 6

Active Directory Security

MICROSOFT EXAM OBJECTIVES COVERED IN THIS CHAPTER:

✓ **Monitor and manage network security. Actions include auditing and detecting security breaches.**

- Configure user-account lockout settings.
- Configure user-account password length, history, age, and complexity.
- Configure Group Policy to run logon scripts.
- Link Group Policy objects.
- Enable and configure auditing.
- Monitor security by using the system security log file.

✓ **Create, manage, and troubleshoot User and Group objects in Active Directory.**

- Create and configure user and computer accounts for new and existing users.
- Troubleshoot groups. Considerations include nesting, scope, and type.
- Configure a user account by using Active Directory Users and Computers. Settings include passwords and assigning groups.
- Perform a search for objects in Active Directory.
- Use templates to create user accounts.
- Reset an existing computer account.

✓ **Manage object and container permissions.**

- Use the Delegation of Control wizard to configure inherited and explicit permissions.

- Configure and troubleshoot object permissions by using object access control lists (ACLs).

✓ **Implement and manage security policies by using Group Policy.**

- Use security templates to implement security policies.
- Analyze the security configuration of a computer by using the secedit command and Security Configuration and Analysis.
- Modify domain security policy to comply with corporate standards.

The "Configure user-account lockout settings" and "Configure user-account password length, history, age, and complexity" subobjectives are covered in Chapter 9, "Managing Client and Server Computers." The "Configure Group Policy to run logon scripts" and "Link Group Policy objects" subobjectives are covered in Chapter 7, "Managing Group Policy."

The "Perform a search for objects in Active Directory" and "Reset an existing computer account" subobjectives are covered in Chapter 5, "Administering Active Directory."

One of the most fundamental responsibilities of any systems administrator is security management. Therefore, all network operating systems offer some way to grant or deny access to resources, such as files and printers. Active Directory is no exception. You can define fundamental security objects through the use of the users, groups, and computers security principals. Then you can allow or disallow access to resources by granting specific *permissions* to each of these objects.

In this chapter, you'll learn how to implement security within Active Directory. Through the use of Active Directory tools, you can quickly and easily configure the settings that you require in order to protect information. Note, however, that proper planning for security permissions is an important prerequisite. If your security settings are too restrictive, users may not be able to perform their job functions. Worse yet, they may try to circumvent security measures. On the other end of the spectrum, if security permissions are too lax, users may be able to access and modify sensitive company resources.

The exam covers several examples of how to use Active Directory to apply permissions to resources on the network. Particular attention is placed on the evaluation of permissions when applied to different groups and the flow of permissions through the OUs via Group Policy, which is discussed in depth in Chapter 7. With all of this in mind, let's start looking at how you can manage security within Active Directory.

In order to complete the exercises in this chapter, you should understand the basics of working with Active Directory objects. If you are not familiar with creating and managing users, groups, computers, and organizational units, you should review the information in Chapter 5 before continuing.

Active Directory Security Overview

Microsoft ✓ ***Exam Objective***

Create, manage, and troubleshoot User and Group objects in Active Directory.

- Troubleshoot groups. Considerations include nesting, scope, and type.

One of the fundamental design goals for Active Directory is to define a single, centralized repository of users and information resources. Active Directory records information about all of the users, computers, and resources on your network. Each domain acts as a security boundary, and members of the domain (including workstations, servers, and domain controllers) share information about the objects within them.

The information stored within Active Directory determines which resources are accessible to which users. Through the use of permissions that are assigned to Active Directory objects, you can control all aspects of network security.

Many security experts state that 20 percent of real-world network security is a technical issue and that 80 percent of it is a process-and-policy one. Don't make the mistake of trying to solve all security problems through system(s) configurations. You also need to establish and enforce business rules, physically secure your resources, and ensure that users are aware of any restrictions.

In this chapter, we'll cover the details of security as it pertains to Active Directory. Note, however, that this is only one aspect of true network security. That is, you should always be sure that you have implemented appropriate access control settings for the file system, network devices, and other resources. Let's start by looking at the various components of network security.

Security Principals

Security principals are Active Directory objects that are assigned security identifiers (SIDs). A SID is a unique identifier that is used to manage any object to which permissions can be assigned. Security principals are assigned permissions to perform certain actions and access certain network resources.

The basic types of Active Directory objects that serve as security principals include the following:

User Accounts   These objects identify individual users on your network. User accounts include information such as the user's name and their password. User accounts are the fundamental unit of security administration.

Groups   There are two main types of groups: *security groups* and *distribution groups*. Both types of groups can contain user accounts. Security groups are used for easing the management of security permissions. Distribution groups, on the other hand, are used solely for the purpose of sending e-mail. Distribution groups are *not* considered security principals. We'll cover the details of groups in the next section.

Computer Accounts   Computer accounts identify which client computers are members of particular domains. Since these computers participate in the Active Directory database, systems administrators can manage security settings that affect the computer. Computer accounts are used to determine whether a computer can join a domain and for authentication purposes. As we'll see later in this chapter, systems administrators can also place restrictions on certain computer settings to increase security. These settings apply to the computer and, therefore, also apply to any user who is using it (regardless of the permissions granted to the user account).

Security principals can be assigned permissions so that they can access various network resources, can be given user rights, and may have their actions tracked (through *auditing*, covered later in this chapter). The three types of security principals—users, groups, and computers—form the basis of the Active Directory security architecture. As a systems administrator, you will likely spend a portion of your time managing permissions for these objects.

It is important to understand that, since a unique SID defines each security principal, deleting a security principal is an irreversible process. For example, if you delete a user account and then later re-create one with the same name, you will need to reassign permissions and group membership settings for the new account.

Note that other objects—such as organizational units (OUs)—do not function as security principals. What this means is that you can apply certain settings (such as Group Policy) on all of the objects within an OU. However, you cannot specifically set permissions with respect to the OU itself. The purpose of OUs is to logically organize other Active Directory objects based on business needs. This distinction is important to remember.

Understanding Users and Groups

The fundamental security principals that are used for security administration include users and groups. In this section, you'll learn how users and groups interact and about the different types of groups that can be created.

Types of Groups

When dealing with groups, you should make the distinction between local security principals and domain security principals. Local users and groups are used for assigning the permissions necessary to access the local machine. For example, we may assign the permissions necessary to restart a domain controller to a specific local group. Domain users and groups, on the other hand, are used throughout the domain. These objects are available on any of the computers within the Active Directory domain and between domains that have a trust relationship.

There are two main types of groups used in Active Directory:

Security Groups   Security groups are considered security principals. They can contain user accounts. To make administration simpler, permissions are usually granted to groups. This allows for changing permissions easily at the Active Directory level (instead of at the level of the resource on which the permissions are assigned).

Security groups can be used for e-mail purposes—that is, a systems administrator can automatically e-mail all of the user accounts that exist within a group. Of course, the systems administrator must specify the e-mail addresses for these accounts.

Active Directory Contact objects can also be placed within security groups, but security permissions will not apply to them.

Distribution Groups   Distribution groups are not considered security principals and are used only for the purpose of sending e-mail messages. You can add users to distribution groups just as you would add them to security groups. Distribution groups can also be placed within OUs for easier management. They are useful, for example, if you need to send e-mail messages to an entire department or business unit within Active Directory.

Understanding the differences between security and distribution groups is important in an Active Directory environment. For the most part, systems administrators use security groups for daily administration of permissions. On the other hand, systems administrators who are responsible for maintaining e-mail distribution lists generally use distribution groups to logically group members of departments and business units.

When working in native-mode domains (domains that support the use of only Windows 2000 domain controllers), security groups can be converted to or from distribution groups. When running in mixed mode (which allows the use of Windows NT domain controllers), group types cannot be changed.

Group Scope

In addition to being classified by type, each group is also given a specific scope. The scope of a group defines two characteristics. First, it determines the level of security that applies to a group. Second, it determines which users can be added to the group. Group scope is an important concept in network environments because it ultimately defines which resources users will be able to access.

The three types of group scope are as follows:

Domain Local   The scope of *domain local groups* extends as far as the local machine. When you're using the Active Directory Users and Computers tool, domain local accounts apply to the computer for which you are viewing information. Domain local groups are used to assign permissions to local resources, such as files and printers. They can contain *global groups*, *universal groups*, and user accounts.

Global   The scope of global groups is limited to a single domain. Global groups may contain any of the users that are a part of the Active Directory domain in which the global groups reside. Global groups are often used for managing domain security permissions based on job functions. For example, if we need to specify permissions for the Engineering department, we could create one or more global groups (such as Engineering-Managers and EngineeringDevelopers). We could then assign security permissions to each group for any of the resources within the domain.

Universal   Universal groups can contain users from any domains within an Active Directory forest. Therefore, they are used for managing security across domains. Universal groups are available only when you're running

Active Directory in native mode. When managing multiple domains, it is often helpful to group global groups within universal groups. For instance, if you have an Engineering global group in Domain 1 and an Engineering global group in Domain 2, you could create a universal AllEngineers group that contains both of the global groups. Now, whenever security permissions must be assigned to all engineers within the organization, you need only assign permissions to the AllEngineers universal group.

In order to process authentication between domains, information about the membership in universal groups is stored in the Global Catalog (GC). Keep this in mind if you ever plan to place users directly into universal groups and bypass global groups because all of the users will be enumerated in the GC, which will impact size and performance.

As you can see, the main properties for each of these group types are affected by whether Active Directory is running in mixed mode or native mode. Each of these scope levels is designed for a specific purpose and will ultimately affect the types of security permissions that can be assigned to them.

There are several limitations on group functionality when running in mixed-mode domains. Specifically, the following limitations exist:

- Universal security groups are not available in mixed-mode domains.

- Changing the scope of groups is not allowed.

- There are limitations to group nesting. Specifically, the only nesting allowed is global groups contained in domain local groups.

When running in native-mode domains, you can make the following group scope changes:

- Domain local groups can be changed to a universal group. This change can be made only if the domain local group does not contain any other domain local groups.

- A global group can be changed to a universal group. This change can be made only if the global group is not a member of any other global groups.

Universal groups themselves cannot be converted into any other group scope type. Changing group scope can be helpful when your security administration or business needs change.

Built-In Local Groups

Built-in local groups are used to perform administrative functions on the local server. Because they have preassigned permissions and privileges, they allow systems administrators to easily assign common management functions. The list of built-in local groups includes the following:

Account Operators   These users are able to create and modify domain user and group accounts. Members of this group are generally responsible for the daily administration of Active Directory.

Administrators   Members of the Administrators group are given full permissions to perform any functions within the Active Directory domain and on the local computer. This includes the ability to access all files and resources that reside on any server within the domain. As you can see, this is a very powerful account.

In general, you should restrict the number of users who are included in this group since most common administration functions do not require this level of access.

Backup Operators   One of the problems associated with backing up data in a secure network environment is that there must be a way to bypass standard file system security in order to copy files. Although you could place users in the Administrators group, this usually provides more permissions than necessary. Members of the Backup Operators group are able to bypass standard file system security for the purpose of backup and recovery only. They cannot, however, directly access or open files within the file system.

Generally, the permissions assigned to the Backup Operators group are used by backup software applications and data.

Guests   The Guests group is typically used for providing access to resources that generally do not require security. For example, if you have a network share that provides files that should be made available to all network users, you can assign permissions to allow members of the Guest group to access those files.

Print Operators   Members of the Print Operators group are given permissions to administer all of the printers within a domain. This includes common functions such as changing the priority of print jobs and deleting items from the print queue.

Replicator   The Replicator group was created to allow the replication of files between the computers in a domain. Accounts that are used for replication-related tasks are added to this group to provide them with the permissions necessary to keep files synchronized across multiple computers.

Server Operators   A common administrative task is managing server configuration. Members of the Server Operators group are granted the permissions necessary to manage services, shares, and other system settings.

Users   The Users group, as shown in Figure 6.1, is often used as a generic grouping for network accounts. Usually, this group is given minimal permissions and is used for the application of security settings that apply to most employees within an organization.

In addition, two main user accounts are created during the promotion of a domain controller. The first is the Administrator account. This account is assigned the password that is provided by a systems administrator during the promotion process and has full permissions to perform all actions within the domain. The second account is Guest, which is disabled by default. The purpose of the Guest account is to provide anonymous access to users who do not have an individual logon and password for use within the domain. Although this might be useful in some situations, it is generally recommended that the Guest account be disabled to increase security.

FIGURE 6.1   Contents of the default Users folder

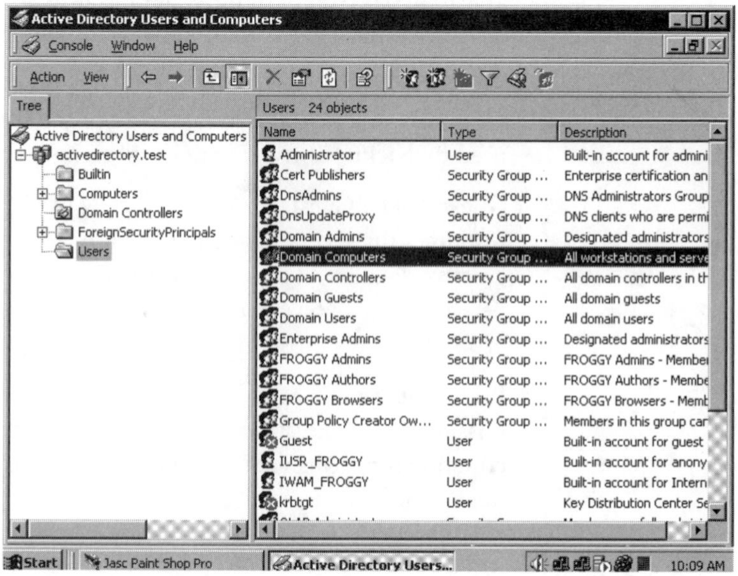

Predefined Global Groups

As we mentioned earlier in this chapter, global groups are used for managing permissions at the domain level. The following predefined global groups are installed in the Users folder:

Cert Publishers   Certificates are used to increase security by allowing for strong authentication methods. User accounts are placed within the Cert Publishers group if they require the ability to publish security certificates. Generally, these accounts are used by Active Directory security services.

Domain Computers   All of the computers that are a member of the domain are generally members of the Domain Computers group. This includes any workstations or servers that have joined the domain but does not include the domain controllers.

Domain Admins   Members of the Domain Admins group have full permissions to manage all of the Active Directory objects for this domain. This is a powerful account; therefore, membership should be restricted to only those users who require full permissions.

Domain Controllers   All of the domain controllers for a given domain are generally included within the Domain Controllers group.

Domain Guests   Generally, members of the Domain Guests group are given minimal permissions with respect to resources. Systems administrators may place user accounts in this group if they require only basic access or require temporary permissions within the domain.

Domain Users   The Domain Users group usually contains all of the user accounts for the given domain. This group is generally given basic permissions to resources that do not require higher levels of security. A common example is a public file share.

Enterprise Admins   Members of the Enterprise Admins group are given full permissions to perform actions within the entire domain forest. This includes functions such as managing trust relationships and adding new domains to trees and forests.

Group Policy Creator Owners   Members of the Group Policy Creator Owners group are able to create and modify *Group Policy* settings for objects within the domain. This allows them to enable security settings on OUs (and the objects that they contain).

Schema Admins   Members of the Schema Admins group are given permissions to modify the Active Directory schema. This, for example, allows them to create additional fields of information for user accounts. This is a very powerful function since any changes to the schema will be propagated to all of the domains and domain controllers within an Active Directory forest. Furthermore, changes to the schema cannot be undone (although additional options can be disabled).

Members of each of these groups are able to perform specific tasks related to the management of Active Directory.

In addition to the groups listed above, new ones might be created for specific services and applications that are installed on the server. Specifically, services that run on domain controllers and servers will be created as security groups with domain local scope. For example, if a domain controller is running the DNS service, the DNSAdmins and DNSUpdateProxy groups will be available. Similarly, installing the DHCP service creates the DHCPUsers and DHCPAdministrators groups. The purpose of these groups varies based on the functionality of the applications being installed.

Foreign Security Principals

In environments that consist of more than one domain, you may need to grant permissions to users that reside in multiple domains. Generally, this is managed through the use of Active Directory trees and forests. However, in some cases, you may want to provide resources to users that are contained in domains that are not part of the same forest.

Active Directory uses the concept of *foreign security principals* to allow permissions to be assigned to users that are not part of the same Active Directory forest. This process is automatic and does not require the intervention of systems administrators. The foreign security principals can then be added to domain local groups, which, in turn, can be granted permissions for resources within the domain.

Managing Security and Permissions

Now that you have a good understanding of the basic issues, terms, and Active Directory objects that pertain to security, it's time to look at how you can apply this information to secure your network resources. The general practice for managing security is to assign users to groups and then grant permissions to the groups so that they can access certain resources.

For ease of management and to implement a hierarchical structure, you can place groups within OUs. You can also assign Group Policy settings to all of the objects contained within an OU. By using this method, you can combine the benefits of a hierarchical structure (through OUs) with the use of security principals. Figure 6.2 provides a diagram of this process.

FIGURE 6.2   An overview of security management

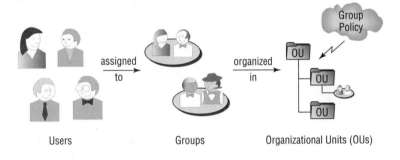

The primary tool used to manage security permissions for users, groups, and computers is the Active Directory Users and Computers snap-in. Using this tool, you can create and manage Active Directory objects and organize them based on your business needs. Common tasks for many systems administrators might include the following:

- Resetting a user's password (for example, in cases where they forget the password)

- Creating new user accounts (when, for instance, a new employee joins the company)

- Modifying group memberships based on changes in job requirements and functions

- Disabling user accounts (when, for example, users will be out of the office for long periods of time and will not require network resource access)

Permissions

Once you've properly grouped your users, you'll need to set the actual permissions that will affect the objects within Active Directory. The actual permissions available vary based on the type of object. Table 6.1 provides an example of some of the permissions that can be applied to various Active Directory objects and an explanation of what each permission does:

TABLE 6.1 Permissions of Active Directory Objects

Permission	Explanation
Control Access	Changes security permissions on the object.
Create Child	Creates objects within an OU (such as other OUs).
Delete Child	Deletes child objects within an OU.
Delete Tree	Deletes an OU and the objects within it.
List Contents	Views objects within an OU.
List Object	Views a list of the objects within an OU.
Read	Views properties of an object (such as a user name).
Write	Modifies properties of an object.

ACLs and ACEs

Each object in Active Directory has an access control list (ACL). The ACL is a list of user accounts and groups that are allowed to access the resource. For each ACL, there is an access control entry (ACE) that defines what a user or a group can actually do at the resource. Deny permissions are always listed first. This means that if users have Deny permissions through user or group membership, they will not be allowed to access the object, even if they have explicit Allow permissions through other user or group permissions. Figure 6.3 shows an ACL for the Sales OU.

Now that you have a good idea of the basis of the Active Directory security architecture, let's move on to covering exactly how security is implemented. We'll cover the steps required to set up permissions in the next section.

FIGURE 6.3   ACL for an OU

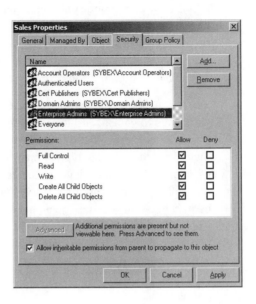

🌐 Real World Scenario

Using Groups Effectively

You are a new systems administrator for a medium-sized organization, and your network spans a single campus-type environment. The previous administrator whom you replaced was the main person who migrated the network from Windows NT to Windows 2000. There are no real complaints with the network, and everyone seems happy with their new workstations. The environment is very collegial, with most communications on a first-name basis, and a great deal of your job is done in the hallway as you bump into people. As you familiarize yourself with the network, you soon realize that the previous administrator had a very ad hoc approach to administration. Many of the permissions to resources had been given to individual accounts as people asked for them. There doesn't seem to be any particular strategy in the design of the directory or allocation of resources.

In one of your meetings with management, you are told that the company has acquired another company, and if this acquisition goes well, there will be several more to follow. You are informed of these sensitive plans because management does not want any hiccups in the information system as these new organizations are absorbed into the existing company.

You immediately realize that management practices of the past for this network have to vanish, and they need to be replaced with the best practices that have been developed for networks over the years. One of the fundamental practices in this type of environment is the use of groups to apply permissions and give privileges to users throughout the network. While it is quite simple to give permissions individually, and in some cases it seems overkill to create a group, give permissions to the group, and then add a user to the group, it really pays off in the long run, regardless of how small your network is today. One constant in the networking world is that networks grow. And when they grow, it much easier to add users to a well-thought-out system of groups and consistently applied policies and permissions.

Don't get caught up in the "easy" way of dealing with each request as it comes down the pike. Take the time to figure out how the system will benefit from a more structured approach. Visualize your network as already large with numerous accounts, even if it is still small, and when it grows, you will be well positioned to keep management of the network as smooth as possible.

Implementing Active Directory Security

You will use the Active Directory Users and Computers tool for configuring most of the Active Directory security settings.

Exercise 6.1 walks you through the steps required to create and manage users and groups. If you are unfamiliar with basic Active Directory administration steps, you will find it useful to review Chapter 5.

Microsoft
Exam
Objective

Create, manage, and troubleshoot User and Group objects in Active Directory.

- Create and configure user and computer accounts for new and existing users.

- Configure a user account by using Active Directory Users and Computers. Settings include passwords and assigning groups.

- Use templates to create user accounts.

Manage object and container permissions.

- Use the Delegation of Control wizard to configure inherited and explicit permissions.

- Configure and troubleshoot object permissions by using object access control lists (ACLs).

EXERCISE 6.1

Creating and Managing Users and Groups

In this exercise, you will create users and groups within Active Directory and then place users into groups.

1. Open the Active Directory Users and Computers tool.

2. Create the following top-level OUs:

    Sales

    Marketing

    Engineering

    HR

3. Create the following User objects within the Sales container (use the defaults for all fields not listed):

    a. First Name: **John**

    Last Name: **Sales**

    User Logon Name: **jsales**

EXERCISE 6.1 *(continued)*

b. First Name: **Linda**

Last Name: **Manager**

User Logon Name: **lmanager**

4. Create the following User objects within the Marketing container (use the defaults for all fields not listed):

a. First Name: **Jane**

Last Name: **Marketing**

User Logon Name: **jmarketing**

b. First Name: **Monica**

Last Name: **Manager**

User Logon Name: **mmanager**

5. Create the following User object within the Engineering container (use the defaults for all fields not listed):

a. First Name: **Bob**

Last Name: **Engineer**

User Logon Name: **bengineer**

6. Right-click the HR container, and select New ≻ Group. Use the name **Managers** for the group, and specify Global for the group scope and Security for the group type. Click OK to create the group.

7. To assign users to the Managers group, right-click the Group object and select Properties. Change to the Members tab, and click Add. From the list, select Linda Manager and Monica Manager, and then click OK. You will see the group membership list. Click OK to finish adding the users to the group.

8. When finished creating users and groups, close Active Directory Users and Computers.

Notice that you can add users to groups regardless of the OU in which they're contained. In Exercise 6.1, for example, we added two user accounts from different OUs into a group that was created in a third OU. This type of flexibility allows you to easily manage user and group accounts based on your business organization.

The Active Directory Users and Computers tool also allows you to perform common functions by simply right-clicking an object and selecting actions from the context menu. For example, we could right-click a user account and select Add Members To Group to quickly change group membership.

Using User Templates

Sometimes you will find it necessary to have several users with the same security settings. Rather than creating each user from scratch and making configuration changes to each one manually, you can create one user template, configure it, and copy it as many times as necessary. Each copy retains the configuration, group membership, and permissions of the original, but you must specify a new username, password, and full name. Exercise 6.2 shows you how to create and use a user template.

EXERCISE 6.2

Creating and Using User Templates

In this exercise, you will create a user template, make configuration changes, and create a new user based on the template. You should have completed the previous exercise before beginning this one.

1. Open Active Directory Users and Computers.

2. Create the following User object within the Sales container (use the defaults for all fields not listed):

   First Name: **Sales User**

   Last Name: **Template**

   User Logon Name: **salesusertemplate**

3. Create a new group called **SalesUsers**, and add salesusertemplate to the group membership.

4. Right-click salesusertemplate and select Copy from the context menu.

5. Enter the username, first name, last name, and password for the new "real" user, and close the dialog box.

EXERCISE 6.2 *(continued)*

6. Right-click the user you created in step 5, select Properties, and click the Member Of tab.

7. Verify that the new user is a member of the SalesUsers group.

Delegating Control of Active Directory Objects

A common administrative function related to the use of Active Directory involves managing objects. OUs can be used to logically group objects so that they can be easily managed. Once you have placed the appropriate Active Directory objects within OUs, you will be ready to delegate control of these objects.

Delegation is the process by which a higher-level security administrator assigns permissions to other users. For example, if Admin A is a member of the Domain Admins group, he will be able to delegate control of any OU within the domain to Admin B. Exercise 6.3 walks through the steps required to delegate control of OUs.

EXERCISE 6.3

Delegating Control of Active Directory Objects

In this exercise, we will delegate control of Active Directory objects. In order to complete the steps in this exercise, you must have already completed Exercise 6.1.

1. Open Active Directory Users and Computers.

2. Create a new user within the Engineering OU, using the following information (use the default settings for any fields not specified):

   a. First Name: **Robert**

   Last Name: **Admin**

   User Logon Name: **radmin**

3. Right-click the Sales OU, and select Delegate Control. This will start the Delegation of Control Wizard. Click Next.

EXERCISE 6.3 *(continued)*

4. To add users and groups to which you want to delegate control, click Add. From the list of users, select Robert Admin. Click OK and then Next to continue.

5. Click the Delegate The Following Common Tasks radio button, and place a check mark next to the following options:

Create, Delete, And Manage User Accounts

Reset Passwords On User Accounts

Read All User Information

Create, Delete, And Manage Groups

EXERCISE 6.3 *(continued)*

Modify The Membership Of A Group

6. Click Next to continue, and then click Finish to save the changes. Now when the user Robert Admin logs on, he will be able to perform common administrative functions for all of the objects contained within the Sales OU.

7. When finished, close Active Directory Users and Computers.

Using Group Policy for Security

Through the use of Active Directory, systems administrators can define Group Policy objects and then apply them to OUs. We'll cover the details of creating, assigning, and managing Group Policy settings later in Chapter 7.

| *Microsoft* ✔ *Exam* *Objective* | **Implement and manage security policies by using Group Policy.** |

Exercise 6.4 walks through the steps required to create a basic Group Policy for the purpose of enforcing security settings.

EXERCISE 6.4

Applying Security Policies by Using Group Policy

In this exercise, you will assign security permissions by using Group Policy. In order to complete the steps of this exercise, you must have already completed Exercise 6.1.

1. Open the Active Directory Users and Computers tool.

2. Right-click the Engineering OU, and select Properties.

3. Change to the Group Policy tab, and click New. Type **Engineering Security Settings** for the name of the new Group Policy.

4. To specify the Group Policy settings, click Edit.

EXERCISE 6.4 *(continued)*

5. In the Group Policy window, open Computer Configuration ➢ Windows Settings ➢ Security Settings ➢ Account Policies ➢ Password Policy.

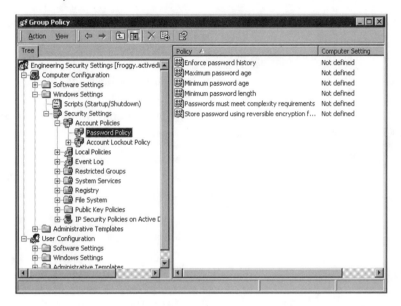

6. In the right-hand pane, double-click the Minimum Password Length setting. In the Security Policy Setting dialog box, place a check mark next to the Define This Policy Setting option. Leave the default value of 7 characters. Click OK.

7. Open User Configuration ➤ Administrative Templates ➤ Control Panel. Double-click Disable Control Panel, select Enabled, and then click OK.

8. Close the Group Policy window to save the settings you chose. Click OK and Close to enable the Security Group Policy for the Engineering OU.

9. To view the security permissions for a Group Policy object, right-click the Engineering OU and select Properties. On the Group Policy tab, highlight the Engineering Security Settings Group Policy object, and select Properties.

10. Select the Security tab. Click Add, and select Linda Manager from the list of users. Click Add and OK. Highlight Linda Manager, and allow this user the Read and Write permissions.

11. Click OK twice to save the changes. Linda Manager will now be able to view and change information for objects in the Sales OU.

12. When finished, close the Active Directory Users and Computers tool.

The settings that you specify will apply to all of the security principals included within the OU to which the Group Policy applies.

Using the Security Configuration and Analysis Utility

The power and flexibility of Windows-based operating systems are both a benefit and a liability. On the plus side, the many configuration options available allow users and systems administrators to modify and customize settings to their preference. On the negative side, however, the full level of functionality can cause problems. For example, novice users might attempt to delete critical system files or incorrectly uninstall programs to free up disk space. So how can you prevent these types of problems? One method is to strictly enforce the types of actions that users can perform. Since most settings for the Windows 2000 interface can be configured in the Registry, you could edit the appropriate settings using the RegEdit command.

Although you could manage security settings manually through the use of Registry changes, this process can become quite tedious. Furthermore, manually modifying the Registry is a dangerous process and one that is bound to cause problems due to human error. In order to make the creation and application of security settings easier, Microsoft has included the Security Configuration and Analysis tool with Windows 2000. This tool can be used to create, modify, and apply security settings in the Registry through the use of security template files. *Security templates* allow systems administrators to define security settings once and then store this information in a file that can be applied to other computers.

These template files offer a user-friendly way of configuring common settings for Windows 2000–based operating systems. For example, instead of

Implement and manage security policies by using Group Policy.

- Use security templates to implement security policies.

- Analyze the security configuration of a computer by using the secedit command and Security Configuration and Analysis.

- Modify domain security policy to comply with corporate standards.

searching through the Registry (which is largely undocumented) for specific keys, a systems administrator can choose from a list of common options. The template file provides a description of the settings, along with information about the Registry key(s) to which the modifications must be made. Templates can be stored and applied to users and computers. For example, we could create three configurations entitled Level 1, Level 2, and Level 3. We may use the Level 3 template for high-level managers and engineers, while the Level 1 and Level 2 templates are used for all other users who require basic functionality.

The overall process for working with the Security Configuration and Analysis tool is as follows:

1. Open or create a security database file.

2. Import an existing template file.

3. Analyze the local computer.

4. Make any setting changes.

5. Save any template changes.

6. Export the new template (optional).

7. Apply the changes to the local computer (optional).

There is no default icon for the *Security Configuration and Analysis utility*. In order to access it, you must manually choose this snap-in from within the Microsoft Management Console (MMC). Exercise 6.5 walks you through the steps required to use the Security Configuration and Analysis utility.

EXERCISE 6.5

Using the Security Configuration and Analysis Utility

In this exercise, you will use the Security Configuration and Analysis utility to create and modify security configurations:

1. Choose Start ➤ Run, type **mmc**, and press Enter. This will open a blank MMC.

2. In the Console menu, select Add/Remove Snap-In. Click Add. Select the Security Configuration And Analysis item, and then click Add. Click Close.

3. You will see that the Security Configuration and Analysis snap-in has been added to the configuration. Click OK to continue.

4. Within the MMC, right-click Security Configuration And Analysis, and select Open Database. Change to a local directory on your computer, and create a new security database file named **SecurityTest.sdb**. Note the location of this file, because you'll need it in later steps. Click OK.

EXERCISE 6.5 *(continued)*

5. Next, you'll be prompted to open a security template file. By default, these files are stored within the `Security\Templates` directory of your Windows 2000 system root. From the list, select DC Security, and place a check mark in the Clear This Database Before Importing box. Click Open to load the template file.

6. Now that we have created a security database file and opened a template, we can start performing useful security tasks. Notice that several tasks are available. To perform an analysis on the security configuration of the local computer, right-click the Security Configuration and Analysis utility, and select Analyze Computer Now. When prompted, enter the path to a local directory with the filename `SecurityTest.log`. Click OK to begin the analysis process.

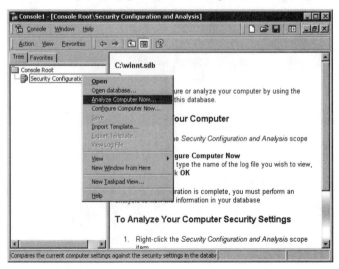

7. You will see the Security Configuration and Analysis utility begin to analyze your computer.

8. When the process has been completed, you will be able to view the current security settings for the local computer. Navigate through the various items to view the current security configuration.

9. To make changes to this template, expand the Password Policy object under the Account Policies object. Double-click the Enforce Password History item. Place a check mark next to the Define This Policy In The Database option, and type **2** for Passwords Remembered. Click OK to make the setting change. Note that this change in setting was not enabled for the local computer—the change was implemented only within the security database file.

10. To save the changes to the security database file, right-click the Security Configuration And Analysis object, and select Save.

11. To export the current settings to a template file, right-click the Security Configuration And Analysis object, and select Export Template. You will be prompted for the location and filename to which these settings should be saved. Be sure to choose a meaningful name so that other systems administrators will understand the purpose of this template.

12. So far, the configuration change we made has not yet been applied to any machines. To apply the change to the local computer, right-click the Security Configuration And Analysis object, and select Configure Computer Now. You will be prompted to enter the path for a log file. Enter any path on the local computer, and specify **SecurityTest2.log** as the filename. Click OK. You will see the settings being applied to the local computer.

13. To quickly view the contents of the log file for the most recent operation, right-click the Security Configuration And Analysis object, and select View Log.

14. When you have finished, exit the Security Configuration And Analysis tool by closing the MMC.

The *Secedit.exe* Command

All of the functionality of the Security Configuration and Analysis utility has also been built into a command-line utility called `secedit.exe`. One advantage of using `secedit.exe` is that you can perform a batch analysis. Just like the Security Configuration and Analysis utility, the command-line utility is database driven, meaning that you can use switches to access database and configuration files. The `secedit.exe` command performs the following high-level functions: analysis, configuration, export function, and validation. Table 6.2 lists the `secedit.exe` switches and their functions.

TABLE 6.2 *Secedit.exe* Switches

Switch	Valid With	Function
/analyze	Function	Analyzes system security.
/configure	Function	Configures system security by applying a stored template.
/refreshpolicy	Function	Reapplies security settings to the GPO.
/export	Function	Exports a template from the database to the template file.
/validate	Function	Validates the syntax of a security template.

TABLE 6.2 *Secedit.exe* Switches *(continued)*

Switch	Valid With	Function
[/DB filename]	/analyze, /configure, /export	Required with the /analyze and /configure commands. Optional with others. Specifies the path to the database file.
[/CFG filename]	/analyze, /configure, /export	Required if a new database file is specified. Specifies the path to a security template to import into the database.
[/log logpath]	/analyze, /configure, /export	Specifies the path to the log file generated during the operation.
[/verbose]	/analyze, /configure, /export	Specifies more detailed progress information.
[/quiet]	/analyze, /configure, /export	Suppresses screen output during the operation.
[/overwrite]	/configure	Optional only if [/CFG filename] is used. Completely overwrites the database rather than appending the database.
[/areas area1 area 2]	/configure, /export	Specifies security areas to be applied to the system. Default is all areas. Options are SECURITYPOLICY, GROUP_MGMT, USER_RIGHTS, REGKEYS, FILESTORE, and SERVICES.

TABLE 6.2   *Secedit.exe* Switches *(continued)*

Switch	Valid With	Function
Machine_policy	/refreshpolicy	Refreshes security settings for the local computer.
User_policy	/refreshpolicy	Refreshes security settings for the current local user account.
/enforce	/refreshpolicy	Refreshes security settings even if no changes have been made to the GPO.
/MergedPolicy	/export	Merges local and domain policy in the export file.
Filename	/validate	Indicates the filename of the template to validate.

🌐 Real World Scenario

Enforcing Consistent Security Policies

You are one of 50 systems administrators for a large, multinational organization. As is the case for most of these administrators, you're responsible for all operations related to a portion of an Active Directory domain. Specifically, your job is to manage all of aspects of administration for objects contained within the Austin OU. The Austin office supports nearly 500 employees. Recently, security has become an important concern because the company is growing quickly and new employees are being added almost daily. In addition, the organization deals with customers' sensitive financial information, and the success of the business is based on this information remaining secure. You've been tasked with creating and implementing an Active Directory security policy for the Austin OU.

At first you start looking into the Group Policy settings that might be appropriate for attaining the desired level of security. You create different levels of security based on users' job functions. Specific policy options include restrictions on when users can access network resources and which resources they can access. You also begin to implement settings that "harden" your production servers, especially those that contain sensitive data.

A few days after your analysis has begun, you join the weekly company-wide IT conference call and learn that you're not alone in this task. It seems that systems administrators throughout the company have been given similar tasks. The only difference is that they're all asked to implement policies only for the specific Active Directory objects for which they're responsible. That gets you thinking about pooling resources: That is, although it might make sense to attack this task for just the Austin OU, wouldn't it be great if the entire organization could implement a consistent and uniform security policy? If every systems administrator decided to implement security policies in a different way, this would compromise consistency and ease of administration within the environment. And it's likely that many systems administrators will create useful security policies that the others overlooked. The idea of "think globally, act locally" may apply here.

The Security Configuration and Analysis tool that is included with Windows 2000 Server is designed to solve exactly this type of problem. You find that by using this tool, you can design a set of security configurations and then apply those policies to various computers within the environment. You decide to begin by creating security templates based on business needs. Since the environment has many different requirements (and some that are specific only to a few offices), your goal is to minimize the number of different security templates that you create while still meeting the needs of the entire organization. Perhaps the best way to proceed in this scenario is to pool resources: Many tech-heads are better than one! However, keep in mind that this will be more of a political task than a technical one, at least until the various administrators can come together. One of the results—and benefits—of Active Directory is that many of these decisions can be centralized so the departmental administrators can spend their time helping users with specific issues rather than on duplication of effort. Regardless, creating the appropriate security policies is unlikely to be an easy task—you'll need to confer with systems administrators throughout the company and you'll need to talk to managers and business leaders as well. However, it will be worth the effort to ensure that the entire organization has implemented consistent security policies. Overall, a little extra work up front can save a lot of headaches in the long run.

If any errors occur during the Security Configuration and Analysis process, the results will be stored in the log file that is created. Be sure to examine this file for any errors that might be present in your configuration.

Implementing an Audit Policy

One of the most important aspects of controlling security in networked environments is ensuring that only authorized users are able to access specific resources. Although systems administrators often spend much time managing security permissions, it is almost always possible for a security problem to occur. Sometimes, the best way to find possible security breaches is to actually record the actions taken by specific users. Then, in the case of a security breach (the unauthorized shutdown of a server, for example), systems administrators can examine the log to find the cause of the problem. The Windows 2000 operating system and Active Directory offer the ability to audit a wide range of actions. In this section, we'll look at how you can implement auditing for Active Directory.

Microsoft ✓ *Exam* *Objective*

Monitor and manage network security. Actions include auditing and detecting security breaches.

- Enable and configure auditing.

- Monitor security by using the system security log file.

Overview of Auditing

The act of auditing relates to recording specific actions. From a security standpoint, auditing is used to detect any possible misuse of network resources. Although auditing will not necessarily prevent the misuse of resources, it will help determine when security violations occurred (or were attempted). Furthermore, just the fact that others know that you have implemented auditing may prevent them from attempting to circumvent security.

There are several steps that you will need to complete in order to implement auditing using Windows 2000. These steps include the following:

- Configuring the size and storage settings for the audit logs

- Enabling categories of events to audit

- Specifying which objects and actions should be recorded in the audit log

In this section, you'll learn how to complete these steps.

Note that there are trade-offs to implementing auditing. First and foremost, recording auditing information can consume system resources. This can decrease overall system performance and use up valuable disk space. Second, auditing many events can make the audit log impractical to view. If too much detail is provided, systems administrators are unlikely to scrutinize all of the recorded events. For these reasons, you should always be sure to find a balance between the level of auditing details provided and the performance-management implications of these settings.

Implementing Auditing

Auditing is not an all-or-none type of process. As is the case with security in general, systems administrators must choose specifically which objects and actions they want to audit.

The main categories for auditing include the following:

- Audit account logon events

- Audit account management

- Audit directory service access

- Audit logon events

- Audit object access

- Audit policy change

- Audit privilege use

- Audit process tracking

- Audit system events

In order to audit access to objects stored within Active Directory, you must enable the Audit Directory Service Access option. Then you must specify which objects and actions should be tracked. Exercise 6.6 walks through the steps required to implement auditing of Active Directory objects on domain controllers.

EXERCISE 6.6

Enabling Auditing of Active Directory Objects

In this exercise, you will enable auditing for an Active Directory domain. In order to complete the steps in this exercise, you must have already completed Exercise 6.1.

1. Open the Domain Controller Security Policy tool.

2. Expand Security Settings ➢ Local Policies ➢ Audit Policy.

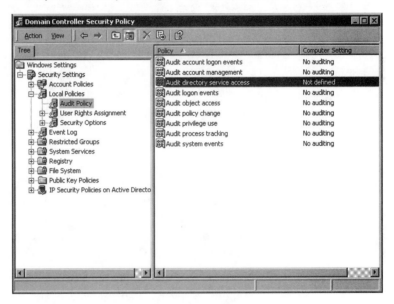

3. Double-click the setting for Audit Directory Service Access. Place a check mark next to the options for Define These Policy Settings, Success, and Failure. Click OK to save the settings.

EXERCISE 6.6

4. Expand Security Settings ≻ Event Log ≻ Settings For Event Logs to see the options associated with the event logs.

5. Double-click the Maximum Security Log Size item, and set the value to 2048KB. Click OK.

6. Double-click the Retain Security Log item, and specify that events should be overwritten after seven days. Click OK. You will be notified that the Retention Method For Security Log option will also be changed. Click OK to accept the changes.

7. When you have finished enabling auditing options, close the Domain Controller Security Policy tool.

Once you have enabled auditing of Active Directory objects, it's time to specify exactly which actions and objects should be audited. Exercise 6.7 walks through the steps required to enable auditing for a specific OU.

EXERCISE 6.7

Enabling Auditing for a Specific OU

In this exercise, you will enable auditing for a specific OU. In order to complete the steps in this exercise, you must have already completed Exercise 6.1 and Exercise 6.6.

1. Open Active Directory Users and Computers.

2. To enable auditing for a specific object, right-click the Engineering OU, and select Properties. Select the Group Policy tab.

3. Highlight the Engineering Security Settings Group Policy object, and select Properties. Select the Security tab, and then click Advanced. Select the Auditing tab. You will see the current auditing settings for this Group Policy object.

4. Click the View/Edit button. Notice that you can view and change auditing settings based on the objects and/or properties. To retain the current settings, click OK. To exit the configuration for the Engineering object, click OK three more times.

5. When you have finished with the auditing settings, close Active Directory Users and Computers.

Viewing Auditing Information

One of the most important aspects of auditing is regularly monitoring the audit logs. If this step is ignored, as it often is in poorly managed environments, the act of auditing is useless. Fortunately, Windows 2000 includes the *Event Viewer* tool that allows systems administrators to quickly and easily view audited events. Using the filtering capabilities of Event Viewer, they can find specific events of interest.

Exercise 6.8 walks through the steps required to generate some auditing events and to examine the data collected for these actions.

EXERCISE 6.8

Generating and Viewing Audit Logs

In this exercise, you will perform some actions that will be audited, and then you will view the information recorded within the audit logs. In order to complete this exercise, you must have already completed the steps in Exercise 6.1 and Exercise 6.7.

1. Open Active Directory Users and Computers.

2. Within the Engineering OU, right-click the Bob Engineer user account, and select Properties. Add the middle initial **A** for this user account, and specify **Software Developer** in the Description box. Click OK to save the changes.

3. Within the Engineering OU, right-click the Robert Admin user account, and select Properties. Add a description of **Engineering IT Admin**, and click OK.

4. Close the Active Directory Users and Computers tool.

5. Open the Event Viewer tool from the Administrative Tools program group. Select the Security item.

EXERCISE 6.8 *(continued)*

6. You will see a list of audited events categorized under Directory Service Access. Note that you can obtain more details about a specific item by double-clicking it.

7. To modify the log file settings, in the right-hand pane of the Computer Management window, right-click the Directory Service Access item, and choose Properties. Change the value for the Maximum Log File Size to **2048KB**, and select the Overwrite Events As Needed option. This will allow you to store more audit events in the log and will ensure that events are cleared out of the log as needed. To save the new settings, click OK.

8. When you have finished viewing the security log, close the Computer Management tool.

Summary

In this chapter, we covered the important topic of security as it pertains to Active Directory. Specifically, we discussed the following:

- The differences between security and distribution groups

- Group scope, including local, global, and universal groups
- Default groups included in Windows 2000 and Active Directory that predefine commonly used sets of permissions
- How permissions can be managed
- How delegation of control can be used to distribute administrative responsibilities
- How Group Policy can be used for security purposes and how the Security Configuration and Analysis utility can ensure consistency
- How and why auditing can be used to increase the security of a networked environment

Thoroughly understanding each of these topics is important when implementing Active Directory in a business environment (and when you're preparing for the exam)!

Exam Essentials

Understand the purpose of security principals.   Security principals are Active Directory objects that can be assigned permissions. Understanding how they work is vital to creating a secure Active Directory environment.

Understand group types and group scope.   The two major types of groups are security and distribution groups, and they have different purposes. Groups can be local, global, or universal.

Understand the purpose and permissions of built-in groups.   The Active Directory environment includes several built-in local and global groups that are designed to simplify common systems administration tasks.

Understand how to use the Delegation of Control wizard to allow distributed administration.   Through the use of this wizard, you can specify which users can control security for particular objects within Active Directory.

Learn how the Security Configuration and Analysis utility can simplify the implementation of security policies.   Through the use of security templates, you can ensure that you are enforcing consistent security policies throughout the environment.

Understand the purpose and function of auditing.   Auditing is helpful in determining the cause of security violations and for troubleshooting permissions-related problems.

Key Terms

Before you take the exam, be certain you are familiar with the following terms:

auditing	Group Policy
delegation	permissions
distribution groups	Security Configuration and Analysis utility
domain local groups	security groups
Event Viewer	security principals
foreign security principals	security templates
global groups	universal groups

Review Questions

1. You are the systems administrator for a medium-sized Active Directory domain. Currently, the environment supports many different domain controllers, some of which are running Windows NT 4 and others that are running Windows 2000. When running in this type of environment, which of the following types of groups *cannot* be used?

   A. Universal security groups

   B. Global groups

   C. Domain local groups

   D. Computer groups

2. Isabel is a systems administrator for an Active Directory environment that is running in native mode. Recently, several managers have reported suspicions about user activities and have asked her to increase security in the environment. Specifically, the requirements are as follows:

   - The accessing of certain sensitive files must be logged.

   - Modifications to certain sensitive files must be logged.

   - Systems administrators must be able to provide information about which users accessed sensitive files and when they were accessed.

   - All logon attempts for specific shared machines must be recorded.

Which of the following steps should Isabel take to meet these requirements? (Choose all that apply.)

A. Enable auditing with the Computer Management tool.

B. Enable auditing with the Active Directory Users and Computers tool.

C. Enable auditing with the Active Directory Domains and Trusts tool.

D. Enable auditing with the Event Viewer tool.

E. View the audit log using the Event Viewer tool.

F. View auditing information using the Computer Management tool.

G. Enable failure and success auditing settings for specific files stored on NTFS volumes.

H. Enable failure and success auditing settings for logon events on specific computer accounts.

3. A systems administrator wants to allow another user the ability to change user account information for all users within a specific OU. Which of the following tools would allow them to do this most easily?

A. Domain Security Policy

B. Domain Controller Security Policy

C. Computer Management

D. Delegation of Control Wizard

4. Minh, an IT manager, has full permissions over several OUs within a small Active Directory domain. Recently, Minh has hired a junior systems administrator to take over some of the responsibilities of administering the objects within these OUs. She gives the new employee access to modify user accounts within two OUs. This process is known as what?

A. Inheritance

B. Transfer of control

C. Delegation

D. Transfer of ownership

5. A systems administrator wants to prevent users from starting or stopping a specific service on domain controllers. Which of the following tools can be used to prevent this from occurring?

   A. Active Directory Users and Computers

   B. Domain Controller Security Policy

   C. Domain Security Policy

   D. Local System Policy

6. As the network administrator of Wanton Accounting Services, you are just getting settled in a comfortable routine. The network was converted from Windows NT and is now deployed as a Windows 2000 network with two sites and one domain. Most of the problems that you have encountered have been from users who needed education on how to search the directory and other nuances on the new system. Recently, you were brought into a meeting with top management and you were told that a few employees who recently left the company joined a competitor. Management wants to know if there were any attempts to obtain information about the company's accounts. They also want to know if anyone internal to the company is trying access the information improperly. When you informed them that you didn't know, the experience was not one that you would want to repeat. Since you are the network administrator, you do not have any control over the perimeter security of the network. What can you audit on the network to make sure that you can answer any future inquiries by management with confidence?

   A. Logon/logoff—success

   B. Logon/logoff—failure

   C. File access and object access—success and failure

   D. Write access for program files—success and failure

   E. User rights—success and failure

7. You are almost finished helping with the migration of a Windows NT network to a Windows 2000 network. There are three locations, and the engineers are creating a single domain for now. There are many rumors that there will be a merger with one of your competitors, and the designers are considering adding a new domain to bring those users into the network. One of your jobs is to help come up with the administrative plans for the designers to manage the users. To outline your task, you are going to build a best-practices approach to giving permissions to resources on your mixed network. Which of the following approaches best suits your situation?

   A. Apply permissions to the domain local groups and add the accounts to this group.

   B. Apply permissions to the domain local groups, add users to global groups, and add the global groups to the domain local groups.

   C. Apply permissions to global groups, add users to universal groups, and place these universal groups into global groups.

   D. Apply permissions to domain local groups, add the users to global groups, add the global groups into universal groups, and add the universal groups into the domain local groups.

8. Which of the following folders in the Active Directory Users and Computers tool is used when users from outside the forest are granted access to resources within a domain?

   A. Users

   B. Computers

   C. Domain Controllers

   D. Foreign Security Principals

9. Lance is a systems administrator for an Active Directory environment that contains four domains. Recently, several managers have reported suspicions about user activities and have asked him to increase security in the environment. Specifically, the requirements are as follows:

- Audit changes to User objects that are contained within a specific OU.

- Allow a special user account called Audit to view and modify all security-related information about objects in that OU.

Which of the following steps should Lance take to meet these requirements? (Choose all that apply.)

A. Convert all volumes on which Active Directory information resides to NTFS.

B. Enable auditing with the Active Directory Users and Computers tool.

C. Create a new Active Directory domain and create restrictive permissions for the suspected users within this domain.

D. Reconfigure trust settings using the Active Directory Domains and Trusts tool.

E. Specify auditing options for the OU using the Active Directory Users and Computers tool.

F. Use the Delegation of Control Wizard to grant appropriate permissions to view and modify objects within the OU to the Audit user account.

10. You are installing a new software application on a Windows 2000 domain controller. After reading the manual and consulting with a security administrator, you find that you have the following requirements:

- The software must run under an account that has permissions to all files on the server on which it is installed.

- The software must be able to bypass file system security in order to work properly.

- The software must be able to read and write sensitive files stored on the local server.

- Users of the software must not be able to view sensitive data that is stored within the files on the server.

You decide to create a new user account for the software and then assign the account to a built-in local group. To which of the following groups should you assign the account?

A. Account Operators

B. Backup Operators

C. Guests

D. Domain Admins

11. Members of which of the following groups have permissions to perform actions in multiple domains?

A. Domain Admins

B. Domain Users

C. Administrators

D. Enterprise Admins

12. The Association of Pipe Builders has offices throughout the United States. It has a Windows 2000 network that is running in mixed mode. The association has confidential information from several companies that needs to be kept that way. You created a shared folder named Confidential and published it in the directory to contain this confidential information. The manager of the department that manages this information has requested that you disable John's access to the share. When checking the properties of the share, you notice that a domain local group called Secret and another domain local group called Temporary have permissions to the Confidential share. You notice that John is the only member of the Temporary group, so instead of modifying John's account directly with a deny to the share, you simply delete the group. You immediately get a call from the manager that he has changed his mind and that John needs access to the resources. You re-create the Temporary group and add John back into the group. The next day you get a call from John telling you that he cannot access the resources. What is the best way for you to provide access for John to the resource?

    A. Add John to the Secret group.

    B. Grant John direct access to the share.

    C. Grant access to the Confidential folder for the Temporary group.

    D. Add the Temporary group into the Secret group.

13. Oscar, a systems administrator, has created a top-level OU called Engineering. Within the Engineering OU, he has created two OUs: Research and Development. Oscar wants to place security permissions on only the Engineering OU. However, when he does so, he finds that the permissions settings automatically applied to the child OUs. Which of the following actions should he take to prevent this from happening?

    A. Block the inheritance of properties for the OUs.

    B. Rename the parent OU.

    C. Delete and re-create the child OUs.

    D. Delete and re-create the parent OU.

14. You are the systems administrator for a small Active Directory domain. Recently, you have hired an intern to assist you with managing user objects within the domain. You want to do the following:

- Provide the intern with permissions to access Active Directory using the Active Directory Users and Computers tool.

- Provide the intern with sufficient permissions to change the properties of user accounts and to create and delete user accounts.

- Provide the intern with the ability to create groups and computers.

- Prevent the intern from being able to make any other changes to the Active Directory environment.

To which of the following groups should you add the user?

A. Backup Operators

B. Account Operators

C. Enterprise Admins

D. Domain Admins

E. Guests

15. You want the security log to overwrite events that are more than nine days old. Looking at the following screen, what would you do next in order to accomplish this task?

A. Double-click Maximum Security Log Size.

B. Double-click Retention Method For Security Log.

C. Double-click Retain Security Log.

D. Right-click Retention Method For Security Log.

Answers to Review Questions

1. A. Because you are supporting Windows NT 4 and Windows 2000 domain controllers, you must run the environment in mixed mode. Universal security groups are not available when running in mixed-mode Active Directory environments.

2. B, E, G, H. The Active Directory Users and Computers tool allows systems administrators to change auditing options and to choose which actions are audited. At the file-system level, Isabel can specify exactly which actions are recorded in the audit log. She can then use Event Viewer to view the recorded information and provide it to the appropriate managers.

3. D. The Delegation of Control Wizard is designed to assist systems administrators in granting specific permissions to other users.

4. C. Delegation is the process of granting permissions to other users. Delegation is often used to distribute systems administration responsibilities. Inheritance is the transfer of permissions and other settings from parent OUs to child OUs.

5. B. The settings made in the Domain Controller Security Policy tool apply only to domain controllers.

6. C. Auditing for the success or failure of file access and object access tells you who is accessing any files that you want to watch. You can then create a report and notify management who has accessed the files and who has tried and failed to access those files. However, since there may be collusion with someone inside the company, the success or failure of logon/logoff will not provide clear results in this situation. User rights refer to changing the authority of a user to system privileges and are not related to this problem. Auditing access for program files is usually associated with determining whether a virus is attempting to embed itself into your program files.

7. B. Since this is still a mixed-mode network, universal groups are not available, so the best practice is to add users to global groups and apply permissions to the domain local groups where the resources reside. Even in a native-mode network, you do not want to place users into a universal group as the contents of universal groups are included in the Global Catalog and therefore will unnecessarily add to its size. When the migration is complete, the universal groups can be used to include global groups from multiple domains and then be placed in domain local groups that have permissions applied to them.

8. D. When resources are made available to users who reside in domains outside the forest, Foreign Security Principal objects are automatically created.

9. B, E, F. The first step is to enable auditing. With auditing enabled, Lance can specify which actions are recorded. To give permissions to the Audit user account, he can use the Delegation of Control Wizard.

10. B. Members of the Backup Operators group are able to bypass file system security in order to back up and restore files. The requirements provided are similar to those for many popular backup software applications.

11. D. Members of the Enterprise Admins group are given full permissions to manage all domains within an Active Directory forest.

12. C. Once you delete a security principal such as a local domain group, it is lost forever, and any new one, even with the same name, needs to have the permissions reapplied to become effective. You could add John to the Secret group, but you don't know what other resources he would get access to by becoming a member of this group. Giving John direct access to the share would work, but it is not the best practice. You should always use groups to apply resources in order to maintain manageability of the network. Since the network is in mixed mode, you cannot nest groups other than adding a global group into a domain local group.

13. A. This flow of permissions (known as inheritance) can be blocked at any level. By blocking inheritance, the permissions will not flow from the Engineering OU to the Research and Development OUs.

14. B. The user should be added to the Account Operators group. Although membership in the Enterprise Admins or Domain Admins group will provide the user with the requisite permissions, these choices will exceed the required functionality.

15. C. The Retain Security Log setting allows you to specify how long the security log should be retained before it gets overwritten.

Chapter

7

Managing Group Policy

MICROSOFT EXAM OBJECTIVES COVERED IN THIS CHAPTER:

✓ **Monitor and manage network security. Actions include auditing and detecting security breaches.**

- Configure user-account lockout settings.
- Configure user-account password length, history, age, and complexity.
- Configure Group Policy to run logon scripts.
- Link Group Policy objects.
- Enable and configure auditing.
- Monitor security by using the system security log file.

✓ **Troubleshoot end-user Group Policy.**

- Troubleshoot Group Policy problems involving precedence, inheritance, filtering, and the No Override option.
- Manually refresh Group Policy.

 The "Configure user-account lockout settings" and "Configure user-account password length, history, age, and complexity" subobjectives are covered in Chapter 9, "Managing Client and Server Computers." The "Enable and configure auditing" and "Monitor security by using the system security log file" subobjectives are covered in Chapter 6, "Active Directory Security."

One of the biggest challenges faced by systems administrators is the management of users, groups, and client computers. It's difficult enough to deploy and manage workstations throughout the environment. When you add in the fact that users are generally able to make system configuration changes, it can quickly become a management nightmare!

One of the most important system administration features in Windows 2000 and Active Directory is the use of *Group Policy*. Through the use of *Group Policy objects (GPOs)*, administrators can quickly and easily define restrictions on common actions and then apply these at the site, domain, or organizational unit (OU) level. In this chapter, we will examine how Group Policies work and then look at how they can be implemented within an Active Directory environment.

An Introduction to Group Policy

One of the strengths of Windows-based operating systems is their flexibility. End users and systems administrators can configure many different options to suit the network environment and their personal tastes. However, this flexibility comes at a price—there are many options that generally should not be changed by end users. For example, TCP/IP configuration and security policies should remain consistent for all client computers.

In previous versions of Windows, System Policies were available for restricting some functionality at the Desktop level. Settings could be made for users or computers. However, these settings focused primarily on preventing the user from performing such actions as changing their Desktop settings. These changes were managed through the modification of Registry keys. This method made it fairly difficult for systems administrators to create and distribute policy settings. Furthermore, the types of configuration options available in the default templates were not always sufficient, and systems administrators often had to dive through cryptic and poorly documented Registry settings to make the changes they required.

Microsoft ✔ **Exam** **Objective**

Monitor and manage network security. Actions include auditing and detecting security breaches.

- Link Group Policy objects.

Troubleshoot end-user Group Policy.

- Troubleshoot Group Policy problems involving precedence, inheritance, filtering, and the No Override option.

Windows 2000's Group Policies are designed to allow systems administrators to customize end-user settings and to place restrictions on the types of actions that users can perform. Group Policies can be easily created by systems administrators and then later applied to one or more users or computers within the environment. Although they ultimately do affect Registry settings, it is much easier to configure and apply settings through the use of Group Policy than it is to manually make changes to the Registry. For ease of management, Group Policy settings can be managed from within the Active Directory environment, utilizing the structure of users, groups, and OUs.

There are several different potential uses for Group Policies. We covered one of them, managing security settings, in Chapter 6, "Active Directory Security." And, we'll cover the use of Group Policies for software deployment in Chapter 8, "Software Deployment through Group Policy." The focus of this chapter is on the technical background of Group Policies and how they apply to general configuration management.

Let's begin by looking at how Group Policies function.

Group Policy Settings

Group Policy settings are based on Group Policy *administrative templates*. These templates provide a list of user-friendly configuration options and specify the system settings to which they apply. For example, an option for a user or computer that reads Require A Specific Desktop Wallpaper Setting would map to a key in the Registry that maintains this value. When the option is set, the appropriate change is made in the Registry of the affected user(s) and computer(s).

By default, Windows 2000 comes with several administrative template files that can be used for managing common settings. In addition, systems administrators and application developers can create their own administrative template files to set options for specific functionality.

Most Group Policy items have three different settings options:

Enabled   Specifies that a setting for this Group Policy object has been enabled. Some settings require values or options to be set.

Disabled   Specifies that this option is disabled for client computers. Note that disabling an option *is* a setting. That is, it specifies that the systems administrator wants to disallow certain functionality.

Not Configured   Specifies that the setting has been neither enabled nor disabled. Not Configured is the default option for most settings. It simply states that this Group Policy does not specify an option and that other policy settings may take precedence.

The specific options available (and their effects) depend on the setting. Often, additional information is required. For example, when setting the Account Lockout policy, you must specify how many bad login attempts may be made before the account is locked out. With this in mind, let's look at the types of user and computer settings that can be managed.

User and Computer Settings

Group Policy settings can apply to two types of Active Directory objects: User objects and Computer objects. Since both users and computers can be placed into groups and organized within OUs, this type of configuration simplifies the management of hundreds, or even thousands, of computers.

The main types of settings that can be made within user and computer Group Policies are as follows:

Software Settings   Software settings apply to specific applications and software that might be installed on the computer. Systems administrators can use these settings to make new applications available to end users and control the default configuration for these applications. For more information on configuring software settings using Group Policy, see Chapter 8.

Windows Settings   Windows settings options allow systems administrators to customize the behavior of the Windows operating system. The specific options that are available here differ for users and computers. For example, the user-specific settings allow the configuration of Internet Explorer (including the default home page and other settings), while the computer settings include security options, such as account policy and event log options.

Administrative Templates   The options available in administrative templates are used to further configure user and computer settings. In addition to the default options available, systems administrators can create their own administrative templates with custom options.

Figure 7.1 provides an example of the types of options that can be configured with Group Policy.

FIGURE 7.1   Group Policy configuration options

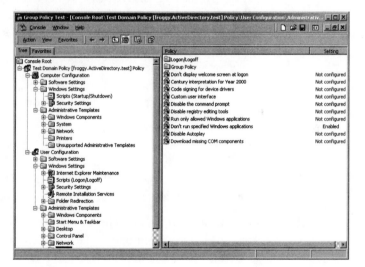

Later in this chapter, we'll look into the various options available in more detail.

Group Policy Objects

So far, we have been talking about what Group Policies are designed to do. Now it's time to drill down into determining exactly how they can be set up and configured.

For ease of management, Group Policies may be contained in items called Group Policy objects (GPOs). GPOs act as containers for the settings made within Group Policy files, which simplifies the management of settings. For example, as a systems administrator, you might have different policies for users and computers in different departments. Based on these requirements, you could create a GPO for members of the Sales department and another for members of the Engineering department. Then you could apply the GPOs to the OU for each department.

Another important concept is that Group Policy settings are hierarchical. That is, Group Policy settings can be linked at three different levels:

Sites   At the highest level, GPOs can be configured to apply to entire sites within an Active Directory environment. These settings apply to all of the domains and servers that are part of a site. Group Policy settings that are managed at the site level may apply to more than one domain. Therefore, they are useful when you want to make settings that apply to all of the domains within an Active Directory tree or forest. For more information on sites, see Chapter 4, "Active Directory's Logical and Physical Structure."

Domains   Domains are the second level to which GPOs can be assigned. GPO settings that are placed at the domain level apply to all of the User and Computer objects within the domain. Usually, systems administrators make master settings at the domain level.

Organizational Units   The most granular level of settings for GPOs is at the OU level. By configuring Group Policy options for OUs, systems administrators can take advantage of the hierarchical structure of Active Directory. If the OU structure is planned well, it will be easy to make logical GPO assignments for various business units at the OU level.

Based on the business need and the organization of the Active Directory environment, systems administrators might decide to configure Group Policy settings at any of these three levels. Since the settings are cumulative by default, a User object might receive policy settings from the site level, from the domain level, and from the organizational units in which it is contained.

Group Policy settings can also be applied to the local computer (in which case Active Directory is not used at all), but this limits the manageability of the Group Policy settings.

Group Policy Inheritance

In most cases, Group Policy settings are cumulative. For example, a GPO at the domain level might specify that all users within the domain must change their passwords every 60 days, and a GPO at the OU level might specify the default Desktop background for all users and computers within that OU. In this case, both settings apply, and users within the OU are forced to change their password every 60 days and have the default Desktop setting.

So what happens if there's a conflict in the settings? For example, suppose a GPO at the site level specifies that users are to change passwords every 60 days while one at the OU level specifies that they must change passwords every 90 days. This raises an important point about *inheritance*. By default, the settings at the most specific level (in this case, the OU, which contains the User object) override those at more general levels.

Although the default behavior is for settings to be cumulative and inherited, systems administrators can modify this behavior. There are two main options that can be set at the various levels to which GPOs might apply:

Block Policy Inheritance The Block Policy Inheritance option specifies that Group Policy settings for an object are not inherited from its parents. This might be used, for example, when a child OU requires completely different settings from a parent OU. Note, however, that blocking policy inheritance should be managed carefully since this option allows other systems administrators to override the settings made at higher levels.

Force Policy Inheritance The Force Policy Inheritance option can be placed on a parent object and ensures that all lower-level objects inherit these settings. In some cases, systems administrators want to ensure that Group Policy inheritance is not blocked at other levels. For example, suppose it is corporate policy that all network accounts are locked out after five incorrect password attempts. In this case, you would not want lower-level systems administrators to override the option with other settings.

This option is generally used when systems administrators want to globally enforce a specific setting. For example, if a password expiration policy should apply to all users and computers within a domain, a GPO with the Force Policy Inheritance option enabled could be created at the domain level.

One final case must be considered: If there is a conflict between the computer and user settings, the user settings will take effect. If, for instance, there is a default Desktop setting applied for the Computer object policy, and there is a different default Desktop setting for the User object policy, the one specified in the User object will take effect. This is because the user settings are more specific, and it allows systems administrators to make changes for individual users, regardless of the computer they're using.

🌐 Real World Scenario

Policy-Based Networking

The West Coast Trading and Collecting Company is an organization that spans the globe. It is really a conglomeration of companies that have been acquired over the years that deal in one-of-a-kind products that are then made available to the public through a catalog. The network that supports this far-flung company has migrated from several different network operating systems including Novell NetWare, Windows NT, and Banyan. The entire network is now based on Windows 2000. As the network administrator, you are responsible for all of the users and applications that the network comprises. Since everything on the network has a history of different systems, there are various ways that have been used to control access to the resource in each region.

The best way to approach a network with this reach is to formulate a process that can be consistently applied to all of the resources in the network without having to be present in all of the locations. The concept behind a consistently applied set of permissions and privileges is *policy-based networking*. With Windows 2000, the administrator can create a hierarchy of groups manifested by the directory tree that represent the administrative tasks and responsibilities necessary to manage each region. Then the administrator can create policies that are contained in Global Policy objects and linked to the appropriate OUs. With this approach, you can then give administrators in each region the permissions for their own region in a consistent manner with the administrators in the other regions.

What is actually happening here is that the administration of the network is abstracted from the technology and allowed to be considered and implemented from a business perspective. The idea of policy-based networking has been a long time in coming and still has quite a way to go. The step in this direction will also be based upon the ability of the directory to represent the Physical layer of the network. This will include the routers and switches that allow the communications of the servers and users to traverse the network. As this method of administration matures, the administrator will be able to manage the bandwidth and accessibility of the network based upon the applications that are running and the type of service the network is providing.

The best way to take advantage of policy-based networking is to build well-thought-out policies with the tools you have today. Even in the smallest network, you want to design your policies with the possibility in mind that your network will continue to expand exponentially. Many times, administrators do not fully take advantage of policy-based networking because it takes time to think out the policies. However, by taking this time, you will certainly reduce the amount of work necessary to administer the network on an ongoing basis.

Implementing Group Policy

Now that we've covered the basic layout and structure of Group Policies and how they work, let's look at how they can be implemented in an Active Directory environment. In this section, we'll start by creating GPOs. Then, we'll apply these GPOs to specific Active Directory objects.

Microsoft ✓ *Exam* *Objective*

Monitor and manage network security. Actions include auditing and detecting security breaches.

- Link Group Policy objects.

Creating GPOs

Although there is only one Group Policy editing application included with Windows 2000, there are several ways to access it. This is because systems administrators may choose to apply the Group Policy settings at different levels within Active Directory. In order to create GPOs at different levels, you can use the following tools:

Active Directory Sites and Services   Used for linking GPOs at the site level.

Active Directory Users and Computers   Used for linking GPOs at the domain or OU level.

MMC Group Policy Snap-In   By directly configuring the Microsoft Management Console (MMC) Group Policy snap-in, you can access and edit GPOs at any level of the hierarchy. This is also a useful option since it allows you to modify the local Group Policy settings and create a custom console that is saved to the Administrative Tools program group.

Exercise 7.1 walks you through the process of creating a custom MMC snap-in for editing Group Policy settings.

You should be careful when making Group Policy settings since certain options might prevent the proper use of systems on your network. Always test Group Policy settings on a small group of users before deploying GPOs throughout your organization. You'll probably find that some settings need to be changed in order to be effective.

EXERCISE 7.1

Creating a Group Policy Object Using the MMC

In this exercise, we will create a custom Group Policy snap-in for managing user and computer settings:

1. Choose Start ➢ Run, type **mmc**, and press Enter.

2. On the Console menu, choose Add/Remove Snap-In.

3. Click the Add button. Select Group Policy from the list, and click Add.

4. For the Group Policy Object setting, click Browse. Note that you can set the scope to Domains/OUs, Sites, or Computers. On the Domains/OUs tab, click the New Policy button (located to the right of the Look In drop-down list).

5. To name the new object, type **Test Domain Policy**. Click OK to open the Policy object.

EXERCISE 7.1 *(continued)*

6. Place a check mark next to the Allow The Focus Of The Group Policy Snap-In To Be Changed When Launching From The Command Line option. This allows the context of the snap-in to be changed when you launch the MMC item.

7. Click Finish to create the Group Policy object. Click Close in the Add Standalone Snap-In dialog box. Finally, click OK to add the new snap-in.

8. Next, we'll make some changes to the default settings for this new GPO. Open the following items: Test Domain Policy ➤ Computer Configuration ➤ Windows Settings ➤ Security Settings ➤ Local Policies ➤ Security Options.

9. Double-click the Do Not Display Last User Name In Logon Screen option. Place a check mark next to the Define This Policy Setting In The Template option, and then select Enabled. Click OK to save the setting.

10. Double-click the Message Text For Users Attempting To Log On option. Place a check mark next to the Define This Policy Setting In The Template option, and then type the following: **By logging onto this domain, you specify that you agree to the usage policies as defined by the IT department.** Click OK to save the setting.

11. Double-click the Message Title For Users Attempting To Log On option. Place a check mark next to the Define This Policy Setting In The Template option, and then type **Test Policy Logon Message**. Click OK to save the setting.

12. Now, to make changes to the user settings, expand the following objects: Test Domain Policy ➢ User Configuration ➢ Administrative Templates ➢ Start Menu & Task Bar.

13. Double-click the Add Logoff To The Start Menu option. Note that you can get a description of the purpose of this setting by clicking the Explain tab. Select Enabled, and then click OK.

14. Expand the following objects: Test Domain Policy ➢ User Configuration ➢ Administrative Templates ➢ System.

15. Double-click the Don't Run Specified Windows Applications option. Select Enabled, and then click the Show button. To add to the list of disallowed applications, click the Add button. When prompted to enter the item, type **wordpad.exe**. To save the setting, click OK three times.

16. To change network configuration settings, choose Test Domain Policy ➢ User Configuration ➢ Administrative Templates ➢ Network ➢ Offline Files. Note that you can change the default file locations for several different network folders.

17. To change script settings (which we will cover later in this chapter), choose Test Domain Policy ➢ Computer Configuration ➢ Windows Settings ➢ Scripts (Startup/Shutdown). Note that you can add script settings by double-clicking either the Startup and/or the Shutdown item.

EXERCISE 7.1 *(continued)*

18. The changes you have made for this GPO are automatically saved. You can optionally save this customized MMC console by selecting Save As from the Console menu. Then provide a name for the new MMC snap-in (such as **Group Policy Test**). You will now see this item in the Administrative Tools program group.

19. When you have finished modifying the Group Policy settings, close the MMC tool.

Note that Group Policy changes do not take effect until the next user logs on. That is, users who are currently working on the system will not see the effects of the changes until they log off and log on again.

Now that we've seen how to create a custom MMC snap-in for modifying Group Policy, let's look at how GPOs can be linked to Active Directory objects.

Linking GPOs to Active Directory

The creation of a GPO is the first step in assigning Group Policies. The second step is to link the GPO to a specific Active Directory object. As mentioned earlier in this chapter, GPOs can be linked to sites, domains, and OUs.

Exercise 7.2 walks through the steps required to assign a GPO to an OU within the local domain.

EXERCISE 7.2

Linking GPOs to Active Directory

In this exercise, we will link the Test Domain Policy GPO to an OU. In order to complete the steps in this exercise, you must have first completed Exercise 7.1.

1. Open the Active Directory Users and Computers tool.

2. Create a new top-level OU called Group Policy Test.

3. Right-click the Group Policy Test OU, and click Properties.

4. Select the Group Policy tab. To add a new policy at the OU level, click Add. In the Look In drop-down list, select the name of the local domain. Select the Test Domain Policy GPO, and then click OK.

5. Note that you can also assign additional GPOs to this OU. When multiple GPOs are assigned, you can control the order in which they apply by using the Up and Down buttons. Finally, you can edit the GPO by clicking the Edit button, and you can remove the link (or, optionally, delete the GPO entirely) by clicking the Delete button.

6. To save the GPO link, click OK. When you have finished, close the Active Directory Users and Computers tool.

Note that the Active Directory Users and Computers tool offers a lot of flexibility in assigning GPOs. We could create new GPOs, add multiple GPOs, edit them directly, change priority settings, remove links, and delete GPOs all from within this interface. In general, creating new GPOs using the Active Directory Sites and Services tool or the Active Directory Users and Computers tool is the quickest and easiest way to create the settings you need.

To test the Group Policy settings, you can simply create a user or computer account within the Group Policy Test OU that we created in Exercise 7.2. Then, using another computer that is a member of the same domain, log on as the newly created user. First, you should see the pre-logon message that we set in Exercise 7.1. After logging on, you'll also notice that the other changes have taken effect. For example, you will not be able to run the WordPad.exe program.

Using Administrative Templates

There are many different options that can be modified by Group Policy settings. Microsoft has included some of the most common and useful items by default, and they're made available when you create new GPOs or when you edit existing ones. You can, however, create your own templates and include them in the list of settings.

By default, there are several templates that are included with Windows 2000. These are as follows:

Common.adm   Contains the policy options that are common to both Windows 95/98 and Windows NT 4 computers.

Inetres.adm   Contains the policy options for configuring Internet Explorer options on Windows 2000 client computers.

System.adm   Includes common configuration options and settings for Windows 2000 client computers.

Windows.adm   Contains policy options for Windows 95/98 computers.

Winnt.adm   Contains policy options that are specific to the use of Windows NT 4.

These administrative template files are stored within the inf subdirectory of the system root directory. It is important to note that the use of the Windows.adm, Winnt.adm, and Common.adm files is not supported in Windows 2000. These files are primarily provided for backward compatibility with previous versions of Windows that used System Policies rather than Group Policies.

The *.adm files are simple text files that follow a specific format that is recognized by the Group Policy editor. Following is an excerpt from the system.adm file:

```
CATEGORY !!WindowsComponents
    CATEGORY !!WindowsExplorer
```

```
KEYNAME "Software\Microsoft\Windows\CurrentVersion
        \Policies\Explorer"

POLICY !!ClassicShell
    EXPLAIN !!ClassicShell_Help
    VALUENAME "ClassicShell"
END POLICY


POLICY !!NoFolderOptions
     EXPLAIN !!NoFolderOptions_Help
     VALUENAME "NoFolderOptions"
END POLICY

POLICY !!NoFileMenu
          EXPLAIN !!NoFileMenu_Help
      VALUENAME "NoFileMenu"
      END POLICY

POLICY !!NoNetConnectDisconnect
            EXPLAIN !!NoNetConnectDisconnect_Help
      VALUENAME "NoNetConnectDisconnect"
END POLICY

POLICY !!NoShellSearchButton
    EXPLAIN !!NoShellSearchButton_Help
    VALUENAME "NoShellSearchButton"
     END POLICY

POLICY !!NoViewContextMenu
          EXPLAIN !!NoViewContextMenu_Help
      VALUENAME "NoViewContextMenu"
      END POLICY
```

Notice that the various options that are available for modification are specified within the administrative template file. If necessary, systems administrators can create custom administrative template files that include more options for configuration.

To add new administrative templates when modifying GPOs, simply right-click the Administrative Templates object and select Add/Remove Templates (see Figure 7.2).

FIGURE 7.2 Adding administrative templates when creating GPOs

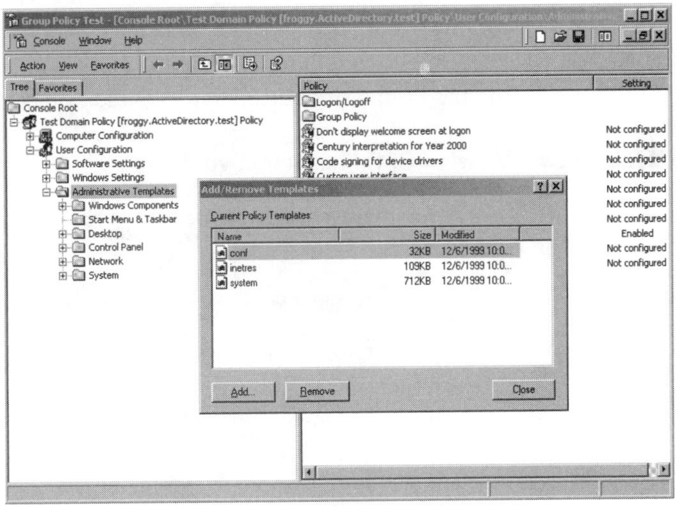

Managing Group Policy

Once you have implemented GPOs and applied them to sites, domains, and OUs within Active Directory, it's time to look at some ways to manage them. In this section, we'll look at how multiple GPOs can interact with one another and ways you can provide security for GPO management. These are very important features of working with Active Directory, and the proper planning of Group Policy can greatly reduce the time the help desk spends troubleshooting common problems.

Microsoft ✓ *Exam* *Objective*

Monitor and manage network security. Actions include auditing and detecting security breaches.

- Configure Group Policy to run logon scripts.

Managing GPOs

One of the benefits of GPOs is that they're modular and can apply to many different objects and levels within Active Directory. This can also be one of the drawbacks of GPOs if they're not managed properly. A common administrative function related to the use of GPOs is finding all of the Active Directory links for each of these objects. This can be done when viewing the properties of a GPO by clicking the Links tab. As shown in Figure 7.3, clicking the Find Now button shows which objects are using a particular GPO.

FIGURE 7.3 Viewing GPO links to Active Directory

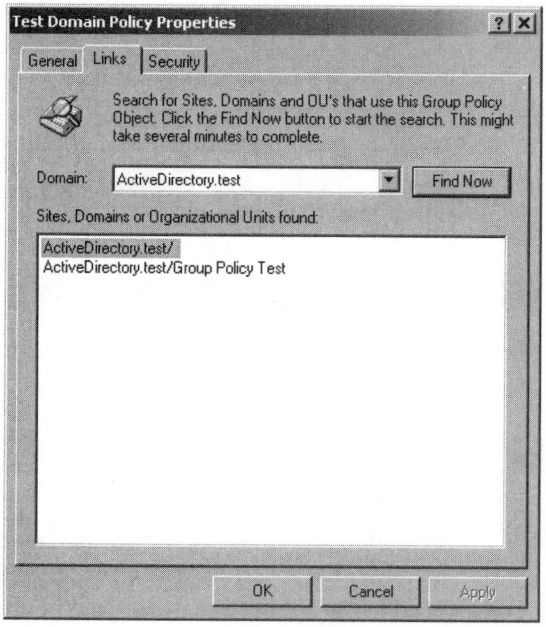

In addition to the common function of delegating permissions on OUs, you can also set permissions regarding the modification of GPOs. One method is to add users to the Group Policy Creator/Owners built-in security group. The members of this group are able to modify security policy.

Filtering Group Policy

Another method of securing access to GPOs is to set permissions on the GPOs themselves. You can do so by selecting the Group Policy tab for an object with the GPO assigned and then choosing Properties. By clicking the

Security tab, you can view the specific permissions that are set on the GPO itself (see Figure 7.4).

FIGURE 7.4 GPO security settings

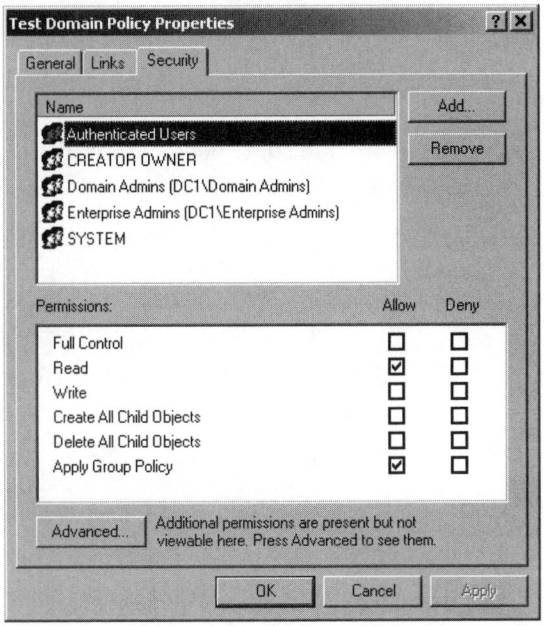

The permissions options include the following:

- Full Control

- Read

- Write

- Create All Child Objects

- Delete All Child Objects

- Apply Group Policy

Of these, the Apply Group Policy setting is particularly important since it is used for filtering the scope of the GPO. *Filtering* is the process by which selected security groups are included or excluded from the effects of the GPOs. To specify that the settings should apply to a GPO, you should grant at least the Apply Group Policy and Read settings. These settings will be applied only if the security group is also contained within a site, domain, or OU to which the GPO is linked. In order to disable GPO access for a group, choose Deny for both of these settings. Finally, if you do not want to specify either Allow or Deny effects, leave both boxes blank. This is effectively the same as having no setting. See Exercise 7.3 for more detailed instructions.

EXERCISE 7.3

Filtering Group Policy Using Security Groups

In this exercise, you will filter Group Policy by using security groups. In order to complete the steps in this exercise, you must have first completed Exercises 7.1 and 7.2.

1. Open the Active Directory Users and Computers administrative tool.

2. Create two new Global Security groups within the Group Policy Test OU, and name them **PolicyEnabled** and **PolicyDisabled**.

3. Right-click the Group Policy Test OU, and select Properties. Select the Group Policy tab.

4. Highlight Test Domain Policy, and select Properties.

5. On the Security tab, click Add, and select the PolicyEnabled and PolicyDisabled groups. Click OK.

6. Highlight the PolicyDisabled group, and select Deny for the Read and Apply Group Policy permissions. This will prevent users in the PolicyDisabled group from being affected by this policy.

7. Highlight the PolicyEnabled group, and select Allow for the Read and Apply Group Policy permissions. This will ensure that users in the PolicyEnabled group will be affected by this policy.

8. Click OK to save the Group Policy settings. You will be warned that Deny takes precedence over any other security settings. Select Yes to continue.

9. Click OK to save the change to the properties of the OU.

10. When finished, close Active Directory Users and Computers.

Through the use of these settings, you can ensure that only the appropriate individuals will be able to modify GPO settings.

Delegating Administrative Control of GPOs

So far, we have talked about how Group Policy can be used to manage user and computer settings. What we haven't done is determine who can modify GPOs themselves. It's very important to establish the appropriate security on GPOs for two main reasons. First, if the security settings aren't set properly, users and systems administrators can easily override them. This defeats the purpose of having the GPOs in the first place! Second, having many different systems administrators creating and modifying GPOs can become extremely difficult to manage. When problems arise, the hierarchical nature of GPO inheritance can make it difficult to pinpoint the problem.

Fortunately, through the use of the Delegation of Control Wizard, determining security permissions for GPOs is a simple task. We looked at the usefulness of the Delegation of Control Wizard in Chapter 5, "Administering Active Directory" and in Chapter 6, "Active Directory Security." Exercise 7.4 walks you through the steps required to grant the appropriate permissions to a user account. Specifically, the process involves delegating the ability to manage Group Policy links on an Active Directory object (such as an OU).

EXERCISE 7.4

Delegating Administrative Control of Group Policy

In this exercise, you will delegate permissions to manage Group Policies of an OU. In order to complete this exercise, you must have first completed Exercises 7.1 and 7.2.

1. Open Active Directory Users and Computers.

2. Expand the local domain, and create a user named **Policy Admin** within the Group Policy Test OU.

3. Right-click the Group Policy Test OU, and select Delegate Control.

4. Click Next to start the Delegation of Control Wizard.

5. On the Users Or Groups page, click Add. Select the Policy Admin account, and click OK. Click Next to continue.

6. On the Tasks To Delegate page, select Delegate The Following Common Tasks, and place a check mark next to the Manage Group Policy Links item. Click Next to continue.

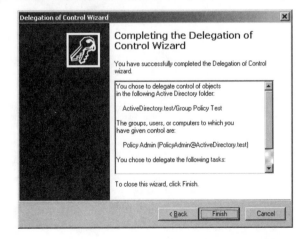

7. Finally, click Finish to complete the Delegation of Control Wizard and assign the appropriate permissions. Specifically, this will allow the Policy Admin user to create GPO links to this OU (and, by default, any child OUs).

8. When finished, close Active Directory Users and Computers.

Controlling Inheritance and Filtering Group Policy

Controlling inheritance is an important function when managing GPOs. Earlier in this chapter, we discussed the fact that, by default, GPO settings flow from higher-level Active Directory objects to lower-level ones. For example, the effective set of Group Policy settings for a user might be based on GPOs assigned at the site level, the domain level, and in the OU hierarchy. In general, this is probably the behavior you would want.

In some cases, however, you might want to block Group Policy inheritance. This can be easily accomplished by selecting the properties for the object to which a GPO has been linked. On the Group Policy tab, you will be able to set several useful options regarding inheritance. The first (and most obvious) option is the Block Policy Inheritance check box located at the bottom of the Group Policy tab (see Figure 7.5). By enabling this option, you are effectively specifying that this object starts with a clean slate. That is, no other Group Policy settings apply to the contents of this Active Directory site, domain, or OU.

FIGURE 7.5 Blocking GPO inheritance

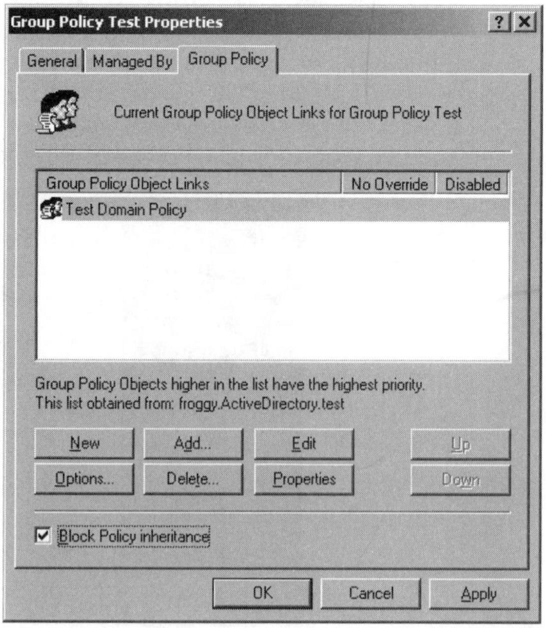

There is, however, a way that systems administrators can force inheritance. This is done using the *No Override* option and is generally set to prevent other systems administrators from making changes to default policies. You can set the No Override option (shown in Figure 7.6) by clicking the Options button on the Group Policy tab for the object to which the GPO applies. Notice that you can also choose to temporarily disable a GPO. This is useful during troubleshooting and when attempting to determine which GPOs are causing certain behavior.

FIGURE 7.6   Setting the No Override GPO option

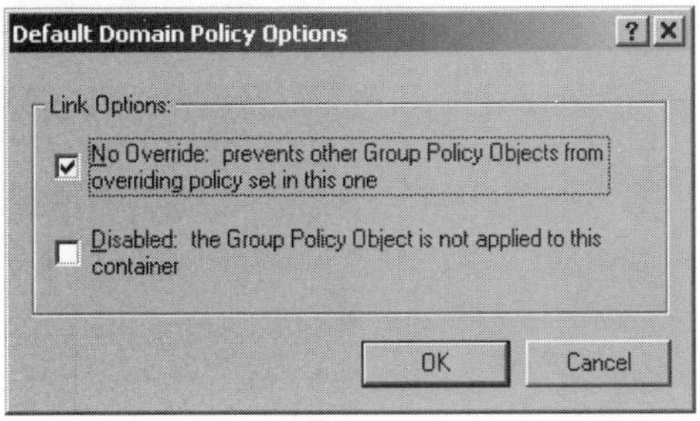

Exercise 7.5 walks through the steps required to manage inheritance and filtering of GPOs.

EXERCISE 7.5

Managing Inheritance and Filtering of GPOs

In this exercise, you will modify the behavior of Group Policy inheritance and filtering:

1. Open the Active Directory Users and Computers administrative tool.

2. Create a top-level OU called **Parent**.

3. Right-click the Parent OU, and select Properties. Select the Group Policy tab, and click the New button to create a new GPO. Name the new object **Master GPO**.

4. Click the Options button. Place a check mark next to the No Override option. This ensures that administrators of OUs contained within the Parent OU will not be able to override the settings defined in this GPO.

5. To save the settings, click OK. Notice that a check mark appears next to the Master GPO in the No Override column in the list of Group Policy object links.

6. Create another GPO for the parent OU, and name it **Optional GPO**. Click the Apply button to save the changes.

7. Within the parent OU, create another OU called **Child**.

8. Right-click the Child OU, and select Properties. Select the Group Policy tab, and place a check mark in the Block Policy Inheritance check box. This option prevents the inheritance of GPO settings from the Parent OU for the Optional GPO settings. Note that since the No Override setting for the Master GPO was enabled on the Parent OU, the settings in the Master GPO take effect on the Child OU regardless of the setting of the Block Policy Inheritance box. Then click OK.

9. When finished, close the Active Directory Users and Computers tool.

Assigning Script Policies

There are several changes and settings that systems administrators might want to make during the startup of a computer or during the logon for a user. Perhaps the most common operation for logon scripts is mapping network drives. Although users can manually map network drives, providing this functionality within logon scripts ensures that mappings stay consistent and that users need only remember the drive letters for their resources.

Script policies are specific options that are part of Group Policy settings for users and computers. These settings direct the operating system to the specific files that should be processed during the startup/shutdown or logon/logoff processes. The scripts themselves may be created through the use of the *Windows Script Host (WSH)* or may be standard batch file commands. WSH is a utility included with the Windows 2000 operating system. It allows developers and systems administrators to quickly and easily create scripts using the familiar Visual Basic Scripting Edition (VBScript) or JScript (Microsoft's implementation of JavaScript). In addition, WSH can be expanded to accommodate other common scripting languages.

To set script policy options, you simply edit the Group Policy settings. As shown in Figure 7.7, there are two main areas for setting script policy settings:

Startup/Shutdown Scripts   These settings are located within the Computer Configuration ➢ Windows Settings ➢ Scripts (Startup/Shutdown) object.

Logon/Logoff Scripts   These settings are located within the User Configuration ➢ Windows Settings ➢ Scripts (Logon/Logoff) object.

FIGURE 7.7   Viewing script policy settings

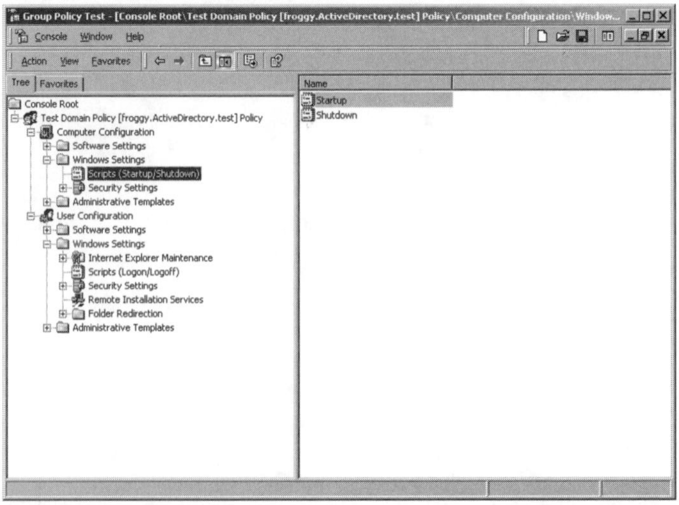

To assign scripts, simply double-click the setting. The Startup Properties dialog box appears, as shown in Figure 7.8. To add a script filename, click the Add button. You will be asked to provide the name of the script file (such as `MapNetworkDrives.vbs` or `ResetEnvironment.bat`). The Show Files button opens the directory folder in which you should store the logon files. In order to ensure that the files are replicated to all domain controllers, you should be sure that you place the files within the `SysVol` share.

FIGURE 7.8   Setting scripting options

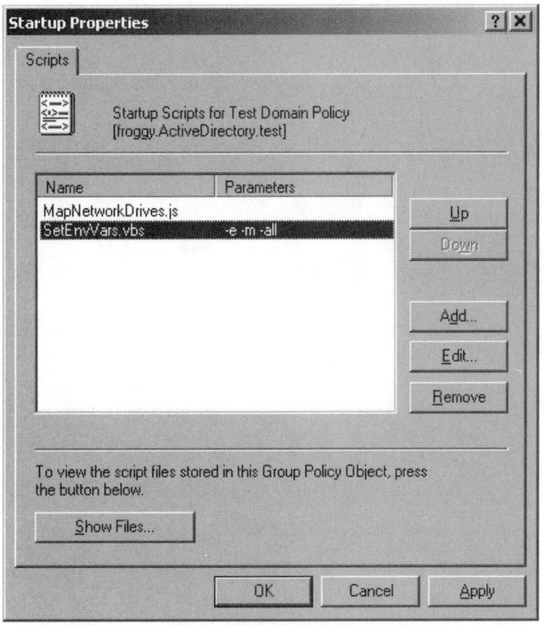

Managing Network Configuration

Group Policies are also useful in network configuration. Although there are many different methods for handling network settings at the protocol level (such as the Dynamic Host Configuration Protocol, or DHCP), Group Policy allows administrators to set which functions and operations are available to users and computers.

Figure 7.9 shows some of the features that are available for managing Group Policy settings. The paths to these settings are as follows:

Computer Network Options   These settings are located within the Computer Configuration ➢ Administrative Templates ➢ Network folder.

User Network Options   These settings are located within the User Configuration ➢ Administrative Templates ➢ Network folder.

FIGURE 7.9   Viewing Group Policy network configuration options

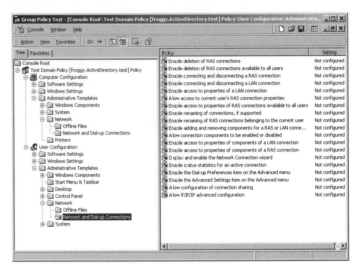

Some examples of the types of settings available include the following:

- The ability to allow or disallow the modification of network settings. In many environments, the improper changing of network configurations and protocol settings is a common cause of help desk calls.

- The ability to allow or disallow the creation of Remote Access Service (RAS) connections. This option is very useful, especially in larger networked environments, since the use of modems and other WAN devices can pose a security threat to the network.

- Setting of offline files and folders options. This is especially useful for keeping files synchronized for traveling users and is commonly configured for laptops.

Through the use of these configuration options, systems administrators can maintain consistency for users and computers and can avoid many of the most common troubleshooting calls.

Troubleshooting Group Policy

Because of the wide variety of configurations that are possible when establishing Group Policy, you should be aware of some common troubleshooting methods. These methods help isolate problems in policy settings or *Group Policy object (GPO) links*.

Microsoft
✓ *Exam*
Objective

Troubleshoot end-user Group Policy.

- Troubleshoot Group Policy problems involving precedence, inheritance, filtering, and the No Override option.

- Manually refresh Group Policy.

A possible problem with GPO configuration is that logons and system startups may take a long time. This occurs especially in large environments when the Group Policy settings must be transmitted over the network and, in many cases, slow WAN links. In general, the number of GPOs should be limited because of the processing overhead and network requirements during logon. By default, GPOs are processed in a synchronous manner. This means that the processing of one GPO must be completed before another one is applied (as opposed to asynchronous processing, where they can all execute at the same time).

Other common issues might include unexpected settings of Group Policy options. When this occurs, there are several options that systems administrators should verify:

Locate Active Directory GPO Links   To find out where GPOs are being used, you can quickly and easily use the Links tab in the Properties dialog box of the GPOs.

Verify GPO Configuration Since GPOs can be assigned to sites, domains, and OUs, systems administrators should be sure to carefully plan for the inheritance of Group Policy settings. And while careful planning and maintenance of GPOs are important, it's just as important to determine the ramifications of moving and reconfiguring Active Directory objects. For example, moving an OU or redefining a site can cause large changes in the effective Group Policy settings.

Attempt to Disable Certain GPOs When certain settings are causing problems, it can be difficult to isolate the GPOs from which the settings are being made. One method for troubleshooting GPO problems is to systematically disable and enable various combinations of GPOs. By doing this, you can determine which GPO(s) is causing the problems.

Manually Refresh Group Policy GPOs automatically refresh every 90 minutes by default, and any policy changes won't take effect until after the refresh. This might make it seem like changes you made to a GPO aren't working. If you want policy changes to take effect immediately, you should use the `secedit /refreshpolicy` command described in Chapter 6.

Interoperability It is also very important to realize that some of the resulting features and functions available within Windows 2000 through GPOs are not available in previous versions. This can have a negative impact on the interoperability during migration periods or if a network is planned to have different versions of Windows NT on the same network. For example there are a couple of GPO templates called Secure Template and Highly Secure Template. These are used to provide uniform security on Windows 2000 Servers, particularly to provide the same level of security between a freshly installed Windows 2000 Server and an upgraded Windows 2000 Server from Windows NT. When you apply the Secure Template to an upgraded Windows 2000 Server, it will then have the same configuration as a freshly installed server. However, if you apply the Highly Secure Template to a Windows 2000 Server, it will then require encryption for network communication. Since this is not available on the Windows NT machines, they will not be able to communicate with the Windows 2000 machines, severing interoperability between them. Make sure that you are aware of how the use of any templates will affect interoperability.

Through the use of these various techniques, you should be able to track down even the most elusive Group Policy problems. Remember, however, that good troubleshooting skills do not replace the need for adequate planning and maintenance of GPO settings!

🌐 Real World Scenario

Troubleshooting Logon Performance Problems

You are the network administrator for a medium-sized Active Directory environment. Several weeks ago, you were asked to design and implement the organization's Group Policy security settings. You spent several days designing a working strategy that was easy to maintain. In order to best suit the needs of your users, you decided to create nine different Group Policy objects. You designed each GPO to contain information about a specific set of permissions. You also had to take into account that the established OU structure within your single Active Directory domain environment consists of a fairly deep hierarchy (for example, many OUs are nested to four levels). In order to work with this system, you linked the nine GPOs you created to these OUs at various levels, which resulted in dozens of links. Before you deployed your solution, you performed several tests to ensure that the resulting policies were what you intended. The settings seemed to work well, and they met the business needs.

Recently, however, you have received several complaints from users throughout the environment; they are complaining about slow performance during logon. Based on their reports, the system seems to hang on the Applying Security Settings dialog box, during which time they cannot access their systems. To determine the cause, you examine the network and find no performance problems. Furthermore, the issue seems to have arisen just after you implemented the GPO links. You determine that the problem must be due to the large number of GPO links. After consulting several resources for more information, your opinion seems to be validated—the issue is likely caused by having so many GPO links. You also find out that the GPOs themselves must be processed synchronously (that is, one after the other). You know that this adds significantly to the logon time, regardless of network and other issues. This is particularly true when users are logging onto the network from remote locations. Remote users always need to be considered in your overall policy plans.

You can solve this problem by reducing the number of GPO links. For example, if users in OUs that are four levels deep within the OU structure have many different GPOs that must be applied during login, perhaps you can consolidate the GPOs into a few more-complicated ones. Or, you can take the settings that you have in some GPOs and repeat them in others (so fewer would have to be applied). Overall, you might sacrifice some of the ease with which you could administer features, but your users could save significant time during logon attempts.

Although the initial GPO policy you established met some of your business requirements (for example, maintaining a good level of security), it failed to meet others (for instance, acceptable performance during logon operations). As is always the case, remember that your technical solutions must always balance business goals, performance issues, and ease of administration. As you can see here, GPO links are no exception. Be sure to adequately test logon performance before you begin your GPO rollout, and don't forget to consider remote users of the network.

Summary

In this chapter, we examined Active Directory's solution to a common headache for many systems administrators: policy settings. Specifically, we discussed the following:

- Group Policies can restrict and modify the actions that are allowed for users and computers within the Active Directory environment.

- Group Policy objects (GPOs) can be linked to Active Directory objects.

- Group Policy object links can interact through inheritance and filtering to result in an effective set of policies.

- Administrative templates can be used to simplify the creation of Group Policy objects.

- Administrators can delegate control over GPOs in order to distribute administrative responsibilities.

A good understanding of Group Policy is very important for both the exam and for working with the Active Directory in the real world.

Exam Essentials

Understand the purpose of Group Policy. Group Policy is used to enforce granular permissions for users in an Active Directory environment.

Understand user and computer settings. Certain Group Policy settings may apply to users, computers, or both. Computer settings affect all users that access the machines to which the policy applies. User settings affect users, regardless of which machines they log on to.

Know the interactions between Group Policy objects and Active Directory. GPOs can be linked to Active Directory objects. This link determines to which objects the policies apply.

Understand filtering and inheritance interactions between GPOs. For ease of administration, Group Policy objects can interact via inheritance and filtering. It is important to understand these interactions when implementing and troubleshooting Group Policy.

Know how Group Policy settings can affect script policies and network settings. Special sets of Group Policy objects can be used to manage network configuration settings.

Understand how delegation of administration can be used in an Active Directory environment. Delegation is an important concept because it allows for distributed administration.

Know the basic steps for troubleshooting Group Policy. When implementing Group Policy, it is possible that the set of applied permissions is not what you expected. In such a case, it's important to understand how a particular Active Directory object obtained these settings and at which levels the settings are applied.

Key Terms

Before you take the exam, be sure you are familiar with the following terms:

administrative templates	inheritance
filtering	no override
Group Policy	script policies
Group Policy object (GPO)	Windows Script Host (WSH)
Group Policy object (GPO) link	

Review Questions

1. A systems administrator is planning to implement GPOs in a new Windows 2000 Active Directory environment. In order to meet the needs of the organization, he decides to implement a hierarchical system of Group Policy settings. At which of the following levels is he able to assign Group Policy settings? (Choose all that apply.)

   A. Sites

   B. Domains

   C. Organizational units (OUs)

   D. Local system

2. Ann is a systems administrator for a medium-sized Active Directory environment. She has determined that several new applications that will be deployed throughout the organization use Registry-based settings. She would like to do the following:

   - Control these Registry settings using Group Policy.

   - Create a standard set of options for these applications and allow other systems administrators to modify them using the standard Active Directory tools.

   Which of the following options can she use to meet these requirements? (Choose all that apply.)

   A. Implement the inheritance functionality of GPOs.

   B. Implement delegation of specific objects within Active Directory.

   C. Implement the No Override functionality of GPOs.

   D. Create administrative templates.

   E. Provide administrative templates to the systems administrators who are responsible for creating Group Policy for the applications.

3. You are the network administrator of a network that is in the process of being upgraded from Windows NT to Windows 2000. There are three Windows NT Servers left in the original domain, with the other four having been migrated to a single-domain Windows 2000 environment. The Windows 2000 domain has one DC and three member servers, one of them containing sensitive information. You have been instructed to make sure that the information on the sensitive server is strongly protected while the migration is under way. In an effort to ensure that the information is protected, you apply the Highly Secure Template on the server. Immediately after you do this, the users from the Windows NT Workstations who need information can no longer access the server. What should you now do to allow these users to once again access the resources on this server?

A. Enable IPSec on the Windows NT Workstations.

B. Apply the Secure Template.

C. Enable NetBIOS on the server you need to access.

D. Re-create the trust relationship between the Windows NT and Windows 2000 domains.

4. John is developing a standards document for settings that are allowed by systems administrators in an Active Directory environment. He wants to maintain as much flexibility as possible in the area of Group Policy settings. In which of the following languages can script policies be written? (Choose all that apply.)

A. Visual Basic Scripting Edition (VBScript)

B. JScript

C. Other Windows Script Host (WSH) languages

D. Batch files

5. You have been brought in as the network administrator of a network that has been completely migrated. During this process, the engineers created local security policies on each computer that were set to allow only three unsuccessful logon attempts before account lockout is enforced. There also exists a Group Policy object linked to the domain that allows five attempts before account lockout. The security policy of your company has finally been completed and published. It allows only three attempts before account lockout. What should you do to be in alignment with the new official policy?

A. Enable No Override on the local account policies.

B. Enable Block Policy Inheritance on the local security policies on the workstations.

C. Remove the local security policies on the workstations.

D. Modify the account lockout threshold policy setting in the GPO to reflect the new policy

6. You are a systems administrator for a medium-sized Active Directory environment. Specifically, you are in charge of administering all objects that are located within the North America OU. The North America OU contains the Corporate OU. You want to do the following:

- Create a GPO that applies to all users within the North America OU except for those located within the Corporate OU.

- Be able to easily apply all Group Policy settings to users within the Corporate OU, should the need arise in the future.

- Accomplish this task with the least amount of administrative effort.

Which two of the following options meet these requirements? (Choose all that apply.)

A. Enable the inheritance functionality of GPOs for all OUs within the North America OU.

B. Implement delegation of all objects within the North America OU to one administrator and then remove permissions for the Corporate OU. Have this administrator link the GPO to the North America OU.

C. Create a GPO link for the new policy at the level of the North America OU.

D. Create special administrative templates for the Corporate OU.

E. Enable the Block Inheritance option on the Corporate OU.

7. You have just been hired as the new network administrator of a Windows 2000 network. The network is unique in that the designers created three domains within one site. Each domain has 750 users and contains five servers. You have discovered that the reason for the multiple domains is that each division of this company has different security requirements and the designers felt that the domain was the best way to accommodate these differences. The old administrator left the company abruptly and did not leave any documentation on how the Global Policies were implemented throughout the domains. You begin to evaluate the network and start looking at the GPOs. After you review some of the GPOs, you decide to make a modification to one of them, but you cannot open it. What is the most likely reason that you cannot open and modify this particular GPO?

   A. The GPO is on an NTFS partition that has permissions that do not allow you to edit it.

   B. The administrator must have Read and Write permissions to edit a GPO.

   C. The GPO is linked to an OU that cannot be edited.

   D. Only the Domain Administrator can edit GPOs.

8. To disable GPO settings for a specific security group, which of the following permissions should be applied?

   A. Deny Write

   B. Allow Write

   C. Enable Apply Group Policy

   D. Disable Apply Group Policy

9. Trent is a systems administrator in a medium-sized Active Directory environment. He is responsible for creating and maintaining Group Policy settings. For a specific group of settings, he has the following requirements:

   ▪ The settings in the Basic Users GPO should remain defined.

   ▪ The settings in the Basic Users GPO should not apply to any users within the Active Directory environment.

   ▪ The amount of administrative effort to apply the Basic Users settings to an OU in the future should be minimal.

Which of the following options can Trent use to meet these requirements?

A. Enable the No Override option at the domain level.

B. Enable the Block Policy Inheritance option at the domain level.

C. Remove the link to the Basic Users GPO from all Active Directory objects.

D. Delete the Basic Users GPO.

E. Rename the Basic Users GPO to break its link with any existing Active Directory objects.

10. A systems administrator wants to ensure that certain GPOs applied at the domain level are not overridden at lower levels. Which option can be used to do this?

A. The No Override option

B. The Block Policy Inheritance option

C. The Disable option

D. The Disable Domain Inheritance option

11. GPOs assigned at which of the following level(s) will override GPO settings at the domain level?

A. OU

B. Site

C. Domain

D. Local

12. A systems administrator wants to ensure that only the GPOs set at the OU level affect the Group Policy settings for objects within the OU. Which option can be used to do this (assuming that all other GPO settings are the defaults)?

A. The No Override option

B. The Block Policy Inheritance option

C. The Disable option

D. The Disable Domain Inheritance option

13. In order to be accessible to other domain controllers, logon/logoff and startup/shutdown scripts should be placed in which of the following shares?

A. Winnt

B. System

C. C$

D. SysVol

14. Matt, a systems administrator, has recently created a new Active Directory domain. The domain forms a tree with the three other domains in the environment, and all of the domains are configured in a single site. He is planning to implement Group Policy and has the following requirements:

- Several GPOs must be created to accommodate five different levels of user settings.

- The GPOs may be assigned at any level within the Active Directory environment.

- All users within the Engineering domain must receive specific GPO assignments.

At which of the following levels can Matt create a single GPO link in order for it to affect all four domains in the environment?

A. Site

B. OU

C. Domain

D. Local computer

E. Domain controller

15. You want to link a GPO to the Group Policy Test OU. You right-click the OU as shown below. In order to accomplish this task, what would you click next?

A. Properties

B. Delegate Control

C. All Tasks

D. Add Members To A Group

Answers to Review Questions

1. A, B, C, D. GPOs can be set at all of the levels listed.

2. D, E. Administrative templates are used to specify the options available for setting Group Policy. By creating new administrative templates, Ann can specify which options are available for the new applications. She can then distribute these templates to other systems administrators in the environment.

3. Answer: B. The Highly Secure Template provides mandatory encryption for network communications. Since only the Windows 2000 Workstations in this scenario support IPSec to provide this encryption, the Windows NT Workstations can no longer communicate with the server. The Secure Template requests encryption but will still communicate with workstations that cannot comply. Once the migration is complete, you can reapply the Highly Secure Template. If NetBIOS were the problem, then it would have been manifested previous to the application of the new template.

4. A, B, C, D. The Windows Script Host (WSH) can be used with any of the above languages. Standard batch files can also be used.

5. D. When account policies are set at the domain level, account policies that may be set at other levels are ignored. Block Policy Inheritance and No Override are options that can be set on GPOs, not in local policies on machines. Removing or modifying the local policies has no effect on the application of GPOs at the domain level.

6. C, E. The easiest way to accomplish this task is to create GPO links at the level of the parent OU (North America) and disable inheritance at the level of the child OU (Corporate).

7. B. One of the ways to delegate administrative capability throughout the network is provide different permissions to different administrators. In order to edit a GPO, the administrators must have Read and Write permissions. The file system is not related to the administrators' ability to edit an object that exists in the directory. The Domain Administrator has the ability to edit all GPOs but is not the only account with the ability to edit GPOs. Linking a GPO to an OU is not related to the administrators' ability to edit it.

8. D. To disable the application of Group Policy on a security group, the Apply Group Policy option should be disabled.

9. C. Systems administrators can disable a GPO without removing its link to Active Directory objects. This prevents the GPO from having any effect on Group Policy but leaves the GPO definition intact so it can be enabled at a later date.

10. A. The No Override option ensures that the Group Policy settings cannot be changed by the settings of lower-level Active Directory objects.

11. A. GPOs at the OU level take precedence over GPOs at the domain level. GPOs at the domain level, in turn, take precedence over GPOs at the site level.

12. B. The Block Policy Inheritance option prevents Group Policies of higher-level Active Directory objects from applying to lower-level objects as long as the No Override option is not set.

13. D. By default, the contents of the SysVol share are made available to all domain controllers. Therefore, scripts should be placed in directories in that share.

14. A. GPO links at the site level affect all of the domains that are part of a site. Therefore, Matt can create a single GPO link at the site level.

15. A. In order to link a GPO to an OU, you would use the Group Policy tab of the OU Properties dialog box. From there, you can create new GPOs, add GPOs to the OU, and configure each GPO.

Software Deployment through Group Policy

MICROSOFT EXAM OBJECTIVES COVERED IN THIS CHAPTER:

✓ **Deploy software by using Group Policy. Types of software include user applications, antivirus software, line-of-business applications, and software updates.**

- Use Windows Installer to deploy Windows Installer packages.
- Deploy updates to installed software including antivirus updates.
- Configure Group Policy to assign and publish applications.

From an end user's viewpoint, it's very easy to take software for granted. For example, many of us have come to expect our computers to run messaging applications and productivity applications. However, from the view of systems administrators and help desk staff, deploying and maintaining software can be a troublesome and time-consuming job. Regardless of how much time is spent installing, updating, reinstalling, and removing applications based on users' needs, there seems to be no end to the process!

Fortunately, Windows 2000 and Active Directory provide many improvements to the process of deploying and managing software. Through the use of Group Policy objects and Microsoft Installer (MSI), it's easy to configure software deployment options. The applications themselves can be made available to any users who are part of the Active Directory environment. Furthermore, systems administrators can automatically assign applications to users and computers and allow programs to be installed automatically when they are needed.

In this chapter, we'll look at how to use Windows 2000 and Active Directory to deploy and manage software throughout the network.

Overview of Software Deployment

One of the key design goals for Active Directory was to reduce some of the headaches involved in managing software and configurations in a networked environment. To that end, Windows 2000 offers several features that can make the task of deploying software easier and less prone to errors. Before we dive into the technical details, though, let's examine the issues related to software deployment.

The Software Management Life Cycle

Although it may seem that the use of a new application requires only the installation of the necessary software, the overall process of managing applications involves many more steps. When managing software applications, there are three main phases to the life cycle of applications:

Deploying Software   The first step in using applications is to install them on the appropriate client computers. Generally, some applications are deployed during the initial configuration of a PC, and others are deployed when they are requested. In the latter case, this often used to mean that systems administrators and help desk staff would have to visit client computers and manually walk through the installation process.

It is very important to understand that the ability to easily deploy software does not necessarily mean that you have the right to do so! Before you install software on client computers, you must make sure that you have the appropriate licenses for the software. Furthermore, it's very important to take the time to track application installations. As many systems administrators have discovered, it's much more difficult to inventory software installations after they've been performed.

Maintaining Software   Once an application is installed and in use on client computers, there's a need to ensure that the software is maintained. Changes due to bug fixes, enhancements, and other types of updates must be applied in order to ensure that programs are kept up-to-date. As with the initial software deployment, software maintenance can be a tedious process. Some programs require that older versions be uninstalled before updates are added. Others allow for automatically upgrading over existing installations. Managing and deploying software updates can consume a significant amount of time for the IT staff.

Removing Software   At the end of the life cycle for many software products is the actual removal of unused programs. Removing software is necessary when applications become outdated or when users no longer require their functionality. One of the traditional problems with uninstalling applications is that many of the installed files may not be removed. Furthermore, the removal of shared components can sometimes cause other programs to stop functioning properly. Also, users often forget to uninstall applications that are no longer needed, and these programs continue to occupy disk space and consume valuable system resources.

Each of these three phases of the software maintenance life cycle is managed by the Microsoft Installer application. Now that we have an overview of the process, let's move on to looking at the actual steps involved in deploying software using Group Policy.

Windows Installer

If you've installed newer application programs, such as Microsoft Office 2000, you probably noticed the updated setup and installation routines. Applications that comply with the updated standard use the *Windows Installer* specification and software packages for deployment. Each package contains information about various setup options and the files required for installation. Although the benefits may not seem dramatic on the surface, there's a lot of new functionality under the hood!

Windows Installer was created to solve many of the problems associated with traditional application development. It has several components, including the Installer service (which runs on Windows 2000 Server and Professional computers), the Installer program (`msiexec.exe`), which is responsible for executing the instructions in a *Windows Installer package*, and the specifications for third-party developers to use to create their own packages. Within each installation package file is a relational structure (similar to the structure of tables in databases) that records information about the programs contained within the package.

In order to appreciate the true value of Windows Installer, let's start by looking at some of the problems with traditional software deployment mechanisms. Then we'll move on and look at how Windows Installer addresses many of these problems.

Application Installation Issues

Before Windows 2000 and Windows Installer, applications were installed using a setup program that managed the various operations required for a program to operate. These operations included copying files, changing Registry settings, and managing any other operating system changes that might be required (such as starting or stopping services). However, this method included several problems:

- The setup process was not robust, and aborting the operation often left many unnecessary files in the file system.

- The process of uninstalling an application often left many unnecessary files in the file system and remnants in the Windows Registry and operating system folders. Over time, this would result in reduced overall system performance and wasted disk space.

- There was no standard method for applying upgrades to applications, and installing a new version often required users to uninstall the old application, reboot, and then install the new program.

- Conflicts between different versions of dynamic link libraries (DLLs)—shared program code used across different applications—could cause the installation or removal of one application to break the functionality of another.

Benefits of Windows Installer

Because of the many problems associated with traditional software installation, Microsoft has created a new standard known as Windows Installer. This new system provides for better manageability of the software installation process and, as we'll see later in this chapter, allows systems administrators more control over the deployment process. Specifically, benefits of Windows Installer include the following:

Improved Software Removal The process of removing software is an important one since remnants left behind during the uninstall process can eventually clutter up the Registry and file system. During the installation process, Windows Installer keeps track of all of the changes made by a setup package. When it comes time to remove an application, all of these changes can then be rolled back.

More Robust Installation Routines If a typical setup program is aborted during the software installation process, the results are unpredictable. If the actual installation hasn't yet begun, then the Installer generally removes any temporary files that may have been created. If, however, the file copy routine starts before the system encounters an error, it is likely that the files will not be automatically removed from the operating system. In contrast, Windows Installer allows you to roll back any changes when the application setup process is aborted.

Ability to Use Elevated Privileges Installing applications usually requires the user to have Administrator permissions on the local computer since file system and Registry changes are required. When installing software for network users, systems administrators thus have two options. The first is to log off the computer before installing the software and then log back on as a user who has Administrator permissions on the local computer. This method is tedious and time-consuming. The second is to temporarily give users Administrator permissions on their own machines. This method could cause security problems and requires the attention of a systems administrator.

Through the use of the Installer service, Windows Installer is able to use temporarily elevated privileges to install applications. This allows users, regardless of their security settings, to execute the installation of authorized applications. The end result is the saving of time *and* the preservation of security.

Support for Repairing Corrupted Applications   Regardless of how well a network environment is managed, critical files are sometimes lost or corrupted. Such problems can prevent applications from running properly and cause crashes. Windows Installer packages support the ability to verify the installation of an application and, if necessary, replace any missing or corrupted files. This saves time and the end-user headaches associated with removing and reinstalling an entire application to replace just a few files.

Prevention of File Conflicts   Generally, different versions of the same files should be compatible with each other. In the real world, however, this isn't always the case. A classic problem in the Windows world is the case of one program replacing DLLs that are used by several other programs. Windows Installer accurately tracks which files are used by certain programs and ensures that any shared files are not improperly deleted or overwritten.

Automated Installations   A typical application setup process requires end users or systems administrators to respond to several prompts. For example, a user may be able to choose the program group in which icons will be created and the file system location to which the program will be installed. They may also be required to choose which options are installed. Although this type of flexibility is useful, it can be tedious when rolling out multiple applications. By using features of Windows Installer, however, administrators are able to specify setup options before the process begins. This allows systems administrators to ensure consistency in installations and saves time for users.

Advertising and On-Demand Installations   One of the most powerful features of Windows Installer is its ability to perform on-demand installations of software. Prior to Windows Installer, application installation options were quite basic—either a program was installed or it was not. When setting up a computer, systems administrators would be required to guess which applications the user *might* need and install them all.

Windows Installer supports a function known as *advertising*. Advertising makes applications appear to be available via the Start menu or the Add/ Remove Programs control panel. However, the programs themselves may not actually be installed on the system. When a user attempts to access an advertised application, Windows Installer automatically downloads the necessary files from a server and installs the program. The end result is that applications are installed only when needed, and the process requires no intervention from the end user. We'll cover the details of this process later in this chapter.

To anyone who has had the pleasure of managing many software applications in a network environment, all of these features of Windows Installer are likely to be welcome ones. They also make life easier for end users and application developers who can focus on the "real work" their jobs demand.

Windows Installer File Types

When performing software deployment with Windows Installer in Windows 2000, there are several different file types you may encounter. These are as follows:

Windows Installer Packages (MSI)   In order to take full advantage of Windows Installer functionality, applications must include Windows Installer packages. These packages are normally created by third-party application vendors and software developers and include the information required to install and configure the application and any supporting files.

Transformation Files (MST)   *Transformation files* are useful when customizing the details of how applications are installed. When a systems administrator chooses to assign or publish an application, he may want to specify additional options for the package. If, for instance, a systems administrator wants to allow users to install only the Microsoft Word and Microsoft PowerPoint components of Office 2000, he could specify these options within a transformation file. Then, when users install the application, they will be provided with only the options related to these components.

Patches (MSP)   In order to maintain software, *patches* are often required. Patches may make Registry and/or file system changes. Patch files are used for minor system changes and are subject to certain limitations. Specifically, a patch file cannot remove any installed program components and cannot delete or modify any shortcuts created by the user.

Initialization Files (ZAP)   In order to provide support for publishing non–Windows Installer applications, *initialization files* can be used. These files provide links to a standard executable file that is used to install an application. An example might be `\\server1\software\program1\setup.exe`. These files can then be published and advertised, and users can access the *Add/Remove Programs* icon to install them over the network.

Please note that ZAP files do not support many of the features of MSI files, so you should use MSI files whenever possible. See technical article Q231747 on Microsoft's TechNet for more information.

Application Assignment Scripts (AAS)   *Application assignment scripts* store information regarding the assignment of programs and any settings that are made by the systems administrator. These files are created when Group Policy is used to create software package assignments for users and computers.

Each of these types of files provides functionality that allows for the customization of software deployment. Windows Installer packages have special properties that can be viewed by right-clicking the file and choosing Properties (see Figure 8.1).

FIGURE 8.1   Viewing the properties of a Windows Installer (MSI) package file

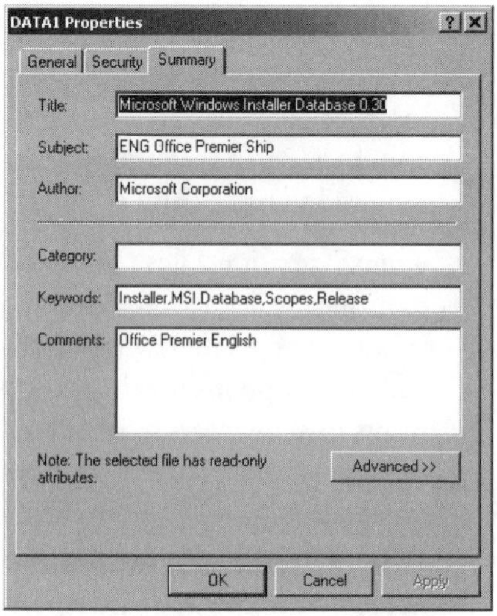

DATA1 Properties

General | Security | Summary

Title: Microsoft Windows Installer Database 0.30

Subject: ENG Office Premier Ship

Author: Microsoft Corporation

Category:

Keywords: Installer,MSI,Database,Scopes,Release

Comments: Office Premier English

Note: The selected file has read-only attributes.

Advanced >>

OK | Cancel | Apply

Deploying Applications

The functionality provided by Windows Installer offers many advantages to end users who install their own software. That, however, is just the tip of the iceberg in a networked environment. As we'll see later in this chapter, the various features of Windows Installer and compatible packages allow systems administrators to centrally determine applications that users will be able to install.

There are two main methods of making programs available to end users using Active Directory. They are *assigning* and *publishing*. In this section, we'll look at how the processes of assigning and publishing applications can make life easier for the IT staff and users alike. The various settings for assigned and published applications are managed through the use of Group Policy objects (GPOs).

Assigning Applications

Software applications can be assigned to users and computers. Assigning a software package makes the program available for automatic installation. The applications advertise their availability to the affected users or computers by placing icons within the Programs folder of the Start menu.

When applications are assigned to a user, programs will be advertised to the user, regardless of which computer they are using. That is, icons for the advertised program will appear within the Start menu, regardless of whether the program is installed on the computer or not. If the user clicks an icon for a program that has not yet been installed on the local computer, the application will automatically be accessed from a server and will be installed on the computer.

When an application is assigned to a computer, the program is made available to any users of the computer. For example, all users who log on to a computer that has been assigned Microsoft Office 2002/XP will have access to the components of the application. If the user did not previously install Microsoft Office, they will be prompted for any required setup information when the program is first run.

Generally, applications such as virus-protection software that are required by the vast majority of users should be assigned to computers. This reduces the amount of network bandwidth required to install applications on demand and improves the end-user experience by preventing the delay involved when installing an application the first time it is accessed. Any applications that may be used by only a few users (or those with specific job tasks) should be assigned to users.

Publishing Applications

When applications are published, the programs are advertised, but no icons are automatically created. Instead, the applications are made available for installation using the Add/Remove Programs icon in Control Panel. Software can be published only to users (not computers). The list of available applications is stored within Active Directory, and client computers can query this list when they need to install programs. For ease of organization, applications can be grouped into *categories*.

Both publishing and assigning applications greatly ease the process of deploying and managing applications in a network environment.

Implementing Software Deployment

So far, we have discussed the issues related to software deployment and management from a high level. Now it's time to drill down into the actual steps required to deploy software using the features of Active Directory. In this section, we will walk through the steps required to create an application distribution share point, to publish and assign applications, and to verify the installation of applications.

Microsoft ✓ *Exam* *Objective*

Deploy software by using Group Policy. Types of software include user applications, antivirus software, line-of-business applications, and software updates.

- Use Windows Installer to deploy Windows Installer packages.

- Deploy updates to installed software including antivirus updates.

- Configure Group Policy to assign and publish applications.

Preparing for Software Deployment

Before you can install applications on client computers, you must make sure that the necessary files are available to end users. In many network environments, systems administrators create shares on file servers that include the installation files for many applications. Based on security permissions, either end users or systems administrators can then connect to these shares from a client computer and install the needed software. The efficient organization of these shares can save the help desk from having to carry around a library of CD-ROMs and can allow for installing applications easily on many computers at once.

One of the problems in network environments is that users frequently install applications whether or not they really require them. They may stumble upon applications that are stored on common file servers and install them out of curiosity. These actions can often decrease productivity and may violate software-licensing agreements. You can help avoid this by placing all of your application installation files in hidden shares (for example, software$).

Exercise 8.1 walks you through the process of creating a software distribution share point.

Creating a Software Deployment Share

In this exercise, you will prepare for software deployment by creating a directory share and placing certain types of files in this directory. In order to complete the steps in this exercise, you must have access to a virus-protection application that supports MSI (via CD-ROM or through a network share).

1. Using Windows Explorer, create a folder called **Software** for use with application sharing. Be sure that the volume on which you create this folder has enough available disk space to install the virus-protection application.

2. Within the `Software` folder, create a folder called `Admin Tools`.

3. Copy the `adminpak.msi` file from the `%systemroot%\system32` folder to the `Admin Tools` folder that you created in step 2.

4. Within the `Software` folder, create a folder called `VirusProtection`.

5. Copy all of the installation files for the virus-protection application from the CD-ROM or network share containing the files to the `VirusProtection` folder that you created in step 4.

6. Right-click the `Software` folder (created in step 1), and select the Sharing tab. Choose Share This Folder, and type **Software** in the Share Name text box and **Software distribution share point** in the Comment text box. Leave all other options as the default, and click OK to create the share.

Once you have created an application distribution share, it's time to actually publish and assign the applications. We'll look at that topic next.

Publishing and Assigning Applications

As we mentioned earlier in this chapter, software packages can be made available to users through the use of publishing and assigning. Both of these operations allow systems administrators to leverage the power of Active Directory and, specifically, Group Policy objects (GPOs) to determine which applications are available to users. In addition, the organization provided by OUs can help group users based on their job functions and software requirements.

The general process involves creating a GPO that includes software deployment settings for users and computers and then linking this GPO to Active Directory objects. If you're unfamiliar with creating and linking GPOs, see Chapter 7, "Managing Group Policy." Exercise 8.2 walks you through the steps required to publish and assign applications.

EXERCISE 8.2

Publishing and Assigning Applications Using Group Policy

In this exercise, you will create and assign applications to specific Active Directory objects using Group Policy objects. In order to complete the steps in this exercise, you must have first completed Exercise 8.1.

1. Open Active Directory Users and Computers from the Administrative Tools program group.

2. Expand the domain, and create a new top-level OU called **Software**.

3. Within the Software OU, create a user named **Jane User** with a login name of **juser** (choose the defaults for all other options).

4. Right-click the Software OU, and select Properties.

5. Select the Group Policy tab, and click New. For the name of the new GPO, type **Software Deployment**.

6. To edit the Software Deployment GPO, click Edit. Expand the Computer Configuration ➢ Software Settings object.

7. Right-click the Software Installation item, and select New ➢ Package. Navigate to the Software share that you created in Exercise 8.1. Within the Software share, double-click the VirusProtection folder, and select the installation file. Click Open.

8. In the Deploy Software dialog box, choose Advanced Published Or Assigned, and click OK. Note that the Published option is unavailable since applications cannot be published to computers.

9. To examine the Deployment options of this package, click the Deployment tab. Accept the default settings by clicking OK.

10. Within the Group Policy Editor, expand the User Configuration ➢ Software Settings object.

11. Right-click the Software Installation item, and select New ➢ Package. Navigate to the Software share that you created in Exercise 8.1. Within the Software share, double-click the Admin Tools folder, and select the adminpak.msi file. Click Open.

12. For the Software Deployment option, select Published and click OK.

13. Close the Group Policy Editor, and then click Close to close the Properties sheet of the Software OU.

The overall process involved with deploying software using Active Directory is quite simple. However, you shouldn't let the intuitive graphical interface fool you—there's a lot of power under the hood of these software-deployment features! Once you've properly assigned and published applications, it's time to see the effects of your work.

Applying Software Updates

The steps described in the previous section work only when you are installing a brand-new application. However, software companies often release updates that need to be installed on top of existing applications. These updates could consist of bug fixes or other changes that are required to keep the software up-to-date. You can apply software updates in Active Directory by using the Upgrades tab of the software package Properties sheet in Group Policy. Exercise 8.3 shows you how to apply a software update.

EXERCISE 8.3

Applying Software Updates

In this exercise, you will apply a software update to an existing application. You should add the upgrade package to the GPO in the same way that you added the original application in steps 7 through 9 of Exercise 8.2. You should also have completed Exercise 8.2 before attempting this exercise.

1. Open Active Directory Users and Computers from the Administrative Tools program group.

2. Right-click the Software OU, and select Properties.

3. To edit the Software Deployment GPO, click Edit. Expand the Computer Configuration ➢ Software Settings object.

4. Right-click the upgrade package (not the original package) and select Properties from the context menu.

5. Select the Upgrades tab and click the Add button.

6. Click the Current Group Policy Object radio button. Select the package to which you want to apply the upgrade. Consult your application's documentation to see if you should choose the Uninstall The Existing Package radio button or the Package Can Upgrade Over The Existing Package radio button.

7. Click OK to close the Add Upgrade Package dialog box.

8. Click OK to save the changes and close the Package Properties dialog box.

You should also understand that not all upgrades make sense in all situations. There may also be some measure of choice among the users regarding which version they use when it doesn't affect the support of the network. Regardless of the underlying reason for allowing this flexibility, you should be aware that there are two basic types of upgrades that are available for administrators to provide to the users.

Mandatory Upgrade Forces everyone who currently has an existing version of the program to be upgraded according to the GPO. Users who have never installed the program for whatever reason will be able to install only the new upgraded version.

Nonmandatory Upgrade Allows users to choose whether they would like to upgrade. This upgrade type also allows users who do not have their application installed to choose which version they would like to use.

Verifying Software Installation

In order to ensure that the settings you made in the GPO for the Software OU have taken place, you can log in to the domain from a Windows 2000 Professional computer that is within the OU to which the software settings apply. When you log in, you will notice two changes. First, Microsoft Office 2000 will be installed on the computer (if it was not installed already). In order to access the Office 2000 applications, all a user would need to do is click one of the icons within the Program group of the Start menu (for example, the Microsoft Word icon). Note also that these applications will be available to any of the users who log on to this machine. Also, the settings apply to any computers that are contained within the Software OU and to any users who log on to these computers.

The second change may not be as evident, but it is equally useful. We assigned the Windows 2000 Administrative Tools program to the Software OU. We also created an account named `juser` within that OU. When you log on to a Windows 2000 Professional computer that is a member of the domain and use the `juser` account, you will be able to automatically install any of the published applications. You can do this by accessing the Add/Remove Programs icon in Control Panel. By clicking Add New Programs, you will see a display similar to that shown in Figure 8.2.

FIGURE 8.2 Installing published applications in Add/Remove Programs

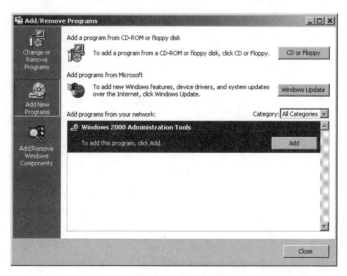

By clicking the Add button, you will automatically begin the installation of the Windows 2000 Administration Tools (see Figure 8.3). This is a useful way of allowing systems administrators to use the Windows 2000 Administration Tools to remotely manage Windows 2000 Server computers.

FIGURE 8.3 The automatic installation of Windows 2000 Administration Tools

---

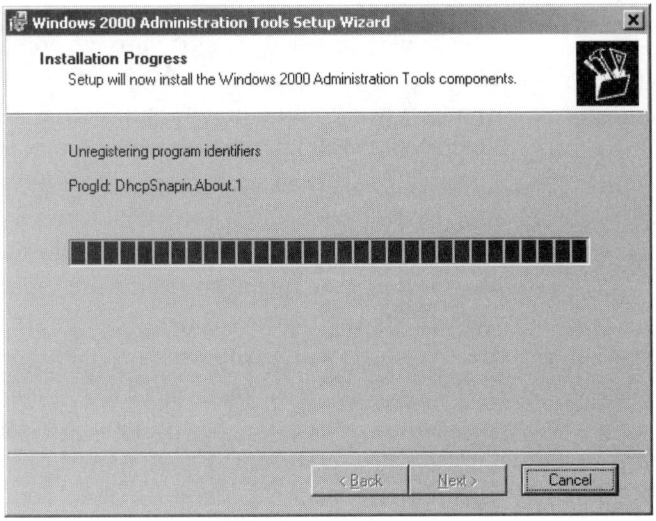

🌐 Real World Scenario

Systematic Software Deployment

As the network administrator of the Foundation Works Company, you have been involved with the migration from Windows NT to Windows 2000. Your role has been to set up the directory tree as designed by the network engineers. The plan was developed in a lab that was used to test replication issues and other architectural concerns. Your company has three sites that are built around the three locations of your company in New York, Chicago, and San Francisco. In the last phase of the migration, you have been testing all of the workstations to verify that the upgrade process has been successful.

The next phase of the migration is the move to a new suite of applications that have been certified by the vendors as Windows 2000–certified. The managers of the departments have been pushing you to get going and arguing that since they are certified, there should be no problem with the upgrades. You are resisting this pressure since the last time you went ahead with a software application install, there were issues surrounding the process that had to be dealt with before it functioned properly. And guess who gets the blame if anything goes wrong?

The best thing to do when you introduce any application to your networking environment is to test the process. You should gain access to the test network and deploy the application in that environment first. Create the packages and GPOs in that environment, and if you come across any problems, they can be resolved with the vendors without impacting any of the users on the network. While this may delay the deployment of applications, it will save you countless hours of unnecessary support calls if you send out packages with problems to your users.

This test environment should be thoroughly documented and published as a best practice in the organization so that you can resist the pressure from the managers who want to get it done as soon as possible. As the administrator, you are not only responsible for the actual manipulation of accounts and resources, but you are also responsible for how smooth the modifications to the system appear to the users. While you may seem invisible when things are working properly, rest assured that you are the most visible target to the user when things go awry.

Configuring Software Deployment Settings

In addition to the basic operations of assigning and publishing applications, there are several other options for specifying the details of how software is deployed. You can access these options from within a GPO by right-clicking the Software Installation item (located within Software Settings in User Configuration or Computer Configuration). In this section, we will examine the various options that are available and their effects on the software installation process.

Microsoft ✓ *Exam* *Objective*	**Deploy software by using Group Policy. Types of software include user applications, antivirus software, line-of-business applications, and software updates.**

Managing Package Defaults

On the General tab of the Software Installation Properties dialog box, you'll be able to specify some defaults for any packages that you create within this GPO. Figure 8.4 shows the General options for managing software installation settings.

FIGURE 8.4   General options for software settings

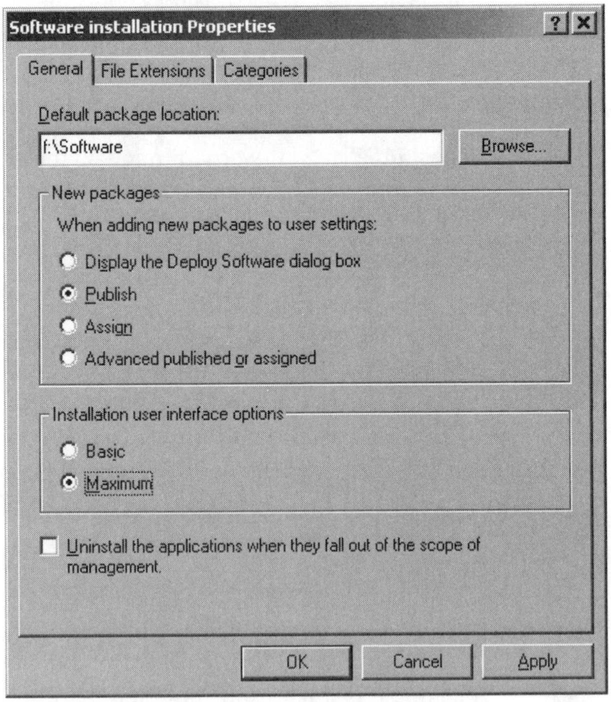

The various options available include the following:

Default Package Location   This setting specifies the default file system or network location for software installation packages. This is useful if you are already using a specific share on a file server for hosting the necessary installation files.

New Packages Options This setting specifies the default type of package assignment that will be used when adding a new package to either the user or computer settings. If you'll be assigning or publishing multiple packages, it may be useful to set a default here.

Installation User Interface Options When an application is being installed, systems administrators may or may not want end users to see all of the advanced installation options. If Basic is chosen, the user will be able to configure only the minimal settings (such as the installation location). If Maximum is chosen, all of the available installation options will be displayed. The specific installation options available will depend on the package itself.

Uninstall The Applications When They Fall Out Of The Scope Of Management So far, we have discussed how applications can be assigned and published to users or computers. But what happens when effective GPOs change? For example, suppose that User A is currently located within the Sales OU. A GPO that assigns the Microsoft Office 2000 suite of applications is linked to the Sales OU. Now I decide to move User A to the Engineering OU, which has no software deployment settings. Should the application be uninstalled, or should it remain?

If the Uninstall The Applications When They Fall Out Of The Scope Of Management option is checked, applications will be removed if they are not specifically assigned or published within GPOs. In our earlier example, this means that Office 2000 would be uninstalled for User A. If, however, the box is left unchecked, the application would remain installed.

Now let's look at some more options that are available for managing software settings.

Managing File Extension Mappings

One of the potential problems associated with the use of many different file types is that it's difficult to keep track of which applications work with which files. For example, if I received a file with the extension .abc, I would have no idea which application I would need to view it. And Windows would not be of much help, either!

Fortunately, through software deployment settings, systems administrators can specify mappings for specific *file extensions*. For example, I could specify that whenever users attempt to access a file with the extension .vsd, the operating system should attempt to open the file using the Visio diagramming software. If Visio is not installed on the user's machine, the computer could automatically download and install it (assuming that the application has been properly advertised).

This method allows users to have applications automatically installed when they are needed. The following is an example of the sequence of events that might occur:

- A user receives an e-mail message that contains an Adobe Acrobat file attachment.

- The Windows 2000 computer realizes that Adobe Acrobat Reader, the appropriate viewing application for this type of file, is not installed. However, it also realizes that a file extension mapping is available within the Active Directory software deployment settings.

- The client computer automatically requests the Adobe Acrobat software package from the server and uses Windows Installer to automatically install the application.

- The Windows 2000 computer opens the attachment for the user.

Notice that all of these steps were carried out without any further interaction with the user! You can manage file extension mappings by viewing the properties for any package that you have defined within the Group Policy settings. Figure 8.5 shows how file extension settings can be managed. By default, the list of file extensions that you'll see is based on the specific software packages you have added to the current GPO.

FIGURE 8.5   Managing file extensions

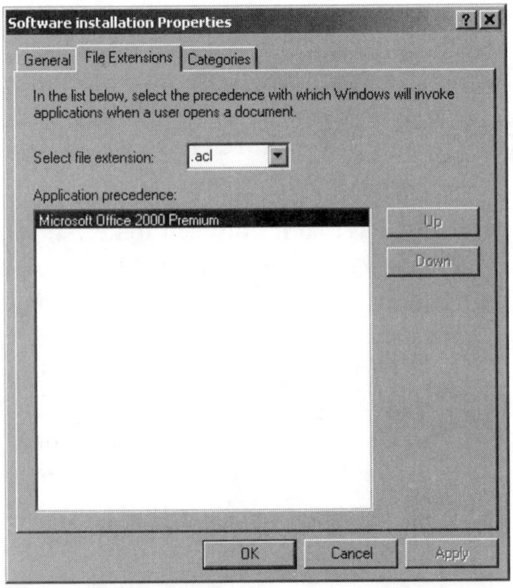

Creating Application Categories

In many network environments, the list of supported applications can include hundreds of items. For users who are looking for only one specific program, searching through a list of all of these programs can be difficult and time-consuming.

Fortunately, there are methods for categorizing the applications that are available on your network. You can easily manage the application categories for users and computers by right-clicking the Software Installation item, selecting Properties, and then clicking the Categories tab. Figure 8.6 shows you how application categories can be created. It is a good idea to use category names that are meaningful to users because it will make it easier for them to find the programs they're looking for.

FIGURE 8.6 Creating application categories

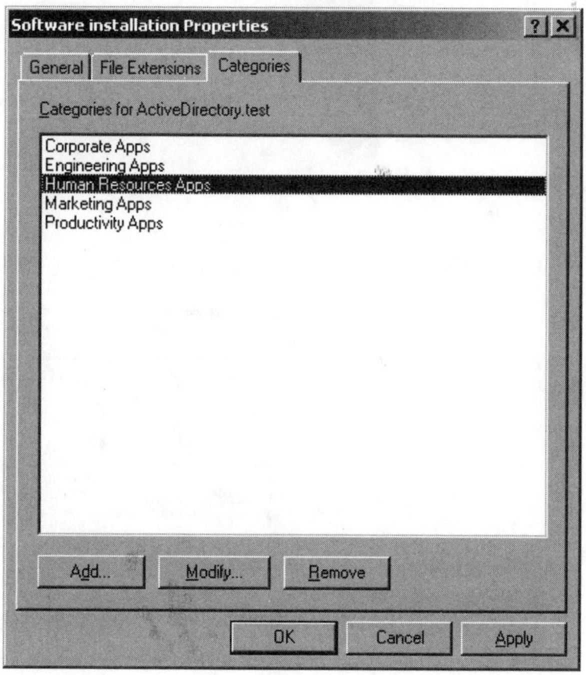

Once the software installation categories have been created, you can view them by choosing the Add/Remove Programs item in Control Panel. When you click Add New Programs, you'll see that there are several options in the

Category drop-down list (see Figure 8.7). Now when you select the properties for a package, you will be able to assign the application to one or more of the categories (as shown in Figure 8.8).

FIGURE 8.7 Viewing application categories in Add/Remove Programs

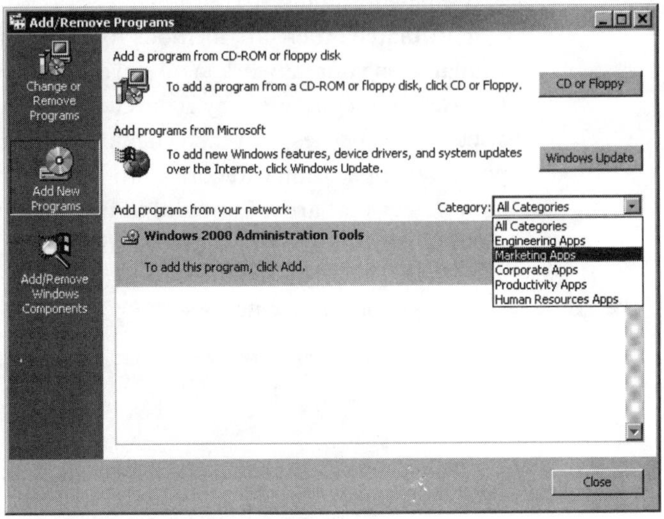

FIGURE 8.8 Specifying categories for application packages

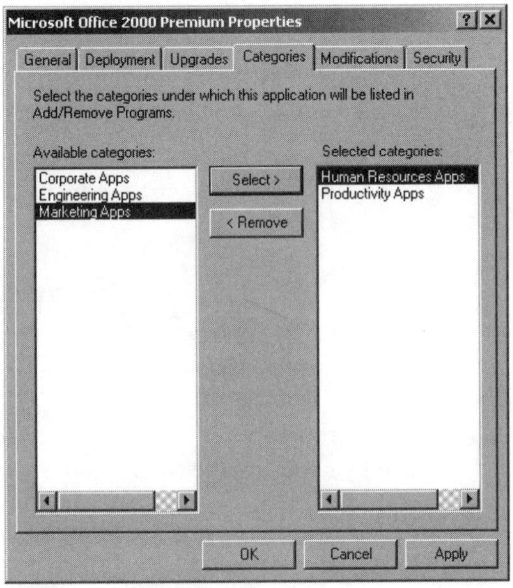

Removing Programs

As we discussed in the beginning of the chapter, an important phase in the software-management life cycle is the removal of applications. Fortunately, using the Active Directory and Windows Installer packages, the process is simple. To remove an application, you can right-click the package within the Group Policy settings and select All Tasks ➤ Remove (see Figure 8.9).

FIGURE 8.9 Removing a software package

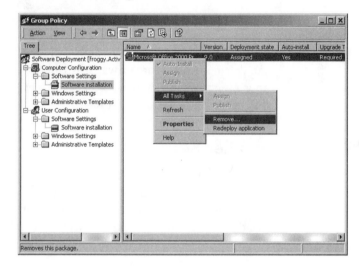

When choosing to remove a software package from a GPO, you have two options:

Immediately Uninstall The Software From Users And Computers Systems administrators can choose this option to ensure that an application is no longer available to users who are affected by the GPO. When this option is selected, the program will be automatically uninstalled from users and/or computers that have the package. This option might be useful, for example, if the licensing for a certain application has expired or if a program is no longer on the approved applications list.

Allow Users To Continue To Use The Software, But Prevent New Installations This option prevents users from making new installations of a package, but it does not remove the software if it has already been installed for users. This is a good option if the company has run out of additional licenses for the software but the existing licenses are still valid.

Figure 8.10 shows the two removal options that are available.

FIGURE 8.10 Software removal options

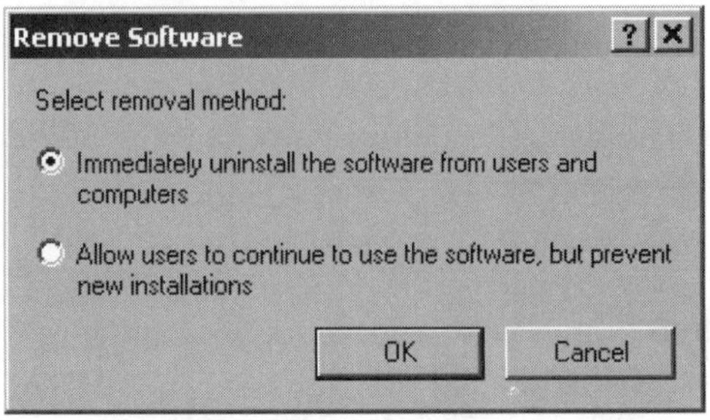

If you no longer require the ability to install or repair an application, you can delete it from your software distribution share point by deleting the appropriate Windows Installer package files. This will free up additional disk space for newer applications.

Windows Installer Settings

There are several options that influence the behavior of Windows Installer that can be set within a GPO. These options are accessed by navigating to User Configuration ≻ Administrative Templates ≻ Windows Components ≻ Windows Installer. The options include the following:

Always Install With Elevated Privileges This policy allows users to install applications that require elevated privileges. For example, if a user does not have the permissions necessary to modify the Registry, but the installation program must make Registry changes, this policy allows the process to succeed.

Search Order This setting specifies the order in which Windows Installer will search for installation files. The options include *n* (for network shares), *m* (for searching removable media), and *u* (for searching the Internet for installation files).

Disable Rollback When this option is enabled, Windows Installer does not store the system state information that's required to roll back the installation of an application. Systems administrators may choose this option to reduce the amount of temporary disk space required during installation and to increase the performance of the installation operation. However, the drawback is that the system cannot roll back to its original state if the installation fails and the application needs to be removed.

Disable Media Source For Any Install   This option disallows the installation of software using removable media (such as CD-ROM, DVD, or floppy disks). It is useful for ensuring that users install only approved applications.

With these options, systems administrators can control how Windows Installer operates for specific users who are affected by the GPO.

Optimizing and Troubleshooting Software Deployment

Although the features in Windows 2000 and Active Directory make software deployment a relatively simple task, there are still many factors that systems administrators should consider when making applications available on the network. In this section, we will discuss some common methods for troubleshooting problems with software deployment in Windows 2000 and optimizing the performance of software deployment.

Microsoft
✔ Exam
Objective

Deploy software by using Group Policy. Types of software include user applications, antivirus software, line-of-business applications, and software updates.

Specific optimization and troubleshooting methods include those that follow:

Test packages before deployment.   The use of Active Directory and GPOs makes publishing and assigning applications so easy that systems administrators may be tempted to make many applications available to users immediately. However, the success of using Windows Installer is at least partially based on the quality of the programming of developers and third-party software vendors.

Before unleashing an application on the unsuspecting user population, you should always test the programs within a test environment using a few volunteer users and computers. The information gathered during these tests can be invaluable in helping the help desk, systems administrators, and end users during a large-scale deployment.

Manage Group Policy scope and links. One of the most flexible aspects of deploying software with Active Directory is the ability to assign Group Policy settings to users and computers. Since it is so easy to set up GPOs and link them to Active Directory objects, it might be tempting to modify all of your existing GPOs to meet the current software needs of your users. Note, however, that this can become difficult to manage.

An easier way to manage multiple sets of applications may be to create separate GPOs for specific groups of applications. For example, one GPO could provide all end-user productivity applications (such as Microsoft Office 2000 and Adobe Acrobat Reader) while another GPO could provide tools for users in the Engineering department. Now whenever the software requirements for a group change, systems administrators can just enable or disable specific GPOs for the OU that contains these users.

Roll out software in stages. Installing software packages over the network can involve high bandwidth requirements and reduce the performance of production servers. If you're planning to roll out a new application to several users or computers, it's a good idea to deploy the software in stages. This process involves publishing or assigning applications to a few users at a time, through the use of GPOs and OUs.

Verify connectivity with the software distribution share. If clients are unable to communicate with the server that contains the software installation files, Windows Installer will be unable to automatically copy the required information to the client computer, and the installation will fail. You should always ensure that clients are able to communicate with the server and verify the permissions on the software installation share.

Organize categories. The list of applications that are available in a typical network environment can quickly grow very large. From standard commercial desktop applications and utilities to custom client-server applications, it's important to organize programs based on functionality. Be sure to group software packages into categories that end users will clearly recognize and understand when searching for applications.

Create an installation log file. By using the `msiexec.exe` command, you can create an installation log file that records the actions attempted during the installation process and any errors that may have been generated.

Reduce redundancy.   In general, it is better to ensure that applications are not assigned or published to users through multiple GPOs. For example, if a user almost always logs on to the same workstation and requires specific applications to be available, you may consider assigning the applications to both the user and the computer. Although this scenario will work properly, it can increase the amount of time spent during logon and the processing of the GPOs. A better solution would be to assign the applications to only the computer (or, alternatively, to only the user).

Manage software distribution points.   When users require applications, they depend on the availability of installation shares. To ensure greater performance and availability of these shares, you can use the Windows 2000 Distributed File System (DFS). The features of DFS allow for fault tolerance and the ability to use multiple servers to share commonly used files from a single logical share point. The end result is increased uptime, better performance, and easier access for end users. In addition, the underlying complexity of where certain applications are stored is isolated from the end user.

Encourage developers and vendors to create Microsoft Installer packages.   Many of the benefits of the software deployment features in Windows 2000 rely on the use of MSI packages. To ease the deployment and management of applications, ensure that in-house application developers and third-party independent software vendors use Microsoft Installer packages that were created properly. The use of MSI packages will greatly assist systems administrators and end users in assigning and managing applications throughout the life cycle of the product.

Enforce consistency using MSI options.   One of the problems with applications and application suites (such as Microsoft Office 2000) is that end users can choose to specify which options are available during installation. While this might be useful for some users, it can cause compatibility and management problems. For example, suppose a manager sends a spreadsheet containing Excel pivot tables to several employees. Some employees are able to access the pivot tables (since they chose the default installation options), but others cannot (since they chose not to install this feature). The users who cannot properly read the spreadsheet will likely generate help desk calls and require assistance to add in the appropriate components.

One way to avoid problems such as these is to enforce standard configurations for applications. For example, we may choose to create a basic and an advanced package for Microsoft Office 2000. The basic package would include the most-used applications, such as Microsoft Word, Microsoft Outlook, and Microsoft Excel. The advanced package would include these applications, plus Microsoft PowerPoint and Microsoft Access.

Create Windows Installer files for older applications.   Although there is no tool included with Windows 2000 to automatically perform this task, it will generally be worth the time to create Windows Installer files for older applications. This is done through the use of third-party applications that are designed to monitor the Registry, file system, and other changes that an application makes during the setup process. These changes can then be combined into a single MSI package for use in software deployment.

By carefully planning for software deployment and using some of the advanced features of Windows 2000, you can make software deployment a smooth and simple process for systems administrators and end users alike.

🌐 Real World Scenario

Understanding Application Architecture and Managing Software Rollouts

The world of computing has moved through various stages and methodologies throughout the past several decades. Real-world business computing began with large, centralized machines called mainframes. In this model, all processing occurred on a central machine and "clients" were little more than keyboards and monitors connected with long extension cords. A potential disadvantage was that clients relied solely on these central machines for their functionality, and the mainframe tended to be less flexible.

Then, with the dramatic drop in the cost of personal computers, the computing industry moved more to a client-based model. In this model, the majority of processing occurred on individual computers. The drawback, however, was that it was difficult to share information (even with networking capabilities), and such critical tasks as data management, backup, and security were challenges.

Since then, various technologies have appeared to try to give us good features from both worlds. A new and promising method of delivering applications has been through the Application Service Provider (ASP) model. In this method, clients are relatively "thin" (that is, they do not perform much processing, nor do they store data); however, users still have access to the tools they need to do their jobs. The software provider is responsible for maintaining the software (including upgrades, backups, security, performance monitoring, etc.), and your company might engage an ASP through a monthly-fee arrangement.

In some respects during the past several years, we've moved back toward housing business-critical functionality on relatively large, central servers. However, we've retained powerful client machines that are capable of performing processing for certain types of applications. In a lot of cases, that makes sense. For example, users of Microsoft Office applications have several advantages if they run their applications on their own machines. Other applications, such as a centralized sales-tracking-and-management tool, might make more sense to reside on a server. However, the fact remains that modern computers are marginally useful without software applications that make practical use of their power and features.

As an IT professional, it's important to understand the business reasons when evaluating an application architecture. Traditionally, the deployment of standard Windows applications was a tedious, error-prone, and inexact process. For example, if a user deleted a critical file, the entire application may have had to be removed and reinstalled. Or, if an application replaced a shared file with one that was incompatible with other applications, you could end up in a situation affectionately referred to as "DLL Hell." Microsoft has attempted to address the sore spot of application deployment and management with the use of the Active Directory and Windows Installer technology. However, it's up to developers and system administrators to take full advantage of these new methods.

As an IT professional, you should urge developers to create installation packages using the Windows Installer architecture. In many ways, it's much simpler to create an Installer package than it is to create the old-style setup programs. On the IT side, be sure that you take advantage of Active Directory's ability to assign and publish applications. And, when it comes time to update a client-side application, be sure to make use of Windows Installer's ability to generate patch files that can quickly and easily update an installation with minimal effort. This method can roll out application updates to thousands of computers in just a few days!

All of these features can cut down on a large amount of support effort that's required when, for example, a user needs to install a file viewer for a file that she received via e-mail. And, for applications that just don't make sense on the desktop, consider the use of Application Service Providers. Outsourced applications can allow you to avoid a lot of these headaches altogether. There's a huge array of options, and it's up to you to make the best choice for your applications!

Summary

The real reason for deploying and managing networks in the first place is to make the applications that they support available. End users are often much more interested in being able to do their jobs using the tools they require than in worrying about network infrastructure and directory services. In the past, software deployment and management have been troublesome and time-consuming tasks.

In this chapter, we covered the following:

- Ways in which new Windows 2000 features can be used to manage the tasks related to software deployment and the benefits of the Windows Installer technology

- How Active Directory, Group Policy objects, and Windows Installer interact to simplify software deployment

- How to publish and assign applications to Active Directory objects

- The tasks associated with deploying, managing, and removing applications using Group Policy

- How to create a network share from which applications can be installed

- How to remotely control software deployment options and configuration through the use of Active Directory administration tools

- How to troubleshoot problems with software deployment

When implemented correctly, the use of the Active Directory software-deployment features can save much time, reduce headaches, and improve the end-user experience.

Exam Essentials

Identify common problems with the software life cycle.   IT professionals face many challenges with client applications, including development, deployment, maintenance, and troubleshooting. Software deployment can be time-consuming and costly, and software can quickly become obsolete, requiring additional maintenance time.

Understand the benefits of Windows Installer.   Windows Installer is an updated way to install applications on Windows-based machines. It offers a more robust method for making the system changes required by applications, and it allows for a cleaner uninstall. Windows Installer–based applications can also take advantage of new Active Directory features.

Understand the difference between publishing and assigning applications.   Some applications can be assigned to users and computers so that they are always available. When you assign an application, an icon for the application is placed in the Start menu, and the first time a user selects the icon, the software is installed automatically. Alternatively, software can be published to users (not computers) so that it may be installed with a minimal amount of effort when a user requires it. The user must use the Add/Remove Programs icon in Control Panel in order to install published software.

Know how to prepare for software deployment. Before your users can take advantage of automated software installation, you must set up an installation share and provide the appropriate permissions.

Know how to configure application settings using Active Directory and Group Policy. Using standard Windows 2000 administrative tools, you can create an application policy that meets your requirements. Features include automatic, on-demand installation of applications when they're needed.

Create application categories to simplify the list of published applications. It's important to group applications by functionality or the users to whom they apply, especially in organizations that support a large number of programs.

Be able to troubleshoot problems with software deployment. There are several methods for deploying applications and for testing to make sure that they are working properly. Should you find a problem with a particular installation of software, you can use various methods to repair and/or remove the specific product.

Key Terms

Before you take the exam, be certain you are familiar with the following terms:

Add/Remove Programs	patches
application assignment scripts	publishing
assigning	transformation files
categories	Windows Installer
file extensions	Windows Installer packages
initialization files	

Review Questions

1. Alicia is a systems administrator for a large organization. Recently, the company moved most of its workstations and servers to the Windows 2000 platform, and Alicia wants to take advantage of the new software-deployment features of Active Directory. Specifically, she wants to do the following:

   - Make applications available to users through the Add/Remove Programs Control Panel applet.

   - Group applications based on functionality or the types of users who might require them.

   - Avoid the automatic installation of applications for users and computers.

   Which of the following steps should Alicia take to meet these requirements? (Choose all that apply.)

   A. Create application categories.

   B. Set up a software installation share and assign the appropriate security permissions.

   C. Assign applications to users.

   D. Assign applications to computers.

   E. Create new file extension mappings.

   F. Create application definitions using the Active Directory and Group Policy administration tools.

2. A systems administrator has created a Software Deployment GPO. Which tool can be used to link this GPO to an existing OU?

   A. Active Directory Users and Computers

   B. Active Directory Domains and Trusts

   C. Add/Remove Programs Control Panel applet

   D. Computer Management

3. Emma wants to make a specific application available on the network. She finds that using Group Policy for software deployment will be the easiest way. She has the following requirements:

- All users of designated workstations should have access to Microsoft Office 2000.

- If a user moves to other computers on which Microsoft Office 2000 is not installed, they should not have access to this program.

Which of the following options should Emma choose to meet these requirements?

A. Assign the application to computers.

B. Assign the application to users.

C. Publish the application to computers.

D. Publish the application to users.

4. A systems administrator wants to ensure that a particular user has access to Microsoft Office 2000 regardless of the computer on which he logs on. Which of the following is the correct solution?

A. Assign the application to all computers within the environment and specify that only this user should have access to it.

B. Assign the application to the user.

C. Publish the application to all computers within the environment and specify that only this user should have access to it.

D. Publish the application to the user.

5. A systems administrator wants to ensure that a particular group of users will be able to install Microsoft Office 2000 by using the Add/Remove Programs applet in Control Panel. He does not want the applications to be automatically installed. Which of the following should he do?

A. Assign the application to their computers.

B. Assign the application to the users.

C. Publish the application to their computers.

D. Publish the application to the users.

6. Charles is the network administrator for the Worldwide Apparel Company. He is responsible for all the accounts in single-domain Windows 2000 network that has two sites; one in Los Angeles and one in New York. He has been told that a new application must be distributed to the designers in each location. It is a Windows 2000–compliant program that has been tested in the lab by the support engineers. He has already created a Designer OU that contains the workstations that need the application. Charles packages the application as an MSI file. He then defines the package in a GPO and links it to the Designer OU. The next day, he gets calls from the users that the promised application is not in their Start menus. What does Charles most likely need to do to deploy the network application to the specified computers?

A. Make a Windows Installer shortcut for the application.

B. Repackage the application as an MSI file and redeploy the application.

C. Apply a transformation file to the installed application on the Designer OU computers.

D. Re-create the ZAP file and then deploy it to the Designer OU.

7. In order to install assigned or published applications, a user must have which of the following permissions?

A. Ability to modify the Registry

B. Local Administrator permissions

C. Ability to create directories

D. Normal logon permissions

8. You are responsible for applications management in your medium-sized network environment. Recently, your organization began deploying a new custom-developed application to your users. On slow client machines, the installation process can take a long time. In some cases, users have chosen to abort the installation process so that they can perform it at a later time. You are now receiving complaints from several users who say that they attempted to cancel the installation process, but the system changes that the application made were not rolled back.

Which of the following Windows Installer settings may be responsible for this?

A. Always Install With Elevated Privileges

B. Disable Rollback

C. Disable Search Order

D. Disallow Uninstall

9. You have recently created a new software-deployment package for installing a new line-of-business application on many users' systems. You have the following requirements:

- You want to use the features of Active Directory and Group Policy to automatically deploy the software.

- The software should be installed on specific machines within the environment only.

- The application must be made available with minimal user intervention.

Which of the following steps must be performed in order to meet these requirements? (Choose all that apply.)

A. Refresh the Active Directory.

B. Synchronize all domain controllers.

C. Rebuild the Global Catalog.

D. Manually copy the required files to an appropriate file share and set the appropriate permissions on the share.

E. Assign the application to the appropriate computers.

F. Publish the application to the appropriate computers.

10. Andrew is a help desk operator for a large organization. Recently, he has been receiving a large number of calls from users who are attempting to open files for which they do not have viewers. For example, one user wants to open a file named `MarketingInfo.ppt`, but she does not have the Microsoft PowerPoint viewer installed. Andrew's boss wants him to meet the following requirements:

- The appropriate application should automatically be installed when a user selects specific file types.

- Applications should not be automatically installed in other circumstances.

- The installation of applications, when they are needed, should require minimal user intervention.

Which of the following Group Policy software-deployment features should Andrew use? (Choose all that apply.)

A. Categories

B. Publishing options

C. Assignment options

D. File extensions

11. You are the network administrator of the Willful Accounting Corporation. You came on board after the migration from Windows NT. The entire company is contained in one domain, although there are three sites that handle the replication between the locations. You have finally gotten a handle on all of the OUs and GPOs that have been created to manage the network. Everything appears to be running smoothly, with most problems simple hardware failures or user misunderstanding. You have just been notified that the company is going to upgrade its core accounting application, and it must be accomplished by the end of the month. You have also been notified that the machines in the Pharmaceutical Division OU cannot be upgraded this month because they are in the middle of an audit that won't be completed until next month. How can you accomplish your overall objective?

    A. At the domain controllers, except the one used by the Pharmaceutical Division, use the accounting application's uninstall program to remove the application. Install the new application on all the servers except for the Pharmaceutical Division.

    B. Create the GPO for the upgrade but remove the Read & Execute permission from the Pharmaceutical Division OU.

    C. Uninstall the application for all of the divisions and then reinstall the old application for the Pharmaceutical Division. Install the new application for the rest of the company, create an upgrade policy for the Pharmaceutical Division, and activate it the following month.

    D. Create a Mandatory Upgrade type for the GPO associated with the Pharmaceutical Division and then associate the new upgrade with the existing software in the Software Installation node of the GPO.

12. How can a systems administrator get more information about a specific Windows Installer setup file?

    A. By right-clicking the file and selecting Properties in Windows Explorer

    B. By issuing a search within Active Directory

    C. By querying the Global Catalog

    D. By viewing the package properties during software deployment

13. Jenny is responsible for application deployment in a medium-sized company that is using Active Directory. She has already configured her Windows 2000 Server computers to automatically deploy new applications (that are packaged using Windows Installer). However, she has recently been tasked with the automatic deployment of some applications that use a legacy installation routine.

How can Jenny create a Windows Installer package from a legacy setup program?

A. By right-clicking the Setup.exe file for the application and choosing Migrate

B. By right-clicking the Setup.exe file for the application and choosing Upgrade To Windows Installer

C. By adding the application to Active Directory

D. By placing the application within a Shared Folder object and then assigning the application to the appropriate client computers

E. By repackaging the legacy setup program for MSI compatibility using third-party software

14. You want to publish an application by using a GPO. In the GPO shown below, what would you do next in order to publish an application?

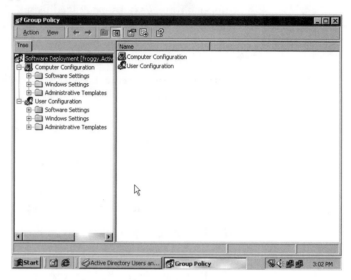

A. Right-click Software Settings under Computer Configuration and select New ➢ Package.

B. Expand Software Settings under Computer Configuration, right-click Software Installation, and select New ➢ Package.

C. Expand Software Settings under User Configuration, right-click Software Installation, and select New ➢ Package.

D. Right-click Software Settings under User Configuration and select New ➢ Package.

15. A new application has been approved for your Windows 2000 network. This approval process included testing the application on a separate network, where it was successfully deployed via GPOs to test OUs. You have been told that the application is to be installed on the machines in the Sales and Marketing OUs, where it will be used for customer contact tasks. You create the MSI package and link it to the Sales and Marketing OUs. The deployment seems to go smoothly, and you move on to other tasks. You then receive a phone call from one of the users in the Sales OU who does not have the application installed on his machine. After some questioning, you determine that the other people in his group did receive the application and it is working fine. What should you do to deploy the application to this user?

A. Re-create the MSI package and relink it to the Sales OU.

B. Re-create the MSI package and relink it to the Sales and Marketing OUs.

C. Make sure that the Windows Installer program is running on the user's machine.

D. Create a ZAP file for this particular user and link it to the Sales OU.

Answers to Review Questions

1. **A, B, F.** Alicia should first create an application share from which programs can be installed. Then she can define which applications are available on the network. The purpose of application categories is to logically group applications in the Add/Remove Programs Control Panel applet. The other options can result in the automatic installation of applications for users and computers (something she wants to avoid).

2. **A.** Group Policy links can be created within the Active Directory Users and Computers tool.

3. **A.** Assigning the application to the computer ensures that all users who access the workstation will have access to Microsoft Office 2000.

4. **B.** Assigning the application to the user ensures that the user has access to Microsoft Office 2000, regardless of the computer used.

5. **D.** When applications are published to users, they can easily install the programs using the Add/Remove Programs applet in Control Panel.

6. **B.** ZAP files cannot be assigned, they must be published, and since the application is Windows 2000 compliant there's no reason not to use an MSI file. ZAP files are created when there is no MSI file available or one cannot be created. These are usually applications that are not Windows 2000–compliant. Transformation files are used to customize a package file to determine which features will be available in the application.

7. **D.** Windows Installer is able to use the Installer service to bypass user permissions for installing software. Therefore, the user performing the installation is not required to have any special permissions other than the ability to log on to the domain.

8. **B.** Disabling a rollback can improve performance and reduce disk space requirements, but this option prevents rolling back from a failed installation.

9. D, E. It is the responsibility of the systems administrator to copy installation files to a software deployment share point and ensure that users can access these files. Once this is done, the applications can be assigned to various computers within the environment.

10. B, D. Publishing makes the applications available for automatic installation. File extension settings can be used to specify the applications that are installed when specific file types are accessed. This method requires minimal user intervention since it occurs automatically in the background.

11. D. Since the software is fundamental to the company, you want to make sure that it is a Mandatory Upgrade. Associating the new upgrade with the existing software will prevent this division from receiving the new software for now. If you removed the Read and Write permissions from the GPO, it would affect the entire GPO, not just this particular application. Installing and uninstalling software manually defeats the purpose of using GPOs.

12. A. Details about MSI files can be viewed by right-clicking the file and selecting Properties. The other options may be available, but only if the software deployment is configured within Active Directory.

13. E. In order to create a Windows Installer package from a legacy setup program, you must repackage the application with a third-party utility. These applications and utilities must be obtained from third-party software vendors and are not included as a supported part of the Windows 2000 operating system.

14. C. Software can be published only to users, not computers. You can assign software to users or computers.

15. C. If the Windows Installer program is not running on the client's workstation, then the MSI instructions cannot execute. Since everyone else's application is installed correctly, it is unlikely that there is anything wrong with the package itself. ZAP files are used only to customize the features that are available within an application.

Managing Client and Server Computers

MICROSOFT EXAM OBJECTIVES COVERED IN THIS CHAPTER:

✓ **Manage data storage. Considerations include file systems, permissions, and quotas.**

- Implement NTFS and FAT file systems.
- Enable and configure quotas.
- Implement and configure Encrypting File System (EFS).
- Configure volumes and basic and dynamic disks.
- Configure file and folder permissions.
- Manage a domain-based distributed file system (DFS).
- Manage file and folder compression.

✓ **Create shared resources and configure access rights. Shared resources include printers, shared folders, and Web folders.**

- Share folders and enable Web sharing.
- Configure shared folder permissions.
- Create and manage shared printers.
- Configure shared printer permissions.

✓ **Monitor and manage network security. Actions include auditing and detecting security breaches.**

- Configure user-account lockout settings.
- Configure user-account password length, history, age, and complexity.

✓ **Install and configure server and client computer hardware.**

- Verify hardware compatibility by using the qualifier tools.
- Configure driver signing options.
- Verify digital signatures on existing driver files.
- Configure operating system support for legacy hardware devices.

✓ **Troubleshoot starting servers and client computers. Tools and methodologies include Safe Mode, Recovery Console, and parallel installations.**

- Interpret the startup log file.
- Repair an operating system by using various startup options.
- Repair an operating system by using the Recovery Console.
- Recover data from a hard disk in the event that the operating system will not start.
- Restore an operating system and data from a backup.

✓ **Monitor and troubleshoot server health and performance. Tools include System Monitor, Event Viewer, and Task Manager.**

- Monitor and interpret real-time performance by using System Monitor and Task Manager.
- Configure and manage System Monitor alerts and logging.
- Diagnose server health problems by using Event Viewer.
- Identify and disable unnecessary operating system services.

✓ **Install and manage Windows 2000 updates. Updates include service packs, hot fixes, and security hot fixes.**

- Update an installation source by using slipstreaming.
- Apply and reapply service packs and hot fixes.
- Verify service pack and hot fix installation.
- Remove service packs and hot fixes.

 Web folders (web sharing) are covered in detail in Chapter 12, "Managing IIS and Terminal Services."

Active Directory is great for network administration, but falls short when it comes to managing individual computers. For example, if a computer won't start up, Active Directory won't do you much good. Installing and configuring new hardware on individual machines can't be accomplished through Active Directory either. In this chapter, we will begin to delve into the issues related to individual computers on the network.

> **NOTE** This chapter represents a review of the topics you have already studied while preparing for the Windows 2000 Professional and Server exams, which are prerequisites for using this book. The information presented here is an indication of things you might see on the Managing a Windows 2000 Network exam. If you need more information on any of these topics, you should see the related sections in either the *MCSE: Windows 2000 Professional Study Guide* or the *MCSE: Windows 2000 Server Study Guide*, 2nd Edition, by Lisa Donald and James Chellis.

This chapter covers myriad issues ranging from hardware installation to boot troubleshooting. Specifically, we discuss the following:

- Installing hardware
- Managing and troubleshooting hardware devices
- Managing disks
- Sharing resources
- Keeping Windows 2000 up-to-date
- Optimizing Windows 2000
- Troubleshooting the Windows 2000 startup process

Installing and Configuring Hardware

Hardware comes in two basic flavors: *Plug and Play* and *non–Plug and Play*. You can just install Plug and Play hardware into the computer (or connect a cable) and the computer will typically take care of everything else for you. You do not have to install drivers or mess with arcane IRQ and DMA settings like you do with non–Plug and Play hardware.

Microsoft ✓ *Exam Objective*

Install and configure server and client computer hardware.

- Verify hardware compatibility by using the qualifier tools.
- Configure driver signing options.
- Verify digital signatures on existing driver files.
- Configure operating system support for legacy hardware devices.

The Hardware Compatibility List (HCL)

Before purchasing or installing any device, you should make sure that your hardware appears on the *hardware compatibility list (HCL)*. The HCL is an extensive list of computers and peripheral hardware that have been tested with the Windows 2000 Server operating system.

The Windows 2000 Server operating system requires control of the hardware for stability, efficiency, and security. The hardware and supported drivers on the HCL have been put through rigorous tests. Microsoft guarantees that the items on the list meet the requirements for Windows 2000 Server and do not have any incompatibilities that could affect the stability of the operating system.

If you call Microsoft for support, the first thing a Microsoft support engineer will ask about is your configuration. If you have any hardware that is not on the HCL, there is no guarantee of support.

To determine if your computer and peripherals are on the HCL, check the most up-to-date list at www.microsoft.com/hcl/.

Installing Plug and Play Hardware

You really don't need to do much in order to install Plug and Play hardware. For example, if you have a Plug and Play PCI modem, all you need to do is turn off the computer, plug the modem into the PCI slot in your motherboard, and turn the computer on. Windows 2000 will automatically detect the modem, allocate resources such as IRQ and DMA channels, and install the appropriate drivers. Depending on the hardware installed, you might need to reboot after Windows has completed the process.

Installing Non–Plug and Play Hardware

Non–Plug and Play hardware is considerably trickier to install and configure than Plug and Play hardware. Whenever possible, you should try to purchase Plug and Play devices for your company's computers, but sometimes specialized legacy devices are needed for specific tasks.

Non–Plug and Play devices require unique IRQs, I/O port addresses, memory addresses, and DMA settings. You should check the devices currently installed on the computer to make sure that you do not have a conflict. In Device Manager, select View ➢ Resources By Connection to see which resources are being used. Make sure that your device has been configured with unique settings that are not already in use by any other device in the machine. You can set these properties on the device itself, typically with jumpers. Refer to the manufacturer's documentation for instructions on how to change these settings. Figure 9.1 shows an example of the resources currently being used by a test computer.

FIGURE 9.1 Viewing resource allocation in Device Manager

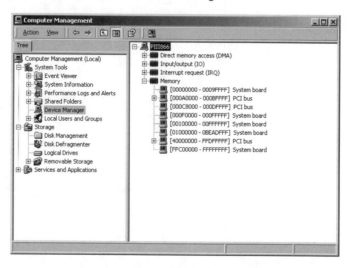

After you physically install the device, you need to install the appropriate device driver. You should use the Add/Remove Hardware applet in the Control Panel, which will automatically start the Add/Remove Hardware Wizard, in order to install the driver. The wizard will walk you through the steps of installing the driver. After you have finished, you will probably need to reboot the computer in order for the device to work properly.

Managing and Troubleshooting Hardware Devices

You typically manage hardware devices through their respective Properties dialog boxes. You can access these dialog boxes either though Device Manager or through individual icons in the Control Panel.

Using Device Manager

You access Device Manager by taking the following steps: Right-click My Computer on the Desktop, select Manage from the context menu, choose System Tools, and then choose Device Manager. The Device Manager window displays a list of all the device categories and devices present in the computer. You can manage a device's properties by double-clicking a device category and then double-clicking a device listed in that category. Figure 9.2 shows the Device Manager window.

FIGURE 9.2 Device Manager

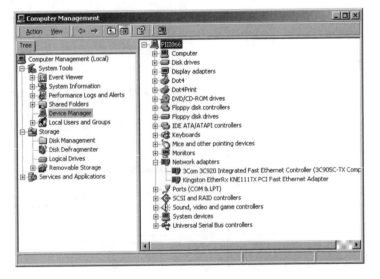

The Properties dialog box can have any number of tabs, depending on the device. The most common tabs are the General tab and the Driver tab. The General tab displays general information related to the device, such as the manufacturer, and informs you whether the device is working properly. You can enable and disable the device using the Device Usage pull-down menu, which is also located on the General tab. The Driver tab lists information about the driver that is currently being used and provides an Update Driver button that you can use to install an updated device driver. An Uninstall button allows you to manually uninstall the driver, and a Driver Details button provides you with more information about the driver. You might also see a Resources tab (which allows you to manually configure IRQ, DMA, etc.), a Power Management tab, an Advanced tab, or any other tab that the device manufacturer feels you might need to configure the device.

Managing Devices in the Control Panel

You can also manage several specific devices through the Control Panel. The Control Panel typically gives you extended functionality beyond what would normally be found in Device Manager. For example, you can set your video card's resolution and bit depth by using the Display applet in the Control Panel, which is something that you cannot do in Device Manager. You can also configure settings for the keyboard, imaging devices, game controllers, modems, printers, and the mouse that you wouldn't be able to configure in Device Manager. Some device manufacturers provide additional Control Panel utilities for specific devices.

Managing Device Drivers

Device drivers sometimes need to be updated. The device manufacturer might have fixed problems with the driver or added functionality to the driver and usually will not provide you with tech support until you have updated the driver. Exercise 9.1 shows you how to update a device driver.

EXERCISE 9.1

Updating a Device Driver

The steps in this exercise show you how to update a device driver. You should have a new driver for a device in your system before attempting this exercise.

EXERCISE 9.1 *(continued)*

1. Right-click My Computer on the Desktop and select Manage from the context menu.

2. Expand System Tools if it is not already expanded, and then choose Device Manager.

3. Double-click the device category that your device is under, and then double-click the device that requires the updated driver.

4. Select the Driver tab in the Properties dialog box.

5. Click the Update Driver button. The Upgrade Device Driver Wizard appears. Click Next to clear the welcome screen and begin the wizard.

6. Click the Search For A Suitable Driver For My Device radio button, and click Next to continue.

7. Choose the option that best describes the location of your new driver. If your driver is on a removable disk, select either Floppy Disk Drive or CD-ROM Drive. If your driver is on the hard disk, select Specify A Location. If you don't have an updated driver but you want Windows to find one for you, select Microsoft Windows Update. Click Next to continue.

8. If you chose the Specify A Location check box in the previous step, then you will need to manually navigate to the driver's location. Click OK when you have finished.

9. The Driver Files Search Results page will appear, showing you the appropriate drivers for the device. Click the driver you want to use, and then click Next to continue. Verify that all of the information is correct on the Completing The Upgrade Device Driver page, and click Finish to end the wizard.

Managing Driver Signing

In the past, poorly written device drivers have caused problems with Windows operating systems. Microsoft is now promoting a mechanism called *driver signing* as a way of ensuring that drivers are properly tested before they are released to the public.

Configuring Driver Signing Options

You can specify how Windows 2000 Server will respond when you choose to install an unsigned driver through the Driver Signing Options dialog box. To access this dialog box, right-click My Computer, select Properties from the context menu, and click the Hardware tab in the System Properties dialog box. Clicking the Driver Signing button in the Device Manager section opens the Driver Signing Options dialog box.

In the Driver Signing Options dialog box, you can select from three options for file system verification:

- The Ignore option has Windows 2000 install all of the files, whether or not they are signed. You will not see any type of message about driver signing.

- The Warn option has Windows 2000 display a warning message before installing an unsigned file. You can then choose to either continue with the installation or cancel it. This is the default setting.

- The Block option has Windows 2000 prevent the installation of any unsigned file. You will see an error message when you attempt to install the unsigned driver, and you will not be able to continue.

If you check the Apply Setting As System Default option, the settings that you apply will be used by all users who log on to the computer.

Verifying a File Signature

Windows 2000 includes a File Signature Verification utility that you can use to verify that system files have been digitally signed. The installation of unsigned drivers can cause random lockups of a server. To run this utility, you issue the `sigverif` command from the Command Prompt window.

If you want to configure advanced verification options, such as advanced search options or logging options, click the Advanced button. When you are ready to check that your files have been digitally signed, click the Start button. The utility will scan all of your system files. When it's finished, it will display the signature-verification results.

In Exercise 9.2, you will check the setting for driver signing and run the File Signature Verification utility.

EXERCISE 9.2

Managing Driver Signing

1. From the Desktop, right-click My Computer and select Properties.

2. In the System Properties dialog box, click the Hardware tab, and then click the Driver Signing button.

3. In the Driver Signing Options dialog box, verify that the Warn radio button is selected and the Apply Setting As System Default check box is checked.

4. Click OK to close the dialog box. Then click OK within the System Properties dialog box.

5. Select Start ➢ Programs ➢ Accessories ➢ Command Prompt.

6. In the Command Prompt window, type **sigverif** and press Enter.

7. In the File Signature Verification window, click the Start button.

8. When the results of the signature verification appear, note whether the utility detected any files that were not digitally signed. Click the Close button.

9. Close the Command Prompt window.

Troubleshooting Devices

If a device is not working properly, the Properties dialog box will sometimes indicate that the device has malfunctioned. You can run the Troubleshooting Wizard to attempt to diagnose the problem and potentially get the device up and running again. Just click the Troubleshooter button on the General tab of the device's Properties dialog box to start the wizard. The wizard will ask you several questions and eventually present you with the most likely cause of the problem.

🌐 Real World Scenario

Network Devices

You have been brought on board at a flooring manufacturing company to help administer their network. The network consists of 1,400 workstations that have been upgraded to Windows 2000 and are now managed by GPOs through Active Directory. The company has three locations that are represented by Windows 2000 sites contained in one domain. After a year in service, the main infrastructure of the network has been fairly well worked out and it functions properly.

One thing that you do notice, however, is that you are starting to get calls regarding problems with several of the users' individual workstations. Some of the users have been adding new devices to their workstations without going through the proper channels, which would include your testing the devices before deploying them. You realize that you need to put some controls over the hardware in addition to deploying applications via the GPOs.

Oftentimes the focus of a systems administrator is on software because people can download it so easily and try to install it on their workstations. But GPOs are also useful for controlling the addition of new hardware. While using GPOS for this purpose is very effective, keep in mind that doing so places a larger burden on the administrator. You want to make sure that all hardware devices are evaluated as diligently as software. Hardware management can be even more time-consuming than software management. You can simply push software down the wire to the workstation, but installing new hardware always means a physical trip to each workstation.

It is important to understand the differences between Plug and Play devices as opposed to legacy devices. It is also important to have written procedures for testing the devices in the workstations. Having a standardized method for troubleshooting the devices in your workstations facilitates the troubleshooting process. It also allows you to delegate the process to others more effectively.

Another aspect of hardware management on the workstation is to create documentation of the interrupt requests (IRQs) and memory consumed by devices. Even though Plug and Play will automatically manage these tasks, there will always be some legacy device that is "essential" to someone on the network and you will have to support it manually. These types of activities can seem quite tedious, but the payoff is in the time saved in dealing with a problem when the productivity of the user is at stake. I can assure you that the user's perspective of productivity will be far different from yours.

Configuring Storage

Disks are first configured during the Windows 2000 installation process. You can't install the operating system without some sort of disk configuration in place. After Windows has been installed, you can use additional tools to configure more complicated and useful disk options. The Windows 2000 installation process is beyond the scope of this book, but you should have already studied that topic while preparing for the Windows 2000 Professional and Server exams.

Microsoft ✓ ***Exam Objective***

Manage data storage. Considerations include file systems, permissions, and quotas.

- Implement NTFS and FAT file systems.

- Enable and configure quotas.

- Implement and configure Encrypting File System (EFS).

- Configure volumes and basic and dynamic disks.

- Configure file and folder permissions.

- Manage a domain-based distributed file system (DFS).

- Manage file and folder compression.

In this section you will learn about file systems, disk configuration, and disk quotas. We will finish the section by discussing NTFS permissions.

Configuring File Systems

Windows uses file systems to format your hard drive in various ways. Each file system has its advantages and disadvantages. Windows 95, 98, and Me can use only the *FAT file system*, so if you want to dual-boot with any of these operating systems then you will need to format your hard drive with FAT. Otherwise, there really isn't any reason not to use *NTFS*. You can convert a FAT partition to an NTFS partition by using the CONVERT command-line utility. The syntax for the CONVERT command is

CONVERT [*drive:*] /fs:ntfs

Table 9.1 shows you the features of each file system that is compatible with Windows 2000.

TABLE 9.1 File System Capabilities

Feature	FAT16	FAT32	NTFS
Operating system support?	Most	Windows 95 OSR2, Windows 98, Windows Me, Windows 2000, and Windows XP	Windows NT, Windows 2000, and Windows XP
Long filename support?	Yes	Yes	Yes
Efficient use of disk space?	No	Yes	Yes
Compression support?	No	No	Yes
Quota support?	No	No	Yes
Encryption support?	No	No	Yes
Local security support?	No	No	Yes
Network security support?	Yes	Yes	Yes
Maximum volume size	2GB	2TB	16EB

Windows 2000 Server also supports *CDFS (Compact Disk File System)*. However, CDFS cannot be managed. It is used only to mount and read CDs.

Disk Configuration

Along with file systems, Windows 2000 supports two types of disk configuration options: *basic storage* and *dynamic storage*. Basic storage uses *partitions* to divide your hard disk into separate drive letters and is compatible with operating systems older than Windows 2000. Dynamic storage uses *volumes* instead of partitions and cannot be used with older operating systems.

Basic Storage

Basic storage uses up to four partitions per physical disk to allocate drive space. Partitions consist of primary partitions and extended partitions, and each physical drive can have only one extended partition. An extended partition can be subdivided into many drive letters, but a primary partition must have only one drive letter assigned to it. The first partition on a disk is always a primary partition. You typically want to use only a single primary partition per physical drive. You might want to add a partition if you need to use two different file systems (such as in a dual-boot configuration).

Dynamic Storage

Dynamic storage is new to Windows 2000 and uses volumes to divide the hard drive into logical components. Volumes are similar to partitions, but they allow for many more configuration options in Windows 2000 than partitions do. You can configure volumes as *simple volumes*, *spanned volumes*, *striped volumes*, *mirrored volumes*, and *RAID-5 volumes*.

Simple Volumes

Simple volumes are almost identical to partitions. They are simply logical divisions of the physical disk that are represented by a drive letter. Figure 9.3 illustrates the use of simple volumes.

FIGURE 9.3 Two simple volumes

Simple Volume C:\
1GB

Simple Volume D:\
1GB

Physical Disk 0
2GB

Spanned Volumes

Spanned volumes are logical drives that span multiple physical disks. Each physical disk must be a dynamic disk, but the drive sizes do not need to be the same. Data is written sequentially to the physical drives. This is very useful if you are running out of disk space. Rather than adding a new disk and creating a separate directory tree on that disk, you can just extend the current volume to span to the new disk. Figure 9.4 shows you how one volume can span multiple physical disks.

FIGURE 9.4 A spanned volume set

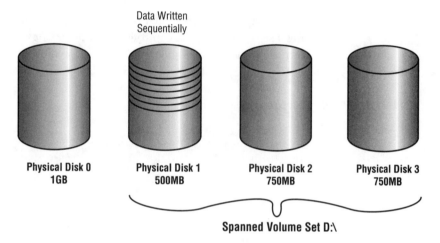

Data Written
Sequentially

Physical Disk 0   Physical Disk 1   Physical Disk 2   Physical Disk 3
1GB   500MB   750MB   750MB

Spanned Volume Set D:\

Striped Volumes

Striped volumes write data to multiple physical disks in stripes, rather than sequentially like spanned volumes. This means that nearly every file in the striped volume is physically stored in multiple locations. Since all of the drives in the stripe set can access their parts of the file simultaneously, this increases the overall speed of the volume. Unfortunately, if one of the drives fails, you cannot access any of the files stored on the volume. Figure 9.5 shows you the stripes that are created across multiple physical disks.

FIGURE 9.5 A striped volume set

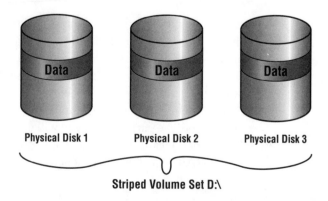

Physical Disk 1   Physical Disk 2   Physical Disk 3

Striped Volume Set D:\

Mirrored Volumes

A mirrored volume automatically writes all of the volume's data to two drives simultaneously. This might seem redundant, but that's exactly the benefit of mirrored volumes. If one of the drives in the mirrored set fails, then you'll always have a backup immediately ready to use. You don't have to spend long hours waiting for your tape backup to restore the information on the failed drive. Disk duplexing is similar to disk mirroring except that each physical disk uses a separate hard disk controller. Disk duplexing is slightly faster than disk mirroring, and you configure the two types of volumes in exactly the same way in Windows 2000. Figure 9.6 illustrates a mirrored volume set.

FIGURE 9.6   A mirrored volume set

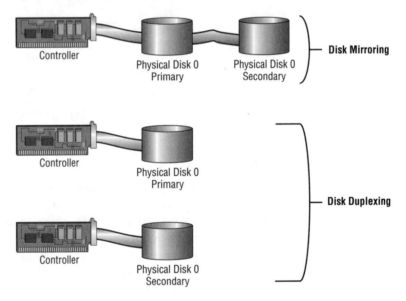

RAID-5 Volumes

RAID-5 combines the speed advantages of striped volumes with the redundancy of mirrored volumes. RAID-5 stripes information across 3 to 32 physical disks but adds a parity stripe as well. The parity stripe contains enough information that if any single drive in the set fails, the entire volume can be restored. If multiple disks fail, then you will still need to turn to your tape backup system in order to restore the lost data. Until the volume has been restored from the parity stripe, you will notice a significant performance hit, so it's a good idea to replace the failed disk as soon as possible. Figure 9.7 shows a RAID-5 volume striped across three physical disks.

FIGURE 9.7 A RAID-5 volume set

FIGURE 9.8 The Disk Management utility

Physical Disk 0   Physical Disk 1   Physical Disk 2   — RAID-5 Volume Set

Using Disk Management

You use the Disk Management utility in Windows 2000 to configure the different types of partitions and volumes discussed above. Disk Management is located under Storage in Computer Management. (Right-click My Computer and select Manage from the context menu in order to access Computer Management.) Figure 9.8 shows you the Disk Management utility.

The main window shows the following information:

- The volumes that are recognized by the computer
- The type of partition, either basic or dynamic
- The type of file system used by each partition
- The status of the partition and whether or not the partition contains the system or boot partition
- The capacity, or amount of space, allocated to the partition

- The amount of free space remaining on the partition
- The amount of overhead associated with the partition

With Disk Management, you can perform a variety of tasks:

- View disk and volume properties
- Add a new disk
- Create partitions and volumes
- Upgrade a basic disk to a dynamic disk
- Change a drive letter and path
- Delete partitions and volumes
- Create extended volumes
- Create spanned volumes
- Create striped volumes
- Create mirrored volumes
- Create RAID-5 volumes

Setting Disk Quotas

As you saw in Table 9.1, one of the features of the NTFS file system is its ability to set *quotas*. Quotas limit the amount of disk space allocated to users. You can either create a blanket quota that applies to all users, or you can set individual quotas that affect all users differently. Disk quotas are configured through the Quotas tab of the NTFS volume Properties dialog box. Disk quotas have the following limitations:

- Disk quotas can be specified only for NTFS volumes.
- Disk quotas apply only at the volume level, even if the NTFS partitions reside on the same physical hard drive.
- Disk usage is calculated on file and folder ownership. When a user creates, copies, or takes ownership of a file, that user is the owner of the file.

- When a user installs an application, the free space that the application sees is based on the disk quota availability, not the actual amount of free space on the volume.

- Disk quota space used is based on actual file size. There is no mechanism to support or recognize file compression.

Disk quotas are not applied to the Administrator account or members of the Administrators group.

Applying NTFS Permissions

Another feature of NTFS that you saw in Table 9.1 was support for local security. All of the folders on a FAT partition are available to all users all the time. However, on an NTFS partition or volume, folders can be locked so that only specific users or groups can access them. These access rights are known as *NTFS permissions*. NTFS offers several different types of permissions, as shown in Table 9.2.

TABLE 9.2   NTFS Permissions

Permission	Access Rights
Full Control	Traverse folders and execute files (programs) in the folders.
	List the contents of a folder and read the data in a folder's files.
	See a folder's or file's attributes.
	Change a folder's or file's attributes.
	Create new files and write data to the files.
	Create new folders and append data to files.
	Delete subfolders and files.
	Delete files.
	Change permissions for files and folders.
	Take ownership of files and folders.

TABLE 9.2 NTFS Permissions *(continued)*

Permission	Access Rights
Modify	Traverse folders and execute files in the folders. List the contents of a folder and read the data in a folder's files. See a folder's or file's attributes. Change a folder's or file's attributes. Create new files and write data to the files. Create new folders and append data to files. Delete files.
Read & Execute	Traverse folders and execute files in the folders. List the contents of a folder and read the data in a folder's files. See a folder's or file's attributes.
List Folder Contents	Traverse folders. List the contents of a folder. See a folder's or file's attributes.
Read	List the contents of a folder and read the data in a folder's files. See a folder's or file's attributes.
Write	Change a folder's or file's attributes. Create new files and write data to the files. Create new folders and append data to files.

You apply NTFS permissions on the Security tab of the affected folder's Properties dialog box.

Inherited and Effective Permissions

In Windows 2000, permissions are inherited from the parent folder to every child folder contained therein. You can disable *inherited permissions* by deselecting the Allow Inheritable Permissions From Parent To Propagate To This Object check box at the bottom of the Security tab of the folder Properties dialog box.

A user's *effective permissions* are the result of multiple permissions due to multiple group membership. In order to determine effective permissions, add up all of the user's allowed permissions according to their various group memberships, and then subtract all denied permissions. This method resolves any potentially conflicting permissions that can arise.

Determining NTFS Permissions for Copied or Moved Files

When you copy or move NTFS files, the permissions that have been set for those files might change. The following guidelines can be used to predict what will happen:

- If you move a file from one folder to another folder on the same volume, the file will retain the original NTFS permissions.

- If you move a file from one folder to another folder between different NTFS volumes, the file is treated as a copy and will have the same permissions as the destination folder.

- If you copy a file from one folder to another folder (on the same volume or on a different volume), the file will have the same permissions as the destination folder.

- If you copy or move a folder or file to a FAT partition, it will not retain any NTFS permissions.

Managing Data Compression

Data compression is the process of storing data in a form that takes less space than uncompressed data does. With Windows 2000 Server, data compression is available only on NTFS partitions. If you copy or move a compressed folder or file to a FAT partition (or a floppy disk), Windows 2000 will automatically uncompress the folder or file.

Both files and folders in the NTFS file system can be compressed or uncompressed. Files and folders are managed independently, which means that a compressed folder could contain uncompressed files, and an uncompressed folder could contain compressed files.

Access to compressed files by DOS or Windows applications is transparent. For example, if you access a compressed file through Microsoft Word, the file will be uncompressed automatically when it is opened and then automatically compressed again when it is closed.

You cannot have a folder or file compressed and encrypted at the same time. Encryption is discussed in the "Managing Data Encryption with EFS" section later in this chapter.

You implement compression through the Windows Explorer utility. Compression is an advanced attribute of a folder's or file's properties.

Exercise 9.3 walks you through the process of compressing folders and files.

EXERCISE 9.3

Compressing Folders and Files

In this exercise, you will learn how to compress folders and files. This exercise assumes that you have completed Exercise 9.1.

1. Select Start ➤ Programs ➤ Accessories ➤ Windows Explorer.

2. In Windows Explorer, find and select a folder on the D: drive. The folder you select should contain files.

3. Right-click the folder and select Properties. In the General tab of the folder Properties dialog box, note the value listed for Size On Disk. Then click the Advanced button.

4. In the Advanced Attributes dialog box, check the Compress Contents To Save Disk Space option. Then click OK. In the folder Properties dialog box, click OK.

<!-- Advanced Attributes dialog box -->
Advanced Attributes [?][x]

Choose the settings you want for this folder
When you apply these changes you will be asked if you want the changes to affect all subfolders and files as well.

Archive and Index attributes
☐ Folder is ready for archiving
☑ For fast searching, allow Indexing Service to index this folder

Compress or Encrypt attributes
☐ Compress contents to save disk space
☐ Encrypt contents to secure data

[OK]   [Cancel]

EXERCISE 9.3 *(continued)*

5. In the Confirm Attribute Changes dialog box, select Apply Changes To This Folder, Subfolder, And Files. (If this dialog box does not appear, click the Apply button in the Properties dialog box to display it.) Then click OK.

Confirm Attribute Changes

You have chosen to make the following attribute change(s):

compress

Do you want to apply this change to this folder only, or do you want to apply it to all subfolders and files as well?

(•) Apply changes to this folder only

( ) Apply changes to this folder, subfolders and files

| OK | Cancel |

6. In the General tab of the folder Properties dialog box, note the value that now appears for Size On Disk. This size should have decreased because you compressed the folder.

You can specify that compressed files be displayed in a different color from uncompressed files. To do so, in Windows Explorer, select Tools ➢ Folder Options ➢ Views. Under Files And Folders, check the Display Compressed Files And Folders With An Alternate Color option.

Managing Data Encryption with EFS

Data encryption is a way to increase data security. Encryption is the process of translating data into code that is not easily accessible. Once data has been encrypted, you must have a password or key to decrypt the data. Unencrypted data is known as plain text, and encrypted data is known as *cipher text*.

The *Encrypting File System (EFS)* is the Windows 2000 technology that is used to store encrypted files on NTFS partitions. Encrypted files add an extra layer of security to your file system. A user with the proper key can transparently access encrypted files. A user without the proper key is denied access. There is a recovery agent that can be used by the Administrator if the owner is unavailable to provide the proper key to decrypt folders or files.

Encrypting and Decrypting Folders and Files

To use EFS, a user specifies that a folder or file on an NTFS partition should be encrypted. The encryption is transparent to the user, who has access to the file. However, when other users try to access the file, they will not be able to decrypt the file—even if those users have Full Control NTFS permissions. Instead, they will receive an error message.

 By default, the Administrator has rights to access the properties of another user's encrypted folder or file and decrypt it. This means that if the user who encrypted a file is unavailable to decrypt the file (for example, because that user left the company), the Administrator can recover it.

Exercise 9.4 walks you through the process of using EFS to encrypt a folder.

EXERCISE 9.4

Using EFS to Manage Data Encryption

In this exercise, you will use EFS to encrypt a folder. This exercise assumes that you have completed Exercise 9.1.

1. Use the Local Users and Groups utility to create the new user **Lauren**. Deselect the User Must Change Password At Next Logon option for this user.

2. Select Start ➤ Programs ➤ Accessories ➤ Windows Explorer.

3. In Windows Explorer, find and select a folder on the D: drive. The folder you select should contain files. Right-click the folder and select Properties.

4. In the General tab of the folder Properties dialog box, click the Advanced button.

5. In the Advanced Attributes dialog box, check the Encrypt Contents To Secure Data option. Then click OK.

EXERCISE 9.4 *(continued)*

6. In the Confirm Attribute Changes dialog box (if this dialog box does not appear, click the Apply button in the Properties dialog box to display it), select Apply Changes To This Folder, Subfolder, And Files. Then click OK.

7. Log off as Administrator and log on as Lauren.

8. Open Windows Explorer and attempt to access one of the files in the folder you encrypted. You should receive an error message stating that the file is not accessible.

9. Log off as Lauren and log on as Administrator.

To decrypt folders and files, repeat the steps above but uncheck the Encrypt Contents To Secure Data option in the Advanced Attributes dialog box.

Managing the Distributed File System

The Distributed File System (Dfs) gives users a central location to access files and folders that are physically distributed across a network. For example, if users in your Sales department need to access files that are stored on several computers in the Sales domain, you can use the Dfs to make it appear as though all of the files reside in the same network share. When you use the Dfs, users won't need to search through multiple computers to find the files or folders they need. Figure 9.9 illustrates how the Dfs works.

A Dfs topology consists of three main components: a *Dfs root*, one or more *Dfs links*, and one or more *Dfs shared folders*, or *replicas*. Each Dfs link points to one shared folder and all of its replicas. You can replicate the Dfs root by creating *root shares* on other member servers in the domain.

Permissions that apply to folders and files are not lost in the Dfs. If a user has access to a specific shared folder, that user will also have access to that folder when using the appropriate Dfs share. If users have access to one Dfs shared folder, they will also be able to see all of the other Dfs shared folders, but they won't be able to use them unless they have the appropriate permissions.

FIGURE 9.9 The Dfs provides a central location for network file and folders.

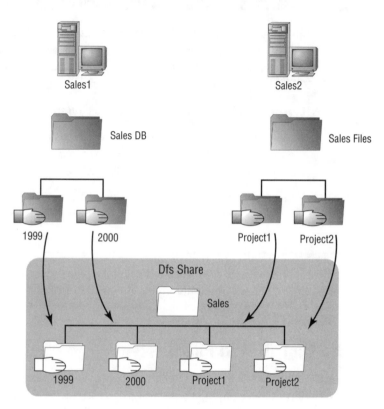

Creating a Dfs Root and Dfs Links

There can be only one Dfs root per server, although there can be unlimited Dfs roots per domain. You should create the Dfs root on an NTFS partition. Automatic replication is available only on the NTFS file system. You can also take advantage of the security features offered by NTFS to control access to Dfs shared folders.

A Dfs link is a link from the Dfs root to one or more shared folders. Dfs links are added at the root of the Dfs topology. You can have up to 1,000 Dfs links assigned to a Dfs root.

Configuring Dfs Replication

Replication ensures that if the host server goes down, the files and folders that are part of the Dfs will be available. Automatic replication can be used only in conjunction with NTFS volumes. If you do not specify automatic replication, you must replicate your Dfs shared folders manually.

You can enable the Dfs to automatically replicate the contents of one or more shared folders using the *File Replication Service (FRS)*. When changes are made to one shared folder, FRS updates the other shared folders to reflect the changes (by default, this happens every 15 minutes). You should specify that all of the shared folders in a Dfs link are replicated automatically, if possible. This ensures that all of the shared folders in a Dfs link are synchronized properly. You must select one of your shared folders to be the Initial Master, which replicates its contents to the other shared folders in the Dfs link the first time the replication policy is set. After the Initial Master is set, the Set Master button will disappear. If the Initial Master goes down, the button will reappear. Also, the Initial Master should be the share with Write access. The Initial Master is the folder that is replicated (in a single-master design); the replica folders require only Read access.

You should not mix and match manual replication with automatic replication. If you do, all of your shared folders may not be synchronized correctly.

Exercise 9.5 walks you through the process of managing Dfs.

EXERCISE 9.5

Managing Dfs

In this exercise, you will create a Dfs root and Dfs links and configure Dfs replication.

1. From your Windows 2000 domain controller, use Windows Explorer to create the `C:\Sales` and `C:\Project1` folders, and share the `Project1` folder as **Project1Share**. On your Windows 2000 member server, create a folder called `C:\2002`. Share this folder as **2002Share**.

2. Select Start ➢ Programs ➢ Administrative Tools ➢ Distributed File System.

3. In the Dfs console, highlight Distributed File System and select Action ➢ New Dfs Root.

4. When the New Dfs Root Wizard starts, click Next.

5. In the Select Dfs Root Type dialog box, verify that the Create A Domain Dfs Root option is selected and click Next.

6. In the Select The Host Domain For The Dfs Root dialog box, confirm that your domain is shown in the Domain Name text box, and click Next.

7. In the Specify The Host Server For The Dfs Root dialog box, verify that your server's name is selected, and click Next.

8. In the Specify The Dfs Root Share dialog box, click the Create A New Share radio button. In the Path To Share text box, type `C:\Sales`. In the Share Name text box, type **Sales**. Click Next.

9. In the Name The Dfs Root dialog box, leave the default Dfs root name and add the comment **This is a test Dfs root**. Click Next.

10. When the Completing The New Dfs Root Wizard dialog box appears, click Finish.

11. Right-click your Dfs root and select New Dfs Link.

12. In the Create A New Dfs Link dialog box, type **Project1** in the Link Name text box. In the Send The User To This Shared Folder text box, specify the UNC path to the `Project1` folder you created in step 1 (`\\computername\Project1Share`). In the Comment text box, type **Data for Sales Project1**. Click OK.

13. In the Dfs console window, right-click your Dfs root and select New Dfs Link.

14. In the Create A New Dfs Link dialog box, type **2002** in the Link Name text box. In the Send The User To This Shared Folder text box, specify the UNC path to the `2002` folder you created in step 1 (`\\computername\2002Share`). In the Comment text box, type **Sales data for 2002**. Click OK.

15. On your member server, create a folder called `C:\Replicate` and share the folder as **ReplDfs**.

16. In the Dfs console, right-click the Dfs link Project1 and select New Replica.

17. In the Add A New Replica dialog box, specify the share you created in step 15 (`\\computername\ReplDfs`) in the Send The User To This Shared Folder text box. For Replication Policy, select the Manual Replication option. Then click OK.

EXERCISE 9.5 *(continued)*

18. Right-click the Dfs link and select Replication Policy.

19. In the Replication Policy dialog box, select the Dfs shared folder
`Project1` as the master folder for the first replication, and click the
Set Master button. Select the `\\computername\Rep1Dfs` shared
folder, and click the Enable button. Click OK.

After you have created the Dfs structure, with a Dfs root and links, users can
access the Dfs root in the same manner that they would access a regular
share.

Sharing Resources

Sharing gives other users on the network access to your files and folders. You can also share a printer that is physically connected to the local
computer. You configure *share permissions* similarly to the way you configure NTFS permissions, but you should make the distinction between the
two. NTFS permissions apply to local users, while share permissions apply
to users out on the network.

Microsoft
Exam
Objective

**Create shared resources and configure access rights. Shared
resources include printers, shared folders, and Web folders.**

- Share folders and enable Web sharing.

- Configure shared folder permissions.

- Create and manage shared printers.

- Configure shared printer permissions.

Creating and Managing Shared Folders

In order to *share* a folder, you must be logged on as an Administrator or a
Power User (on a member server), or as an Administrator or a Server Operator

(on a domain controller). In the folder Properties dialog box, shown in Figure 9.10, select the Sharing tab and click the Share This Folder radio button to begin sharing the folder. You will need to enter a share name in the Share Name field (this could be the same name as the folder, but doesn't need to be), and you can specify an optional comment in the Comment field. You can also limit the number of users simultaneously accessing the folder.

FIGURE 9.10 The Sharing tab of the folder Properties dialog box

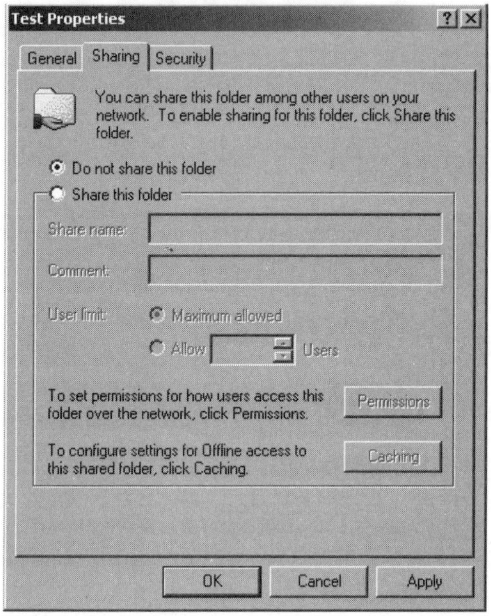

Shared Folder Permissions

Clicking the Permissions button on the Sharing tab of the folder Properties dialog box opens the Share Permissions dialog box, as shown in Figure 9.11. From here you can add users or groups in order to grant or deny access to the share, as well as set the specific permissions for the users or groups you add. By default, the Everyone group is granted the Full Control permission, so you will probably want to make any changes to sensitive share folders right away.

FIGURE 9.11 The Share Permissions dialog box

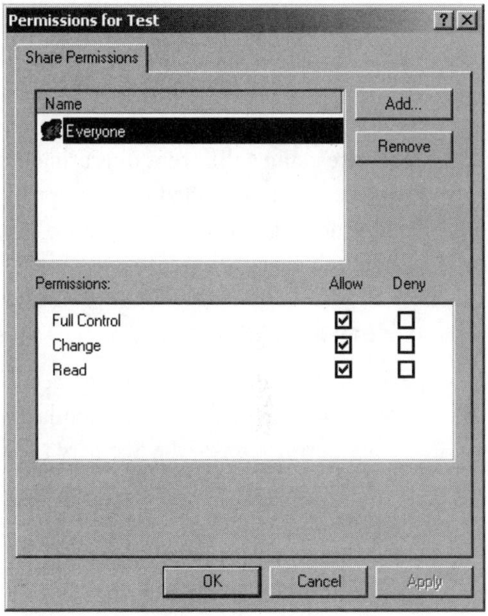

Table 9.3 explains the three share permissions and their function.

TABLE 9.3 Share Permissions

Permission	Access Rights
Full Control	Have full access to the shared folder.
Change	Change data in a file or delete files.
Read	View and execute files.

Shared folders do not use the same concept of inheritance as NTFS folders. If you share a folder, there is no way to block access to lower-level resources through share permissions.

Printer Sharing

Printer sharing is very similar to folder sharing. Once the printer has been installed on the local machine, you can share it through the Sharing tab of the printer Properties dialog box. You will have the option of specifying additional drivers that remote users can download from your computer in case they are using a different operating system or computer type than the printer was originally installed on. The print driver that is used in Windows 2000 might not work for users running Windows 98, so this function makes sharing much easier.

Print Permissions

Print permissions are set on the Security tab of the printer Properties dialog box. Don't be misled by the similarity to the Security tab that is used to set NTFS permissions—the Security tab of the printer Properties dialog box controls local as well as network access to the printer. Print permissions are distinct from shared folder permissions because printing is a much different task than working with folders. Table 9.4 shows the three print permissions and what they mean.

TABLE 9.4 Print Permissions

Print Permission	Description
Print	Allows a user or group to connect to a printer and send print jobs to the printer.
Manage Printers	Allows administrative control of the printer. With this permission, a user or group can pause and restart the printer, change the spooler settings, share or unshare a printer, change print permissions, and manage printer properties.
Manage Documents	Allows users to manage documents by pausing, restarting, resuming, and deleting queued documents. Users cannot control the status of the printer.

Managing Password and Account Lockout Policies

In Chapter 6, "Active Directory Security," you learned how to create and configure user accounts in Active Directory. You learned how to create and configure local users and groups when you studied for the Windows 2000 Professional and Server exams, which are prerequisites for using this book. We will now re-examine two issues from those exams that you will find relevant for the MCSA exam: password and account lockout policies.

Microsoft ✓ *Exam* *Objective*	**Monitor and manage network security. Actions include auditing and detecting security breaches.** • Configure user-account lockout settings. • Configure user-account password length, history, age, and complexity.

Account policies are used to specify the user account properties that relate to the logon process. They allow you to configure computer security settings for passwords, account lockout specifications, and Kerberos authentication within a domain.

Open the MMC snap-in for Group Policy, and you will see an option for Local Computer Policy. To access the Account Policies folders, expand Local Computer Policy ➢ Computer Configuration ➢ Windows Settings ➢ Security Settings ➢ Account Policies.

If you are on a Windows 2000 member server, you will see two folders: Password Policy and Account Lockout Policy. If you are on a Windows 2000 Server computer that is configured as a domain controller, you will see three folders: Password Policy, Account Lockout Policy, and Kerberos Policy. The account policies available for member servers and domain controllers are described in the following sections.

Setting Password Policies

Password policies ensure that security requirements are enforced on the computer. It is important to note that the password policy is set on a per-computer basis; it cannot be configured for specific users.

The password policies that are defined on Windows 2000 member servers are described in Table 9.5. On Windows 2000 domain controllers, all of these policies are configured as "not defined."

TABLE 9.5 Password Policy Options

Policy	Description	Default	Minimum	Maximum
Enforce Password History	Keeps track of user's password history.	Remember 0 passwords.	Same as default.	Remember 24 passwords.
Maximum Password Age	Determines maximum number of days user can keep valid password.	Keep password for 42 days.	Keep password for 1 day.	Keep password for 999 days.
Minimum Password Age	Specifies how long password must be kept before it can be changed.	0 days (password can be changed immediately).	Same as default.	999 days.
Minimum Password Length	Specifies minimum number of characters password must contain.	0 characters (no password required).	Same as default.	14 characters.
Passwords Must Meet Complexity Requirements	Allows you to install password filter.	Disabled.	Same as default.	Enabled.
Store Password Using Reversible Encryption For All Users In The Domain	Specifies higher level of encryption for stored user passwords.	Disabled.	Same as default.	Enabled.

The password policies are used as follows:

- The Enforce Password History option is used so that users cannot reuse the same password. Users must create a new password when their password expires or is changed.

- The Maximum Password Age option is used so that after the maximum number of days has passed, users are forced to change their password.

- The Minimum Password Age option is used to prevent users from changing their password several times in rapid succession in order to defeat the purpose of the Enforce Password History policy.

- The Minimum Password Length option is used to ensure that users create a password as well as to specify that it must meet the length requirement. If this option isn't set, users are not required to create a password at all.

- The Passwords Must Meet Complexity option is used to prevent users from using items found in a dictionary of common names as passwords.

- The Store Password Using Reversible Encryption For All Users In The Domain option is used to provide a higher level of security for user passwords.

Exercise 9.6 takes you through the steps to configure password policies for your computer. This and the remaining exercises in this chapter assume that you have created a Security Management console.

EXERCISE 9.6

Setting Password Policies

In this exercise, you will configure password policies for your computer.

1. Select Start ➤ Programs ➤ Administrative Tools ➤ Security, and expand the Local Computer Policy snap-in.

2. Expand the folders as follows: Computer Configuration ➢ Windows Settings ➢ Security Settings ➢ Account Policies ➢ Password Policy.

3. Open the Enforce Password History policy. In the Effective Policy Setting field, specify **5** passwords remembered. Click OK.

4. Open the Maximum Password Age policy. In the Local Policy Setting field, specify that the password will expire in **60** days. Click OK.

5. Select Start ➢ Programs ➢ Accessories ➢ Command Prompt. At the command prompt, type `secedit /refreshpolicy machine_policy` and press Enter.

6. At the command prompt, type `exit` and press Enter.

Setting Account Lockout Policies

The *account lockout policies* are used to specify how many invalid logon attempts should be tolerated. You configure the account lockout policies so that after x number of unsuccessful logon attempts within y number of minutes, the account will be locked for a specified amount of time or until the Administrator unlocks the account.

The account lockout policies are described in Table 9.6.

TABLE 9.6 Account Lockout Policy Options

Policy	Description	Default	Minimum	Maximum	Suggested
Account Lockout Threshold	Specifies number of invalid attempts allowed before account is locked out.	0 (disabled, account will not be locked out)	Same as default	999 attempts	5 attempts
Account Lockout Duration	Specifies how long account will remain locked if Account Lockout Threshold is exceeded.	0; but if Account Lockout Threshold is enabled, 30 minutes	Same as default	99,999 minutes	5 minutes

TABLE 9.6   Account Lockout Policy Options *(continued)*

Policy	Description	Default	Minimum	Maximum	Suggested
Reset Account Lockout Counter After	Specifies how long counter will remember unsuccessful logon attempts.	0, but if Account Lockout Threshold is enabled, 5 minutes	Same as default	99,999 minutes	5 minutes

Exercise 9.7 shows you how to configure account lockout policies and test their effects.

EXERCISE 9.7

Setting Account Lockout Policies

In this exercise, you will configure account lockout policies and test their effects.

1. Select Start ➢ Programs ➢ Administrative Tools ➢ Security and expand the Local Computer Policy snap-in.

2. Expand the folders as follows: Computer Configuration ➢ Windows Settings ➢ Security Settings ➢ Account Policies ➢ Account Lockout Policy.

3. Open the Account Lockout Threshold policy. In the Local Policy Setting field, specify that the account will lock after **3** invalid logon attempts. Click OK.

4. The Suggested Value Changes dialog box will appear. Accept the default values for Account Lockout Duration and Reset Account Lockout Counter by clicking OK.

5. Log off as Administrator. Try to log on as Emily with an incorrect password three times.

6. After you see the error message stating that account lockout has been enabled, log on as Administrator.

7. To unlock Emily's account, open the Local Users and Groups snap-in in the MMC, expand the Users folder, and double-click user Emily. In the General tab of Emily's Properties dialog box, click to remove the check from the Account Is Locked Out check box. Then click OK.

Optimizing Windows 2000

Windows 2000, like almost every other software package, was not perfect right out of the box. Microsoft periodically releases updates called *service packs* that address bugs and provide new features. You should always install the latest service pack as soon as it becomes available. Windows 2000 also includes the Windows Update utility that makes it easy to download and install other minor fixes that might not be included with a full service pack.

To have an optimized system, you must monitor its performance. The tools for monitoring Windows 2000 Server are System Monitor, Performance Logs and Alerts, and Task Manager. With these tools, you can track memory, processor activity, the disk subsystem, the network subsystem, and other computer subsystems.

You should also keep an eye on the various services running on your computers. You might consider disabling or removing services that hog an inordinate amount of system resources in order to improve system performance.

Keeping Windows 2000 Up-to-Date

One way to make sure that your Windows 2000 system is working at its best is to keep it up-to-date. Using the Windows Update utility, you can check for and download the latest software, such as updates, patches, and drivers. You'll also want to install Windows 2000 Server service packs as they become available, in order to fix bugs and sometimes add new features.

Microsoft
✓ *Exam*
Objective

Monitor and troubleshoot server health and performance. Tools include System Monitor, Event Viewer, and Task Manager.

- Monitor and interpret real-time performance by using System Monitor and Task Manager.
- Configure and manage System Monitor alerts and logging.
- Diagnose server health problems by using Event Viewer.
- Identify and disable unnecessary operating system services.

Install and manage Windows 2000 updates. Updates include service packs, hot fixes, and security hot fixes.

- Update an installation source by using slipstreaming.
- Apply and reapply service packs and hot fixes.
- Verify service pack and hot fix installation.
- Remove service packs and hot fixes.

Using the Windows Update Utility

The *Windows Update utility* makes it easy to download and install the latest Windows 2000 patches and update files. Minor revisions are usually included in small hot fixes, and major changes are rolled into larger service packs. You must be connected to the Internet to use Windows Update. Just select Windows Update from the Start menu to launch the utility. Windows Update will automatically find the appropriate page on the Microsoft website. At the time of this writing, you must click the Product Updates link in order to continue to the Microsoft Windows Update page. The website will scan your copy of Windows 2000 and recommend any update files that you are missing. Click each update to download and install it. You can typically remove these features using the Add/Remove Programs applet in the Control Panel, just as you would for Desktop applications.

Using Windows 2000 Service Packs

The latest Windows 2000 *service pack* will appear on the Windows Update website if you have not already installed it. Click the Download link and follow the instructions provided in order to install the service pack.

Windows 2000 service packs use a new feature called *slipstream*. Under Windows NT 4, any time you installed a driver for a new device or added any other sort of software component, you would need to reapply the latest service pack. Slipstream technology allows you to bypass this annoying extra step. Slipstream is seamless and requires no configuration.

You can determine if any service packs have been installed on your computer by using the `winver` command, as shown in Figure 9.12. To issue this command, select Start ➢ Programs ➢ Accessories ➢ Command Prompt. In the Command Prompt window, type **winver** and press Enter. You will see a dialog box that shows which service packs are currently installed.

FIGURE 9.12 Response to the *winver* command

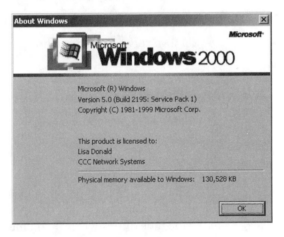

When you install a new Windows 2000 service pack, you are given the option of backing up the files that will be changed or removed. If you deselect this option, you will not be able to uninstall the new service pack. If you have problems with a new service pack, you might want to revert the system to its original state. You can use the Add/Remove Programs applet in the Control Panel to remove the service pack as long as you enabled the backup option.

Determining System Performance

Using Windows Update will sometimes solve performance issues, but in order to really fine-tune Windows 2000, you will need to use the built-in optimization tools: System Monitor and Performance Logs and Alerts. While these tools cannot solve performance issues directly, they can help you determine the spots where your computer is slowest so that you can take effective steps to make the computer run at its best.

Creating Baselines

Baseline reports tell you how the computer is performing at a certain point in time. If you think that the computer is running more slowly than normal, you can compare a current baseline report to one that was taken when you thought the computer was running normally. Most performance changes should be readily apparent when you compare the reports, allowing you to determine exactly which resources are slowing down the system. You should always take baseline reports before and after adding hardware so that you can see objectively the performance gained or lost by adding the new equipment.

You create baselines by using the Counter Log and Trace Log features of Performance Logs and Alerts. You can access Performance Logs and Alerts by selecting Start ➤ Programs ➤ Administrative Tools ➤ Performance, and clicking Performance Logs And Alerts in the Performance window.

Identifying System Bottlenecks

The slowest component of your computer is called a *system bottleneck*. Computers always have bottlenecks. No matter how much you've spent on your machine, there will always be a slowest component. One of the keys to optimization is to make the slowest component fast enough that your computer performs at an acceptable level. Often, the type of software that you use will determine the bottleneck. If your applications typically require large amounts of memory but very little processing power, then you can almost be certain that memory is your bottleneck. In order to truly be certain, you should use System Monitor to determine the source of your bottleneck.

Using Task Manager

Task Manager displays the applications and processes currently running and gives you some control over these elements. Notably, you can kill any applications or processes that are not responding to the system. Task Manager also provides a sort of mini System Monitor that displays only CPU and memory usage. This can be useful to get a quick look at two key performance indicators without having to open System Monitor and configure counters. You can open Task Manager in one of three ways: press Ctrl+Alt+Delete and click the Task Manager button, right-click an empty part of the taskbar and select Task Manager from the context menu, or hold down Shift+Ctrl and press Esc.

The Applications Tab

The Applications tab of the Task Manager window lists all of the currently running applications. Anything that you see on the taskbar is displayed in the Applications tab. The Status column indicates whether an application is Running or Not Responding. You can select an application in the list and then click the End Task button to kill it, the Switch To button to bring the application to the front, or the New Task button to start running a new task.

The Processes Tab

The Processes tab lists all of the processes currently running on the machine. You can quickly see each unique process ID, as well as each process's CPU usage, CPU time, and memory usage. Figure 9.13 shows the Processes tab.

FIGURE 9.13 The Processes tab of the Task Manager window

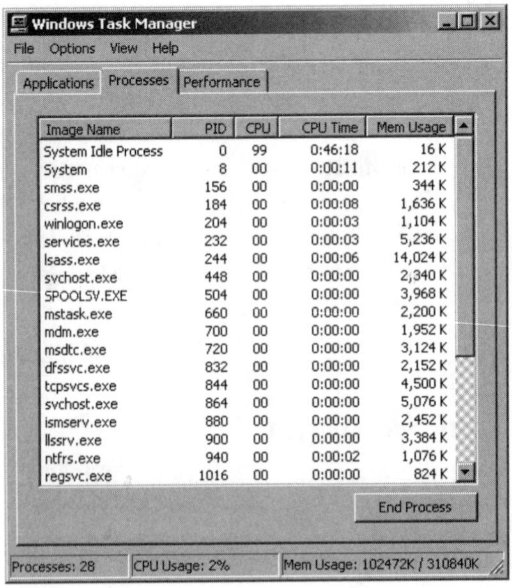

You can manage a process by right-clicking it and selecting one of the following options from the context menu: End The Process, End The Process Tree, or Set The Priority Of The Process.

Real World Scenario

System Performance

You are a network administrator of an 800-user network based in four locations across the country. The offices are in Atlanta, Philadelphia, Dallas, and Denver, with half the users in Atlanta and the rest roughly equally divided among the other cities. There are two domain controllers, a DNS server, and an Exchange server in each location. The locations are connected by routers and are appropriately configured as sites for Active Directory replication. Everything has been fairly stable until recently. You have been getting calls from the users in the Atlanta office, complaining that the network has been slow lately. Since the complaints have been vague, you need to go on a troubleshooting expedition to determine what is causing the problem.

Obviously, the first thing you need to do is talk to the users and determine exactly what the users mean by "slow." Is this logging on to the network? Is this running applications on the workstations? Figuring this out can be more difficult than it may seem because many people pay little attention to their computers until they break and they also do not understand the difference between their computer and the network that connects all the computers together. To be effective, then, your job skills must transcend the technical and reach the interpersonal.

The next thing you need is something that should have already been done. You need to have baseline measurements that can be used to measure current performance against a known quantity. This is critical because if you have nothing to measure against, then how do you really know if the performance is healthy?

If you do have these baselines, then dig in for a little deeper level of work. You can determine performance metrics in some areas by measuring the absolute performance of some systems. For example, if the CPU is at 100 percent sustained utilization, it doesn't matter what the baseline was last month. Taking these measurements can help with obvious problems, but it does leave a little in the shadows with slower degradation of performance.

> Another best practice is to take periodic measurements that become a series of baselines. These can be done over time, and if you are diligent, you can determine a growing problem before the users even notice it. You, in effect, remain invisible to the user, which is right where they prefer you…and where you should prefer yourself. No one calls the support department just to say hello.

Using Event Viewer

You can use the *Event Viewer* utility to track information about your computer's hardware and software, as well as to monitor security events. The information that is tracked is stored in three types of log files:

- The *System log* tracks events that are related to the Windows 2000 operating system.

- The *Security log* tracks events that are related to Windows 2000 auditing.

- The *Application log* tracks events that are related to applications that are running on your computer.

On Windows 2000 domain controllers, Event Viewer also includes Directory Service, DNS Server, and File Replication Service logs. Depending on how your server is configured, you may also have other Event Viewer logs.

You can access Event Viewer by selecting Start ➤ Programs ➤ Administrative Tools ➤ Event Viewer. Alternatively, right-click My Computer, select Manage from the context menu, and access Event Viewer under System Tools. From Event Viewer, select the log you want to view. Figure 9.14 shows Event Viewer with the System log displayed.

In the log file, you will see all of the events that have been recorded. By default, you see the oldest events at the bottom of the screen and the newest events at the top of the screen. This can be misleading in troubleshooting, since one error can precipitate other errors. You should always resolve the oldest errors first. To change the default listing order, click one of the three logs and select View ➤ Oldest First.

FIGURE 9.14   A System log in Event Viewer

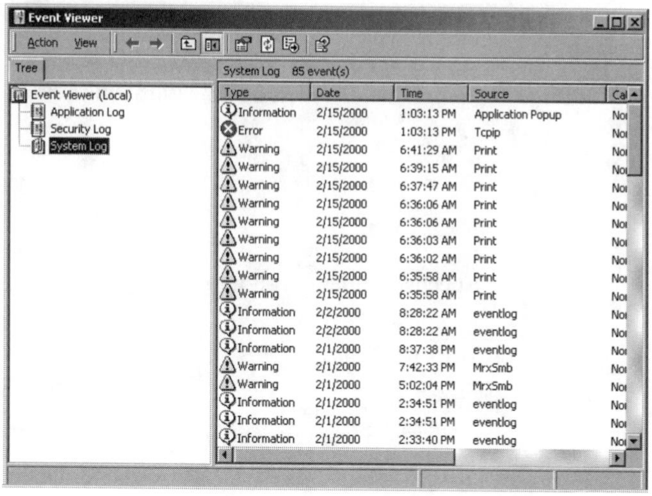

Reviewing Event Types

The Event Viewer logs display five event types, denoted by their icons. Table 9.7 describes each event type.

TABLE 9.7   Event Viewer Log Events

Event Type	Icon	Description
Information	White bubble with blue i	Informs you of the occurrence of a specific action, such as a system shutting down or starting. Information events are logged for informative purposes.
Warning	Yellow triangle with black exclamation point	Indicates that you should be concerned with the event. Warning events may not be critical in nature but may be indicative of future errors.

TABLE 9.7 Event Viewer Log Events *(continued)*

Event Type	Icon	Description
Error	Red circle with white X	Indicates the occurrence of an error, such as a driver failing to load. You should be very concerned with Error events.
Success Audit	Yellow key	Indicates the occurrence of an event that has been audited for success. For example, a Success Audit event is a successful logon when system logons are being audited.
Failure Audit	Yellow lock	Indicates the occurrence of an event that has been audited for failure. For example, a Failure Audit event is a failed logon due to an invalid username and/or password when system logons are being audited.

Clicking an event in an Event Viewer log file brings up the Event Properties dialog box, which shows details about the event.

Managing Log Files

Over time, your log files will grow, and you will need to decide how to manage them. You can clear a log file for a fresh start. You may want to save the existing log file before you clear it, to keep that log file available for future reference or further analysis.

To clear all log file events, right-click the log you wish to clear and choose Clear All Events from the context menu. Then specify whether or not you want to save the log before it is cleared.

If you just want to save as existing log file, right-click that log and choose Save Log File As. Then specify the location and name of the file.

To open an existing log file, right-click the log you wish to open and choose Open Log File. Then specify the name and location of the log file and click the Open button.

Setting Log File Properties

Each Event Viewer log has two sets of properties associated with it:

- General properties control items such as the log filename, its maximum size, and the action to take when the log file reaches its maximum size.

- Filter properties specify which events are displayed.

To access the log Properties dialog box, right-click the log you want to manage and select Properties from the context menu.

In Exercise 9.8, you will use Event Viewer to view individual events and set up an event filter.

EXERCISE 9.8

Using Event Viewer

In this exercise you will see how to use Event Viewer.

1. Select Start ➤ Programs ➤ Administrative Tools ➤ Event Viewer.

2. Click System Log in the left pane of the Event Viewer window to display the System log events.

3. Double-click the first event in the right pane of the Event Viewer window to see its Event Properties dialog box. Click the Cancel button to close the dialog box.

4. Right-click System Log in the left pane of the Event Viewer window and select Properties.

5. Click the Filter tab. Clear all the check marks under Event Types except those in the Warning and Error check boxes, and then click OK. You should see only Warning and Error events listed in the System log.

6. To remove the filter, return to the Filter tab of the log Properties dialog box, click the Restore Defaults button at the bottom of the dialog box, and click OK. You should see all of the event types listed again.

7. Right-click System Log and select Clear All Events.

8. You'll see a dialog box asking if you want to save the System log before clearing it. Choose Yes. Specify the path and filename for the log file, and then click Save. All the events should be cleared from the System log.

Managing Windows 2000 Services

A *service* is a program, routine, or process that performs a specific function within the Windows 2000 operating system. You can access the Services utility in a variety of ways, including through the Computer Management utility (right-click My Computer, select Manage ➤ Services and Applications, ➤ Services), through Administrative Tools, or as an MMC snap-in.

For each service, the Services window listing shows the name, a short description, the startup type, and the logon account that is used to start the service. To configure the properties of a service, double-click it to open its Properties dialog box. This dialog box contains four tabs of options for services, which are described in the following sections.

Configuring General Service Properties

The General tab of the service Properties dialog box allows you to view and configure the following options:

- The service display name
- A description of the service
- The path to the service executable
- The startup type, which can be automatic, manual, or disabled
- The current service status
- Startup parameters that can be applied when the service is started

The buttons across the lower part of the dialog box allow you to start, stop, pause, or resume the service.

Configuring Service Log On Properties

The Log On tab of the service Properties dialog box allows you to configure the logon account that will be used to start the service. You can choose to use the local system account or specify another logon account.

At the bottom of the Log On tab, you can select hardware profiles to associate the service with. For each hardware profile, you can set the service as Enabled or Disabled.

Configuring Service Recovery Properties

The Recovery tab of the service Properties dialog box allows you to configure what action will be taken if the service fails to load. For the first, second, and subsequent failures, you can select from the following actions:

- Take No Action

- Restart The Service

- Run A File

- Reboot The Computer

If you choose to run a file, you then specify the file and any command-line parameters. If you choose to reboot the computer, you can then configure a message that will be sent to users who are connected to the computer before it is restarted.

Checking Service Dependencies

The Dependencies tab of the service Properties dialog box lists any services that must be running in order for the specified service to start. If a service fails to start, you can use this information to determine what the dependencies are and then make sure that each dependency service is running.

At the bottom of the Dependencies tab, you can see if any other services depend on this service. You should verify that there are no services that depend on a service that you are about to stop.

Removing Unnecessary Services

By analyzing System Monitor and Task Manager, you might be able to pinpoint certain services that are hogging resources. Unless you absolutely need these services, you should either disable them or remove them entirely. You can disable a service by opening its Properties dialog box and selecting either Disabled or Manual from the Startup Type drop-down menu. Alternatively, you might be able to remove the service by using the Add/Remove Programs applet in the Control Panel.

Troubleshooting the Windows 2000 Startup Process

Troubleshooting a computer that won't start can be a difficult task. Luckily, Windows 2000 includes a few tools to help you with this. However, it's useful to understand the boot sequence before delving into these diagnostic tools.

Microsoft ✓ *Exam* *Objective*

Troubleshoot starting servers and client computers. Tools and methodologies include Safe Mode, Recovery Console, and parallel installations.

- Interpret the startup log file.
- Repair an operating system by using various startup options.
- Repair an operating system by using the Recovery Console.
- Recover data from a hard disk in the event that the operating system will not start.

The Normal Boot Process

You must understand the normal boot process before attempting to solve problems related to an abnormal boot process. The boot sequence consists of the five following steps:

1. The preboot sequence

   2. The boot sequence

   3. Kernel load

   4. Kernel initialization

   5. Logon

The Preboot Sequence

The preboot sequence occurs before the proper boot sequence begins. During this process, the onboard BIOS runs its system checks and the computer accesses the NTLDR file. The preboot sequence consists of the following steps:

   1. The computer runs the power-on self-test (POST) routine in order to determine the nature of the computer's hardware.

   2. The BIOS loads the Master Boot Record (MBR) from the boot device.

   3. The MBR locates the active partition and loads the boot sector into memory. The boot sector is then executed.

   4. The boot sector locates and executes the NTLDR file, which in turn initializes and begins the Windows 2000 boot process.

The preboot sequence has very little to do with Windows 2000 itself. However, errors can certainly occur during this phase, so you should be aware of the potential problems shown in Table 9.8.

TABLE 9.8 Preboot Sequence Errors

Symptom	Possible cause
Improperly configured hardware	If the POST cannot recognize your hard drive, the preboot stage will fail. This error is most likely to occur in a computer that is still being initially configured. If everything has been working properly and you have not made any changes to your configuration, a hardware error is unlikely.
Corrupt MBR	Viruses that are specifically designed to infect the MBR can corrupt it. You can protect your system from this type of error by using virus-scanning software. Also, most virus-scanning programs can correct an infected MBR.

TABLE 9.8 Preboot Sequence Errors *(continued)*

Symptom	Possible cause
No partition marked as active	This can happen if you used the FDISK utility and did not create a partition from all of the free space. If the partition is FAT16 or FAT32 and on a basic disk, you can boot the computer to DOS or Windows 9x with a boot disk, run FDISK, and mark a partition as active. If you created your partitions as a part of the Windows 2000 installation and have dynamic disks, marking an active partition is done for you during installation.
Corrupt or missing NTLDR file	If the NTLDR file does not execute, it may have been corrupted or deleted (by a virus or malicious intent). You can restore this file using the Emergency Repair Disk (ERD), which is covered later in this chapter.
Windows starts DOS or Windows 9x/Me rather than Windows 2000	The NTLDR file may not execute because the SYS program was run from DOS or Windows 9x after Windows 2000 was installed. If you have done this, the only solution is to reinstall Windows 2000.

The Boot Sequence

As you saw in the preboot sequence, the NTLDR file activates the boot sequence. The boot sequence consists of the following steps:

1. The NTLDR file switches the processor into 32-bit flat memory mode and starts the mini file system (FAT16, FAT32, or NTFS, depending on the way the drive is formatted) drivers.

2. The computer reads the BOOT.INI file and determines how many operating systems are installed on the machine. If more than one operating system is installed, the OS selection screen appears and presents the options listed in the BOOT.INI file. If only one operating system is installed, then the BOOT.INI file automatically loads the OS.

3. The NTDETECT.COM file detects your computer's hardware and passes the information along to the HKEY_LOCAL_MACHINE key in the Registry.

Table 9.9 lists some common causes for errors during the boot stage.

TABLE 9.9 Boot Sequence Errors

Symptom	Possible Cause
Missing or corrupt boot files	If NTLDR, BOOT.INI, BOOTSECT.DOS, NTDETECT.COM, or NTOSKRNL.EXE is corrupt or missing (by a virus or malicious intent), the boot sequence will fail. You will see an error message that indicates which file is missing or corrupt. You can restore these files through the ERD, which is covered later in this chapter.
Improperly configured BOOT.INI file	If you have made any changes to your disk configuration and your computer will not restart, chances are your BOOT.INI file is configured incorrectly.
Unrecognizable or improperly configured hardware	If you have serious errors that cause NTDETECT.COM to fail, you should resolve the hardware problems. If your computer has a lot of hardware, remove all of the hardware that is not required to boot the computer. Add each piece of hardware one at a time and boot the computer. This will help you identify which piece of hardware is bad or is conflicting for a resource with another device.

The Kernel Load Sequence

In the kernel load sequence, the Hardware Abstraction Layer (HAL), computer control set, and low-level device drivers are loaded. The following steps take place during the kernel load sequence:

1. Control passes from the NTDETECT.COM file (explained in the previous section) to the NTOSKRNL.EXE file, and the kernel load process begins.

2. The HAL, which Windows 2000 uses to support multiple platform architectures, is loaded.

3. The current control set is loaded. The control set is a list of drivers and other configuration information that Windows needs to run properly.

4. Low-level drivers are loaded. Low-level drivers include such things as disk drivers.

If a problem occurs during the kernel load sequence, there's not much you can do other than reinstall the operating system.

The Kernel Initialization Sequence

In the kernel initialization sequence, the HKEY_LOCAL_MACHINE\HARDWARE Registry and clone control set are created, device drivers are initialized, and high-order subsystems and services are loaded.

The kernel initialization sequence consists of the following steps:

1. The HKEY_LOCAL_MACHINE\HARDWARE key is created in the Registry and determines the configuration of the various hardware devices installed in the computer.

2. The clone control set is loaded. The clone control set is an exact copy of the control set that has not been affected by the boot sequence.

3. The low-level device drivers that were loaded in step 4 of the previous section are initialized.

4. Higher-level device drivers and services are loaded.

The Last Known Good Configuration might be able to help you if you are experiencing trouble with the kernel initialization sequence. If that doesn't work, then you will probably need to reinstall the operating system to fix the problem.

The Logon Sequence

The user logs on to the computer and any remaining services are started during the logon sequence. Specifically, the following steps occur during the logon sequence:

1. The Log On To Windows dialog box appears after the kernel initialization sequence is finished. You must enter a valid username and password to continue.

2. Any remaining services are loaded, and Windows 2000 begins normal operation.

Most errors in the logon sequence are related to an invalid username or password. In a domain environment, you won't be able to log on if the computer cannot reach a domain controller.

You might also get errors if services fail to load, but typically this doesn't prevent Windows from loading. When errors of this nature occur, you can usually check the event log to see exactly what the problem is.

Using Advanced Startup Options

You will notice that for a few seconds during the boot process you will be prompted to hit F8 to configure advanced startup options. Typically, you don't need to use this feature unless you are having problems booting Windows 2000. The advanced startup options are as follows:

- Safe Mode
- Safe Mode with Networking
- Safe Mode with Command Prompt
- Enable Boot Logging
- Enable VGA Mode
- Last Known Good Configuration
- Directory Services Restore Mode
- Debugging Mode
- Boot Normally

Safe Mode, Safe Mode with Networking, and Safe Mode with Command Prompt

Safe Mode loads only the drivers and services that are absolutely necessary to get Windows 2000 up and running. This enables you to get into the operating system and make any changes that you think will make it possible to boot normally again. If even Safe Mode doesn't work, then you know that the problem lies somewhere in the low-level system functions. A computer booted to Safe Mode shows *Safe Mode* in the four corners of the Desktop, as shown in Figure 9.15.

FIGURE 9.15 A computer running in Safe Mode

Safe Mode with Networking is similar to Safe Mode, except that it loads the drivers and services that are used to connect to the network. Safe Mode with Command Prompt boots Windows 2000 directly into the command prompt, bypassing the graphical user interface altogether. You should use this method only if you are very familiar with the command prompt.

Enabling Boot Logging

Selecting Boot Logging from the Advanced Startup menu loads Windows 2000 normally. In addition, a boot log file, also known as a Startup log, is created that documents each step of the boot process. This file is stored as \Windir\ntbtlog.txt. After the boot process has completed, you can examine the boot log file to determine the cause of the problem. If the problem prevents Windows from booting completely, you can enable the boot log until the computer hangs and then restart the machine and examine the boot log file in Safe Mode. A sample of the ntbtlog.txt file is shown in Figure 9.16.

The boot log file contains a list of the drivers and services that loaded successfully and those that failed to load. This can help you determine which drivers or services might be the cause of the boot failure.

FIGURE 9.16 The Windows 2000 boot log file

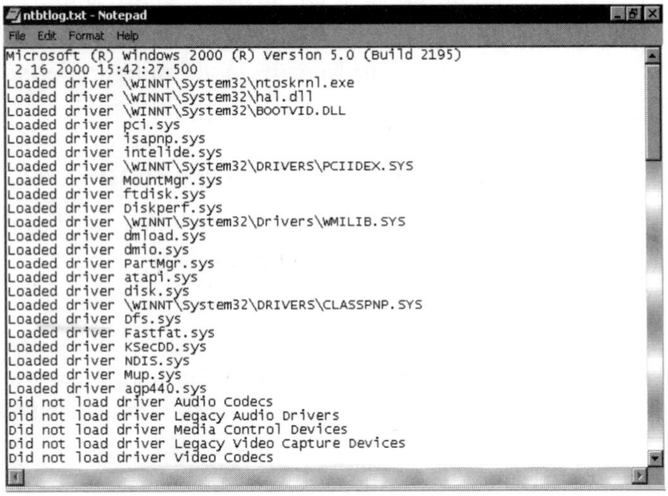

```
ntbtlog.txt - Notepad
File  Edit  Format  Help
Microsoft (R) Windows 2000 (R) Version 5.0 (Build 2195)
 2 16 2000 15:42:27.500
Loaded driver \WINNT\System32\ntoskrnl.exe
Loaded driver \WINNT\System32\hal.dll
Loaded driver \WINNT\System32\BOOTVID.DLL
Loaded driver pci.sys
Loaded driver isapnp.sys
Loaded driver intelide.sys
Loaded driver \WINNT\System32\DRIVERS\PCIIDEX.SYS
Loaded driver MountMgr.sys
Loaded driver ftdisk.sys
Loaded driver Diskperf.sys
Loaded driver \WINNT\System32\Drivers\WMILIB.SYS
Loaded driver dmload.sys
Loaded driver dmio.sys
Loaded driver PartMgr.sys
Loaded driver atapi.sys
Loaded driver disk.sys
Loaded driver \WINNT\System32\DRIVERS\CLASSPNP.SYS
Loaded driver Dfs.sys
Loaded driver Fastfat.sys
Loaded driver KSecDD.sys
Loaded driver NDIS.sys
Loaded driver Mup.sys
Loaded driver agp440.sys
Did not load driver Audio Codecs
Did not load driver Legacy Audio Drivers
Did not load driver Media Control Devices
Did not load driver Legacy Video Capture Devices
Did not load driver Video Codecs
```

Enabling VGA Mode

VGA Mode should be used when you suspect that the problem lies with the video card settings. For example, if you set the refresh rate out of the range that your monitor can handle, you won't be able to see anything on the screen. Enabling VGA mode loads Windows 2000 with the most basic video settings so that you can open the Display applet in the Control Panel and make any changes that need to be made.

 When you boot to any Safe Mode, you automatically use VGA Mode (640 X 480 with 16 colors).

Last Known Good Configuration

The Last Known Good Configuration option loads the settings that were saved the last time Windows successfully booted. This can be extremely useful if you made a configuration change that prevents the computer from booting. Last Known Good Configuration won't work in some instances: For example, if you load a new driver and completely erase the old driver, Last Known Good Configuration won't be able to revert to the old driver. In addition, Last Known Good Configuration won't repair a problem once you successfully log on to the workstation.

Directory Services Restore Mode

Directory Services Restore Mode is used to restore Active Directory information on a domain controller.

Debugging Mode

Debugging Mode runs the kernel debugger utility if it has been installed on the machine. The details of the kernel debugger utility are beyond the scope of the MCSA exam.

Boot Normally

The Boot Normally option boots Windows 2000 as if you had never hit F8 in the first place. This option is useful if you just wanted to take a look at the Advanced Startup menu or if you accidentally hit the F8 key during the boot process.

Using Startup and Recovery Options

The Startup And Recovery dialog box lets you specify the default operating system (as selected from the entries in the BOOT.INI file) and gives you control over how Windows should respond to system failures. To open the Startup And Recovery dialog box, select Start ➢ Settings ➢ Control Panel ➢ System ➢ Advanced ➢ Startup And Recovery, or right-click My Computer, select Properties, click the Advanced tab, and click the Startup And Recovery button. Figure 9.17 shows the Startup And Recovery dialog box.

FIGURE 9.17   The Startup And Recovery dialog box

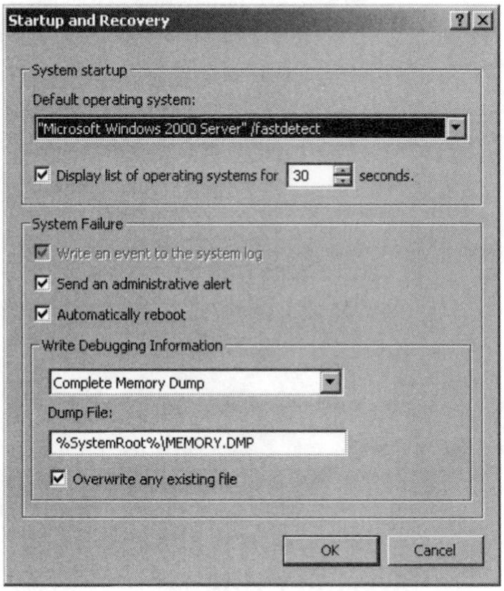

Using the Recovery Console

If your computer will not start, and you have tried to boot to Safe Mode with no luck, there's one more option you can try. The *Recovery Console* is an option designed for administrators and advanced users. It allows you limited access to FAT16, FAT32, and NTFS volumes without starting the Windows 2000 Server graphical interface.

Through the Recovery Console, you can perform the following tasks:

- Copy, replace, or rename operating system files and folders. You might do this if your boot failure was caused by missing or corrupt files.

- Enable or disable the loading of services when the computer is restarted. If a particular service may be keeping the operating system from booting, you could disable the service. If a particular service is required for successful booting, you want to make sure that service loading is enabled.

- Repair the file system boot sector or the MBR. You might use this option if a virus may have damaged the system boot sector or the MBR.

- Create and format partitions on the drives. You might use this option if your disk utilities will not delete or create Windows 2000 partitions. Normally, you would use a disk-partitioning utility for these functions.

Starting the Recovery Console

If you have created the Windows 2000 Server Setup disks, you can start the Recovery Console from them. Alternatively, you can add the Recovery Console to the Windows 2000 startup options, but you would need to configure this prior to the failure.

In Exercise 9.9, you will add the Recovery Console to the Windows 2000 startup options. You will need the Windows 2000 Server CD for this exercise.

EXERCISE 9.9

Adding the Recovery Console to the Windows 2000 Startup Options

In this exercise, you will install the Recovery Console and make it available in the Windows 2000 startup options.

1. Insert the Windows 2000 Server CD in your CD-ROM drive. Hold down the Shift key as the CD is read to prevent auto-play.

2. Select Start ➢ Programs ➢ Accessories ➢ Command Prompt.

3. Change the drive letter to your CD-ROM drive.

4. From the CD drive letter prompt (*x:*\>), type **CD I386** and press Enter.

5. From *x:\I386>*, type **WINNT32 /CMDCONS**.

6. In the Windows 2000 Setup dialog box, click the Yes button to confirm that you want to install the Recovery Console.

7. After the installation files are copied to your computer, a dialog box appears to let you know that the Recovery Console has been successfully installed. Click OK.

8. Shut down and restart your computer. In the startup selection screen, select the option for Microsoft Windows 2000 Recovery Console.

9. At the command prompt, type **exit** to close the Recovery Console. The system reboots.

Using the Recovery Console

The Recovery Console presents you with a command prompt and very limited access to system resources. This keeps unauthorized users from using the Recovery Console to access sensitive data. The following are the only folders you can access through the Recovery Console:

- The root folder
- The Windir folder and the subfolders of the Windows 2000 Server installation
- The CMDCONS folder
- Removable media drives such as CD-ROM drives

If you try to access any other folders besides the ones listed above, you will receive an "access denied" error message.

In the Recovery Console, you cannot copy files from a local hard disk to a floppy disk. You can copy only files from a floppy disk or CD to a hard disk, or from one hard disk to another hard disk. This is for security purposes.

You should use the Recovery Console with extreme caution. Improper use may cause even more damage than the problems you are trying to fix.

If your computer dual-boots with other Windows 2000 operating systems, the first option you must specify is which Windows 2000 operating system you will log on to. Next, you must specify the Administrator password for the system you are logging on to.

When the Recovery Console starts, you can use the commands listed in Table 9.10.

TABLE 9.10 Commands Available with the Recovery Console

Command	Description
ATTRIB	Used to set file attributes. You can set file attributes for Read-only (R), System (S), Hidden (H), or Compressed (C).
BATCH	Used to execute commands in a specified input file.

TABLE 9.10 Commands Available with the Recovery Console *(continued)*

Command	Description
CHDIR (CD)	Used to navigate the directory structure. If executed without a directory name, the current directory is displayed. (CHDIR and CD work the same way.)
CLS	Used to clear any text that is currently displayed on the console.
CHKDSK	Used to check the disk and display a disk status report.
COPY	Used to copy a single file from one location to another. COPY does not support wildcards and does not copy files to removable media (such as floppy disks).
DELETE (DEL)	Used to delete a single file. Wildcards are not supported. (DELETE and DEL work the same way.)
DIR	Used to display lists of files and subdirectories in the current directory.
DISABLE	Used to disable Windows 2000 system services and drivers.
DISKPART	Used to manage disk partitions. If executed without a command-line argument, a user interface is displayed.
ENABLE	Used to enable Windows 2000 system services and drivers.
EXIT	Used to quit the Recovery Console and restart the computer.
EXPAND	Used to expand compressed files.
FIXBOOT	Used to write a new boot sector onto the computer's system partition.
FIXMBR	Used to repair the MBR of the computer's boot partition.

TABLE 9.10 Commands Available with the Recovery Console *(continued)*

Command	Description
FORMAT	Used to prepare a disk for use with Windows 2000 by formatting the disk as FAT16, FAT32, or NTFS.
HELP	Used to display help information for Recovery Console commands.
LISTSVC	Used to list all available services and drivers on the computer, as well as the current status of each service and driver.
LOGON	If the computer is configured for dual-booting or multi-booting, used to log on to other installations as the local administrator.
MAP	Used to display the current drive letter mappings.
MKDIR (MD)	Used to create new directories. (MKDIR and MD work the same way.)
MORE	Used to display a text file on the console screen. (Same as TYPE.)
RENAME (REN)	Used to rename a single file. (RENAME and REN work the same way.)
RMDIR (RD)	Used to delete directories. (RMDIR and RD work the same way.)
SYSTEMROOT	Used to specify that the current directory is the system root.
TYPE	Used to display a text file on the console screen. (Same as MORE.)

Creating a Parallel Installation

If you have an extra partition available, you might want to create a parallel installation of Windows 2000 that you can boot to in case your main installation fails. Theoretically, you could install both installations in separate directories on the same partition, but this can cause problems when both installations copy information to the same Program Files and Documents and Settings folders.

If your main Windows 2000 installation fails because of system file corruption, you can boot the parallel installation. From there you can restore the corrupted files, and with any luck boot to the main installation again.

Restoring the Operating System from Backup

If none of the procedures in the previous section fix the problem, you will probably need to restore the operating system from backup. The *Windows 2000 Backup* utility allows you to create and restore backups and create an *Emergency Repair Disk (ERD)*. Backups protect your data in the event of system failure by storing the data on another medium, such as another hard disk or a tape. If your original data is lost due to corruption, deletion, or media failure, you can restore the data using your backup. The ERD is a subset of a backup that you can use to restore configuration information quickly.

Microsoft ✓ Exam Objective

Troubleshoot starting servers and client computers. Tools and methodologies include Safe Mode, Recovery Console, and parallel installations

- Restore an operating system and data from a backup.

Creating and Using an ERD

You can use the ERD to repair and restart Windows 2000 Server in the event that your computer will not start or if the system files have been damaged. You should create an ERD when the computer is installed and then update the ERD after making any changes to the configuration of your computer. This option does not back up any system data.

You can repair the following items with the ERD:

- The basic system
- System files
- The partition boot sector
- The startup environment
- The Registry (return the Registry to its original configuration)

Preparing an ERD

To create an ERD, click the Emergency Repair Disk button in the opening Backup Utility window. This brings up the Emergency Repair Disk dialog box, which asks you to insert a blank, formatted floppy disk into drive A:. At this point, you can also specify whether you want to back up the Registry to the ERD. If the Registry will fit onto your ERD, you should select this option. When you click OK, the system data will be copied to the ERD.

The ERD is not a bootable disk and can be accessed only by using the Windows 2000 Server Setup CD or the Windows 2000 Server Setup disks that are created from the CD.

You should update your ERD after you make any major configuration changes to your computer.

Exercise 9.10 takes you through the steps required to create an ERD. You will need a blank, formatted, high-density floppy disk for this exercise.

EXERCISE 9.10

Creating an Emergency Repair Disk

In this exercise, you will create an ERD.

1. Select Start ➤ Programs ➤ Accessories ➤ System Tools ➤ Backup.

2. Click the Emergency Repair Disk button.

3. The Emergency Repair Disk dialog box appears. Insert a blank, formatted floppy disk into drive A:.

EXERCISE 9.10 *(continued)*

4. Select the Also Back Up The Registry To The Repair Directory option.

5. Click OK. The system data will be copied to the ERD.

6. A confirmation dialog box appears. Click OK to close this dialog box.

Using the Backup Wizard

The *Backup Wizard* takes you through all of the steps that are required for a successful backup. Before you start the Backup Wizard, you should be logged on as an Administrator or a member of the Backup Operators group.

In Exercise 9.11, you will use the Backup Wizard. You will need a blank, formatted, high-density floppy disk for this exercise.

EXERCISE 9.11

Using the Backup Wizard

In this exercise, you will use the Backup Wizard to make a successful backup.

1. Create a folder on your D: drive called **DATA**. Create some small text files in this folder. The size of all of the files combined should not exceed 1MB.

2. Select Start ➢ Programs ➢ Accessories ➢ System Tools ➢ Backup.

3. In the opening Backup window, click the Backup Wizard button.

4. In the Welcome To The Windows 2000 Backup And Recovery Tools dialog box, click Next.

5. In the What To Back Up dialog box, click the Back Up Selected Files, Drives, Or Network Data radio button. Then click Next.

6. In the Items To Back Up dialog box, select My Computer, expand D:, and check the DATA folder. Click Next.

7. In the Where To Store The Backup dialog box, click the Browse button. In the Open dialog box, select Floppy (A:). For the filename, enter the date (in the *mmddyy* format). Then click Open.

EXERCISE 9.11 *(continued)*

8. In the Where To Store The Backup dialog box, click Next.

9. Verify your selections in the Completing The Backup Wizard dialog box. Then click the Finish button.

10. When the Backup Wizard completes, click the Report button in the Backup Progress dialog box. This will show the backup log in a Notepad window. Close this window when you have finished viewing the report.

11. Close all the Backup Wizard dialog boxes.

Managing System State Data

System state data refers to a collection of system-specific configuration information. You can manage the availability of system state data by using the Backup utility to back up this information on a regular basis.

On any Windows 2000 computer, system state data consists of the Registry, the COM+ Class Registration database, and the system boot files. On Windows 2000 Server computers, system state data also includes the Certificate Services database (if the server is configured as a certificate server). On Windows 2000 Server computers that are domain controllers, system state data also includes the Active Directory services database and the SYSVOL directory, which is a shared directory that stores the server copy of the domain's public files.

If you need to restore system state data on a domain controller, you should restart your computer with the advanced startup option Directory Services Restore Mode. This allows the Active Directory services database and the SYSVOL directory to be restored. If the system state data is restored on a domain controller that is a part of a domain where data is replicated to other domain controllers, you must perform an authoritative restore. For an authoritative restore, you use the Ntdsutil.exe command and then restart the computer.

If you have a backup device attached to your computer, you can follow the steps in Exercise 9.12 to back up your system state data. This information will not fit on a single floppy disk.

EXERCISE 9.12

Backing Up System State Data

In this exercise, you will back up your system state data to a backup device.

1. Select Start ≻ Programs ≻ Accessories ≻ System Tools ≻ Backup.

2. In the opening Backup window, click the Backup tab.

3. Under My Computer, click the System State check box and select the backup medium or filename that will be used for the backup.

4. Click the Start Backup button.

5. When the backup is complete, click the Report button in the Backup Progress dialog box.

6. The backup log appears in a Notepad window. Close this window when you have finished viewing the report.

7. Close all of the Backup dialog boxes.

Using the Restore Wizard

Having a complete backup won't help you when your system fails unless you can successfully restore that backup. To be sure that you can restore your data, you should test the restoration process before anything goes wrong. You can use the *Restore Wizard* for testing purposes, as well as when you actually need to restore your backup.

Exercise 9.13 walks you through the steps of the Restore Wizard. You will need the floppy disk that you created in Exercise 9.11 for this exercise.

EXERCISE 9.13

Using the Restore Wizard

In this exercise, you will use the Restore Wizard to restore your data.

1. Select Start ➤ Programs ➤ Accessories ➤ System Tools ➤ Backup.

2. In the opening Backup window, click the Restore Wizard button.

3. In the Welcome To The Restore Wizard dialog box, click Next.

4. In the What To Restore dialog box, click the filename of the backup session that you created in Exercise 9.11. Click the D: drive to put a check mark in the box. Click Next.

5. In the Completing The Restore Wizard dialog box, verify that everything is configured properly. Then click Finish.

6. In the Enter The Backup File Name dialog box, verify that the filename for the backup session is the same file you specified in Exercise 9.11. Then click OK.

7. When the Restore Wizard completes, click the Report button in the Restore Progress dialog box. Close the Notepad window when you have finished viewing the report.

8. Close all the Restore and Backup dialog boxes.

Summary

Client and server computers sometimes need to be configured individually without the help of Active Directory. We looked at the most common configuration issues that you as an administrator will need to deal with in the real world. You have already seen many of these concepts in the MCSE Windows 2000 Professional and Server Study Guides, but you will be required to remember most of this information for the MCSA exam.

We started with a review of installing and configuring hardware devices in Windows 2000. We also explained how to manage device drivers. The next section dealt with configuring storage devices and disk subsystems. We reviewed the file systems available in Windows 2000, basic and dynamic storage, NTFS permissions, disk quotas, encryption and compression, and the distributed file system. Next, we reviewed sharing as it applies to files, folders, and printers.

The MCSA exam focuses primarily on management through Active Directory, but you should also be familiar with local administration as well. In this chapter, we reviewed a couple of key concepts related to local user management: password and account lockout policies. We finished the chapter with reviews of optimizing and troubleshooting Windows 2000.

Exam Essentials

Be able to configure hardware devices.   Be aware of the different utilities that are used to install and configure hardware devices. Be able to successfully install Plug and Play hardware as well as non–Plug and Play hardware.

Understand how to update device drivers.   Understand the process of updating Windows 2000 device drivers. Know how to recover from failure due to updated drivers.

Be able to successfully troubleshoot hardware errors.   Understand what causes hardware failure and be able to list common problems that cause hardware errors. Be able to successfully troubleshoot and correct hardware errors.

Understand the disk configurations that are used by Windows 2000.   Define the differences between basic and dynamic disks. Be able to configure options such as simple, spanned, striped, mirrored, and RAID-5 volumes. Be able to define the characteristics of each volume configuration.

Know how to set and manage disk quotas.   Be able to specify the purpose of disk quotas and successfully set disk quotas.

Be able to define local NTFS security options and to configure local security.   Be able to list NTFS permissions and understand how they work together when combined (especially Deny). Know who can manage NTFS permissions and how they are applied.

Be able to create network shares and apply share permissions. Know which group memberships can create network shares and be able to apply share permissions.

Be able to deploy service packs. Understand the purpose of service packs. Know how to successfully deploy them and how to verify that they are installed correctly.

Be able to monitor and troubleshoot Windows 2000 performance. Know which utilities can be used to track Windows 2000 performance events and issues. Know how to track and identify performance problems related to memory, the processor, the disk subsystem, and the network subsystem. Be able to correct system bottlenecks when they are identified.

Be able to manage processes. Know how to manage processes including identifying which resources are used by a process, how to stop and start processes, and how to assign priorities to processes.

Know how to manage the Windows 2000 boot process. List the files required within the Windows 2000 boot process. Be able to troubleshoot the boot process in the event of failure. Know the options that are configured within BOOT.INI and how the BOOT.INI file is configured. Be able to recover the boot files in the event of corruption.

Be able to use the Windows 2000 advanced startup options. List the Windows 2000 advanced startup options and under what circumstances it is appropriate to use each one.

Key Terms

Before you take the exam, be certain you are familiar with the following terms:

account lockout policies	basic storage
account policies	CDFS
Application log	cipher text
Backup Wizard	Compact Disk File System
baseline reports	device drivers

Dfs links

Dfs root

Dfs shared folders

driver signing

dynamic storage

effective permissions

EFS

Emergency Repair Disk

Encrypting File System

ERD

Event Viewer

FAT file system

File Replication Service (FRS)

hardware compatibility list (HCL)

inherited permissions

mirrored volumes

non–Plug and Play

NTFS

NTFS permissions

partitions

Password policies

Plug and Play

quotas

RAID-5 volumes

Recovery Console

replicas

Restore Wizard

root shares

Security log

service pack

share

share permissions

simple volumes

spanned volumes

striped volumes

system bottleneck

System log

Task Manager

volumes

Windows 2000 Backup

Windows Update utility

Review Questions

1. A workstation is running slowly, the processor is pegged at 100 percent, and the disk light is almost always on when applications are running. What is the best thing you could do to solve this problem?

   A. Upgrade the processor.

   B. Move the paging file from the system partition to another partition.

   C. Increase the size of the paging file.

   D. Add memory to the workstation.

2. What account would you use to run a System Monitor script on a domain controller in a remote site?

   A. System account

   B. Administrator account

   C. The user's account for that server

   D. The Guest account

3. What should you use to repair a Windows 2000 workstation if you receive a message at bootup that the NTLDR file is missing?

   A. Recovery Console

   B. Last Known Good Configuration

   C. Safe Mode

   D. Emergency Repair Process

   E. Reinstall with the upgrade option to maintain configuration information

4. You have just been hired as the network administrator for a network that is in the process of migrating from Windows NT to Windows 2000. The company has four locations that are currently separate domains. The network engineers have designed a network with one Windows 2000 domain that that will control the other domains. Part of your responsibility is to test applications that are running under Windows NT and see if they will run properly under Windows 2000. To test these applications, you have configured a workstation that is shared by two people to dual-boot between the two operating systems. Windows 2000 is installed on disk 0 and used by Sam. Windows NT is installed on disk 1 and used by Laura, with both disks formatted with NTFS. You have applied the latest service pack to Windows NT so it will support the new NTFS. Even though this is a test, the work these people do is important to them and they do not want their work to be inadvertently deleted by the other person. What steps should you take to ensure that each user can read from both drives but neither user has the ability to delete files from each other's drive? (Choose all that apply.)

A. Allow Modify permissions for Laura on disk 1 and Read permissions on disk 0.

B. Allow Modify permissions for Sam on disk 0 and Read permissions on disk 1.

C. Remove the Everyone group from both disks.

D. Allow Read-only permissions to the Everyone group on both disks.

E. Configure disk 1 as dynamic.

F. Configure disk 0 as dynamic.

5. The migration to Windows 2000 from Windows NT is behind you now. You have been spending most of your time stabilizing and fine-tuning the GPOs that are applied to the various OUs for the users and workstations. During the migration, the company bought all new equipment to support the new operating system, which made it very straightforward to support the drivers for the workstation devices such as network interface cards (NICs). Recently, you had a NIC failure, and the vendor sent you a newer driver, which you used to fix the problem workstation. When you were prompted to reboot the workstation, it locked up when you entered your name and password. Since you haven't logged in yet, you try the Last Known Good Configuration, expecting the problem to be resolved. However, it still locks up at the logon screen. You want to use the older driver with the card to get back to a functional machine. What is the next step in the troubleshooting process?

A. Use the Emergency Repair Disk.

B. Use the Recovery Console.

C. Reinstall Windows 2000.

D. Boot up in Safe Mode.

6. You've established your network infrastructure and now you can begin to focus on the applications. You have just been given an application that has been tested by the network engineers that renders graphics and processes photographs used by the Product Design department. You create a package for the application and link its GPO to the Marketing department OU. The application is successfully deployed, and you don't receive any trouble calls regarding the installation of the program. However, you later begin to get calls from users complaining about the performance of their workstation. You notice that all of the calls are coming from the Marketing department. You run System Monitor on the workstations while the new application is running, and you observe that the Processor: % Processor Time counter is maxed out and the System: Processor Queue Length is over 3. You also notice that there is a great deal of disk activity. What can you do to resolve the problem?

A. Add a second processor.

B. Add more memory to the workstation.

C. Modify the priority of the new application.

D. Increase the size of the paging file.

7. You have a sound card that you want to install on your server that does not support Plug and Play. Which utility should you use to install the sound card?

   A. Device Manager

   B. System Information

   C. Control Panel ➢ Sound Cards

   D. Control Panel ➢ Add/Remove Hardware

8. You are installing Windows 2000 Server on a computer with the configuration shown in the following exhibit. You want to make sure that you use the maximum amount of disk space with the fastest access. What configuration should you use?

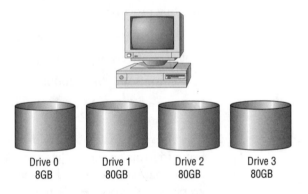

| Drive 0 | Drive 1 | Drive 2 | Drive 3 |
| 8GB | 80GB | 80GB | 80GB |

   A. Install Windows 2000 Server on the 8GB drive. Create a spanned volume set with the three remaining drives.

   B. Install Windows 2000 Server on the 8GB drive. Create a striped volume set with the three remaining drives.

   C. Install Windows 2000 Server on the 8GB drive. Create a RAID-3 volume set with the three remaining drives.

   D. Install Windows 2000 Server on the 8GB drive. Create a RAID-5 volume set with the three remaining drives.

9. You have a mirrored volume set on your Windows 2000 Server computer. You open Disk Management and realize that the secondary drive in the mirrored set has failed. You make a full backup at the end of each day. Which of the following courses of action should you take?

    A. Remove the mirror, replace the failed drive, and re-create the mirrored set.

    B. Replace the failed drive, right-click the mirrored set, and choose to regenerate the mirrored set.

    C. Replace the failed drive, right-click the mirror set, and choose to repair the volume. On the drive you replaced, select to regenerate mirrored set.

    D. Replace the failed drive, rescan the disks, and restore the volume set from tape backup.

10. You have a RAID-5 volume set on your Windows 2000 Server computer. You open Disk Management and realize one of the drives in the RAID-5 set has failed. Which of the following courses of action should you take?

    A. Remove the RAID-5 volume set, replace the failed drive, and re-create the RAID-5 volume set.

    B. Replace the failed drive, right-click the RAID-5 volume set, and choose to reactivate the mirrored set.

    C. Replace the failed drive, right-click the RAID-5 volume set, and choose to repair the volume. On the drive you replaced, select to regenerate the RAID-5 set.

    D. Replace the failed drive and select to rescan the disks.

11. Michael has just installed a service pack on his Windows 2000 Server. After he installed the service pack, he added the DHCP service. He notices that the new service runs without a hitch, even though he didn't reapply the service pack. Which of the following options allows you to install service packs just once, without having to reapply them after installing new services?

    A. MSI packages

    B. The chcksp command-line utility

    C. The verifysp command-line utility

    D. Slipstream technology

12. James wants to run the `BigProcessorDrain.exe` program on Windows 2000 Server. He notices that when this program is run at the server, the server slows down significantly. Which of the following utilities can he use to set the priority of the `BigProcessorDrain.exe` program to low?

    A. Performance Monitor

    B. System Monitor

    C. Task Manager

    D. Service Manager

13. You are a consultant who has been called in to troubleshoot a Windows 2000 Server that is not functioning properly. You suspect that some of the services are not loading properly during the boot sequence. What can you use to see a list of drivers and services that were loaded on your computer during the boot sequence?

    A. Configure Startup and Recovery options to enable boot logging.

    B. Press F5 during the boot sequence to see each driver and service as it is loading.

    C. Configure the `BOOT.INI` file with the `/enablelog` switch and reboot the computer.

    D. Use the advanced startup option Enable Boot Logging during the boot process.

14. You use a custom application on your Windows 2000 Server. The application requires that you manually edit the Registry to add a key and edit another key. When you restart the server, you see a blue screen and are unable to access the logon screen. Which recovery option should you try first?

    A. Boot the computer in Safe Mode and fix the Registry settings.

    B. Boot the computer with the Last Known Good Configuration option.

    C. Use the last full backup you made to restore the server.

    D. Use the ERD that was created when the server was installed to restore the Registry.

15. You've just updated one of your drivers, and now your computer won't restart. How can you access the Last Known Good Configuration option?

A. Press the spacebar when prompted during the boot sequence.

B. Access the Advanced Options menu by pressing F8 when prompted during the boot sequence.

C. Access the Advanced Options menu by pressing F6 when prompted during the boot sequence.

D. There is no Last Known Good Configuration option in Windows 2000.

Answers to Review Questions

1. D. The easiest thing to do first is to increase the size of the paging file, which will prevent thrashing, but this is a temporary solution at best. The best long-term solution is probably to increase the memory so as to reduce paging. The CPU is probably being utilized because of the swapping and thrashing. Moving the paging file may also help, but without increasing its size, the impact will probably be minimal.

2. B. The Task Scheduler allows you to run remote commands within an account context, but you should always use the Administrator account to do this. You shouldn't allow users to log on to a domain controller, and the System account is used for services to run in the Windows 2000 environment. The Guest account is never used for administering a domain controller.

3. D. If the NTLDR file is missing, then the machine will not boot to a point where the Last Known Good Configuration or Safe Mode will be available. The Emergency Repair Disk contains the NTLDR and other boot files that can be transferred to the crippled workstation. You could run the Recovery Console from the startup floppies or the CD, but that would not be the most efficient solution.

4. A, B, D. Laura needs to be able to access the OS and her files on disk 1, and Sam needs to be able to access the OS and his files on disk 0. The Everyone group includes Sam and Laura, so any permissions here would impact the specific permissions given to the individual users. Dynamic disks are supported only in Windows 2000, so either disk configured in this manner would preclude the Windows NT OS from working.

5. D. Using Safe Mode will put the workstation through the boot process without loading the network drivers. This will allow you to log on to the workstation locally, remove the new driver, and install the old one or an even newer driver from the vendor. The Recovery Console will allow you to access the machine, but it is not as straightforward as Safe Mode, so it should not be tried first. The Emergency Repair Disk is used to replace boot and system files and will not address the NIC driver problem. While reinstalling the OS is an option, it certainly entails a great deal more work than booting in Safe Mode.

6. A. A second processor, or at least a faster one, is in order here. The processor time is maxed out, and the queue of instructions is filling up, which means that there are instructions to be executed but the processor cannot keep up. Adding to the paging file will not help the CPU gain performance. Adding RAM will not totally alleviate the CPU activity problem.

7. D. You use Control Panel ➢ Add/Remove Hardware to add any hardware that does not support Plug and Play. Any device that you install should have a Windows 2000–compatible device driver.

8. B. You should create a striped volume set if you want to maximize the amount of storage and increase performance. A spanned volume set will not increase performance, and a RAID-5 volume set will not maximize space. Windows 2000 Server does not support RAID-3.

9. A. If a mirrored set fails, you must right-click the mirrored volume in Disk Management and remove the mirror. Then select the disk that has failed. The remaining disk will become a simple volume. Replace the failed drive, and then use Disk Management to re-create the mirrored volume. If you restore the set from backup, you will lose any of the data that had been created or edited since the last backup.

10. C. If a drive in a RAID-5 volume set fails, you should take the following steps to re-create the data through the parity on your other drives: Replace the failed hardware. Open the Disk Management utility, right-click the failed RAID-5 volume set (marked as Failed Redundancy), and choose Repair Volume from the context menu. In the Repair RAID-5 Volume dialog box, choose the drive that has been replaced, and click OK to regenerate the RAID-5 volume set.

11. D. Windows 2000 service packs use slipstream technology. With slipstream technology, when a service pack is installed, the service pack files are written to the Windows 2000 distribution files. If you add a new service, the correct files with the service pack are applied, and there is no need to reapply service packs (as was necessary with previous versions of Windows NT).

12. C. The Processes tab of Task Manager can be used to manage process priorities. To change the priority of a process that is already running, right-click the process you want to manage and select Set Priority

13. D. When the computer restarts, press F8 when prompted during the boot process. Select the Enable Boot Logging option. The log file will be written to \\`Windir`.

14. B. You use the Last Known Good Configuration if you made changes to your computer and are now having problems. Last Known Good Configuration is an Advanced Options menu item that you can select during startup. It loads the configuration that was used the last time the computer booted successfully.

15. B. In Windows NT 4, you access the Last Known Good Configuration option by pressing the spacebar when prompted during the boot sequence. In Windows 2000, the Last Known Good Configuration option is on the Advanced Options menu, which you access by pressing F8 during the boot sequence.

Managing Remote Access

MICROSOFT EXAM OBJECTIVES COVERED IN THIS CHAPTER:

✓ **Configure and troubleshoot remote access and virtual private network (VPN) connections.**

- Configure and troubleshoot client-to-server PPTP and L2TP connections.
- Manage existing server-to-server PPTP and L2TP connections.
- Configure and verify the security of a VPN connection.
- Configure client computer remote access properties.
- Configure remote access name resolution and IP address allocation.

✓ **Troubleshoot a remote access policy.**

- Diagnose problems with remote access policy priority.
- Diagnose remote access policy problems caused by user account group membership and nested groups.
- Create and configure remote access policies and profiles.
- Select appropriate encryption and authentication protocols.

VPNs are discussed in Chapter 11, "Configuring Advanced Remote Access Features."

Some Windows 2000 features are only thinly disguised retreads from Windows NT and its various service and option packs. Others are wholly new. The remote access service component of the Routing and Remote Access Service (RRAS) falls somewhere in between—RRAS itself dates back to the NT 4 Option Pack, but the Windows 2000 implementation of remote access adds a ton of new features not present in the older version.

Before you can get into the details of what these features do and how you configure them to provide remote access for your network, you need to understand some of the terms and concepts specific to RRAS remote access. That's where you'll begin in this chapter, and then you'll move on to reviewing the features and configuration settings that you need to understand to meet the exam objectives.

Learning Remote Access Buzzwords

At the very least, remote access services provide another way, in addition to LANs, to carry the network protocols you're already using. In the case of RRAS, they also provide some security services necessary to effectively provide remote access. For example, you'll probably want to have the ability to restrict user dial-up access by group membership, time of day, or other factors, and you'll need a way to specify the various callback, authentication, and encryption options that the protocols support.

Security Goodies

In the bad old days, remote access was seldom a part of most networks. It was too hard to implement, too hard to manage, and too hard to secure. It's reasonably easy to secure your networks from unauthorized physical access, but doing so for remote access was perceived (rightly or wrongly) as being much harder. There are a number of security policies, protocols, and technologies that have been developed to ease this problem.

User Authentication

One of the first steps in establishing a remote access connection involves allowing the user to present some credentials to the server. This is like showing your invitation to the doorkeeper at a fancy party; some parties have more elaborate authentication mechanisms than others. The same is true of remote access; you can use any or all of the following five authentication protocols that Windows 2000 supports.

Password Authentication Protocol (PAP) *Password Authentication Protocol (PAP)* is the simplest—and least secure—authentication protocol. It transmits all authentication information in clear text with no encryption, which makes it vulnerable to snooping. In addition, it has no way for a client and server to authenticate each other. Since other protocols offer better security, PAP is falling out of favor, and Microsoft recommends turning it off unless you have clients that cannot use a more secure protocol.

Shiva Password Authentication Protocol (SPAP) *Shiva Password Authentication Protocol (SPAP)* is a slightly more secure version of PAP that's primarily intended for talking to remote-access hardware devices made by Shiva (which is now owned by Intel). It's included for backward compatibility, but isn't in wide use.

Challenge Handshake Authentication Protocol (CHAP) *Challenge Handshake Authentication Protocol (CHAP)* (sometimes called MD5-CHAP because it uses the RSA MD5 hash algorithm) has a major security advantage over PAP: It doesn't transmit password information in the clear. Instead, the server sends a challenge encrypted with the DES algorithm to the client, which must decrypt it and return the correct response. This allows the server to verify the user's credentials without sending those credentials across an insecure link.

Although NT's RAS client can use MD5-CHAP when dialing into a third-party device, an unmodified NT RAS server will not support MD5-CHAP clients. This is because MD5-CHAP requires that the server store passwords in clear text. For security purposes, the Security Account Manager (SAM) database stores NT passwords as a hash, never in clear text.

Microsoft CHAP (MS-CHAP)   Microsoft has extended the CHAP protocol to allow the use of Windows authentication information. (Among other things, that's what the Log On With Dial-Up Networking check box in the Windows 2000 logon dialog box does.) There are actually two separate versions of *MS-CHAP*. Version 2 is much more secure than version 1, and all Microsoft operating systems support version 2. Some other operating systems support MS-CHAP version 1 as well.

Extensible Authentication Protocol (EAP)   *Extensible Authentication Protocol (EAP)* is pretty nifty. Instead of hardwiring any one authentication protocol, a client-server pair that understands EAP can negotiate an authentication method. The computer that asks for authentication is called the *authenticator*. The authenticator is free to ask for several different pieces of information, making a separate query for each one. This allows the use of almost any authentication method, including secure access tokens like SecurID, one-time password systems like S/Key, or ordinary username/password systems.

Each authentication scheme supported in EAP is called an *EAP type*. Each EAP type, in turn, is implemented as a plug-in module. Windows 2000 can support any number of EAP types at once; the RRAS server can use any EAP type to authenticate if you've allowed that module to be used and the client has the module in question. Windows 2000 actually comes with the following two EAP types:

- EAP MD5-CHAP implements the version of CHAP that uses the MD5 hash algorithm. The EAP version of CHAP is identical to the regular version, but the challenges and responses are packaged and sent as EAP messages. This means that if you turn on EAP MD5-CHAP and disable regular CHAP on the server, plain CHAP clients won't be able to authenticate.

- EAP Transport Level Security (TLS) allows you to use public-key certificates as an authenticator. TLS is very similar to the familiar Secure Sockets Layer (SSL) protocol used for web browsers. When EAP TLS is turned on, the client and server send TLS-encrypted messages back and forth. EAP TLS is the strongest authentication method you can use; as a bonus, it supports smart cards. However, EAP TLS requires your RRAS server to be part of a Windows 2000 domain.

There's a third EAP authentication method included with Windows 2000, but it's not really an EAP type. EAP-RADIUS is a fake EAP type that passes any incoming message to a RADIUS server for authentication. (*RADIUS* stands for *Remote Authentication Dial-In User Service*.)

Connection Security

There are some additional features you can use to provide connection-level security for your remote access clients. The Callback Control Protocol, or CBCP, allows your RRAS servers or clients to negotiate a callback with the other end. When CBCP is enabled, either the client or the server can ask the server to call the client back at a number supplied by the client or a prearranged number stored on the server.

Another nifty option is that the RRAS server can be programmed to accept or reject calls based on the Caller ID or Automatic Number Identification (ANI) information transmitted by the phone company. For example, you can instruct your primary RRAS server to accept calls from only your home analog line; while this keeps you from calling it when you're on the road, it also keeps the server from talking to strangers.

Finally, you can specify various levels of encryption to protect your connection from interception or tampering; the exact type and kind of encryption used will vary according to the options you specify.

Access Control

Apart from the connection-level tricks you can use to prohibit outside callers from talking to your servers, you can restrict which users can make remote connections in a number of ways. First of all, you can allow or disallow remote access from individual user accounts. This is the same limited control you have in Windows NT, but it's just the start for Windows 2000.

Besides turning dial-in access on or off for a single user, you can use *remote access policies* to control whether users can get access or not. Like Group Policies, remote access policies give you an easy way to apply a consistent set of policies to groups of users. However, the policy mechanism is a little different: You create rules that include or exclude the users you want in the policy. Unlike Group Policies, remote access policies are available only in native Windows 2000 domains (that is, in domains where there are no Windows NT domain controllers present). That means that you may not have the option to use remote access policies until your Windows 2000 deployment is further along.

What Multilink Is All About

Many parts of the world don't have high-speed broadband access yet. In fact, many places don't have ISDN or even phone lines that support 56K modems. Wouldn't it be nice if there were some way to aggregate multiple analog or ISDN lines to make them act like one faster connection? In fact, there is. The multilink extensions to the Point-to-Point Protocol (PPP) provide a way to gang up several independent PPP connections so that they act as a single connection. For example, if I use two phone lines and modems to place a two-line multilink call to my ISP, instead of getting the usual 48Kbps connection, I end up with an apparent bandwidth of 96Kbps. The multilink PPP software on my Windows 2000 machine and on the ISP's router takes care of stringing all of the packets together to make this process seamless.

Windows 2000's RRAS supports multilink PPP for inbound and outbound calls, and the dial-up networking client supports it, too. The primary drawbacks to multilink calls: They take up more than one phone line apiece and they don't support callback authentication.

Installing Remote Access

The RRAS installation process is driven by the Routing and Remote Access Server Setup Wizard. Exercise 10.1 leads you through the process of configuring an RRAS server using the wizard.

Microsoft ✓ Exam Objective

Configure and troubleshoot remote access and virtual private network (VPN) connections.

EXERCISE 10.1

Installing a Routing and Remote Access Service Server

Follow these steps to install an RRAS remote access server:

1. Open the RRAS MMC console by selecting Start ➢ Programs ➢ Administrative Tools ➢ Routing and Remote Access.

2. Select the server you want to configure in the left pane of the MMC. Right-click the server and choose Configure And Enable Routing And Remote Access from the context menu. The RRAS Setup Wizard appears. Click the Next button.

3. In the Common Configurations page of the wizard, select the Remote Access Server radio button, and then click Next.

4. The Remote Client Protocols page appears, listing the protocols available for remote access clients. If you need to add another protocol to the list, click the No, I Need To Add Protocols button; if all the protocols you want to use are on the list, leave the Yes, All Of The Required Protocols Are On This List button selected. Click Next. If you indicate that you need to add additional protocols, the wizard will stop. If the protocols you need are already present, it will continue.

Routing and Remote Access Server Setup Wizard

Remote Client Protocols
The protocols required for remote client access must be available on this server.

Verify that the protocols required on this server for remote clients are listed below.

Protocols:

AppleTalk
IPX
NetBEUI
TCP/IP

● Yes, all of the required protocols are on this list
○ No, I need to add protocols

< Back   Next >   Cancel

5. The Macintosh Guest Authentication page appears. The Mac OS allows anonymous remote access. If you want your RRAS server to imitate this behavior, click the Allow Unauthenticated Access For All Remote Clients button. Click Next. (Please note that this will occur only if Macintosh File and Print services are loaded.)

6. The IP Address Assignment page appears. If you want to use DHCP (either a DHCP server on your network or the built-in address allocator), leave the Automatically radio button selected. If you want to pick out an address range, select the From A Specified Range Of Addresses button. Click Next. (If you choose to use static addressing, at this point the wizard will give you the opportunity to define one or more address ranges to be assigned to remote clients.)

7. The Managing Multiple Remote Access Servers page appears. You use this page to configure your RRAS server to work with other RADIUS-capable servers on your network. In this case, you don't want to use RADIUS, so leave the No, I Don't Want To Set Up This Server To Use RADIUS Now button selected, and then click Next.

8. The Wizard Summary page appears. Click the Finish button to start RRAS and prepare your server to be configured. If RRAS is running on the same server as a DHCP server, you'll see a message indicating that you need to configure the DHCP relay agent (more on that later).

Configuring Your Remote Access Server

Most of the configuration necessary for a remote access server happens at the server level. In particular, you use the server's Properties dialog box to control whether the server allows remote connections at all, what protocols and options it supports, and so forth. You also have to configure settings for your users, which you'll read about in the next section.

To open the RRAS server's Properties dialog box, pick the server you're interested in and choose Action ➢ Properties (or the Properties option on the context menu).

Microsoft
✓ *Exam*
Objective

Configure and troubleshoot remote access and virtual private network (VPN) connections.

- Configure remote access name resolution and IP address allocation.

Troubleshoot a remote access policy.

- Diagnose problems with remote access policy priority.

- Diagnose remote access policy problems caused by user account group membership and nested groups.

- Create and configure remote access policies and profiles.

- Select appropriate encryption and authentication protocols.

Setting General Configuration Options

The General tab of the server Properties dialog box (see Figure 10.1) has only one check box of interest for remote access configurations. When checked, the Remote Access Server check box allows RRAS to act as a remote access server. You need to know this so that you can switch remote access capability on and off without deactivating and reactivating RRAS, which causes the service to erase its settings.

FIGURE 10.1 The General tab of the RRAS server Properties dialog box

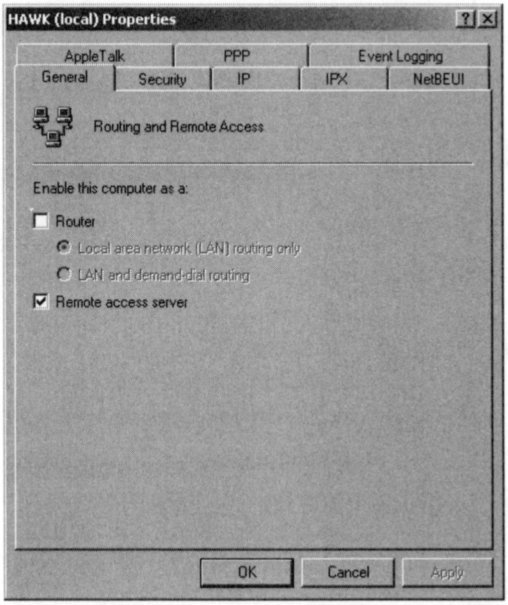

The other tabs in this dialog box control specific settings for different protocols. Note that the tabs you see depend on which protocols you have installed; for example, on a server that doesn't have IPX installed, you won't have the IPX tab. The other tabs available from this dialog box include the following:

- The Security tab lets you specify which authentication providers and settings you want the server to use. The controls on this tab are covered in the "Configuring Security" section later in the chapter.

- The next four tabs—IP, IPX, NetBEUI, and AppleTalk—control the specific settings applied to each protocol you have installed. In particular, these tabs govern whether or not the associated protocol can be used for remote access clients as well as whether remote clients can reach the entire network or only the remote access server itself. The next section, "Configuring Inbound Connections," discusses each of these tabs independently.

- The PPP tab controls which PPP protocols—including multilink—the clients on this server are allowed to use. The "Configuring PPP Options" section discusses these settings in detail.

- The Event Logging tab controls what level of log detail is kept for incoming connections. The section on monitoring your RRAS servers more fully discusses these controls.

Configuring Inbound Connections

The whole point behind using an RRAS server is to allow remote clients to call it, but it's not an all-or-nothing proposition. You can set separate options for each protocol that the server supports; since all of those protocols are carried via PPP, there are some generic PPP options you can set, as well.

Configuring PPP Options

The PPP tab of the RRAS server Properties dialog box (see Figure 10.2) lets you control the PPP-layer options available to clients that call in. The settings you specify here control whether or not the related PPP options are available to clients; remote access policies can be used to control whether individual connections make use of them or not. There are a total of four check boxes on this tab:

- The Multilink Connections check box, which is on by default, controls whether or not the server will allow clients to establish multilink connections when they call in.

- The Bandwidth Allocation Protocol (BAP) and Bandwidth Allocation Control Protocol (BACP) allow a client and server to dynamically add or remove links during a multilink session. This is handy because it lets you throttle the amount of available bandwidth up or down on demand—provided you have the Dynamic Bandwidth Control Using BAP Or BACP check box turned on. It's available only when you have the Multilink Connections check box enabled.

- The PPP Link Control Protocol (LCP) is used to establish a PPP link and negotiate its settings. There are a variety of LCP extensions defined in various RFCs; these extensions allow a client and server to dynamically agree on exactly which protocols are being passed back and forth, among other things. The Link Control Protocol (LCP) Extensions check box controls whether or not these extensions are available. Windows 9x, NT, and 2000 clients depend on the LCP extensions, so you should leave this check box enabled.

- The Software Compression check box controls whether RRAS will allow a remote client to use the Compression Control Protocol (CCP) to compress PPP traffic. In some cases, hardware compression at the modem level is more efficient, but not everyone has a compression-capable modem. Leave this check box turned on as well.

FIGURE 10.2 The PPP tab of the RRAS server Properties dialog box

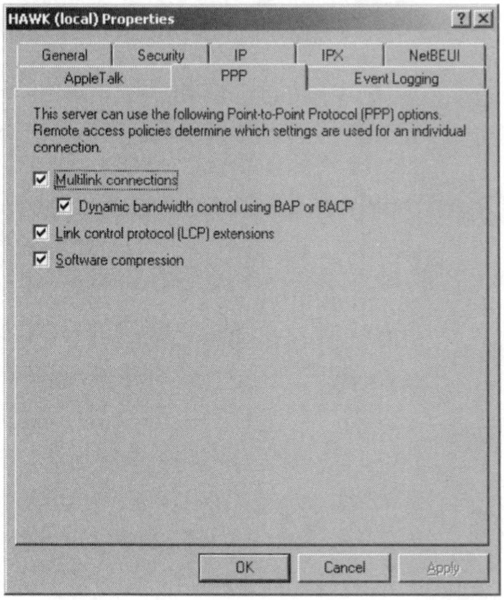

It doesn't make sense to enable multilink connections if you have only one phone line; in addition, you may want to turn them off to keep a small number of users from hogging all your lines. Exercise 10.2 takes you through the process of controlling multilink for incoming calls.

EXERCISE 10.2

Controlling Multilink for Incoming Calls

To control whether multilink is turned on or off, follow these steps:

1. Open the RRAS MMC console (Start ➢ Programs ➢ Administrative Tools ➢ Routing and Remote Access).

2. Right-click the server you want to configure in the left pane of the MMC, and then choose the Properties command. The server Properties dialog box appears.

3. Switch to the PPP tab by clicking it.

4. To turn multilink capability off, make sure the Multilink Connections check box is turned off. To turn it back on, simply check the appropriate check box.

5. If you decide to turn multilink capability on, you should also enable the use of BAP/BACP to make it easier for your server to adjust to the load placed on it. To do so, make sure the Dynamic Bandwidth Control Using BAP Or BACP check box is marked.

6. Click OK to enable these settings.

Configuring IP-Based Connections

TCP/IP is far and away the most commonly used remote access protocol; coincidentally, it's also the most configurable of the protocols that Windows 2000 supports. Both of these facts are reflected in the IP tab of the server Properties dialog box (see Figure 10.3).

FIGURE 10.3   The IP tab of the RRAS server Properties dialog box

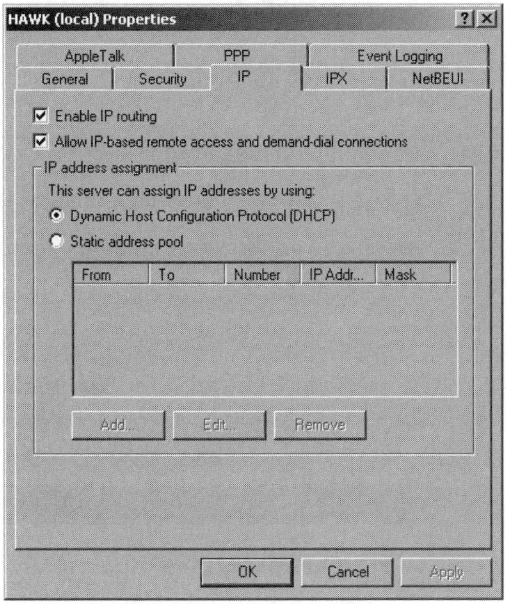

The controls on this tab do the following:

- The Enable IP Routing check box controls whether or not RRAS will route IP packets between the remote client and other interfaces on your RRAS server. When this box is checked, as it is by default, remote clients' packets can go to the RRAS server or to any other host to which the RRAS server has a route. To limit clients to only accessing resources on the RRAS server itself, uncheck this box.

- The Allow IP-Based Remote Access And Demand-Dial Connections check box controls whether clients may use IP over PPP. It might seem odd to have this choice since the overwhelming majority of PPP connections use IP, but if you want to limit your server to NetBEUI, IPX, or AppleTalk remote clients, you can do so by making sure this box is unchecked.

- The IP Address Assignment control group lets you specify how you want remote clients to get their IP addresses. The default setting here will vary, depending on what you told the RRAS Server Setup Wizard during setup. If you want to use a DHCP server on your network as the source of IP addresses for remote clients, select the DHCP radio button (making sure, of course, that you have the DHCP relay agent installed and running). If you'd rather use static address allocation, select the Static Address Pool button, and then use the controls beneath the address list to specify which IP address ranges you want issued to clients.

If you choose to use static addressing, be sure that you don't use any address ranges that are part of a DHCP server's address pool. Better still, you can add the ranges you want reserved for remote access as excluded ranges in the DHCP snap-in.

In Exercise 10.3, you're going to configure your RRAS server so that it accepts only inbound calls that use the IP protocol. You may have to skip some steps (as noted) if you don't have all four network protocols loaded.

EXERCISE 10.3

Configuring Incoming Connections

Follow these steps to configure your RRAS server to accept only incoming calls that use the IP protocol:

1. Open the RRAS MMC console (Start ➢ Programs ➢ Administrative Tools ➢ Routing and Remote Access).

2. Right-click the server you want to configure in the left pane of the MMC, and then choose the Properties command. The server Properties dialog box appears.

3. Switch to the IP tab by clicking it. Verify that both the Enable IP Routing and the Allow IP-Based Remote Access And Demand-Dial Connections check boxes are marked.

4. Switch to the IPX tab if you have one. Uncheck the Allow IPX-Based Remote Access And Demand-Dial Connections check box.

5. If your Properties dialog box has a NetBEUI tab, switch to it, then uncheck the Allow NetBEUI-Based Remote Access Clients To Access check box.

EXERCISE 10.3

6. If your Properties dialog box has an AppleTalk tab, switch to it, and then uncheck the Enable AppleTalk Remote Access check box.

7. Click OK. After a brief pause, the Properties dialog box disappears and your changes take effect.

Configuring IPX-Based Connections

You may recall from Chapter 1, "Installing and Configuring Network Protocols," that IP and IPX are very similar in many respects. Even though the particulars differ, they both involve addresses that must be assigned to every device on the network. Accordingly, the IP and IPX tabs of the server Properties dialog box aren't as different as you might expect. The IPX tab (see Figure 10.4) includes two controls that give you power over whether this server speaks IPX or not.

FIGURE 10.4 The IPX tab of the RRAS server Properties dialog box

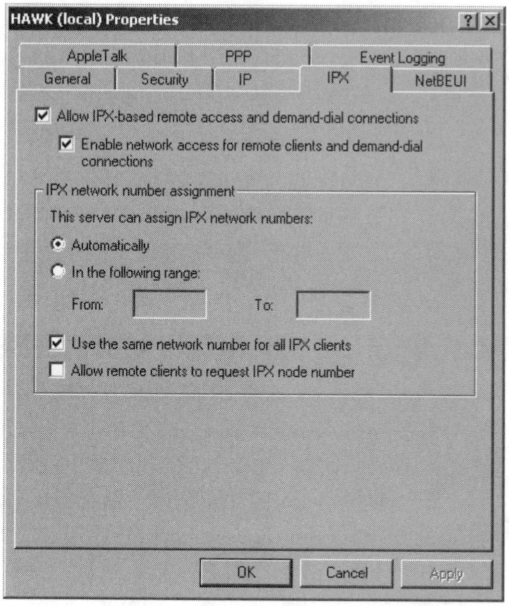

The IPX tabs include the following:

- The Allow IPX-Based Remote Access And Demand-Dial Connections check box controls whether this server accepts IPX connections or not.

- The Enable Network Access For Remote Clients And Demand-Dial Connections check box controls whether IPX clients can reach only this server or other IPX-capable servers on your network.

Notice that each protocol tab has a check box like this, but that each one is labeled differently. Make sure you get their names straight for the exam.

In addition, the IPX Network Number Assignment control group gives you a way to have this server automatically assign IPX network numbers to dial-up clients. Your best bet is to leave the Automatically radio button selected, which tells the server to pass out numbers as it sees fit. If necessary, you can manually assign numbers in a specified range. The two other check boxes give you some additional control:

- The Use The Same Network Number For All IPX Clients check box, on by default, indicates whether you want all IPX clients to get the same network number or not. Normally, you'll want this to be on so that all your IPX resources are immediately visible to clients.

- The Allow Remote Clients To Request IPX Node Number check box is normally off by default, because it's a potential security hole. When this check box is on, clients can request a particular IPX node number; in theory, this could allow a malicious remote client to impersonate another IPX device. Leave this box unchecked.

Configuring AppleTalk and NetBEUI Connections

The AppleTalk and NetBEUI tabs control whether or not your server will accept remote connections using those protocols. Since AppleTalk and NetBEUI are both pretty simple, there aren't really any configuration options on the tabs—just check boxes that you use to specify whether your server will allow incoming connections or not. The AppleTalk check box is labeled Enable AppleTalk Remote Access, while its NetBEUI counterpart reads Allow NetBEUI-Based Remote Access Clients To Access. The NetBEUI version also has an associated pair of radio buttons that regulate whether NetBEUI clients can see only the RRAS server or the entire network.

Configuring User Access

Now that you've set up the server to accept incoming calls, it's time to determine who can actually *use* it. You do this in two ways: by setting up *remote access profiles* on individual accounts and by creating and managing remote access policies that apply to groups of users. This distinction is subtle but important because you manage and apply profiles and policies in different places.

Using User Profiles

Windows 2000 stores a ton of information for each user account. Collectively, this information is known as the account's profile, and it's normally stored in Active Directory. Some settings in the user's profile are available through the two user-management snap-ins—Active Directory Users and Computers or Local Users and Groups—depending on whether or not your RRAS server is part of an Active Directory domain. In either case, the interesting part of the profile is the Dial-In tab of the user's Properties dialog box (see Figure 10.5). It turns out that this tab has a number of controls that regulate how the user account may be used for dial-in access.

FIGURE 10.5 The Dial-In tab of the user's Properties dialog box

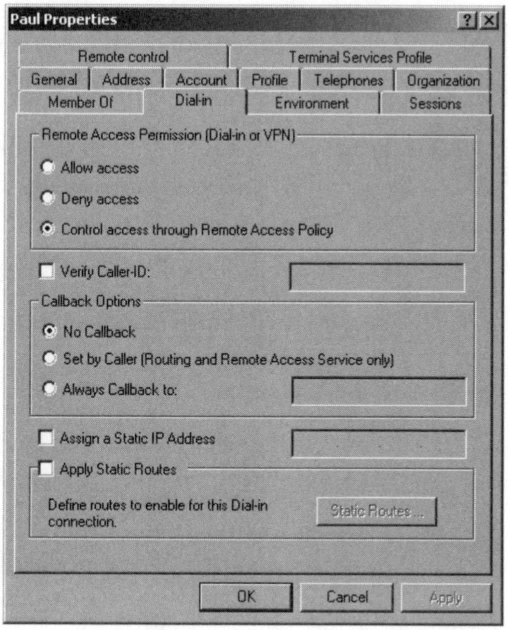

These controls include the following:

The Remote Access Permission (Dial-In Or VPN) Control Group   The
first, and probably most familiar, controls on this tab are in the Remote
Access Permission control group; they control whether this account has
dial-in permission or not. They're similar to the controls you may remember from the Windows NT User Manager; however, Windows 2000 has
a new wrinkle. In addition to explicitly allowing or denying access (with
the Allow and Deny radio buttons, of course), you can leave the access
decision up to a remote access policy, provided you're using Windows 2000
in native mode.

The Verify Caller-ID Check Box   If you like, you can force RRAS to
verify the user's Caller ID information and use the results of that verification to decide whether the user gets access. When you check the Verify
Caller-ID check box and enter a phone number in the field, you're explicitly telling RRAS to reject a call from anyone who provides that username
and password but whose Caller ID information doesn't match what you
enter. That means you need to be careful to get the number right!

The Callback Options Control Group   The Callback Options control
group gives you three choices for regulating callback. The first (and
default setting) is the No Callback radio button. When this button is
selected, the server never honors callback requests from this account. If
you choose the Set By Caller radio button instead, the calling system can
specify a number where it wants to be called, and the RRAS server will
call the client back at that number. The final choice, Always Callback To,
allows you to enter a number that the server will call back no matter from
where the client's actually calling. This is less flexible, but more secure,
than the second option.

The Assign A Static IP Address Check Box   If you want one particular
user to always get the same static IP address, you can arrange it by checking the Assign A Static IP Address check box and then entering the desired
IP address. This allows you to set up non-dynamic DNS records for individual users, guaranteeing that their machines always have a usable DNS
entry. On the other hand, this is much more error-prone than the dynamic
DNS-DHCP combination you *could* be using instead.

The Apply Static Routes Control Group   In an ordinary LAN, you
don't have to do anything special to clients to enable them to route packets—just configure them with a default gateway, and the gateway handles

the rest. For dial-up connections, though, you may want to define a list of static routes that will enable the remote client to reach hosts on your network, or elsewhere, without requiring that packets be sent to a gateway in between. If you want to define a set of static routes on the client, you'll have to do it manually. If you want to assign static routes on the server, check the Apply Static Routes check box, and then use the Static Routes button to add and remove routes as necessary.

Remember that these settings apply to individual users, so you can assign different routes, caller ID, or callback settings to each user.

You might not want to do this on your production systems since it may reduce your ability to dial in and fix problems.

Using Remote Access Policies and Profiles

Windows 2000 includes support for two additional configuration systems: remote access policies and remote access profiles. Policies determine who may and may not connect; you define rules with conditions that the system evaluates to see whether a particular user can connect or not. Profiles contain settings that determine what happens during call setup and completion. (Don't confuse remote access profiles with the dial-in settings associated with a user profile.)

You can have any number of policies in a native Windows 2000 domain; each policy may have exactly one profile associated with it.

Settings in an individual user's profile override settings in a remote access policy.

You manage remote access policies through the Remote Access Policies folder in the RRAS snap-in. By default, there's only one policy listed there: Allow Access If Dial-In Permission Is Enabled. That should give you a clue as to how policies work; they contain conditions that you pick from a list. When a caller connects, the policy's conditions are evaluated, one by one, to see whether the caller gets in or not. *All* of the conditions in the policy must match for the user to gain access. If there are multiple policies, they're evaluated according to an order you specify.

Creating a New Policy

To create a policy, just right-click the Remote Access Policies folder and use the New Remote Access Policy command. This command starts the Add Remote Access Policy Wizard, which uses a series of steps to help you define the policy. First stop: the Policy Name page (see Figure 10.6), in which you define a friendly name for the policy. This is the name that appears in the snap-in's policy list.

FIGURE 10.6   The Policy Name page of the Add Remote Access Policy Wizard

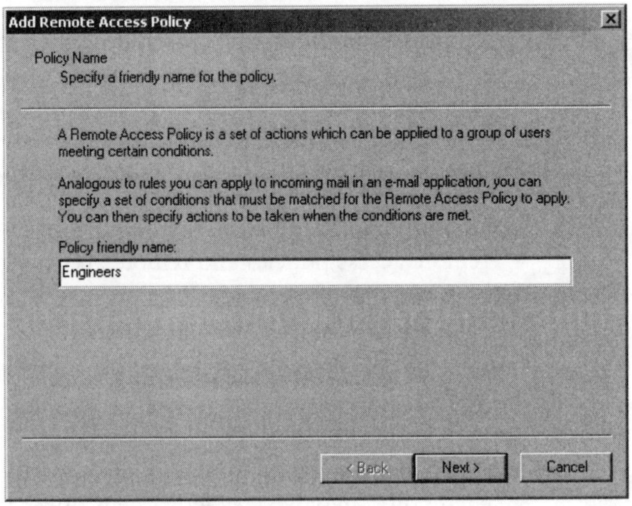

Next, you'll see a page listing the conditions for this policy (see Figure 10.7). Since you're just defining the policy, this page will initially be blank. Since this isn't very helpful, you'll need to use the Add button to create a condition for the policy. Clicking the Add button displays the Select Attribute dialog box, which is much more interesting.

If you want to restrict dial-in access based on an account's group membership, check out the Windows Groups attribute.

FIGURE 10.7   The Conditions page of the Add Remote Access Policy Wizard

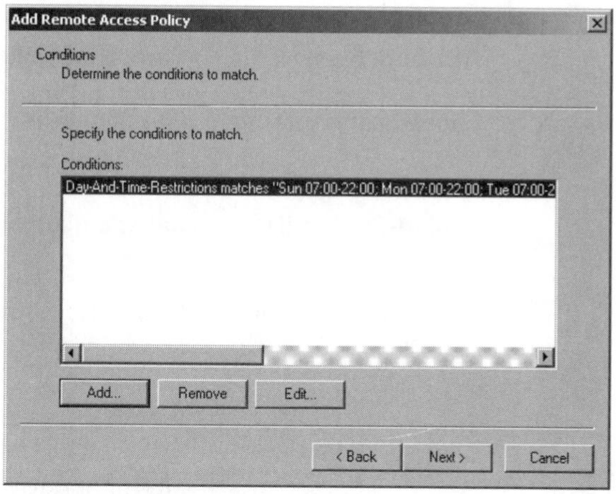

The Select Attribute dialog box (see Figure 10.8) lists all of the attributes that you can evaluate in a policy (see Table 10.1; attributes marked as "IAS only" work only with the Internet Authentication Service, which will not be discussed here). These attributes are drawn from the RADIUS standards, so you can (and in some cases, should) intermix your Windows 2000 RRAS servers with RADIUS servers. Once you choose an attribute and click the Add button, another dialog box appears, which you use for editing the value of the attribute. For example, when you select the Day-and-Time-Restrictions attribute, it pops up a calendar grid that lets you select which days and times are available for logging on. Each attribute has its own unique editor, which makes sense when you consider the wide range of attribute values. After you select an attribute and give it a value, you can add more attributes or move on to the next wizard step by clicking the Next button.

FIGURE 10.8   The Select Attribute dialog box

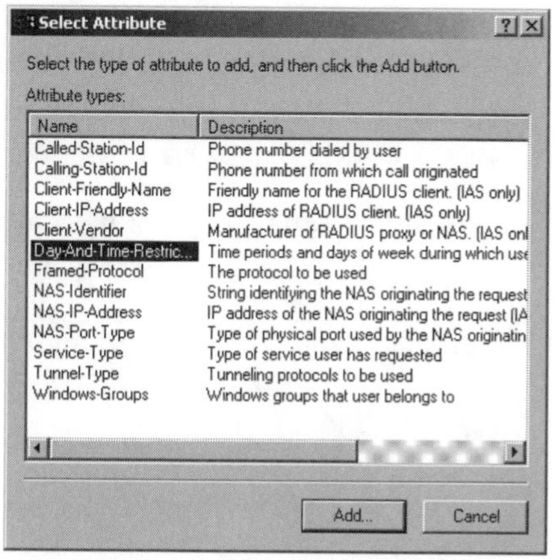

TABLE 10.1 Remote Access Policy Attributes

Attribute Name	What It Specifies
Called-Station-ID	Phone number of the remote access port called by the caller
Calling-Station-ID	Caller's phone number
Client-Friendly-Name	(IAS only) Name of the RADIUS server that's attempting to validate the connection
Client-IP-Address	(IAS only) IP address of the RADIUS server that's attempting to validate the connection
Client Vendor	(IAS only) Vendor of remote access server that originally accepted the connection; used to set different policies for different hardware
Day-and-Time-Restriction	Weekdays and times when connection attempts are accepted or rejected
Framed-Protocol	Protocol to be used for framing incoming packets (e.g., PPP, SLIP, etc.)
NAS-Identifier	(IAS only) Friendly name of the remote access server that originally accepted the connection
NAS-IP-Address	(IAS only) IP address of the remote access server that originally accepted the connection
NAS-Port-Type	Physical connection (e.g., ISDN, POTS) used by the caller
Service-Type	Framed (for PPP) or login (telnet)

TABLE 10.1 Remote Access Policy Attributes *(continued)*

Attribute Name	What It Specifies
Tunnel-Type	Which tunneling protocol should be used (L2TP or PPTP)
Windows-Groups	List of groups that the caller is a member of

The Permissions page of the wizard has only two radio buttons, but they're important because they specify whether the policy you create allows or prevents users from connecting. The two buttons, Grant Remote Access Permissions and Deny Remote Access Permissions, do what their names imply. Once you choose one of these permissions and click Next, the User Profile page appears. Its primary characteristic is the Edit Profile button, which you click to edit the user profile attached to the policy. You don't have to edit the profile when you create the policy; you can always come back to it later. Once you create the policy, it appears in the snap-in and you can manage it independently of the other policies.

In Exercise 10.4, you'll create an adjunct policy that adds time and day restrictions to the default policy.

EXERCISE 10.4

Creating a Remote Access Policy

This exercise requires you to be in a native-mode Windows 2000 domain.

1. Open the RRAS MMC snap-in (Start ➢ Programs ➢ Administrative Tools ➢ Routing and Remote Access).

2. Expand the server you want to configure in the left pane of the MMC.

3. Select the Remote Access Policies folder. The right pane of the MMC displays a single policy, Allow Access If Dial-In Permission Is Enabled.

4. Select Action ➤ New Remote Access Policy. The Add Remote Access Policy Wizard starts.

5. In the Policy Name page, type **Working hours restrictions**, and then click Next.

6. In the Conditions page, click the Add button. The Select Attributes dialog box appears.

7. Select the Day-and-Time-Restrictions attribute, and then click the Add button.

8. The Time Of Day Constraints dialog box appears. Use the calendar controls to allow remote access Monday–Saturday from 7 A.M. to 7 P.M., and then click OK.

9. The Conditions page reappears, this time with the new condition listed. Click the Next button.

10. The User Profile page appears. Click the Finish button (you'll edit the profile in the next exercise).

Working with Existing Policies

After you complete Exercise 10.4, you'll be better equipped to see a couple of additional policy-management features. To begin, you can reorder policies by right-clicking a policy in the MMC window and using the Move Up and Move Down commands. Since policies are evaluated in the order of their appearance in the snap-in and since all conditions of all policies must match for a user to get access, this is a good way to establish a set of policies that filter out some users. For example, you could create one policy that allows only members of the Marketing department to dial in between 8 A.M. and 5 P.M. and then add another that allows engineers free rein to dial in anytime.

In addition, when you open the policy's Properties dialog box (see Figure 10.9), you can add and remove conditions to the policy, change the policy's name, or control whether a user whose connection matches the policy's conditions will be granted or denied access.

Of course, you can always delete a policy you no longer need by right-clicking it and choosing Delete; the snap-in will prompt you for confirmation before it removes the policy.

FIGURE 10.9   The policy's Properties dialog box

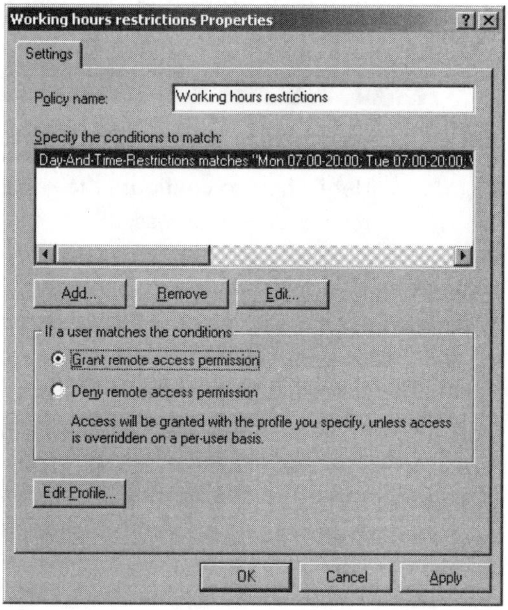

Using Remote Access Profiles

Remote access profiles are an integral part of remote access policies. Each policy has a profile associated with it; the profile determines what settings will be applied to connections that meet the conditions stated in the policy. You can create one profile for each policy, either when you create the policy or later (by using the Edit Profile button in the policy's Properties dialog box). The profile contains settings that fit into six distinct areas; each area has its own tab in the profile Properties dialog box. These tabs include the Dial-In Constraints tab, the IP tab, the Multilink tab, the Authentication tab, the Encryption tab, and the Advanced tab.

For security reasons, it's usually a good idea to limit access to the administrative accounts on your network. In particular, I usually tell clients to restrict remote access for the Administrator account; that way, the potential exposure from a dial-up compromise is somewhat reduced.

Exercise 10.5 walks through the process of configuring the Administrator account's user profile to restrict dial-up access.

EXERCISE 10.5

Configuring a User Profile for Dial-In Access

Here's how to configure the Administrator account's user profile to restrict dial-up access:

1. Log on to your computer using an account that has administrative privileges.

2. Open the Active Directory Users and Computers snap-in (Start ≻ Programs ≻ Administrative Tools ≻ Active Directory Users and Computers) if you're using an RRAS server that's part of an AD domain. If not, open the Local Users and Groups snap-in (Start ≻ Programs ≻ Administrative Tools ≻ Local Users and Groups) instead.

3. Expand the Users folder. Right-click the Administrator account in the right-hand pane, and choose Properties. The Administrator Properties dialog box appears.

4. Switch to the Dial-In tab by clicking it. On machines that participate in Active Directory, the Permission group should have the Control Access Through Remote Access Policy radio button set.

5. Click the Deny Access radio button to prevent the use of this account over a dial-in connection.

6. Click OK.

The Dial-In Constraints Tab

The Dial-In Constraints tab (see Figure 10.10) has most of the settings that you think of when you consider dial-in access controls. The controls here allow you to adjust how long the connection may be idle before it gets dropped, how long it can be up, which dates and times the connection may be established, and which dial-in port and medium can be used to connect.

FIGURE 10.10   The Dial-In Constraints tab of the Edit Dial-In Profile Properties dialog box

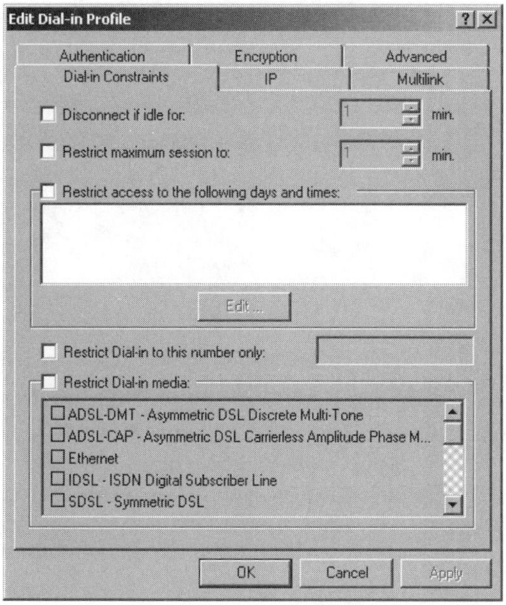

The IP Tab

The IP tab (see Figure 10.11) gives you control over the IP-related settings associated with an incoming call. If you think back to the server-specific settings covered earlier in the chapter, you'll remember that the server preferences include settings for other protocols besides IP; this is not so in the remote access profile. In the remote access profile, you can specify where the client gets its IP address. As a bonus, you can define IP packet filters that screen out particular types of traffic to and from the client.

The Multilink Tab

The profile mechanism also gives you a degree of control over how the server handles multilink calls; you exert this control through the Multilink tab (see Figure 10.12) of the profile Properties dialog box. Your first choice is to decide whether to allow such calls at all and, if so, how many ports you want to allow a single client to use at once. Normally, this setting is configured so that the server-specific settings take precedence, but you can override them.

FIGURE 10.11 The IP tab of the Edit Dial-In Profile Properties dialog box

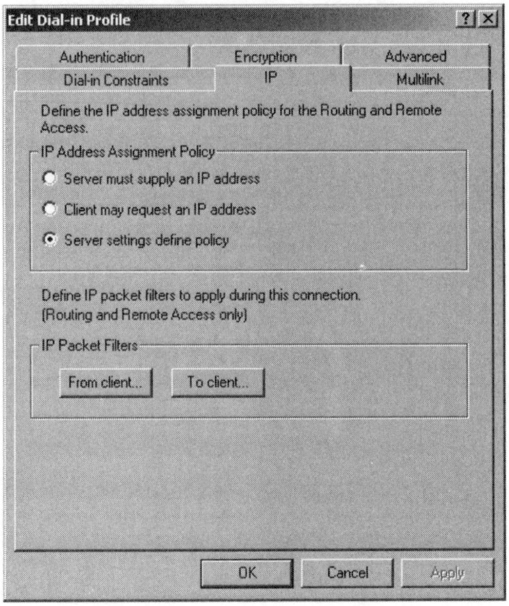

FIGURE 10.12 The Multilink tab of the Edit Dial-In Profile Properties dialog box

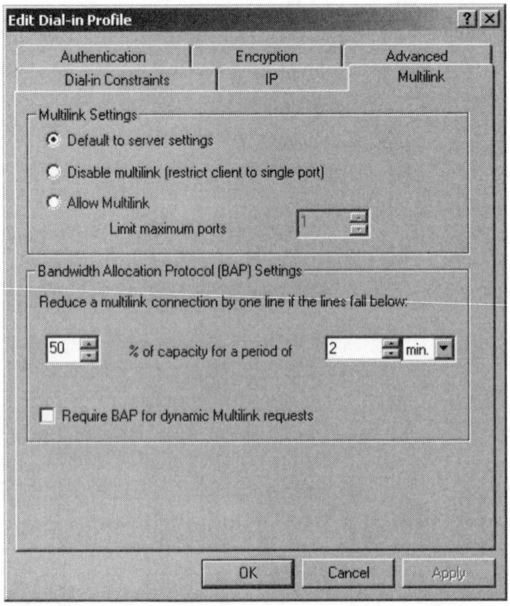

The Bandwidth Allocation Protocol (BAP) Settings control group gives you a way to control what happens during a multilink call when the bandwidth usage drops below a certain threshold. For example, why tie up three analog lines to provide 120Kbps of bandwidth when the connection is using only 85Kbps? You can tweak the capacity and time thresholds; by default, a multilink call drops one line every time the bandwidth usage falls below 50 percent of the available bandwidth and stays there for two minutes. The Require BAP For Dynamic Multilink Requests check box allows you to refuse calls from clients that don't support BAP; this is an easy way to make sure that no client can hog your multilink bandwidth.

The settings you specify on the Multilink tab will be ignored unless you have multilink and BAP/BACP enabled on the server.

The Authentication Tab

The Authentication tab (see Figure 10.13) allows you to specify which authentication methods you're willing to allow on this specific policy. Note that these settings, like the other policy settings, are useful only if the server's settings match. For example, if you turn EAP authentication off in the server Properties dialog box, turning it on in the Authentication tab of the profile Properties dialog box has no effect.

Speaking of EAP authentication (as well as CHAP, MS-CHAP, and PAP/SPAP), each authentication method has a check box. Check the appropriate boxes to control the protocols that you want this profile to use. If you enable EAP, you can also choose which specific EAP type you want the profile to support. You can also choose to allow totally unauthenticated access; thankfully, this option is off by default.

FIGURE 10.13 The Authentication tab of the Edit Dial-In Profile Properties dialog box

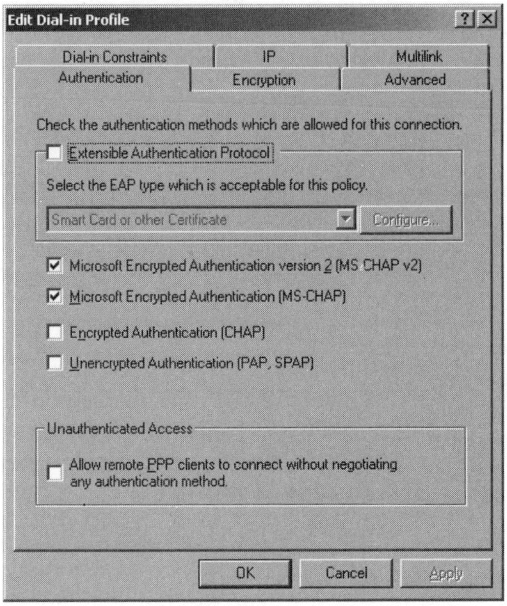

The Encryption Tab

The Encryption tab (see Figure 10.14) controls to which type of encryption you want your remote users to have access.

Unfortunately, instead of labeling the tab's check boxes with algorithm names and key lengths, Microsoft labels them with the following adjectives:

- The No Encryption check box means what it says. When this box is checked, users can connect using no encryption at all; when it's unchecked, a remote connection must be encrypted or it will be rejected.

- The Basic check box means single DES for IPSec or 40-bit Microsoft Point-to-Point Encryption (MPPE) for PPTP.

- The Strong check box means 56-bit encryption (single DES for IPSec; 56-bit MPPE for PPTP).

- The Strongest check box means triple DES for IPSec or 128-bit MPPE for PPTP connections. This option is available only on Windows 2000 installations that use the full-strength High Encryption Pack.

FIGURE 10.14 The Encryption tab of the profile Properties dialog box

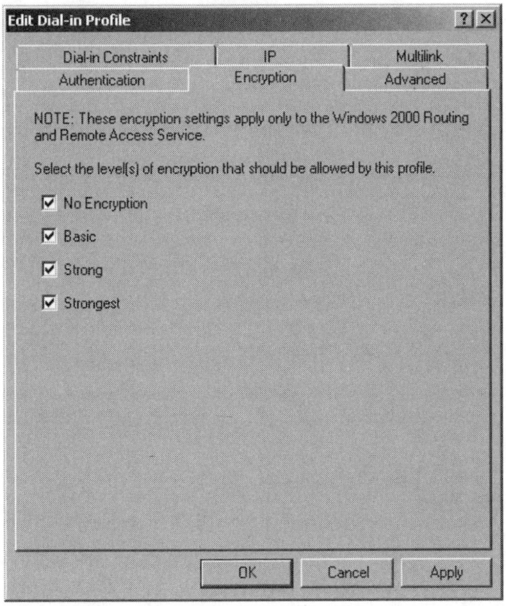

In Exercise 10.6, you'll force all connections to your server to use encryption. Any client that can't use encryption will be dropped; accordingly, don't do this on your production RRAS server unless you're sure that all of your clients are encryption-capable.

EXERCISE 10.6

Configuring Encryption

Follow these steps to require that connections to your server use encryption:

1. Open the RRAS snap-in (Start ➢ Programs ➢ Administrative Tools ➢ Routing and Remote Access).

2. Expand the server you want to configure in the left pane of the MMC.

3. Select the Remote Access Policies folder. The right pane of the MMC displays the policies defined for this server. Select the Allow Access If Dial-In Permission Is Enabled policy.

4. Choose Action ➤ Properties. The policy Properties dialog box appears.

5. Click the Edit Profile button. The Edit Dial-in Profile dialog box appears (refer back to Figure 10.10 from earlier in this chapter).

6. Switch to the Encryption tab (see Figure 10.14 shown previously).

7. Uncheck the No Encryption check box. Make sure that the Basic, Strong, and Strongest (if present) check boxes are all marked.

8. Click OK. When the policy Properties dialog box reappears, click OK again.

The Advanced Tab

The Advanced tab (see Figure 10.15) is primarily useful if you want your RRAS server to interoperate with RADIUS equipment from other vendors. You use the tab to specify additional attributes you want incorporated into the profile. When you first open the tab, you'll see only two attributes specified: a Service-Type attribute of Framed and a Framed-Protocol attribute of PPP. That combination allows the RRAS server to tell its peers that it's handling a framed PPP connection. There are several dozen additional attributes available through the Add button; some are defined in the RADIUS standard, while others are specific to particular vendors. It's not necessary to know what attributes are on this list, only that you use the Advanced tab to add additional attributes when combining RRAS with third-party RADIUS-based solutions.

FIGURE 10.15 The Advanced tab of the profile Properties dialog box

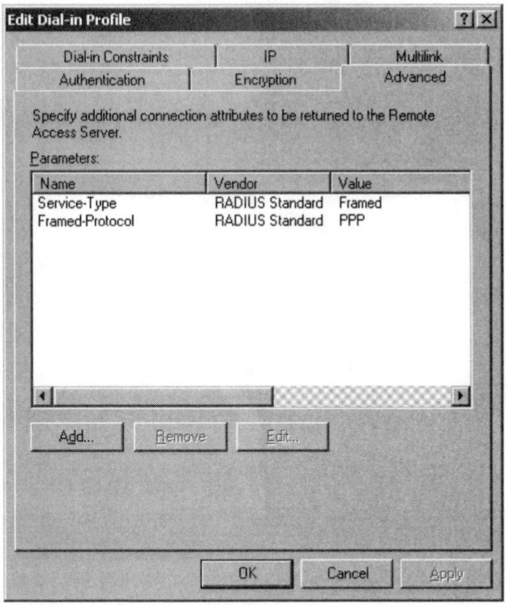

Real World Scenario

Remote Access Is More than Technology

You are the network administrator of a Windows 2000 network that supports the sales organization of a national training company. In an effort to cut costs, your management wants the sales representatives to work out of their homes and on the road. You jump to the task with the immediate intention of implementing RRAS, which you know has the necessary components to provide secure remote access.

However, one thing you want to keep in mind is that the simplicity of RRAS creates a tendency for administrators to rely too much on the technology and to take their eyes off the ball of proper processes and procedures. If your users can get into your network, then unauthorized intruders will surely try to do so. The first step in dealing with the losers and maladjusted purveyors of mischief is to prepare a properly detailed written remote access policy. This should include a description of how you want to enable remote access, what resources should be available, and what consistent type of technical mechanism you will deploy to facilitate remote access. There is no one right or wrong answer for every organization, but there needs to be a thought-out rationale for how you deploy remote services. As you can see, this is not simply a technical problem to solve.

The approach to this remote access policy should be based on an analysis of risk and liability. This analysis should cover what the implications would be if various levels of information were breached. Then the cost necessary to protect the resource could be objectively determined. This determination will affect all decisions regarding the variety of technologies that are included with RRAS, such as types of authentication, control of who can access the network remotely, encryption levels, and callback. Failure to complete a process of this nature will most likely result in a situation where unauthorized access results in damage to your network—and, by extension, damage to your career.

Configuring Security

Remote access security is a touchy topic in some quarters, probably because no one wants to admit not having it. There are several different aspects involved with remote access security configuration, the most fundamental of which involves configuring the types of authentication and encryption the server will use when accepting client requests.

Controlling Server Security

The Security tab of the server's Properties dialog box (see Figure 10.16) allows you to specify which authentication and accounting methods RRAS uses.

You can choose one of two authentication providers by using the Authentication Provider drop-down list. Your choices include the following:

- Windows Authentication is what Microsoft calls the built-in authentication suite included with Windows 2000.

- RADIUS Authentication allows you to send all authentication requests heard by your server on to a RADIUS server for approval or denial.

FIGURE 10.16 The Security tab of the RRAS server Properties dialog box

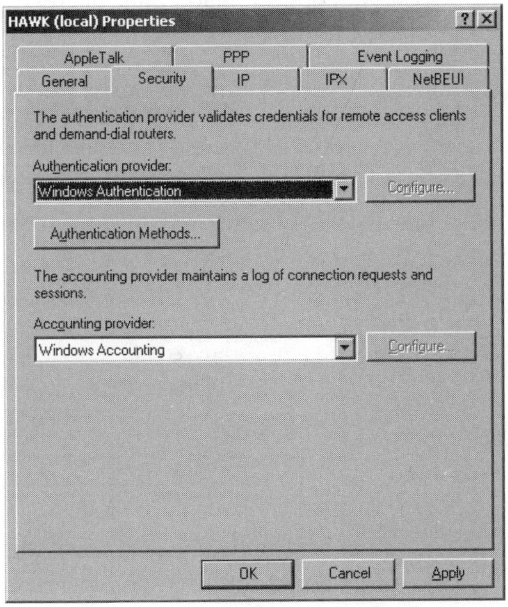

As a bonus, you can use the Accounting Provider drop-down list on the Security tab to choose between Microsoft-style accounting, in which connection requests are maintained in the event log, and RADIUS accounting, in which all accounting events are sent to a RADIUS server for action.

What if you want to change the set of authentication methods that a particular server will allow? You might think that you'd do it with the Configure button next to the Authentication Provider drop-down list, but that's actually used to set up communications with RADIUS servers when using RADIUS authentication. To configure the server by telling it which authentication methods you want it to use, you have to use the Authentication

Methods button, which displays the Authentication Methods dialog box (see Figure 10.17). If you look back over the list of authentication protocols earlier in the chapter, you'll find that each one has a corresponding check box here: EAP, MS-CHAP v2, MS-CHAP, CHAP, SPAP, and PAP are all represented. If you're feeling *really* adventurous, you can turn on totally unauthenticated access by checking the Allow Remote Systems To Connect Without Authentication check box, but that's a really, really bad idea since it allows literally anyone to connect to, and use, your server (and thus by extension your network)!

FIGURE 10.17 The Authentication Methods dialog box

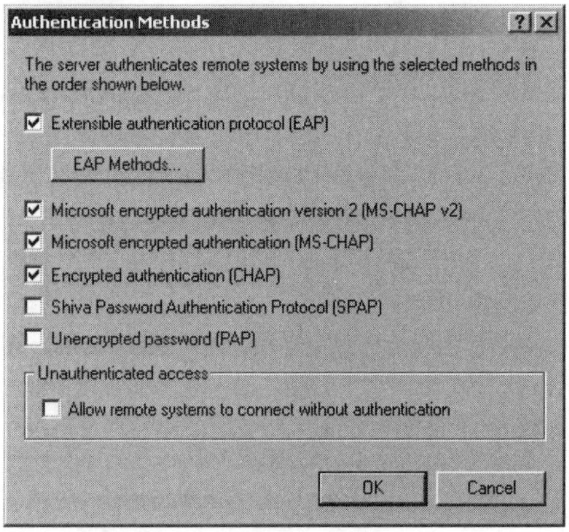

There's actually a special set of requirements for using CHAP since it requires access to each user's encrypted password. Windows 2000 normally doesn't store user passwords in a format that CHAP can use, so you have to take some additional steps if you want to use CHAP. First, enable CHAP at the server and policy levels. Next, you need to edit the default domain GPO's Password Policy object to turn on the Store Password Using Reversible Encryption For All Users policy setting. After you've done that, each user's password must be either reset or changed, which forces Windows 2000 to store the password in reversibly encrypted form. After these steps are completed for an account, that account can be used with CHAP. These steps aren't required for MS-CHAP or MS-CHAP v2; for those protocols, you just enable the desired version of MS-CHAP at the server and policy levels.

In Exercise 10.7, you're going to configure your RRAS server so that it accepts only inbound calls that use the IP protocol. You may have to skip some steps (as noted) if you don't have all of the four network protocols loaded.

EXERCISE 10.7

Configuring Authentication Protocols

Follow these steps to configure your RRAS server to accept only inbound calls using IP:

1. Open the RRAS MMC snap-in (Start ➢ Programs ➢ Administrative Tools ➢ Routing and Remote Access).

2. Navigate to the server whose authentication support you want to change. Select the server, and then choose Action ➢ Properties to open the server Properties dialog box.

3. Switch to the Security tab (refer back to Figure 10.16). Make sure that Windows Authentication is selected in the Authentication Provider drop-down list.

4. Click the Authentication Methods button. The Authentication Methods dialog box appears.

5. Select the Extensible Authentication Protocol (EAP) check box.

6. Select the two MS-CHAP check boxes.

7. Select the CHAP check box.

8. Clear the SPAP and PAP check boxes.

9. Clear the Allow Remote Systems To Connect Without Authentication check box.

10. Click OK; when the server Properties dialog box reappears, click OK again.

Controlling Security at the Policy Level

You can apply authentication restrictions at the policy level, too. As you saw in the preceding sections, policy-level settings don't exactly override the server settings. For example, you could configure your server to allow CHAP, MS-CHAP, and MS-CHAP v2 and then set up a policy that would prevent some users from using CHAP. On the other hand, if you disable CHAP at the server level, you can't build a policy that will magically allow it.

Having said that, the trick to remember is to configure your server with the *sum* of the authentication methods you want to be able to use and then create specific policies that limit which authentication methods (and other settings, particularly dial-in constraints) individuals or groups can use on that server.

Configuring Dial-Up Networking Clients

The Network and Dial-Up Connections folder is home base for *all* network connections, whether they're made through the *Dial-Up Networking (DUN)* subsystem or directly through some kind of network adapter.

Microsoft ✓ *Exam Objective*

Configure and troubleshoot remote access and virtual private network (VPN) connections.

- Configure client computer remote access properties.

Creating New Connections

Windows 2000 creates separate files for each connection you create; this helps keep related settings together. To create a new connection, you use the Make New Connection icon in the Network and Dial-Up Connections folder. This activates the Network Connection Wizard. This particular wizard leads you through the process of setting up a new network connection, beginning with a meaningless introductory page (not shown here). The first "real" page of the wizard gives you five radio-button choices (as shown in Figure 10.18).

FIGURE 10.18   The Network Connection Type page of the Network Connection Wizard

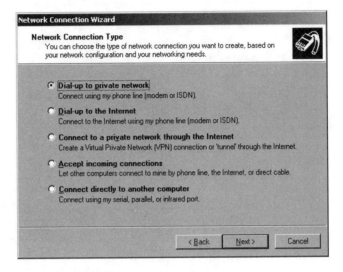

The following list includes all five radio-button choices, but only the first three are covered in this chapter.

Dial-Up To Private Network   Allows you to establish a dial-up connection to a host somewhere on someone else's network.

Dial-Up To The Internet   Establishes vanilla dial-up connections to a host that speaks the *Point-to-Point Protocol (PPP)*.

Connect To A Private Network Through The Internet   Allows you to create a virtual private network (VPN) connection on top of an established PPP session. You'll see more about VPNs in Chapter 11.

Accept Incoming Connections   Allows you to set up your system to accept incoming connections.

Connect Directly To Another Computer   Makes it possible to establish a direct peer-to-peer connection to another Windows 2000 machine using a serial, parallel, or infrared connection.

The first step toward creating a new connection on a Windows 2000 client machine is to pick one of the first two radio buttons. Creating an Internet connection requires you to use the Internet Connection Wizard, and that's not part of the test objectives. Instead of describing that wizard, the next section will explain what happens when you select the first button, Dial-Up To Private Network.

Since the connections are files, you can copy them from Windows Explorer. The fastest way to create several connections is to create one, copy it, and modify the copy's properties.

Specifying the Phone Number

Once you click Next on the Network Connection Type page, the next thing you'll see is the Phone Number To Dial page (shown in Figure 10.19). You use this page to specify the area code, phone number, and country code of the network into which you're dialing. The fields are all self-explanatory, except for the Area Code field. It's disabled by default, unless you check the Use Dialing Rules check box to indicate that you want to use the *dialing rules* set up in the Modem applet of the Control Panel. These rules allow you to tell DUN what country and region you're in so that it knows to add the appropriate long-distance codes, area codes, and calling card numbers when it's dialing. Click Next once you've entered the calling information you want to use for this connection.

FIGURE 10.19 The Phone Number To Dial page of the Network Connection Wizard

Network Connection Wizard

Phone Number to Dial
You must specify the phone number of the computer or network you want to connect to.

Type the phone number of the computer or network you are connecting to. If you want your computer to determine automatically how to dial from different locations, check Use dialing rules.

Area code:
`256`

Phone number:
`2337075`

Country/region code:
`United States of America (1)`

☑ Use dialing rules

< Back   Next >   Cancel

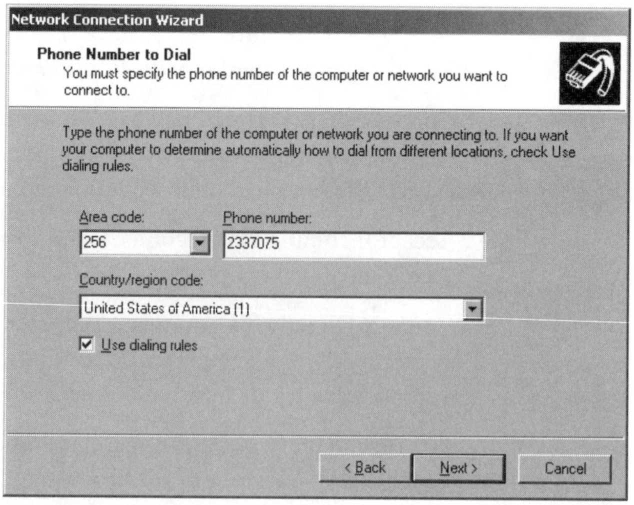

Sharing the Dial-Up Connection with Other Users

The next page of the Network Connection Wizard is where you specify whether this particular connection should be available to all users on the machine or just to you. This is a handy way for administrators to quickly set up a connection that any user on a particular client machine can use—selecting the For All Users button makes the connection available, while the Only For Myself button restricts its availability to the currently logged-on user.

The next page you'll encounter (see Figure 10.20) gives you two more sharing-related options. The first is a check box labeled Enable Internet Connection Sharing For This Connection. As you might suspect from its label, this check box turns on Internet Connection Sharing, or ICS, for this dial-up connection. ICS is really just a watered-down version of Network Address Translation (NAT), and it's covered as part of the discussion of NAT later in this chapter. For now, all you need to know about ICS is that the second check box, Enable On-Demand Dialing, tells the ICS code that it's allowed to bring up the connection when another network user wants to send some packets out to the Internet.

You can use ICS on Windows 2000 Server, not just on Professional. However, NAT is available only on the Server products.

FIGURE 10.20 The Internet Connection Sharing page of the Network Connection Wizard

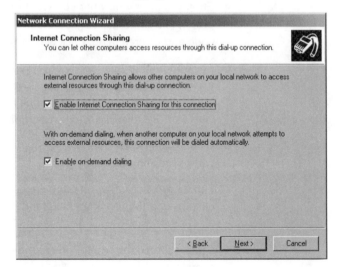

Naming Your Connection

The completion page of the Network Connection Wizard asks you to identify this connection by giving it a name. The name you supply will be used to identify the connection in the Network and Dial-Up Connections folder, so make sure you give it a name that will help you remember what the connection's for! When you click the Finish button, the connection information is stored on disk, and the Connection dialog box appears so you can test the new connection.

Exercise 10.8 outlines the process of configuring a Windows Professional client for dial-up networking.

EXERCISE 10.8

Configuring a Windows Professional Client for Dial-Up Networking

Follow these steps to configure a Windows Professional client for dial-up networking:

1. Choose Start ➢ Settings ➢ Network and Dial-Up Connections.

2. Double-click the Make New Connection icon. The Network Connection Wizard appears. Click Next.

3. Click the Dial-Up To Private Network button and click Next.

4. Enter the phone number you want this connection to dial. If you prefer, you can check the Use Dialing Rules box and enter a country code and/or area code. Click Next when you've finished.

5. The Connection Availability page appears. If you want to make this connection available to all users, choose the For All Users radio button. If this connection should be available only to you, choose Only For Myself. Click Next when finished.

6. When the Internet Connection Sharing page appears, click Next without turning on ICS.

7. The wizard's completion page appears. Type a name for this connection into the provided field, and then click Finish.

8. The Connect dialog box appears. Enter a username and password; if necessary, adjust the phone number, and click the Dial button to connect.

Setting Connection Properties

Once you've created a connection, you can change its properties at any time by opening its Properties dialog box. The Dial-Up Connection Properties dialog box has a total of five tabs that let you adjust all the pertinent settings for each individual connection. Don't confuse these settings with the ones present in the Local Area Connection Properties dialog box; they're entirely different.

The General Tab

The General tab of the Dial-Up Connection Properties dialog box (see Figure 10.21) is where you specify the modem and phone number to use with this particular connection. In this tab, as with the other tabs in this dialog box, you may recognize the filled-in fields when you use the Network Connection Wizard.

In this dialog box, you can do the following:

- Change the modem this connection uses, or settings for the modem you already have, with the Configure button. Note that you can also use the Phone and Modem Options applet of the Control Panel to adjust a broader range of modem settings.

- Change the phone number, area code, or country code used to dial this number.

- Change whether or not dialing rules (e.g., I Am Now In Area Code 770) are used when DUN decides how to dial the number for this connection. When the Use Dialing Rules check box is enabled, the Rules button becomes active, allowing you to define new locations and edit the dialing rules attached to each.

- Change whether or not the connection shows a status/progress icon in the system tray whenever the connection is active. By default, dial-up connections have the Show Icon In Taskbar When Connected check box turned on.

FIGURE 10.21   The General tab of the Dial-Up Connection Properties dialog box

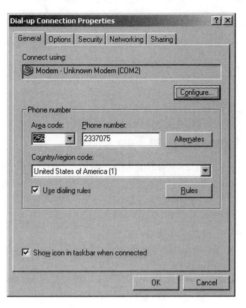

The Options Tab

The Options tab (see Figure 10.22) holds settings that control how DUN dials and redials the connection. If the General tab is like the listing in a phone book, the Options tab is the equivalent of teaching your babysitter how to use the PBX in your house. (What do you mean, you don't have a PBX in your house?) The controls in this dialog box are segregated into two groups: the Dialing Options group holds controls that govern DUN's interface behavior while dialing, and the Redialing Options group controls whether or not and how DUN will redial if it doesn't immediately connect. (There's also a button labeled X.25; not surprisingly, you use it to change the settings of your X.25 PAD if you're using one.)

FIGURE 10.22 The Options tab of the Dial-Up Connection Properties dialog box

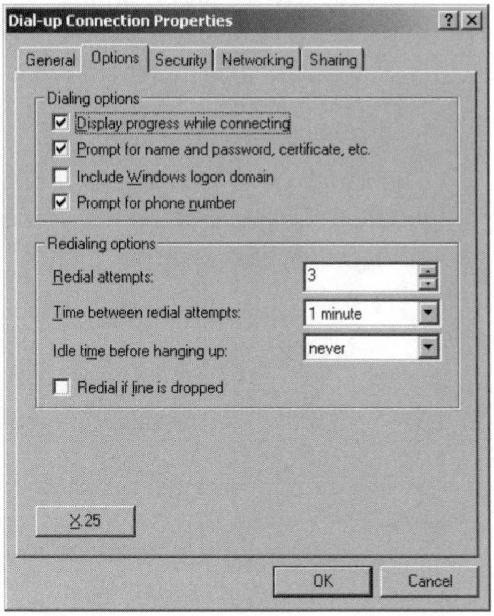

Dialing Options

There are four separate dialing options available in the Dialing Options group:

- The Display Progress While Connecting check box (on by default) instructs DUN to keep you updated on its progress as it attempts to raise the connection.

- The Prompt For Name And Password, Certificate, Etc. check box is also on by default. When it's on, Windows 2000 will prompt you for any credentials it needs to authenticate your connection to the remote server. This may be a username, a password, a public-key certificate, or some combination of the three, depending on what the remote end requires.

- The Include Windows Logon Domain check box is off by default; it forces DUN to include the domain name of the domain you're logged on to as part of the authentication credential. Leave this turned off unless you're dialing in to a Windows NT/2000 network that has a trust relationship with your logon domain.

- The Prompt For Phone Number check box (normally on) tells DUN to display the phone number in the Connection dialog box. This gives you a chance to edit it before dialing; you may want to uncheck it if you (or your users) are prone to accidental changes.

Redialing Options

The settings in the Redialing Options group control how DUN will attempt to redial the specified number if the remote end is busy or doesn't answer with a recognizable carrier tone. These settings include the following:

- The Redial Attempts field controls how many attempts DUN will make to raise the other end before giving up. The default value is 3, but you can set any value from 0 (meaning that DUN won't attempt to redial) to the ridiculous value of 999,999,999.

- The Time Between Redial Attempts pull-down menu controls how long DUN will wait after each failed call before it tries again. Values in the pull-down menu range from 1 second all the way to 10 minutes, with various increments in between.

- The Idle Time Before Hanging Up pull-down menu lets you specify an inactivity timer. If your connection is idle for longer than the specified period, your client will terminate the call. Note that the remote end may drop the call sooner than your client, depending on how it's configured. By default, this pull-down menu is set to Never, meaning that your client will never drop a call. If you want an inactivity timer, you can pick values ranging from 1 minute to 24 hours.

- The Redial If Line Is Dropped check box is a welcome Windows 2000 feature if you frequently have to use flaky telephone lines or service providers. Our experience has been that hotels in the U.S. have worse phone lines, on average, than anyplace else.

The Security Tab

How useful you find the Security tab depends on whom you're calling. The default settings it provides will work fine with most Internet service providers and corporate dial-up facilities, but Windows 2000 has a broad range of security settings you can change if you need to. Figure 10.23 shows the Security tab; the Security Options group contains controls that directly affect the security of your connection, while the Interactive Logon And Scripting group controls which canned script (if any) your client uses when connecting.

FIGURE 10.23 The Security tab of the Dial-Up Connection Properties dialog box

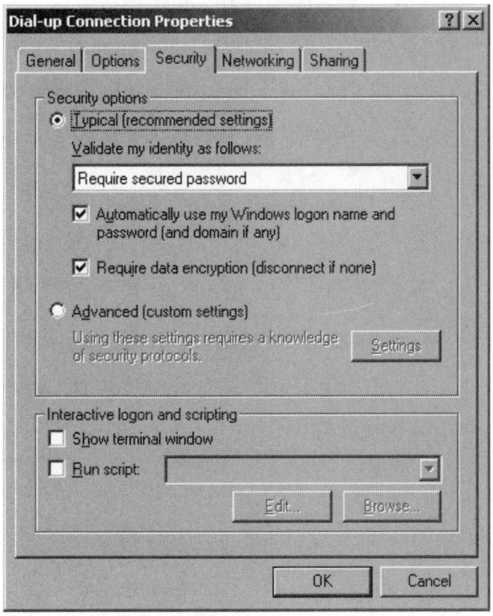

Security Options

The security options themselves are pretty straightforward; Microsoft has done a good job of labeling them clearly so that non-security weenies can understand what they mean. Here's the scoop: The security settings in effect for this connection are governed by your choice between the Typical (Recommended Settings) and Advanced (Custom Settings) radio buttons. Normally, your best bet is to stick with the typical settings and use its subordinate controls to pick a canned setting that matches your needs. These subordinate controls include the following:

- The Validate My Identity As Follows pull-down menu lets you choose among unsecured passwords (the default, and the only type of authentication that most networks support), secured passwords, and smart card authentication (useful only when calling another Windows 2000 network).

▪ If you choose to require a secured password, the Automatically Use My Windows Logon Name And Password check box instructs DUN to offer the logon credentials you used to log on to the computer or domain to the remote end. Obviously this is useful only if you're dialing into a network that has access to your domain authentication information.

▪ If you require a secured password or smart card authentication, the Require Data Encryption check box allows you to have either an encrypted connection or none at all. If you check this box, your client and the remote server will attempt to negotiate a common encryption method. If they can't (perhaps because the remote end doesn't offer encryption), your client will hang up.

Advanced Security Settings

If you select the Advanced (Custom Settings) radio button and then click the Settings button, you'll see the Advanced Security Settings dialog box shown in Figure 10.24. Its controls are more complex than the ones on the Security tab, so they bear a little more explanation.

FIGURE 10.24 The Advanced Security Settings dialog box

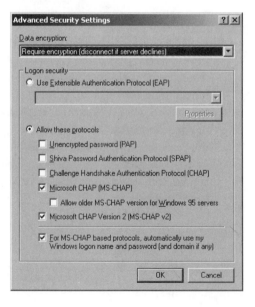

The first field is the Data Encryption pull-down menu. Windows 2000 offers you the opportunity to encrypt both sides of network connections using IPSec. This capability extends to dial-up connections, too. The pull-down menu gives you the following four choices:

- No Encryption Allowed means that the server will drop your call if it requires encryption, since you can't provide it.

- Optional Encryption tells the client to request encryption but to continue the call if it's not available.

- Require Encryption tells the client to request encryption and to refuse to communicate with servers that don't support it.

- Maximum Strength Encryption tells the client to communicate only with servers that offer the same strength encryption it does. For example, with this setting in force, a North American Windows 2000 machine with the High Encryption pack won't talk to a French Windows 2000 machine, since the French machine uses the weaker exportable encryption routines.

The Logon Security group controls which authentication protocols this client is willing to admit it knows. The default setting, Use Extensible Authentication Protocol (EAP), is what you use if you want to use standard Windows 2000 authentication (using the MD5-Challenge method) or certificate-based authentication (using the Smart Card Or Other Certificate choice in the pull-down menu). Certificate-based authentication is fascinating but not on the MCSE exam, so it will not be discussed further in this book.

The other radio button, Allow These Protocols, is followed by a laundry list of authentication protocols. While the specifics of how they work are different, the basic idea behind each of these protocols is the same: Provide a secure way for a client to prove its identity to a server. By selecting the appropriate check boxes, you can make your client speak the same protocols as the remote end. The authentication protocols were described at the beginning of this chapter.

Which protocols should you pick? We generally recommend avoiding PAP and SPAP unless you *must* talk to some elderly device that doesn't speak CHAP or MS-CHAP. If possible, allow only CHAP and MS-CHAP version 2 on your clients and servers. By default, when you turn on the Allow These Protocols button, CHAP, MS-CHAP, and MS-CHAP version 2 will be enabled. This gives you the best mix of flexibility and security.

The Networking Tab

You use the Networking tab (see Figure 10.25) to control which protocols your client will attempt to use when communicating with other servers. With power comes responsibility, though—you have to tell DUN what kind of server it's calling in the first place, using the Type Of Dial-Up Server I Am Calling field. Your choices are PPP or SLIP (the Serial Line Internet Protocol, now relegated to ancient Unix boxes and dial-up hardware). By default, PPP will be selected, and it's unlikely that you'll need to change it.

FIGURE 10.25 The Networking tab of the Dial-Up Connection Properties dialog box

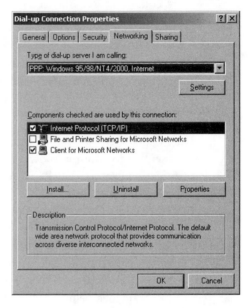

The list box in the middle of the tab shows the network protocols installed on the client. Protocols marked with a check are available for use with this connection. Normally, you'll see Internet Protocol (TCP/IP) and Client For Microsoft Networks marked, which indicates that those two protocols can be used over the connection. The Install, Uninstall, and Properties buttons work just as they do in the Local Area Connection Properties dialog box—by using them you can control which protocols live on your machine and what their settings are.

It's worth mentioning that selecting Internet Protocol (TCP/IP) in the protocols list and opening its Properties dialog box gives you access to a set of properties that are completely distinct from any TCP/IP settings that may apply to your LAN interfaces. Normally, the dial-up TCP/IP settings are configured to obtain an IP address and DNS information from the remote server, although if you need to you can override these settings.

The Sharing Tab

The Sharing tab contains only two controls, and as it happens, they're the same ones you saw earlier in Figure 10.20: Enable Internet Connection Sharing For This Connection and Enable On-Demand Dialing.

Managing Your Remote Access Server

RRAS server management is generally pretty easy since in most cases there's not much to manage. You set up the server, it answers calls, and life is good. You'll probably find it necessary to monitor the server's ongoing activity, and you may find it necessary to log activity for accounting or security purposes.

Microsoft ✓ *Exam* *Objective*

Configure and troubleshoot remote access and virtual private network (VPN) connections.

- Configure remote access name resolution and IP address allocation.

Seeing What's Going On

You can monitor your server's activity in a number of ways, including having the server keep local copies of its logs or having it send logging data to a remote RADIUS server. In addition, you can always monitor the current status of any of the ports on your system. Microsoft's documentation distinguishes between event logging, which records significant things that happen like startup and shutdown of the RRAS service, and authentication and accounting logging, which tracks things like when user X logged on and logged off. The settings for both types of logging are intermingled in the RRAS snap-in.

Monitoring Overall Activity

The Server Status node in the RRAS snap-in shows you a summary of all the RRAS servers known to the system. Depending on whether or not you use the features to manage multiple RRAS servers from one console, you may see only the local server's information here. When you select the Server Status item, the right-hand pane of the MMC lists each known RRAS server; each entry in the list tells you whether the server is up or not, what kind of server it is, how many ports it has, how many ports are currently in use, and how long the server's been up. You can right-click any Windows 2000 RRAS server in this view to start, stop, restart, pause, or resume its RRAS, disable RRAS on the server, or remove the server's advertisement from Active Directory (provided, of course, that you're using AD).

Controlling Remote Access Logging

A vanilla RRAS installation will always log *some* data locally, but that's pretty worthless unless you know what gets logged and where it goes. Each RRAS server on your network has its own set of logs, which you manage through the Remote Access Logging folder. Within that folder, you'll normally see a single item labeled Local File, which is the log file stored on that particular server.

If you don't have Windows accounting or Windows authentication turned on, you won't have a local log file. Depending on whether or not you're using RADIUS accounting and logging, you may see additional entries. However, the rest of this section will stick with local file logging.

Setting Server Logging Properties

The first place where you can control server logging is at the server level; you use the Event Logging tab (see Figure 10.26) to control what level of detail you want in the server's event log. Bear in mind that these controls regulate *all* logging by RRAS, not just remote access log entries. You have four choices for the level of logged detail:

- The Log Errors Only radio button instructs the server to log errors and nothing else. This gives you adequate indication of problems *after* they happen, but it doesn't point out potential problems noted by warning messages.

- The Log Errors And Warnings radio button is the default choice. This forces the server to log error and warning messages to the event log, giving you a nice balance between information content and log volume.

- The Log The Maximum Amount Of Information radio button causes the RRAS service to log mass quantities of messages, covering literally everything the server does. While this voluminous output is useful for troubleshooting (or even for getting a better understanding of how remote access works), it's overkill for everyday use.

- The Disable Event Logging radio button turns off all events logging for RRAS. *Don't use this option.* It will disallow you from reviewing the service's logs in case of a problem.

FIGURE 10.26   The Event Logging tab of the server Properties dialog box

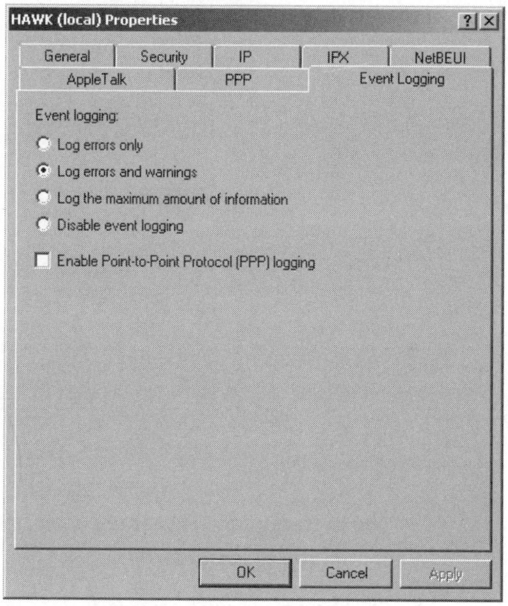

The Enable Point-to-Point Protocol (PPP) Logging check box allows you to turn on logging of all PPP negotiations and connections. This can provide valuable information when you're trying to figure out what's wrong, but it adds a lot of unnecessary bulk to your log files. Don't turn it on unless you're trying to pin down a problem.

Setting Log File Properties

You can select an individual log file in the snap-in to control what that log file contains. More precisely, you can control what events should be logged in that file from the time of the change forward. You make these changes by selecting the log file and choosing Action ➢ Properties (or one of its equivalents) to open the log file Properties dialog box. This dialog box has two tabs: The Settings tab (see Figure 10.27) controls what gets logged in the file, and the Local File tab controls the format of the file itself.

FIGURE 10.27 The Settings tab of the Local File Properties dialog box

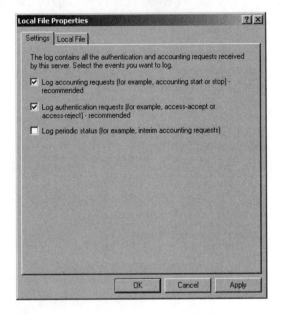

The Settings tab has three check boxes that control what gets logged. They include the following:

- The first, Log Accounting Requests, should always be checked since it governs whether events related to the accounting service itself are logged (as well as accounting data).

- The second, Log Authentication Requests, should also remain checked—it adjusts whether successful and failed logon requests are logged or not.

- The third, Log Periodic Status, should normally remain off; it controls whether or not interim accounting packets are permanently stored on disk.

The Local File tab (see Figure 10.28) controls how the log file is written to disk. You use this tab to designate three things:

- The Log File Format field determines the format of the log file. By default, RRAS uses the old-school Internet Authentication Service (IAS) format, which was originally used by the IAS component included as part of the Windows NT Option Pack. You can instead choose to use the database-compatible file format, which is available only in Windows 2000. This format makes it easy for you to take log data and store it in a database, enabling more sophisticated post-processing for things like billing and charge-backs.

- The New Log Time Period field controls how often new log files are created. For example, some administrators prefer to get a new log file each week or each month, while others are content to let the log file grow without end. You can choose to have RRAS start new log files each day, each week, each month, or when the log file reaches a certain size.

- The Log File Directory field shows where the log file is stored. By default, each server logs its data in `%systemroot%\system32\LogFiles\iasLog.log`. By using the Log File Directory field, you can change this location to wherever you want.

FIGURE 10.28 The Local File tab of the Local File Properties dialog box

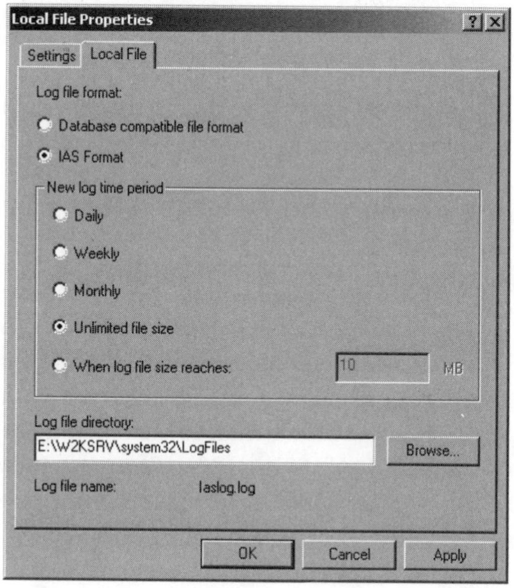

Having correct accounting and authorization data is critical to maintaining a good level of security. Exercise 10.9 walks you through configuring remote access logging.

EXERCISE 10.9

Changing Remote Access Logging Settings

Follow these steps to change your remote access logging settings:

1. Open the RRAS MMC snap-in (Start ➤ Programs ➤ Administrative Tools ➤ Routing and Remote Access).

2. Navigate to the server whose logging settings you want to change. Expand the target server, and then select the Remote Access Logging node. The right-hand MMC pane lists the log files on that server.

3. Locate the log file named Local log file, and then open its Properties dialog box by right-clicking it and choosing Properties.

4. The Local File Properties dialog box appears. Make sure the Log Accounting Requests and Log Authentication Requests check boxes are marked.

5. Switch to the Local File tab. Select an appropriate time period for log rollover by choosing one of the radio buttons in the New Log Time Period control group.

6. Click OK to accept the new settings.

Reviewing the Remote Access Event Log

You use the Local File tab to find out exactly where the log file lives, but what do you do with it then? Windows 2000 online help has an exhaustive list of all the fields logged for each connection attempt and accounting record; you don't need to have all those fields memorized, and you don't have to know how to make sense of the log entries. The Windows 2000 Resource Kit includes a handy utility called *iasparse* that will digest an RRAS log in IAS or in database formats and then produce a readable summary.

Why bother reviewing the logs? One nice feature is that each entry in the authentication log indicates which remote access policy applied (either to accept or reject the connection). This is a good way to identify problems with policies since sometimes multiple policies can combine to have an effect you didn't expect. Furthermore, if it's desirable in your environment, you can use the logged data to generate accounting reports to tell you things like the average utilization of your dial-in ports, the top 10 users of dial-in connect time, or how much online time the accounts in a certain Windows group used. Unfortunately, though, you're on your own when it comes to building tools to generate reports that will tell you whatever it is you want to know—there aren't any reporting tools included with Windows 2000.

Monitoring Ports and Port Activity

You can monitor port status and activity from the RRAS snap-in, too. The Ports folder under the server contains one entry for each defined port; when you select the Ports folder, then you'll see a list of the ports and their current status. The list indicates whether each port is a dial-in or VPN port and whether or not it's active, so you can get a quick summary of your server's workload at any time.

Double-clicking an individual port displays the Port Status dialog box (see Figure 10.29). This dialog box shows you pretty much everything you'd care to know about an individual port, including its line speed, the amount of transmitted and received data, and the network addresses for each protocol being carried on the port. This is a useful tool for verifying whether a port is in active use or not, and the Errors control group gives you a count of the number of transmission and reception errors on the port.

FIGURE 10.29 The Port Status dialog box

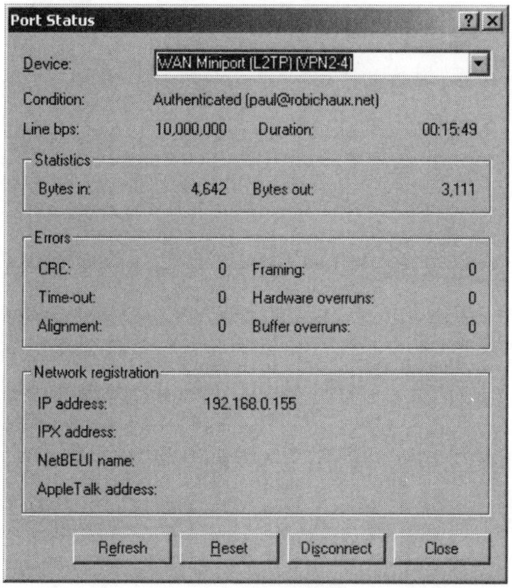

Integrating RRAS with DHCP

If you want your RRAS clients to use a DHCP server on your network, you may need to do a little fancy dancing to get things working properly. By design, the DHCP protocol is intended to allow clients and servers on the same IP network to communicate. RFC 1542 sets out how the Bootstrap Protocol (BootP), on which DHCP is based, should work in circumstances where the client and server are on different IP networks. If there's no DHCP server available on the network where the client's located, you can use a *DHCP relay agent* to forward DHCP messages from the client to the DHCP server's network. The relay agent acts like a radio repeater, listening for DHCP client requests and retransmitting them on the server's network.

The bottom line is that each network that has a DHCP client on it must have either a DHCP server or a DHCP relay agent. Otherwise, the client has no way to reach a DHCP server and get a lease.

What does this mean for your remote access deployment? It depends on your network configuration, as described by the following:

- On a small or simple network, you may choose to use static IP addressing and assign each dial-in client a fixed IP address. In this case, you don't have to fool with DHCP at all.

- If your RRAS server is also a DHCP server, you're okay since dial-in clients will get an IP address from that server's address pool.

- If your RRAS server is on a different IP network from your DHCP servers, or if you want to assign client addresses out of an address range that's not part of any DHCP scope, you need a relay agent.

The RRAS package includes a DHCP relay agent that you install as an additional routing protocol; once you install and configure it, it can tie your remote access clients to whatever DHCP infrastructure you want to use.

Installing the DHCP Relay Agent

First, a couple of caveats: You can't install the relay agent on a computer that's already acting as a DHCP server, nor can you install it on a system running Network Address Translation (NAT) with the addressing component installed. (See the section on NAT later in this chapter for more on NAT and automatic addressing.) As long as you meet these requirements, the actual installation process is easy (see Exercise 10.10). Once you have the agent installed, you're ready to configure it to forward requests when and where you want them to be relayed.

Configuring the DHCP Relay Agent

As is typical of other RRAS components, you actually configure the DHCP relay agent in two places: from the Relay Agent Properties dialog box and again on each individual interface. The configuration settings required for each of these two places are different.

Setting DHCP Relay Agent Properties

When you select the DHCP Relay Agent item under the IP Routing node and open its Properties dialog box, you'll see the contents of Figure 10.30. The only thing you can do here is to specify to which DHCP servers you want *this particular* DHCP relay agent to forward requests. The only restriction is that the RRAS server that's running the DHCP relay agent must be able to route IP packets to the destination network. The servers you specify here apply to all network interfaces to which you attach the relay agent; there's no way to configure independent forwarding addresses for individual network interfaces.

Exercise 10.10 shows you how to install the DHCP relay agent on an RRAS server.

FIGURE 10.30   The DHCP Relay Agent Properties dialog box

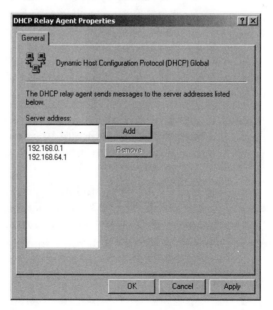

EXERCISE 10.10

Installing the DHCP Relay Agent on an RRAS Server

Follow these steps to install the DHCP relay agent on an RRAS server:

1. Open the Routing and Remote Access snap-in (Start ➢ Programs ➢ Administrative Tools ➢ Routing and Remote Access).

2. Locate the server on which you want to install the DHCP relay agent.

3. Expand the server's configuration until you see the General node (*ServerName* ➢ IP Routing ➢ General).

4. Right-click the General node and choose New Routing Protocol. The New Routing Protocol dialog box appears.

5. Select DHCP Relay Agent from the list of routing protocols, and then click OK.

6. The IP Routing node will now have a child node named DHCP Relay Agent. Select it and use the Properties command to open its Properties dialog box.

7. In the DHCP Relay Agent Global Properties dialog box, add the IP addresses of the DHCP servers you want DHCP requests forwarded to, and then click OK.

Assigning the Relay Agent to Specific Interfaces

Once you've configured the list of servers to which you want DHCP requests forwarded, you still have to attach the relay agent to particular network interfaces. You use the following procedure to create a relay agent interface: Right-click the DHCP Relay Agent item and choose New Interface. When the New Interface For DHCP Relay Agent dialog box appears, select the network interface to which you want the relay agent bound. Once you do, the interface-specific Properties dialog box (which you're about to meet) appears.

Setting Interface Properties

Each relay agent–enabled interface has its own set of properties, which are exposed through the interface-specific relay agent Properties dialog box (see Figure 10.31). The topmost control, the Relay DHCP Packets check box, lets you control whether DHCP relaying is active on this interface or not—you can turn it on or off without restarting RRAS.

The other two controls affect how long relayed DHCP requests will bounce around your network. The Hop-Count Threshold controls the number of intervening routers between the client and the DHCP server that the DHCP traffic can traverse, and the Boot Threshold controls how long the relay agent waits before forwarding any DHCP messages it hears. If you want to give a local DHCP server first crack at incoming requests, adjust the Boot Threshold upward so that the local server has a chance to respond before the message is forwarded.

FIGURE 10.31 The interface-specific DHCP relay agent Properties dialog box

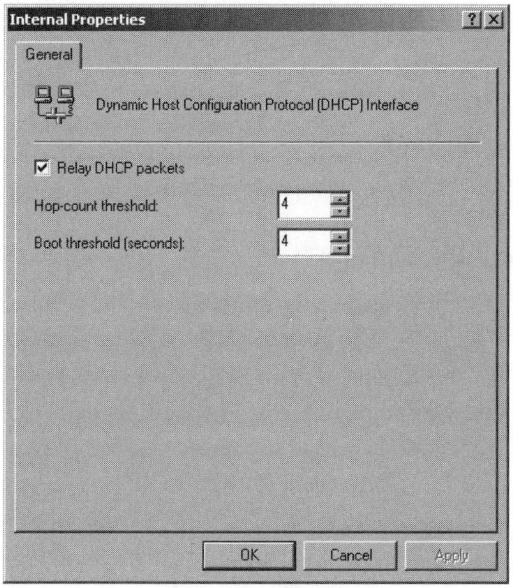

In Exercise 10.11, you'll add a new DHCP relay agent interface for your LAN connection and then specify configuration parameters for it. In practice, you'd need to add the DHCP relay agent to whichever interface remote clients use, but since I can't assume anything about the configuration of your lab machine, this lab is simplified somewhat.

EXERCISE 10.11

Configuring the DHCP Relay Agent on a Network Interface

Follow these steps to add a DHCP relay agent interface for a LAN connection:

1. Install the DHCP relay agent on your server according to the instructions in Exercise 10.10.

2. Right-click the DHCP Relay Agent item and choose New Interface.

3. The New Interface For DHCP Relay Agent dialog box appears, listing each of the interfaces to which you could attach the relay agent. Select Local Area Connection and click OK.

4. The interface-specific Properties dialog box (refer back to Figure 10.31) appears. If you have a DHCP server on your local network, increase the Boot Threshold value to 5 seconds; if you don't, decrease it to 0.

5. Click OK. Note that the list of DHCP relay agent interfaces has been updated to reflect the new interface.

Summary

Remote access is an increasingly important topic as more and more users need to access the network from the road or from home. This chapter explained in detail how to set up a RAS server, how to configure RAS clients, and how to use remote access policies.

We started the chapter by discussing all of the terms associated with remote access. You then saw how to install and configure a remote access server. You also learned how to implement remote access policies to restrict RAS. Next you saw how to configure special security settings that apply only to remote access. You also learned how to configure a remote access client machine. We then discussed the details of managing and monitoring the RAS server, as well as integrating RAS with DHCP.

Exam Essentials

Know the five user-authentication protocols supported by Windows 2000.
You can enable any or all of the five authentication protocols that Windows 2000 supports: Password Authentication Protocol (PAP), Shiva Password Authentication Protocol (SPAP), Challenge Handshake Authentication Protocol (CHAP), Microsoft CHAP (MS-CHAP), and Extensible Authentication Protocol (EAP).

Understand how multilink works. The multilink extensions to the Point-to-Point Protocol (PPP) provide a way to combine several independent PPP connections so that they act as a single connection. Windows 2000's RRAS supports multilink PPP for inbound and outbound calls.

Know how to install and configure RAS at the server level. The RAS installation process is driven by the Routing and Remote Access Server Setup Wizard, which you use to set up a dial-up server. You can specify whether the server acts as a remote access server, specify which authentication providers and settings you want the server to use, control the specific settings applied to each protocol you have installed, specify which PPP protocols, including multilink, the clients on this server are allowed to use, and control what level of log detail is kept for incoming connections.

Know how to use remote access policies. Policies determine who may and may not connect; you define rules with conditions that the system evaluates to see whether a particular user can connect or not. You manage remote access policies through the Remote Access Policies folder in the RRAS snap-in. Policies contain conditions that you pick from a list. When a caller connects, the policy's conditions are evaluated, one by one, to see whether the caller gets in or not.

Know how to use remote access profiles. Each remote access policy has a profile associated with it; the profile determines which settings will be applied to connections that meet the conditions stated in the policy. The settings fit into six distinct areas, and each area has its own tab in the profile Properties dialog box. These tabs are named Dial-In Constraints, IP, Multilink, Authentication, Encryption, and Advanced.

Know how to configure remote access security. There are several different aspects involved with remote access security configuration, the most fundamental of which involves configuring the types of authentication and encryption the server will use when accepting client requests.

You can choose one of two authentication providers by using the Authentication Provider drop-down list: Windows Authentication and RADIUS. You can apply authentication restrictions at the policy level, too.

Know the different components you can use to manage the remote access server. The Server Status node in the RRAS snap-in shows you a summary of all the RRAS servers known to the system. Each RRAS server on your network has its own set of logs, which you manage through the Remote Access Logging folder. You can monitor port status and activity from the RRAS snap-in, too. The Ports folder under the server contains one entry for each defined port; when you select the Ports folder, you'll see a list of the ports and their current status.

Know how to integrate RRAS with DHCP. If there's no DHCP server available on the network where the client is located, you can use a DHCP relay agent to forward DHCP messages from the client to the DHCP server's network. The relay agent acts like a radio repeater, listening for DHCP client requests and retransmitting them on the server's network.

Key Terms

Before you take the exam, be sure you're familiar with the following terms:

Challenge Handshake Authentication Protocol (CHAP)	Password Authentication Protocol (PAP)
DHCP relay agent	Point-to-Point Protocol (PPP)
dialing rules	RADIUS
Dial-Up Networking (DUN)	remote access policies
EAP type	remote access profiles
Extensible Authentication Protocol (EAP)	Remote Authentication Dial-In User Service
iasparse	Shiva Password Authentication Protocol (SPAP)
MS-CHAP	

Review Questions

1. You have just been hired as the administrator of a Windows 2000 network that has offices in two locations, one in New York and the other in Los Angeles. Each network has only about 200 local workstations in each city, and a single router connects them. There are several application servers in each location, but the heart of the network is a transactional database that is located in New York and available to Los Angeles. This database is an order-tracking system that support over 500 remote salespeople who use laptops to enter orders remotely into the system. They also connect to the system while they are calling on customers as part of the company's relationship-building strategy. There has been a recent barrage of inappropriate attempts to enter the system, and the president of the company directed the CIO to add another layer of security to the system. The CIO responded by having a hardware-based RADIUS server installed to intercept all remote authentication chores. Each salesperson has been assigned a smart card that is verified by the RADIUS server. As the network administrator, your task is configure the RRAS server to interoperate with the RADIUS server. Which authentication protocol should you configure on the RRAS server to support this situation?

   A. MS-CHAP

   B. PAP

   C. EAP

   D. CHAP

2. You are the network administrator of the New Products Development Company, which has offices in southern California. The employees at the corporate office are a combination of administrative support staff and technical engineers in the lab. The engineers also frequently work from home at all hours of the night, and they are supported via RRAS. You were involved with the migration of the network from a hodge-podge of different network operating systems, but predominately Windows clients and a smattering of Macintosh client computers. The CIO decided that the network operating system would be based upon Windows 2000 and that the Novell and Banyan hardware would be removed. This was completed last year, and everything appears to be fine. Recently, and increasingly, you have been getting calls from development engineers who are working with the Linux operating system complaining that they cannot connect to the RAS server. You are now told that even though the fundamental network for the company will remain Windows 2000–based, it is still important to support the work of the development engineers. What steps do you need to take in order for the Linux clients to be able to connect to the RRAS servers so that they can securely access resources at the office from home?

   A. Select Store Passwords using reversible encryption for the engineers.

   B. Select The User Must Change Password At Next Logon for the engineers.

   C. Reset the passwords for the engineers.

   D. Enable PAP on RRAS and in the engineers' remote access policy.

   E. Enable MS-CHAP v2 on RRAS and in the engineers' remote access policy.

   F. Enable CHAP on RRAS and in the engineers' remote access policy.

3. The Risk Assessment Insurance Company has five main offices across the United States. The cities are Los Angeles, Dallas, Atlanta, Chicago, and New York. Each city acts as the hub for the many individual sales offices each agent represents in their respective region. You have been involved in the migration from Windows NT to Windows 2000 over the last year. The main reason for the migration as directed by the CIO was to reduce administrative costs, a benefit promised by the new operating system platform. The migration has been completed, and the domain has finally been switched over from mixed node to native node. While the software has been upgraded across all the workstations and servers, you still have not taken full advantage of the administrative opportunities available with the system. You still spend a great deal of time managing all of the remote connections used by the agents from their home offices. You are instructed to reduce the amount of time you spend supporting these tasks. What should you do to accomplish this?

A. Create and implement consistent remote access rules for the agents in a Group Policy object and place it in the root domain of the forest with the No Override option set.

B. Create and implement consistent remote access rules for the agents in a Group Policy object and place it in each domain of the forest with the No Override option set.

C. Create a master remote access policy and implement it systematically on each RRAS server.

D. Implement Internet Authentication Service and configure all of the RRAS servers to participate.

4. You have a local DHCP server for your dial-in clients, but you also want to use the DHCP relay agent to forward requests to a remote DHCP server if the local server doesn't answer a request. To do this, you must do which of the following?

A. Add a static route to the remote server.

B. Adjust the boot threshold on the DHCP relay agent interface for the remote network so that the local server has enough time to respond.

C. Adjust the DHCP Forwarding Time parameter in the Registry.

D. Adjust the forwarding time in the DHCP Relay Agent Global Properties dialog box.

5. You are the network administrator for Worldwide Sales Organization, Inc., and you have hundreds of salespeople who need to connect to the network from all over the world. The sales representatives' computers all have smart cards that they use with a Cisco RADIUS server for authentication into the network. The network consists of a Windows NT LAN as well as several Unix servers and a mainframe. You are in the process of migrating the Windows NT portion of the network to Windows 2000. You have included Windows 2000 RRAS, and you want to incorporate the RADIUS authentication for use with the RRAS server. Which authentication protocol should you select for the RRAS server to use the RADIUS server?

   A. MS-CHAP

   B. Kerberos

   C. EAP

   D. PAP

6. You receive a phone call from Carlos, the new network administrator for the Enterprise Shoe Sales to Your Door Company. The majority of the users are the hundreds of remote salespeople who connect throughout the day to the network to update and track sales orders. For quite a while, they have been experiencing intermittent problems, which have actually grown since the previous administrator left the company. Carlos attempted to modify the default remote access policy with little success, so he decided to begin from scratch. In order to make sure that no one is negatively affected by the modifications, he deleted the now-confusing default remote access policy that he was trying to modify. During his telephone call, Carlos asks for your help in building the new remote access policy. What will happen to the remote users until the new remote policy is created?

   A. Only users who have standard remote access permission set to Allow Access will be able to connect to the server.

   B. All connection attempts will be rejected.

   C. Anyone who dials the server will be connected.

   D. Only users in Active Directory will be connected.

   E. All users will be connected except those who are configured to be allowed access through the remote access policy.

7. Your sales force consists of 1,000 people who use laptops that are standardized on Windows 98 and Windows NT Workstation. In a migration that's well under way, you have already upgraded all your servers and services to Windows 2000, and one-half of your internal Windows NT and Windows 98 machines to Windows 2000 Professional. As soon as you finish the internal migration, you'll begin to bring all the remote users up to Windows 2000 Professional. Recently, you were told that your CEO is concerned with network security, and you were ordered to make sure that all of your external network connections are secure and that any data paths outside your network are encrypted. Which of the following steps can you take to follow these new requirements? (Choose all that apply.)

    A. Configure IPSec for all of your network communications.

    B. Upgrade all of your remote users immediately to Windows 2000 Professional.

    C. Configure your RRAS servers to use MS-CHAP.

    D. Configure your RRAS servers to accept only PPTP and MPPE connections.

    E. Disable remote connections until you complete the Windows 2000 migration.

8. Rick needs to set up RRAS callbacks for a single group of users who work from home. He could accomplish this by enabling callbacks for each individual user in that user's Properties dialog box *or* by doing which of the following?

    A. Creating a Windows 2000 security group, and then configuring a remote access policy for the group

    B. Creating a remote access profile for the group

    C. Moving the users to a server that has callbacks enabled

    D. Enabling callbacks on the server

9. You are building a dial-up ISP around the technology available with Windows 2000. You are marketing personalized services that will ultimately allow you to provide voice, data, and video services to your customers by integrating Active Directory with the infrastructure of the network. For example, you plan to sell bandwidth on demand based on the customer's account in Active Directory. Your long-range plans notwithstanding, you start providing basic services to your customers by offering both dynamic and static IP addressing. Most ISPs offer static IP addresses based on a particular machine, but you want to provide a particular address based on the individual user. How can you provide this level of service for the users?

   A. Create an IP address reservation for each user in the Windows 2000 DHCP server.

   B. Assign a unique IP address to the user account in Active Directory.

   C. Create a remote access policy that provides an assigned static IP address to the appropriate users.

   D. You can't provide a static IP address per user using Windows 2000 services.

10. Hannah's manager has asked her to configure a remote access server so that it restricts what times of day users can dial in. She creates a remote access policy that contains time-of-day restrictions, but it doesn't work. What is the most likely cause?

    A. The time-of-day policy hasn't been replicated throughout the domain.

    B. The time-of-day policy doesn't have a high enough priority.

    C. The time-of-day policy has a priority that's too high.

    D. The time-of-day policy is not linked to an active remote access profile.

11. Your company has offices in five locations around the country. Most of the users' activity is local to their own network. Occasionally, some of the users in one location need to send confidential information to one of the other four locations or to retrieve information from one of them. Since the communication between the remote locations is sporadic and relatively infrequent, you have configured RRAS to use demand-dial lines to set up the connections. Management's only requirement is that any communication between the office locations be encrypted and authenticated. Which of the following steps should you take to ensure compliance with this requirement? (Choose all that apply.)

    A. Configure CHAP on all the RRAS servers.

    B. Configure PAP on all the RRAS servers.

    C. Configure MPPE on all the RRAS servers.

    D. Configure L2TP on all the RRAS servers.

    E. Configure MS-CHAP on all the RRAS servers.

12. You are using a RRAS server to manage remote access to your small Windows 2000 network that serves a single location. RRAS provides access to several remote users and to the people who have machines on the local network but occasionally want to access the network from home or from hotels when on the road. Regardless of the category of user, everyone is authenticated through Active Directory. You haven't spent much time reviewing the use of this remote connectivity since you configured the system, but now there is a concern about unauthorized users and as well as intermittent problems that remote users are experiencing when connecting to the network. You've been asked to prepare a report for management, describing the extent of these problems in the company. You recall that when you set up the system, you configured the logging to track all connection attempts using local Windows accounting. Where will you find the logging information that you need for preparing your report?

    A. The Performance Monitor log

    B. Active Directory

    C. The `%systemroot%\System32\LogFiles` folder

    D. The System event log

    E. The RRAS authentication log

13. You have already upgraded all your network servers and the services that run on them, including RRAS, to Windows 2000. You are responsible for building the remote access system for all your remote users. The requirements are that you must support Windows 98, Windows NT, Windows 2000 Professional, and also the growing number of Linux machines that the users are authorized to use from home or on the road. Since most of the users have machines on the local network as well as the need to connect from home, another requirement is that all authentications use encrypted passwords to protect the passwords from use across the Internet and the ISP networks through which users connect to the RRAS servers. What authentication protocol should you use to satisfy these requirements?

A. MS-CHAP v1

B. MS-CHAP v2

C. CHAP

D. PAP

E. EAP

14. You are the network administrator for the Beach Party Bingo Apparel Company. You serve offices in three cities, with support people for the network in each location. The support people occasionally need to access the network from home when they get paged for network problems during weekends and evenings. You also have more than 100 salespeople who travel constantly as they try to get your company's product in boutiques across the country. They need to access the network on a regular basis. You want all remote communication to be logged so that for security purposes you can track the locations where connections originate. How can you configure the RRAS server to accommodate these requirements?

A. Configure Set By Caller for the sales staff and No Callback for the support staff.

B. Configure Set By Caller for the sales staff and for the support staff.

C. Configure Set By Caller for the sales staff and Always Callback To for the support staff.

D. Configure No Callback for the sales staff and Set By Caller for the support staff.

E. Configure Set By Caller for the sales staff.

15. You are configuring RAS on your network, and you have installed RRAS on a Windows 2000 Server. Users can dial in to one of two phone numbers, 420-4200 and 420-4201, in order to establish RAS connectivity. The Remote Access Permission for each user is set to Control Access through Remote Access Policy.

You are required to apply the following rules:

- Administrators and Power Users can connect at any time, but power users must dial in to 420-4200.

- If a user is a member of both the Administrators group and the Power Users group, that user must be treated as an Administrator. *Admin overrules power user*

- Members of the Domain Users group can connect only between the hours of 5 p.m. and 11 p.m. but may connect to either phone number.

Using the following exhibit, design the simplest remote access policies possible by selecting the items in the Choices column and placing them in the appropriate empty boxes. Policy A is always processed first, and Policy C is always processed last. The default remote access policy has been deleted. Use the Default item if the default setting is required for an element. If no setting is required, then leave its box blank. Note that some items might be used more than once, and some items might not be used at all.

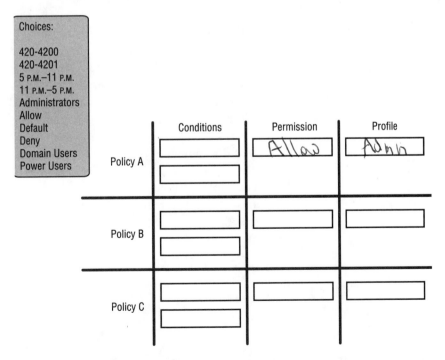

Choices:

420-4200
420-4201
5 P.M.–11 P.M.
11 P.M.–5 P.M.
Administrators
Allow
Default
Deny
Domain Users
Power Users

Answers to Review Questions

1. C. The Extensible Authentication Protocol (EAP) allows Windows 2000 to support authentication protocols that are used by other vendors. Smart cards, for example, generally use EAP-TLS. The RAS client can use this protocol to format the authentication request in a manner that the RADIUS server understands. Windows 2000 can be used as RADIUS server via the IAS protocol. However, in this scenario, the CIO has installed a dedicated RADIUS server. CHAP and PAP work with clear-text passwords, and MS-CHAP is a Microsoft proprietary protocol.

2. A, C, F. PAP uses clear-text passwords and MS-CHAP supports only Microsoft clients, so they are not options for the Linux clients. CHAP supports encryption across the wire but not in storage, so the encryption must be reversible. Selecting this option does not affect existing passwords, so after you select this option, you need to reset the engineers' passwords. However, if you select the option that forces a password change at the next login, then the engineers will be unable to access the system in the first place from their Linux machines as CHAP does not support this feature.

3. D. The Windows 2000 RRAS server can be configured to behave as a RADIUS server. This allows configuration information to be shared by multiple machines through the Internet Authentication Service. In this configuration, when the RRAS server receives a request, it forwards that request to the IAS server for processing and authorizes or denies access based upon a centralized policy. Remote access polices cannot be set in GPOs. The problem of creating a master policy and trying to keep all of the RRAS servers in sync will expand geometrically as the number of servers you are trying to manage increases.

4. B. The boot threshold for an interface controls how long the relay agent will wait before forwarding DHCP requests it hears on that interface.

5. C. RRAS supports multiple authentication methods that can be used for different purposes. The Extensible Authentication Protocol (EAP) allows requests to the RRAS server to be properly formatted and forwarded to the RADIUS server. MS-CHAP is the Microsoft Challenge Handshake Authentication Protocol, which is used in a pure Microsoft environment. Kerberos is a standard that's used to authenticate a user to the Active Directory. PAP stands for Password Authentication Protocol, a simple protocol that provides little security and does not forward requests to third-party authentication authorities.

6. B. Without a default remote access policy, no user will be allowed access through the RRAS server. All connection requests are evaluated against the criteria contained in the remote access policy. If there is no remote access policy, there are no conditions to compare, and any request is thereby denied. Removing the remote access policy does not leave the remote connection to your network open. Therefore, partial connectivity to your network is not possible if there is no remote access policy. The options are either granularity of access through policy or no access at all with no policy.

7. C, D. Since all of your client machines are Windows clients, you can use MS-CHAP to provide password encryption when establishing a connection to the network. PPTP and MPPE provide encryption of data between the client machine and the RRAS server. IPSec provides encryption from the client all the way to the resource it's connecting to, which is more than what is required by the directives. Upgrading the remote clients will not, by itself, provide the encryption required, and the Windows NT clients already support MS-CHAP. Disabling all remote connections until you finish the migration isn't necessary, since the pieces are already in place to satisfy the requirements.

8. A. Remote access policies allow you to create policies that target specific groups (provided you're in Windows 2000 native mode).

9. B. In Active Directory, dial-in users can be assigned a static IP address associated with their user account. You need to make sure that you have removed these IP addresses from any scope that is being delivered through DHCP so that you won't create conflicts. DHCP delivers addresses based on the machine, and reservations are assigned based on a particular MAC address. Remote policy doesn't allow you to deliver a unique IP address.

10. B. Policies are evaluated in order, so if the time-of-day restrictions have too low a priority, another policy may allow the connection to proceed instead of stopping it.

11. C, E. MS-CHAP provides encrypted and mutual authentication between the respective RRAS locations. MPPE works with MS-CHAP and provides encryption for all the data between the locations. CHAP provides encrypted authentication, but MS-CHAP is needed for MPPE to work. PAP is the lowest level of authentication providing passwords, but in clear text. L2TP needs to team up with IPSec to provide the data encryption for the secure transfer of information between the locations.

12. C. When you use Windows accounting, the local Windows account logs are found in the `%systemroot%\System32\LogFiles` folder. These logs can be stored in either an Open Database Connectivity (ODBC) or in Internet Authentication Service format for later analysis. Performance Monitor is the tool that came with Windows NT, and it has been replaced with the System event log. This is used for global service errors such as initialization failures and service starts and stops. There is no RRAS authentication log. You do have RADIUS logging available; when it's used, the log files are stored on the RADIUS servers. This is very useful when you have multiple RRAS servers, since you can centralize RRAS authentication requests. Active Directory is not used to log events from the various services in Windows 2000.

13. C. The Challenge Handshake Authentication Protocol (CHAP) is a standard remote-access authentication that is available on Microsoft and non-Microsoft clients. It provides the use of encrypted passwords. The MS-CHAP protocol is based on CHAP but is not available for non-Microsoft clients. If MS-CHAP is the only authentication protocol available on the RRAS server, the Linux clients won't be able to connect to the server. PAP is available on Linux clients, but it doesn't provide the encryption that you need. EAP is an authentication protocol that allows RRAS to interact with other authentication enforcement entities such as RADIUS servers.

14. C. Setting the Set By Caller option for the sales staff will allow them
to travel around the country and enter the number where they are at
any given time for the callback, thereby allowing you to keep records
of all connections. Setting the Always Callback option for the support
staff will ensure that their remote connections are always made from
their homes. Using No Callback would allow anyone configured with
this option to call from anywhere and connect to the system without
any callback requirements.

15. See the following exhibit.

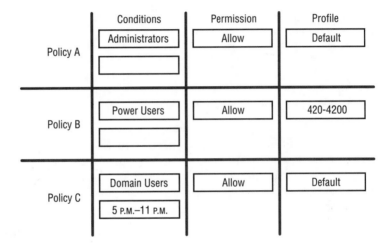

Administrators need to be able to connect to either line at any time of
the day, so this policy should be listed first. The policy allowing members of the Power Users group to connect should come second; this
will make it possible for members of both the Administrators and the
Power Users groups to take advantage of the unlimited access enjoyed
by administrators. The policy that applies to Domain Users needs to
come last; otherwise, users who are members of both Power Users and
Domain Users would be allowed to dial in to 420-4201.

Configuring Advanced Remote Access Features

MICROSOFT EXAM OBJECTIVES COVERED IN THIS CHAPTER:

✓ **Configure and troubleshoot remote access and virtual private network (VPN) connections.**

- Configure and troubleshoot client-to-server PPTP and L2TP connections.

- Manage existing server-to-server PPTP and L2TP connections.

- Configure and verify the security of a VPN connection.

- Configure client computer remote access properties.

- Configure remote access name resolution and IP address allocation.

✓ **Configure and troubleshoot Network Address Translation (NAT) and Internet Connection Sharing.**

- Configure Routing and Remote Access to perform NAT.

- Troubleshoot Internet Connection Sharing problems by using the ipconfig and ping commands.

In the previous chapter, you learned how to configure standard dial-up remote access connections on the server and the client. However, there are a couple of important features of RRAS that we didn't discuss in that chapter: *virtual private networks (VPNs)* and *Network Address Translation (NAT)*.

VPNs provide remote access to private networks across public connections. Clients can dial in to an ISP and connect to your private network across the Internet. The main benefit of this is reduced cost, since long-distance calls are unnecessary.

NAT, and its little brother Internet Connection Sharing (ICS), allows you to hide many machines behind a single IP address. This is particularly useful if you have only one public IP address and every machine on the network needs to access the Internet.

Managing Virtual Private Networking

Virtual private networks (VPNs) are increasingly popular because they essentially give you something for nothing. If you have users outside your network boundary (whether they're telecommuting, traveling, or permanently located where they can't reach your network), VPNs give you an easy-to-implement, easy-to-manage solution to the problem of how you allow these remote users access.

Conventional dial-up access still works fine, but it can be expensive to implement, painful to manage, and vulnerable to attack. VPNs offer a way around these problems by offering low initial and ongoing cost, easy management, and excellent security. Windows 2000's Routing and Remote Access Service (RRAS) component includes two complete VPN implementations: one using Microsoft's *Point-to-Point Tunneling Protocol (PPTP)* and one using a combination of the Internet-standard IPSec protocol and the *Layer 2 Tunneling Protocol (L2TP)*.

Microsoft **Configure and troubleshoot remote access and virtual private**
Exam **network (VPN) connections.**
Objective

- Configure and troubleshoot client-to-server PPTP and L2TP connections.

- Manage existing server-to-server PPTP and L2TP connections.

- Configure and verify the security of a VPN connection.

In this section, you'll learn how to set up and configure RRAS as a VPN server using PPTP and L2TP + IPSec (which we'll lump together and call L2TP from now on).

Comparing PPTP and L2TP

Since you can choose between two different VPN protocols, how do you know which one is the proper choice in a given situation? If you know the differences and similarities between the two, you'll be better prepared to make the right choice. To make it easier, the following list summarizes the most important points of interest:

- PPTP and L2TP both depend on the PPP protocol to move data (note that this doesn't mean that either requires a dial-up PPP connection, though).

- PPTP requires an IP connection. L2TP can use PPP over IP, Frame Relay, X.25, or ATM.

- L2TP supports header compression; PPTP doesn't.

- L2TP connections can be encrypted and authenticated, but PPTP connections are only encrypted.

- L2TP must be used with IPSec, which requires a certificate server (though IPSec can be used alone). PPTP always uses Microsoft Point-to-Point Encryption (MPPE).

Installing a VPN

To get any use from your VPN, you need two pieces: a VPN client and a VPN server. In Windows 2000's case, having a VPN server means that you're very likely to be using RRAS. Since we already explained how to install RRAS in Chapter 10, "Managing Remote Access and Related Services," this chapter will give a bare-bones explanation just as a refresher.

Starting from Scratch

If you don't have RRAS installed at all, you'll need to install it, activate it, and configure it as a VPN server. The easiest way to do this is with the RRAS Setup Wizard. You may remember that the wizard gives you a page with several radio buttons that you use to select the kind of server you want to set up. What you may not know is that if you followed the instructions in Exercise 10.1 ("Installing a Routing and Remote Access Service Server"), you actually already *have* a VPN server—when you install RRAS as a remote access server, the wizard automatically sets up VPN ports for you. Just in case you didn't follow the exercise steps, though, Exercise 11.1 goes through them again from the standpoint of how things look when you explicitly choose to build a VPN server.

EXERCISE 11.1

Installing the Routing and Remote Access Service as a VPN Server

Follow these steps to install a RRAS VPN server:

1. Open the RRAS MMC console (Start ➤ Programs ➤ Administrative Tools ➤ Routing and Remote Access).

2. Select the server you want to configure in the left pane of the MMC. Right-click the server and choose Configure And Enable Routing And Remote Access. The RRAS Setup Wizard appears. Click Next.

3. In the Common Configurations page of the wizard, make sure that the Virtual Private Network (VPN) Server radio button is selected, and then click Next.

4. The Remote Client Protocols page appears, listing the protocols available for remote access clients. If you need to add another protocol to the list, click the No, I Need To Add Protocols button; if all the protocols you want to use are on the list, leave the Yes, All Of The Required Protocols Are On The List button selected. Click Next.

5. If you indicate that you need to add additional protocols, the wizard stops. If the protocols you need are already present, it continues.

6. The Internet Connections page appears next. This page lists all of the demand-dial and permanent network interfaces known to RRAS; you have to choose an interface to serve as the incoming "phone number" for VPN connections. Pick an interface, and then click Next.

7. The IP Address Assignment page appears. If you want to use DHCP (either a DHCP server on your network or the built-in address allocator), leave the Automatically radio button selected. If you want to pick out an address range, select the From A Specified Range Of Addresses button. Click Next.

   If you choose to use static addressing, at this point the wizard will give you the opportunity to define one or more address ranges to be assigned to remote clients.

8. The Managing Multiple Remote Access Servers page appears. You use this page to configure your RRAS server to work with other RADIUS-capable servers on your network. In this case, you still don't want to use RADIUS, so leave the No, I Don't Want To Set Up This Server To Use RADIUS Now button selected, and then click Next.

9. The wizard summary page appears. Click the Finish button to start RRAS and prepare your server to be configured. If RRAS is running on the same server as a DHCP server, you'll see a message indicating that you need to configure the DHCP relay agent (more on that later).

Once you've completed this exercise, you'll have a complete, ready-to-go VPN server that will start accepting connections immediately. (Try it if you don't believe it!) However, you may want to configure the available ports to meet your VPN needs; we'll get to that in a minute.

If You're Already Using RRAS

If you're already using RRAS for IP routing or remote access, you can enable it as a VPN server without reinstalling. (Of course, if you want to start from scratch, you can always right-click the server and use the Disable Routing And Remote Access command to wipe out the server's configuration.)

The General tab of the Server Properties dialog box contains controls that you use to specify whether your RRAS server is a router, a remote access server, or both. The first step in converting your existing RRAS server to handle VPN traffic is to make sure that the Remote Access Server check box is marked on this tab. Making this change requires you to stop and restart RRAS, but that's okay because the snap-in will do it for you. (There are some additional configuration steps you can take; to find out what they are, read on!)

Configuring a VPN

VPN configuration is extremely simple, at least for PPTP. Either a server can accept VPN calls or it can't. If it can, it will have a certain number of VPN ports, all of which are configured identically. There's very little that you *have* to change or tweak to get a VPN server set up, but there are a few things you can adjust as you like.

Configuring VPN Ports

The biggest opportunity to configure your VPN server is to adjust the number and kind of VPN ports available for clients to use. The initial release of Windows 2000 supports up to 1,000 simultaneous connections, though this may be more than your hardware can handle. In addition, you can enable or disable either PPTP or L2TP, depending on what you want your remote users to have access to. You accomplish this magic through the Ports Properties dialog box (see Figure 11.1).

For conventional remote access servers, this dialog box shows you a long list of hardware ports, but for servers that support VPN connections, there are some extra goodies: two WAN Miniport devices, one for PPTP and one for L2TP. These aren't really devices, of course. They're actually virtual ports maintained by RRAS for accepting VPN connections. You configure these ports with the Configure button, which displays the Configure Device dialog box (see Figure 11.2). This is where the VPN rubber actually meets the road.

FIGURE 11.1 The Ports Properties dialog box

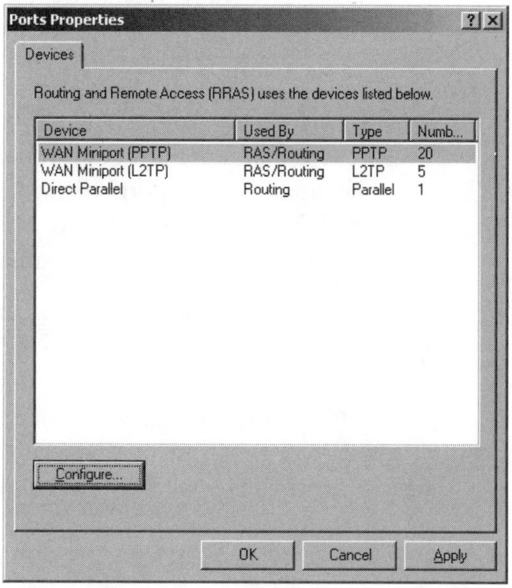

FIGURE 11.2 The Configure Device dialog box

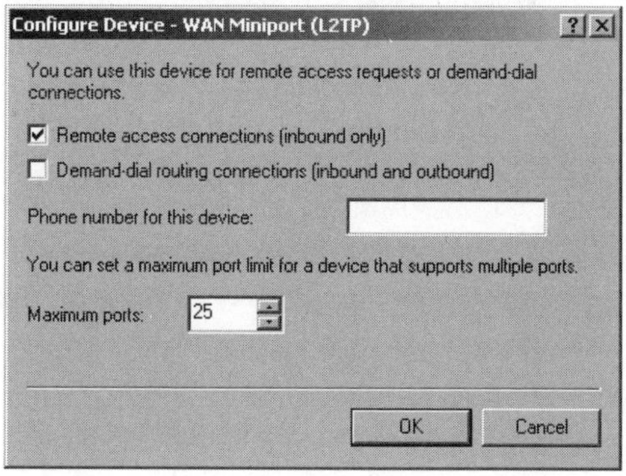

The three controls pertinent to a VPN configuration are the following:

- The Remote Access Connections (Inbound Only) check box must be activated in order to accept VPN connections with this port type. To disable a VPN type (say, if you wanted to turn off L2TP), uncheck this box in the corresponding device's Configure Device dialog box.

- The Demand-Dial Routing Connections (Inbound And Outbound) check box controls whether or not this VPN type can be used for demand-dial connections. By default, this box is checked; you'll need to turn it off if you don't want to use VPN connections to link your network with other networks.

- The Maximum Ports control lets you set the number of inbound connections that this port type will support. By default, you get five PPTP and five L2TP ports when you install RRAS; you can use from zero to 1,000 ports of each type by adjusting the number here.

You can also use the Phone Number For This Device field to enter the IP address of the public interface to which VPN clients connect. You might want to do this if your remote access policies accept or reject connections based on the number called by the client. Since you can assign multiple IP addresses to a single adapter, you can control VPN traffic by throttling which clients can connect to which addresses through a policy.

Setting Up a VPN Remote Access Policy

Previously, you learned how to use the remote access policy mechanism on a Windows 2000 native-mode domain. Now it's time to apply what you've learned to the VPN world. Recall that there are two ways to control which specific users can access a remote access server: You can grant dial-up permission to individual users in each user's Properties dialog box, or you can create a remote access policy that embodies whatever restrictions you want to impose. It turns out that you can do the same thing for VPN connections, but there are a few additional twists to consider.

Granting Per-User Access

To grant or deny VPN access to individual users, all you have to do is make the appropriate change on the Dial-In tab of each user's Properties dialog box. While this is the easiest method to understand, it gets tedious quickly if you need to change VPN permissions for more than a few users. Furthermore, there's no way to distinguish between dial-in and VPN permissions.

Creating a Remote Access Policy for VPNs

You may find it helpful to create remote access policies that enforce the permissions you want end users to have. There are a number of ways to accomplish this result; which one you use depends on your overall use of remote access policies. The simplest way is to create a policy that allows all of your users to use a VPN. In Chapter 10, you learned how to create remote access policies and specify settings for them; one thing you may have noticed was that there's a NAS-Port-Type attribute that you can use in the policy's conditions. That attribute is the cornerstone of building a policy that allows or denies remote access via VPN, since you use it to accept or reject connections arriving over a particular type of VPN connection. For best results, you'll use Tunnel-Type in conjunction with the NAS-Port-Type attribute, as described in Exercise 11.2.

Remember that you can use remote access policies only if you're in a native-mode Windows 2000 domain.

EXERCISE 11.2

Creating a VPN Remote Access Policy

Follow these steps to create a remote access policy that governs VPN use:

1. Open the RRAS MMC console (Start ➤ Programs ➤ Administrative Tools ➤ Routing and Remote Access).

2. Navigate to the server on which you want to create the policy; then expand the server node until you see the Remote Access Policies node.

3. Right-click the Remote Access Policies folder and choose New Remote Access Policy. This starts the Add Remote Access Policy Wizard.

4. Name the policy **VPN Access** or something else that clearly indicates what it's for, and then click Next.

5. When the Conditions page of the wizard appears, click the Add button to add this condition: NAS-Port-Type Attribute Set To "Virtual (VPN)."

   If you want to restrict VPN users to either PPTP or L2TP, add this other condition: Tunnel-Type Attribute Set To The Appropriate Protocol.

EXERCISE 11.2 *(continued)*

6. In the Permissions page of the wizard, make sure the Grant Remote Access Permission radio button is selected (unless you're trying to *prevent* VPN users from connecting). Click Next when finished.

7. The User Profile page appears next. If you want to create a specific profile (perhaps to restrict which authentication types VPN clients may use), click the Edit Profile button to specify them. At a minimum, you should clear the No Encryption option on the Encryption tab of the remote access profile. When you've finished tweaking the profile, click Finish to create and activate the policy.

If you don't want to grant VPN access to everyone, there are some changes you can make to the above process to fine-tune it. When you add the policy described in the exercise, it will end up after the default Allow Access If Dial-In Permission Is Enabled policy. This means that the default policy will take effect before the VPN-specific policy, so you'll probably want to move the VPN policy to the top of the list.

Let's say you want to allow everyone dial-up access, but you also want VPN capability to be reserved for a smaller group. The easiest way to accomplish this is to create an Active Directory group and put your VPN users in it. You can then create a policy using the two conditions outlined in the exercise *plus* a condition that uses the Windows-Groups attribute to specify the new group. As with the ordinary VPN policy in the exercise, if you create a policy using the Windows-Groups attribute, make sure to put it ahead of the default policy.

You can also delete the default remote access policy if you don't need it for dial-in users.

🌐 Real World Scenario

Planning VPN Security

The CEO of your company has just returned from a seminar that promised lower communication costs through the magic of VPNs tunneled through the Internet. She can't wait to start ripping out the fixed leased lines so that she can see the saved dollars move down to the bottom line. As the network administrator, you are now charged with implementing VPNs to provide secure communications across the network.

You know that along with the increase of mobile computing there has been a correlating increase in the use of VPNs. This trend has been, and will continue to be, a boon to productivity. This growth is akin to the benefit that the public highway system has provided to private organizations for their economic activities. For this reason, VPNs will continue to grow in importance in the explosion of remote communication that's taking place today.

However, you know that a VPN is only a part of an overall security implementation for a network; you can't assume that a company's communications are secure simply because it's using a VPN. As mentioned previously, a written remote access policy needs to include a written security policy that is based on an analysis of risk and liability. You can make all the effort to create a VPN solution for the users on your network, but they may have NetBIOS enabled on their network connection, with file and printer sharing enabled. With this type of configuration, you may have secure communications with your network, but any confidential company information that the users have downloaded to their computers is now exposed to the Internet.

Other things to consider are that clients may download Java applets and ActiveX controls that have the ability to run their own remote control activities, hidden from view, or that hackers may use your system to gain access to your network so that they can use it as a platform for a future Denial of Service (DoS) attack on another network.

Ensure that you have considered as many aspects as possible when you are planning your remote systems. As you deploy VPNs to secure your company's communications, make sure that you aren't plugging one narrow crack in your system while leaving another gaping hole that's too big to see.

Server-to-Server VPN Connections

For the most part, you will use a VPN to connect remote users to your company's network. An alternate use for VPNs is to connect physically separate networks (also known as an internetwork) without the expense of a leased WAN connection. This can be especially useful if you plan on having little network traffic because typical dial-up or even broadband Internet connections can't handle the kind of traffic generated by most corporate networks.

In a server-to-server VPN implementation, both sides of the internetwork have a VPN server, and the VPN servers always connect to each other, similarly to routers. The only step you need to perform in addition to the typical RAS VPN implementation is to establish a demand-dial interface on each VPN server

You create new demand-dial interfaces with the Demand Dial Interface Wizard, which you activate with the New Demand-Dial Interface command (available when you right-click the Routing Interfaces node in the RRAS console).

Naming the Interface

The first step in the wizard is the Interface Name page, where you specify the name you want the new interface to have. This is the name you'll see in the RRAS console, so you should choose some name that identifies the source and destination of the connection (for example, HSV-ATL for a connection between Huntsville and Atlanta). This is particularly useful when you want to use one RRAS console somewhere on a network to manage many RRAS servers—having an easy way to see which link you're working with can be very valuable.

Choosing a Connection Type

Demand-dial interfaces can use a physical device (such as a modem or an ISDN adapter) or in our case, a VPN connection. For example, you can have a demand-dial connection that opens a VPN tunnel to a remote network when it sees traffic destined for that network.

Connecting via a VPN

If you specify that you want to use a VPN connection, the next step is to indicate what type of VPN connection to use. You do this through the VPN Type page, which offers you the following three choices:

- The Automatic radio button tells RRAS to figure out the connection type when negotiating with the remote server. This is the most flexible choice, so it's selected by default.

- The Point-to-Point Tunneling Protocol (PPTP) radio button tells RRAS that this connection will always use PPTP.

- The Layer 2 Tunneling Protocol (L2TP) radio button indicates that you want this connection to always use L2TP.

The next step is the Network Address page. On this page, you should enter the IP address of the remote VPN server.

Next comes the Protocols And Security page, which contains five configuration check boxes. They are the following:

- The Route IP Packets On This Interface and Route IPX Packets On This Interface check boxes control whether this interface will handle the specified packet types or not. By default, IP routing is enabled but IPX routing isn't.

- If you want to add a user account so that a remote server (running RRAS or not) can dial in, check the Add A User Account So A Remote Router Can Dial In check box. When this check box is active, you can also choose to require that the remote server authenticate itself (using the same credentials) when you call it—just check the Authenticate Remote Router When Dialing Out check box.

- Some servers can handle PAP, CHAP, or MS-CHAP authentication, but others can handle only PAP. If your remote partner falls into this latter group, make sure that Send A Plain-Text Password If That Is The Only Way To Connect is checked.

- If the system that your RRAS server is calling isn't running RRAS, it may expect you to manually interact with it, perhaps through a terminal window. This is what the last check box, Use Scripting To Complete The Connection With The Remote Router, is for—check it and you'll get a terminal window after the modem connects so you can provide whatever commands or authenticators you need.

Setting Dial-In Credentials

If you choose to allow remote routers to dial in to the RRAS machine you're setting up, you'll have to create a user account with appropriate permissions. The Demand Dial Interface Wizard handles the account-creation process for you, assuming that you fill out the Dial-In Credentials page. Microsoft recommends that you pick a username that makes evident which routers use the link. You can use ICAO airport identifiers, city names, or whatever else you like, as long as you can figure out what's what.

Setting Dial-Out Credentials

If you want your router to initiate calls to another router, you'll need to tell your local RRAS installation what credentials to use when it makes an outgoing call. Unlike the Dial-In Credentials page, RRAS makes no attempt to do anything with the credentials you provide on this page. (Actually, it does check the two password fields to make sure you've typed the same password into each one, but that's it.) The credentials you provide here must match the credentials the remote router expects to see, or your router won't be able to authenticate itself to the remote end.

Troubleshooting VPNs

The two primary VPN problems are the inability to establish a connection at all and the inability to reach some needed resource once connected. There's a lot of common ground between the process of troubleshooting a VPN connection and an ordinary remote access connection.

Verifying the Simple Stuff

"Is it plugged in?" That's one of the first questions that support techs at mass-market vendors like Gateway and Packard Bell ask customers who call to report a dead computer. In the same vein, there are some extremely simple—but sometimes overlooked—things to check when your VPN clients can't connect.

This list presupposes that your client can make the underlying connection to the ISP.

Check the following things:

- Is the RRAS server installed and configured on the server?

  - Is the server configured to allow remote access? Check the General tab of the server Properties dialog box.

  - Is the server configured to allow VPN traffic? Check the Ports Properties dialog box to make sure that the appropriate VPN protocol is enabled and that the number of ports for that protocol is greater than zero.

  - Are there any available VPN ports? If you have only 10 L2TP ports allocated, caller #11 will be out of luck.

- Do the client and server match?

  - Is the VPN protocol used by the client enabled on the server? Windows 2000 clients will try L2TP first and switch to PPTP as a second choice; however, clients on other operating systems (including Windows NT) can normally expect either L2TP or PPTP.

  - Are the network protocols for all clients enabled on the server? This is particularly good to check if you have some IPX-using clients lurking in the woodpile.

- What about authentication?

  - Here's a favorite: Are the username and password correct? If not, don't expect to get a VPN connection.

  - Does the user account in question have remote access permissions, either directly on the account or through a policy?

  - Speaking of policy, do the authentication settings in the server's policies (if any) match the supported set of authentication protocols?

The Slightly More Esoteric Problems

If you check all the simple stuff and find nothing wrong, it's time to move on to some slightly more sophisticated problems. These tend to affect more than one user, as opposed to the simple (and generally user-specific) issues outlined above. The problems include the following:

Policy Problems   If you're using a native-mode Windows 2000 domain, and you're using policies, those policies may have some subtle problems that show up under some circumstances.

- Are there any policies whose Allow or Deny settings conflict with each other? Remember that all conditions of all policies must match to gain user access; if any condition of any policy fails, or if there are any policies that deny access, it's "game over" for that connection.

- Does the user match all of the necessary conditions that are in place, such as Time and Date?

Network Stuff   If you're using static IP addressing, are there any addresses left in the pool? If the VPN server can't assign an address, it won't accept the connection.

If you're using IPX, be sure that the client and server settings that control whether or not the client can ask for its own node number match; if the server disallows it, the client won't be able to connect unless it already has an assigned number.

Domain Stuff   Windows 2000 RRAS servers can coexist with Windows NT RRAS servers, and both of them can interoperate with RADIUS servers from Microsoft and other vendors. Sometimes, though, this interoperation doesn't work exactly as you'd expect.

- Is the RRAS server's domain membership correct? Your RRAS servers don't have to be domain members unless you want to use native-mode features like remote access policies.

- If you're in a domain, are the server's group memberships correct? The server account must be a member of the RAS and IAS Servers security group.

Managing Network Address Translation

Until recently, Microsoft didn't offer a way for more than one person to share a single connection to the Internet. As part of Windows 98 Second Edition, Microsoft included a feature called *Internet Connection Sharing (ICS)*. The idea behind ICS is simple: If you have more than one computer and they're networked together, one computer can act as a gateway to the Internet.

ICS actually implements a service called Network Address Translation (NAT). Since every IP packet contains address information, you can probably guess how NAT got its name: It's a service that translates between your own network's addresses and addresses usable on the Internet. With either ICS or NAT, your entire network uses only a single IP address on the Internet. All outgoing traffic passes through the NAT machine on its way out. All inbound traffic is likewise addressed to the NAT machine, which is responsible for passing it back to the proper computer on your local network.

Microsoft ✔ *Exam* *Objective*	**Configure and troubleshoot Network Address Translation (NAT) and Internet Connection Sharing.** ■ Configure Routing and Remote Access to perform NAT. ■ Troubleshoot Internet Connection Sharing problems by using the `ipconfig` and `ping` commands.

NAT Fundamentals

The job of a NAT server seems simple enough at first glance: Allow a bunch of computers to masquerade behind a single IP address. However, there are some subtleties that make it more complex than a first glance would indicate. You can start exploring the process by looking at a simple representation of a network using NAT to connect to the Internet (see Figure 11.3). In this network, there are six workstations and a NAT server, each with addresses in the 10.10.1.*x* range. Notice that the only machine connected to the Internet is the NAT server and that it actually has a second IP address assigned—those are both small but very important details, as you'll see shortly.

In the rest of this section, we'll use NAT to refer to the protocol used by both the ICS and NAT services in Windows 2000, but we'll call those components by their correct names.

FIGURE 11.3 A small NAT network

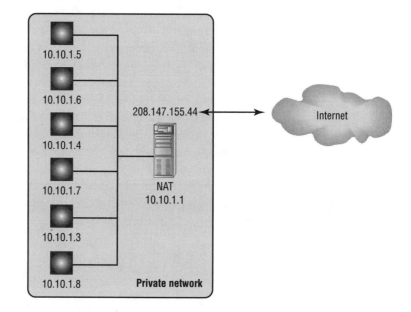

Private Addressing Made Simple

As a workaround to the problem of a limited number of IP addresses, the Internet Network Information Center (InterNIC), in conjunction with the Internet Assigned Numbers Authority (IANA), designated some address ranges as *private addresses*. These addresses cannot receive traffic from or send traffic to the Internet. In every other respect, though, they're just ordinary IP addresses. The idea behind private addresses is that you can use them to configure a network that's not connected to the Internet. That seems like a useful idea, until you want to hook your network up to the Internet. That's where NAT comes in: It translates between public and private addresses.

RFC 1597, "Address Allocation for Private Internets," designates the three private address ranges:

- 10.0.0.0 with a subnet mask of 255.0.0.0
- 172.16.0.0 with a subnet mask of 255.240.0.0
- 192.168.0.0 with a subnet mask of 255.255.0.0

You can use any of these address spaces with impunity, since no router is allowed to route Internet traffic to or from those addresses. If you remember that Figure 11.3 shows a second IP address assigned to the computer running NAT, now you know why: The NAT server uses a public IP address to communicate with the Internet and a private IP address for the local network.

How NAT Works

For NAT to work, the NAT server must be able to do a number of things:

- Maintain two interfaces, one with a private IP address and one with a public IP address, and route packets between them.

- Determine where outbound packets are going and then edit their address data so that replies come back to the NAT box (after all, Internet servers can't send data back to the original clients).

- Receive replies sent in response to outbound packets and then re-address them to the correct client on the private network.

You can follow each of these steps to see what really happens when a client makes a request for some data on an Internet server. For this exercise, you can say that a client with a private IP address of 10.10.1.5 is trying to fetch a web page from www.robichaux.net (216.92.40.80). The NAT router has two IP addresses: 10.10.1.1 on the private side and 208.170.118.207 on the Internet.

Maintaining Multiple Interfaces

Windows 2000 already understands how to route data between multiple IP addresses on the same computer—it just uses the same static routing code included with Windows NT. Static routing just moves packets among multiple interfaces that you define yourself. In reality, though, you have to install and configure the Routing and Remote Access Service to use NAT on a Windows 2000 Server (more on that a little later). ICS, though, doesn't require RRAS, even though it does the same kind of routing.

Deciding Where Outbound Packets Are Going

Take a look at Figure 11.4 to see what happens to the outbound packet. Here's the scoop:

1. The client generates its request and sends it to its default gateway—the NAT server. The packet's addressed to port 80 at IP address 216.92.40.80, the machine you're trying to reach.

2. The NAT server receives the packet and examines it to determine where it's bound. It creates an entry in its NAT table that ties the real destination address and port number to its origin and to a substitute port number it chooses at random. It also replaces the original source address of the packet with its own address, so that replies from the target machine will come back to the NAT machine.

3. The NAT server sends the rewritten packet over its external interface to the Internet, where it's routed and handled normally. At this point, there's essentially no way to tell that the request came from a computer behind the NAT server, since all the network's Internet traffic originates from, and is returned to, the NAT machine.

The NAT table is the key to this whole process, since it associates the original source address and port with the destination address and port. That way, when an incoming packet arrives, the NAT software can scan the table to identify the original source for the packet.

FIGURE 11.4 An outbound packet's journey through NAT

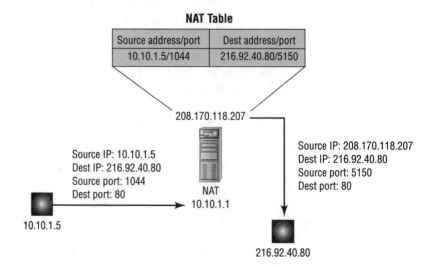

Accepting and Distributing Inbound Packets

So far, you've seen the outgoing packet get rewritten so that it appears to be a request from port 5150 on a machine at 208.170.118.207 to port 80 on the machine at 216.92.40.80. You can assume that the packet reaches the destination machine without incident and that it's able to generate a reply packet containing the requested data. This packet is addressed to 208.170.118.207, port 5150. What happens when the packet reaches the NAT machine?

Figure 11.5 holds the answer. The web server sends a packet back to the source address of the original request, which happens to be the address of the NAT server. When the NAT server receives the packet, it uses its table of port and address mappings to determine that the incoming packet is arriving in response to an outgoing packet sent from a particular address. In this case, the table tells the NAT software that an incoming packet addressed to port 5150 at 208.170.118.207 was sent in response to an outbound packet that reached the NAT server from 10.1.1.5's port 1044. In other words, the NAT table maps the original client address and source port to the destination address plus the source port that NAT used when it rewrote the packet.

FIGURE 11.5   An inbound packet's journey through NAT

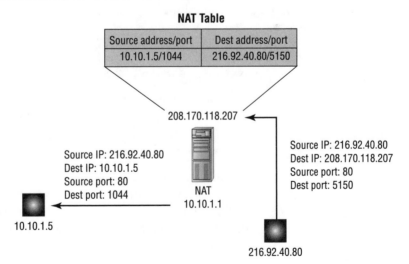

The NAT server can use this information to readdress the packet to the original source address (10.1.1.5) and port (1044). When that machine receives the packet, it appears to have come directly from the requested host. As far as the client and remote server can tell, NAT never even happened.

NAT Editors

The approach described above works fine for data where the IP address information is all in the packet headers, but it falls down for protocols that embed addressing information in the packet payload. For example, the File Transfer Protocol (FTP) embeds IP address data in the payload, as do Net-BIOS over TCP/IP and the Point-to-Point Tunneling Protocol. The approved solution is for the NAT machine to inspect the packet payloads and change any addressing data it finds. However, this works only with certain data types; a special component called a *NAT editor* is responsible for changing data in the protocols it supports. Windows 2000 includes NAT editors for FTP, PPTP, NBT, and the Internet Control Message Protocol (ICMP). It also includes a similar capability called *NAT proxying* for videoconferencing (the H.323 protocol) and the Windows Remote Procedure Call (RPC) interprocess communications tool.

The Difference between ICS and NAT

Up to this point, we've treated ICS and NAT as though they are identical. That's because they're extremely similar: They both implement NAT but with differing levels of bells and whistles. However, Microsoft expects you to know the differences between the two, including the following:

- What they run on: NAT requires Windows 2000 Server or Advanced Server, while ICS is available on every version of Windows since Windows 98 SE.

- How you configure them: Checking one check box on the Sharing tab of a network adapter configures ICS. NAT requires you to use the Routing and Remote Access snap-in, and there are lots more configuration options available.

- How many public IP addresses they can use: With ICS, you expose a single public IP address (e.g., the address that your ISP assigns you). NAT can expose a number of public IP addresses, which is useful if you want to tie specific public IP addresses to individual machines on your LAN.

- How many networks they can link: ICS links one LAN to one public IP address, but NAT can link many LANs (provided they each have their own interfaces) to many public IP addresses.

Using Internet Connection Sharing

ICS is simple to install and use, provided you make the right decisions during installation. It's easy to configure, too; this ease of use and management comes at the expense of some functionality, though.

Installing ICS

Unlike almost every other service you've seen in this book, you don't install ICS using the Windows Components Wizard. All you do is check one box on a Properties dialog box, and the installation process is invisible after that—save for the changes ICS makes to your existing TCP/IP configuration.

Who Should Install ICS

ICS is primarily intended for connecting small office/home office (SOHO) networks to the Internet. In particular, it's designed for small networks that don't already have a full network infrastructure and that have a single connection to the Internet. Because ICS installs its own DHCP server (more on that in a minute) and it requires you to use the 192.168.* address block, it's not suitable for networks that already have their own DHCP server, that use static IP addresses, or that run DNS servers or Windows 2000 domain controllers.

Assuming you still want to install ICS, you must have administrative privileges on the target machine to do so.

What Happens When You Install ICS

Now that you understand how the underlying protocol works, you might be curious to see what happens on a machine when you install Internet Connection Sharing. ICS is a NAT implementation all right, but it leaves out some of the more powerful features included in the full-blown NAT version.

As an example, say you have a Windows 2000 Professional machine that's connected to your cable modem via an Ethernet NIC. You decide to install ICS so that you can add network connections for two other machines in your house, so you buy the necessary supplies and hardware to construct a LAN for your house. As part of that process, you add a second NIC to your Windows 2000 machine so it can run ICS. While this isn't strictly required, ICS *does* require you to have two independent network interfaces. One can be a modem or a NIC; the other must be a NIC.

When you install ICS, you attach it to one of the adapters—the one that's connected to the Internet. When you do so, some things change in your machine and adapter configurations:

- The *other* adapter (i.e., the one connected to your LAN) gets a new IP address of 192.168.0.1 and a subnet mask of 255.255.255.0.

- The Internet Connection Sharing service is started and set to run automatically at boot time.

- The DHCP address allocator service is enabled. The allocator gives out IP addresses in the range 192.168.0.1–192.168.0.254, using the standard 255.255.255.0 subnet mask. Think of it like a baby DHCP server, since there's no way to configure any of the options you learned about in Chapter 2, "Managing the Dynamic Host Configuration Protocol."

- If you're using a dial-up connection on the Internet-connected adapter, automatic dialing is enabled.

These changes don't do anything special to the clients on your network; you must manually configure each of them to use DHCP so they can get the necessary settings from the *DHCP allocator*. ICS also doesn't make any changes to the adapter connected to the Internet. If you need to make changes (for example, because your ISP wants you to use DHCP with your cable modem), make them to the Internet adapter, *not* the LAN adapter.

The ICS Installation Process

Installing ICS is easy, as you'll see in Exercise 11.3: It's literally a one–check box operation. When you open the Network And Dial-Up Connections window, you'll see one icon for each adapter (whether real or dial-up) that you have installed. Find the adapter that you normally connect to the Internet with and right-click it, choosing the Properties command from the context menu. When the Properties dialog box opens, click the Sharing tab, and you'll see the controls shown in Figure 11.6.

To enable ICS, just click the check box labeled Enable Internet Connection Sharing For This Connection, and that's it! If you want Internet traffic from other computers on your LAN to automatically bring up the connection (as you normally will), make sure the Enable On-Demand Dialing check box is selected, too. That's all you have to do to set up a basic ICS configuration, apart from configuring each client to use DHCP.

WARNING

Installing ICS interrupts any TCP/IP connection you have set up, so don't do it in the middle of any operations you don't want interrupted.

FIGURE 11.6   The Sharing tab

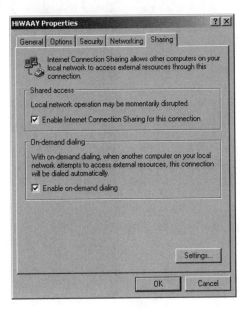

EXERCISE 11.3

Installing Internet Connection Sharing

Follow these steps to install ICS. Note that you can do this on Windows 2000 Professional, Server, or Advanced Server.

1. Open the Network And Dial-Up Connections window (Start ➢ Settings ➢ Network and Dial-Up Connections).

2. Right-click the icon for the adapter that's connected to the Internet (bearing in mind that you can share a dial-up or VPN connection, too), and then choose the Properties command.

3. The adapter's Properties dialog box appears. Click the Sharing tab. If you don't see the tab, it's probably because you're trying to share an unshareable connection, like the Local Area Connection, or because you're not logged on as an administrator.

EXERCISE 11.3 *(continued)*

4. On the Sharing tab, make sure the Enable Internet Connection Sharing For This Connection check box is on. If you want demand dialing turned on, make sure the Enable On-Demand Dialing check box is on, as well.

5. Click OK.

Configuring ICS Options

Once you enable ICS, you'll have access to the Settings button at the bottom of the Sharing tab. This button allows you to configure two separate, but related, groups of settings that have to do with which entries are preloaded into the NAT table on your ICS computer. These settings include the following:

- The Applications tab controls *outbound port mapping*. Changing the settings here allows you to add entries to the NAT table so that computers on your network can make connections to remote services out on the Internet.

- The Services tab controls *inbound port mappings*; by adjusting settings here, you can control where requests from outside your network should be routed.

The Applications Tab

The Applications tab (see Figure 11.7) allows you to create predefined routings for Internet services that you want your users to be able to access. For example, you might want to let users on your network access streaming audio and video sent from servers using Apple's QuickTime. QuickTime implements the Internet-standard Real Time Streaming Protocol (RTSP, defined in RFC 2326), but you have to make some adjustments to your NAT server to allow RTSP traffic to come inside. RTSP uses TCP port 554 and UDP ports 6970 through 6999. To make this work, you click the Add button on the Applications tab, which then displays the Internet Connection Sharing Application dialog box shown in Figure 11.8.

FIGURE 11.7 The Applications tab

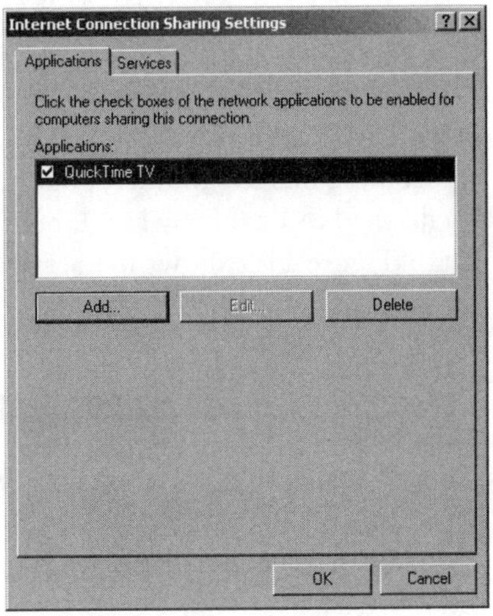

FIGURE 11.8 Adding a new application using the Internet Connection Sharing Application dialog box

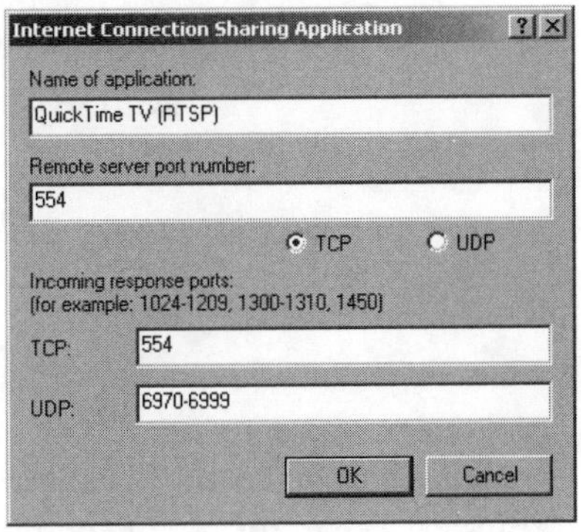

Fill out the dialog box like this:

- Use the Name Of Application field to specify some meaningful name that you'll recognize later.

- Use the Remote Server Port Number field (and the TCP and UDP radio buttons) to specify the port number and type that your machines will use when making connections to the outside world.

- Use the Incoming Response Ports fields to specify which TCP and UDP ports outside servers will use when sending data back to a client on your network.

The Services Tab

The Services tab allows outside computers to access some of the services on your network. For example, say you've set up a small home office and you're using ICS to connect it to the Internet. By making the appropriate entries in the NAT table, you can redirect incoming web requests to one machine, incoming mail to another, and incoming FTP requests to a third. You can't edit the NAT table by hand, but you can achieve the same effect with this tab. Figure 11.9 shows the Services tab.

FIGURE 11.9   The Services tab

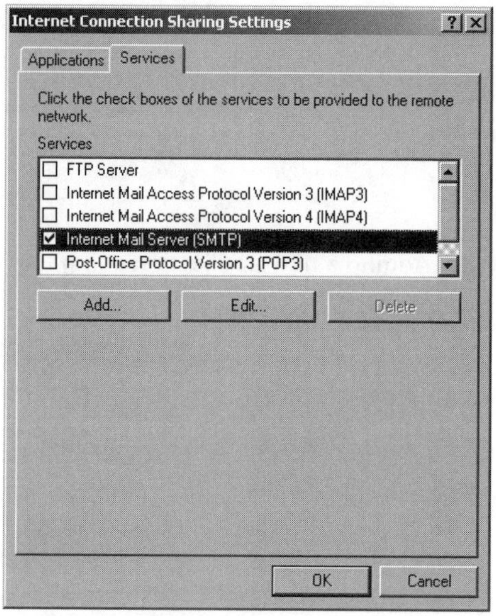

Microsoft helpfully added the six most common services: FTP for file transfer; Telnet for remote administration; IMAP3, IMAP4, and POP3 for remote mail access; and SMTP for sending and receiving mail. Since these services all use well-known port numbers, you must first check the box next to the services you want to enable. That in and of itself probably won't be sufficient since checking the boxes doesn't specify which computer on your LAN should get the traffic. To do that, you need to click the Edit button, which displays the dialog box shown in Figure 11.10. By specifying the local DNS name (e.g., **exchange**, not **exchange.robichaux.net**) or its IP address, you're instructing the NAT software to route incoming packets for that port to the server you specify.

FIGURE 11.10 Editing a predefined service

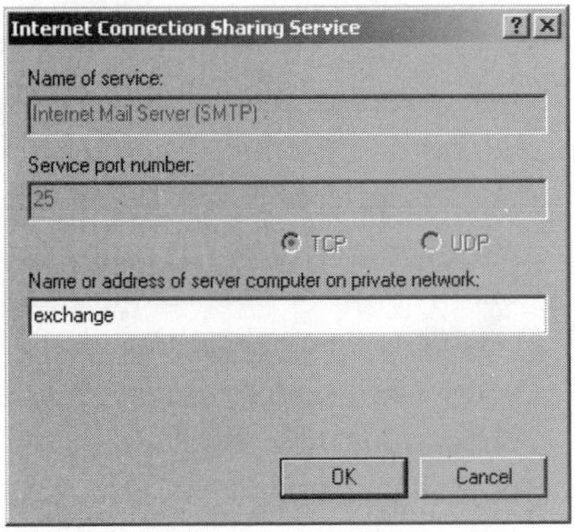

You can also add new services. For example, say you're using Exchange 5.5 as a Network News Transfer Protocol (NNTP) server, and you want outside hosts to be able to reach it. NNTP uses TCP port 119, so you'd click the Add button and fill out the resulting dialog box.

Troubleshooting ICS with *Ipconfig* and *Ping*

As with all network-related problems, you should always check your physical connection first. If a cable is unplugged, then you're definitely going to have problems. You should also verify the TCP/IP configuration on the ICS computer and the ICS client computers, but with ICS you should be aware of some specific points.

The first thing to do when troubleshooting ICS problems is to verify that the ICS computer can make the initial connection to the Internet and that it can actually browse web pages. You might make the connection to the ISP and assume that everything is working properly, but if your DNS configuration is incorrect, then the ICS computer and the clients will have difficulty surfing the net. You then need to make sure that the Internet connection is shared and that the LAN connection is working properly.

As always, you can quickly get a snapshot of the local machine's IP information for all of it's network interfaces using the `ipconfig /all` command. This will show you your configuration on the Internet interface and the LAN interface. If everything looks good, then it's time to start checking the ICS clients for problems.

ICS clients should always be configured as if they are connected to a DHCP server. This means that you must select the Obtain An IP Address Automatically option in the TCP/IP properties dialog box.

If you can't make a connection to the Internet from an ICS client, you should attempt to ping both of the ICS computer's IP addresses. If neither ping is successful, then you should run the `ipconfig /renew` command to renew your IP address. If you still can't ping either of the ICS computer's IP addresses, then there is either a physical connection problem or the ICS computer is misconfigured. If you can ping only one of the ICS computer's addresses, then you know that the ICS computer is not configured properly, but the physical connection is probably okay. If both of these pings are successful, try pinging an outside address. If this is unsuccessful, then the ICS computer is not connected to the Internet. If this ping is successful, but you still can't browse websites, then the ICS computer's DNS information is probably incorrect.

Using Network Address Translation

It's fair to describe ICS as "NAT Lite" since it offers many of the same features in a pretty, not-so-filling package. Earlier on, we saw that the primary differences between the ICS and NAT implementations in Windows 2000 are related to scale and scope. The good news is that the actual configuration isn't that much more difficult; there's just more of it.

Installing NAT

"Installing" NAT is a little bit of a misnomer because NAT is actually treated as another routing protocol you install under the aegis of the Routing and Remote Access Service (RRAS). In that light, when you install NAT what you're really doing is activating some components that provide services within the RRAS framework. Of course, you must install and run RRAS before you install NAT (but more on that in a minute).

What You Get When You Install NAT

Microsoft's documentation discusses three separate, but related, components that contribute to the NAT implementation. It's important to understand these components so that you'll understand the buzzwords used in their docs and on the exams. They include the following:

The Translation Component No, it's not one of those little hand-held gizmos you see in old *Star Trek* episodes. The translation component handles the NAT functions themselves, including maintaining the NAT table for inbound and outbound connections.

The Addressing Component This is what Microsoft calls the "DHCP address allocator" in its ICS documentation. Like the DHCP allocator, the *addressing component* is just a stripped-down DHCP server that assigns an IP address, a subnet mask, a default gateway, and the IP address of a DNS server.

The Name Resolution Component When you install and configure NAT, it begins to act as a DNS server for the other machines on the local network. That service is provided by the *name resolution component*; when a client resolver makes a DNS query, it goes to the name resolution component on the NAT server, which forwards it to the DNS server defined on the Internet-connected adapter and returns the reply. Think of this as a proxy for DNS.

Of course, just because you install these components doesn't mean you'll have to use them all. You always need the translation component since it actually implements the NAT functionality. If you're running a DHCP server *or* the DHCP relay agent on your private LAN, you can't concurrently use the NAT addressing component. Likewise, if you're running an internal DNS server, you may not use the name resolution component. Don't worry; you'll see how to turn these off in a bit.

The Overall NAT Installation Process

ICS hides a lot of the necessary gory details from you, but Microsoft assumes if you're confident enough to run NAT that you can take a little extra time to do some of the things ICS does for you. Here's what you need to do:

1. Install RRAS and enable it. If you use the RRAS Server Setup Wizard (described in the next section), this is your last step. The wizard will take care of the other steps for you. If not (e.g., if you're installing NAT on an existing RRAS box, or if you just like to know what the wizard is doing behind your back), read on.

2. If you're not using a permanent connection (that is, not something that's always up like a dedicated analog line, ISDN line, DSL, or cable modem connection), you need to configure your dial-up connection to reach your ISP using these steps:

   a. Create a demand-dial interface to reach your ISP using the Demand Dial Wizard.

   b. Use RRAS to make the dial-up port routable.

3. Configure the local network adapter properly. This means that you need to give it an appropriate private IP address and network mask, and you need to make sure there's no default gateway specified.

4. Add a static IP route on the adapter that's connected to the Internet. The destination address must be 0.0.0.0, and the subnet mask should also be 0.0.0.0. This forces RRAS to send all traffic across that interface, which is what you want for Internet connectivity.

5. Add NAT as a routing protocol inside RRAS.

6. Add two NAT interfaces: one for your Internet adapter and one for the local network adapter.

7. If you want to use the addressing or name resolution components, you have to configure them.

Activating RRAS

As it turns out, RRAS is installed by default with Windows 2000 Server and Advanced Server, but it's not activated. There are two ways to set up NAT: You can use the Routing and Remote Access Server Setup Wizard to lead you through the process, or you can start up a bare-bones RRAS server and add NAT manually.

In either case, here's what you need to do:

1. Open the Routing and Remote Access Service snap-in (Start ➤ Programs ➤ Administrative Tools ➤ Routing and Remote Access).

2. When the RRAS snap-in opens, navigate to the server you want to manage. If you see a little red spot on the computer icon, that means RRAS is inactive on that machine.

3. Right-click the inactive machine, and then choose Configure And Enable Routing And Remote Access. This command starts the Routing and Remote Access Server Setup Wizard.

4. Dismiss the first page of the wizard by clicking Next.

5. On the Common Configurations page of the wizard, you'll see radio buttons that let you choose which role you want this server to play. If you want to manually configure the server later, choose the Manually Configured Server radio button. If you want the wizard to lead you through the process, make sure the Internet Connection Server radio button is selected, and then click Next.

STEP 1: CHOOSING ICS OR NAT

Once you complete the previous five steps, the next question is simple: The Internet Connection Server Setup page asks you to specify whether you want to set up ICS or NAT. If you select the ICS radio button, a snippy little dialog box tells you to set it up using the Network and Dial-Up Connections folder (but you already knew that, since you've read this far). To set up NAT properly then, you must make sure that the Set Up A Router With The Network Address Translation (NAT) Routing Protocol radio button is selected. Then click Next.

STEP 2: SELECTING A CONNECTION TO SHARE

The next step in the wizard requires you to pick the connection that you want to share. As you can see in Figure 11.11, you can choose how you want the connection to be made. Your two choices are to use an existing Internet connection or to create a new demand-dial connection.

FIGURE 11.11   The Internet Connection page of the Routing and Remote Access Server Setup Wizard

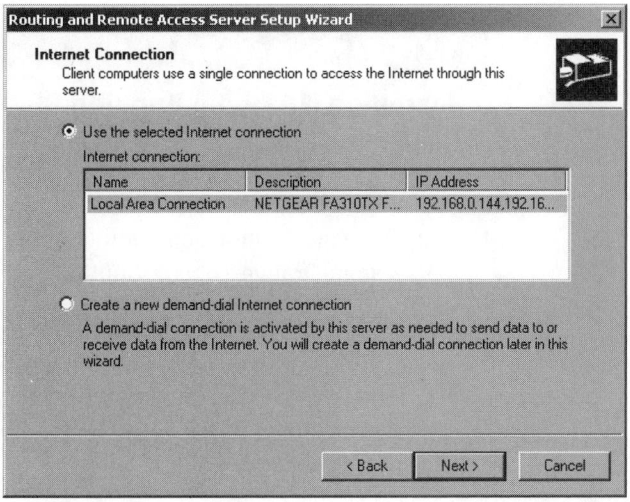

Here's what those options *really* mean:

- The Use The Selected Internet Connection radio button and the corresponding list of adapters that Windows 2000 thinks are connected to the Internet allow you to choose an adapter to share. Choosing this radio button and selecting an adapter is roughly equivalent to picking an adapter in the Network and Dial-Up Connections folder, opening its Properties dialog box, and clicking the ICS check box on its Sharing tab. Notice that it will display dial-up connections even though the dialog says "adapter." Therefore, this is the button to use if you want to press an existing VPN or dial-up connection into service.

- The Create A New Demand-Dial Internet Connection button tells the wizard that you want to create a brand-new, demand-dial connection to use as your Internet pipeline. When you choose this option, it triggers the Demand Dial Interface Wizard. Once you complete the wizard, it will automatically add a NAT interface for the new demand-dial connection (but you'll see in a minute how to do so manually).

Installing NAT When RRAS Is Already Running

If you've already configured RRAS to handle IP or IPX routing, you'll probably want to know how to configure NAT without deactivating RRAS (which wipes out its configuration information) and reactivating it to start the wizard. The steps required to do this are described in Exercise 11.4; note that this covers only the installation and not the process of adding a NAT interface and configuring it.

EXERCISE 11.4

Installing NAT on a Running RRAS Server

Follow these steps to install NAT on a previously installed RRAS server:

1. Open the Routing and Remote Access snap-in (Start ➤ Programs ➤ Administrative Tools ➤ Routing and Remote Access).

2. Locate the server on which you want to enable NAT. If its icon has a little red down-pointing arrow, right-click it and choose Enable And Configure Routing And Remote Access Service, and then proceed with the RRAS Server Setup Wizard as described in the preceding section.

3. Expand the server's configuration until you see the General node (*serverName* ➤ IP Routing ➤ General).

4. Right-click the General node and choose New Routing Protocol. The New Routing Protocol dialog box appears.

5. Select Network Address Translation from the list of routing protocols, and then click OK. The IP Routing node now has a child node named Network Address Translation.

Adding and Removing NAT Interfaces

You have to add an interface in RRAS before it can do anything with packets bound to or from that interface. NAT is no different; before you can use NAT on your local network, you must add a *NAT interface* by using the RRAS interface. The actual process of adding a new NAT interface, detailed in Exercise 11.5, is fairly simple provided you know on which adapter to put the interface.

Adding a NAT Interface

Just as with ICS, you have to distinguish between adapters that are connected to your local network and those connected (or that can connect) to the Internet. NAT links these two interfaces, so you actually need to create both of them. ICS is smart enough to automatically create both interfaces for you, but RRAS requires you to do it yourself. There's a simple process to follow:

1. Create an interface for your local network adapter, specifying it as such.

2. Create the Internet adapter interface. If you're using a dial-up connection, you need to also add some routing information.

EXERCISE 11.5

Adding and Configuring a Public NAT Interface

Follow these steps to add a NAT interface:

1. Open the Routing and Remote Access snap-in (Start ➤ Programs ➤ Administrative Tools ➤ Routing and Remote Access).

2. Expand the RRAS tree until you see the Network Address Translation node (RRAS ➤ *serverName* ➤ IP Routing ➤ Network Address Translation).

3. Right-click Network Address Translation and choose New Interface.

4. The New Interface For Network Address Translation dialog box appears. Select the adapter you want to use and click OK.

5. The NAT Properties dialog box (covered later; see Figure 11.12 below) appears. Select Public Interface Connected To The Internet and click OK.

6. (Optional) If you want to specify an address pool for NAT clients, switch to the Address Pool tab and click Add. In the Add Address Pool dialog box, specify the starting address and subnet mask to be used for the pool, and then click OK.

7. (Optional) If you want to create port-mapping entries (as described later in this chapter), switch to the Special Ports tab and click Add to create them.

Removing NAT Interfaces

As it turns out, you can easily remove any NAT interface—just select it and choose Action ➢ Delete (or the corresponding command on the context menu). RRAS asks you to confirm that you want to remove the interface. If you remove an interface that has active connections, they'll be immediately closed, so don't do this if you (or your network users) are in the middle of something you don't want interrupted.

Setting NAT Interface Properties

Each NAT interface has its own set of properties. Unsurprisingly, you can edit these properties by right-clicking an interface and choosing Properties on the context menu.

THE GENERAL TAB

The General tab lets you designate what kind of NAT interface this is. Normally, you'll need to add a pair of NAT interfaces: one for the adapter that's connected to the Internet and the other for your local adapter. That means you'll have reason to use both of the radio buttons on the General tab (Figure 11.12):

- The Private Interface Connected To Private Network button is what you use to specify that this interface is bound to the adapter on your local network.

- The Public Interface Connected To The Internet button specifies that this adapter is connected to the Internet. That means (duh!) that you use it only on the adapter that you use to connect to the Internet, whatever type of adapter it is.

The Translate TCP/UDP Headers check box controls whether the built-in NAT editors do their thing on IP address data in the packet headers. If you turn this option off, other clients on your local network won't be able to exchange data with Internet hosts. This should always be turned on for a public interface.

FIGURE   11.12   The General tab

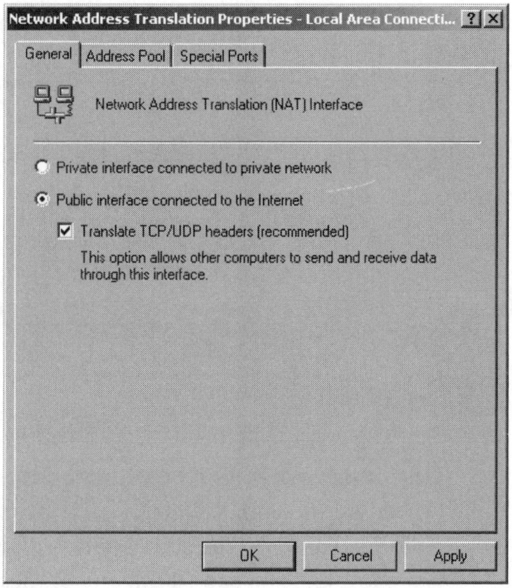

THE ADDRESS POOL TAB

Remember from earlier in this chapter that the number of supported IP addresses is one of the differences between NAT and ICS? The Address Pool tab is where you inform NAT of which IP addresses it should expect traffic to come from. You can assign *address pool* information as a range or as a collection of individual addresses. No matter how deep the pool is, you manage it from this dialog box (see Figure 11.13) by using the list of addresses (or ranges) and the Add, Edit, Remove, and Reservations buttons.

FIGURE 11.13 The Address Pool tab

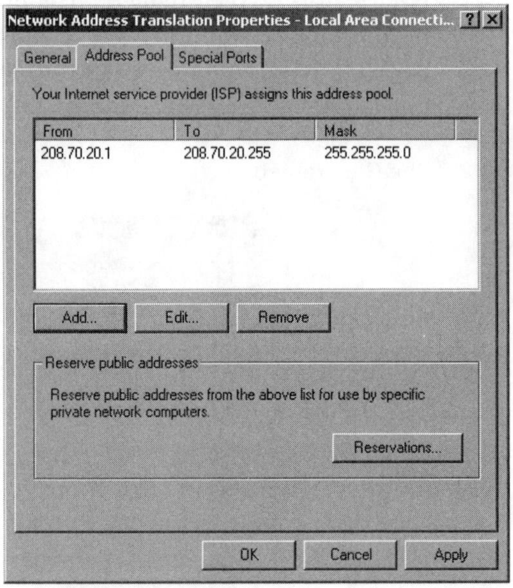

Network Address Translation Properties - Local Area Connecti... [?][X]

General | Address Pool | Special Ports |

Your Internet service provider (ISP) assigns this address pool.

From	To	Mask
208.70.20.1	208.70.20.255	255.255.255.0

Add...   Edit...   Remove

Reserve public addresses

Reserve public addresses from the above list for use by specific private network computers.

Reservations...

OK   Cancel   Apply

When you add a new range of addresses, you specify the starting address, the subnet mask, and the ending address. If you're using a single address, just specify it alone. RRAS tries to be helpful and calculate the correct ending address based on the start address and subnet mask you specify. When you edit a range, you can tweak any of these settings; removing a range from the address pool removes it as part of the public IP address set that can be used to reach machines on your internal LAN.

WARNING Removing an address from the address pool *does not* prevent outside hosts from reaching your NAT server; it just prevents the NAT server from routing packets any further on your LAN.

The Reservations button allows you to reserve individual IP addresses from the public range and add static mappings in the NAT table that point to particular hosts on the inside of your network. This adds a degree of efficiency to the NAT process. For example, let's say that you have a web server whose private IP address is 192.168.0.146. By adding a reserved address that maps that private IP to a single external public IP (say, 208.70.14.212, if that were in your address pool), you could register a DNS record for www.robichaux.net (or whatever other name you wanted it to have). The NAT table would contain a predefined entry that would map any traffic bound for 208.70.14.212 to 192.168.0.146. The only tricky part of adding a reservation is getting the matching addresses into the Add Reservation dialog box (see Figure 11.14). You need to specify a single public IP address that maps to a single private IP address. If you want incoming traffic to reach through the NAT box and to the target machine, you must also check the Allow Incoming Sessions To This Address check box.

FIGURE 11.14   The Add Reservations dialog box

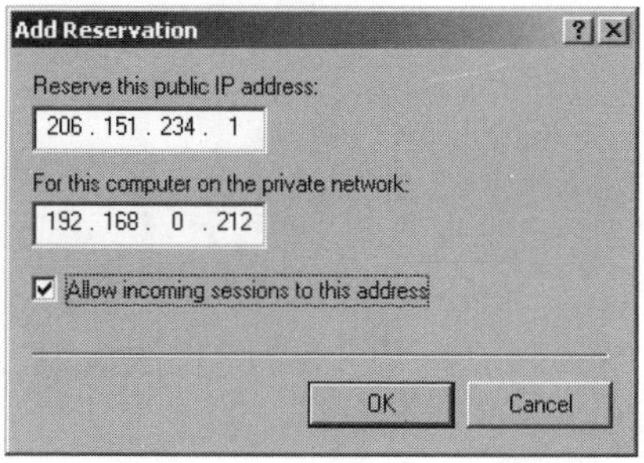

THE SPECIAL PORTS TAB

You can also edit the NAT table in a second way: You can specify which ports inbound traffic should be mapped to. This allows you to take traffic coming to any port on any of your public IP addresses and direct it to the port you wish on any machine on your private network. For example, you could channel any incoming web requests to a single machine by mapping port 80 on the public interface to port 80 on your internal web server. Of course, you could do the same with SMTP or any other TCP or UDP protocol if you wish. All of this flexibility is yours for the asking, thanks to the Special Ports tab (see Figure 11.15). In the example here, the Secure Sockets Layer (SSL) port is mapped to 192.168.0.240 so that any SSL connection attempt from the outside world will automatically be channeled to a single machine on the private network. The *Special Ports tab* lists the *port mappings* you have in effect, and you can add, edit, and remove them using the buttons at the bottom of the tab.

FIGURE 11.15 The Special Ports tab

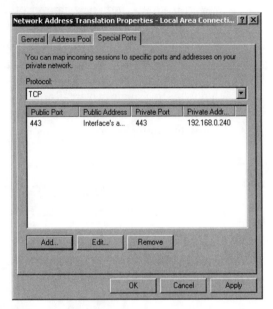

When you add or edit a special port, you'll see a dialog box like the one shown in Figure 11.16. You use the controls in this dialog box to set up the special port mapping you want to take effect:

- The Public Address group lets you specify what public address can receive traffic for this specific port. The On This Interface radio button (the default choice) accepts traffic on the specified port for all public IP addresses in the address pool. If you instead select the On This Address Pool Entry radio button, the public IP address you provide is the only one for which this port mapping will be active.

- Specify the port number the outside world will be using in the Incoming Port field.

- Use the Private Address field to specify the private address to which incoming traffic on the magic port will go.

- Use the Outgoing Port field to select the port that will be used for outbound traffic generated by hosts on your local network.

FIGURE 11.16   The Edit Special Port dialog box

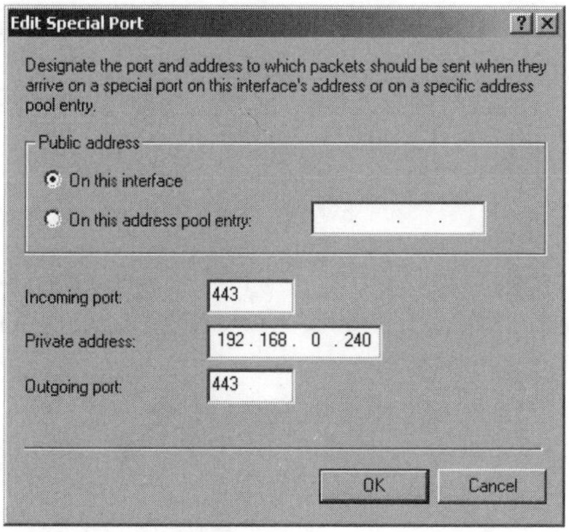

Configuring NAT Properties

Totally apart from configuring the interfaces themselves, there are some properties that pertain to all NAT interfaces and connections on your RRAS NAT server. You modify these settings through the NAT Properties dialog box, which you get by right-clicking the Network Address Translation node in the RRAS console and choosing Properties. The Properties dialog box has four tabs: the General tab, the Translation tab, the Address Assignment tab, and the Name Resolution tab.

The General Tab

The General tab (see Figure 11.17) is pretty uninteresting; it simply allows you to change the amount of event logging information that the NAT software writes to the system event log. The default is set to log errors only, but you can choose from three other levels: no logging at all, logging of errors and warnings, and logging of *everything*. The more detailed log information is useful when you're trying to troubleshoot a problem, but it can bulk up your event log quickly, so don't turn up logging unless you're trying to find and fix a problem.

FIGURE 11.17 The General tab of the NAT Properties dialog box

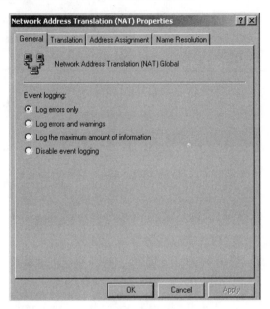

The Translation Tab

The Translation tab (see Figure 11.18) is a little more interesting. It allows you to set scavenging times for port mappings, and it gives you access to an application mapping dialog box very much like the one you saw earlier in Figure 11.8. The controls in the Translation tab do the following:

- The Remove TCP Mapping After and Remove UDP Mapping After fields allow you to control how long entries remain in the NAT table after their last use. The default behavior is to keep TCP mappings for 1440 minutes (24 hours) and UDP mappings for 1 minute.

- The Applications button allows you to open the Applications dialog box so you can add, remove, or edit application mappings. Any mappings you create with ICS are preserved for NAT and vice versa. This helps smooth the way if you start off with ICS and later migrate to a more sophisticated NAT implementation.

FIGURE 11.18 The Translation tab of the NAT Properties dialog box

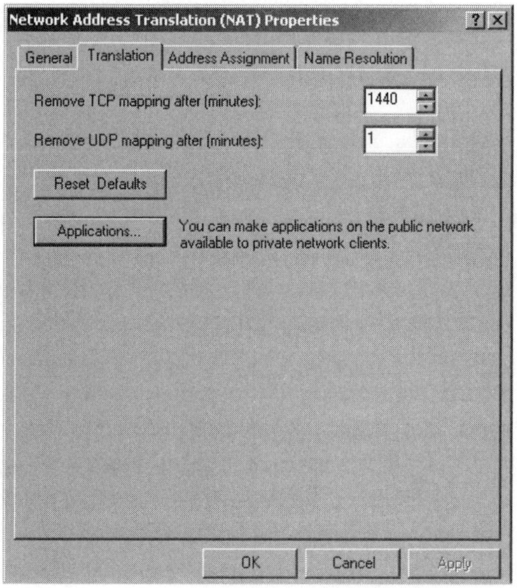

The Address Assignment Tab

The Address Assignment tab (see Figure 11.19) controls whether the NAT addressing component is used or not. Recall that the NAT addressing component is just a baby DHCP server; it's not necessary to use it if you already have a DHCP server on your private network, but you can use it if you want to streamline the number and kind of services you have installed. The controls in this dialog box are simple: The Automatically Assign IP Addresses By Using DHCP check box controls whether the addressing component is active or not. If it is, the IP Address and Mask fields control the address range that's handed out. There's no way to change the default gateway address (it's always the private IP address of the NAT machine), default DNS server, or any of the other DHCP options.

You can, however, exclude IP addresses that you don't want assigned by the allocator. You do this with the Exclude button on the Address Assignment tab, which displays the Exclude Reserved Addresses dialog box (see Figure 11.20). In this dialog box, you'll see a list of any reserved IP addresses, and you can modify the list contents with the ever-present Add, Edit, and Remove buttons. This is functionally equivalent to creating an exclusion range in the DHCP snap-in when you're using the "real" DHCP server.

FIGURE 11.19 The Address Assignment tab of the NAT Properties dialog box

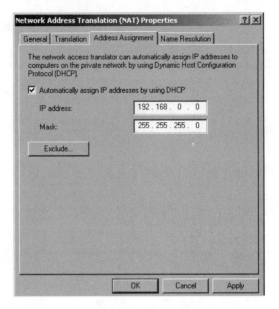

To allow inbound connections from the Internet, you need to exclude the IP address of the target machine here and then assign that IP address statically to the target. Once you've done so, you'll be able to configure a special port pointing to the target.

FIGURE 11.20 The Exclude Reserved Addresses dialog box

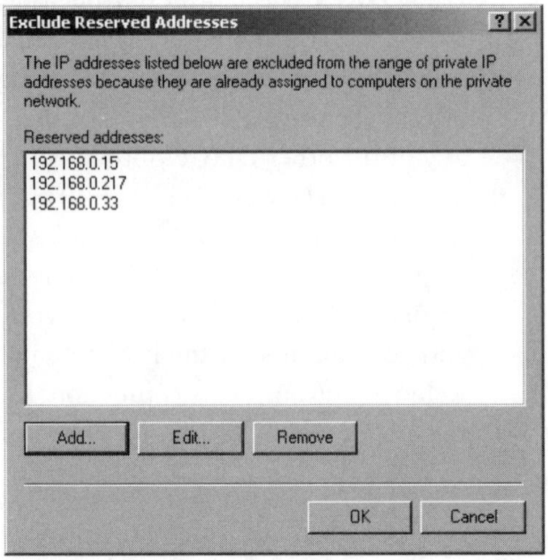

The Name Resolution Tab

You can choose to use the NAT name resolution component, or not, with the Name Resolution tab. When you turn on the component, its address is passed out by the addressing component, and client computers send all their DNS queries to the NAT computer that acts as a DNS proxy. You can still configure each individual client with the IP address of an external DNS server, but then you may not be able to resolve the names of hosts on your private LAN.

The Name Resolution tab (see Figure 11.21) has two check boxes that control how resolution works. The first, Clients Using Domain Name System (DNS), is normally checked—a good thing since it controls whether the name resolution component is active or not. The second check box, Connect To The Public Network When A Name Needs To Be Resolved, specifies whether or not you want the Internet connection brought up just for DNS queries. The Demand-Dial Interface pull-down list lets you select which demand-dial interface, if any, you want brought up when a DNS query requires bringing the link up.

FIGURE 11.21 The Name Resolution tab of the NAT Properties dialog box

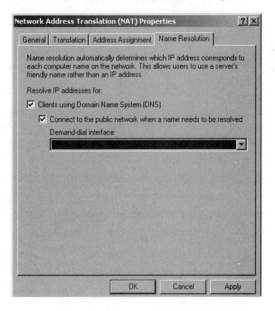

In Exercise 11.6, you'll set the logging level for the NAT components to a more reasonable value. You'll also turn on client name resolution.

EXERCISE 11.6

Configuring NAT Properties

To configure NAT properties on a server, do the following:

1. Open the Routing and Remote Access snap-in (Start ➤ Programs ➤ Administrative Tools ➤ Routing and Remote Access).

2. Expand the RRAS tree until you see the Network Address Translation node (RRAS ➤ *serverName* ➤ IP Routing ➤ Network Address Translation).

3. Right-click Network Address Translation and choose Properties.

4. In the General tab, change the logging setting by selecting the Log Errors And Warnings radio button.

5. Switch to the Name Resolution tab, and then check the Clients Using Domain Name System (DNS) check box.

6. Click OK.

🌐 Real World Scenario

The Expanding Global Network

Your company has a Class C address that it acquired years ago when it had 50 employees and a few network servers. Now the company has grown to over 300 employees, all of whom want to access the Internet. You have been dealing with this by running NWLink for internal traffic, using TCP/IP only for Internet traffic, and allowing only some of the users to connect to the Internet. So far, you have had enough address space for your Internet traffic, but because you see more growth ahead, you realize that your current solution will no longer work. As the network administrator, you have been told that everyone must have unfettered access to the Internet. Rather that chase down more Class C public addresses, you decide to implement Windows 2000 NAT.

This stretching of the address space is particularly useful for small- to medium-sized companies that cannot even acquire a public Class C address for their own private address space. When these small companies go to their ISPs, they have the opportunity to acquire a rather small block of IP addresses, commonly in the range of 4 to 32 individual addresses. For the most part, this still leaves too few addresses to uniquely identify all the devices within a given network. NAT is often seen as the solution for the addressing problem, and it obviously addresses the problem rather well.

IP v6 is poised to resolve these addressing issues and other problems with a more robust protocol stack and a 128-bit address space. But even as wide-scale implementation approaches, the movement to IP v6 will be cascading from the backbone, with a slow radiation down to the client devices on the edge of the network. Even after the address space squeeze is solved, the rationale for NAT will still be there because of the other benefits it provides for access control in your network. One thing it offers is another characteristic to the network architecture that provides another type of security. NAT can also be used to control the manageability of the enterprise network.

Summary

This chapter began by discussing how to manage Virtual Private Networking. You learned about the differences between PPTP and L2TP, and then you quickly moved on to learning how to actually install a VPN server. Next you saw how to configure VPN ports, and you learned about the specific details of VPN remote access policies. We finished the section on Virtual Private Networking with a discussion of troubleshooting.

Next we looked at Network Address Translation and Internet Connection Sharing, two related services. First you got an overview of Network Address Translation, and you learned about the private address scheme. Before installing NAT, you learned how to install ICS, which is a much simpler version of NAT. Then you got into the heart of this section, which dealt with the slightly more complex issue of NAT configuration.

Exam Essentials

Know the similarities and differences between PPTP and L2TP. Both PPTP and L2TP depend on the PPP protocol to move data. PPTP requires an IP connection; L2TP can use PPP over IP, Frame Relay, X.25, or ATM. L2TP supports header compression; PPTP doesn't. L2TP connections can be encrypted and authenticated, but PPTP connections are only encrypted. L2TP must be used with IPSec (although IPSec can be used alone); PPTP always uses MPPE.

Know how to install and configure a VPN server. If you don't have RRAS installed, you'll need to install it, activate it, and configure it as a VPN server. If you're already using RRAS for IP routing or remote access, you can enable it as a VPN server without reinstalling. VPN configuration is extremely simple, at least for PPTP. Either a server can accept VPN calls or it can't. If it can, it will have a certain number of VPN ports, all of which are configured identically.

Know how to create a remote access policy for VPNs. The simplest way is to create a policy that allows all your users to use a VPN. To allow VPN access to a smaller group, create an Active Directory group and put your VPN users in it. You can then create a policy using the following conditions: Set the NAS-Port-Type attribute to Virtual (VPN), set the Tunnel-Type attribute to the appropriate protocol, and use the Windows-Groups attribute to specify the new group.

Know how to troubleshoot a VPN. Verify that the RRAS server is installed and configured on the server, that the client and server protocols match, and that authentication is working properly. Then check for policy problems, network problems, and domain problems.

Understand the difference between ICS and NAT. NAT requires Windows 2000 Server or Advanced Server, while ICS is available on Windows 2000 Professional and the various versions of Windows 2000 Server. ICS is much simpler to install. ICS links one LAN to one public IP address, but NAT can link many LANs (provided each has its own interface) to many public IP addresses.

Understand what happens when you install ICS. When you install ICS, you attach it to one of the adapters—the one that's connected to the Internet. The other adapter (i.e., the one connected to your LAN) gets a new IP address of 192.168.0.1 and a subnet mask of 255.255.255.0. The ICS service is started and set to run automatically at boot time. The DHCP address allocator service is enabled. If you're using a dial-up connection on the Internet-connected adapter, automatic dialing is enabled. The only thing you need to do is configure the machines on the LAN to use DHCP.

Understand the different components of NAT.   The translation component handles the NAT functions themselves, including maintaining the NAT table for inbound and outbound connections. The addressing component is just a stripped-down DHCP server that assigns an IP address, a subnet mask, a default gateway, and the IP address of a DNS server. The name resolution component acts as a DNS server for the other machines on the local network.

Know how to install and configure NAT.   First, install RRAS and enable it. Then configure the local network adapter properly. Add a static IP route on the adapter that's connected to the Internet. Add NAT as a routing protocol inside RRAS. Add two NAT interfaces: one for your Internet adapter and one for the local network adapter. Configure the addressing or name resolution components as needed.

Key Terms

Before you take the exam, be sure you're familiar with the following terms:

address pool	NAT proxying
addressing component	Network Address Translation (NAT)
DHCP allocator	outbound port mapping
inbound port mappings	Point-to-Point Tunneling Protocol (PPTP)
Internet Connection Sharing (ICS)	port mappings
Layer 2 Tunneling Protocol (L2TP)	private addresses
name resolution component	Special Ports tab
NAT editor	virtual private networks (VPNs)
NAT interface	

Review Questions

1. Snappy Lens is a camera and photo-processing company based in one location in Santa Fe, New Mexico. There are 35 Windows 2000 Professional workstations and two Windows 2000 Servers, which together comprise a peer-to-peer network. All of the machines are configured individually with an IP address, and APIPA is disabled. One of the Windows 2000 Servers is used for storing images for customers, and the other supports the working files that the graphic artists use to generate and touch up customers' images. Five of the computers are independently connected to the Internet through dial-up modems, but you are getting requests from everyone wanting an Internet connection. Because you don't want the expense of more connections, you install a second NIC in your image server, open a DSL account, and enable ICS on the public side of the NIC. You modify the Windows 2000 Professional machines to connect to the Internet through the LAN. Now no one can access the Internet. What is the cause of this problem?

   A. You have not configured a WINS server.

   B. You have static IP addresses.

   C. You need to install ICS on the NIC that connects to the public side of the network, not the private side.

   D. APIPA is not enabled.

2. The Land for Sale Real Estate Company has been in business for many years. All the staff—15 agents and a receptionist—work out of the same office. The firm is finally going high tech and has installed a Windows 2000 network consisting of 16 Windows 2000 Professional workstations and one Windows 2000 Server. All the agents are thrilled because they will at last get to use the Internet to check out the competition and look at properties throughout the region. When you set up this system for them, you enabled ICS on the Windows 2000 Server with a cable modem to the ISP. Everything worked fine for a while, but now some websites include audio and video tours of upscale homes, and the agents can't view them. What should you do to resolve this problem?

A. Install NAT instead of ICS.

B. Configure the Windows 2000 clients to support streaming media.

C. Specify ports through the Applications tab.

D. Specify ports through the Services tab.

3. Your NAT configuration is shown in the following diagram. One of the computers that is behind the NAT server is requesting data on port 80 from a web server that has the IP address 216.30.210.110. Select the IP addresses and port numbers in the Choices column and place them in the appropriate positions in the diagram. Note that any of the items can be used more than once or not at all.

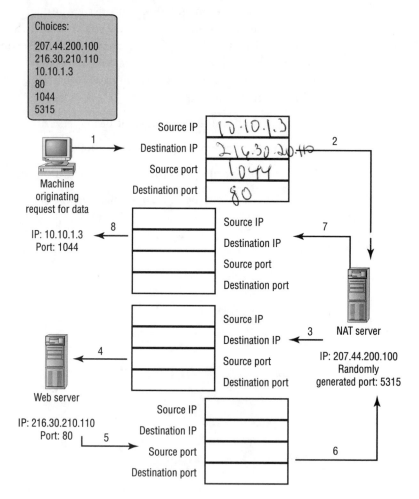

Choices:

207.44.200.100
216.30.210.110
10.10.1.3
80
1044
5315

Source IP: 10.10.1.3
Destination IP: 216.30.20.110
Source port: 1044
Destination port: 80

Machine originating request for data

IP: 10.10.1.3
Port: 1044

Source IP
Destination IP
Source port
Destination port

Source IP
Destination IP
Source port
Destination port

NAT server

IP: 207.44.200.100
Randomly generated port: 5315

Web server

IP: 216.30.210.110
Port: 80

Source IP
Destination IP
Source port
Destination port

4. Monica wants to set up VPN access for her users, who are spread all over North America. There is no central Windows 2000 domain for her users. Which of the following VPN solutions is the most appropriate one for Monica's situation?

   A. L2TP

   B. PPTP

   C. IPSec

   D. ATM

5. One of the employees of your company is trying to connect to the network through the VPN. She complains that she can't access any of the resources on the network. You determine that none of the VPN ports are free. What is happening?

   A. The connection has been refused.

   B. The connection is held in a pending state until there's a free port.

   C. The connection is accepted, but network services are suspended until a port is free.

   D. The user will have to wait a few minutes before she can access the network, because new ports take time to be allocated.

6. A user is attempting to connect to the network through the VPN. He can't seem to get anything to work. You determine that free ports are available. What else should you verify? (Choose all that apply.)

   A. The user must have dial-in permission.

   B. The user must be using compatible authentication and VPN protocols.

   C. The user account must match all conditions in at least one remote access policy.

   D. The user must supply correct credentials.

7. Mildred's Natural Pharmaceuticals is in the process of gobbling up other health food and homeopathic companies and integrating them into a national organization. Because many of the companies that are coming on board haven't completed the acquisition process, you don't want them to have complete access to your network. Your company is halfway through a migration from Windows NT to Windows 2000 at the corporate level. You are still running the Windows 2000 network using Active Directory running in mixed mode. Most of the new locations are small, mom-and-pop health food stores, and many of them aren't computerized at all. You are in the process of sending out stand-alone Windows 2000 Servers so that each of those locations can connect to the corporate RRAS server. The other locations represent a mix of Windows 95, Windows 98, and Windows NT workstations. You want to use VPNs to enable each location to connect to the corporate network through the location's local Internet connection. What is the best way for you to grant and control VPN access to the RRAS server for all the locations that have completed the acquisition process?

   A. Use the default remote access policy for VPN.

   B. Grant access per user.

   C. Create a remote access policy with a NAS port type that uses the Tunnel-Type attribute.

   D. Create an Active Directory group containing your VPN users, add a condition that uses the Windows-Groups attribute, and put this policy ahead of the default remote access policy in order to ensure execution.

8. Your company's 150 sales reps are finally going to receive laptops so that they can communicate with the corporate office whenever they need information stored on the corporate network. The corporate network is fully upgraded to Windows 2000, including the default configuration of the RRAS server for remote connectivity over VPNs. You have installed Windows 2000 Professional with the default configuration on all the laptops and have added the sales reps to a special group in Active Directory. After testing the laptops, everything appears to work fine. You ship them out, and as they reach the sales reps, you monitor their initial connections. During the next few days, you begin receiving support calls from people complaining that they cannot connect to the network. What is the most likely cause of the problem?

   A. The Windows 2000 clients are not configured to support VPNs.

   B. The default RRAS configuration does not support VPNs.

   C. The default RRAS configuration does not support enough VPN connections.

   D. The default RRAS configuration does not support L2TP.

   E. The Windows 2000 client default configuration does not support L2TP.

9. The following diagram shows how VPN traffic flows between the client and the corporate network. Select the items in the Choices box and place them in the correct positions in the diagram so that the VPN configuration will work properly.

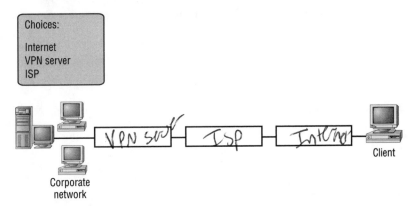

Choices:

Internet
VPN server
ISP

Corporate
network

Client

10. Your Windows 2000 network has 350 Windows 2000 Professional workstations and five Windows 2000 servers. You had a Class C address that you acquired from the InterNIC, but you released it when you went to a national ISP. The cost of having almost 400 IP addresses from your ISP continues to rise, and your manager has told to reduce this cost. You decide to implement NAT and use a statically configured private address space, 172.16.0.0/12, while obtaining a single public address and DNS service from your ISP. You install another NIC in one of your Windows 2000 Servers and configure the public NIC with the provided address. When you try to reach the Internet from any of the machines except the NAT server, your attempt fails. What is most likely causing this problem?

    A. You didn't create any address reservations.

    B. You don't have proper name resolution.

    C. You didn't enable TCP and UDP header translation.

    D. You didn't create the range of ports needed for the translation.

11. Arlene wants to set up NAT so that the public IP address A.ʻ.C.D points to a machine on her LAN with the private address 192.168.15.212. To do this, which of the following must she do?

    A. Create a special port.

    B. Create a reserved address.

    C. Install a packet filter.

    D. Turn off the NAT addressing component.

12. Rainbow Software has been working on products for a couple of years, and as the network administrator, you have been responsible for the network. You have upgraded the Windows NT network that you inherited and have moved completely over to Windows 2000 Servers and Professional workstations, all with static private IP addresses. After the migration, you implemented a NAT server so that everyone could access the Internet. Your manager just told you that one of the company's business partners needs to access an FTP server on your private network. What do you need to do to allow the clients outside the network to access this server through the NAT server?

   A. Create a security filter to allow the traffic to come through.

   B. Install DNS on the NAT server so that the FTP name requests can be translated to the internal network.

   C. Create a special port on the public side of the NAT server to map to the internal ftp server.

   D. Configure the web server with an external address from your ISP.

13. You administer a small network, and you want all your computers to share an Internet connection. You have only one public IP address, and you don't want to spend a lot of time with configuration. What method should you use?

   A. Install NAT.

   B. Install ICS.

   C. Install both NAT and ICS.

   D. You can't use NAT or ICS with only one public IP address.

14. Your Windows 2000 network has 100 Windows 2000 Professional workstations and five Windows 2000 Servers. You have deployed DHCP and DNS so that you can use Active Directory to help manage the network. In your DHCP server, you have implemented a private IP addressing scheme; it is delivering the addresses to the clients, and all the machines are interoperating appropriately. After your users pressure you to allow them to access the Internet, your manager finally relents and allows Internet access from the workplace. You add another NIC to one of your Windows 2000 Servers and configure one of the NICs with the public address that was given to you by your ISP. The other NIC is given an address from your DHCP server. You then open the Network And Dial-Up Connections windows and edit the Properties tab of the public interface to enable Internet connection sharing. Even though you have completed this configuration, no one can browse the Internet—and, in fact, no one can even access the server that's running ICS. What is most likely causing this problem?

A. You need to configure the ICS server with the private address that you are using.

B. You need to run NAT if you need to support the full version of DHCP or DNS.

C. You need to install NAT first and then enable ICS.

D. You need to renew all of the IP address leases.

15. Jerry configured NAT on his network. Users are now complaining that they can't use MSN Instant Messenger. Assuming that Jerry wants to fix this problem, what should he do?

A. Open the necessary ports at the firewall.

B. Add an outbound NAT mapping for the required ports.

C. Add an inbound NAT mapping for the required ports.

D. Set up a proxy server.

Answers to Review Questions

1. B. ICS has a built-in DHCP service that it uses to provide internal addresses that map to the public address. If you have static addresses, ICS cannot use the addresses. WINS is not involved in the ICS service or process. ICS is supposed to be installed on the private side of the network.

2. C. The Applications tab allows you to create routings for Internet services that users need to access through ICS. For example, QuickTime uses TCP port 554 and UDP ports 6970 through 6999. You can use the Applications tab to create both a label to recognize the application and a place to enter the ports that the application uses for communication. You don't need the full version of NAT in order to provide application access through the ICS. Windows 2000 already supports streaming media; if you want to use a different type of streaming media, you can download the application automatically as the client tries to view the files. The Services tab is used for computers outside your network to access services on your network.

3. See the following diagram.

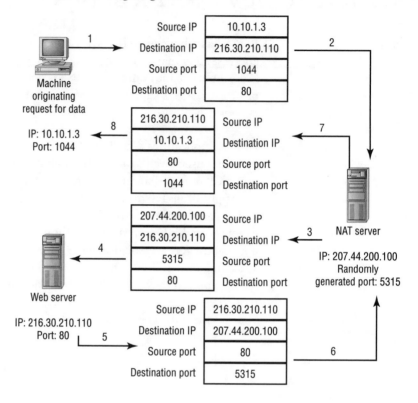

The client generates its request and sends it to the NAT server. The NAT server receives the packet and examines it to determine its destination. It creates an entry in its NAT table that ties the real destination address and port number to the packet's origin and to a substitute port number that it chooses at random. The NAT server also replaces the original source address of the packet with its own address, so that replies from the target machine will come back to the NAT machine. The NAT server sends the rewritten packet over its external interface to the Internet, where it is routed and handled normally. The web server sends a packet back to the source address of the original request, which happens to be the address of the NAT server. When the NAT server receives the packet, it uses its table of port and address mappings to determine that the incoming packet is arriving in response to an outgoing packet sent from a particular address.

4. B. L2TP requires machine certificates, which means that Monica would have to set up and maintain a certificate authority (CA) and public-key infrastructure. PPTP will be much easier to implement, given her constraints.

5. A. The connection is not accepted.

6. A, B, C, D. All four of these conditions must be met for the connection to be accepted.

7. B. In this situation, you are forced to grant access per user because you can implement remote access policies only if you are running your Windows 2000 Active Directory network in native mode. Ideally, you would use Active Directory and create groups so that you could manage access to the network via remote access policies, but this solution doesn't apply in this situation.

8. C. The default configuration for RRAS supports five PPTP ports and five L2TP ports. With up to 150 sales reps trying to connect to the server, only the first 10 will be able to connect. You have to increase the number of ports available, up to 1,000, by using the Ports Properties dialog box. The Windows 2000 Professional clients are by default ready to support VPNs; they will first try L2TP and then switch over to PPTP if ports are unavailable.

9. See the following diagram.

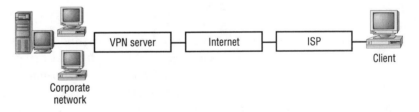

The client establishes a connection to the Internet through the ISP. The VPN server is the means by which Internet traffic can access the corporate network, provided that the client has the correct credentials.

10. C. When you have fewer public addresses than private addresses, NAT performs Port Address Translation (PAT), which uses port numbers to keep track of individual sessions. This is done through the ability of the NAT server to translate the TCP or UDP headers that address the packets. Address reservations are used when you want to map a specific private internal address to a specific public external address consistently. The NAT server provides the name resolution for the private clients using the ISP DNS server.

11. B. Creating a reserved address binds a public IP address to a specific internal machine.

12. C. A NAT server is designed to allow internal traffic to be mapped on outbound connections that are tracked by ports assigned by the server. To enable an external client to reach a private address behind the NAT server, you need to have a public address mapped to a special port on the NAT server so that traffic addressed to it can be sent to the FTP server. A security filter is set on a machine to allow or deny traffic by address, but it's not used on ports to protect a machine behind the NAT server. Name resolution won't allow external traffic to establish a connection to an internal machine. Configuring your internal FTP server with a public address not only will expose it to the public through the NAT, but will prevent it from communicating with the rest of the internal private network as well.

13. B. ICS uses only one public IP address and is very easy to install and configure.

14. B. ICS comes with built-in DNS and DHCP services. However, these cannot be configured like the full-featured versions. If you have an internal DNS or DHCP server that's running, you should run NAT instead of ICS. ICS is a version of NAT that is designed for small LANs and is easy to configure. It fact, it's designed to be automatic. You enable ICS on the NIC that's connected to the Internet and then check the Enable Internet Connection Sharing For This Connection box. The other step for using ICS is to configure all your Windows 2000 Professional clients to use DHCP. You can then configure ICS to allow certain programs and services to pass through ICS.

15. B. Outbound NAT mappings allow outbound traffic to be answered back to the original client machines.

Managing Terminal Services and IIS

MICROSOFT EXAM OBJECTIVES COVERED IN THIS CHAPTER:

✓ **Create shared resources and configure access rights. Shared resources include printers, shared folders, and Web folders.**

- Share folders and enable Web sharing.
- Configure shared folder permissions.
- Create and manage shared printers.
- Configure shared printer permissions.

✓ **Configure and troubleshoot Internet Information Services (IIS).**

- Configure virtual directories and virtual servers.
- Troubleshoot Internet browsing from client computers.
- Troubleshoot intranet browsing from client computers.
- Configure authentication and SSL for Web sites.
- Configure FTP services.
- Configure access permissions for intranet Web servers.

✓ **Implement and troubleshoot Terminal Services for remote access.**

- Configure Terminal Services for remote administration or application server mode.
- Configure Terminal Services for local resource mapping.
- Configure Terminal Services user properties.

Only the web sharing part of the "Create shared resources and configure access rights. Shared resources include printers, shared folders, and Web folders" objective is covered in this chapter. The rest of that objective and its subobjectives were covered earlier in this book.

This final chapter wraps up the book with a discussion of two services that could almost be considered separate products from the Windows 2000 operating system: Terminal Services and Internet Information Services (IIS).

You learned how to use Terminal Services when you prepared for the Windows 2000 Server exam. The MCSA exam will ask you several questions on Terminal Services, so we will review the terms and concepts in this chapter.

IIS is Microsoft's version of an Internet server. You also saw IIS when you studied for the Windows 2000 Server exam, so you should be familiar with many of its features and configuration options. In this chapter we will review these concepts as well as introduce new things that you will be tested on in the MCSA exam.

Overview of Terminal Services

Windows 2000 includes a feature called *Terminal Services* that provides thin client support to the Windows 2000 environment. Rather than install a full version of Windows 2000 on an expensive computer, you can deploy inexpensive *thin clients* (essentially networked computers stripped of most hardware devices, or inexpensive full-featured computers) that use Terminal Services to attach to a Windows 2000 Server computer. The thin client receives monitor signals from the Terminal Services server and sends mouse and keyboard signals back to the server. Everything that you see on a thin client's screen is actually stored and executed on the Windows 2000 Server machine that the thin client is attached to.

Terminal Services consists of two components: the server and the client. The server component runs only on Windows 2000 Server and gives clients access to every function of the server machine. Clients can run applications on the server and administer the server, and they can even use Terminal Services as a remote access method. Terminal Services uses the Remote Desktop Protocol (RDP) to send and receive data between the server and clients.

The Terminal Services client software is very simple and provides just enough functionality to receive monitor signals and send mouse and keyboard signals between the client and server machines. Terminal Services can be run across any type of TCP/IP connection, including LAN, WAN, and VPN. The client software can run on any of the following types of computer:

- Embedded Windows-based terminals

- Computers running Windows 3.11, Windows 95, 98, and Me, Windows NT 3.1, 3.5, 3.51, and 4, and Windows 2000 and XP.

- Macintosh and Unix computers, with third-party client software

Terminal Services can be run in either remote administration mode or application server mode. The following sections describe these modes in more detail.

Remote Administration Mode

Remote administration mode gives Terminal Services clients access to all of the administrative functions on the Windows 2000 Server computer. This includes configuring permissions, altering the Registry, and configuring Active Directory. Only two clients may simultaneously connect to the Terminal Services server in remote administration mode.

If you install the Terminal Services server in remote administration mode, the computer does not install the application-sharing components of Terminal Services described in the next section. The advantages of remote administration mode are that it places very little strain on the Terminal Services server and you do not need to configure licensing (described later).

Application Server Mode

Application server mode creates unique sessions for thin clients and grants them access to applications that run on the Terminal Services server. Each client can see only its own individual session. Only one copy of each application needs to be installed on the Terminal Services server, even if many clients will run that application simultaneously. Terminal Services uses a feature called *application sharing* to run the single application in several sessions.

You do need to configure licensing with a license server in order to run Terminal Services in application server mode. Terminal Services clients need a Windows 2000 Server Client Access License (CAL) and either a Windows 2000 Professional license or a Terminal Services CAL, and they can receive them only from a license server. Terminal Services Licensing is described in the next section.

Terminal Services Licensing

If you plan on using Terminal Services in application server mode, then you will need to install *Terminal Services Licensing* in addition to Terminal Services itself. Terminal Services clients that want to connect to an application server need to get a license first, and only a Terminal Services License Server can provide that license.

When you install the Terminal Services License Server, you must choose between an enterprise server and a domain server. An enterprise server can span Windows 2000–based domains but cannot be used with workgroups or non-Windows 2000–based domains. A domain server can serve licenses within only one domain but does not have the limitations of an enterprise server.

In order to deploy Terminal Services, you will be required to obtain server and client licenses. The licenses you may need are described in Table 12.1.

TABLE 12.1 Terminal Services Licenses

License	Description
Windows 2000 Server license	This server license is included when you purchase Windows 2000 Server.
Windows 2000 Server Client Access license	This license is required for all computers or Terminal Services clients that connect to a Windows 2000 Server. This license is required by all connecting computers to use file, print, and other network services, regardless of whether they are using Terminal Services.

TABLE 12.1 Terminal Services Licenses *(continued)*

License	Description
Windows 2000 Terminal Services Client Access license or Windows 2000 Professional license	Every Terminal Services client needs to have a Windows 2000 Terminal Services Client Access license in addition to a Windows 2000 Server Client Access license. This license gives each Terminal Services client the right to connect to a Terminal Services server and run applications on the server. Windows 2000 Professional machines that are used as Terminal Services clients are automatically licensed to connect to Terminal Services.
Windows 2000 Terminal Services Internet Connector license	This license can be purchased and used separately from the client access licenses described above. This license allows up to 200 clients to connect anonymously from the Internet. This is useful for providing Windows-based applications to the public without porting them to a web-based format.
Work at Home Windows 2000 Terminal Services Client Access license	This license is required for users who want to use Terminal Services to access the Windows 2000 Desktop and applications from home. You can purchase a Work at Home Windows 2000 Terminal Services Client Access license for each Terminal Services Client Access license owned. The Work at Home license includes a Windows 2000 Server Client Access license but does not include application licenses, which must be purchased separately.

Installing and Configuring Windows 2000 Terminal Services

Terminal Services should be installed on the server first and then installed on all of the clients. After installing the Terminal Services server, you can manage Terminal Services settings with the Terminal Services Server Configuration utility and the Terminal Services Manager.

Microsoft ✓ *Exam Objective*

Implement and troubleshoot Terminal Services for remote access.

- Configure Terminal Services for remote administration or application server mode.
- Configure Terminal Services for local resource mapping.
- Configure Terminal Services user properties.

Installing Terminal Services on the Server

The Terminal Services server component is installed through the Add/Remove Programs utility in the Control Panel on Windows 2000 Server computers. Exercise 12.1 shows you how to install Terminal Services in remote administration mode.

EXERCISE 12.1

Installing Terminal Services in Remote Administration Mode

In this exercise, you will install Terminal Services on the server in remote administration mode. You can perform this exercise only on a Windows 2000 Server computer.

1. Choose Start ➢ Settings ➢ Control Panel ➢ Add/Remove Programs.

2. Click the Add/Remove Windows Components button.

3. Check the Terminal Services check box, and click Next to continue.

4. Verify that the Remote Administration Mode radio button is selected, and click Next to continue.

5. Insert the Windows 2000 Server CD-ROM if prompted. The computer will copy the necessary files to the hard drive.

6. Click Finish to close the wizard.

7. Click Yes to restart the computer and enable Terminal Services.

After the computer reboots, you will notice that three items have been added to the Administrative Tools program group: *Terminal Services Client Creator*, *Terminal Services Configuration*, and *Terminal Services Manager*. The Terminal Services Client Creator is used to create floppy disks with the Terminal Services client software. The Terminal Services Configuration utility is used to configure Terminal Services settings, and the Terminal Services Manager is used to monitor and manage individual sessions attached to the Terminal Services server.

Installing a Terminal Services License Server

When a client connects to a Terminal Services server in application server mode for the first time, the server will recognize that the client does not have a license. The server will locate a license server (typically the license server is separate from the Terminal Services server), and the license server will issue a license to the client. The license server will contact the Microsoft Clearinghouse across the Internet and receive a license for every Terminal Services client that it serves. Each client retains its license forever and cannot share the license with any other client for any reason.

Exercise 12.2 shows you how to install a Terminal Services License Server.

EXERCISE 12.2

Installing the Terminal Services License Server

In this exercise you will install a Terminal Services License Server. You must perform these steps on a Windows 2000 Server machine.

1. Choose Start ➤ Settings ➤ Control Panel ➤ Add/Remove Programs.

2. Click the Add/Remove Windows Components button.

3. Check the Terminal Services Licensing check box, and click Next to continue.

4. The Terminal Services Setup dialog box appears. Verify that Terminal Services is set up in application server mode, and click Next to continue.

5. The Terminal Services Licensing Setup dialog box appears. Specify an enterprise or domain Terminal Services License Server, and click Next to continue.

6. Insert the Windows 2000 Server CD-ROM if prompted, and wait for the computer to copy the necessary files to the hard drive. Close the Control Panel when you have finished.

You must activate the license server within 90 days of installing Terminal Services in application server mode. You can do this by selecting Start ➤ Programs ➤ Administrative Tools ➤ Terminal Services Licensing and starting the Licensing Wizard. The wizard guides you through the steps necessary to activate the license server.

You must also install the licenses through the Terminal Services Licensing administrative tool. Once all of these steps are complete, you can begin using Terminal Services in application server mode.

Configuring Terminal Services User Properties

You manage Terminal Services user properties in Active Directory Users and Computers in the same way that you learned in Chapter 6, "Active Directory Security." Four tabs of the standard user Properties dialog box contain settings pertinent to Terminal Services:

- The Environment tab enables and disables starting specific programs at logon, connecting client drives and printers at logon, and defaulting to the main client printer.

- The Sessions tab allows you to configure timeout and reconnection settings.

- The Remote Control tab allows you to enable and disable remote control, which allows the user to observe or control another user's session.

- The Terminal Services Profile tab allows you to specify a specific profile for that user for use with Terminal Services only.

Creating a Terminal Services Client Disk

After you install Terminal Services on the server, you should use the Terminal Services Client Creator to create a floppy disk containing the client software. Alternatively, you can share the `\%systemroot%\system32\clients` `sclient` folder on the server and have the clients access the share for the client installation software. If your clients cannot access the network on their own, you will need to create a disk with the client software, as described in Exercise 12.3.

EXERCISE 12.3

Creating a Terminal Services Client Disk

In this exercise, you will create a Terminal Services client disk. You will need a blank floppy disk, and you must have completed Exercise 12.1 in order to perform this exercise.

1. Select Start ➤ Programs ➤ Administrative Tools ➤ Terminal Services Client Creator.

2. The Create Installation Disks dialog box appears. Select either 16 bit (for pre-Windows 95/NT4 machines) or 32 bit (for Windows 95/NT4 and later machines).

3. Select the drive letter of your floppy disk, and click OK.

4. If prompted, insert the floppy disk and click OK. The Client Creator will copy the files to the disk. Remove the disk from the drive when the process is complete.

After you have created a client floppy, you can use it to install the software on the client machines.

Connecting to the Server

Connecting to the server is fairly straightforward once everything is set up correctly. Exercise 12.4 shows you how to install the client software and connect the client to the server.

Connecting to the Terminal Services Server

In this exercise, you will install the Terminal Services client software from a network share and connect to the Terminal Services server. You should have completed Exercise 12.1 before performing this exercise. In addition, you should share the %systemroot%\system32\ clientssclient folder on the server. You should perform this exercise on a separate machine from the server.

1. Make sure that you are logged on as an Administrator, and select Start ➢ Run.

2. Enter \\[servername]\[drivesharename]\%systemroot%\ system32\clients\tsclient\net\win32 in the Run field, and click OK.

3. A folder window appears containing the files in the \\[servername]\ [drivesharename]\%systemroot%\system32\clients\tsclient\ net\win32 folder. Double-click the Conman icon to display the Client Connection Manager.

4. Click New Connection.

5. The Client Connection Manager Wizard appears. Click Next at the Welcome screen to continue.

6. Enter a name for the connection, and specify either the IP address or the name of the server. Click Next to continue.

7. Select the Log On With This Information Automatically check box. Enter the name of a valid Administrator account in the User Name field, and enter that user's password in the Password field. Enter the name of your domain in the Domain field, and click Next to continue.

8. Select a valid screen resolution, and click Next to continue.

9. Select the Enable Data Compression and Cache Bitmaps check boxes, and click Next to continue.

10. Click Next to step through the last few screens, leaving any settings at the default. Click Finish when you have finished.

11. The new connection appears in the Client Configuration Manager window. Double-click the connection to begin the terminal session.

12. You will be prompted to enter the password for the Administrator account you entered in step 7. After you log in, you will see the Desktop of the server machine, and you will be able to perform any administrative action that you would normally be able to perform if you were sitting in front of the server. Leave the terminal session running so that you can perform the next exercise in this chapter.

Managing Terminal Services Sessions

The Terminal Services Manager utility controls specific sessions. With this tool, you can view information about active servers, sessions, users, and processes, as well as connect, disconnect, reset, and monitor sessions. You can also send messages to users, log off users, and terminate application processes. The Terminal Services Manager window is shown in Figure 12.1.

FIGURE 12.1 The Terminal Services Manager window

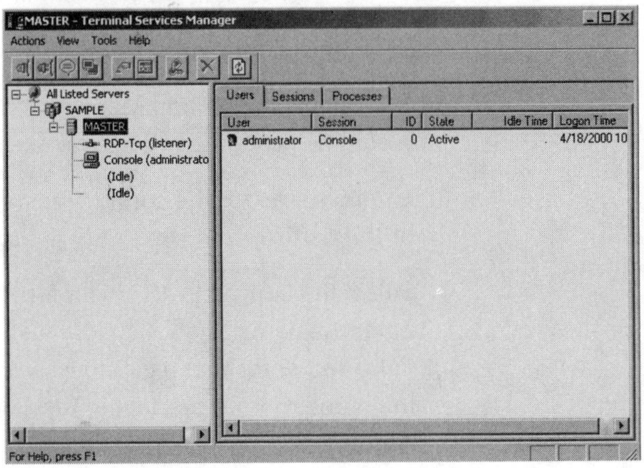

Right-clicking a session, user, or process reveals a context menu with some of the options listed in Table 12.2, depending on what you clicked.

TABLE 12.2 Terminal Services Manager Menu Options

Action	Description	Permission Required
Connect	Allows a user to connect to a session from another session. This option can be used only from a session; it cannot be used from the console.	Full Control or User Access
Disconnect	Disconnects a user from a session. The session is saved, and all running applications continue to run.	Full Control
Send Message	Allows a user to send a message to any or all sessions.	Full Control or User Access

TABLE 12.2   Terminal Services Manager Menu Options *(continued)*

Action	Description	Permission Required
Remote Control	Allows a user to use the session to view or control another user's session. Sessions cannot be controlled from the console.	Full Control
Reset	Immediately ends a session. Any unsaved data will be lost.	Full Control
Status	Displays information about a session, such as bytes sent and received.	Full Control or User Access
Log Off	Logs off a user from a session.	Full Control
End Process	Ends a process on a session. This is useful if a program has crashed and is no longer responding.	Full Control

Overview of IIS

Internet Information Services (IIS) supports four high-level protocols, which in turn interface with TCP/IP to provide web services to client computers. These protocols use *port mappings* to specify which application is sending the TCP/IP requests to the web server. Port mappings are standardized numbers that are typically always the same around the world, although they can be changed.

You do not need to know how to change port mapping for the exam, but you will need to know the standard ports for each of the four protocols listed in Table 12.3.

Table 12.3 shows the details of each of these protocols.

TABLE 12.3 Protocols Supported by IIS

Protocol	Port	Function
HTTP	80	Standard protocol of the World Wide Web. Handles the publishing of static and dynamic web content.
FTP	21	Enables users to transfer files across the Internet. Allows users to upload and download files to and from an FTP server.
SMTP	25	Used for transferring e-mail from one SMTP host to another.
NNTP	119	Forms the basis of the Usenet system for viewing and posting to newsgroups.

Installing IIS

Even though IIS is built into Windows 2000 Server, it is not installed by default. You install IIS through the Add/Remove Programs utility in the Control Panel. Exercise 12.5 shows you how to install IIS.

EXERCISE 12.5

Installing IIS

In this exercise, you will install IIS. You must perform these steps on a Windows 2000 Server computer.

1. Select Start ➢ Settings ➢ Control Panel ➢ Add/Remove Programs.

2. Click the Add/Remove Windows Components button.

3. Select Internet Information Services from the list, and click Next to continue.

4. Insert the Windows 2000 Server CD-ROM into the drive if prompted. After the computer finishes copying the files, click the Finish button.

5. Close the Add/Remove Programs window.

Configuring IIS

After you install IIS, you should notice that a new item has been added to the Administrative Tools program group. Select Start ➢ Programs ➢ Administrative Tools ➢ Internet Services Manager to open the *Internet Services Manager* window, where you control IIS.

Five items are installed by default: Default FTP Site, Default Web Site, Administration Web Site, Default SMTP Virtual Server, and Default NNTP Virtual Server. In the following sections, we will focus on the Default Web Site and the Default FTP Site items.

Microsoft ✓ *Exam Objective*

Create shared resources and configure access rights. Shared resources include printers, shared folders, and Web folders.

- Share folders and enable Web sharing.

Configure and troubleshoot Internet Information Services (IIS).

- Configure virtual directories and virtual servers.
- Configure authentication and SSL for Web sites.
- Configure FTP services.
- Configure access permissions for intranet Web servers.

Configuring the Default Web Site

In order to configure a website (including the Default Web Site), right-click the website in the Internet Services Manager window and select Properties from the context menu. This brings up the Web Site Properties dialog box, which contains several tabs. Most of the tabs can be left at the default settings, but you should know how to make certain changes for the exam.

Configuring Home Directory Options

The Home Directory tab, shown in Figure 12.2, contains some of the most useful configuration options in the Properties dialog box. The most obvious option is the location of the *home directory* for the website content. You can specify either a local directory or a share folder on another machine, or you can automatically redirect site traffic to another location entirely. Whichever option you choose, you will need to specify either a local directory, the UNC path to a share on the LAN, or the URL to another website, respectively.

FIGURE 12.2 The Home Directory tab of the Default Web Site Properties dialog box

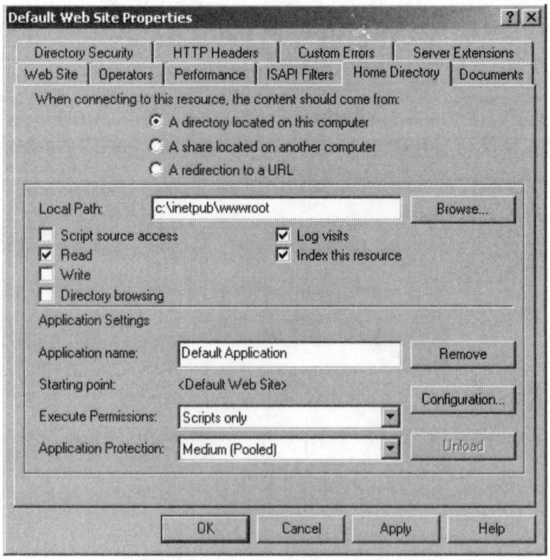

Another useful feature of the Home Directory tab is access control. By default, users have Read access to the website, but you can also permit additional access options, as shown in Table 12.4.

TABLE 12.4 Access Permissions and Content Control Options

Option	Description
Script Source Access	Allows users to access source code for scripts, such as ASP (Active Server Pages) applications, if the user has either Read or Write permission.
Read	Allows users to read or download files located in your home folder. This is used if your folder contains HTML files. If your home folder contains CGI applications or ISAPI applications, you should uncheck this option so that users can't download your application files.
Write	Allows users to modify or add to your web content. This access should be granted with extreme caution.
Directory Browsing	Allows users to view website directories. This option is not commonly used because it exposes your directory structure to users who access your website without specifying a specific HTML file.
Log Visits	Allows you to log access to your website. In order to log access, the Enable Logging box in the Web Site tab of the Properties dialog box also must be checked.
Index This Resource	Allows you to index your home folder for use with the Microsoft Indexing Service.

Web service access permissions and NTFS permissions work together. The more restrictive of the two permissions will be the effective permission.

You can also define application settings, which go beyond the scope of the exam.

Configuring Authentication and SSL

You might find the need to restrict your website content. You can use websites for more than just public information over the Internet. Many companies use intranets, which are basically mini-Internets that run on the local network. You might also want to support an Internet website for employees on the road, and this information would probably be sensitive enough to require some form of authentication. The Directory Security tab of the Properties dialog box, shown in Figure 12.3, provides you with settings necessary for configuring authentication, SSL, and other methods of restricting website content.

FIGURE 12.3 The Directory Security tab of the Default Web Site Properties dialog box

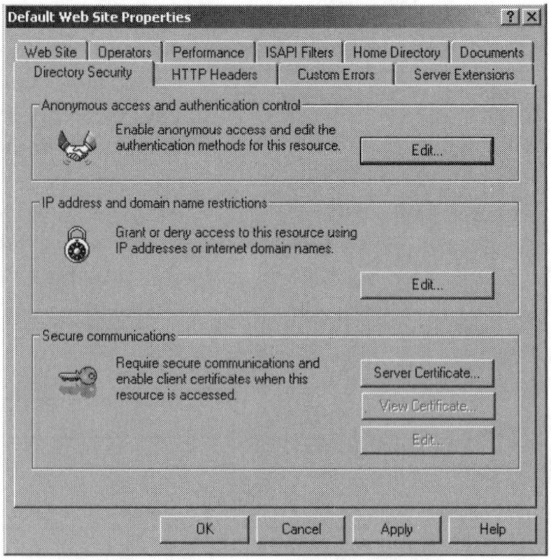

Click the Edit button in the Anonymous Access And Authentication Control section to reveal the Authentication Methods dialog box shown in Figure 12.4. By default, anonymous users have access to the website. This makes sense since typically you want everyone on the Internet (or your private intranet) to be able to see your content. By default, the user account associated with anonymous users is IUSR_*computername*. If you need to restrict access to certain users, then deselect this option. If you want some parts of the website to be restricted, but other parts to be available to everyone, then you should apply NTFS permissions to the restricted content and leave the Account Used For Anonymous Access check box selected. If you want to restrict the entire website, then you should choose one of the three authentication methods available to you. Typically, you should use Integrated Windows Authentication because it provides the highest level of secure authentication.

FIGURE 12.4   The Authentication Methods dialog box

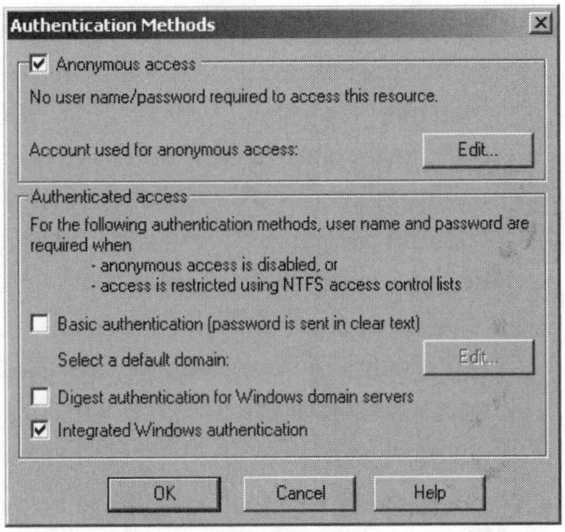

You can also restrict website access to certain IP addresses or domain names. Click the Edit button in the IP Address And Domain Name Restrictions section to bring up the IP Address And Domain Name Restrictions dialog box, shown in Figure 12.5. You must specify whether the listed IP addresses and domain names should be granted or denied access; then you can create a list with the Add button.

FIGURE 12.5 The IP Address And Domain Name Restrictions dialog box

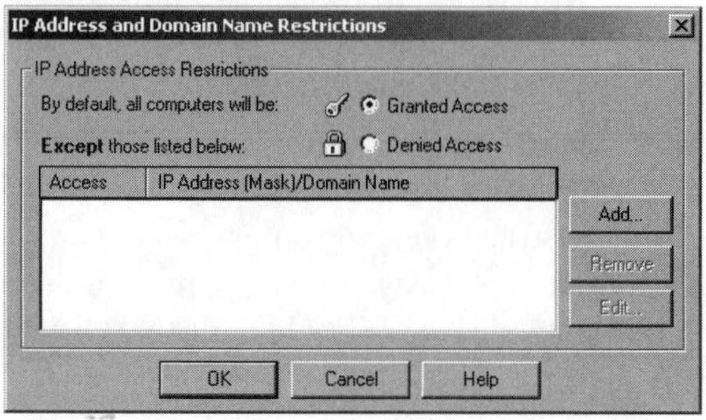

You can also use Secure Socket Layer (SSL) to encrypt data sent between the web server and the client machines. SSL is typically used by banks and online merchants that require you to send your credit card number across the Internet. When you connect to an SSL-enabled site with Internet Explorer, you will notice a small lock icon at the bottom of the window, indicating that all data sent to and from the server is encrypted.

In order to enable SSL on your website, you must have a server certificate. You can obtain a server certificate through either a third party or Certificate Services, a feature of Windows 2000 Server that goes way beyond the scope of this exam. You can configure and enable a certificate for your website by clicking the Server Certificate button in the Secure Communications section of the Directory Security tab.

This opens the Web Server Certificate Wizard which walks you through the process of enabling a certificate for your web server. You must have access to a Certificate Authority in order to establish a certificate.

Configuring Virtual Directories

In the previous section, you saw how to specify a home folder for your website. The home folder could become inconvenient if you have lots of files and folder that need to be published on the website. Every file would need to be copied to the home folder in order to be used by the website.

Fortunately, IIS includes support for *virtual directories*, which allow you to publish website content from any folder on the network. The content stays in the remote folder and appears as a subfolder of the main website. For example, you could create a virtual directory that has a sales alias and points to the \computer1\documents\htmldata\ network share. If your main website was located at http://www.mycompany.com, then the new virtual directory would look like http://www.mycompany.com/sales to the end user. The content of the http://www.mycompany.com/sales URL is still stored in the \computer1\documents\htmldata\ network share, so you must make sure that computer1 is available any time users need access to that content.

You can configure virtual directories in two ways. You can use Internet Services Manager or you can use web sharing in Windows Explorer. Exercise 12.6 shows you how to create a virtual directory in Internet Services Manager.

EXERCISE 12.6

Creating a Virtual Directory in Internet Services Manager

In this exercise, you will create a virtual directory in Internet Services Manager. You should have completed Exercise 12.5 before beginning this exercise.

1. Select Start ➤ Programs ➤ Administrative Tools ➤ Internet Services Manager.

2. Right-click Default Web Site and select New ➤ Virtual Directory.

3. The Virtual Directory Creation Wizard appears. Click Next at the Welcome screen to continue.

4. Enter the name of the alias that users will see in the URL. Click Next to continue.

5. Enter the path to a local directory in the Directory field. Click Next to continue.

6. Specify permissions for the virtual directory, and click Next to continue.

7. Click Finish to close the wizard and enable the new virtual directory.

Alternatively, you can use *web sharing* in Windows Explorer to create a virtual directory. This can be more convenient than using Internet Services Manager, but you can use web services only on the physical computer that is running IIS. You cannot use web sharing for folders on other machines on the network, even if they are running IIS. Exercise 12.7 shows you how to create a virtual directory using web sharing.

EXERCISE 12.7

Using Web Sharing to Create a New Virtual Directory

In this exercise, you will create a new virtual directory using web services in Windows Explorer. You should have completed Exercise 12.5 before attempting this exercise.

1. Select Start ➢ Programs ➢ Accessories ➢ Windows Explorer.

2. Navigate to a folder on your hard drive that you want to share. Right-click the folder and select Properties from the context menu.

3. Click the Web Sharing tab.

4. Select Default Web Site from the Share On pull-down menu.

5. Select Share This Folder, and click the Edit Properties button.

6. Enter the alias for the share in the Alias field, and select applicable permissions. Click OK when you have finished.

7. If you want to provide more than one alias for the directory, you can click the Add button and enter as many aliases as you want. Each alias will point to the same content.

8. Click OK to close the Properties dialog box. The virtual directory will appear in Internet Services Manager just as if you had created it according to the steps in Exercise 12.6.

Configuring an FTP Site

Websites and FTP sites are actually very similar from the administrator's point of view. Both provide access to files, but one displays them in a browser and the other saves them to disk. Consequently, most of the administrative tasks associated with websites are similar to those associated with FTP sites. You should understand how to create a new FTP site for the exam, so you will learn how to do this in Exercise 12.8.

EXERCISE 12.8

Creating a New FTP Site

In this exercise, you will create a new FTP site. You must have completed Exercise 12.5 before attempting this exercise.

1. Select Start ➢ Programs ➢ Administrative Tools ➢ Internet Services Manager.

2. Right-click the name of the server, and select New ➢ FTP Site.

3. The FTP Site Creation Wizard appears. Click Next at the Welcome screen to continue.

4. Enter the name for the FTP site as you wish it to appear in the Internet Services Manager window, and click Next.

5. Leave the IP Address and Port settings at the default, and click Next.

6. Enter the path to a local directory to use for the FTP site's home directory. This directory should be different from your website's home directory. Click Next to continue.

7. Specify any permissions that you require for the FTP site, and click Next.

8. Click Finish to close the wizard. You should see the new FTP site in the list in the Internet Services Manager window.

Troubleshooting IIS

In some ways, troubleshooting IIS is similar to troubleshooting any other network problem. Common sense and thorough analysis of the situation are always good practices when troubleshooting any situation. However, there are some things that you should pay special attention to whenever clients report problems connecting to your web and FTP sites.

Microsoft ✓ **Exam Objective**

Configure and troubleshoot Internet Information Services (IIS).

- Troubleshoot Internet browsing from client computers.
- Troubleshoot intranet browsing from client computers.

When troubleshooting client web connectivity, you should first determine if the problem is with the client or the server. If the client can connect to every website except for one, then that website's server is probably to blame. If the client cannot connect to any web server then the client is probably at fault. When a remote web server goes down there's not much you can do to fix it, but if the problem lies with the client you can use the troubleshooting steps outlined in Chapter 1 to fix the basic client network configuration. Be sure that the IP address, subnet mask, gateway address, and DNS name server addresses are correct, or that the client is receiving the correct information from a DHCP server. This should solve most client-related Internet connectivity problems.

Of course, if your clients are on an intranet and only one web server is present, it can be a bit trickier to determine if the problem is with the client or the server. As with any network problem, you should always make sure that the client can physically connect to the server. This means that you should use the `ping` utility to see if the client can even send a packet to the server. If this doesn't work, then the problem probably isn't with IIS but rather with the connection between the client and the IIS server.

If the client and server are able to connect physically, but the client still cannot view the IIS server's web pages, then you should probably start thinking about your IIS configuration. One of the first things to check is the port number that your web and FTP services are using. If you specified anything other than the default, then clients won't be able to view web pages or FTP directories. If you must use alternate port numbers on the server side, then you must tell your clients to specify the correct port number in the URL. If your HTTP port number is 83, then you must tell users to use the following syntax:

```
http://www.mycompany.com:83
```

If you haven't specified anonymous access, then anonymous users won't be able to connect to your website. You must either enable anonymous access or provide proper authentication to users who need it.

If the website contains scripts or programs, then you must make sure that permissions are properly configured to allow users to use scripts and programs.

Finally, if your site uses SSL, you should make sure the users know that the URL must begin with `https://` rather than `http://`.

Summary

Terminal Services and IIS could almost be considered add-on products for Windows 2000, but Microsoft has taken steps to integrate these features into the operating system. You already saw both of these things when you studied for the Windows 2000 Server exam, but it is useful to review the concepts because you will be tested on them in the MCSA exam as well.

In the first part of this chapter, you learned how to install and configure Terminal Services on both the server and client machines. You also learned how to make a connection between a client and server and saw how to monitor these connections using Terminal Services Manager.

Next we covered IIS, Microsoft's full-featured Internet server. You saw how to install IIS, configure the Default Web Site, set up virtual directories, create a new FTP site, and troubleshoot client connection problems.

Exam Essentials

Know the difference between remote administration mode and application server mode.   Remote administration mode allows administrators to administer a server from a remote location. Only two concurrent connections are allowed, and you do not need to use a license server. Application server mode provides access to applications running on the server to Terminal Services clients. Terminal Services shares a single application so that it can run in many sessions simultaneously. You must use a license server in order to use application server mode.

Understand how Terminal Services Licensing works.   If you run Terminal Services in application server mode, you need to use a license server. The license server provides both a Terminal Services license and a Windows 2000 license to each client machine.

Know how to install Terminal Services and Terminal Services Licensing on the server.   Terminal Services and Terminal Services Licensing are installed using the Add/Remove Windows Components portion of the Add/Remove Programs utility in the Control Panel. These services can be installed only on Windows 2000 Server machines.

Know how to configure Terminal Services user properties.   You manage Terminal Services user properties in the standard user Properties dialog box accessed through Active Directory Users and Computers. The tabs relevant to Terminal Services are the Environment tab, the Sessions tab, the Remote Control tab, and the Terminal Services Profile tab.

Know how to create a Terminal Services client disk.   If your client machines cannot run the client software from a network share, you must create a client disk. You use the Terminal Services Client Creator to create a floppy containing the client software.

Know how to connect a client to a Terminal Services server.   Using the Terminal Services client software, you will need to create a new connection. The Client Connection Manager Wizard walks you through the steps of creating a new connection. Once the connection is saved, you can connect automatically by double-clicking the connection icon in Client Connection Manager.

Know how to observe and control sessions.   The Terminal Services Manager utility gives you control over individual sessions connected to the Terminal Services server. You can simply observe the sessions in the window, and you can connect, disconnect, and reset a session. You can also send messages to users, take control of a user's session, log off a user, or end a process in use by a session.

Understand the protocols supported by IIS and know their default port numbers.   IIS supports four high-level protocols: HTTP on port 80, FTP on port 21, SMTP on port 25, and NNTP on port 119.

Know how to install IIS.   You install IIS in much the same way that you install Terminal Services. IIS is an option in the Add/Remove Windows Components section of the Add/Remove Programs utility in the Control Panel.

Know how and why you should configure home directory options. The Home Directory tab of the website Properties dialog box contains many useful options such as the location of the home directory and access permissions. Access permissions restrict how users interact with the website.

Know how to configure authentication and SSL for your website.   The Security tab of the website Properties dialog box provides you with all of the options you need to configure authentication and encryption through SSL. You can either allow or disallow anonymous access and specify what type of authentication to use. If you want to use SSL, you need a server certificate provided by either a third party or your own certificate server.

Know how to configure virtual directories.   Virtual directories provide web access for folders outside of the home directory. You can configure virtual directories either in Internet Services Manager or through web sharing in Windows Explorer.

Know how to create a new FTP site.   You create new sites by right-clicking the server in Internet Services Manager and selecting New ➢ Site from the context menu. A Site Creation Wizard will walk you through the steps of creating the new site.

Know how to troubleshoot IIS.   Troubleshooting IIS is similar to troubleshooting other network problems because both mainly require common sense and thorough analysis of the problem. You should understand your IIS configuration and make sure that clients are able to physically connect to the server.

Key Terms

Before you take the exam, be sure you're familiar with the following terms:

application server mode	Terminal Services Client Creator
home directory	Terminal Services Configuration
Internet Information Services (IIS)	Terminal Services Licensing
Internet Services Manager	Terminal Services Manager
port mappings	thin clients
remote administration mode	virtual directories
Terminal Services	web sharing

Review Questions

1. You are installing Terminal Services on your network for the first time. You successfully used the Add/Remove Windows Components section of the Add/Remove Programs utility in the Control Panel to install the server, but Terminal Services isn't an option on the client machines. What is most likely the problem?

   A. You need the Terminal Services client CD-ROM in order for Terminal Services to show up in the Add/Remove Windows Components section of the Add/Remove Programs utility in the Control Panel.

   B. You need to create a Terminal Services client disk in order for Terminal Services to appear in the Add/Remove Windows Components section of the Add/Remove Programs utility in the Control Panel.

   C. The Terminal Services client software isn't installed through the Add/Remove Windows Components section of the Add/Remove Programs utility in the Control Panel.

   D. You don't need to install any client software in order to use Terminal Services.

2. Your company has grown quite large and spans multiple domains. You are installing Terminal Services in application server mode for the first time. You must provide access to every user in your company. Which option should you choose when installing the Terminal Services License server?

   A. Domain server

   B. Enterprise server

   C. Certificate server

   D. Internet Information server

3. Several users complain that their Terminal Services connections time out after only one minute of idle time, but other users say that they don't have this problem. Where should you change the timeout setting?

A. Active Directory Users and Computers

B. Terminal Services Management

C. Terminal Services Configuration

D. Terminal Services Connection Manager

4. Your manager asked you to change the port mapping for HTTP to 82. What must now be done in order for clients to browse your web pages?

A. Each client must change its default HTTP port mapping to 82 in the network Properties dialog box.

B. You must change the port mapping back to the default.

C. You must add a virtual directory that also uses port 82.

D. You must tell the users to add :82 to the end of the URL when they attempt to access the website.

5. You work for an online merchant, and you need to set up a secure server so that customers can send you their credit card numbers without worrying that a hacker will steal them. You decide to implement SSL on the web server. What else must you do in order for the secure transactions to work properly?

A. You must install certificate services on the machine running IIS.

B. You must obtain a certificate from either a third party or from a certificate server.

C. You must use authentication settings and require customers to enter a password when they want to make purchases.

D. You must configure a virtual directory that stores the credit card numbers.

6. You have configured a virtual directory that points to a computer other than the web server. It had been working fine, but lately users have been complaining that the virtual directory is inaccessible most of the time. The rest of the website is okay. What is most likely the problem?

   A. The computer that the virtual directory is pointing to has either been shut down or disconnected from the network.

   B. The web server has either been shut down or disconnected from the network.

   C. The virtual directory's alias is incorrect.

   D. The virtual directory's UNC path is incorrect.

7. You have a website that provides anonymous access and has been working perfectly until yesterday. One of your users complains that he can't access the intranet at all. No one else has this problem. What is most likely the cause of the problem?

   A. The user doesn't have correct permissions.

   B. The user's idle timeout setting has disconnected his session.

   C. The user is probably having general network connectivity problems.

   D. The user's virtual directory was deleted.

8. You want to use Terminal Services for clients that are not able to run Windows 2000 applications through their native platform. You install a Terminal Services server on a Windows 2000 Server in application server mode. Which of the following clients not are supported through this service?

   A. Windows 3.11

   B. Windows 3.1

   C. Unix

   D. Macintosh

9. You are using Terminal Services in application server mode. You will have 100 various clients accessing the Terminal Services server. You want to ensure that you meet the licensing requirements for all of the Terminal Services clients. Who must you contact in order to activate a license server?

   A. A system administrator

   B. The Microsoft Clearinghouse

   C. A Microsoft License Center

   D. The Terminal Services clients

10. You use Terminal Services to provide Windows 2000 application support for clients that are not able to run Windows 2000 applications natively. One of your users runs an application and leaves for home without closing the terminal session. Where in Windows 2000 Server do you end Terminal Services sessions?

   A. Terminal Services Manager

   B. Terminal Services Configuration

   C. Terminal Services Client Creator

   D. Internet Services Manager

11. You are evaluating Terminal Services as a way of managing the clients that will attach to your Windows 2000 Servers. As a part of your research, you come across a utility called Terminal Services Client Creator. What is the primary purpose of this utility?

   A. Establishing new client sessions to the Terminal Services server

   B. Purchasing Terminal Client licenses online

   C. Buying new client machines online

   D. Creating Terminal Services client disks

12. You have just installed a Windows 2000 member server and want to take advantage of as many features of Windows 2000 as possible. Which of the following configuration options are associated with Terminal Services? (Choose all that apply.)

    A. Remote administration mode

    B. Application server mode

    C. Network management mode

    D. Protocol analysis mode

13. You host multiple web servers through a Windows 2000 Server that is connected to a high-speed link that attaches to the Internet. Some of your web servers are designed for specific users who require authenticated logon requests. Other servers will be used for public access, and you have no way of knowing who will access these servers. Which user account is used by default in order to enable public access to a website?

    A. IUSR_Anonymous

    B. IUSR_*computername*

    C. IUSR_IIS

    D. IIS_Anonymous

14. You need to provide Internet access to corporate data sheets that are used by your customers. You need to ensure that HTTP requests can be passed through your firewall. What port is used to support HTTP requests by default?

    A. Port 21

    B. Port 23

    C. Port 62

    D. Port 80

15. You are creating a home directory for the Goobedup.com website. When you create the home directory, which of the following options can't be used to specify the location of the home directory?

    A. A directory on the local computer

    B. A share on another computer

    C. A folder that is located on a NetWare server

    D. A redirection to a resource using a URL

Answers to Review Questions

1. C. You access the Terminal Services client software with either a client disk or through a network share. You do not install it through the Add/Remove Windows Components section of the Add/Remove Programs utility in the Control Panel like you do the server component.

2. B. You must install the Terminal Services License server as an enterprise server because only enterprise servers can provide licenses across domains.

3. A. Terminal Services user properties are configured in the user Properties dialog box. The Sessions tab allows you to configure timeout settings.

4. D. Web browsers use the default port mappings unless you specify alternate mappings. You can do this by adding :*newmapping* to the end of the URL in the web browser.

5. B. You must obtain a certificate from either a third party or from a certificate server in order to use SSL. The certificate server does not need to be running on the same machine as IIS.

6. A. Since the virtual directory had been working properly, and the question doesn't say that you made changes, options C and D aren't correct. The rest of the website is working fine, so option B isn't correct. Most likely the computer that the virtual directory is pointing to has either been shut down or disconnected from the network.

7. C. You should first make sure that such problems aren't related to general network connectivity. You can use the `ping` utility to verify that the user can even connect to the web server at all. If not, then you should perform additional troubleshooting steps as outlined in Chapter 1.

8. B. In order to access a Terminal Services server, the client has to be able to attach to the network through a TCP/IP connection. Windows 3.1 does not support networking. Macintosh clients and Unix clients are supported only through third-party software.

9. B. You need to contact the Microsoft Clearinghouse by telephone, fax, the Internet, or the World Wide Web in order to activate your license server.

10. A. You can end sessions in Terminal Services Manager.

11. D. The Terminal Services Client Creator utility is used to create floppies that contain the client software so that Terminal Services clients can connect to Terminal Services servers.

12. A, B. Terminal Services can be used in remote administration mode or application server mode. In remote administration mode, administrators can perform administrative tasks from virtually any client on the network. In application server mode, users have remote access to applications running on the server. Using this mode, Terminal Services delivers the Windows 2000 Desktop environment to computers that might not otherwise be able to run Windows 2000 because of hardware or other limitations.

13. B. If your website is available for public use, you will most likely use anonymous access. If you allow anonymous access, by default, your computer will use the IUSR_*computername* user account. You can limit the access the Anonymous user account has by applying NTFS permissions to your web content.

14. D. Common ports that are used by IIS and can be modified for additional security include FTP on port 21, Telnet on port 23, and HTTP on port 80.

15. C. The home directory is used to provide web content. The default directory is called `inetpub\wwwroot`. You have three choices for the location of the home directory: a directory on the local computer, a share on another computer (stored on the local network and identified by a UNC name), or a redirection to a resource using a URL.

Glossary

A

Active Directory A directory service available with the Windows 2000 Server platform. Active Directory stores information in a central database and allows users to have a single user account (called a domain user account or Active Directory user account) for the network.

Active Directory replication A method by which Active Directory domain controllers synchronize information. See also *replication, intersite* and *replication, intrasite*.

Active Directory Services Interface (ADSI) Code component that can be used for accessing information from various types of directory services, such as Active Directory, Windows NT, Novell Directory Services, and Lightweight Directory Access Protocol (LDAP) sources. ADSI can be accessed from within various programming languages, including Java, Visual Basic, and Visual C++.

Active Directory Users and Computers Windows 2000 administrative tool used for managing objects within Active Directory.

Add/Remove Programs Control Panel applet that allows for installing and uninstalling software applications and components of the Windows 2000 operating system.

address pool The range of IP addresses that the DHCP server can actually assign in a scope.

addressing component A portion of the Internet Connection Sharing or Network Address Translation service that assigns IP addresses to clients; takes the place of a DHCP server.

administrative templates Templates that specify additional options that can be set using the Group Policy Editor.

application assignment scripts Script files that specify which applications are assigned to users of Active Directory.

application server mode A *Terminal Services* mode that gives users remote access to applications running on the server. Using this mode, Terminal Services delivers the Windows 2000 *Desktop* environment to computers that might not otherwise be able to run Windows 2000 because of hardware or other limitations.

assigning The process by which applications are made available to computers and/or users.

auditing The act of recording specific actions that are taken within a secure network operating system. Auditing is often used as a security measure to provide for accountability. Typical audited events include logon and logoff events, as well as accessing files and objects.

B

baseline report A snapshot record of a computer's current performance statistics that can be used for performance analysis and planning purposes.

basic storage A disk-storage system supported by Windows 2000 that consists of *primary partitions* and *extended partitions*.

bridgehead server Used in Windows 2000 replication to coordinate the transfer of replicated information between Active Directory sites.

C

caching-only DNS server   See *DNS server*, *caching-only*.

capture buffer   A resizable storage area in memory to copy frames that are captured by Network Monitor. The default size is 1MB; you can adjust the size manually as needed. The buffer is a memory-mapped file and occupies disk space.

capture filter   This configuration of Network Monitor is used to either collect or reject frames based upon specific criteria.

category   A grouping of applications that are available for installation by users through the Add/Remove Programs applet in the Control Panel. Categories are useful for managing large lists of available applications.

Challenge Handshake Authentication Protocol (CHAP)   Remote access authentication protocol that uses encrypted challenge and response messages instead of sending passwords and usernames in plain text.

child domain   A relative term that describes a subdomain of another domain.

Comma-Separated-Value Directory Exchange (CSVDE)   A Windows 2000 command-line utility for exchanging information between comma-separated-value files and Active Directory.

Compact Disk File System (CDFS)   A *file system* used by Windows 2000 to read the file system on a CD-ROM.

Computer object   An Active Directory object that is a security principal and that identifies a computer that is part of a domain.

Connection object   An object that can be defined as part of the Active Directory's replication topology using Active Directory Sites and Services. Connection objects are automatically created to manage Active Directory replication, and administrators can use them to manually control details about how and when replication operations occur.

Contact object   An Active Directory object that stores contact information.

D

default gateway   A TCP/IP configuration option that specifies the gateway that will be used if the network contains routers.

default subnet mask   Network IDs and host IDs within an IP address are distinguished by using a subnet mask. The default subnet mask is assigned to a Class A, B, or C address. These addresses are characterized by 8, 16, or 24 bits to specify the network number in the address.

delegation   The process by which a user who has higher-level security permissions grants certain permissions over Active Directory objects to users who are lower-level security authorities. Delegation is often used to distribute administrative responsibilities in a network environment.

Delegation of Control Wizard A Windows 2000 tool used for delegating permissions over Active Directory objects. See also *delegation*.

device driver Software that allows a specific piece of hardware to communicate with the Windows 2000 operating system.

DHCP allocator An addressing component that is a simplified DHCP server, which assigns an IP address, a subnet mask, a default gateway, and the IP address of a DNS server.

DHCP authorization The process of enabling a DHCP server to lease addresses by registering the server in Active Directory.

DHCP integration Feature that allows you to pass out addresses to DHCP clients while still maintaining the integrity of your DNS services.

DHCP relay agent To enable DHCP on a multisegment network, you can use a DHCP relay agent or proxy to forward requests.

distinguished name The fully qualified name of an object within a hierarchical system. Distinguished names are used for all Active Directory objects and in the Domain Name System (DNS). No two objects in these systems should have the same distinguished name.

Distribution group A collection of Active Directory users that is used primarily for e-mail distribution.

DNS namespace A hierarchical network-naming structure that is designed to resolve hostnames to IP addresses. Typical DNS names within a namespace are hierarchical, ranging from most specific on the left to least specific on the right (e.g., `server1.mycompany.com`).

DNS server, caching-only A DNS server that is not the authority for any specific zone but can resolve DNS queries. Caching-only DNS servers are used to improve performance.

DNS server, master A DNS server that is responsible as an authority for name resolution within a DNS zone. Each DNS zone can have only one master DNS server.

DNS server, primary A DNS server that is authoritative for a zone and that is able to receive updates of DNS information.

DNS server, secondary A DNS server that is used to resolve DNS names to TCP/IP addresses. Secondary servers contain a read-only copy of the DNS database.

domain In Microsoft networks, an arrangement of client and server computers referenced by a specific name that shares a single security permissions database. On the Internet, a domain is a named collection of hosts and sub-domains, registered with a unique name by the InterNIC.

domain controller A Windows 2000 Server computer that includes a copy of the Active Directory data store. Domain controllers contain the security information required to perform services related to Active Directory.

Domain Local group An Active Directory security or distribution group that can contain Universal groups, Global groups, or accounts from anywhere within an Active Directory forest.

Domain Name System (DNS)   The TCP/IP network service that translates textual Internet network addresses into numerical Internet network addresses.

dynamic storage   A Windows 2000 disk-storage system that is configured as *volumes*. Windows 2000 Server dynamic storage supports *simple volumes*, *spanned volumes*, *striped volumes*, *mirrored volumes*, and *RAID-5 volumes*.

E

EAP type   Authentication scheme supported in EAP. See also *Extensible Authentication Protocol (EAP)*.

effective permission   The permission that a user actually has to a file or folder. To determine a user's effective permission, add all of the permissions that have been allowed through the user's assignments based on that user's username and group associations. Then subtract any permissions that have been denied the user through the username or group associations.

Event Viewer   A Windows 2000 utility that tracks information about the computer's hardware and software, as well as security events. This information is stored in three log files: the Application log, the Security log, and the System log.

Exclusion   Any IP addresses within the scope range that you *never* want the DHCP server to automatically assign.

Extensible Authentication Protocol (EAP)
A protocol that allows third parties to write modules that implement new authentication methods and retrofit them to fielded servers.

F

FAT16   The 16-bit version of the *File Allocation Table (FAT)* system, which was widely used by DOS and Windows 3.*x*. The file system is used to track where files are stored on a disk. Most operating systems support FAT16.

FAT32   The 32-bit version of the *File Allocation Table (FAT)* system, which is more efficient and provides more safeguards than *FAT16*. Windows 9*x* and Windows 2000 support FAT32. Windows NT does not support FAT32.

File Allocation Table (FAT)   The *file system* used by *MS-DOS* and available to other operating systems such as Windows (all versions) and OS/2. FAT, now known as *FAT16*, has become something of a mass-storage compatibility standard because of its simplicity and wide availability. FAT has fewer fault tolerance features than the *NTFS* file system and can become corrupted through normal use over time.

file extension   The three-letter suffix that follows the name of a standard file-system file. Using Group Policy and software management functionality, systems administrators can specify which applications are associated with which file extensions.

filtering   The process by which permissions on security groups are used to identify which Active Directory objects are affected by Group Policy settings. Through the use of filtering, systems administrators can maintain a fine level of control over Group Policy settings.

foreign security principals   Active Directory objects used to give permissions to other security principals that do not exist within an Active Directory domain. Generally, foreign security principals are automatically created by the services of Active Directory.

forest   A collection of Windows 2000 domains that do not necessarily share a common namespace. All of the domains within a forest share a common schema and Global Catalog, and resources can be shared between the domains in a forest.

forward lookup zone   A DNS zone that is used for resolving DNS names to TCP/IP addresses.

forwarding   The process by which a DNS server sends a request for name resolution to another DNS server. Forwarding is often used to improve performance and to restrict network traffic over slow connections.

G

Global Catalog   A portion of Active Directory that contains a subset of information about all of the objects within all domains of the Active Directory data store. The Global Catalog is used to improve performance of authentications and for sharing information between domains.

Global Catalog server   A Windows 2000 Active Directory domain controller that hosts a copy of the Global Catalog. See also *Global Catalog*.

Global group   An Active Directory security group that contains accounts only from its own domain.

Group Policy   Settings that can affect the behavior of, and the functionality available to, users and computers.

Group Policy object (GPO)   A collection of settings that control the behavior of users and computers.

Group Policy object (GPO) link   A link between a Group Policy object and the Active Directory objects to which it applies. Group Policy objects can be linked to sites, domains, organizational units, and other Active Directory objects.

H

hierarchical address   Instead of treating an IP address's entire 32 bits as a unique identifier, one part of the IP address is designated as the network address and the other part as a node address, giving the address a layered, hierarchical structure.

home directory   The default location for content in IIS.

Hosts file   Manually maps DNS names to IP addresses. Entries in the Hosts file take priority over DNS queries.

I

iasparse   A utility (included in the Windows 2000 Resource Kit) that digests an RRAS log, in IAS or database formats, and then produces a readable summary.

inbound port mapping   Controls where requests from outside your network should be routed.

inheritance   The process by which settings and properties defined on a parent object implicitly apply to a child object.

inherited permissions   Parent folder permissions that are applied to (or inherited by) files and subfolders of the parent folder. In Windows 2000, the default is for parent folder permissions to be applied to any files or subfolders in that folder.

initialization files   Files used to specify parameters that are used by an application or a utility. Initialization files are often used by setup programs to determine application installation information.

Internet Connection Sharing (ICS)   A Windows 2000 feature that allows a small network to be connected to the Internet through a single connection. The computer that dials into the Internet provides network address translation, addressing, and name resolution services for all of the computers on the network. Through Internet connection sharing, the other computers on the network can access Internet resources and use Internet applications, such as Internet Explorer and Outlook Express.

Internet Control Message Protocol (ICMP)   Protocol designed to pass control and status information between TCP/IP devices.

Internet Information Services (IIS)   Software that serves Internet higher-level protocols like *HTTP* and *FTP* to clients using web browsers and FTP client software. The IIS software that is installed on a Windows 2000 Server computer is a fully functional web server and is designed to support heavy Internet usage.

Internet Protocol (IP)   The Network layer protocol upon which the Internet is based. IP provides a simple connectionless packet exchange. Other protocols such as TCP use IP to perform their connection-oriented (or guaranteed delivery) services.

Internet Services Manager   A Windows 2000 utility used to configure the protocols that are used by *Internet Information Services (IIS)* and Personal Web Services (PWS).

ipconfig   A command used to display a Windows NT or 2000 computer's IP configuration.

iteration   The incremental process by which DNS names are resolved to IP addresses.

L

Layer 2 Tunneling Protocol (L2TP)
A generic tunneling protocol that allows encapsulation of one network protocol's data within another protocol. Used in conjunction with IPSec to enable VPN access to Windows 2000 networks.

LDIF Directory Exchange (LDIFDE)   A command-line utility that is used to transfer Active Directory objects between LDIF files and Active Directory. LDIF files can be read and modified through the use of LDIF-compatible tools.

Lightweight Directory Access Protocol (LDAP)   A protocol used for querying and modifying information stored within directory services. Active Directory can be queried and modified through the use of LDAP-compatible tools.

Lmhosts file   A file that consists of NetBIOS computer name–to–IP address mappings. Used in name resolution if the broadcast doesn't generate a useful answer or if a WINS query is unsuccessful.

LostandFound container   Active Directory places orphaned objects into a special container called the LostandFound container, which can be accessed through Active Directory Sites and Services.

M

master DNS server   See *DNS server, master*.

member server   A server that participates in the security of Active Directory domains but does not contain a copy of the Active Directory data store.

mirrored volume   A *volume* set that consists of copies of two simple volumes stored on two separate physical partitions. A mirrored volume set contains a primary drive and a secondary drive. The data written to the primary drive is mirrored to the secondary drive. Mir-rored volumes provide fault tolerance, because if one drive in the mirrored volume fails, the other drive still works without any interruption in service or loss of data.

Multicast Address Dynamic Client Allocation Protocol (MADCAP)   A protocol that issues leases for multicast addresses only.

multicast scope   Range in which multicast addresses may be assigned.

N

name resolution component   The component that acts as a DNS server for other machines on the local network; this works as a "proxy" for DNS.

NAT editor   A component responsible for changing data in the protocols it supports.

NAT interface   Network interface that supports Network Address Translation services for LAN clients.

nbtstat   The nbtstat command can help you diagnose and correct errors that occur in NBT.

NetBIOS Extended User Interface (NetBEUI)   A simple Network layer transport protocol developed to support NetBIOS installations. NetBEUI is not routable, and so it is not appropriate for larger networks. NetBEUI is the fastest transport protocol available for Windows 2000.

NetBIOS over TCP/IP (NBT)   NBT provides NetBIOS name resolution over TCP/P. This solves the inherent problem that NetBIOS is not routable.

network address   Each TCP/IP host is identified by a logical IP address. This address is unique for each host that communicates by using TCP/IP. Each 32-bit IP address identifies a location of a host system on the network in the same way that a street address identifies a house on a city street. Also called node address.

Network Address Translation (NAT)   A service that allows multiple LAN clients to share a single public IP address and Internet connection by translating and modifying packets to reflect the correct addressing information.

New Technology File System (NTFS)   A secure, transaction-oriented file system developed for Windows NT and Windows 2000. NTFS offers features such as *local security* on files and folders, *data compression*, *disk quotas*, and *data encryption*.

non–Plug and Play   A hardware device that does not support Plug and Play is known as non–Plug and Play. See also *Plug and Play*.

NTFS permissions   Permissions used to control access to *NTFS* folders and files. Access is configured by allowing or denying NTFS permissions to users and groups.

NWLink IPX/SPX/NetBIOS Compatible Transport   Microsoft's implementation of the Novell IPX/SPX protocol stack.

O

organizational units (OUs)   Used to logically organize the Active Directory objects within a domain.

outbound port mappings   Outbound filters are applied to traffic leaving a computer toward a destination, triggering a security negotiation that takes place before traffic is sent. See also *port mappings*.

P

parent domain   A relative term that describes a domain that is a parent of another domain. Parent domains may contain child domains (also called subdomains).

partition   A section of a hard disk that can contain an independent *file system volume*. Partitions can be used to keep multiple operating systems and file systems on the same hard disk.

Password Authentication Protocol (PAP)   The simplest and least-secure authentication protocol; it transmits all authentication information in clear text, which makes it vulnerable to snooping.

patch   A Windows Installer file that updates application code. Patches can be used to ensure that new features are installed after an application has already completed installation.

permissions   Security constructs used to regulate access to resources by username or group affiliation. Permissions can be assigned by administrators to allow any level of access, such as Read Only, Read/Write, or Delete, by controlling the ability of users to initiate object services. Security is implemented by checking the user's security identifier (SID) against each object's access control list (ACL).

ping Command used to send an Internet Control Message Protocol (ICMP) echo request and echo reply to verify that a remote computer is available.

Plug and Play A technology that uses a combination of hardware and software to allow the operating system to automatically recognize and configure new hardware without any user intervention.

Point-to-Point Tunneling Protocol (PPTP) A Microsoft-specific VPN protocol that encapsulates IP, IPX, or NetBEUI information inside IP packets, hiding data from onlookers.

port mappings TCP and UDP use ports to specify which program running on the system is sending or receiving the data. NAT can map ports from one interface to another to allow a particular service to work properly through NAT. Port mappings are also used in IIS to specify which application is sending the TCP/IP requests to the web server.

primary DNS server See *DNS server, primary.*

Printer object An Active Directory object that identifies printers that are published within domains.

Printer sharing Provides network access to a printer.

private addresses These addresses cannot receive traffic from, or send traffic to, the Internet. In every other respect, though, they're just ordinary IP addresses. The idea behind private addresses is that you can use them to configure a network that's not connected to the Internet. If you wish to connect these machines

to the Internet, you can use NAT to translate between public and private addresses.

promiscuous mode Mode in which a node on a network accepts all packets, regardless of their destination addresses.

publishing Making applications available for use by users through Group Policy and Software Installation settings. Published applications can be installed on demand or when required by end users through the use of the Add/Remove Programs applet in the Control Panel.

Q

quota, disk A Windows 2000 feature used to specify how much disk space a user is allowed to use on specific *NTFS volumes.* Disk quotas can be applied for all users or for specific users.

R

RAID-5 volume A *volume* set that stripes the data over multiple disk channels. RAID-5 volumes place a parity stripe across the volume. RAID-5 volumes are fault tolerant.

recursion The process by which DNS servers or clients use other DNS servers to resolve DNS names to TCP/IP address queries.

remote access policies Like Group Policies, remote access policies allow the administrator to control whether users can get access or not. Unlike Group Policies, remote access policies are available only in native Windows 2000 domains.

remote access profiles Allow an administrator to determine who can actually use dial-up capabilities. Remote access profiles work on individual accounts, whereas remote access policies work on groups of users.

Remote Access Service (RAS) A service that allows network connections to be established over a modem connection, an Integrated Services Digital Network (ISDN) connection, or a null-modem cable. The computer initiating the connection is called the RAS client; the answering computer is called the RAS server.

remote administration mode A *Terminal Services* mode that allows administrators to perform administrative tasks from virtually any client on the network.

Remote Authentication for Dial-In User Service (RADIUS) A common authentication scheme, used by (for example) ISPs using non-Microsoft systems.

Remote Procedure Call (RPC) protocol A protocol used to allow communications between system processes on remote computers. Active Directory uses the RPC protocol for intrasite replication. See also *intrasite replication*.

replication, intersite The transfer of information between domain controllers that reside in different Active Directory sites.

replication, intrasite The transfer of information between domain controllers that reside within the same Active Directory site.

replication latency The time between scheduled Active Directory replication events.

reservation An IP-to-MAC mapping that allows a DHCP server to always give the same IP address to a DHCP client.

resource record (RR) A DNS entry that specifies the availability of specific DNS services. For example, an MX record specifies the IP address of a mail server, and Host (A) records specify the IP addresses of workstations on the network.

reverse lookup zone A DNS zone that is used to resolve a TCP/IP address to a DNS name.

root domain In DNS, the name of the top of the Internet domain hierarchy. Although the root domain does not have a name, it is often referred to as ".".

Routing and Remote Access Service (RRAS) Windows 2000 component that provides multi-protocol routing and dial-up access.

S

scope Contiguous range of addresses used by DHCP.

script policy Setting within Group Policy objects that specifies logon, logoff, startup, and shutdown script settings.

secondary DNS server See *DNS server, secondary*.

Security Configuration and Analysis A Windows 2000 utility used for creating security profiles and managing security settings across multiple machines.

Security groups Active Directory objects that can contain users or other groups and that are used for the management and assignment of permissions. Users are placed into Security groups, and then permissions are granted to these groups. Security groups are considered to be security principals.

security principals An Active Directory object that is used for the assignment and maintenance of security settings. The primary security principals are users, groups, and computers.

security templates Files used by the Security Configuration and Analysis tool for defining and enforcing security settings across multiple computers.

service pack An update to the Windows 2000 operating system that includes bug fixes and enhancements.

share A *resource* such as a folder or printer shared over a network.

share permissions Permissions used to control access to shared folders. Share permissions can be applied only to folders, as opposed to *NTFS permissions*, which are more complex and can be applied to folders and files.

Shared Folder object An Active Directory object that specifies the name and location of specific shared resources that are available to users of Active Directory.

Simple Mail Transfer Protocol (SMTP) A TCP/IP-based protocol that is primarily used for the exchange of Internet e-mail. SMTP can also be used by Active Directory to manage intersite replication between domain controllers. See also *replication, intersite*.

simple volume A *dynamic disk* volume that contains space from a single disk. The space from the single drive can be contiguous or non-contiguous. Simple volumes are used when the computer has enough disk space on a single drive to hold an entire volume.

site A collection of well-connected TCP/IP subnets. Sites are used for defining the topology of Active Directory replication.

site link bridge A connection between two or more Active Directory site links. A site link bridge can be used to create a transitive relationship for replication between sites. See also *site* and *site link*.

spanned volume A *dynamic disk* volume that consists of disk space on 2 to 32 dynamic drives. Spanned volume sets are used to dynamically increase the size of a dynamic volume. With spanned volumes, the data is written sequentially, filling space on one physical drive before writing to space on the next physical drive in the spanned volume set.

Special Ports tab Lists the port mappings you have in effect; you can add, edit, and remove them using buttons at the bottom of the tab.

striped volume A *dynamic disk* volume that stores data in equal stripes between 2 and 32 dynamic drives. Typically, administrators use striped volumes when they want to combine the space of several physical drives into a single logical volume and increase disk performance.

subnet   If an organization is large and has numerous computers, or if its computers are geographically dispersed, it makes good sense to divide its colossal network into smaller ones connected together by routers. These smaller nets are called subnets.

subnet address   Subnetting is the process of carving a single IP network into smaller logical subnetworks. This trick is achieved by dividing the host portion of an IP address to create something called a subnet address.

subnet mask   A number mathematically applied to IP addresses to determine which IP addresses are a part of the same subnetwork as the computer applying the subnet mask.

superscope   Allows you to group two or more DHCP scopes together even though they're actually separate.

system bottleneck   A system *resource* that is inefficient compared with the rest of the computer system as a whole. The bottleneck can cause the rest of the system to run slowly.

T

Task Manager   A Windows 2000 utility that can be used to start, end, or prioritize applications. Task Manager shows the applications and *processes* that are currently running on the computer, as well as *CPU* and *memory* usage information.

Terminal Services   A Windows 2000 Server service that allows *thin clients* to connect to a *Terminal Services server* and access many Win-

dows 2000 features. In Terminal Services application server mode, clients can access the Windows 2000 *Desktop* environment and run applications. In Terminal Services remote administration mode, administrators can perform server administrative tasks remotely from a client.

Terminal Services Client Creator   A Windows 2000 Server utility used to create 32-bit and 16-bit *Terminal Services client* software disks for use with client machines.

Terminal Services Configuration   A Windows 2000 Server utility used to change the properties of the *RDP-TCP* connection that is created when *Terminal Services* is installed and to add new connections.

Terminal Services license server   A server that issues licenses to *Terminal Services clients*. This license is a digitally signed certificate that will remain with the client and cannot be used by any other client.

Terminal Services Manager   A Windows 2000 Server utility used to manage and monitor users, *sessions*, and *processes* that are connected to or running on any *Terminal Services server* on the network.

thin client   A client that has minimal requirements. With *Terminal Services*, a thin client can be run on a variety of machines, including older computers and terminals that would not otherwise be able to run Windows 2000.

tracert   A tool used to report the path that the packets are taking as they flow to a remote system.

transformation file   A type of file used by Windows Installer to modify the behavior of the application-installation process.

Transmission Control Protocol (TCP)   A Transport layer protocol that implements guaranteed packet delivery using the IP protocol.

tree   A set of Active Directory domains that share a common namespace and are connected by a transitive two-way trust. Resources can be shared between the domains in an Active Directory tree.

trust   A relationship between domains that allows for the sharing of resources.

U

Unicast scope   DHCP scope used to assign unicast (point-to-point) addresses. Compare with *Multicast Address Dynamic Client Allocation Protocol (MADCAP)*.

Universal group   An Active Directory Security or Distribution group that can contain members from, and be accessed from, any domain within an Active Directory forest. A domain must be running in native mode to use Universal groups.

User object   An Active Directory object that is a security principal and that identifies individuals who can log on to a domain.

V

virtual directory   Virtual directories allow you to publish website content from any folder on the network. The content stays in the remote folder and appears as a subfolder of the main website.

virtual private network (VPN)   A private network that uses links across private or public networks (such as the Internet). When data is sent over the remote link, it is encapsulated, encrypted, and requires authentication services.

volume   A storage area on a Windows 2000 *dynamic disk*. Dynamic volumes cannot contain *partitions* or *logical drives*. Windows 2000 Server dynamic storage supports five dynamic volume types: *simple volumes, spanned volumes, striped volumes, RAID-5 volumes*, and *mirrored volumes*. Dynamic volumes are accessible only to Windows 2000 systems.

W

web sharing   Web sharing allows you to create a virtual directory within Windows Explorer, bypassing the need to create virtual directories in Internet Services Manager.

Windows Installer   A Windows service that provides for the automatic installation of applications through the use of compatible installation scripts.

Windows Installer packages   Special files that include the information necessary to install Windows-based applications.

Windows Internet Name Service (WINS)
A network service for Microsoft networks that provides Windows computers with IP addresses for specified NetBIOS computer names, facilitating browsing and intercommunication over TCP/IP networks.

Windows Script Host (WSH) A utility for running scripts on Windows-based computers. By default, WSH includes support for the VBScript and JScript languages. Through the use of third-party extensions, scripts can be written in other languages.

Windows Update A utility that connects the computer to Microsoft's website and checks the files to make sure that they are the most up-to-date versions.

Z

zone A portion of the DNS namespace that is managed by a specific group of DNS servers.

zone transfer The synchronization of information between DNS servers that are responsible for servicing the same DNS zone.

Index

Note to the reader: Throughout this index **boldfaced** page numbers indicate primary discussions of a topic. *Italicized* page numbers indicate illustrations.

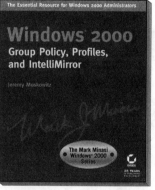
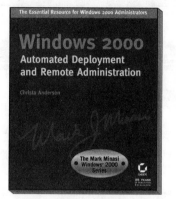
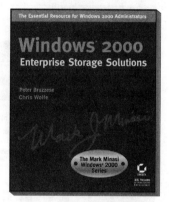

TELL US WHAT YOU THINK!

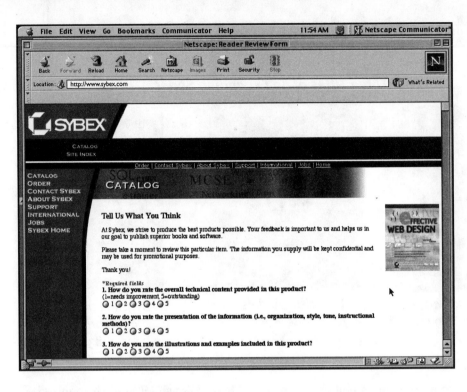

Your feedback is critical to our efforts to provide you with the best books and software on the market. Tell us what you think about the products you've purchased. It's simple:

1. Visit the Sybex website
2. Go to the product page
3. Click on **Submit a Review**
4. Fill out the questionnaire and comments
5. Click **Submit**

With your feedback, we can continue to publish the highest quality computer books and software products that today's busy IT professionals deserve.

www.sybex.com

SYBEX Inc. • 1151 Marina Village Parkway, Alameda, CA 94501 • 510-523-8233

Sybex– the Leaders in Certification

Whether you're searching for a new career opportunity in the IT industry or looking to strengthen an already solid resume, working toward your first certification or your tenth, beginning your studies or doing last-minute review before sitting for an exam, Sybex has the resources you need.

From self-study texts to advanced computer-based training, quick review guides to simulated testing programs, Sybex has the most complete MCSA/MCSE training solution on the market. And all of our products are competitively priced to make it easier for you to concentrate on acquiring Windows 2000 skills instead of worrying about how you'll pay for all the necessary training.

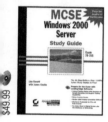

$49.99

Study Guides

Designed for optimal learning, *Sybex Study Guides* provide you with comprehensive coverage of all exam objectives. Hands-on exercises and review questions help reinforce your knowledge.

STUDY

- In-depth coverage of exam objectives
- Hands-on exercises
- CD includes: test engine, flashcards for PCs and Palm devices, PDF version of entire book
- Insights and tips from expert instructors

$39.99

Virtual Trainers™
software

Based on the content of the *Study Guides*, *Virutal Trainers* offer you advanced computer-based training, complete with animations and customization features. Self-assessment and study planning features put you on the fast track to success.

- Customizable study planning tools
- Narrated instructional animations
- Preliminary assessment tests
- Results reporting

$32.45

Virtual Test Centers™
software

Powered by an advanced testing engine, Sybex's new line of *Virtual Test Centers* give you the opportunity to test your knowledge before sitting for the real exam.

PRACTICE

- Hundreds of challenging questions
- Computer adaptive testing
- Support for drag-and-drop and hot-spot formats
- Detailed explanations and cross-references

$24.99

Exam Notes™

Organized according to the official exam objectives, Sybex *Exam Notes* help reinforce your knowledge of key exam topics and identify potential weak areas requiring further study.

REVIEW

- Excellent quick review before the exam
- Concise summaries of key exam topics
- Tips and insights from experienced instructors
- Definitions of key terms and concepts

25 Years of Publishing Excellence

The Complete MCSA/MCSE Solution

The Microsoft® Certified Systems Administrator (MCSA) is a new certification from Microsoft developed to address demands from the IT industry for a mid-level Microsoft certification. No matter what combination of exams you decide to take, Sybex has the study tools you need so you can approach the exams with confidence.

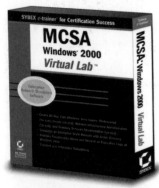

MCSA Virtual Lab software
by James Chellis
ISBN: 0-7821-3030-5
US $199.99

MCSA/MCSE: Windows® 2000 Network Management Study Guide
by Michael Chacon, James Chellis, Anil Desai, and Matthew Sheltz
ISBN: 0-7821-4105-6 • US $49.99

MCSA: Microsoft Certified Systems Associate Exam Requirements

Pass ONE Client OS Exam

70-210	Installing, Configuring and Administering Microsoft Windows 2000 Professional
	— OR —
70-270	Installing, Configuring and Administering Microsoft Windows XP Professional

Pass TWO Networking System Exams

70-215	Installing, Configuring and Administering Microsoft Windows 2000 Server
	— OR —
70-275	Installing, Configuring and Administering Microsoft Windows .NET Server (available late 2002)
70-218	Managing a Microsoft Windows 2000 Network Environment
	— OR —
70-278	Managing a Microsoft Windows .NET Server Network Environment (available late 2002)

Pass ONE Elective Exam

70-216	Implementing and Administering a Microsoft Windows 2000 Network Infrastructure
70-028	Installing, Configuring, and Administering Microsoft SQL Server 2000
70-224	Installing, Configuring, and Administering Microsoft Exchange 2000 Server
70-227	Installing, Configuring, and Administering Microsoft ISA Server 2000
70-244	Supporting and Maintaining a Microsoft Windows NT Server 4.0 Network
220-201 220-202 N10-002	CompTIA's A+ and Network+ Combination
220-201 220-202 SK0-001	CompTIA's A+ and Server+ Combination

For a list of all Sybex products that will help prepare you for any of the MCSA exams, visit www.sybex.com, or train online at www.sybexetrainer.com.